Records of North American Sheep, Rocky Mountain Goats and Pronghorn

Records of North American Sheep, Rocky Mountain Goats and Pronghorn

A book of the Boone and Crockett Club containing tabulations of
wild sheep, Rocky Mountain goats and pronghorn
of North America as compiled from data in
the Club's Big Game Records Archives.

Edited by Jack and Susan Reneau

First Edition
1996
The Boone and Crockett Club
Missoula, Montana

Records of North American Sheep, Rocky Mountain Goats and Pronghorn

First Edition - 1996

Library of Congress Catalog Card Number: 96-084238
ISBN Number for softcover: 0-940864-26-6
ISBN Number for hardcover: 0-940864-28-2

Published October 1996

Published in the United States of America
by the
Boone and Crockett Club
250 Station Drive
Missoula, MT 59801

(406) 542-1888
(406) 542-0784 (fax)

Prologue
A Tribute by the Boone and Crockett Club

Paul D. Webster

The seeds of this book were sown more than two decades ago when interest grew for increasing populations of wild sheep, goats, and pronghorn. The Boone and Crockett Club co-sponsored a ground-breaking symposium on wild sheep at the University of Montana in June 1974 with the Wildlife Management Institute and the National Audubon Society to draw attention to declining numbers of wild sheep and to formulate a strategy to increase wild sheep populations. A book published by the Boone and Crockett Club in 1975 titled, *The Wild Sheep in Modern North America*, edited by Club member James B. Trefethen, was the end result of this historic workshop that brought together leading wildlife researchers and sheep enthusiasts from around North America who united with a common cause to reestablish dwindling sheep populations.

Much has been accomplished for wildlife over the years since the Boone and Crockett Club, America's first and oldest conservation organization, was founded in 1887. Among the organizations that followed in its footsteps is the Foundation for North American Wild Sheep (FNAWS), founded in 1977, that is dedicated to "putting sheep on the mountains." The One-Shot Hunt, established in 1940, led to the establishment of the One-Shot Antelope Hunt Foundation in 1975, the Water for Wildlife Program in 1976, and the Water for Wildlife Foundation in 1991. Wildlife researchers such as Drs. Bruce L. Smith, Valerius Geist, and Bart W. O'Gara, who contributed chapters in this book, provide valuable information to these organizations and to game managers who use their data to manage these species. Dedicated volunteer work and financial support by a few men and women have resulted in habitat improvements that have led to the steady growth of wild sheep, goat, and pronghorn populations since the start of the 20th century.

Records of North American Sheep, Rocky Mountain Goats and Pronghorn is a permanent testimonial to the contributions of private conservation organizations, as well as hunters who have financed the operations of state and provincial game and fish departments throughout Canada, the United States, and Mexico through their purchases of hunting licenses. The statistics contained in this first edition recognize some of the finest examples of wild sheep, goats, and pronghorn ever produced. The vital populations of horned animals are now at such numbers that extinction is not considered as it once was by Boone and Crockett Club members in the early 1900s.

When William T. Hornaday and fellow Boone and Crockett Club member Theodore Roosevelt established the National Collection of Heads and Horns at New York's Bronx Zoo in 1906, they dedicated it to the "vanishing big game of the world." They firmly believed it was only a matter of years before sheep, goats, pronghorn, and all other native North American big-game species would no longer exist in the wild. Members of the Boone and Crockett Club established the Bronx Zoo and the National Bison Range, the National Elk Refuge, and other wildlife refuges because of this underlying fear their children and grandchildren would never experience the surefootedness of the wild sheep and mountain goats and the fleetness and curiosity of the pronghorn in their natural habitat. If those early Boone and Crockett Club founders could witness the status of wildlife populations today, they would be justly proud of their legacy.

Records of North American Sheep, Rocky Mountain Goats and Pronghorn pays tribute to the thousands of men and women who serve as wildlife biologists, game managers, and fish and game administrators for state, provincial, and federal governments in the United States, Canada, and Mexico. Without these professionals, and the support of hunters who buy licenses and hunting equipment, much of the wildlife heritage we now take for granted would not exist.

Paul D. Webster of Wayzata, Minnesota, is the current president of the Boone and Crockett Club and the Boone and Crockett Foundation. He served as its treasurer from 1993 to 1994 and is active in all aspects of the Club and Foundation. Paul is president of Webster Industries Incorporated, managing partner of Webster Wood Preserving Company and president of Bangor Equipment Company. He is a sustainer of the World Wildlife Fund and life member of the Foundation for North American Wild Sheep, The Grand Slam Club, International Sheep Hunters Association, Amateur Trapshooting Association, National Skeet Shooting Association, Rocky Mountain Elk Foundation and Texas Bighorn Society. Paul also supports and is active in many other wildlife conservation and hunting organizations.

Contents

Illustrations

Photographs of Wild Sheep Record Trophies

STATE/PROVINCE/MEXICO	BIGHORN SHEEP	DESERT SHEEP
Arizona	60	122
California	—	134
Colorado	62	—
Idaho	64	—
Montana	68	—
Nevada	—	138
New Mexico	84	146
North Dakota	86	—
Oregon	88	—
South Dakota	90	—
Texas	—	148
Utah	92	—
Washington	94	—
Wyoming	96	—
Alberta	100	—
British Columbia	116	—
Mexico	—	150

STATE/PROVINCE	DALL'S SHEEP	STONE'S SHEEP
Alaska	164	—
British Columbia	178	190
Northwest Territories	180	—
Yukon Territory	184	208

Photographs of Rocky Mountain Goat Record Trophies
STATE/PROVINCE

Photographs of Pronghorn Record Trophies
STATE/PROVINCE/MEXICO

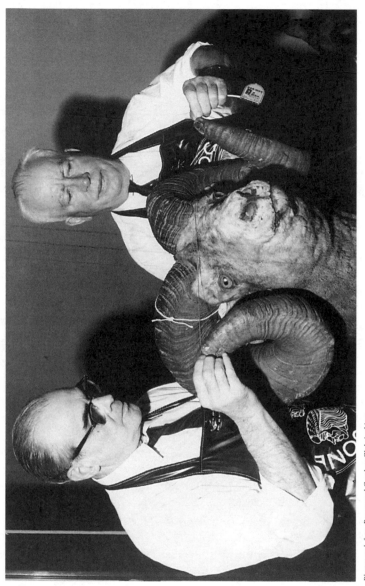

Edward McGuire, left, and John E. Hammett take the tip to tip spread measurement on Clarence Baird's World's Record bighorn sheep (208-1/8 points) at the 12th Competition (1964-1965) held at the Carnegie Museum, Pittsburgh, Pennsylvania. This outstanding Alberta trophy was destroyed in a fire.

Introduction
The Making of This Book

Jack and Susan Reneau

Some of the most elusive and challenging big-game species to hunt are among the horned animals of North America. Wild sheep and Rocky Mountain goats beckon men and women who long to experience rugged terrain, high altitudes, steep cliffs, spectacular mountain vistas, and memorable hunting opportunities. The wily pronghorn with its keen eyesight offers a unique challenge to one's stalking abilities on the sage and grass-covered plains.

It's no wonder the members and staff of the Boone and Crockett Club thought it appropriate to dedicate an entire book to six of North America's most outstanding big-game species. The data and photographs filling this 420-page book offers the reader concise, accurate and entertaining information about six of the most challenging big game animals to hunt.

With total Boone and Crockett Club listings of 709 bighorn sheep, 544 desert sheep, 339 Stone's sheep, and 336 Dall's sheep, this book draws attention to the health of the herds. From 1974 to 1994, a span of 20 short years, the number of trophy bighorns accepted in the Club's Awards Programs increased from three entries per year to 30. These figures are even more astounding when considering the fact that during the Club's most recent Awards Program, ending December 31, 1994, the top six award-winning bighorn sheep trophies exceeded 200 points, and all took their rightful place in the all-time top ten.

The increase in desert sheep during this same time period has not been as dramatic, but has increased from 10 per year during the 16th Awards Program (1974-1976) to 14 per year during the 22nd Awards Program (1992-1994). While the desert sheep statistics don't appear dramatic at first glance, the real story is that the majority of desert sheep currently being entered are coming from the United States where desert sheep management is paying big dividends. Mexico was the leading producer of trophy desert sheep during the 1960s and 1970s, but its contribution to the B&C records books is not as significant at this time.

More modest gains in accepted trophies also have been recorded in the Dall's and Stone's sheep categories. In the same time period, B&C Dall's sheep entries only rose from 13 during the 16th Awards Program to 14 in the 22nd Awards Program. Stone's sheep entries in the 16th Awards Program totaled 11 and rose to 16 by the end of the 22nd Awards Program in 1994. Tables 1, 2, 3, and 4 illustrate the increase in B&C sheep entries.

Rocky Mountain goat and pronghorn increases in B&C trophy listings are just as impressive. The total number of goats accepted since the Boone and Crockett Club first copyrighted its scoring system in 1950 is 601 animals. Pronghorn trophies listed in this book total 1,412. Tables 5 and 6 illustrate the dramatic increases in the numbers of goat and pronghorn entries accepted during the last twenty years. None of these tables include trophies listed in this book at the lower awards minimums because these awards minimums weren't established until near the end of the 18th Awards Program and would skew the data.

Wildlife management success aside, *Records of North American Sheep, Rocky Mountain Goats and Pronghorn* offers the avid hunter a concise guide to where such outstanding trophies live, where they were taken, and who took them. The listings are broken down by the state or province where the trophy was taken and ranked by final score. Key horn measurements, such as horn lengths, basal circumferences, and greatest spreads, are also included in the listings. The state or provincial ranking, as well as the all-time rank of each trophy, is included so the reader can compare one state or province with another, or one trophy with another.

Added to the enjoyment of this book are the score charts of the World's Record Stone's sheep, taken in 1936 by L.S. Chadwick with a final score of 196-6/8 points; the World's Record Rocky Mountain goat, taken in 1949 by E.C. Haase with a final score of 56-6/8 points; and the World's Record pronghorn, taken in 1985 by Michael J. O'Haco, Jr., with a final score of 93-4/8 points. Hunters can use these same score charts to compare their trophies to the World's Records – and dream.

Boone and Crockett Club Records Books

The Boone and Crockett Club has published books on wildlife conservation, hunting and records keeping since 1893 when founding member George Bird Grinnell initiated the Club's book publishing program.

Table 1

Bighorn Sheep Meeting or Exceeding B&C All-Time Minimum Entry Score of 180 Points.

1974 - 1994

Awards Program	Years	Totals
16th	1974-76	9
17th	1977-79	29
18th	1980-82	36
19th	1983-85	56
20th	1986-88	55
21st	1989-91	107
22nd	1992-94	102

Table 4

Stone's Sheep Meeting or Exceeding B&C All-Time Minimum Entry Score of 170 Points.

1974 - 1994

Awards Program	Years	Totals
16th	1974-76	11
17th	1977-79	9
18th	1980-82	8
19th	1983-85	9
20th	1986-88	11
21st	1989-91	14
22nd	1992-94	16

Table 2

Desert Sheep Meeting or Exceeding B&C All-Time Minimum Entry Score of 168 Points.

1974 - 1994

Awards Program	Years	Totals
16th	1974-76	29
17th	1977-79	51
18th	1980-82	54
19th	1983-85	51
20th	1986-88	58
21st	1989-91	56
22nd	1992-94	42

Table 5

Rocky Mountain Goats Meeting or Exceeding B&C All-Time Minimum Entry Score of 50 Points.

1974 - 1994

Awards Program	Years	Totals
16th	1974-76	28
17th	1977-79	25
18th	1980-82	26
19th	1983-85	44
20th	1986-88	44
21st	1989-91	33
22nd	1992-94	45

Table 3

Dall's Sheep Meeting or Exceeding B&C All-Time Minimum Entry Score of 170 Points.

1974 - 1994

Awards Program	Years	Totals
16th	1974-76	13
17th	1977-79	11
18th	1980-82	6
19th	1983-85	12
20th	1986-88	12
21st	1989-91	10
22nd	1992-94	14

Table 6

Pronghorn Meeting or Exceeding B&C All-Time Minimum Entry Score of 82 Points.

1974 - 1994

Awards Program	Years	Totals
16th	1974-76	74
17th	1977-79	75
18th	1980-82	108
19th	1983-85	143
20th	1986-88	109
21st	1989-91	232
22nd	1992-94	239

The specialty records books, dedicated to one or two popular species, first began in 1986 with the first edition of *Records of North American Whitetail Deer*. This book, which was an instant success, focused on the typical and non-typical whitetail and Coues' deer accepted in the Club's archives through the 19th Awards Program that ended December 31, 1985. A second edition of this book was released in 1991. A third edition, which was released in 1995, includes all trophies accepted through the 22nd Awards Program that ended December 31, 1994. All three editions of the whitetail deer book include the statistics on B&C trophies listed by the state or province in which they were taken. As with the book, *Records of North American Sheep, Rocky Mountain Goats and Pronghorn*, the whitetail books include the final score and all-time rank of each trophy, the date and location of kill, the hunter and owner of each trophy, and key trophy measurements. The whitetail deer records books are available from the Boone and Crockett Club along with all the other Club books.

A second specialty records book, *Records of North American Elk and Mule Deer*, was published by B&C in 1991, and a second edition was published in 1996. Both editions of the elk and mule deer records book are organized like the whitetail book but feature the statistics of typical and non-typical American elk, Roosevelt's elk, typical and non-typical mule deer, Sitka blacktail deer, and Columbia blacktail deer. As with the whitetail deer book, the elk and mule deer book includes hundreds of full-page photographs of top-ranked trophies and their hunters, plus official score charts with actual measurements of World's Records.

The all-time records book, *Records of North American Big Game*, has been published by the Boone and Crockett Club since 1932 when Prentiss N. Gray was its first editor. The 10th edition is now available and includes statistics, photographs, and score charts of all big-game trophies accepted in 35 categories through December 31, 1991. The 11th edition of *Records of North American Big Game* will be published in 1999.

An awards book is published at the close of each triennial Awards Program to highlight the most outstanding big-game trophies accepted during that three-year period. The first awards book, *Boone and Crockett Club's 18th Big Game Awards*, featured all the entries accepted during the 18th Awards Program (1980-1982). Similar awards books were published at the close of the 19th, 20th, 21st, and 22nd Awards Programs. The 23rd Awards book will be published in the fall of 1998 after the final judging takes place for top trophies accepted from 1995 to 1997. The awards books are unique in that they include a full-page portrait photograph and hunting story of each award-winning trophy as provided by the hunters who took them. All trophies accepted above the lower awards minimums (e.g., whitetail awards with minimums of 160 or better) are included in these books. The 18th, 19th, 20th, and 22nd Awards books are available for sale through the Boone and Crockett Club's national headquarters while supplies last.

Scoring of Trophies

The famous B&C scoring system dates from 1950 when it was officially adopted by the Club's Records Committee and copyrighted. The system has been in continuous usage – without major change since that date – which underscores its reliable methods of measurement. Skulls, antlers, or horns are measured, depending upon the category of big-game animal being scored. Scores can be replicated using the Club's copyrighted system because of the enduring nature of trophy material. Had body length or weight been used to judge the size of an animal, the flesh and muscle would decompose, rendering remeasurement and verification of scores impossible. That sense of understanding by hunters and official measurers on how to score a trophy aids in making the Boone and Crockett Club's scoring system the universally accepted method for evaluating the size of native North American big game.

Scoring a trophy begins by first studying the score charts and reading the instructions printed elsewhere in this book. If a hunter or trophy owner finds his or her rough score to be close to or above the minimum entry score for B&C, he or she should call the Club's office in Missoula, Montana, at (406) 542-1888 to obtain a list of entry requirements and the names of official measurers in his or her state or province.

No official measurement of a trophy can take place until it has air dried 60 days under normal atmospheric conditions. Antlered trophies in velvet must have the velvet removed before official measurements are taken. Doing a preliminary measurement of the trophy using this book or a score chart ordered from the Boone and Crockett Club helps the official measurer determine if his or her time is needed to do the official scoring.

Official measurers are volunteers who do not charge for their services, so hunters or owners need to deliver their trophies to measurers at a mutually agreed upon time and location. If the official measurer determines that the hunter or owner has a B&C trophy, he or she will assist the hunter or owner with entering their trophy. A trophy is not a B&C specimen unless it is officially accepted into an Awards Program.

The entry process requires a completed official score chart, signed by an official measurer; a completed hunter, guide and hunt information form; a completed Fair Chase Statement; a copy of the hunting license; and photographs of the front, left and right sides of the trophy (top of skull photograph for bears and cats). The entry fee is $25. Trophies accepted in any B&C Awards Program are sent a handsome acceptance certificate that can be displayed with the trophy. Beginning in 1996, the Club offers an acceptance plaque that is available at a nominal price for trophy owners who wish to memorialize their accomplishment in their home or office.

The Boone and Crockett Club's Awards Programs

The Club's first competition was held in 1947. The first three competitions were annual events until the fourth competition in 1951 when they became biennial events. The biennial competitions continued until the 14th Competition in 1968 when they became triennial activities. The competitions were renamed Awards Programs beginning with the 15th Awards Program (1971-1973) to better reflect the Club's intent. The Club has completed twenty-two Competitions/Awards Programs since 1947, and is currently in the middle of the 23rd Awards Program.

Only a few top-ranking trophies accepted in each category during each three-year Awards Program are recognized with medals and/or certificates. Owners of the top-ranking trophies in each big-game category are invited to send their antlers, skulls, and horns to a triennial Awards Program for judging. At the Awards Program a select panel of B&C official measurers, called judges, remeasure and certify the invited trophies and recognize them with place awards depending upon their final scores. If trophy owners do not send their invited trophy to the Judges' Panel, their respective records book listing will be unranked and asterisked in the all-time records book, pending submission of additional verifying measurements by other official measurers. In the case of a potential World's Record, the trophy must come before the Judges' Panel to be certified as the new World's Record. There is no exception to this rule.

Trophies invited to an Awards Program are displayed for an extended period of time at a public museum or exhibit hall preceding the Awards

Banquet. Displays are often held at natural history museums in major metropolitan areas where tens of thousands of people view the trophies before they are returned to their owners, never to be seen assembled together again.

Records of North American Sheep, Rocky Mountain Goats and Pronghorn is a collection of the photographs and statistics that pays tribute to these spectacular examples of North American big game and offers hours of reading enjoyment to wildlife biologists, hunters, game managers, and wildlife researchers who appreciate the wild.

Jack Reneau is director of big game records for the Boone and Crockett Club, a position he has held since January 1983. He is a certified wildlife biologist with The Wildlife Society and holds a B.S. from Colorado State University and a M.S. from Eastern Kentucky University in wildlife management. From 1976 to 1979, Jack was an information specialist for the National Rifle Association's Hunter Services Division and was responsible for the day-to-day paperwork of the Boone and Crockett Club's records keeping activities at a time when NRA and B&C cosponsored the North American Big Game Awards Program. He is co-author of the book, Colorado's Biggest Bucks and Bulls, *and co-editor and designer of sixteen Boone and Crockett Club books.*

Susan Reneau is the author of The Adventures of Moccasin Joe: True Life Story of Sgt. George S. Howard, 1872 to 1877, *and co-author of* Colorado's Biggest Bucks and Bulls. *She is co-editor and designer of seven Boone and Crockett Club books and 28 books for other publishers. She also produces three to five hours of live radio shows per day for Super News Talk 1290 KGVO Radio in Missoula, Montana. She holds a B.A. in education and speech communication from the University of Northern Colorado and a M.S. in business marketing and public relations from American University. Jack and Susan live in Missoula, Montana, with their three teen-age sons and two black Labrador retrievers.*

Photograph from Boone & Crockett Club Archives

Ram River, Alberta, produced this bighorn ram, scoring 187-6/8 points, for famed sheep hunter George W. Parker on October 16, 1961. The increase of B&C rams is testament to the strength of the herd.

Making Mountain Sheep Common

Valerius Geist, Ph.D.

There has been an astonishing rise in the number of record class bighorn rams taken between 1974 and 1994 (Table 1). It is a success worth celebrating. The same cannot be said of desert bighorns or any of the northern thinhorn sheep. These have, apparently, retained fairly constant populations throughout, but the number of high-quality bighorn trophies has expanded dramatically.

The conservation of mountain sheep indeed has had some encouraging success in the past decades, in part due to good science being sensibly turned into good management. It is a fine example of how new insights derived from field research have changed the views of managers about mountain sheep and how to safeguard them. To safeguard a species it is necessary to increase its numbers, expand its geographic distribution, and elevate the quality of its populations so that robust adults produce abundant, viable offspring. The effort put into research has paid off in more and better mountain sheep, with the primary beneficiary being Rocky Mountain bighorns. Quality sheep management, clearly, is here to stay. To understand how it works; that is, how to make mountain sheep common and healthy, one needs to know how they disperse in space and time. In this aspect of their biology, mountain sheep differ greatly from whitetail deer, for instance. It's a contrast in need of closer examination.

Whitetail deer are the primary big-game animal in North America. As a consequence, they are a subject of constant inquiry and discussion among wildlife managers, researchers, and the public. Little wonder, therefore, that – previously – managers applied what they had learned about whitetail deer to other big-game species. That's perfectly understandable in the absence of sound knowledge about other big-game species. However, whitetail deer differ profoundly from mountain sheep, and early attempts to manage bighorns as if they were whitetail deer could not lead to anything but disappointment. Here is why.

Whitetail deer evolved as specialists in quickly exploiting forage resources on sites disturbed by fire, floods, and storms. They are ecological opportunists, a "weed species," and they have been supremely good at it for about four million years. They co-evolved with specialists in forage competition; that is, in the removal of all high-quality plant food. The former competitors of whitetail deer virtually all went extinct at the end of the last ice age. They had formed for more than two million years several successions of species – rich faunas in North America, composed of many species of horses, camels, guanacos, bison, forest and mountain muskox, bighorns, mountain goats, elephants, mastodons, ground sloths, pronghorns, and other deer species. Whitetail deer prospered by fitting "between the cracks" of the food specialists, by quickly finding the high-quality forages on disturbed sites, and skimming the very best food to quickly turn it into more whitetail deer. They evolved excellent means of detecting places where fires, storms, and floods had torn holes into climax plant communities, and where early succession plants flourished until they were replaced again with climax plant species. In the meantime, the forbs, shrubs, and baby trees that grew on the disturbed site offered a high-quality forage that whitetail deer exploited. Consequently, whitetail deer have an inherently high reproductive rate. Females may give birth to twins, even triplets. On excellent forage females grow rapidly to large body size and mature early; some breed as young as six months old, giving birth when they are only one-year-old. Before giving birth, pregnant females disperse the fawns of the previous year, or may move out themselves to give birth in a new, superior locality. The fawns hide after birth, a most successful (and thus common) survival strategy of deer that allows fawns to be rather small at birth and to grow relatively slowly to survivable size. A big investment in large fawns is thus not needed for success by whitetail deer. The fawns see relatively little of their mothers and come equipped by nature with a package of excellent survival instincts. While whitetails have very clever instincts, as individuals they are not very clever – despite what frustrated hunters might think.

In addition to an intrinsically high reproductive rate and social behavior that helps disperse yearlings, whitetail deer readily roam on their own and are ready to abandon a home range if unfavorable circumstances so warrant. While as yet unstudied in whitetail deer, it was shown in the related roe deer that the bigger the yearlings grow in body size, the wider they dispersed geographically. Therefore, the better the food resource the higher the reproduction and the wider the dispersal.

The down side of this is, of course, that whitetail deer are very poor competitors. They are readily displaced by other species, such as sika deer or red deer. This explains the many failures at introducing whitetail

2

deer in New Zealand and in Europe. While whitetail deer flourish in Finland, they do so in the absence of competing deer species and on agricultural and closely managed (disturbed) forest lands. It also explains why the archeological record shows a sharp increase in deer numbers following the post-glacial extinction of North America's native specialist fauna about 10,000 years ago. When this fauna was still intact, whitetail deer were very rare. When their competitors died out, whitetails exploded in numbers and expanded their range. They flourished not only post-glacially, but also with native horticulture and the skilled fire-management by native North Americans in pre-Colombian times. That is, native people may have managed the land so as to deliberately increase the numbers of whitetail deer. Today's abundance of whitetail deer is largely a function of massive surface disturbances by agriculture, forestry, and urban development. From the ecological perspective, cropping, logging, and city building sets back ecological succession, and whitetails are designed by nature to take advantage of just that.

What does this have to do with mountain sheep? Plenty! To manage for deer you need to create habitat, and deer will, normally, quickly take you up on it. That is, create habitat and whitetail deer will follow automatically. The major problem then is likely to be too may deer, rather than too few. Deer, after all, do cause traffic problems and may become a pest in suburbs and on crop land. Wildlife managers are likely to fight for more liberal kills of deer by hunters, against prevailing public opinion that wants to protect deer as most persons never see enough of them. With disperser-type species such as whitetail deer, cotton-tails, pheasants, or ptarmigan, hunting mortality is largely compensatory, and has normally little impact on populations. This type of management, however, would spell disaster for North American mountain sheep – as some mangers noted with distress about four decades ago.

What was the problem? The problem lay in several unknowns in the biology of mountain sheep. Mountain sheep were apparently not capable dispersers. Some relict populations occupied only a fraction of the available habitat, while areas that looked equally good as sheep habitat lay abandoned. This was odd in view of the huge areas sheep had colonized in prehistoric times. Yet ecological information suggested early on that mountain sheep could not be good dispersers, given the nature of plant communities they exploited. Normally, bighorns live on patches of permanent grassland. Such can be occasionally expanded at the edges by forest fires, but normally mountain sheep habitat consists of patches of grassland and alpine tundra and the distribution and size of these patches is pretty well fixed. In the immediate future the problem a mountain sheep population faces is to retain the scattered pieces of habitat within one whole, functional home range.

Sheep must establish mental maps of where and when to go from patch to patch. They do so by carefully choosing as youngsters whom to follow. Young rams, notoriously, follow large horned rams. This is eminently sensible. Large horns are a function of the amount and quality of food a ram has eaten. The better the food, the larger the horns. Alternatively, horns may grow large with age. That can only happen if their bearer occupies superior security terrain on his seasonal home ranges. Since body and horn size are vitally important in ranking males before breeding, the larger the horns and body, the disproportionately greater the chances of breeding females. Consequently, following a large-horned ram reveals to the young male either better places to eat or safer places, quite acceptable alternatives. That is, home range in mountain sheep is normally not something obtained through individual exploration, as in whitetail deer, but obtained as a cultural inheritance from the population of older sheep. Therefore, having good sheep habitat is, by itself, not enough to generate a good sheep population. Sheep have, normally, no ready mechanism to find abandoned or man-created patches of habitat. We have to lead them there – or place them there. One thus needs, in addition to sheep habitat, skills at introducing bighorns to unoccupied habitat.

Once this was understood by researchers and managers, it was self-evident that to safeguard mountain sheep it was necessary to re-introduce sheep to abandoned ranges. We know now that, normally, it is futile to sit and wait hoping that mountain sheep will colonize these empty ranges. Multiplying sheep became a matter of re-introducing sheep to historic habitat that stood empty.

That was not the whole story, but before turning to it, why should mountain sheep act so different from whitetail deer? Bighorns are primarily grazers and good competitors. They are tied psychologically to "safe terrain" – steep slopes, ragged cliffs, occasionally dense forests – where they can readily escape predators. Within the proximity of that terrain they graze out the food reserves. Thus they stay normally only short times – two to four weeks – on seasonal home ranges before moving on to another seasonal range. Good sheep habitat is quite rare during warm inter-glacial periods such as we live in currently. During interglacial

Photograph Courtesy of Chris L. Mostad

Chris L. Mostad with one of the 121 bighorn sheep accepted in B&C Club's 20th Awards Program (1986-1988). Chris took this outstanding 8-year-old ram on Petty Creek in Missoula County, Montana, during the 1990 hunting season. It scores 190-5/8 points.

periods forests surged over areas previously covered by open grass land. This obliterates much sheep habitat and fragments the rest. The scattered patches, however, are retained in the population memory by sheep and the animals visit these dispersed patches in a regular, predictable fashion during the yearly cycle. Therefore, in undisturbed regions, sheep regularly visit widely scattered patches, making use of a maximum of the available habitat patches. Thus, for sheep to find unknown habitat is unlikely. That is, even if a ram bent on exploration did find one of the rare habitat patches, chances are that it is already occupied by other sheep and used regularly within an annual tradition of movements. Such roaming is also very dangerous, as the exploring sheep may be surprised by a predator in dense cover, and caught for lack of escape terrain. For young sheep it is, therefore, safer and more rewarding to follow older sheep and learn from them about good places to feed and live secure from predators.

During the last glacial period, when huge continental glaciers covered northern North America, huge, long-legged bighorn sheep lived on open glacial loess steppe and periglacial tundra in the West. During that time forests were reduced to small patches and mountain sheep could roam freely over large areas without being confined by huge tracts of forest, as they are today. The warm interglacial climates changed all that as forests expanded, covering and fracturing sheep habitat into small, disjunct patches. Sheep, however, continued to migrate between the shrinking patches, stitching such together into large, viable home ranges. That's why following others with superior habitat knowledge is a safe bet for young bighorns.

This paradigm of sheep biology poses several problems, but also opportunities for conservation. The mountain sheep manager must think not only about habitat, but also about how to keep sheep from wandering off if disturbed or how to restore them to vacant habitat. Harassment that alienates mountain sheep from critical habitat patches can lead to sheep permanently abandoning those patches. That may spell the end of a herd and most certainly leads to shrinkage in sheep numbers. Harassment and re-introductions are subjects that bighorn sheep managers must be routinely concerned with, but which managers of whitetail deer need not worry about too much.

Moreover, bighorns have a lower intrinsic rate of reproduction than do whitetail deer. Our mountain sheep, normally, give birth to one young only. The lamb follows its dam almost constantly. When it does separate from its mother after weaning it does so gradually. As a yearling it is kept in the company of other sheep. Older, barren ewes make a point of attracting yearlings to themselves, while their mothers go off to lamb in hiding. Yearlings may also temporarily follow rams, or stay in the company of other yearlings. They do not roam about, and if they do, it is to look for other sheep. It is as if bighorn society is "designed" to closely retain yearlings, where as whitetail deer society has evolved to disperse theirs.

Once that insight became common currency, it justified vigorous reintroduction programs. These led, of necessity, to large-horned rams and record trophies during the early growth phases of introduced sheep populations. It so happens that in probably all vertebrate species, individuals change in size and body proportions with the quality of their environment, in particular, with the quality and quantity of their food. The more abundant, but above all, the higher the protein levels in the ingested food, the larger the lambs, the richer the milk, and the bigger the adults. Moreover, the sheep not only change physically, but also in their behavior. The bigger they get the more likely they explore and disperse. Consequently, one has in newly established, fast-growing young populations big-dispersal-type individuals and in old, mature populations with shortages of high-quality food, one has small-maintenance type sheep. While mountain sheep in maintenance-type populations do not disperse readily, they will do some surprising dispersal in populations of dispersal types. Therefore, a vigorous program of reintroductions not only increases sheep numbers, but also leads to unexpected dispersal and colonization, as well as to – initially – big-bodied sheep that grow large, heavy horns.

One can, of course, increase sheep populations by changing forest to open grassland using control burning. Vegetation on control burns will almost certainly be of higher quality than on established, well-used ranges. This will give a boost to both reproduction by females and horn-growth by males. However, one can go even further. One can create custom sheep habitat.

An opportunity to create mountain sheep habitat may exist in strip mines close to where sheep occur naturally. Instead of filling in the deep cuts, one can re-engineer the land surface so that rock faces serve as escape terrain and vegetated slopes close by are converted to forage sites. One such experiment in Alberta is now generating not only an abundance of bighorns, but also the body size of the bighorns is steadily increasing while the biodiversity of the rehabilitated strip mine is also increasing year by year. These bighorns are becoming the largest in Alberta, and the end is not in sight. One can thus create a wildlife oasis, an artificial one for sure, but one that attracts not only bighorn sheep, but also elk, deer, grizzly bears, wolves, wolverine, marmots, and an ever-increasing number of bird species. A few bighorns that lived within the scenic mountains of Jasper National Park did find our artificial sheep habitat in the reclaimed mine site and refused to leave it. This was proof positive that we had built habitat highly attractive to bighorns, but it also got us into trouble with the park authorities. Creating custom wildlife habitat out of strip mines may also be cheaper than conventional mine rehabilitation.

Some environmentalists resent the aesthetics of the artificial sheep habitat and have subsequently condemned it as producing "domestic" bighorns. This is nonsense as the bighorns using these mines are everything but domestic. Moreover, what is the alternative? Growing trees on artificial surfaces? If so, why not grow wildlife on artificial surfaces – unless the critics prefer the aesthetics and ecology of an unreclaimed strip mine. Some strip mines may thus become mountain sheep habitat and produce vigorous populations of large sheep. Such are expected to generate trophy rams.

Good science thus can take the mystery out of mountain sheep management and may improve the success of ongoing efforts. And so it is with introductions or reintroductions. The study of mountain sheep biology teaches that young sheep accept the home range knowledge of older sheep by following them. If so, catching bands of sheep, corralling them on the release site, and then letting them go will, theoretically, only colonize the patch of habitat on which the sheep were liberated. The released sheep are expected to explore the new site to the limits of open habitat and not go beyond. In practice, some dispersal may occur if the sheep population grows steeply after introduction and large-bodied dispersal-type sheep are grown. Is it possible to mimic nature's way and give reintroduced sheep an opportunity to accept home range knowledge by following a knowledgeable leader? After all, that's what happens naturally. Why not mimic nature on this point?

To do that would require mapping disjunct pieces of potential habitat; hiking between these to establish short, safe routes for sheep to follow; then having a researcher act as an adult sheep surrogate by leading lambs over these trails to the disjunct patches. Theoretically, this ought to be a superior method of establishing sheep populations. Yet there are drawbacks: it will leave thoroughly tame sheep on the mountains that will seek out human company. Tame bighorn rams may be dangerous during the rut and can certainly knock out humans and inflict injuries as I am able to attest. Tame sheep may follow passing hikers to unexpected places. Certainly, the bighorns I studied would follow me anywhere once they knew and trusted me, including through long stretches of dense forest that were strange to them.

We also know more today about livestock diseases that can be transmitted to mountain sheep. These may suffer severe mortality if they come close to domestic sheep. This insight has also become basic to choosing sites for the reintroduction of bighorn sheep.

As long as there is historical mountain sheep habitat unoccupied by sheep, as long as there is industrial land that can be skillfully converted to high-quality sheep habitat, there is the potential to produce huge trophy rams. Such rams arise within rapidly growing new herds. Maintenance-type bighorn populations are not expected to grow record size heads, as are dispersal-type populations. The rapid increase in large trophy rams taken in the past 20 years is thus a sign that reintroductions to former sheep habitat and the reclamation of spent strip mines are generating fine, rapidly growing bighorn populations. It's a good sign. It suggests that the transplants are taking well. There will be more bighorns living in the future than there are alive today. Let us hope that science can help other wild sheep, such as the struggling desert bighorns, to form large, secure populations.

Valerius Geist, Ph.D., is Professor Emeritus of Environmental Science at The University of Calgary in Alberta, Canada. He has authored or edited twelve books and has written more than a hundred refereed papers and a greater number of popular articles, book chapters and encyclopedia entries. His research and technical writing has won several awards by professional societies, including the 1971 Book of the Year award by The Wildlife Society for Mountain Sheep. *Dr. Geist has been an editorial consultant to various encyclopedias, as well as to several book and television productions for the National Geographic Society. His latest books are* Buffalo Nation, Moose *and* The Deer of the World.

Photograph Courtesy of Foundation for North American Wild Sheep

The Southeast Oregon bighorn sheep restoration project is one of the many outstanding projects funded by FNAWS with the goal "to put sheep on the mountains."

Foundation For North American Wild Sheep

Daniel A. Pedrotti

Man's admiration of the magnificent wild sheep of North America dates back 12,000 years ago to the age of the nomadic tribes of our earliest inhabitants, as seen from paleoliths found in caves and primitive shelters depicting rams, ewes, and lambs. Modern man's fascination with wild sheep began with our earliest settlers and explorers. Today's awareness and desire for these beautiful rams can be traced to the writings of such great hunters as Elgin Gates, Elmer Keith, Charles Sheldon, and Jack O'Connor and his wife Eleanore.

That we have huntable numbers of this species today must be attributed to the early conservation efforts of the Boone and Crockett Club and more recently to the work of the Foundation for North American Wild Sheep (FNAWS).

The 22nd Awards Program of the Boone and Crockett Club covering the years 1992, 1993 and 1994 recognized five bighorn rams taken in Montana with official scores in excess of 200. This is a remarkable statistic when one considers the fact that as of 1980 there were only ten rams listed from Montana that exceeded a score of 190, yet today more than 75 are listed and all came from reintroduced populations.

As native habitat for all North American big-game species continued to shrink during the late 1970s, 1980s, and into the first half of the 1990s, due to human encroachment, a remarkable phenomenon occurred – wild sheep numbers actually increased. New herds were established in many of the ancestral ranges where native populations had disappeared decades before. Existing herds became stronger and many more sheep hunting opportunities became available.

It is not a mere coincidence that in 1974 a group of dedicated sheep hunters met at Mt. Horeb, Wisconsin, to discuss ways that they could conserve the magnificent wild sheep for themselves and future generations to hunt and enjoy. A second meeting was held in Des Moines, Iowa, in 1976 and this led to the formation of The Foundation for North American Wild Sheep in 1977, for the express purpose of putting wild sheep on the mountains of North America. The first formal FNAWS convention met in Memphis, Tennessee, on February 2-4, 1978. This meeting drew 400 participants and raised $44,000 for sheep projects.

Word of the new sheep organization was spread to all sheep hunters by Bob Householder, founder of the North American Sheep Hunter's Association and the Grand Slam Club. Bob edited and published the Grand Slam Club bulletin that contained sheep hunting stories and maintained a file on all hunters who had taken the four species of North American wild sheep.

Membership numbers grew rapidly so that by the 1980 convention in Houston, Texas, more than 800 were present. This year marked the beginning of the sheep horn plugging program and also was the inaugural year for governors' permits to be utilized as fund raisers for wild sheep.

The governors of Utah and Wyoming each set aside a special sheep hunting opportunity to be sold at the FNAWS convention to raise money for wild sheep. The governor of Utah offered a sheep permit to the first person to donate $20,000 to the Foundation for sheep work in Utah. Fred L. Morris of Salt Lake City stepped forward and received the first "Governor's Permit." The Wyoming permit was put in the live auction and Dr. George Vogt of Houston, Texas, bought it with a bid of $23,000.

The Wyoming permit, given to FNAWS every year by the governor, is unique in that all of the proceeds go to FNAWS to be used at its discretion for Grant-In-Aid projects. This permit sold for $55,000 in 1993 and has led thirteen other states and the country of Mexico to become active participants in this program. The all-time record price for a governor's permit was paid in San Antonio in 1994 when Jerry Fletcher of Phoenix, Arizona, donated $310,000 for the right to hunt a ram in any of the sheep hunting areas of Montana. Jerry saw many sheep but chose not to take one in 1994.

The first chapter of the Foundation, the Iowa Chapter, was chartered in 1979 and today boasts 165 members. The International Sheep Hunters Association and the Utah Bighorn Sheep Society were the first affiliates. The Arizona Desert Bighorn Sheep Society (ADBSS) joined FNAWS in 1980. This affiliate, with 1,500 members, has directed more than $2.5 million plus an inordinate amount of hard work, management skills, and political clout for the benefit of the desert bighorn sheep of Arizona, surrounding states, and Mexico. FNAWS now has ten chapters and ten affiliates with more than 5,000 members.

The Texas Chapter of FNAWS, disturbed by the impending

de-emphasis of the sheep program in Texas, met at the Phoenix Convention in 1981 and determined to do something about the situation. This group organized The Texas Bighorn Society for the express purpose of restoring desert sheep to the mountains of West Texas. Headed by such avid hunters and aggressive personalities as Dr. Red Duke, Bill Leech, Gib Lewis, Edwin L. Cox, and many others, this affiliate set out to lobby the Texas Legislature to keep the sheep program alive and then proceeded to raise more than $200,000, including help from FNAWS, to build the Sierra Diablo Brood Facility near Van Horne, Texas, to propagate desert bighorn lambs. With brood stock provided by Arizona, Nevada, and Utah, Texas can now count more than 500 wild sheep in five different mountain ranges. Texas has provided three governor's permits for auction at FNAWS conventions that have generated a total of $208,000 for wild sheep projects.

The Arizona convention in 1981 provided the membership with their first opportunity to do hands-on work for wild sheep. ADBSS, along with the Arizona Fish and Game Department, sponsored the "Betty Lou Tank," a water development project in the Plomosa Mountains. More than 135 workers turned out, including 45 visiting FNAWS members. They spent two nights on the desert floor and in two days created a water hole that to this day still provides critical water for sheep and other wildlife. Each year FNAWS members travel to Arizona to be a part of the ongoing water development program and in 1995 prior to the convention in Phoenix, a group of FNAWS members again participated in the construction of a water hole project.

The foregoing paragraphs provide some examples of how FNAWS and its founders have created an atmosphere of awareness that prompted wildlife departments and wildlife conservation groups throughout North America, along with big-game hunters worldwide, to do something about declining wild sheep populations. Big-game outfitters, wildlife artists, biologists, hunters, and benefactors have been mobilized and continue to raise funds in huge amounts to "Put Sheep on the Mountains."

FNAWS, a 99 percent volunteer group of hunters and conservationists, moved to its present headquarters in Cody, Wyoming, in the spring of 1987. This organization, run by Executive Director Karen Werbelow, six full-time employees and an all-volunteer 11-member board of directors, honestly can boast that it returns the largest percentage of gross revenues to wildlife projects of all the conservation groups in America.

Wild Sheep, an excellent quarterly magazine and the official FNAWS

Photograph Courtesy of Foundation for North American Wild Sheep

Volunteers repair a big-game guzzler as part of a project funded by FNAWS in San Bernardino County, California. Their efforts are paying big dividends as five desert sheep, ranging in scores from 167-7/8 to 175-1/8 points, have been accepted from this area in B&C's archives since 1992.

14

publication, is collated and edited by the staff. All other communications with the members, directors, advertisers, donors, and others are handled in Cody by this efficient team. Merchandise sales, convention planning, chapter liaison, outfitter problems, public relations, budgeting, and all other FNAWS business falls under the supervision of the executive director, who serves subject to the approval of the Board of Directors.

FNAWS will celebrate the 20th anniversary of its charter at the annual convention in Philadelphia, Pennsylvania, in February of 1997. During these twenty years, more than $18 million has been funded directly for sheep projects. These funds are generated primarily at annual conventions, lotteries, fund-raising banquets by chapters and affiliates, and through the sale of special sheep hunting permits granted by governors of various states with huntable sheep populations. Distribution of these funds is controlled by the Board of Directors through approved Grant-In-Aid and chapter and affiliate funding. The proceeds from special state permits are returned to the states to be used solely for sheep projects.

In addition, hundreds of volunteers, working with state wildlife departments and federal agencies, provide countless hours for "on-the-ground" projects such as water development, sheep transplants, surveys, habitat enhancement, predator control, and a myriad of other important tasks beneficial to wild sheep. The volunteer work during and prior to conventions also numbers into thousands of hours. All of this is accomplished by an organization of just over 6,000 dedicated members, united by the lofty purposes of wild sheep conservation and preservation of our rights to hunt these awe inspiring creatures.

Had this group, composed primarily of hunters, not wished to put something back on the mountains in return for the many wonderful hours of quality experiences that had been theirs to enjoy because of the privilege to hunt the wild sheep of North America, who knows what the condition of all North American wildlife and their habitat might look like today. The recovery of wild sheep to their indigenous range, in abundance and health, is without a doubt the wildlife success story of this century.

FNAWS is presently in the process of examining its history, resources, and potential in order to embark on a process that will revisit its "Vision" as a prelude to developing a comprehensive "Strategic Plan" for the next century. How many sheep would we like to think could exist on the mountains 100 years from now and what do we have to do in the next year, in the next five years, and in the next ten years to have a chance for this vision to be realized? How many members do we need and how much money must we raise to accomplish this? How do we secure the immortality of FNAWS beyond a time when there may not be sheep hunters in sufficient numbers to provide for the species? These are the burning questions that must be answered not only by FNAWS but also by all hunter-conservation-oriented organizations as earth's human population explodes during the next 50 years.

A historical opportunity to "Put Sheep on the Mountain" has presented itself in the northwestern United States that may lead FNAWS to the answer to some of these questions. Three states – Washington, Oregon, and Idaho – share a common border known as Hell's Canyon where the majestic Snake River has created more than two million acres of pristine sheep habitat. That this is indeed indigenous sheep country is attested to by pictographs drawn in caves by America's earliest hunters.

In recent years, herds of wild sheep, transplanted into Hell's Canyon through the efforts of FNAWS, in cooperation with the various wildlife agencies, the U.S. Bureau of Land Management, and the U.S. Forest Service, have thrived for a time and then declined due to stress and disease, presumably acquired through contact with domestic sheep. As of this writing, the last domestic sheep allotment in Hell's Canyon is being negotiated in exchange for an allotment outside the canyon. This sets the stage for a project to restore wild sheep in numbers equaling the 15,000 estimated to have originally occupied the canyon.

Though this appears to be an awesome undertaking, there exist unique circumstances favoring a resounding success. For the first time, all the federal, state, and local agencies involved, along with FNAWS and its chapters, have come together with a commonality of purpose. There is a genuine determination on the part of all concerned to finally succeed in a conservation effort that will establish the parameters for the 21st century and beyond.

FNAWS has chosen the Hell's Canyon initiative as the first landmark project of its relatively short life. Through the efforts of our past president, Pete Cimellaro, our staff, our Board, and myself personally, FNAWS has pledged to support the states and agencies involved to the fullest extent of our resources. A fund-raising program is underway that will solicit donations in the form of endowments, research grants, specific project funding, and both restricted and unrestricted gifts to be utilized directly in the Hell's Canyon project and/or to fund an endowment to guarantee the survival of FNAWS itself.

Photograph Courtesy of Foundation for North American Wild Sheep

This drop net in Whiskey Basin is an integral part of a bighorn sheep reintroduction project funded by FNAWS in Wind River Canyon, Wyoming.

The Hell's Canyon initiative will provide corporate America, foundations, and individuals an exceptional opportunity to be part of one of the great conservation efforts of modern time. The project can be broken into segments fully sponsored by one entity or by a group of smaller donors collectively. It will provide high visibility, prominent recognition, and the satisfaction of being a part of this great undertaking.

Hell's Canyon has already attained national recognition due to the recent highly publicized wild sheep die-off seemingly caused by pasturella, the dreaded disease often caused by contact with domestic sheep. The massive effort to capture and treat the remaining diseased sheep, sponsored by FNAWS in cooperation with the state, local, and federal agencies involved, drew nationwide television and newspaper coverage.

Despite the disappointment to all Hell's Canyon participants, there is a positive fall out from this incident. Literally hundreds of sheep tissue and blood samples were collected by fish and game personnel from the states involved during the disease outbreak. These samples from both healthy and diseased sheep are safely stored at the Caldwell Research Center laboratories in Idaho. It is believed that the cause and ultimately the cure for these pasturella-induced disease outbreaks will be found through intensive research utilizing the Hell's Canyon samples. FNAWS has already committed to fund a full-time molecular biologist at the Caldwell Center to work with this vast data bank utilizing the most modern technology available to seek the clues that may lead to a cure.

Hell's Canyon is indeed a landmark project for FNAWS but it is not to be considered unique. Instead it represents a major step in the growth of an idea generated a short 24 years ago by believers in their ability to make a difference. Based upon these results other projects of landmark proportions will surely follow.

You are welcomed and encouraged to join this great endeavor by becoming a member of FNAWS and/or making your tax-deductible donations directly to the Foundation or specifically to the Hell's Canyon Initiative by contacting the headquarters at the following address: The Foundation for North American Wild Sheep, 720 Allan Avenue, Cody, WY 82414; Phone: (307) 527-6261, FAX: (307) 527-7117.

Strengthened by the successes described above, we must face the seemingly insurmountable challenges ahead that may be brought on by unchecked population growth, habitat destruction, and the anti-hunting movement with dauntless courage. Remember that in 1887 Teddy Roosevelt and his fellow hunter-conservationists, fearing that big-game in North America would become extinct, chartered the Boone and Crockett Club to prevent such a catastrophe. As a result of this effort, today we have more big game animals roaming the continent than existed 100-years ago.

Who is to say we can't have a 100-year vision for wildlife to be enjoyed by generations not yet even imagined in the minds of man?

Daniel A. Pedrotti, a geologist, is president of an independent oil and gas exploration company, Suemaur Exploration, Inc., in Corpus Christi, Texas. He is the current president of the Foundation for North American Wild Sheep, having served six years as a director. He became a regular member of the Boone and Crockett Club in 1989, chaired the Editorial and Historical Committee in 1993, and oversaw the publication of Records of North American Big Game, 10th Edition, *in 1993. He became vice president of communications in 1994 and has served as first vice president of the Boone and Crockett Club since 1995. Daniel is a founder and past president of the Texas Bighorn Society and a director of the International Sheep Hunters Association.*

Photograph by Bruce L. Smith

Rocky Mountain goats can be exceptionally curious if carefully stalked. This adult male, from a hunted population, approached within ten meters of the author.

The American Mountain Goat: Ace of Alpinists

Bruce L. Smith, Ph.D.

It wasn't until February 9, 1811, at the present location of Kootenay Park in Canada, that the first white man saw the American goat-antelope with characteristics of both, yet closely related to neither. Its closest relatives are the European chamois and the Asiatic gorals and serows. The only member of its genus, *Oreamnos,* has been called white goat, Old Man of the Mountains, American chamois, and Rocky Mountain goat. I prefer American mountain goat (or just mountain goat) because its specific name is *americanus,* and it inhabits both the coastal and Rocky Mountain ranges of the United States and Canada.

Although it occurs only in North America, the mountain goat evolved in Asia and is one of the Pleistocene immigrants to our continent across the Bering Land Bridge at a time when the waters of the Pacific Ocean were 300-400 feet lower than at present. It arrived perhaps 100,000 years ago, and survived south of the Cordilleran ice sheet at the peak of the massive Wisconsin glaciation. Fossils of its ancestors have been found as far south as California and Nevada.

By definition, the mountain goat is a mountain dwelling ruminant, physically adapted for rock climbing and surviving arctic alpine weather conditions, with a highly diverse diet. It has a social structure consisting of a well-defined dominance hierarchy organized into loosely associated female-subadult groups. Males are solitary or found in small bachelor groups during much of the year.

Without question, the mountain goat is the ace of alpinists. North American sheep, although agile in the mountains by ungulate (hoofed animal) standards, possess neither the unique physical adaptations nor the raw ability of the mountain goat on cliffs and crags. While sheep bound crisply across mountain slopes and outcrops, the goat is more of a plodder and inclined to stick to steeper terrain. Leverage, friction, and balance are the tools of his trade. The sheep are free-climbing scramblers; the goat is a technician.

Specialization begins with the hooves. Unlike mountain sheep or any other North American ungulate, the mountain goat has hooves superbly adapted to a life on the rocks. The outer portion of the hoof is a hard, bony material; but the bottom surface of the hoof is a pliable pad, convex in shape. It conforms to uneven surfaces, providing gripping ability. The four "toes" (digits two and three comprising the cloven hoof, and digits one and four being the elevated "dew claws" on the rear of the foot) are large for the goat's body size. These provide a large surface area for traction on rock and support on snow. Digits two and three of the cloven hoof are more flexible than in other ungulates. As the goat descends a rocky face or steep snowfield, the toes spread apart improving balance and providing friction in an outward as well as downward direction. During descents, the goat lowers its hindquarters to reduce its center of gravity and to bring the large dew claws into contact with the substrate, increasing friction and control.

Specialized hooves are only the beginning of the mountain goat's adaptations. Its overall build includes short, stocky legs set relatively close together, and a compact torso with the forequarters decidedly larger than the hindquarters. Although it may trot or lope when startled, this is not an animal built for speed. The compact, short-legged body provides a low center of gravity, balance, and uncanny agility on narrow ledges with nothing but thin air below. The heavily muscled shoulders and forelegs help it trudge through deep snow.

I've watched a goat climb to the top of a dizzying pinnacle and stand – all four feet together – on a summit measuring only eight inches square. Then he raised a hind foot, scratched behind an ear, and shook the dust from his coat.

Rock climbing requires a combination of strength, skill, and confidence (mental attitude). To successfully spend a ten- to twelve-year life span on cliffs requires one other ingredient: patience. Natural selection and good parental training have given mountain goats remarkable patience. Goats "choose" their routes. Their climbing is methodical, even painstaking. They are not averse to abandoning a route and seeking an alternative should the footing become treacherous. Goats are renowned for performing "walk-overs" when a cliff ledge narrows to nothingness. A quick lurch to position their forefeet against the cliff face, followed by walking the feet above the head across the face, and they're ambling back along the ledge nibbling on sedges and groundsels.

While studying mountain goats in Montana's Selway-Bitterroot Wilderness, again and again I was amazed by their patience. High on the cliffs one winter day, I stalked a nanny I wanted to immobilize with my dart gun. I planned my stalk from the canyon bottom to the ledge where she was feeding some 1,000 feet of elevation above me. An hour later, she and I met on the ledge. Startled, she ran out of sight before I could get off a shot. I waited several minutes, then followed. Just beyond an angle in the cliff where the ledge ended in a 75-foot vertical drop, she stood facing me. I couldn't immobilize her there for fear she would plummet from the ledge when she lost control of her limbs. So I retreated some 50 yards and sat, dart gun ready, behind a boulder. Surely she would retrace her steps and I'd dart her as she passed by. Three hours later, with the sun sinking into Idaho, my hands and feet numb, and my patience played out, she remained at the same location. I bid her good night before descending in the twilight. The next morning I spotted her grazing near the boulder where I had waited.

Beyond its specializations for climbing, the mountain goat's most obvious adaptation is its coat. The coarse outer "guard" hairs shed wind and snow and provide the distinctive "goat-like" appearance. Longest on the lower legs, sides of the lower jaw, and along the back (where they stand erect over the shoulders), the six- to seven-inch guard hairs provide the Old Man of the Mountains with pantaloons, beard, and shoulder hump. Beneath the guard hair is an underfur of wool as luxurious as cashmere. This dense layer (goats patented the idea of layering for warmth) insulates him from subzero temperatures and winds of six-month winters. During particularly wet weather, the lee side of outcrops, overhangs, and caves offer goats refuge. Goat caves I've found in Montana's Bitterroot Range and Glacier National Park were carpeted with a decomposing layer of goat dung.

During May, June, and July, goats seem to metamorphose from shaggy beasts of winter into the close-cropped attire they sport in summer. The guard hair of the rump, pantaloons, and front of the beard are often last to shed. With a fresh half-inch of wool adorning the rest of the body, the American mountain goat looks less than elegant, if not comical, as the molt progresses.

The white coat reflects rather than absorbs solar radiation on summer days, enabling them to remain in the security of steep, exposed terrain, rather than seeking the coolness of forests below. Still, on August afternoons, goats may retreat to the shade of cliffs or lounge on remnant snowfields to stay cool.

The ruminant digestive system of the mountain goat and other members of the cattle and deer families, with its four-chambered stomach,

Photograph by Bruce L. Smith

An adult nanny goat and her nine-month-old kid during early spring. Kids generally remain with their mothers for 11 to 12 months. Female subadult groups are composed of adult nannies, their kids, yearlings, and two-year olds of both sexes.

is highly efficient compared to the simple digestive systems of other mammals such as humans and horses. Their digestive efficiency permits mountain goats to utilize a variety of coarse plants in winter when the availability of nutritious green forage is limited in temperate and subarctic regions. Although a specialist in many ways, the goat is a generalist in diet. Winter fare includes grasses and sedges, shrubs, forbs, twigs of deciduous and coniferous trees, mosses, ferns (including rhizomes that are pawed from the soil), and lichens stripped from trees and nibbled from rock surfaces. The diet composition of each food item varies with location across the mountain goat's range, with snow depth, and with stage of growth or curing of each plant.

Finally, I should add a few words about the mountain goat's horns. They are black, upright, dagger-like, and are eight to eleven inches long in adults. The horns are neither spiralled (as in true goats) nor arced (as in wild sheep). They appear similar in both sexes (fact is, there is little difference in appearance between the sexes). The horns constitute formidable weapons when the head is lowered against a would-be predator. However, their primary function is associated with dominance establishment and maintenance in the goat's social hierarchy. A high social position confers breeding rights, access to optimum feeding sites, and relative freedom from challenges by other group and herd members.

The annual cycle of the mountain goat begins with the birth of offspring during late May and early June on winter ranges. A nanny will isolate herself from other goats and produce a single snow-white kid, or rarely twins. Kids are born in particularly rugged, steep terrain, probably as an anti-predator strategy. From the moment of birth, their surroundings are seen as vertical, and this may leave a lasting impression of the way their environment should be oriented.

Newborn kids weigh just six to seven pounds, but are quite precocious. Just thirty minutes after its birth, I watched a kid scrambling to follow its mother across a fell field strewn with bathroom-sized boulders. Being born into such an environment means more than a few bumps on the chin, but predators are relatively few on the cliffs and nannies are doting mothers. When moving across steep slopes, nannies often position themselves just downslope of their kids, presumably to protect against miscues by their youngsters.

Newborns quickly gain strength. Within a week or two of birth, the spring migration to summer range begins as winter's snow recedes from the high country. Summer range offers abundant, nutritious forage (grasses, sedges, and forbs), enabling goats to recover from the previous winter, produce milk for their young, and to lay on fat for the coming winter.

Summers are short in the mountain goat's domain, and the fall migration precedes or coincides with the November breeding season. Heavy snows precipitate the return to winter range.

Fidelity to seasonal ranges – particularly winter ranges – is characteristic of goat herds. Radio-collared individuals have frequented the same section of cliffs year after year, even returning to favored bed sites. Recently introduced goats may exhibit some tendency to wander since they do not have traditional ties to seasonal ranges in their new homes. For example, mountain goats introduced to Montana's Absaroka Mountains in 1960 have colonized contiguous portions of Yellowstone National Park. Likewise, goats transplanted to Idaho's Palisades Range have been observed 20 to 44 airline miles to the north in Grand Teton National Park. This creates a dilemma for Park Service managers, because mountain goats are not native to Grand Teton and Yellowstone. Had colonizing goats originated from pioneering native populations, they would have been welcome. Instead, they are considered exotic species. Government efforts to control goats transplanted to Olympic National Park have met with limited success and significant public opposition, despite National Park Service concerns that endemic plants of the Park are threatened by feeding and dust-bathing activities of mountain goats.

Mountain goats are polygamous, but males do not gather harems. In romance too, patience is virtuous. Billies cautiously approach and sniff females to determine their reproductive status. Submissive posturing is characteristic of male advances. Females not in estrus will threaten or charge their suitors once their personal space of six to eight feet is violated.

The peak of mating occurs near Thanksgiving Day. Once mating is accomplished, males wander off to spend much of winter solitarily or in bachelor groups.

Females, their kids, and subadults (yearlings and two-year-olds) associate in small groups of changing membership. The nanny-kid bond is the only enduring union in goat society, lasting 11 to 12 months. In general, adult females with kids are at the top of the dominance hierarchy, followed by barren females, two-year-olds, and yearlings. Dominance is established and maintained in the pecking order by ritualized displays, postures, and threats. The most intense involve horn contact, which can cause serious injury or death. Displays and avoidance therefore settle most issues of social order.

Despite the much larger size of adult males (150-200 pounds compared to about 125 pounds for adult females in the lower 48 states), billies assume a subdominant role when they encounter female-subadult groups. As a result they often occupy habitat peripheral to the rest of a herd. This reserves the best habitat and food resources for the reproductive segment of the herd and their offspring.

Mountain goats find security in steep rocky terrain and they are seldom far from it. Their evolved survival strategy includes patterned behaviors that enhance security on the cliffs. As Montana goat researcher Douglas Chadwick explained: "The normal activities of mountain goats are interspersed with behavior patterns that have developed as anti-predator devices. These include: the habit of raising the head to look around at intervals while feeding, a proclivity for walking on the outside edges of ledges and overhanging snow cornices to gain a better view of the situation below, pausing on high vantage points during feeding and traveling to gaze for long periods of time and test the wind before going on, the selection of bed sites that overlook the landscape and have a high wall behind them, a routine of carefully surveying their surroundings for several minutes before bedding down, and rising and turning every half hour or so to scan the terrain anew and then re-bedding to face a different direction than before (though this is probably for the sake of relieving stiffness too)."

As its behavior suggests, the mountain goat relies mainly on sight and smell for detection of danger. In the goat's noisy environment of wind, falling rock, cascading water, and snowslides, small noises rarely draw its attention. With a cliff at the goat's back that only it can climb, it seldom looks for danger above. Furthermore, daytime air currents generally carry upslope. Herein lies his vulnerability. Most of my successful stalks, whether for observation, photography, or immobilizing animals, were approaches from above. More often than not, this involves a climb up the cliffs out of view of the stalkee, a traverse, and then descent to the last observed location. Sometimes the fruits of this labor are warm droppings in an abandoned bed site. However, this technique often rewards the stalker.

Despite this vulnerability to approach from above, successful attack on this ledge-dweller is quite another proposition. Predation is a relatively unimportant source of mortality in most goat herds. Likewise competitors are scarce in the goat's chosen habitat. On winter ranges, mule deer are

Table 7. Hunting Regulations for Rocky Mountain Goats

State/ Province	Hunting Permits in 1996	Range of Permits Since 1986	Goat Age Restrictions	Goat Sex Restrictions	Application Limitations	Harvest Criteria
Alaska	662[A]	452-662[A]	None	Encourage taking males	None	2-10% of observed goats[B]
Colorado	112	82-120	Encourage taking mature goats	None	5-year wait to reapply if harvest a goat	5-8% of population
Idaho	59	64	None	Nannies with kids are protected	Can harvest only one goat in lifetime	Less than 5% of non-kid goats[C]
Montana	283	280-330	None	Encourage taking males	7-year wait to draw again	None[D]
Oregon	2	E	None	Encourage taking adult males	Can draw only one permit in lifetime	None
South Dakota	5	4-5	None	Encourage taking adult males	Can draw only one permit in lifetime	Less than 5% of known population
Utah	20	10-20	None	Encourage taking adult males	Can draw only one permit in lifetime	None[D]
Washington	106	106-325	Minimum 4" horn length	Encourage not taking nannies with kids	None, preference points awarded	Less than 4% of known population
Wyoming	12	8-12	None	Encourage taking males	5-year wait to draw again	None
Alberta	0[F]	0-35	Not applicable	Not applicable	Not applicable	Not applicable
British Columbia	3,268[G]	2,024-3,268[G]	None	Encourage taking males	None	2-5% of estimated population
Northwest Territories	H	H	None	None	None	None
Yukon	3[I]	3[I]	Kids are protected	Nannies with kids are protected	None	None

[A] Alaska offers three types of goat permits: drawing permits (numbers shown in this column, drawn by lottery); registration permits, which can be obtained directly at specified vendors and have ranged from 1,882-2,237 in recent years; and limited numbers of tier II permits for subsistence hunting, which have ranged from 46-105 in recent years.
[B] Varies with productivity of individual herds.
[C] Also up to 5% of non-kid goats can be harvested if twinning rate exceeds 50% of females; and only herds with at least 50 goats are subject to harvest.
[D] Varies with population productivity.
[E] Goats only previously hunted during 1965-1968.
[F] Mountain goat season has been closed since 1987.
[G] British Columbia offers limited entry permits (numbers shown in this column), and general open season permits (no limitations on permit numbers) in the northern third of the province.
[H] No restrictions on permit numbers but very little interest in goat hunting in Northwest Territories.
[I] The Yukon offers limited entry permits (numbers shown in this column), and general open season permits (57-95 issued annually during past 10 years) for very inaccessible areas.

occasionally seen. Mountain sheep may occur in the same general area but prefer windblown ridges rather than cliffs. However, where mountain goats have been transplanted to ranges with limited cliffy terrain, they may compete with native sheep herds.

Mountain lions, golden eagles, and occasionally even bears and wolverines may prey upon this gentle mountaineer. The primary sources of natural mortality among goats, however, are the perils of spending winter in steep, snowbound habitats. Winter tends to weed out the weak and less fit of most species in northern latitudes. Winters are just a little longer and more treacherous if you are a mountain goat. As snow blankets winter ranges, food becomes scarce, and the goats must expend more energy to travel and paw for their next meal. Thus their catholic diet.

Prime feeding sites are on steep slopes and narrow ledges where radiant energy and gravity remove snow. Food occurs in small patches. Given the rigid organization within goat society, it is impractical for large groups to exploit patchy food sources on cliffs. As winter progresses, snow crusts. Pawing becomes difficult. Forage becomes depleted. More calories are expended to fill the rumen. And the nutritional quality of the diet declines. If the weather does not break by early spring, malnutrition begins to affect some animals.

Kid goats enter winter weighing a mere 30-40 pounds – considerably smaller than young of any of our other northern latitude ungulates. At this size, the surface to volume ratio (and therefore heat loss) is high; stamina to paw for food is limited; and legs are too short to move efficiently through deep snow. Kids are dependent on their mothers to break trail; to paw feeding craters; to provide protection from larger, more dominant goats; and for some measure of body heat and wind protection when bedded. Still survival can be problematic when you're 35 pounds and winter lasts six months. Annual winter mortality among kids ranges from 30 percent to 60 percent in studied goat herds. The more severe the winter, the higher the death rate.

Yearlings fare only slightly better. At only half of adult size, and no longer enjoying the social rank of a protective mother, they must remain alert to aggression from all other members of female-subadult groups. During one winter in Montana's Selway-Bitterroot Wilderness, over-winter mortality of yearlings was 29 percent.

Once winter subsides in late March and April, the mountain goat is not over the hump. In fact, spring can be the most treacherous time of year for young and old, male and female alike. This is the season of avalanches. The sliding of snow on goat winter ranges can be an awesome spectacle when conditions are right. During the day, exposed rock absorbs solar heat and melts adjacent snow, which flows and freezes under large snowfields. Fluctuation of temperatures around the freezing point causes slabs of snow, both small and immense, to slide off ledges, crash over cliffs, and plunge down debris chutes, carrying ice, rock, and vegetation along for the ride. This is not a good time to live on a cliff.

But the shedding of snow by the mountains is both a blessing and a curse. Avalanches expose new patches of food to winter-weary goats. But they are also the single greatest cause of goat mortality. Many researchers have found the crumpled remains of goats in avalanche debris in spring. The carcasses serve as carrion for bears, coyotes, ravens, and other scavengers.

Thus, the Old Man of the Mountain pays a price for his security in the cliffs. The hoary marmot, the mammal with which the mountain goat's distribution most closely coincides, avoids the perils of winter by hibernating from October to June. Far beneath winter's white blanket, it lives off stored fat manufactured from last summer's crop of glacier lilies and sheep fescue. It never hears the avalanches that thunder down the mountains as it hunkers against the cliffs.

Despite the rigors of long winters and perilous springs, the mountain goat has roamed the North American cordilleras since his ancestors crossed the Bering Land Bridge from Asia. Today it inhabits most of his historic range. Transplants have expanded this range to the states of Colorado, Nevada, Oregon, South Dakota, and Utah.

Until midway through this century, there was so little concern for goats' welfare that only two studies had been conducted on the species. The possible misconception that mountain goats were safe from exploitation, due to the inaccessibility of their habitat and their relatively poor table fare, resulted in their neglect as a species to be "managed."

Studies in the 1970s and 1980s in Canada and the United States showed that: (1) harvest of females (either-sex harvest had been the rule in all states and provinces with huntable goat populations) may reduce productivity and recruitment in mountain goat populations; and (2) removal of goats from a population by hunting increases overall mortality, rather than substituting for other kinds of losses. This latter point requires some explanation.

For most hoofed big-game species, wildlife managers recognize that a harvestable surplus exists. In place of the natural mortality that would occur, they plan to remove the annual surplus by hunting. Some animals still die in winter because hunters cannot necessarily select the old, weak, or less fit. With bighorn sheep, females, young, and subadults are subject to harvest in only the most productive populations. This is the case because of the species relatively low reproductive rate and high winter mortality. By protecting the reproductive segment of the herd, managers can provide for a harvest without reducing herd size over time.

Like bighorn, mountain goats have low reproductive rates and high natural mortality – primarily among kids and yearlings. But unlike bighorns, the sexes are not readily distinguishable in the field without training and practice. As a result, harvests of goats were traditionally not restricted to males, and often removed nearly as many females as males. Because the mountain goat is considered a trophy species, hunters primarily kill adults, which have larger horns and bodies than subadults. Thus, harvests erode some of the reproductive potential of herds and do not compensate for natural mortality, which is concentrated in younger age classes. This factor combined with historically liberal hunting regulations, uneven distribution of harvest among individual goat herds within large hunting units, expanded road access to goat ranges, and management prescriptions based primarily on harvest trends led to declines in mountain goat populations throughout North America during this century.

Hunter success – an important ingredient in designing seasons for plains and forest-dwelling ungulates – can be a weak and misleading indication of population trend and well-being of goats. Three particular characteristics of mountain goats account for this: (1) their rigid social hierarchy in which dominant females occupy prime habitats, (2) fidelity of herds and their offspring to seasonal ranges, and (3) the goat's reluctance to colonize new habitats. Where hunting occurs on or adjacent to winter ranges, hunters tend to frequent the most accessible areas where they have seen the most goats. These are generally habitats occupied by female-subadult groups. Males may associate with females if the rut is in progress and some hunters work to distinguish and bag a billy. However, females are inevitably harvested also, under either-sex harvest regulations. Removal of several females vacates prime habitats, which are then occupied by the next most dominant animals – other adults and two-year-old females. Those may be harvested in future years as they and the hunters return to prime goat habitats. Hunter success may remain high, but the herd is shrinking. Natural mortality continues among juveniles.

With fewer females in the herd, the number of kids born each year declines. Harvest of nannies may also reduce the chances of over-winter survival of their kids. Thus wildlife managers now recognize the importance of surveying goat populations to estimate population size, trend, reproduction, and the recruitment of last year's kids into the yearling age class.

In 1996, nine states and three Canadian provinces supported huntable goat populations. Outside of British Columbia, which harbors more goats, by far, than any other province or state (about 50,000), wildlife managers either encourage or require the harvest of male goats or at least discourage the harvest of females with kids at heel. Brochures and classes help hunters learn distinguishing characteristics of the sexes. Except in some productive, introduced herds, harvest rates are generally held to 5 percent or less of pre-season goat numbers.

Range expansion has been accomplished in recent decades solely as a result of transplants. Transplanted into suitable ranges, mountain goats can do very well and reproduce at a higher rate than native herds. This has occurred, for example, since the introduction of 12 goats between 1969 and 1971 into the Snake River Range of eastern Idaho. By 1983, the herd had grown to 142 animals and 29 percent of the nannies produced twin offspring that year. The lesson from past introductions into unexploited habitat is that an initial boom is followed by an eventual bust. The population declines dramatically and is slow to recover – if it does. Instituting well-conceived annual harvests before a population approaches the carrying capacity of its habitat can avert this outcome. In 1983, the first hunting season was implemented in the Snake River Range to try to stem the herd's rapid growth. The herd has since been hunted annually, now numbers about 250, and also serves as transplant stock for depleted native herds in central Idaho.

Even when modestly harvested, native goat herds tend not to over-populate their range as can occur with pronghorn antelope and deer family members. Mother Nature continues to regulate herd sizes through the delicate interworkings of social behavior, fidelity to seasonal habitats, and the hardships of winter. The stability of populations in the U.S. and Canadian national parks suggests that populations are self-regulating, left undisturbed on historically occupied ranges. However, alterations of their habitat can upset that stability. Energy development and logging have directly or indirectly precipitated declines in remote goat herds in Alberta, Idaho, and Montana. The inaccessibility of resources in goat country has historically protected them from extinction. However, creating access adjacent to goat cliffs can be as devastating to a herd as actual loss of habitat. In more than one case, overharvest and poaching have followed after a gravel road replaced a pack trail to a herd's winter range. Roads punched along ridge tops above goat cliffs render goats particularly vulnerable.

Because of their specialized niche, mountain goats can't just "go somewhere else" when their wilderness haunts are tamed by human enterprise. "Somewhere else" will likely not be suited to their specialized lifestyle and may well subject these cliff dwellers to additional stresses in habitats to which they are not adapted. Goat ranges are unique wilderness areas inhabited by this unique wilderness beast.

After observing, photographing, and studying mountain goats during the past three decades, I'm still inspired and amazed by them. Their placid nature, superb adaption to a vertical and often inhospitable environment, doting maternal care of their young, respect of social position, and independent spirit make them a very special part of North America's wildlife heritage. In many ways, the mountain goat is a symbol of the American wilderness, and like wilderness, presents a clear challenge to us. The future of both are braided together – to conserve the animal, we must conserve the wild places it cannot do without.

Bruce L. Smith of Jackson, Wyoming, has a B.S. and M.S. degree in wildlife biology from the University of Montana. For his master's degree he studied winter ecology of mountain goats in Montana's Selway-Bitterroot Wilderness Area for three years. Bruce received his doctorate in zoology from the University of Wyoming in 1994. His research concerned population regulation of the Jackson, Wyoming, elk herd. He has been employed by the U.S. Fish and Wildlife Service for eighteen years, including four years as the wildlife biologist on the Wind River Indian Reservation and fourteen years as the wildlife biologist at the National Elk Refuge and ungulate ecologist in Grand Teton National Park. He is currently the wildlife biologist for the National Elk Refuge, Jackson, Wyoming. He has authored more than 25 technical and popular papers dealing primarily with American mountain goats, elk and moose.

Photograph by Bart W. O'Gara

Groups of does are collected by individual bucks, with the number of does in a harem depending on the aggressiveness and vigor of a particular male. Here, a buck stands watch.

Speed and Beauty on the Western Plains

Bart W. O'Gara, Ph.D.

The pronghorn (*Antilocapra americana* Ord) evolved during the Pleistocene epoch and is endemic to North America. Coronado and his men saw pronghorn on the plains of Kansas in 1535, but it was the reports of Lewis and Clark and a specimen collected by them that made the animal known to science and led George Ord to describe and name it in 1818.

Before the arrival of the white man, pronghorn – often called antelope – roamed a great expanse of prairie and semi-desert west of the Mississippi River from central Mexico into the prairie provinces of Canada. They apparently equaled or even surpassed the buffalo (*Bison bison*) in numbers. It has been estimated that there were once 40 million pronghorn in North America. Subsequent to 1870, the white man's occupation of the open range depleted the herds. By the early 1900s, only about 30,000 remained, and extinction of the species seemed imminent. The decline was halted, but increases were slow until the early 1940s, when transplanting programs returned pronghorn to many suitable but unoccupied ranges.

About a million pronghorn now roam the West. This has been a remarkable achievement, reflecting the resilience of the species and the ability of management to permit recovery from the virtual brink of extinction to sustainable, harvestable abundance within the span of a human lifetime. Without the cooperation of many ranchers and money provided by sportsmen through licenses and the federal aid in the Wildlife Restoration Act (Pittman-Robertson) funds, it would not have happened.

The vast majority of pronghorn are on the mixed sagebrush grasslands of the Great Plains. Lesser numbers, and densities, occur in the intermountain valleys of the Rocky Mountains, Great Basin, and hot deserts of the southwestern United States and northwestern Mexico. Succulent spring forbs and grasses on the Great Plains allow pronghorn does to raise about twice as many fawns there than in the drier areas. The tolerance of ranchers and the policies of the U.S. Bureau of Land Management will determine, to a great extent, how many pronghorn can be maintained.

Five subspecies of pronghorn generally were recognized before the advent of modern techniques. More than 90 percent of pronghorn belong to the type subspecies *A.a. americana*. Recent DNA studies indicate animals formerly recognized as *A.a. oregona* are similar to *A.a. americana*, but that *A.a. mexicana* is a legitimate subspecies. Too few specimens are available for study to determine if *A.a. peninsularis* or *A.a. sonoriensis* are valid subspecies.

Pronghorn are not large animals. The largest does usually weigh between 100 and 110 pounds and the bucks between 120 and 135 pounds. The basic body color is cinnamon buff with black and white markings on the head and neck. A black line that distinguishes the male of all ages outlines the edge of the lower jaw below the ear and covers a scent gland used to mark vegetation and attract does. In both sexes, the belly and lower sides are creamy white. The short tail is surrounded by a large, white rump patch. Hairs of the rump patch can be erected at will and serve as a visual signal to other animals in the vicinity. Rump glands release a pungent odor when the rump patch is erected. A mane, which can be erected, is present along the back of the neck. The eyes are large, black, and lustrous with heavy, jet-black eyelashes that act as sun shades. In summer the hair of the pronghorn is smooth and flexible, but as winter approaches it lengthens, and each hair, composed of many air cells, becomes thick and spongy. The hair is so loose and brittle that it falls out or breaks off at the least pressure.

Pronghorn are the only hoofed animals in America that do not have dew claws. Their absence is an adaptation for fast running in open country. These animals do not hide. They remain in open country and rely on eyesight and speed for protection. Their eyesight has been compared to a man equipped with eight-power binoculars, and they have been clocked at speeds up to 55 miles per hour. A highly developed sense of curiosity prompts the pronghorn to investigate anything unusual in its territory. Before the advent of long-range rifles, hunters often took advantage of this characteristic.

Pronghorn feed on a seemingly endless variety of plants. Studies have shown that forbs and browse, especially sagebrush, are the principal food during summer and winter, respectively. Grass is consumed in quantity only during spring green-up. Cacti are usually eaten in substantial quantities where they are available. Other strange preferences include many weeds and plants that are poisonous to livestock. Pronghorn feed extensively on wheat and barley shoots and, to some extent, on the ripe grain. Few farmers object to the amount of grain these animals eat, but a large herd running through a field of ripe grain can do extensive damage.

During spring and early summer, bucks may be found alone or in small herds. The breeding season is short, generally beginning in September and continuing into October. Groups of does are collected by individual bucks, with the number of does in a harem depending on the aggressiveness and vigor of a particular male. Fighting, which can be deadly, is most prevalent prior to the breeding season when supremacy is determined.

Breeding behavior studies have described the pronghorn as having a harem-type mating system in which dominant bucks control and defend does during the rut without regard to a specific location. Other studies have indicated that dominant bucks were territorial, defending a specific area throughout summer and holding a harem on that territory during the rut. These dissimilar social organizations are not caused by differences in specific behaviors in particular areas. Rather, social organization is influenced by the environment, and flexibility aids in adapting to specific areas and to changing environmental conditions. Territorial bucks are vulnerable to hunting because they remain in a given location day after day. When driven from its territory by a hunter, a territorial buck generally will be back in less than half a day. Heavy hunting pressure during the rut can shift a population from territorial to harem-type breeding strategies.

In late fall and early winter, northern pronghorn gather into large herds that generally move to areas where snow depths are not extreme and browse is readily available. Does often become solitary when kids are dropped in the spring but band together in small groups shortly after the youngsters are old enough to follow. Newly born fawns generally weigh six to nine pounds and resemble their parents in color, but are more drab. They begin walking less than an hour after birth and can outrun a man when they are several days old. The greater portion of their first three weeks of life is spent hidden, and they rise only to nurse. In many areas, predation, especially from coyotes (*Canis latrans*), is extensive during the first month of life.

Rivers and small mountain ranges are not barriers to pronghorn. They can pass under or through most barbed wire fences, but woven wire topped with barbed wire or seven-strand barbed wire fences, constructed with the bottom close to the ground, form barricades that pronghorn are unable to cross. Their movements appear critically curtailed in some areas because highway rights-of-ways are being fenced. Some herds may have

Photograph by Bart W. O'Gara

Fighting, which can be deadly, is most prevalent prior to the breeding season when supremacy is determined.

to be reduced to levels that would allow a particular range to be adequate for both summer and winter use.

Pronghorn have a number of unique characteristics. Their common name is derived from the best known of these, the branching or pronged horns. These are true horns composed of keratinized epithelial cells forming a black outer sheath over a bony core. Both sexes have horns. Those of mature bucks average about twelve to fifteen inches in length, while those of the does are one to five inches in length and usually do not have prongs. About one third of the does do not have horn sheaths, even though small nipple-like cores can be felt under the skin. The outer sheaths of the bucks' horns are shed annually, usually in November. Those of the does are shed but not at a definite time of year. Early authors reported that the horns were made of hair. A great deal of hair, which may lend considerable structural support, is indeed embedded in the keratinized epidermis.

Although twin births are the rule, three to seven embryos begin development. Pronghorn have an unusually long gestation period for their size that lasts about 250 days. Females usually breed at the age of about 16 months. Occasionally a four- to six-month-old female will breed and produce fawns at slightly over one year of age. On a good range, where food is plentiful, adult does produce twins about 98 percent of the time, but fewer first births involve twins.

Unregulated hunting, along with loss and deterioration of habitat, once took pronghorn dangerously near extinction. The species now thrives and provides extensive hunting opportunities despite continuing loss of habit. However, freedom of movement over the prairies is a thing of the past. If the animals were not managed by hunting, crop damage would be high and die-offs during severe winters or droughts would eliminate some populations or reduce them to low numbers. More than 100,000 pronghorn are now being harvested annually, and more than four million have been legally harvested since 1934. They provide the only prairie hunting available to many American big-game hunters.

Crawling over a landscape covered with cacti, sagebrush, sharp rocks, and an occasional rattlesnake to get close enough for a shot can be exciting. Shots often must be taken at fairly long ranges and the prairie wind will do its part to foil the marksman. Despite all this, the success rate is higher for pronghorn than for other big game, usually in the 75 percent to 90 percent range. Under most circumstances, even the inept hunter will see lots of game and have a memorable experience.

The most satisfying way to pursue pronghorn is on foot and this involves more than simply walking around the countryside. Hunters must remember that the game has better senses of sight, hearing, and smell than they do. It then goes without saying that a successful nimrod avoids being seen, heard, or smelled by the quarry.

Those who cannot spend the time or do not have the physical stamina to hunt all day on foot miss much of the thrill and satisfaction of hunting. Yet, a sporting hunt still is possible without chasing animals or shooting from vehicles. Glassing from high points on roads and taking short walks to check the other sides of ridges often will reveal pronghorn.

Under the right conditions, stalking, flagging, walking-down, and waiting at crossings, green fields, or water holes all can afford shots at standing pronghorn. But, stalking is by far the most sporting and enjoyable way to hunt these prairie speedsters.

The hunter who sees game before being seen holds the trump cards. To accomplish this, avoid the tops of ridges and hills. The stalker should cross ridges in saddles or notches, using bushes or rocks for cover, and crawling, if necessary, because pronghorn notice objects on the skyline at tremendous distances. Watch carefully while crossing because game may be just over any ridge.

Never glass from the tops of ridges; cross them first, then settle down behind or against rocks or bushes, and glass all of the terrain in sight. Take ample time; frightened pronghorn flash white, but bedded ones are hard to see. Although the country may look flat, small draws and undulations can hide whole herds. The longer one glasses, the greater the chances of an animal moving out of such places. Setting up a spotting scope is worthwhile for scanning distant ground.

The person who rushes from ridge to ridge spreads fear and is sure to get more exercise than game. But a slow-moving hunter, who stops often to use binoculars, sounds much like a feeding animal. If they do not see or smell anything strange, pronghorn sometimes investigate unfamiliar sounds.

Theodore Roosevelt observed, "It is a queer animal, with keen senses, but with streaks of utter folly in its character."

Once pronghorn are located, the hunter should watch them long enough to determine what they are doing and whether a particular animal among them warrants a stalk. If the group is moving, a quick stalk-and-wait interception often is possible. If the animals are bedded, it is time to

The strength of the pronghorn population today is evidenced by the quantity and quality of trophy bucks taken by hunters throughout its range. Charlinda Webster took this outstanding B&C pronghorn in Apache County, Arizona, on September 20, 1991. It scores 84 points.

plan the stalk. Once a route is selected, do not dally. The game may move any time. Stalking with the rising sun at one's back can be effective.

Undulations in the ground usually will allow a circuitous approach out of sight of the animals and into or across wind. Walking almost any distance while screened from pronghorn will prove more effective than trying to cross even small openings within their sight. Crawling on hands and knees, or even one's belly, is fine for the final 200 yards or so, but it is tiring and time consuming to crawl for a longer distance. After just a short crawl, the average hunter will be too out of breath for a steady shot, and it takes some moments while lying in a cramped position to get one's breath back.

Often, a hunter can get within shooting distance on hands and knees – a fairly fast mode of travel if one is wearing knee pads and leather gloves. Crossing an opening in sight of pronghorn can only be done flat on one's belly and slowly. Watching a cat stalk a bird gives an idea of how slow movements should be. Resist the temptation to lift your head for a look or to raise your buttocks for faster crawling.

A pronghorn hunt is the ideal situation for teaching a young sportsman hunting ethics, the close stalk, and clean kill. It is deplorable that many neophytes are introduced to chasing animals with vehicles and long-range flock shooting. Living in open country, pronghorn are easy to see and easy to chase with a vehicle. Their habit of running in wide arcs around pursuers instead of straight away, racing and crossing in front of moving objects, reluctance to jump fences, and penchant for open ground all serve to make them easy prey to vehicular pursuit. The use of a vehicle is considered unfair chase by the Boone and Crockett Club, and trophies taken by such methods are ineligible for entry into the Club's records keeping program.

Stalking pronghorn is fun. The hunter can count on seeing many animals, and excitement builds as one sneaks up on a trophy buck or an animal for the table. A quick, clean kill may leave the sportsman momentarily sad at the death of a beautiful animal, but a good, honest satisfaction soon sets in from knowing the game was played by the rules, and played well. Those who chase these interesting animals with a vehicle and who shoot at running herds not only risk damaging landowner/ sportsman relations, crippling animals, and lending needless credibility to the propaganda of individuals and groups who are inclined to label all hunting as unfair and inhumane; but they also miss one of the greatest thrills in North American hunting.

Bart W. O'Gara, Ph.D., of Lolo, Montana, is a certified wildlife biologist and Wildlife Professor Emeritus of the University of Montana, Missoula, Montana. Bart was a wildlife biologist from 1968 to 1992 for the U.S. Fish and Wildlife Service at the Montana Cooperative Wildlife Research Unit. He has studied pronghorn biology and management for more than 30 years. He earned a doctorate in zoology from the University of Montana and a B.S. in fish and wildlife biology from Montana State University, Bozeman. He has authored dozens of articles on birds, mammals, and wildlife management and is currently working on a book about pronghorn for the Wildlife Management Institute.

Photograph Courtesy of Ruby W. Dahl

Harold Evans and Harold Dahl, Sr., co-founders of the One-Shot Antelope Hunt.

The Lander One-Shot Antelope Hunt

Ruby W. Dahl

Every September in Lander, Wyoming, a unique hunt is conducted. The pronghorn, commonly called antelope, is the quarry, and each hunter is allowed only one cartridge in his gun. The event is the One-Shot Antelope Hunt.

The One-Shot Antelope Hunt is a world-renowned hunting organization founded in 1940 by the late Harold Evans of Lander, Wyoming, and the late Harold Dahl, Sr., of Golden, Colorado, two hunting companions who dreamed up the idea while on a bear hunt in Wyoming. While waiting for the bear to take the bait, they talked of how the Indians had only one shot with their bow and arrow. This led to considering how limited the chances of modern-day man would be with only one shot. The two friends challenged each other to such a hunt and chose the wily, swift pronghorn as the game to pursue with one bullet. From this conversation grew the One-Shot Antelope Hunt.

The first One-Shot Antelope Hunt took place on Labor Day weekend of 1940 in the Lander, Wyoming, area. In this first hunt there were two teams, one from Colorado, and one from Wyoming. Five men were on each team. In 1941, three teams representing Colorado, Wyoming, and Texas were organized. The hunt has been held ever since in September in Lander except for the World War II years of 1942 to 1945. The hunt is composed of several teams and each hunter is allowed only one cartridge. With this one cartridge, the hunter must make a successful shot. A wounding shot does not count and the guide dispatches the animal.

Sportsmen from all over the world and all walks of life have participated in the hunt. Governors and senators of many states, movie stars, opera singers, astronauts, cosmonauts, royalty from Europe and India, and many people who are just interested in this unusual hunt have participated.

Some of the famous shooters include Gen. H. Norman Schwarzkopf, Gen. Chuck Yeager, and Gen. Curtis LeMay. The renowned tenor from the Metropolitan Opera, Lauritz Melchior, first attended the hunt in 1949 and was so entranced with the challenge of the hunt and the friendliness of the Lander people that he returned every year thereafter until his death. He always sang at the Victory Banquet, to the delight of all his friends. Roy Rogers, singing cowboy of the films, has also been a faithful participant and supporter of the hunt, returning many times.

When the hunt first started, the Wyoming Game and Fish Department furnished guides and wardens to monitor the teams, but in the late 1940s they discontinued this service and the Wyoming governor said he would no longer furnish licenses for the participants. The local sponsors were undecided as to how to go about continuing the event. A group of local people met and decided to form a club of 100 members to perpetuate the hunt. On August 23, 1949, the One-Shot Antelope Hunt Club was incorporated. This membership of 100 is still maintained today, with a limited number of associate members.

The hunt has had very few changes since its inception. The number of team members varied greatly until 1966 when it was decided to limit a team to three hunters with one alternate. In the early years, the victory banquets were held in a big tent. Attendance at these banquets has grown each year and now tops 500 people. The banquets now are held in the community center. During the banquets, awards are given to hunters and Past Shooters for their prowess in the competition shooting held the previous day and all hunters have the chance to tell the audience about their successful or losing shot made during the hunt. Only 33 percent of the hunters who participate ever down a pronghorn buck with a single shot, so there are lots of excuses to share.

Successful hunters are awarded a plastic encased silver bullet. A pronghorn plaque is awarded to those hunters who miss on their first shot.

The rules are designed to promote the ideals of good sportsmanship and game conservation, placing much emphasis on comradeship, ability in the field, and accuracy with a big-game rifle. Hunting teams are selected to participate on the basis of challenges issued either to the One-Shot Club's 14-member board of directors or through the governor of Wyoming. Three teams from Wyoming, Colorado, and Past Shooters are automatic entries in each year's hunt. Hunters must meet qualifications and can read about the qualifications by writing to the Lander One-Shot Club, P.O. Box 95, Lander, Wyoming 82520.

The president is elected for a two-year term and, with the board of directors, coordinates all the activities related to the actual hunt each year. Rule changes in recent years have established three men per team with anywhere from six to eight teams in the one-day hunt. The hunt is always held on the opening day of pronghorn season near Lander, with all team members gathering on the day before the hunt.

Pre-hunt ceremonies include the sighting in of rifles, friendly competition shooting, and an evening Indian ceremony where hunters learn the Legend of the Hunt. Hunters are made blood brother members of the Shoshone Tribe and each hunter is given an Indian name that usually corresponds to his vocation. Each hunter is given a sacred Indian medicine bag and has the single bullet blessed for the hunt.

Hunters go to bed early and begin their one-day, one-shot hunt at 4:30 a.m. for breakfast. The hunt starts at sunrise around 6:30 a.m. within 50 miles of Lander. Two vehicles, each with a hunter and guide, comprise a hunting party. Since the two hunters in each party are on different teams, they are indirectly competing with each other. A drawing is held to determine which hunter shoots first. If the first hunter has not had a shot within the first hour, then the second hunter gets a turn to shoot. The two hunters alternate each hour until one of them gets a shot. If the hunter has taken a shot, whether he has been successful or not, the other hunter has the shooting privilege for the rest of the day. At sundown, the hunt ends for another year.

Because of a continuing interest, many hunters have returned year after year to attend the hunt and to participate in all the activities. These hunters are known as Past Shooters. By September 2, 1955, the number of returning Past Shooters had grown enough to warrant the forming of an organization. It was called the Past Shooters Club. Harrison Johnson was elected the first president. George Case of Lander was elected secretary-treasurer. This office eventually became the paid position of executive vice-president. The headquarters is always located in Lander. Their purpose was and is to support the hunt and to enjoy each other's fellowship.

Besides the annual One-Shot Antelope Hunt, the Past Shooters Club usually meets for the Spring Foo Foo Rah based on the tradition of the frontier trappers, traders, and Indians of the 19th century. The president of the club arranges the location and facilities. A weekend is devoted to fun and competitive shooting events.

In 1979 the Wyoming legislature granted the One-Shot Hunt a percentage of pronghorn licenses in the areas around Lander. Those not needed by the One-Shot are made available to Past Shooters and their guests. Past Shooters who don't get a pronghorn license in the drawing

Photograph Courtesy of John P. Poston

The winning team members at the 1988 One-Shot Antelope Hunt were Boone and Crockett Club members (l. to r.) William L. Searle, William I. Spencer and John P. Poston. Norden van Horne, a member of B&C and the One-Shot Antelope Hunt Club, stands at far right.

may be able to get one through the Past Shooters Club.

In the late 1960s and early 1970s, the Past Shooters Club decided that their energies and efforts should be directed to the establishment of a separate organization that in turn could pursue goals in a variety of new directions. The One-Shot Antelope Hunt Foundation was formally incorporated on May 1, 1975. This foundation is composed of the Past Shooters of the One-Shot Antelope Hunt. The board of directors of this new group is composed of twelve trustees.

In 1962 Norden van Horne, an ardent sportsman, hunter, and Boone and Crockett Club member, was invited to attend the Lander One-Shot Hunt by then Colorado Governor Steve McNichols. Norden was taken out to hunt by Wyoming Game Warden Bill Crump. They talked of many things on the hunt and one topic was the needs of pronghorn and how man could return something to the pronghorn in exchange for the pleasures derived from hunting the animal. Crump said one of the greatest needs of the antelope and for most wild game was water. Great expanses of the West are very dry. Norden returned to the hunt year after year because of his fascination with the One-Shot Hunt. In 1975 Norden shot on the Safari Club International team.

Through these years Norden continued studying the possibilities of providing water for wildlife and every year he tried to interest the people who were running the hunt in such a program. It took several years, but finally in 1971 he was successful in getting Jim Guschewsky, Frank Bandy, and Harold Mares, all Past Shooters, interested in the idea, and they began to work towards establishing such a program. Mares named the program Water for Wildlife. Much study was given to the best way to provide water for wildlife. Studies conducted by the Wyoming Game and Fish Department concluded the largest single factor in fawn survival of any species was water.

Money was, of course, needed to get the program going and members of the Past Shooters Club provided the funds to start the operation. The program was supported by individuals, conservation groups, the U.S. Bureau of Land Management, and the Wyoming Game and Fish Department. Since its inception in 1976, the Water for Wildlife program has benefited many other animals such as bighorn sheep, mule deer, wild horses, grouse, rabbits, partridge, chukars, and doves, and recently provided for the introduction of bighorn sheep to a new area. By 1983, the One-Shot Foundation had completed more than 20 water projects in Wyoming, Colorado, and Idaho, with future projects proposed by a variety of agencies in many bordering states. The program was off to an unprecedented beginning.

Water sources are from wells developed from oil and gas drillings where they found water but not commercial oil, wells drilled and powered by windmills, and reservoir improvements at springs or artesian wells. Guzzlers are used where there has been no source of groundwater. These devices are designed to collect and hold rain or snow and then release it into a reservoir as needed through the use of a float valve.

The Wyoming Game and Fish Department has prepared a Water for Wildlife program outline that explains how water sources are located, the criteria for qualifications as an acceptable site, the procedure for authorization to complete the project, and the provisions for ongoing maintenance.

The Water for Wildlife Foundation was established in 1991 as a tax-exempt, non-profit organization to benefit the program, thanks in large part to the legal services of a Denver attorney and judge, Leonard Sutton. All financial donations receive an IRS tax receipt. Funding of this foundation comes from hundreds of private individuals and organizations from around the world. The Union Pacific Foundation gave the first large financial grant to the newly formed foundation. By 1995, the new foundation had approved for funding 172 water development projects in twelve different states, primarily in the arid western and southwestern United States. There is also, thus far, one international program. The cost of a water development project varies but the average cost per project is approximately $4,000.

The founders of the One-Shot Foundation had long nurtured another major dream – to establish a museum to preserve the traditions of the One-Shot Hunt. In 1978, the Evans-Dahl Memorial Museum became a reality. Under the dedicated supervision of Frank H. Bandy, the museum was constructed and donated to the Fremont County Commissioners as an addition to the existing Fremont County Pioneer Museum in Lander. The museum is dedicated to the preservation of Native American cultures and heritage and to the preservation of artifacts relating to the One-Shot Antelope Hunt. The public is welcome to visit the museum and learn more about the Lander One-Shot Club and its many worthwhile programs.

The on-going efforts of the Water for Wildlife Foundation, itself an outgrowth of the Past Shooters Club and the Lander One-Shot Antelope Hunt, are providing an assured future for this fleet sentinel of the plains, the pronghorn.

Ruby W. Dahl of Golden, Colorado, is the author of the book, The Lander One-Shot Antelope Hunt. *She is the daughter-in-law of the late Harold W. Dahl, Sr., who co-founded the Lander One-Shot Antelope Hunt with Harold Evans of Lander, Wyoming. Ruby's family has been active in the One-Shot Hunt from its beginning. Harold Dahl, Ruby's husband, has attended the One-Shot Hunt every year since he first shot in 1949. Ruby is a graduate of the University of Colorado. Harold is a hunter of note and she has accompanied him on many hunts for deer and antelope and has gone on safari in Africa. Her book is available through the One-Shot Antelope Hunt Foundation, 545 Main Street, P.O. Box 13, Lander, Wyoming 82520. Their telephone number is (307) 332-3356. To contact the Water for Wildlife Foundation, call (800) 768-7743. The One Shot Past Shooter's Club can be reached by calling (307) 332-8190.*

Records of North American
Big Game

BOONE AND CROCKETT CLUB

250 Station Drive
Missoula, MT 59801
(406) 542-1888

Minimum Score:	Awards	All-time
bighorn	175	180
desert	165	168
Dall's	160	170
Stone's	165	170

SHEEP

Kind of Sheep: __Stone's__

Measure to a
Point in Line
With Horn Tip

SEE OTHER SIDE FOR INSTRUCTIONS		Column 1	Column 2	Column 3
A. Greatest Spread (Is Often Tip to Tip Spread)	31	Right Horn	Left Horn	
B. Tip to Tip Spread	31			Difference
C. Length of Horn		50 1/8	51 5/8	
D-1. Circumference of Base		14 6/8	14 6/8	--
D-2. Circumference at First Quarter		14 1/8	14 2/8	1/8
D-3. Circumference at Second Quarter		11 7/8	12 1/8	2/8
D-4. Circumference at Third Quarter		6 6/8	7	2/8
TOTALS		97 5/8	99 6/8	5/8

ADD	Column 1	97 5/8	Exact Locality Where Killed: Muskwa River, B.C.
	Column 2	99 6/8	Date Killed: 1936 Hunter: L.S. Chadwick
	SUBTOTAL	197 3/8	Owner: B & C National Collection
SUBTRACT Column 3		5/8	Owner's Address:
			Guide's Name and Address:
			Remarks: (Mention Any Abnormalities or Unique Qualities)
FINAL SCORE		196 6/8	

I certify that I have measured this trophy on ___10 April___ 19 51
at (address) __American Museum of Natural History__ City __New York__ State __NY__
and that these measurements and data are, to the best of my knowledge and belief, made in
accordance with the instructions given.

Witness: _____Samuel B. Webb_____ Signature: ___Grancel Fitz___

B&C Official Measurer

I.D. Number

INSTRUCTIONS FOR MEASURING SHEEP

All measurements must be made with a 1/4-inch wide flexible steel tape to the nearest one-eighth of an inch. Wherever it is necessary to change direction of measurement, mark a control point and swing tape at this point. Enter fractional figures in eighths, without reduction. Official measurements cannot be taken until horns have air dried for at least 60 days after the animal was killed.

A. Greatest Spread is measured between perpendiculars at a right angle to the center line of the skull.

B. Tip to Tip Spread is measured between tips of horns.

C. Length of Horn is measured from the lowest point in front on outer curve to a point in line with tip. Do not press tape into depressions. The low point of the outer curve of the horn is considered to be the low point of the frontal portion of the horn, situated above and slightly medial to the eye socket (not the outside edge). Use a straight edge, perpendicular to horn axis, to end measurement on "broomed" horns.

D-1. Circumference of Base is measured at a right angle to axis of horn. Do not follow irregular edge of horn; the line of measurement must be entirely on horn material, not the jagged edge often noted.

D-2-3-4. Divide measurement C of longer horn by four. Starting at base, mark both horns at these quarters (even though the other horn is shorter) and measure circumferences at these marks, with measurements taken at right angles to horn axis.

FAIR CHASE STATEMENT FOR ALL HUNTER-TAKEN TROPHIES

FAIR CHASE, as defined by the Boone and Crockett Club, is the ethical, sportsmanlike and lawful pursuit and taking of any free-ranging wild game animal in a manner that does not give the hunter an improper or unfair advantage over such game animals.
Use of any of the following methods in the taking of game shall be deemed **UNFAIR CHASE** and unsportsmanlike:

I. Spotting or herding game from the air, followed by landing in its vicinity for the purpose of pursuit and shooting;

II. Herding, pursuing, or shooting game from any motorboat or motor vehicle;

III. Use of electronic devices for attracting, locating, or observing game, or for guiding the hunter to such game;

IV. Hunting game confined by artificial barriers, including escape-proof fenced enclosures, or hunting game transplanted solely for the purpose of commercial shooting;

V. Taking of game in a manner not in full compliance with the game laws or regulations of the federal government or of any state, province, territory, or tribal council on reservations or tribal lands;

VI. Or as may otherwise be deemed unfair or unsportsmanlike by the Executive Committee of the Boone and Crockett Club.

I certify that the trophy scored on this chart was taken in **FAIR CHASE** as defined above by the Boone and Crockett Club. In signing this statement, I understand that if the information provided on this entry is found to be misrepresented or fraudulent in any respect, it will not be accepted into the Awards Program and all of my prior entries are subject to deletion from future editions of *Records of North American Big Game* and future entries may not be accepted.

Date: _____ Signature of Hunter:_____
(Signature must be witnessed by an Official Measurer or a Notary Public.)

Date: _____ Signature of Notary or Official Measurer:_____

Records of North American
Big Game

BOONE AND CROCKETT CLUB

250 Station Drive
Missoula, MT 59801
(406)542-1888

Minimum Score: Awards All-time   **ROCKY MOUNTAIN GOAT**
47   50

SEE OTHER SIDE FOR INSTRUCTIONS		Column 1	Column 2	Column 3
A. Greatest Spread	9 2/8	Right Horn	Left Horn	
B. Tip to Tip Spread	9			Difference
C. Length of Horn		12	12	--
D-1. Circumference of Base		6 4/8	6 4/8	--
D-2. Circumference at First Quarter		4 7/8	4 6/8	1/8
D-3. Circumference at Second Quarter		3 2/8	3 1/8	1/8
D-4. Circumference at Third Quarter		2	2	--
TOTALS		28 5/8	28 3/8	2/8

ADD	Column 1	28 5/8	Exact Locality Where Killed: Babine Mountains, B.C.	
	Column 2	28 3/8	Date Killed: 1949 Hunter: E.C. Haase	
	Subtotal	57	Owner: B & C National Collection	
	SUBTRACT Column 3	2/8	Owner's Address:	
			Guide's Name and Address: Allen Fletchers	
			Remarks: (Mention Any Abnormalities or Unique Qualities)	
	FINAL SCORE	56 6/8		

I certify that I have measured this trophy on _____ 28 January _____ 19 50 __
at (address) American Museum of Natural History City New York _____ State NY __
and that these measurements and data are, to the best of my knowledge and belief, made in
accordance with the instructions given.

Witness: _____ Samuel B. Webb _____ Signature: _____ Grancel Fitz _____

B&C Official Measurer

I.D. Number

54

INSTRUCTIONS FOR MEASURING ROCKY MOUNTAIN GOAT

All measurements must be made with a 1/4-inch wide flexible steel tape to the nearest one-eighth of an inch. Wherever it is necessary to change direction of measurement, mark a control point and swing tape at this point. Enter fractional figures in eighths, without reduction. Official measurements cannot be taken until horns have air dried for at least 60 days after the animal was killed.

A.   Greatest Spread is measured between perpendiculars at a right angle to the center line of the skull.

B.   Tip to Tip spread is measured between tips of the horns.

C.   Length of Horn is measured from the lowest point in front over outer curve to a point in line with tip.

D-1.   Circumference of Base is measured at a right angle to axis of horn. Do not follow irregular edge of horn.

D-2-3-4.   Divide measurement C of longer horn by four. Starting at base, mark both horns at these quarters (even though the other horn is shorter) and measure circumferences at these marks.

FAIR CHASE STATEMENT FOR ALL HUNTER-TAKEN TROPHIES

FAIR CHASE, as defined by the Boone and Crockett Club, is the ethical, sportsmanlike and lawful pursuit and taking of any free-ranging wild game animal in a manner that does not give the hunter an improper or unfair advantage over such game animals.
Use of any of the following methods in the taking of game shall be deemed **UNFAIR CHASE** and unsportsmanlike:

I.   Spotting or herding game from the air, followed by landing in its vicinity for the purpose of pursuit and shooting;

II.   Herding, pursuing, or shooting game from any motorboat or motor vehicle;

III.   Use of electronic devices for attracting, locating, or observing game, or for guiding the hunter to such game;

IV.   Hunting game confined by artificial barriers, including escape-proof fenced enclosures, or hunting game transplanted solely for the purpose of commercial shooting;

V.   Taking of game in a manner not in full compliance with the game laws or regulations of the federal government or of any state, province, territory, or tribal council on reservations or tribal lands;

VI.   Or as may otherwise be deemed unfair or unsportsmanlike by the Executive Committee of the Boone and Crockett Club.

I certify that the trophy scored on this chart was taken in **FAIR CHASE** as defined above by the Boone and Crockett Club. In signing this statement, I understand that if the information provided on this entry is found to be misrepresented or fraudulent in any respect, it will not be accepted into the Awards Program and all of my prior entries are subject to deletion from future editions of *Records of North American Big Game* and future entries may not be accepted.

Date: _____ Signature of Hunter:_____
                                        (Signature must be witnessed by an Official Measurer or a Notary Public.)

Date: _____ Signature of Notary or Official Measurer:_____

Records of North American
Big Game

BOONE AND CROCKETT CLUB

250 Station Drive
Missoula, MT 59801
(406) 542-1888

Minimum Score: Awards All-time
          80   82

PRONGHORN

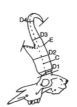

SEE OTHER SIDE FOR INSTRUCTIONS		Column 1	Column 2	Column 3
A. Tip to Tip Spread	8 1/8	Right Horn	Left Horn	Difference
B. Inside Spread of Main Beams	12 5/8			
C. Length of Horn		17 6/8	17 4/8	2/8
D-1. Circumference of Base		6 7/8	7	1/8
D-2. Circumference at First Quarter		6 7/8	7 2/8	3/8
D-3. Circumference at Second Quarter		4 3/8	4 4/8	1/8
D-4. Circumference at Third Quarter		3 1/8	3 2/8	1/8
E. Length of Prong		8	8 2/8	2/8
TOTALS		47	47 6/8	1 2/8

ADD	Column 1	47	Exact Locality Where Killed: Coconino Co., Arizona
	Column 2	47 6/8	Date Killed: 20 Sept 1985 Hunter: Michael J. O'Haco, Jr.
	Subtotal	94 6/8	Owner: Michael J. O'Haco, Jr.
	SUBTRACT Column 3	1 2/8	Owner's Address:
			Guide's Name and Address:
			Remarks: (Mention Any Abnormalities or Unique Qualities)
	FINAL SCORE	93 4/8	

I certify that I have measured this trophy on _____ 13 May _____ 19 86

at (address) Nevada State Museum _____ City Las Vegas _____ State NV
and that these measurements and data are, to the best of my knowledge and belief, made in
accordance with the instructions given.

Witness: _____ George Tsukamoto _____ Signature: ____ Walter H. White ____

B&C Official Measurer

I.D. Number

INSTRUCTIONS FOR MEASURING PRONGHORN

All measurements must be made with a 1/4-inch wide flexible steel tape to the nearest one-eighth of an inch. Wherever it is necessary to change direction of measurement, mark a control point and swing tape at this point. Enter fractional figures in eighths, without reduction. Official measurements cannot be taken until horns have air dried for at least 60 days after the animal was killed.

A. Tip to Tip Spread is measured between tips of horns.

B. Inside Spread of Main Beams is measured at a right angle to the center line of the skull, at widest point between main beams.

C. Length of Horn is measured on the outside curve on the general line illustrated. The line taken will vary with different heads, depending on the direction of their curvature. Measure along the center of the outer curve from tip of horn in line with the lowest edge of the base, using a straight edge to establish the line end.

D-1. Measure around base of horn at a right angle to long axis. Do not follow irregular edge of horn.

D-2-3-4. Divide measurement C of longer horn by four. Starting at base, mark both horns at these quarters (even though the other horn is shorter) and measure circumferences at these marks. If the prong interferes with D-2, move the measurement down to just below the swelling of the prong. If the prong interferes with D-3, move the measurement up to just above the swelling of the prong.

E. Length of Prong: Measure from the tip of the prong along the upper edge of the outer curve to the horn; then continue around the horn to a point at the rear of the horn where a straight edge across the back of both horns touches the horn, with the latter part being at a right angle to the long axis of horn.

FAIR CHASE STATEMENT FOR ALL HUNTER-TAKEN TROPHIES

FAIR CHASE, as defined by the Boone and Crockett Club, is the ethical, sportsmanlike and lawful pursuit and taking of any free-ranging wild game animal in a manner that does not give the hunter an improper or unfair advantage over such game animals.

Use of any of the following methods in the taking of game shall be deemed **UNFAIR CHASE** and unsportsmanlike:

I. Spotting or herding game from the air, followed by landing in its vicinity for the purpose of pursuit and shooting;

II. Herding, pursuing, or shooting game from any motorboat or motor vehicle;

III. Use of electronic devices for attracting, locating, or observing game, or for guiding the hunter to such game;

IV. Hunting game confined by artificial barriers, including escape-proof fenced enclosures, or hunting game transplanted solely for the purpose of commercial shooting;

V. Taking of game in a manner not in full compliance with the game laws or regulations of the federal government or of any state, province, territory, or tribal council on reservations or tribal lands;

VI. Or as may otherwise be deemed unfair or unsportsmanlike by the Executive Committee of the Boone and Crockett Club.

I certify that the trophy scored on this chart was taken in **FAIR CHASE** as defined above by the Boone and Crockett Club. In signing this statement, I understand that if the information provided on this entry is found to be misrepresented or fraudulent in any respect, it will not be accepted into the Awards Program and all of my prior entries are subject to deletion from future editions of *Records of North American Big Game* and future entries may not be accepted.

Date: _____ Signature of Hunter:_____
                       (Signature must be witnessed by an Official Measurer or
                       a Notary Public.)

Date: _____ Signature of Notary or Official Measurer:_____

TOP 5 BIGHORN SHEEP LISTINGS INDEX

TOP 5 DESERT SHEEP LISTINGS INDEX

TOP 5 DALL'S SHEEP LISTINGS INDEX

TOP 5 STONE'S SHEEP LISTINGS INDEX

Tabulations of Recorded Bighorn, Desert, Stone's and Dall's Sheep

The trophy data shown on the following pages are taken from score charts in the records archives of the Boone and Crockett Club.

The wild sheep of North America belong in only two species, the thin-horned sheep of northern British Columbia northward (*Ovis dalli*), and the bighorn sheep ranging from central British Columbia to Baja California (*Ovis canadensis*). Dall's sheep (or white) range over much of Alaska, most of Yukon Territory, the Mackenzie Mountains of Northwest Territories, and a small area of British Columbia. Stone's sheep primarily occur in northern British Columbia. Thin-horned sheep with black hairs on the body, except for the tail, are classified as Stone's sheep. In cases where the pelage is white, except for black hairs on the tail, the trophy is considered a Dall's sheep.

Bighorn sheep are separable into Rocky Mountain bighorns and desert bighorns. Desert bighorns are found in Nevada, Mexico, Arizona, New Mexico, California, and extreme western Texas. Rocky Mountain bighorns are found from Alberta and British Columbia southward to Arizona and New Mexico.

The scores and ranks shown are final, except for the trophies shown with an asterisk (*). The asterisk identifies entry scores subject to final certification by an Awards Panel of Judges. The asterisk can be removed (except in the case of a potential World's Record) by the submission of two additional, independent scorings by Official Measurers of the Boone and Crockett Club. The Records Committee of the Club will review the three scorings available (original plus two additional) and determine which, if any, will be accepted in lieu of the Judges' Panel measurement. When the score has been accepted as final by the Records Committee, the asterisk will be removed in future editions of this book and the all-time records book, *Records of North American Big Game*. In the case of a potential World's Record, the trophy must come before a Judges' Panel at the end of an entry period. Only a Judges' Panel can certify a World's Record and finalize its score. Asterisked trophies are unranked at the end of their category.

Photograph Courtesy of Timothy R. Lacy, Sr.

**ARIZONA STATE RECORD
BIGHORN SHEEP
SCORE: 181⁴⁄₈**
Locality: Greenlee Co. Date: 1991
Hunter: Timothy R. Lacy, Sr.

ARIZONA

BIGHORN SHEEP

Score	Length of Horn		Circumference of Base		Circumference at Third Quarter		Greatest Spread	Tip-to-Tip Spread	All-Time Rank	State Rank
	R	L	R	L	R	L				
♦ Locality / Hunter / Owner / Date Killed										
181⁴⁄₈	38³⁄₈	31¹⁄₈	17	17	9	9	23⁵⁄₈	19³⁄₈	507	1
♦ Greenlee County / Timothy R. Lacy, Sr. / Timothy R. Lacy, Sr. / 1991										
180³⁄₈	35¹⁄₈	37²⁄₈	15⁵⁄₈	15⁴⁄₈	9⁴⁄₈	9⁷⁄₈	24		15⁶⁄₈	596	2
♦ Greenlee County / James A. Gerrettie II / James A. Gerrettie II / 1988										
180³⁄₈	41⁵⁄₈	36	16	16	9	7⁶⁄₈	23⁴⁄₈	16⁶⁄₈	596	2
♦ Greenlee County / Hoover L. Lee / Hoover L. Lee / 1993										

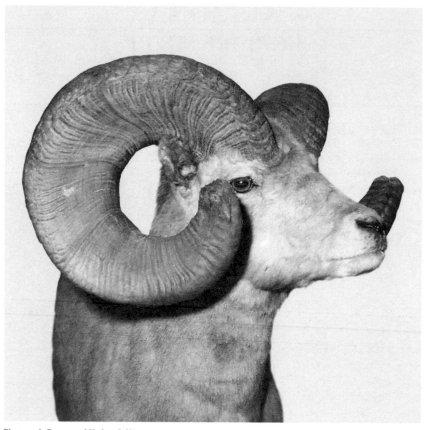

Photograph Courtesy of Herbert J. Havemann

COLORADO STATE RECORD
BIGHORN SHEEP
SCORE: 193⅝
Locality: Cameron Pass   Date: 1954
Hunter: F. Cotter
Owner: Herbert J. Havemann

COLORADO
BIGHORN SHEEP

Score	Length of Horn		Circumference of Base		Circumference at Third Quarter		Greatest Spread	Tip-to-Tip Spread	All-Time Rank	State Rank
	R	L	R	L	R	L				

♦ Locality / Hunter / Owner / Date Killed

Score	R	L	R	L	R	L	Spread	Spread	Rank	Rank
$193\frac{6}{8}$	41	42	16	16	$10\frac{5}{8}$	$10\frac{2}{8}$	24	$18\frac{1}{8}$	61	1
$191\frac{7}{8}$	$40\frac{4}{8}$	$41\frac{1}{8}$	15	15	$11\frac{1}{8}$	$11\frac{6}{8}$	$23\frac{3}{8}$	$21\frac{4}{8}$	89	2
$187\frac{5}{8}$	$39\frac{6}{8}$	$37\frac{7}{8}$	$15\frac{6}{8}$	$15\frac{5}{8}$	$9\frac{3}{8}$	$9\frac{3}{8}$	$22\frac{6}{8}$	$20\frac{5}{8}$	197	3
187	$36\frac{6}{8}$	38	$15\frac{6}{8}$	$15\frac{7}{8}$	$10\frac{3}{8}$	$10\frac{6}{8}$	$23\frac{4}{8}$	$22\frac{7}{8}$	219	4
$185\frac{3}{8}$	$39\frac{5}{8}$	39	16	16	$9\frac{6}{8}$	$9\frac{1}{8}$	21	$20\frac{5}{8}$	293	5
$185\frac{2}{8}$	$38\frac{1}{8}$	$37\frac{5}{8}$	$16\frac{5}{8}$	$16\frac{5}{8}$	$9\frac{1}{8}$	$8\frac{5}{8}$	$22\frac{4}{8}$	21	299	6
$184\frac{7}{8}$	$37\frac{6}{8}$	$37\frac{7}{8}$	15	$15\frac{3}{8}$	$10\frac{4}{8}$	$10\frac{2}{8}$	$22\frac{3}{8}$	20	316	7
$184\frac{3}{8}$	$37\frac{4}{8}$	$37\frac{7}{8}$	$15\frac{2}{8}$	$15\frac{4}{8}$	$10\frac{2}{8}$	11	$21\frac{6}{8}$	$13\frac{7}{8}$	337	8
$183\frac{1}{8}$	$34\frac{7}{8}$	36	$16\frac{2}{8}$	$16\frac{2}{8}$	$9\frac{7}{8}$	$10\frac{1}{8}$	$24\frac{5}{8}$	20	406	9
$182\frac{4}{8}$	$35\frac{4}{8}$	$35\frac{2}{8}$	$16\frac{4}{8}$	$16\frac{4}{8}$	10	$9\frac{4}{8}$	24	$22\frac{5}{8}$	436	10
182	$39\frac{4}{8}$	$38\frac{6}{8}$	15	15	$8\frac{7}{8}$	9	24	24	466	11
$181\frac{6}{8}$	$38\frac{2}{8}$	$36\frac{4}{8}$	17	$16\frac{7}{8}$	$8\frac{4}{8}$	$8\frac{4}{8}$	$23\frac{4}{8}$	$20\frac{6}{8}$	488	12
$181\frac{4}{8}$	$36\frac{3}{8}$	$35\frac{7}{8}$	$15\frac{1}{8}$	$15\frac{1}{8}$	$10\frac{7}{8}$	$10\frac{6}{8}$	$22\frac{5}{8}$	18	507	13
$181\frac{3}{8}$	$37\frac{2}{8}$	$36\frac{7}{8}$	17	17	8	$8\frac{1}{8}$	$20\frac{4}{8}$	$15\frac{4}{8}$	525	14
$180\frac{6}{8}$	35	$34\frac{2}{8}$	$15\frac{2}{8}$	$15\frac{2}{8}$	$11\frac{2}{8}$	$10\frac{6}{8}$	$22\frac{5}{8}$	17	563	15
$180\frac{1}{8}$	$36\frac{4}{8}$	$34\frac{5}{8}$	$15\frac{2}{8}$	$15\frac{1}{8}$	$10\frac{3}{8}$	$10\frac{7}{8}$	$22\frac{1}{8}$	$18\frac{4}{8}$	631	16
$180\frac{1}{8}$	$37\frac{4}{8}$	$37\frac{3}{8}$	$15\frac{2}{8}$	$15\frac{2}{8}$	$9\frac{2}{8}$	9	$22\frac{7}{8}$	$18\frac{2}{8}$	631	16
$191\frac{3}{8}$	$42\frac{3}{8}$	$42\frac{2}{8}$	$15\frac{5}{8}$	$15\frac{4}{8}$	$9\frac{1}{8}$	$9\frac{1}{8}$	24	$20\frac{1}{8}$	*	*

♦ Cameron Pass / F. Cotter / Herbert J. Havemann / 1954

♦ Lake County / Emory Whilton / Kern Co. (Calif.) Mus. / 1901

♦ El Paso County / Picked Up / Michael D. Swanson / 1988

♦ Colorado / Picked Up / E.H. Brown / PR 1964

♦ Fremont County / Leonard L. Kiser / Leonard L. Kiser / 1955

♦ Fremont County / Robert W. Wallace / Robert W. Wallace / 1978

♦ Glenwood Springs / Picked Up / Mark E. Cook / 1960

♦ Gunnison County / Billy Prior / Daniel C. Harrington / 1915

♦ S. Platte Canyon / Harold C. Eastwood / Harold C. Eastwood / 1957

♦ Waterton / William D. Jenkins / William D. Jenkins / 1956

♦ Saguache County / Ralph G. Hejny / Ralph G. Hejny / 1992

♦ Gunnison County / Paula D. Darner / Paula D. Darner / 1986

♦ Saguache County / Darrel L. Moberly / Darrel L. Moberly / 1994

♦ Park County / Richard L. Rudeen / Richard L. Rudeen / 1963

♦ Texas Creek / Picked Up / Jack Putnam / PR 1963

♦ Sugarloaf Mt. / Picked Up / Henry Zietz / 1947

♦ Clear Creek County / Charles W. Hanawalt / Charles W. Hanawalt / 1990

♦ El Paso County / Raymond E. Moore / Raymond E. Moore / 1983

Photograph by Curtis S. Chastain

IDAHO STATE RECORD
BIGHORN SHEEP
SCORE: 196
Locality: Nez Perce Co.   Date: 1994
Hunter: Richard N. Aznaran

IDAHO
BIGHORN SHEEP

Score	Length of Horn		Circumference of Base		Circumference at Third Quarter		Greatest Spread	Tip-to-Tip Spread	All-Time Rank	State Rank
	R	L	R	L	R	L				
◆ Locality / Hunter / Owner / Date Killed										
196	45 3/8	43 3/8	16 5/8	16 5/8	9 1/8	7 7/8	22 6/8	22 6/8	44	1
◆ Nez Perce County / Richard N. Aznaran / Richard N. Aznaran / 1994										
187 6/8	43 4/8	44 2/8	14 7/8	14 7/8	8 4/8	8 2/8	24 2/8	24 2/8	191	2
◆ Salmon River / Picked Up / Dwight Smith / 1951										
186 5/8	42 6/8	42 1/8	15	15	8 3/8	8 2/8	25 6/8	25 6/8	242	3
◆ Shell Rock / Lea J. Bacos / Lea J. Bacos / 1953										
185 5/8	40 5/8	40	15 2/8	15 2/8	8 7/8	9	23 4/8	23 4/8	282	4
◆ Lemhi County / W.R. Franklin / W.R. Franklin / 1963										
185 2/8	38 1/8	37 1/8	16	15 5/8	10 4/8	9 7/8	20 1/8	20 1/8	299	5
◆ Big Creek / Edson Piers / Edson Piers / 1962										
184 7/8	40 4/8	39 5/8	14 6/8	14 7/8	9 5/8	9 4/8	23 5/8	23 5/8	316	6
◆ Westhorse Mts. / Cecil Dodge / Cecil Dodge / 1953										
184 5/8	38 5/8	37 4/8	15 6/8	15 7/8	9 4/8	9 4/8	22 3/8	20 7/8	324	7
◆ Salmon River / Ted Biladeau / Ted Biladeau / 1939										
184 4/8	38 7/8	39 5/8	16	16 1/8	8 5/8	8 4/8	22 4/8	18 5/8	331	8
◆ Custer County / Stanley V. Potts / Stanley V. Potts / 1981										
184	40 5/8	37 7/8	14 6/8	14 7/8	9 2/8	9 4/8	22 4/8	22 3/8	349	9
◆ Valley County / Picked Up / LaVarr Jacklin / 1949										
183 7/8	38 1/8	39	16	16 2/8	8 4/8	8 4/8	20 5/8	20 2/8	356	10
◆ Nez Perce County / Michael L. Lohman / Michael L. Lohman / 1993										
183 6/8	39	37 6/8	15 2/8	15 2/8	9 7/8	9 6/8	23 5/8	17 7/8	363	11
◆ Lewis County / Earl G. Lunceford, Jr. / Earl G. Lunceford, Jr. / 1993										
183 5/8	38 2/8	39 3/8	15 6/8	15 5/8	9 2/8	9 2/8	19 4/8	18 7/8	374	12
◆ Marble Creek / Joseph T. Pelton / Joseph T. Pelton / 1961										
182 6/8	39 6/8	38	14 3/8	14 4/8	10 2/8	10	22 4/8	18	421	13
◆ Salmon River / Picked Up / Wayne Demaray / 1963										
182 6/8	40 4/8	40 4/8	14 6/8	14 5/8	9	9 1/8	22 6/8	22 6/8	421	13
◆ Lower Salmon River / Glenn H. Schubert / Deloras A. Schubert / 1970										
182 1/8	41 5/8	39	12 7/8	13 1/8	11 6/8	11 5/8	22 6/8	22 6/8	461	15
◆ Salmon River / Picked Up / Anson Eddy / PR 1959										
182 1/8	35 4/8	39 3/8	15 2/8	15 2/8	11 2/8	9 2/8	24 6/8	24 6/8	461	15
◆ Lemhi County / Leonard C. Miller, Sr. / Leonard C. Miller, Sr. / 1963										
182	40	41	14 5/8	14 7/8	8 5/8	8 7/8	24	24	466	17
◆ Salmon River / Picked Up / Elmer Keith / 1957										
181 5/8	39	38 1/8	15 3/8	15 2/8	9 7/8	9 2/8	22 6/8	20	493	18
◆ Lemhi County / David Freel / David Freel / 1986										

IDAHO BIGHORN SHEEP *(continued)*

Score	Length of Horn R	Length of Horn L	Circumference of Base R	Circumference of Base L	Circumference at Third Quarter R	Circumference at Third Quarter L	Greatest Spread	Tip-to-Tip Spread	All-Time Rank	State Rank
♦ *Locality / Hunter / Owner / Date Killed*										
180 5/8	38	39 3/8	14 3/8	14 3/8	9 6/8	10 3/8	19 4/8	19 4/8	574	19
♦ *Salmon River / Emerson Hall / Emerson Hall / 1968*										
180 5/8	38 7/8	40 2/8	14 4/8	14 2/8	9 5/8	10	21 6/8	21	574	19
♦ *Lemhi County / Eugene L. Chesler / Eugene L. Chesler / 1990*										
180 4/8	40 2/8	40	14 3/8	14 4/8	8 4/8	8 4/8	23 1/8	23	583	21
♦ *Lemhi County / Maxallen D. Jackson / Maxallen D. Jackson / 1993*										
180 3/8	36 6/8	36 1/8	16 2/8	16 2/8	9 2/8	9	22 4/8	16 7/8	596	22
♦ *Nez Perce County / Don R. Scoles / Don R. Scoles / 1994*										
180 2/8	39 3/8	38 1/8	14 1/8	14 1/8	10 6/8	10	20 7/8	20 3/8	619	23
♦ *Salmon River / Ralph Puckett / Ralph Puckett / 1958*										
180 2/8	39	39 2/8	15	15 1/8	8 3/8	8 2/8	25 4/8	25 4/8	619	23
♦ *Lemhi County / Picked Up / Thomas C. Pike / 1993*										
180 1/8	39 5/8	40 2/8	14 7/8	15	8 3/8	8 5/8	23	23	631	25
♦ *Salmon River / C.A. Schwope / C.A. Schwope / 1959*										
180 1/8	39 4/8	38 5/8	15	15	8 5/8	8 2/8	23 1/8	20 7/8	631	25
♦ *Custer County / Leland S. Speakes, Jr. / Leland S. Speakes, Jr. / 1987*										
180 1/8	40	39 5/8	14 1/8	14 2/8	9 3/8	9 1/8	22 6/8	22 4/8	631	25
♦ *Lemhi County / JoAnn Basso / JoAnn Basso / 1990*										
180	40 5/8	40 1/8	14 4/8	14 4/8	8 4/8	8 6/8	20 7/8	19 5/8	651	28
♦ *Lemhi County / A. Oscar Carlson / A. Oscar Carlson / 1993*										
177 4/8	38 6/8	38 2/8	14 7/8	14 7/8	9	8 5/8	22 6/8	19 4/8	688	29
♦ *Valley County / R. Barry Wood / R. Barry Wood / 1985*										
175 7/8	37 3/8	39 2/8	14	14	9	9	21 2/8	19	698	30
♦ *Lemhi County / Penny L. Brown / Penny L. Brown / 1988*										

Photograph Courtesy of Hoover L. Lee

While Arizona is most noted for healthy desert sheep populations, it also shares a population of bighorn sheep with neighboring New Mexico. Here, Hoover L. Lee poses with one of only three bighorns listed in the records book from Arizona. Taken in Greenlee County in 1993, it scores 180-3/8 points.

Photograph by Mike Biggs

**MONTANA STATE RECORD
BIGHORN SHEEP
SCORE: 204⅞**
Locality: Granite Co.   Date: 1993
Hunter: James R. Weatherly

MONTANA
BIGHORN SHEEP

Score	Length of Horn R	L	Circumference of Base R	L	Circumference at Third Quarter R	L	Greatest Spread	Tip-to-Tip Spread	All-Time Rank	State Rank
				♦ Locality / Hunter / Owner / Date Killed						
204⁷⁄₈	43¹⁄₈	41⁶⁄₈	17¹⁄₈	16⁷⁄₈	11⁴⁄₈	11⁷⁄₈	23⁴⁄₈	18⁶⁄₈	4	1
	♦ Granite County / James R. Weatherly / James R. Weatherly / 1993									
203⁵⁄₈	43²⁄₈	41⁵⁄₈	17²⁄₈	17⁴⁄₈	11³⁄₈	10²⁄₈	20⁷⁄₈	23⁴⁄₈	6	2
	♦ Beaverhead County / Picked Up / MT Dept. Fish, Wildl. & Parks / 1992									
202³⁄₈	41	40⁷⁄₈	17²⁄₈	17²⁄₈	11	11	25³⁄₈	26²⁄₈	8	3
	♦ Granite County / Richard B. Wiant / Richard B. Wiant / 1992									
200⁷⁄₈	45⁷⁄₈	49²⁄₈	15²⁄₈	15²⁄₈	9²⁄₈	9¹⁄₈	28⁵⁄₈	28³⁄₈	13	4
	♦ Deer Lodge County / Lester A. Kish / Lester A. Kish / 1990									
200²⁄₈	42⁴⁄₈	43⁶⁄₈	16⁷⁄₈	16⁷⁄₈	9²⁄₈	9⁶⁄₈	23⁷⁄₈	23⁷⁄₈	15	5
	♦ Blaine County / Eugene R. Knight / Eugene R. Knight / 1991									
200¹⁄₈	44	44¹⁄₈	16¹⁄₈	16²⁄₈	10⁴⁄₈	10¹⁄₈	23³⁄₈	22⁶⁄₈	16	6
	♦ Granite County / Mavis M. Lorenz / Mavis M. Lorenz / 1993									
199⁶⁄₈	42⁶⁄₈	43⁶⁄₈	16²⁄₈	16⁴⁄₈	9⁶⁄₈	9⁷⁄₈	22⁷⁄₈	21⁶⁄₈	20	7
	♦ Granite County / Kevin E. Williams / Kevin E. Williams / 1993									
199³⁄₈	42⁴⁄₈	45³⁄₈	16	16	10	11	22²⁄₈	20⁶⁄₈	21	8
	♦ Sanders County / Michael D. Turner / Michael D. Turner / 1992									
197⁷⁄₈	42⁵⁄₈	42⁶⁄₈	16⁵⁄₈	16⁴⁄₈	9⁴⁄₈	9⁵⁄₈	23⁴⁄₈	23¹⁄₈	25	9
	♦ Sanders County / Daniel R. Schwenk / Daniel R. Schwenk / 1992									
197⁵⁄₈	41¹⁄₈	42⁴⁄₈	15⁷⁄₈	16¹⁄₈	11¹⁄₈	11	22³⁄₈	22³⁄₈	27	10
	♦ Deer Lodge County / Arthur R. Dubs / Arthur R. Dubs / 1987									
197¹⁄₈	44³⁄₈	45⁴⁄₈	15⁷⁄₈	15⁵⁄₈	8⁵⁄₈	9⁴⁄₈	28⁷⁄₈	28⁷⁄₈	30	11
	♦ Sanders County / Armand H. Johnson / Armand H. Johnson / 1979									
197¹⁄₈	42	41⁵⁄₈	16⁵⁄₈	16⁴⁄₈	10⁵⁄₈	10⁶⁄₈	23⁵⁄₈	23²⁄₈	30	11
	♦ Granite County / Lee Hart / Lee Hart / 1990									
197¹⁄₈	41²⁄₈	40⁷⁄₈	16⁵⁄₈	16⁶⁄₈	10⁴⁄₈	10²⁄₈	20⁷⁄₈	18⁴⁄₈	30	11
	♦ Granite County / Mary E. Schroeder / Mary E. Schroeder / 1992									
196⁷⁄₈	43	40⁷⁄₈	16³⁄₈	16²⁄₈	9⁷⁄₈	10¹⁄₈	20²⁄₈	20	33	14
	♦ Granite County / Keith J. Koprivica / Keith J. Koprivica / 1990									
196⁵⁄₈	45²⁄₈	44³⁄₈	14⁵⁄₈	14⁶⁄₈	10⁴⁄₈	10⁴⁄₈	24⁵⁄₈	24⁴⁄₈	37	15
	♦ Sun River / Don Anderson / Don Anderson / 1961									
196⁴⁄₈	40⁴⁄₈	45	16	15⁶⁄₈	10¹⁄₈	10⁵⁄₈	24²⁄₈	21⁴⁄₈	40	16
	♦ Silver Bow County / Verne O. Barnett / Verne O. Barnett / 1991									
196²⁄₈	44⁶⁄₈	43⁶⁄₈	14⁷⁄₈	14⁶⁄₈	11	11²⁄₈	22²⁄₈	22¹⁄₈	42	17
	♦ Sanders County / Earl V. Cole / Earl V. Cole / 1993									
195⁷⁄₈	45⁴⁄₈	44³⁄₈	15⁵⁄₈	15⁶⁄₈	9²⁄₈	8⁶⁄₈	24	24	46	18
	♦ Montana / Unknown / Dole & Bailey, Inc. / 1890									

Score	Length of Horn		Circumference of Base		Circumference at Third Quarter		Greatest Spread	Tip-to-Tip Spread	All-Time Rank	State Rank
	R	L	R	L	R	L				
♦ Locality / Hunter / Owner / Date Killed										
195 3/8	44 5/8	43 4/8	15 4/8	15 7/8	9	9	24 7/8	23 2/8	49	19
♦ Missoula County / Leonard G. Thompson / Leonard G. Thompson / 1990										
195 3/8	40 4/8	41 7/8	16 3/8	16 1/8	10 2/8	11 2/8	22 3/8	21 3/8	49	19
♦ Granite County / Craig R. Johnson / Craig R. Johnson / 1994										
195	44 2/8	38 4/8	15 5/8	16 4/8	11	11 6/8	26 7/8	26 7/8	52	21
♦ Sun River / Gold White / Lee M. Ford / 1911										
194 7/8	40 4/8	39 5/8	16 2/8	16 2/8	10 3/8	10 3/8	23 7/8	22 4/8	53	22
♦ Granite County / Rick L. Barkell / Rick L. Barkell / 1992										
194 3/8	44 2/8	41 3/8	15 3/8	15 6/8	10 5/8	10 3/8	22 4/8	20 6/8	56	23
♦ Beaverhead County / Glenn M. Smith / Glenn M. Smith / 1992										
193 6/8	40 4/8	39 6/8	16 5/8	16 4/8	9 7/8	9 7/8	23 7/8	22 7/8	61	24
♦ Granite County / Michael L. Girard / Michael L. Girard / 1986										
193 6/8	40 2/8	42	15 6/8	15 7/8	11 1/8	10 6/8	22 6/8	20 1/8	61	24
♦ Granite County / Kenneth L. Getz / Kenneth L. Getz / 1992										
193 5/8	42 2/8	43 3/8	16 4/8	16 3/8	8 3/8	8 4/8	23	23	66	26
♦ Lincoln County / Al Bratkovich / Al Bratkovich / 1993										
193 4/8	39	39 4/8	16 4/8	16 3/8	10 6/8	10 7/8	26 7/8	23 2/8	68	27
♦ Silver Bow County / Thomas R. Webster / Thomas R. Webster / 1990										
193 2/8	39 7/8	39 7/8	16 5/8	16 4/8	10	10	22 4/8	19 1/8	70	28
♦ Sanders County / Jerry Landa / Jerry Landa / 1989										
193 1/8	41 7/8	43 4/8	15 1/8	15 5/8	9 7/8	9 7/8	23 6/8	21 4/8	72	29
♦ Missoula County / Bonnie A. Ford / Bonnie A. Ford / 1982										
193	39 2/8	41 2/8	16 3/8	16 4/8	9 6/8	9 7/8	23	21 7/8	75	30
♦ Granite County / Phillip S. Benson / Phillip S. Benson / 1992										
192 7/8	40 6/8	41 3/8	16 2/8	16 3/8	10	9 5/8	21 3/8	21 3/8	77	31
♦ Granite County / Raymond J. Dvorak / Raymond J. Dvorak / 1989										
192 5/8	42 7/8	44 2/8	14 3/8	14 2/8	10 6/8	10 3/8	24	24	79	32
♦ Sun River / Unknown / Leyton Z. Yearout / 1963										
192 3/8	40 6/8	40 7/8	15 4/8	15 5/8	10 5/8	10 5/8	20 5/8	17 6/8	81	33
♦ Granite County / Robert L. Sandman / Robert L. Sandman / 1991										
192 2/8	45 2/8	43	16	15 6/8	8 3/8	8 3/8	21	21	83	34
♦ Sanders County / Richard W. Browne / Richard W. Browne / 1968										
192 2/8	40 5/8	40 5/8	16 7/8	16 7/8	8 6/8	9 2/8	22	17 6/8	83	34
♦ Sanders County / Michael A. Jorgenson / Michael A. Jorgenson / 1978										
192 2/8	43 3/8	41 7/8	16 2/8	16 1/8	8 4/8	9 1/8	22 2/8	21 3/8	83	34
♦ Granite County / John P. Steele / John P. Steele / 1991										
192 1/8	42 7/8	42 4/8	16	16 2/8	9 1/8	8 6/8	22 4/8	19 1/8	86	37
♦ Deer Lodge County / Mitchell A. Thorson / Mitchell A. Thorson / 1987										

Score	Length of Horn R	L	Circumference of Base R	L	Circumference at Third Quarter R	L	Greatest Spread	Tip-to-Tip Spread	All-Time Rank	State Rank
191⁷⁄₈	44	41⁷⁄₈	15³⁄₈	15³⁄₈	9⁶⁄₈	8⁷⁄₈	24⁴⁄₈	22²⁄₈	89	38

♦ *Lake County / Picked Up / Univ. Mont. Mus. / 1961*

| 191⁷⁄₈ | 41³⁄₈ | 40⁴⁄₈ | 16 | 15⁷⁄₈ | 10¹⁄₈ | 9⁵⁄₈ | 24 | 24 | 89 | 38 |

♦ *Granite County / Steven L. Gingras / Steven L. Gingras / 1984*

| 191⁷⁄₈ | 41³⁄₈ | 40⁶⁄₈ | 15⁶⁄₈ | 15⁷⁄₈ | 8⁶⁄₈ | 9⁴⁄₈ | 24³⁄₈ | 21⁷⁄₈ | 89 | 38 |

♦ *Missoula County / Carl W. Schmidt / Carl W. Schmidt / 1989*

| 191⁶⁄₈ | 41⁷⁄₈ | 41⁵⁄₈ | 16 | 16¹⁄₈ | 9¹⁄₈ | 9 | 25 | 23⁶⁄₈ | 94 | 41 |

♦ *Silver Bow County / James G. Dennehy / James G. Dennehy / 1992*

| 191⁶⁄₈ | 41⁶⁄₈ | 41⁴⁄₈ | 16²⁄₈ | 16³⁄₈ | 8⁴⁄₈ | 8⁵⁄₈ | 24⁵⁄₈ | 23⁶⁄₈ | 94 | 41 |

♦ *Missoula County / Shelley Goodman / Shelley Goodman / 1993*

| 191⁴⁄₈ | 42⁴⁄₈ | 41⁴⁄₈ | 14⁶⁄₈ | 15 | 10²⁄₈ | 9⁷⁄₈ | 22⁶⁄₈ | 22³⁄₈ | 98 | 43 |

♦ *Lincoln County / Picked Up / Ed Boyes / PR 1961*

| 191³⁄₈ | 40 | 39³⁄₈ | 15⁷⁄₈ | 15⁷⁄₈ | 10³⁄₈ | 10⁴⁄₈ | 21 | 19 | 100 | 44 |

♦ *Sanders County / Robert A. Larsson / Robert A. Larsson / 1994*

| 191 | 40 | 39²⁄₈ | 16⁵⁄₈ | 16⁵⁄₈ | 9¹⁄₈ | 9 | 24 | 22²⁄₈ | 112 | 45 |

♦ *Granite County / Harry W. Miller / Harry W. Miller / 1985*

| 190⁷⁄₈ | 39⁶⁄₈ | 41⁵⁄₈ | 15⁷⁄₈ | 16 | 9⁴⁄₈ | 10 | 23⁴⁄₈ | 18⁷⁄₈ | 114 | 46 |

♦ *Sanders County / Terri Stoneman / Terri Stoneman / 1988*

| 190⁷⁄₈ | 42⁵⁄₈ | 40⁴⁄₈ | 15⁴⁄₈ | 15⁴⁄₈ | 9⁷⁄₈ | 9⁷⁄₈ | 25²⁄₈ | 24⁷⁄₈ | 114 | 46 |

♦ *Lewis & Clark County / Rodney H. Eaton / Rodney H. Eaton / 1992*

| 190⁶⁄₈ | 42³⁄₈ | 41⁵⁄₈ | 15⁵⁄₈ | 15⁵⁄₈ | 8⁷⁄₈ | 8⁷⁄₈ | 25⁵⁄₈ | 25⁷⁄₈ | 116 | 48 |

♦ *Missoula County / Arthur R. Dubs / Arthur R. Dubs / 1986*

| 190⁶⁄₈ | 40⁶⁄₈ | 39⁴⁄₈ | 15⁶⁄₈ | 15⁷⁄₈ | 10³⁄₈ | 9⁷⁄₈ | 23 | 17³⁄₈ | 116 | 48 |

♦ *Granite County / Scott A. Campbell / Scott A. Campbell / 1990*

| 190⁶⁄₈ | 41¹⁄₈ | 40⁵⁄₈ | 15⁷⁄₈ | 15⁷⁄₈ | 9⁴⁄₈ | 9²⁄₈ | 24⁷⁄₈ | 22²⁄₈ | 116 | 48 |

♦ *Sanders County / H. Gene Warren / H. Gene Warren / 1991*

| 190⁵⁄₈ | 43⁵⁄₈ | 43²⁄₈ | 15⁶⁄₈ | 15⁵⁄₈ | 8⁶⁄₈ | 8⁴⁄₈ | 24⁵⁄₈ | 24⁵⁄₈ | 121 | 51 |

♦ *Missoula County / John J. Ottman / John J. Ottman / 1985*

| 190⁵⁄₈ | 40⁴⁄₈ | 42⁵⁄₈ | 15⁶⁄₈ | 16¹⁄₈ | 9²⁄₈ | 9²⁄₈ | 24²⁄₈ | 23⁴⁄₈ | 121 | 51 |

♦ *Missoula County / Chris L. Mostad / Chris L. Mostad / 1986*

| 190³⁄₈ | 39²⁄₈ | 39¹⁄₈ | 16 | 16 | 10⁴⁄₈ | 10³⁄₈ | 21⁷⁄₈ | 21⁷⁄₈ | 124 | 53 |

♦ *Sun River / F.P. Murray / F.P. Murray / 1957*

| 190²⁄₈ | 39²⁄₈ | 37⁶⁄₈ | 16⁵⁄₈ | 16⁴⁄₈ | 10²⁄₈ | 9⁷⁄₈ | 22⁴⁄₈ | 18¹⁄₈ | 126 | 54 |

♦ *Sanders County / Duane Dauenhauer / Duane Dauenhauer / 1992*

| 190²⁄₈ | 44⁶⁄₈ | 41²⁄₈ | 14⁷⁄₈ | 14⁵⁄₈ | 9⁴⁄₈ | 9²⁄₈ | 23³⁄₈ | 22⁵⁄₈ | 126 | 54 |

♦ *Sanders County / Scott W. Johnson / Scott W. Johnson / 1994*

| 190¹⁄₈ | 41⁶⁄₈ | 40³⁄₈ | 15⁷⁄₈ | 16¹⁄₈ | 9²⁄₈ | 9²⁄₈ | 23⁴⁄₈ | 21 | 128 | 56 |

♦ *Missoula County / Joseph C. Turner / Joseph C. Turner / 1987*

Score	Length of Horn R	L	Circumference of Base R	L	Circumference at Third Quarter R	L	Greatest Spread	Tip-to-Tip Spread	All-Time Rank	State Rank
190	40 5/8	40 1/8	16	15 4/8	10 5/8	10 2/8	22 6/8	22	129	57
Granite County / Rick L. Williams / Rick L. Williams / 1991										
189 5/8	39 4/8	42 3/8	15 4/8	15 3/8	9 7/8	10 1/8	22 3/8	21 4/8	136	58
Deer Lodge County / Lawrence A. Jany / Lawrence A. Jany / 1990										
189 3/8	40 7/8	40 4/8	16 6/8	16 4/8	8 4/8	8 5/8	23	19 1/8	140	59
Teton County / R.L. Kennedy / R.L. Kennedy / 1983										
189 2/8	40 7/8	40 3/8	16 6/8	16 6/8	8 1/8	8 2/8	26	25 6/8	144	60
Sanders County / Linda Phillips / Linda Phillips / 1989										
189	40 1/8	41 5/8	15 3/8	15 4/8	9 5/8	9 3/8	21 3/8	20 5/8	149	61
Granite County / Mark M. Morgan / Mark M. Morgan / 1991										
188 7/8	41 2/8	44 5/8	15 1/8	15	9	8 7/8	24 4/8	23 6/8	151	62
Gallatin Range / Alden B. Walrath / Alden B. Walrath / 1965										
188 7/8	44 7/8	39 6/8	15 7/8	15 7/8	8 4/8	8 2/8	26 6/8	26 4/8	151	62
Silver Bow County / Jerry J. Joseph / Jerry J. Joseph / 1990										
188 6/8	40	40	15 4/8	15 4/8	10 3/8	10 5/8	21 7/8	20 6/8	157	64
Deer Lodge County / Mike J. Bartoletti / Mike J. Bartoletti / 1991										
188 5/8	38 7/8	39 4/8	15 6/8	15 6/8	9 6/8	10 1/8	21 4/8	19 2/8	160	65
Sun River / Bruce McCracken / Bruce McCracken / 1955										
188 5/8	40 5/8	39 2/8	15 2/8	15 3/8	10 3/8	10 2/8	20 6/8	18 2/8	160	65
Sanders County / Richard L. Grimes / Richard L. Grimes / 1990										
188 4/8	39	40 4/8	15 7/8	15 7/8	9 5/8	10	22 4/8	22 4/8	165	67
Rivalli Creek / Sandy Rose / Sandy Rose / 1978										
188 4/8	40 4/8	37 4/8	15 7/8	15 7/8	10	9 5/8	23 6/8	17 4/8	165	67
Blaine County / Lanny L. Walker / Lanny L. Walker / 1991										
188 3/8	40	40 7/8	15 5/8	15 4/8	9 6/8	9 7/8	24	23 1/8	169	69
Deer Lodge County / Paul J. Druyvestein / Paul J. Druyvestein / 1986										
188 3/8	40 4/8	39 3/8	15 2/8	15 4/8	10 7/8	11	23 6/8	20 6/8	169	69
Granite County / Larry J. Antonich / Larry J. Antonich / 1990										
188 2/8	40	40 6/8	15 4/8	15 1/8	9 3/8	10 4/8	21 4/8	19	177	71
Sun River / Bruce Neal / Bruce Neal / 1912										
188 2/8	40 4/8	40 6/8	15 1/8	15	10	10 5/8	22 4/8	21 1/8	177	71
Sun River / J.R. Pfeifer / J.R. Pfeifer / 1958										
188 2/8	43	42 2/8	15 6/8	15 5/8	7 7/8	8 1/8	24 3/8	24 3/8	177	71
Deer Lodge County / Walter F. Smith / Walter F. Smith / 1986										
188 2/8	39 4/8	42	15 5/8	15 7/8	9 1/8	9 5/8	25 6/8	25 2/8	177	71
Beaverhead County / Corey J. Buhl / Corey J. Buhl / 1992										
188 2/8	40 6/8	40 4/8	17	17	8	8	25 4/8	25 3/8	177	71
Granite County / Donald O. Cure / Donald O. Cure / 1994										

MONTANA BIGHORN SHEEP *(continued)*

Score	Length of Horn		Circumference of Base		Circumference at Third Quarter		Greatest Spread	Tip-to-Tip Spread	All-Time Rank	State Rank
	R	L	R	L	R	L				
$188\frac{1}{8}$	$44\frac{3}{8}$	$42\frac{2}{8}$	$14\frac{3}{8}$	$14\frac{7}{8}$	$9\frac{6}{8}$	$9\frac{2}{8}$	$25\frac{3}{8}$	$25\frac{3}{8}$	185	76
◆ Lincoln County / Alfred E. Journey / Alfred E. Journey / 1980										
$188\frac{1}{8}$	$38\frac{5}{8}$	$39\frac{4}{8}$	$16\frac{6}{8}$	$16\frac{5}{8}$	9	$9\frac{2}{8}$	$26\frac{4}{8}$	21	185	76
◆ Sanders County / Patti L. Lewis / Patti L. Lewis / 1984										
$188\frac{1}{8}$	$40\frac{1}{8}$	$40\frac{4}{8}$	$15\frac{1}{8}$	$15\frac{2}{8}$	$10\frac{1}{8}$	10	$23\frac{4}{8}$	$23\frac{4}{8}$	185	76
◆ Blaine County / Curtis L. Kostelecky / Curtis L. Kostelecky / 1991										
$187\frac{6}{8}$	$39\frac{4}{8}$	42	$15\frac{6}{8}$	$15\frac{6}{8}$	$8\frac{7}{8}$	$8\frac{7}{8}$	$23\frac{2}{8}$	$23\frac{1}{8}$	191	79
◆ Deer Lodge County / William H. Shurte / William H. Shurte / 1984										
$187\frac{5}{8}$	$39\frac{3}{8}$	$40\frac{4}{8}$	$15\frac{2}{8}$	$15\frac{2}{8}$	$9\frac{6}{8}$	$9\frac{6}{8}$	$21\frac{2}{8}$	$21\frac{2}{8}$	197	80
◆ Glacier Natl. Park / Olmstead, Dow, & Hawley / Mont. Dept. Fish, Wildl., & Parks / 1956										
$187\frac{4}{8}$	35	$37\frac{4}{8}$	$16\frac{1}{8}$	$16\frac{2}{8}$	$10\frac{7}{8}$	$10\frac{7}{8}$	$24\frac{4}{8}$	$23\frac{5}{8}$	202	81
◆ Deer Lodge County / Dorothy A. Pennington / Dorothy A. Pennington / 1991										
$187\frac{2}{8}$	$39\frac{2}{8}$	$40\frac{4}{8}$	$15\frac{7}{8}$	$15\frac{7}{8}$	$8\frac{6}{8}$	$8\frac{6}{8}$	$23\frac{1}{8}$	$22\frac{6}{8}$	208	82
◆ Granite County / Donald A. Chamberlain / Donald A. Chamberlain / 1987										
$187\frac{2}{8}$	$42\frac{4}{8}$	$39\frac{4}{8}$	$15\frac{7}{8}$	$15\frac{5}{8}$	$8\frac{3}{8}$	$8\frac{7}{8}$	$22\frac{2}{8}$	$21\frac{5}{8}$	208	82
◆ Granite County / Chuck Houtz / Chuck Houtz / 1988										
$187\frac{2}{8}$	$40\frac{3}{8}$	$41\frac{1}{8}$	16	$16\frac{1}{8}$	$8\frac{4}{8}$	$8\frac{7}{8}$	$21\frac{1}{8}$	$20\frac{2}{8}$	208	82
◆ Beaverhead County / Charles R. Moe / Charles R. Moe / 1994										
$187\frac{1}{8}$	$40\frac{7}{8}$	$40\frac{4}{8}$	$14\frac{5}{8}$	$14\frac{4}{8}$	$10\frac{5}{8}$	$10\frac{3}{8}$	$23\frac{4}{8}$	$23\frac{4}{8}$	215	85
◆ Deer Lodge County / David J. Etzwiler / David J. Etzwiler / 1985										
187	$40\frac{6}{8}$	$40\frac{6}{8}$	$15\frac{5}{8}$	$15\frac{5}{8}$	$8\frac{4}{8}$	$8\frac{6}{8}$	$22\frac{2}{8}$	$20\frac{7}{8}$	219	86
◆ Sanders County / Bruce L. Hartford / Bruce L. Hartford / 1978										
187	$37\frac{4}{8}$	$38\frac{4}{8}$	$16\frac{3}{8}$	$16\frac{5}{8}$	$9\frac{4}{8}$	$9\frac{7}{8}$	25	$22\frac{4}{8}$	219	86
◆ Sanders County / Richard F. Lukes / Richard F. Lukes / 1980										
187	$40\frac{6}{8}$	$40\frac{4}{8}$	$16\frac{4}{8}$	$16\frac{4}{8}$	$7\frac{6}{8}$	8	$21\frac{6}{8}$	$21\frac{6}{8}$	219	86
◆ Deer Lodge County / Wayne E. Bousfield / Wayne E. Bousfield / 1985										
187	$41\frac{3}{8}$	$41\frac{3}{8}$	16	$15\frac{6}{8}$	$8\frac{2}{8}$	$8\frac{2}{8}$	$24\frac{4}{8}$	$24\frac{4}{8}$	219	86
◆ Sanders County / Mark S. Eaton / Mark S. Eaton / 1985										
187	$39\frac{3}{8}$	$39\frac{7}{8}$	16	$15\frac{7}{8}$	$8\frac{7}{8}$	$8\frac{5}{8}$	22	$22\frac{4}{8}$	219	86
◆ Granite County / Norman C. Dunkle / Norman C. Dunkle / 1989										
187	39	$38\frac{4}{8}$	$15\frac{2}{8}$	$15\frac{2}{8}$	$10\frac{3}{8}$	11	$22\frac{1}{8}$	$22\frac{1}{8}$	219	86
◆ Sanders County / William V. Kuchera / William V. Kuchera / 1990										
187	$40\frac{4}{8}$	$39\frac{4}{8}$	$15\frac{5}{8}$	$15\frac{5}{8}$	10	$9\frac{6}{8}$	$20\frac{4}{8}$	$17\frac{4}{8}$	219	86
◆ Granite County / Pearl Foust / Pearl Foust / 1991										
$186\frac{6}{8}$	$39\frac{1}{8}$	$37\frac{5}{8}$	$15\frac{2}{8}$	$15\frac{3}{8}$	$11\frac{1}{8}$	$10\frac{5}{8}$	$22\frac{3}{8}$	$20\frac{4}{8}$	234	93
◆ Sanders County / Bill Mitchell / Bill Mitchell / 1988										
$186\frac{6}{8}$	$41\frac{1}{8}$	$41\frac{1}{8}$	$15\frac{4}{8}$	$15\frac{4}{8}$	$8\frac{5}{8}$	$8\frac{6}{8}$	$22\frac{3}{8}$	$21\frac{6}{8}$	234	93
◆ Granite County / Carol K. Chudy / Carol K. Chudy / 1991										

Score	Length of Horn		Circumference of Base		Circumference at Third Quarter		Greatest Spread	Tip-to-Tip Spread	All-Time Rank	State Rank
	R	L	R	L	R	L				
♦ *Locality / Hunter / Owner / Date Killed*										
$186\frac{5}{8}$	41	$40\frac{7}{8}$	$16\frac{1}{8}$	$16\frac{1}{8}$	8	$8\frac{6}{8}$	$23\frac{6}{8}$	$23\frac{6}{8}$	242	95
♦ *Beaverhead County / Gary L. Peltomaa / Gary L. Peltomaa / 1989*										
$186\frac{5}{8}$	$37\frac{5}{8}$	$38\frac{4}{8}$	$15\frac{7}{8}$	$15\frac{6}{8}$	$9\frac{7}{8}$	$9\frac{6}{8}$	$22\frac{3}{8}$	$16\frac{3}{8}$	242	95
♦ *Sanders County / Robert G. Blenker / Robert G. Blenker / 1991*										
$186\frac{1}{8}$	$43\frac{2}{8}$	$44\frac{5}{8}$	$16\frac{4}{8}$	$16\frac{5}{8}$	$6\frac{5}{8}$	$6\frac{7}{8}$	$24\frac{5}{8}$	$24\frac{5}{8}$	264	97
♦ *Yellowstone Park / William H. Dirrett / James K. Weatherford / 1913*										
$186\frac{1}{8}$	$41\frac{5}{8}$	$41\frac{2}{8}$	$15\frac{3}{8}$	$15\frac{4}{8}$	$8\frac{2}{8}$	$8\frac{5}{8}$	$20\frac{7}{8}$	$19\frac{1}{8}$	264	97
♦ *Sun River Canyon / Glen Roberts / Glen Roberts / 1961*										
$186\frac{1}{8}$	$41\frac{4}{8}$	$36\frac{7}{8}$	16	$16\frac{1}{8}$	$9\frac{1}{8}$	$9\frac{2}{8}$	$22\frac{1}{8}$	18	264	97
♦ *Fergus County / Henry M. Kengerski / Henry M. Kengerski / 1993*										
186	$39\frac{4}{8}$	39	$14\frac{6}{8}$	$14\frac{6}{8}$	$10\frac{6}{8}$	$10\frac{6}{8}$	21	21	270	100
♦ *Granite County / Dale W. Hoth / Dale W. Hoth / 1981*										
$185\frac{7}{8}$	35	$37\frac{3}{8}$	$14\frac{4}{8}$	$14\frac{4}{8}$	13	13	$20\frac{3}{8}$	$17\frac{5}{8}$	274	101
♦ *Ural / Curtis Gatson / Curtis Gatson / 1962*										
$185\frac{6}{8}$	$39\frac{6}{8}$	$38\frac{4}{8}$	$15\frac{2}{8}$	$15\frac{2}{8}$	$9\frac{7}{8}$	$9\frac{6}{8}$	$20\frac{4}{8}$	20	279	102
♦ *Granite County / James M. Milligan / James M. Milligan / 1990*										
$185\frac{6}{8}$	$38\frac{4}{8}$	$36\frac{6}{8}$	$15\frac{6}{8}$	16	$10\frac{6}{8}$	$10\frac{2}{8}$	21	$18\frac{3}{8}$	279	102
♦ *Granite County / Donald A. Dwyer / Donald A. Dwyer / 1992*										
$185\frac{4}{8}$	$39\frac{7}{8}$	$38\frac{3}{8}$	$16\frac{6}{8}$	$16\frac{3}{8}$	$8\frac{2}{8}$	$8\frac{2}{8}$	$27\frac{3}{8}$	$27\frac{3}{8}$	284	104
♦ *Granite County / Lawrence R. Simkins / Lawrence R. Simkins / 1986*										
$185\frac{4}{8}$	$40\frac{5}{8}$	$39\frac{3}{8}$	$16\frac{4}{8}$	$16\frac{3}{8}$	$8\frac{7}{8}$	$8\frac{3}{8}$	$21\frac{7}{8}$	$21\frac{7}{8}$	284	104
♦ *Deer Lodge County / Douglas C. Landers / Douglas C. Landers / 1987*										
$185\frac{4}{8}$	$40\frac{7}{8}$	$40\frac{3}{8}$	$14\frac{5}{8}$	$14\frac{6}{8}$	$9\frac{7}{8}$	$10\frac{2}{8}$	$20\frac{5}{8}$	$20\frac{3}{8}$	284	104
♦ *Lewis & Clark County / Darlene K. Kechely / Darlene K. Kechely / 1992*										
$185\frac{4}{8}$	$41\frac{1}{8}$	$39\frac{3}{8}$	$15\frac{6}{8}$	$15\frac{7}{8}$	$8\frac{7}{8}$	$8\frac{3}{8}$	25	$22\frac{2}{8}$	284	104
♦ *Missoula County / Thomas J. Dux / Thomas J. Dux / 1993*										
$185\frac{3}{8}$	$39\frac{4}{8}$	$38\frac{3}{8}$	$14\frac{7}{8}$	$15\frac{1}{8}$	$10\frac{2}{8}$	$10\frac{2}{8}$	22	$17\frac{4}{8}$	293	108
♦ *Lewis & Clark County / Richard Tyler / Richard Tyler / 1954*										
$185\frac{3}{8}$	$38\frac{1}{8}$	$40\frac{6}{8}$	$15\frac{7}{8}$	$15\frac{7}{8}$	$9\frac{4}{8}$	$9\frac{3}{8}$	$22\frac{6}{8}$	$17\frac{6}{8}$	293	108
♦ *Sanders County / Chad R. Jones / Chad R. Jones / 1990*										
$185\frac{2}{8}$	$38\frac{5}{8}$	$41\frac{3}{8}$	$15\frac{5}{8}$	$15\frac{1}{8}$	$8\frac{6}{8}$	$9\frac{2}{8}$	$21\frac{4}{8}$	$20\frac{4}{8}$	299	110
♦ *Teton County / Picked Up / Tim French / 1980*										
$185\frac{2}{8}$	$39\frac{2}{8}$	38	15	$15\frac{2}{8}$	$11\frac{3}{8}$	$10\frac{3}{8}$	$22\frac{7}{8}$	17	299	110
♦ *Phillips County / Patrick R. Trujillo / Patrick R. Trujillo / 1992*										
$185\frac{1}{8}$	38	$38\frac{5}{8}$	$16\frac{4}{8}$	$16\frac{2}{8}$	$8\frac{5}{8}$	9	$25\frac{1}{8}$	$22\frac{4}{8}$	305	112
♦ *Blaine County / Mark K. Weiser / Mark K. Weiser / 1989*										
$185\frac{1}{8}$	41	$40\frac{1}{8}$	$14\frac{2}{8}$	$14\frac{1}{8}$	11	$10\frac{7}{8}$	21	$17\frac{6}{8}$	305	112
♦ *Lewis & Clark County / Eugene R. Lewis / Eugene R. Lewis / 1990*										

MONTANA BIGHORN SHEEP *(continued)*

Score	Length of Horn R	Length of Horn L	Circumference of Base R	Circumference of Base L	Circumference at Third Quarter R	Circumference at Third Quarter L	Greatest Spread	Tip-to-Tip Spread	All-Time Rank	State Rank
♦ *Locality / Hunter / Owner / Date Killed*										
185 1/8	38	39 1/8	16 2/8	16 3/8	9	9	22 2/8	18 2/8	305	112
♦ *Sanders County / Marcus M. Nichols / Marcus M. Nichols / 1994*										
185	40	41	14 7/8	15	10	10	23 3/8	18 1/8	311	115
♦ *Sanders County / Patrick M. Woolard / Patrick M. Woolard / 1992*										
184 6/8	41 2/8	41 2/8	14 4/8	14 4/8	9 6/8	9 4/8	21	20 6/8	318	116
♦ *Castle Mt. / E.L. Anderson / E.L. Anderson / 1954*										
184 6/8	37 7/8	37 3/8	15 4/8	15 4/8	10 1/8	10 2/8	19 7/8	18 4/8	318	116
♦ *Sanders County / William J. Alexander / William J. Alexander / 1991*										
184 4/8	39 5/8	38 5/8	14 4/8	14 4/8	10 1/8	10 1/8	21 5/8	17 7/8	331	118
♦ *Sun River / Picked Up / W.H. Stecker / 1948*										
184 4/8	36 7/8	37 5/8	15 7/8	15 4/8	10 1/8	10 5/8	24 6/8	23 7/8	331	118
♦ *Granite County / Kevin R. Bouley / Kevin R. Bouley / 1988*										
184 3/8	39 6/8	39 7/8	14 1/8	14	11	11 6/8	22	21	337	120
♦ *Carbon County / Picked Up / Monte Berzel / 1977*										
184 3/8	42 4/8	41 7/8	15 3/8	15 4/8	7 4/8	7 4/8	24 2/8	23 7/8	337	120
♦ *Sanders County / Charles Hall / Charles Hall / 1992*										
184 1/8	39	38 1/8	16	15 7/8	9 5/8	9 5/8	25	23 5/8	344	122
♦ *Silver Bow County / John D. Truzzoline / John D. Truzzoline / 1990*										
184	39 1/8	39 1/8	14 7/8	14 7/8	10 1/8	10 3/8	21 6/8	21 6/8	349	123
♦ *Sun River / Carl Mehmke / Carl Mehmke / 1957*										
184	37 5/8	39 5/8	16 4/8	16 3/8	8 2/8	8 7/8	21	20	349	123
♦ *Sanders County / Don Robinson / Don Robinson / 1980*										
184	40 4/8	43 4/8	15	15	8 2/8	8 3/8	25 5/8	25 5/8	349	123
♦ *Deer Lodge County / Dave Bisch / Dave Bisch / 1988*										
184	39	40 2/8	14 4/8	14 4/8	10 2/8	10 4/8	22	19 7/8	349	123
♦ *Mineral County / Ronald A. Snyder / Ronald A. Snyder / 1991*										
183 7/8	43 5/8	35 2/8	17	17	7 5/8	6 6/8	24 4/8	23	356	127
♦ *Beaverhead County / James C. Garrett / James C. Garrett / 1983*										
183 7/8	41	41 1/8	15 1/8	15 1/8	8 4/8	8 2/8	24 3/8	24 3/8	356	127
♦ *Sanders County / Lyndell C. Stahn / Lyndell C. Stahn / 1988*										
183 7/8	39 1/8	39 2/8	15 6/8	15 5/8	8 7/8	8 6/8	23 7/8	21 6/8	356	127
♦ *Granite County / Gordon H. Brandenburger / Gordon H. Brandenburger / 1992*										
183 7/8	37 4/8	37 1/8	16 4/8	16 4/8	9	9	23 2/8	23	356	127
♦ *Beaverhead County / Arthur E. Nuthak / Arthur E. Nuthak / 1993*										
183 6/8	37 6/8	36 4/8	16 5/8	16 6/8	9	9	23 4/8	23 4/8	363	131
♦ *Ravalli County / Sandra L. Gann / Les Towner / 1985*										
183 6/8	37 4/8	37 4/8	16	16	9 3/8	9 4/8	24	22 4/8	363	131
♦ *Silver Bow County / Emmett O. Riordan / Emmett O. Riordan / 1986*										

Score	Length of Horn		Circumference of Base		Circumference at Third Quarter		Greatest Spread	Tip-to-Tip Spread	All-Time Rank	State Rank
	R	L	R	L	R	L				
◆ Locality / Hunter / Owner / Date Killed										
183$\frac{6}{8}$	36	36	16$\frac{2}{8}$	16$\frac{2}{8}$	9$\frac{5}{8}$	10$\frac{1}{8}$	21$\frac{7}{8}$	15$\frac{3}{8}$	363	131
◆ Teton County / Greg D. Gilbert / Greg D. Gilbert / 1992										
183$\frac{6}{8}$	37$\frac{1}{8}$	36$\frac{1}{8}$	17$\frac{2}{8}$	17$\frac{2}{8}$	8$\frac{1}{8}$	8	21$\frac{4}{8}$	21	363	131
◆ Blaine County / John H. Miller / John H. Miller / 1992										
183$\frac{6}{8}$	38$\frac{5}{8}$	40$\frac{3}{8}$	14$\frac{7}{8}$	14$\frac{7}{8}$	9$\frac{6}{8}$	9$\frac{7}{8}$	23$\frac{6}{8}$	17$\frac{6}{8}$	363	131
◆ Granite County / Janice J. Kauffman / Janice J. Kauffman / 1993										
183$\frac{5}{8}$	36$\frac{7}{8}$	37	16$\frac{1}{8}$	16$\frac{1}{8}$	9$\frac{6}{8}$	9$\frac{5}{8}$	24$\frac{7}{8}$	24$\frac{7}{8}$	374	136
◆ Granite County / Sandy C. Antonich / Sandy C. Antonich / 1982										
183$\frac{5}{8}$	38$\frac{3}{8}$	37$\frac{6}{8}$	16$\frac{5}{8}$	16$\frac{5}{8}$	8$\frac{4}{8}$	8$\frac{5}{8}$	21$\frac{6}{8}$	21$\frac{2}{8}$	374	136
◆ Phillips County / Dee Strickler / Jack F. Strickler / 1993										
183$\frac{4}{8}$	33$\frac{4}{8}$	39	15$\frac{6}{8}$	16	10$\frac{4}{8}$	10$\frac{4}{8}$	22$\frac{3}{8}$	18$\frac{2}{8}$	379	138
◆ Sweetgrass County / Basil C. Bradbury / Basil C. Bradbury / 1965										
183$\frac{4}{8}$	38$\frac{4}{8}$	37$\frac{6}{8}$	15$\frac{4}{8}$	15$\frac{6}{8}$	9$\frac{5}{8}$	9$\frac{4}{8}$	20$\frac{4}{8}$	20$\frac{4}{8}$	379	138
◆ C. M. R. Game Range / Mrs. Gordon Pagenkopf / Mrs. Gordon Pagenkopf / 1970										
183$\frac{4}{8}$	38$\frac{2}{8}$	39$\frac{2}{8}$	16$\frac{1}{8}$	16$\frac{2}{8}$	8$\frac{6}{8}$	8$\frac{1}{8}$	18	13$\frac{7}{8}$	379	138
◆ Granite County / Karen Throckmorton / Karen Throckmorton / 1987										
183$\frac{4}{8}$	39	39$\frac{6}{8}$	16	16	8$\frac{2}{8}$	8	21$\frac{2}{8}$	20$\frac{3}{8}$	379	138
◆ Lewis & Clark County / Lynn E. Valtinson / Lynn E. Valtinson / 1991										
183$\frac{3}{8}$	41	38$\frac{1}{8}$	16	15$\frac{6}{8}$	8	8$\frac{3}{8}$	24$\frac{1}{8}$	23$\frac{5}{8}$	386	142
◆ Lewis & Clark County / John Coston / John Coston / 1961										
183$\frac{3}{8}$	38$\frac{7}{8}$	39$\frac{4}{8}$	16$\frac{4}{8}$	16$\frac{6}{8}$	7$\frac{7}{8}$	8$\frac{2}{8}$	21	15$\frac{6}{8}$	386	142
◆ Sanders County / John P. Dilley / John P. Dilley / 1981										
183$\frac{3}{8}$	42$\frac{7}{8}$	42$\frac{4}{8}$	15$\frac{2}{8}$	15$\frac{2}{8}$	7$\frac{4}{8}$	6$\frac{7}{8}$	27$\frac{4}{8}$	27$\frac{4}{8}$	386	142
◆ Sanders County / Edward W. Blackwood / Rocky Mtn. Elk Foundation / 1985										
183$\frac{3}{8}$	40$\frac{4}{8}$	41$\frac{1}{8}$	15$\frac{6}{8}$	15$\frac{4}{8}$	7$\frac{5}{8}$	7$\frac{4}{8}$	21$\frac{5}{8}$	21$\frac{5}{8}$	386	142
◆ Sanders County / Ilse R. Knight / Ilse R. Knight / 1986										
183$\frac{3}{8}$	37$\frac{5}{8}$	37$\frac{4}{8}$	16$\frac{1}{8}$	16$\frac{1}{8}$	9$\frac{5}{8}$	9$\frac{6}{8}$	22$\frac{6}{8}$	19$\frac{4}{8}$	386	142
◆ Silver Bow County / Travis R. Schuessler / Travis R. Schuessler / 1990										
183$\frac{2}{8}$	39$\frac{4}{8}$	38$\frac{4}{8}$	14$\frac{6}{8}$	14$\frac{7}{8}$	9$\frac{7}{8}$	9$\frac{6}{8}$	23$\frac{2}{8}$	23$\frac{2}{8}$	393	147
◆ Sun River / Earl Hofland / Earl Hofland / 1957										
183$\frac{2}{8}$	38$\frac{4}{8}$	40$\frac{2}{8}$	15$\frac{6}{8}$	15$\frac{6}{8}$	8	8$\frac{4}{8}$	22$\frac{3}{8}$	18$\frac{4}{8}$	393	147
◆ Granite County / John L. Wozniak / John L. Wozniak / 1984										
183$\frac{2}{8}$	41	42$\frac{6}{8}$	15$\frac{2}{8}$	15$\frac{2}{8}$	7$\frac{4}{8}$	7$\frac{7}{8}$	23$\frac{7}{8}$	23$\frac{7}{8}$	393	147
◆ Deer Lodge County / Phillip Demers / Phillip Demers / 1985										
183$\frac{2}{8}$	41$\frac{4}{8}$	40$\frac{2}{8}$	16$\frac{2}{8}$	16$\frac{2}{8}$	7$\frac{3}{8}$	7$\frac{6}{8}$	22$\frac{2}{8}$	21$\frac{1}{8}$	393	147
◆ Sanders County / Alma E. Arnold / Alma E. Arnold / 1986										
183$\frac{2}{8}$	40$\frac{2}{8}$	40$\frac{2}{8}$	15$\frac{7}{8}$	15$\frac{4}{8}$	8$\frac{1}{8}$	8$\frac{1}{8}$	23$\frac{6}{8}$	23$\frac{3}{8}$	393	147
◆ Sanders County / Thorne R. Johnson / Thorne R. Johnson / 1987										

Score	Length of Horn		Circumference of Base		Circumference at Third Quarter		Greatest Spread	Tip-to-Tip Spread	All-Time Rank	State Rank
	R	L	R	L	R	L				
◆ *Locality / Hunter / Owner / Date Killed*										
$183\frac{2}{8}$	$39\frac{5}{8}$	$36\frac{3}{8}$	$16\frac{2}{8}$	$16\frac{3}{8}$	$8\frac{7}{8}$	$8\frac{5}{8}$	$28\frac{2}{8}$	$28\frac{2}{8}$	393	147
◆ *Granite County / Scott R. Rossow / Scott R. Rossow / 1988*										
$183\frac{1}{8}$	$36\frac{1}{8}$	$40\frac{2}{8}$	16	$15\frac{7}{8}$	$8\frac{7}{8}$	9	$20\frac{3}{8}$	$20\frac{2}{8}$	406	153
◆ *Deer Lodge County / Jeffrey R. Shellenberg / Jeffrey R. Shellenberg / 1990*										
$183\frac{1}{8}$	$39\frac{6}{8}$	$39\frac{5}{8}$	$15\frac{4}{8}$	$15\frac{4}{8}$	9	$8\frac{5}{8}$	$22\frac{7}{8}$	$20\frac{4}{8}$	406	153
◆ *Granite County / Stephen E. Brown / Stephen E. Brown / 1993*										
$183\frac{1}{8}$	$41\frac{1}{8}$	$39\frac{6}{8}$	$14\frac{6}{8}$	$14\frac{5}{8}$	$9\frac{5}{8}$	$9\frac{4}{8}$	22	$18\frac{4}{8}$	406	153
◆ *Sanders County / Robert A. Parker / Robert A. Parker / 1993*										
$182\frac{6}{8}$	$40\frac{6}{8}$	$39\frac{2}{8}$	$16\frac{1}{8}$	16	$7\frac{6}{8}$	$7\frac{7}{8}$	$22\frac{6}{8}$	$19\frac{6}{8}$	421	156
◆ *Sanders County / Terrence Pond / Terrence Pond / 1978*										
$182\frac{6}{8}$	42	$40\frac{4}{8}$	16	16	7	$7\frac{1}{8}$	$25\frac{7}{8}$	$25\frac{3}{8}$	421	156
◆ *Deer Lodge County / Kirk G. Stovall / Kirk G. Stovall / 1990*										
$182\frac{6}{8}$	$40\frac{1}{8}$	$40\frac{3}{8}$	15	$15\frac{2}{8}$	9	$8\frac{4}{8}$	23	$22\frac{1}{8}$	421	156
◆ *Ravalli County / Robert S. Wood / Robert S. Wood / 1993*										
$182\frac{5}{8}$	$42\frac{1}{8}$	$40\frac{4}{8}$	$15\frac{2}{8}$	$15\frac{2}{8}$	$7\frac{5}{8}$	$7\frac{3}{8}$	$20\frac{2}{8}$	20	429	159
◆ *Sun River / Martin Alzheimer / Martin Alzheimer / 1955*										
$182\frac{4}{8}$	$39\frac{3}{8}$	$39\frac{3}{8}$	$15\frac{5}{8}$	$15\frac{5}{8}$	$9\frac{7}{8}$	$8\frac{4}{8}$	$21\frac{5}{8}$	19	436	160
◆ *Sanders County / Thorne R. Johnson / Thorne R. Johnson / 1989*										
$182\frac{3}{8}$	$38\frac{7}{8}$	$38\frac{2}{8}$	$15\frac{4}{8}$	$15\frac{3}{8}$	$9\frac{1}{8}$	$9\frac{5}{8}$	20	$18\frac{1}{8}$	447	161
◆ *Montana / Unknown / Joseph P. Scurti / PR 1949*										
$182\frac{3}{8}$	$37\frac{2}{8}$	$37\frac{3}{8}$	$15\frac{3}{8}$	$15\frac{2}{8}$	$10\frac{4}{8}$	$10\frac{4}{8}$	$21\frac{7}{8}$	17	447	161
◆ *Teton River / Geoffrey A. Morrison / Geoffrey A. Morrison / 1969*										
$182\frac{2}{8}$	$37\frac{5}{8}$	$39\frac{1}{8}$	$14\frac{5}{8}$	$14\frac{7}{8}$	$10\frac{1}{8}$	$10\frac{1}{8}$	$22\frac{5}{8}$	$21\frac{3}{8}$	452	163
◆ *Park County / Rodney W. Cole / Rodney W. Cole / 1985*										
$182\frac{2}{8}$	$39\frac{3}{8}$	$39\frac{7}{8}$	$15\frac{7}{8}$	$16\frac{1}{8}$	8	$7\frac{7}{8}$	$23\frac{1}{8}$	$23\frac{5}{8}$	452	163
◆ *Beaverhead County / Raymond L. Cote / Raymond L. Cote / 1989*										
$182\frac{2}{8}$	$38\frac{5}{8}$	$38\frac{7}{8}$	$15\frac{1}{8}$	$15\frac{1}{8}$	$9\frac{3}{8}$	$9\frac{6}{8}$	$19\frac{7}{8}$	$19\frac{1}{8}$	452	163
◆ *Silver Bow County / John T. LaPierre / John T. LaPierre / 1990*										
$182\frac{1}{8}$	39	$39\frac{3}{8}$	$16\frac{1}{8}$	$16\frac{1}{8}$	$7\frac{6}{8}$	$7\frac{6}{8}$	$22\frac{4}{8}$	$22\frac{4}{8}$	461	166
◆ *Silver Bow County / Eric L. Jacobson / Eric L. Jacobson / 1990*										
182	$39\frac{1}{8}$	$41\frac{7}{8}$	15	15	$8\frac{3}{8}$	$7\frac{6}{8}$	$23\frac{5}{8}$	$23\frac{3}{8}$	466	167
◆ *Lewis & Clark County / Allan L. Davies / Allan L. Davies / 1981*										
182	37	$38\frac{6}{8}$	$15\frac{3}{8}$	$15\frac{1}{8}$	$10\frac{4}{8}$	$9\frac{6}{8}$	$22\frac{1}{8}$	$20\frac{2}{8}$	466	167
◆ *Deer Lodge County / George A. Kovacich / George A. Kovacich / 1988*										
182	$39\frac{4}{8}$	$39\frac{6}{8}$	15	$15\frac{1}{8}$	$8\frac{7}{8}$	$9\frac{4}{8}$	$20\frac{1}{8}$	$19\frac{1}{8}$	466	167
◆ *Sanders County / Kevin K. Harris / Kevin K. Harris / 1988*										
182	$38\frac{3}{8}$	$38\frac{1}{8}$	$15\frac{2}{8}$	$15\frac{2}{8}$	$9\frac{4}{8}$	$9\frac{5}{8}$	$21\frac{1}{8}$	$17\frac{2}{8}$	466	167
◆ *Missoula County / Jeff S. Putnam / Jeff S. Putnam / 1993*										

Score	Length of Horn		Circumference of Base		Circumference at Third Quarter		Greatest Spread	Tip-to-Tip Spread	All-Time Rank	State Rank
	R	L	R	L	R	L				
◆ Locality / Hunter / Owner / Date Killed										
181⅞	36⅛	38²⁄₈	16	16	8⁴⁄₈	8⅝	23²⁄₈	21⅞	479	171
◆ Granite County / Don Syvrud / Don Syvrud / 1991										
181⅞	38⅝	39⁴⁄₈	15⅜	15⅜	9	8⁴⁄₈	22	20²⁄₈	479	171
◆ Teton County / Deborah Conway / Deborah Conway / 1991										
181⁶⁄₈	38⅜	39⅞	14⅞	14⅞	9⅛	8⁴⁄₈	22²⁄₈	22²⁄₈	488	173
◆ Blaine County / Betty L. Ramsey / Betty L. Ramsey / 1989										
181⅝	39⅛	37	15⁶⁄₈	15⁶⁄₈	8⁴⁄₈	9⅜	23²⁄₈	21²⁄₈	493	174
◆ Custer County / Picked Up / W.S. Maloit / 1959										
181⅝	39⁶⁄₈	40⅛	15⅝	15⅜	8⁴⁄₈	7⁶⁄₈	22⅞	22⅞	493	174
◆ Sun River / Walter L. Bodie / Walter L. Bodie / 1965										
181⅝	36²⁄₈	35⅝	16	16	9⅝	10⁴⁄₈	23⅜	22⅝	493	174
◆ Lewis & Clark County / Pamela J. Bennett / Pamela J. Bennett / 1989										
181⅝	39	39⅛	15⅜	15²⁄₈	9	9⅜	24⁴⁄₈	23⁴⁄₈	493	174
◆ Deer Lodge County / Roy A. Wiant / Roy A. Wiant / 1990										
181⅝	39⅛	38²⁄₈	15⁶⁄₈	15⁴⁄₈	8⁴⁄₈	8⅞	21²⁄₈	20⅛	493	174
◆ Teton County / Neil L. Hamm / Neil L. Hamm / 1990										
181⁴⁄₈	43	43⁴⁄₈	16	16	6⅞	6²⁄₈	29⁴⁄₈	29⁴⁄₈	507	179
◆ Gallatin County / Richard D. Gilman / Richard D. Gilman / 1967										
181⁴⁄₈	41⅜	39⅞	15²⁄₈	15²⁄₈	8	7⅞	22⅝	22⅝	507	179
◆ Lewis & Clark County / Picked Up / William L. Wesland / 1973										
181⁴⁄₈	41	41²⁄₈	16⅛	16	6⅝	6⁶⁄₈	21⁴⁄₈	21⁴⁄₈	507	179
◆ Deer Lodge County / Gerald P. Wendt / Gerald P. Wendt / 1978										
181⁴⁄₈	37	39	16²⁄₈	16⅜	8⁴⁄₈	8⅜	24⅜	24⅜	507	179
◆ Lewis & Clark County / Donel G. Hayes / Donel G. Hayes / 1980										
181⁴⁄₈	38⅜	41⅜	16²⁄₈	16⅜	6⅞	6⅞	24	24	507	179
◆ Granite County / Michael B. Murphy / Michael B. Murphy / 1987										
181⁴⁄₈	35⅞	36⅞	16⅜	16⅜	8⅝	9²⁄₈	22⅜	21	507	179
◆ Granite County / Bronwyn M. Price / Bronwyn M. Price / 1989										
181⁴⁄₈	38⅛	38⅝	16²⁄₈	16⁴⁄₈	8⅛	8⅛	20⁴⁄₈	18⁴⁄₈	507	179
◆ Granite County / Jacob A. Streitz / Jacob A. Streitz / 1992										
181⁴⁄₈	40⁴⁄₈	40²⁄₈	15²⁄₈	15²⁄₈	8²⁄₈	8²⁄₈	22⅛	21⅝	507	179
◆ Sanders County / Thomas L. Judge / Thomas L. Judge / 1992										
181⅜	38⅜	38⁴⁄₈	15	14⅞	9⅝	9⅝	21⁴⁄₈	15	525	187
◆ Beartooth Plateau / Olav E. Nelson / Olav E. Nelson / 1970										
181⅜	39	39⅝	15⁴⁄₈	15⅝	8⅜	8²⁄₈	22⅜	19⁴⁄₈	525	187
◆ Lincoln County / Lowell Olin / Lowell Olin / 1977										
181⅜	38⁴⁄₈	39⅝	14⁶⁄₈	14⅞	9⅜	9	20⁶⁄₈	20⅜	525	187
◆ Lake County / Picked Up / J. Michael Conoyer / 1978										

Score	Length of Horn R	L	Circumference of Base R	L	Circumference at Third Quarter R	L	Greatest Spread	Tip-to-Tip Spread	All-Time Rank	State Rank
					♦ Locality / Hunter / Owner / Date Killed					
181³⁄₈	39⅛	41²⁄₈	15⅝	15⁶⁄₈	8⅛	7⅞	21²⁄₈	20⅝	525	187
♦ Granite County / David D. Rittenhouse / David D. Rittenhouse / 1980										
181³⁄₈	39	38³⁄₈	15⁶⁄₈	15⅝	8²⁄₈	8⅝	21²⁄₈	20⅝	525	187
♦ Lewis & Clark County / Elmer T. Crawford / Elmer T. Crawford / 1986										
181²⁄₈	40³⁄₈	40³⁄₈	14³⁄₈	14³⁄₈	8⅞	9	23⅞	23⅞	538	192
♦ Lewis & Clark County / Brandon C. Johns / Brandon C. Johns / 1987										
181²⁄₈	41³⁄₈	39⅝	15⁴⁄₈	15³⁄₈	7⅝	7⁶⁄₈	21	21	538	192
♦ Granite County / Tom J. Lewis / Tom J. Lewis / 1989										
181²⁄₈	37⅛	37³⁄₈	15⁴⁄₈	15⅝	9⁴⁄₈	9⅝	20⅞	20⁴⁄₈	538	192
♦ Fergus County / Leda R. McReynolds / Leda R. McReynolds / 1991										
181⅛	38²⁄₈	38⅝	14	14²⁄₈	11	10³⁄₈	20²⁄₈	15⅛	546	195
♦ Cooke City / Larry L. Altimus / Larry L. Altimus / 1969										
181⅛	39⁴⁄₈	39³⁄₈	14⅝	14⁴⁄₈	9⅝	9⁴⁄₈	22⅝	22⅝	546	195
♦ Deer Lodge County / Thomas R. Puccinelli / Thomas R. Puccinelli / 1984										
181⅛	39³⁄₈	39²⁄₈	16⁴⁄₈	16³⁄₈	7⅞	7⁴⁄₈	22	21	546	195
♦ Sanders County / David O. Conrad / David O. Conrad / 1993										
181	39⁴⁄₈	39⁶⁄₈	14⅞	14⁶⁄₈	8³⁄₈	8³⁄₈	23⅝	17⁶⁄₈	552	198
♦ Lincoln County / Hal Kanzler / Hal Kanzler / 1960										
180⅞	40⅝	37⁴⁄₈	16	16³⁄₈	7⅞	7⁶⁄₈	25⅝	25³⁄₈	558	199
♦ Sanders County / Raymond J. Smith / Raymond J. Smith / 1990										
180⅞	41	40³⁄₈	14⁶⁄₈	14⁶⁄₈	8⁴⁄₈	7⅞	24⁴⁄₈	24⁴⁄₈	558	199
♦ Deer Lodge County / Jack D. Shanstrom / Jack D. Shanstrom / 1991										
180⁶⁄₈	39⁶⁄₈	39⁴⁄₈	15	15	8⅞	8⁴⁄₈	22	19⅛	563	201
♦ Mineral County / Roberta A. Hartford / Roberta A. Hartford / 1982										
180⁶⁄₈	38⅞	37⅞	16²⁄₈	16²⁄₈	7⅝	7⁶⁄₈	24⁴⁄₈	24	563	201
♦ Sanders County / Bob L. Jacks / Bob L. Jacks / 1990										
180⅝	38⅛	38²⁄₈	14⁶⁄₈	14⁶⁄₈	10⅛	10	21⅛	21⅛	574	203
♦ Sun River / Robert W. Boucher / Robert W. Boucher / 1966										
180⅝	40⅝	39⁴⁄₈	15³⁄₈	15⁴⁄₈	8⅛	7⁶⁄₈	20	18⁶⁄₈	574	203
♦ Lewis & Clark County / William J. McRae / William J. McRae / 1980										
180⅝	41⁴⁄₈	41⅞	14⅞	14⅞	7⅝	7⁶⁄₈	27²⁄₈	27⅛	574	203
♦ Sanders County / Raymond J. Baenen / Raymond J. Baenen / 1986										
180⅝	39⁴⁄₈	38⅞	15⅝	15³⁄₈	8²⁄₈	8⅛	21²⁄₈	19⁶⁄₈	574	203
♦ Blaine County / Mark D. Farnam / Mark D. Farnam / 1990										
180⁴⁄₈	40⁶⁄₈	38²⁄₈	14⅝	14⅝	9²⁄₈	9³⁄₈	23²⁄₈	22⁶⁄₈	583	207
♦ Deer Lodge County / Jan J. Henry / Jan J. Henry / 1983										
180⁴⁄₈	39⅛	37⅝	14⁶⁄₈	14⅞	9⁴⁄₈	9	25²⁄₈	24⁶⁄₈	583	207
♦ Sanders County / Terry F. Brown / Terry F. Brown / 1991										

Score	Length of Horn		Circumference of Base		Circumference at Third Quarter		Greatest Spread	Tip-to-Tip Spread	All-Time Rank	State Rank
	R	L	R	L	R	L				
◆ Locality / Hunter / Owner / Date Killed										
180³⁄₈	40⁷⁄₈	40²⁄₈	14⁴⁄₈	14⁶⁄₈	8⁵⁄₈	8³⁄₈	22⁷⁄₈	22⁷⁄₈	596	209
◆ Lemhi County / Picked Up / R. Munn & F. Porter / 1982										
180³⁄₈	35⁵⁄₈	38²⁄₈	16³⁄₈	16⁴⁄₈	8²⁄₈	8³⁄₈	24⁴⁄₈	21⁵⁄₈	596	209
◆ Silver Bow County / Robert C. Carlson / Robert C. Carlson / 1983										
180³⁄₈	39⁴⁄₈	39¹⁄₈	15³⁄₈	15³⁄₈	8⁵⁄₈	8¹⁄₈	22⁵⁄₈	19⁶⁄₈	596	209
◆ Mineral County / J. Ray Lake / J. Ray Lake / 1984										
180³⁄₈	37⁵⁄₈	41⁴⁄₈	15²⁄₈	15³⁄₈	7⁷⁄₈	8³⁄₈	23⁴⁄₈	23⁴⁄₈	596	209
◆ Silverbow County / Scott A. Shuey / Scott A. Shuey / 1985										
180³⁄₈	37¹⁄₈	38	15⁴⁄₈	15⁵⁄₈	9	8⁶⁄₈	21	19	596	209
◆ Sanders County / Calvin L. Pomrenke / Calvin L. Pomrenke / 1986										
180³⁄₈	38	38¹⁄₈	15⁵⁄₈	15⁵⁄₈	8³⁄₈	9³⁄₈	19³⁄₈	19³⁄₈	596	209
◆ Ravalli County / Terry Frey / Terry Frey / 1988										
180³⁄₈	40⁴⁄₈	40³⁄₈	14⁶⁄₈	15	8¹⁄₈	8	25⁶⁄₈	25⁶⁄₈	596	209
◆ Chouteau County / Scott D. Rubin / Scott D. Rubin / 1989										
180³⁄₈	41⁶⁄₈	32⁵⁄₈	16⁴⁄₈	16⁴⁄₈	9¹⁄₈	7³⁄₈	25	22⁴⁄₈	596	209
◆ Beaverhead County / James M. Linscott / James M. Linscott / 1990										
180³⁄₈	38⁴⁄₈	38⁵⁄₈	15¹⁄₈	15³⁄₈	8⁷⁄₈	8⁷⁄₈	23¹⁄₈	22⁴⁄₈	596	209
◆ Deer Lodge County / Max E. Leishman / Max E. Leishman / 1990										
180²⁄₈	39¹⁄₈	39¹⁄₈	14⁵⁄₈	14⁴⁄₈	9¹⁄₈	9¹⁄₈	22	20²⁄₈	619	218
◆ Lincoln County / Bradley S. Osler / Bradley S. Osler / 1989										
180²⁄₈	36⁵⁄₈	40³⁄₈	15⁴⁄₈	15⁴⁄₈	8²⁄₈	8²⁄₈	26²⁄₈	26²⁄₈	619	218
◆ Missoula County / Joel D. Cusker / Joel D. Cusker / 1994										
180¹⁄₈	36¹⁄₈	40⁶⁄₈	15⁴⁄₈	15²⁄₈	8⁵⁄₈	8³⁄₈	20⁴⁄₈	18	631	220
◆ Sun River / Dennis Reichelt / Dennis Reichelt / 1958										
180¹⁄₈	37⁶⁄₈	38¹⁄₈	15⁷⁄₈	15⁷⁄₈	8¹⁄₈	8	18⁶⁄₈	18⁶⁄₈	631	220
◆ Nye / Ira H. Kent / Ira H. Kent / 1974										
180¹⁄₈	37⁵⁄₈	37⁴⁄₈	16⁴⁄₈	16⁴⁄₈	8¹⁄₈	8	20	20	631	220
◆ Sanders County / Gene N. Meyer / Gene N. Meyer / 1976										
180¹⁄₈	41³⁄₈	41⁴⁄₈	15	15	7	7²⁄₈	28⁶⁄₈	28⁶⁄₈	631	220
◆ Deer Lodge County / Arden Holden / Arden Holden / 1979										
180¹⁄₈	38⁵⁄₈	42⁶⁄₈	15⁷⁄₈	15⁷⁄₈	6³⁄₈	6³⁄₈	24³⁄₈	24³⁄₈	631	220
◆ Granite County / Leonard W. Bowen / Leonard W. Bowen / 1985										
180¹⁄₈	38	37¹⁄₈	16⁴⁄₈	16⁴⁄₈	7⁶⁄₈	7⁵⁄₈	19³⁄₈	19³⁄₈	631	220
◆ Sanders County / Bruce P. Allen / Bruce P. Allen / 1986										
180¹⁄₈	36²⁄₈	38¹⁄₈	15⁴⁄₈	15⁴⁄₈	9⁵⁄₈	9⁶⁄₈	19²⁄₈	17⁴⁄₈	631	220
◆ Granite County / Scott M. Willumsen / Scott M. Willumsen / 1989										
180	38⁵⁄₈	41¹⁄₈	14⁵⁄₈	14⁵⁄₈	8³⁄₈	8⁴⁄₈	24	23⁴⁄₈	651	227
◆ Lewis & Clark County / James G. Braddee, Jr. / James G. Braddee, Jr. / 1978										

Score	Length of Horn		Circumference of Base		Circumference at Third Quarter		Greatest Spread	Tip-to-Tip Spread	All-Time Rank	State Rank
	R	L	R	L	R	L				
	Locality / Hunter / Owner / Date Killed									
180	40²/₈	37²/₈	15³/₈	15⁴/₈	8²/₈	8⁷/₈	22⁶/₈	22⁶/₈	651	227
	Granite County / Jerry E. Gallagher / Jerry E. Gallagher / 1980									
180	39⁷/₈	40¹/₈	15⁵/₈	15⁵/₈	7⁵/₈	7⁴/₈	22²/₈	22²/₈	651	227
	Granite County / Jim A. Crepeau / Jim A. Crepeau / 1986									
180	37¹/₈	39⁵/₈	15⁶/₈	15⁶/₈	7⁷/₈	8¹/₈	21⁶/₈	21⁶/₈	651	227
	Beaverhead County / Kory McGavin / Kory McGavin / 1988									
180	38²/₈	40	14⁴/₈	14⁶/₈	9²/₈	9¹/₈	21²/₈	20⁶/₈	651	227
	Lewis & Clark County / Brian J. Boehm / Brian J. Boehm / 1989									
180	38¹/₈	37⁵/₈	15³/₈	15²/₈	9¹/₈	9	23¹/₈	22⁴/₈	651	227
	Deer Lodge County / Michael P. Lorello / Michael P. Lorello / 1990									
180	37⁴/₈	37	15³/₈	15⁵/₈	9²/₈	9¹/₈	21	17⁴/₈	651	227
	Granite County / Thomas I. Jenni / Thomas I. Jenni / 1991									
179⁶/₈	36⁴/₈	37	15⁴/₈	15⁵/₈	9	9³/₈	21⁶/₈	18⁷/₈	667	234
	Granite County / G.C. Hart / G.C. Hart / 1993									
179⁵/₈	34⁷/₈	37	15⁷/₈	15⁷/₈	10	9⁵/₈	22	17⁵/₈	668	235
	Granite County / Blake A. Trangmoe / Blake A. Trangmoe / 1994									
179²/₈	39³/₈	39⁵/₈	15	15	7⁶/₈	7⁵/₈	21⁷/₈	21⁵/₈	673	236
	Sanders County / Everett A. Robbins / Everett A. Robbins / 1991									
179¹/₈	37⁷/₈	37⁶/₈	15	15¹/₈	9²/₈	9⁴/₈	20³/₈	21⁴/₈	675	237
	Deer Lodge County / Chad Gochanour / Chad Gochanour / 1988									
178⁷/₈	38	38⁵/₈	15¹/₈	15¹/₈	8⁶/₈	9	22³/₈	21²/₈	677	238
	Sanders County / Aivars O. Berkis / Aivars O. Berkis / 1989									
178⁵/₈	40¹/₈	38⁶/₈	14	14	8⁷/₈	8⁷/₈	23²/₈	23²/₈	679	239
	Park County / Craig L. Leerberg / Craig L. Leerberg / 1985									
178²/₈	39⁴/₈	40⁴/₈	15²/₈	15²/₈	7⁷/₈	7⁶/₈	20⁴/₈	19⁷/₈	682	240
	Granite County / Daniel A. Pletscher / Daniel A. Pletscher / 1994									
177⁶/₈	35²/₈	36	15²/₈	15²/₈	9⁴/₈	9⁵/₈	22³/₈	22³/₈	685	241
	Lewis & Clark County / Rusten L. Barnes / Rusten L. Barnes / 1990									
176⁵/₈	40¹/₈	41²/₈	14⁶/₈	14⁶/₈	6⁷/₈	7²/₈	21¹/₈	20⁴/₈	694	242
	Sanders County / Melvin J. Wojcik / Melvin J. Wojcik / 1991									
176⁴/₈	38³/₈	38³/₈	15	15¹/₈	8¹/₈	8⁴/₈	20⁷/₈	19¹/₈	695	243
	Sanders County / Dino V. Seppi / Dino V. Seppi / 1987									
175¹/₈	34²/₈	39³/₈	15	14⁷/₈	8⁶/₈	8²/₈	21⁵/₈	22⁵/₈	701	244
	Sanders County / Picked Up / Patrick J. Gilligan / 1992									
199	43²/₈	43²/₈	15⁶/₈	16¹/₈	10⁷/₈	10⁵/₈	23⁷/₈	23⁷/₈	*	*
	Granite County / Larry D. Smith / Larry D. Smith / 1984									
196	44⁷/₈	41³/₈	15⁷/₈	16	10¹/₈	9⁷/₈	22⁷/₈	20	*	*
	Missoula County / Claude I. Burlingame / Claude I. Burlingame / 1984									

Score	Length of Horn		Circumference of Base		Circumference at Third Quarter		Greatest Spread	Tip-to-Tip Spread	All-Time Rank	State Rank
	R	L	R	L	R	L				
♦ *Locality / Hunter / Owner / Date Killed*										
195 4/8	46 2/8	41	16 1/8	16 3/8	9	8 4/8	29 6/8	29 6/8	*	*
♦ *Deer Lodge County / Thomas J. Matosich / Thomas J. Matosich / 1986*										
194 3/8	42 3/8	43 2/8	16	16 2/8	9 1/8	9	26 4/8	26 4/8	*	*
♦ *Deer Lodge County / Norman F. Lesh / Norman F. Lesh / 1987*										
191 5/8	41 7/8	42 6/8	16 2/8	16	8 6/8	8 2/8	23	22 6/8	*	*
♦ *Sanders County / Bryan G. Nelson / Bryan G. Nelson / 1982*										

Charles R. Moe passed up 35 different rams in 1994 before squeezing the trigger on this Montana bighorn, scoring 187-2/8 points, from Beaverhead County.

Photograph Courtesy of Clyde Reed

**NEW MEXICO STATE RECORD
BIGHORN SHEEP
SCORE: 186⅜**
Locality: Grant Co.   Date: 1992
Hunter: Clyde Reed

NEW MEXICO

BIGHORN SHEEP

Score	Length of Horn		Circumference of Base		Circumference at Third Quarter		Greatest Spread	Tip-to-Tip Spread	All-Time Rank	State Rank
	R	L	R	L	R	L				
♦ Locality / Hunter / Owner / Date Killed										
186 3/8	43 4/8	40 5/8	14 1/8	14 1/8	10 2/8	9 7/8	23 3/8	23	250	1
♦ Grant County / Clyde Reed / Clyde Reed / 1992										
181 7/8	35 5/8	36 2/8	15	14 6/8	12	12	21 2/8	16 4/8	479	2
♦ Taos County / Reuben R. Tipton III / Reuben R. Tipton III / 1994										
181 3/8	39 3/8	39	15	15 1/8	10 2/8	9 6/8	23 3/8	21 4/8	525	3
♦ Grant County / Dan Pocapalia / Dan Pocapalia / 1990										
180 3/8	37 6/8	36 5/8	15 2/8	15 2/8	10	10	19 5/8	17 6/8	596	4
♦ Mora County / Ronald D. Rod / Ronald D. Rod / 1992										
176 1/8	38	39 7/8	15	15 1/8	8	8	19 3/8	19 1/8	696	5
♦ Rio Arriba County / Kevin L. Reid / Kevin L. Reid / 1994										

Photograph by Alex Rota

NORTH DAKOTA STATE RECORD
BIGHORN SHEEP
SCORE: 196⅛
Locality: Badlands   Date: 1880
Hunter: Howard Eaton
Owner: Richard K. Mellon

NORTH DAKOTA

BIGHORN SHEEP

Score	Length of Horn		Circumference of Base		Circumference at Third Quarter		Greatest Spread	Tip-to-Tip Spread	All-Time Rank	State Rank
	R	L	R	L	R	L				
♦ Locality / Hunter / Owner / Date Killed										
196⁶⁄₈	41²⁄₈	40⁴⁄₈	16⁴⁄₈	16⁴⁄₈	9⁷⁄₈	10¹⁄₈	22⁶⁄₈	19⁴⁄₈	35	1
♦ *Badlands / Howard Eaton / Richard K. Mellon / 1880*										

Photograph Courtesy of Oregon Department of Fish & Wildlife

OREGON STATE RECORD
BIGHORN SHEEP
SCORE: 197⅞
Locality: Wallowa Co.   Date: Picked Up 1986
Owner: Oregon Department of Fish & Wildlife

OREGON

BIGHORN SHEEP

Score	Length of Horn R	Length of Horn L	Circumference of Base R	Circumference of Base L	Circumference at Third Quarter R	Circumference at Third Quarter L	Greatest Spread	Tip-to-Tip Spread	All-Time Rank	State Rank
♦ *Locality / Hunter / Owner / Date Killed*										
197 7/8	43 2/8	42 7/8	14 7/8	15	11 4/8	11 5/8	21 6/8	21 2/8	25	1
♦ *Wallowa County / Picked Up / Oreg. Dept. Fish & Wildl. / 1986*										
192	43 3/8	42 7/8	15 5/8	15 6/8	9	9 6/8	24 2/8	24 2/8	87	2
♦ *Wallowa County / H. James Tonkin / H. James Tonkin / 1991*										
191 4/8	44 3/8	39 3/8	15 7/8	16	9 6/8	9 3/8	23 6/8	20 3/8	98	3
♦ *Wallowa County / Sam Jaksick, Jr. / Sam Jaksick, Jr. / 1987*										
188 7/8	40 5/8	40 4/8	14 6/8	14 7/8	10 6/8	10 5/8	22	22	151	4
♦ *Wallowa County / Nick J. Gianopoulos / Nick J. Gianopoulos / 1986*										
183 6/8	38 4/8	39	15 6/8	15 6/8	8 7/8	8 6/8	23 2/8	14 4/8	363	5
♦ *Wallowa County / Tom R. Croswell / Tom R. Croswell / 1992*										
182 4/8	38 6/8	35 6/8	15 3/8	15 5/8	11 1/8	10 1/8	23 2/8	23 2/8	436	6
♦ *Wallowa County / Randy Craddock / Randy Craddock / 1981*										
182	40 7/8	39 5/8	16 2/8	16 3/8	7 1/8	7 3/8	22 5/8	22 2/8	466	7
♦ *Wallowa County / Dale R. Dotson / Dale R. Dotson / 1988*										
181 3/8	38 5/8	40 2/8	14 5/8	14 7/8	9 2/8	9 1/8	22 6/8	22 1/8	525	8
♦ *Wallowa County / Michael L. Taylor / Michael L. Taylor / 1987*										
180 3/8	39 5/8	39 4/8	14 6/8	15	8 7/8	9	23 2/8	23 2/8	596	9
♦ *Wallowa County / Kirk W. Jones / Kirk W. Jones / 1979*										
180	39 6/8	39 2/8	15 3/8	15 3/8	8	8	22 4/8	20 6/8	651	10
♦ *Wallowa County / F. Carter Kerns / F. Carter Kerns / 1978*										
180	40 2/8	40 2/8	14 5/8	14 5/8	8 4/8	8 4/8	25	25	651	10
♦ *Wallowa County / Jerome V. Epping / Jerome V. Epping / 1984*										
179 7/8	36	35 7/8	16 3/8	16 4/8	9 1/8	8 5/8	21 2/8	19	666	12
♦ *Wallowa County / Jim A. Turcke / Jim A. Turcke / 1982*										
179 5/8	36	36 3/8	15 6/8	15 6/8	10 1/8	9 3/8	21 7/8	19 6/8	668	13
♦ *Wallowa County / Susan L. Shriner / Susan L. Shriner / 1993*										
176	36 6/8	36 2/8	15	15 1/8	9	9 1/8	22 5/8	21 2/8	697	14
♦ *Harney County / Red Iler / Red Iler / 1991*										
198	42 4/8	43 4/8	16 5/8	16 5/8	10	9 4/8	25	18 4/8	*	*
♦ *Wallowa County / Todd B. Jaksick / Todd B. Jaksick / 1988*										

SOUTH DAKOTA STATE RECORD
BIGHORN SHEEP
SCORE: 196⁴/₈
Locality: Badlands National Park   Date: Picked Up 1984
Owner: South Dakota Game, Fish & Parks Department

SOUTH DAKOTA
BIGHORN SHEEP

Score	Length of Horn		Circumference of Base		Circumference at Third Quarter		Greatest Spread	Tip-to-Tip Spread	All-Time Rank	State Rank
	R	L	R	L	R	L				
♦ Locality / Hunter / Owner / Date Killed										
196⁴⁄₈	40⁶⁄₈	40²⁄₈	15⁴⁄₈	15⁴⁄₈	12	12	24	19²⁄₈	40	1
♦ Badlands Natl. Park / Picked Up / S.D. Dept. Game, Fish & Parks / 1984										

Photograph Courtesy of Stephen C. Walker

**UTAH STATE RECORD
BIGHORN SHEEP
SCORE: 186⅜**
Locality: Emery Co.   Date: 1992
Owner: Stephen C. Walker

UTAH

BIGHORN SHEEP

Score	Length of Horn		Circumference of Base		Circumference at Third Quarter		Greatest Spread	Tip-to-Tip Spread	All-Time Rank	State Rank
	R	L	R	L	R	L				
♦ Locality / Hunter / Owner / Date Killed										
186⅜	39	40⅛	14⁶⁄₈	14⁶⁄₈	10⁴⁄₈	10⁶⁄₈	23⅝	19⁴⁄₈	250	1
♦ Emery County / Stephen C. Walker / Stephen C. Walker / 1992										
179	35⁴⁄₈	37⁶⁄₈	15²⁄₈	15²⁄₈	9⅜	9⁶⁄₈	22⅛	19⁴⁄₈	676	2
♦ Grand County / H. James Tonkin, Jr. / H. James Tonkin, Jr. / 1991										

Photograph Courtesy of Edwin L. Harris

WASHINGTON STATE RECORD
BIGHORN SHEEP
SCORE: 189⅜
Locality: Asotin Co.   Date: 1987
Hunter: Edwin L. Harris

WASHINGTON

BIGHORN SHEEP

Score	Length of Horn R	Length of Horn L	Circumference of Base R	Circumference of Base L	Circumference at Third Quarter R	Circumference at Third Quarter L	Greatest Spread	Tip-to-Tip Spread	All-Time Rank	State Rank
♦ *Locality / Hunter / Owner / Date Killed*										
189 3/8	40 1/8	41 4/8	16 6/8	16 6/8	8 5/8	8	23 2/8	21 6/8	140	1
♦ *Asotin County / Edwin L. Harris / Edwin L. Harris / 1987*										
187 2/8	41 1/8	38 3/8	17	17	7 7/8	7 7/8	24 2/8	20 1/8	208	2
♦ *Asotin County / Roger S. Brazier / Roger S. Brazier / 1986*										
186 7/8	40 1/8	39 4/8	15 1/8	15	10 2/8	10 2/8	22 1/8	21 4/8	231	3
♦ *Asotin County / Ron Willenborg / Ron Willenborg / 1991*										
186 6/8	41 7/8	42 7/8	15 7/8	15 7/8	7 3/8	7 4/8	22 3/8	21 6/8	234	4
♦ *Whitman County / Picked Up / Inland Empire Big Game Council / 1983*										
184 5/8	41 6/8	37 7/8	16	16 3/8	9 1/8	7 7/8	21 3/8	22 1/8	324	5
♦ *Asotin County / Thomas J. Pawlacyk / Thomas J. Pawlacyk / 1994*										
183 7/8	39 2/8	39 3/8	16	16 1/8	8 2/8	8 2/8	21 5/8	18 3/8	356	6
♦ *Garfield County / Klaus H. Meyn / Klaus H. Meyn / 1990*										
180 3/8	40 4/8	38 3/8	16 1/8	15 5/8	7 6/8	8 3/8	23 1/8	21 2/8	596	7
♦ *Asotin County / Brian Greenhaw / Brian Greenhaw / 1993*										
198 2/8	40 6/8	44 4/8	17 2/8	17 4/8	8 6/8	9	23 6/8	18 6/8	*	*
♦ *Asotin County / Michael W. Houser / Michael W. Houser / 1989*										

Photograph by Bill Hepworth

WYOMING STATE RECORD
BIGHORN SHEEP
SCORE: 200
Locality: Wind River Range   Date: 1883
Hunter: Crawford
Owner: Duncan Weibel

WYOMING

BIGHORN SHEEP

Score	Length of Horn		Circumference of Base		Circumference at Third Quarter		Greatest Spread	Tip-to-Tip Spread	All-Time Rank	State Rank
	R	L	R	L	R	L				
◆ *Locality / Hunter / Owner / Date Killed*										
200	40 6/8	41 6/8	16 4/8	16 3/8	11 2/8	11 2/8	22	19 6/8	19	1
◆ *Wind River Range / Crawford / Duncan Weibel / 1883*										
191 5/8	40 2/8	40 3/8	15 6/8	15 6/8	10 2/8	10 1/8	22 1/8	15	97	2
◆ *Dinwoody Creek / Oris Miller / Oris Miller / 1954*										
189 4/8	41	40 4/8	14 5/8	14 7/8	11 4/8	11 2/8	23 3/8	21	138	3
◆ *Park County / Picked Up / Dale McWilliams / 1975*										
188 7/8	40 1/8	41	14 6/8	14 6/8	10 6/8	10 6/8	24	17	151	4
◆ *Gannet Peak / James Huffman / James Huffman / 1962*										
187 5/8	42 4/8	39 5/8	16 1/8	16	8 7/8	8	26 1/8	25 4/8	197	5
◆ *Teton County / William R. Flagg / William R. Flagg / 1967*										
187 4/8	39 5/8	43 1/8	15 5/8	15 4/8	9	8 4/8	26 4/8	19	202	6
◆ *Crystal Creek / Picked Up / Melvin R. Fowlkes / 1970*										
187	39	39 4/8	15	15	10 5/8	10 4/8	22 6/8	17 4/8	219	7
◆ *Wind River Mts. / Ralph E. Platt / Ralph E. Platt / 1963*										
186 3/8	41	41 7/8	14 1/8	14	10 6/8	11 1/8	22 1/8	17 6/8	250	8
◆ *Ventre-Flat / John Evasco / John Evasco / 1953*										
185 4/8	42 6/8	41	13 6/8	14	10	9 7/8	21 2/8	21 2/8	284	9
◆ *Wind River Mts. / Elgin T. Gates / Elgin T. Gates / 1954*										
185 1/8	41 3/8	40 6/8	14 5/8	14 4/8	9 3/8	9 6/8	22 7/8	19 2/8	305	10
◆ *Dubois / B.N. Lively / B.N. Lively / 1953*										
185	39 1/8	39 1/8	14 7/8	14 7/8	10 4/8	10 4/8	23	17 6/8	311	11
◆ *Green River / Floyd J. Stalnaker / Elsie Stalnaker / 1913*										
184 6/8	40	40 4/8	14 2/8	14 2/8	10 2/8	10 5/8	23 7/8	21 6/8	318	12
◆ *Jackson Hole / Johnny Kretschman / Johnny Kretschman / 1962*										
184 2/8	37 6/8	37 6/8	15 4/8	15 4/8	10 1/8	10 7/8	24	24	342	13
◆ *Middle Mts. / William Underwood / William Underwood / 1959*										
183	39 4/8	38	16 2/8	16 2/8	8 2/8	8 4/8	21 4/8	17 6/8	414	14
◆ *Teton Basin / William A. Baillie-Grohman / John H. Batten / 1876*										
182 4/8	37	35 4/8	15 4/8	15 3/8	11 2/8	10 4/8	23	21	436	15
◆ *Wind River / Hubert Weibel / Hubert Weibel / 1956*										
182 4/8	38 3/8	37 5/8	15	14 6/8	10 6/8	10 5/8	22 1/8	18 2/8	436	15
◆ *Turtle Creek / Russell C. Cutter / Russell C. Cutter / 1968*										
182 2/8	40 3/8	40 1/8	14 5/8	14 5/8	9 7/8	9 6/8	21 4/8	21	452	17
◆ *Shoshone N. Fork / Herb Klein / Herb Klein / 1934*										
182 2/8	40 7/8	40 1/8	15	15	8 7/8	8 6/8	23 4/8	20 4/8	452	17
◆ *Dubois / George Pate / Larry Pate / 1960*										

Score	Length of Horn		Circumference of Base		Circumference at Third Quarter		Greatest Spread	Tip-to-Tip Spread	All-Time Rank	State Rank
	R	L	R	L	R	L				
	♦ *Locality / Hunter / Owner / Date Killed*									
181 6/8	40 5/8	39 5/8	15 2/8	15 2/8	8 4/8	8	26	24 4/8	488	19
	♦ *Teton County / Richard L. Grabowski / Richard L. Grabowski / 1989*									
181 5/8	38 4/8	39 3/8	14 4/8	14 6/8	9 2/8	9 6/8	23 5/8	19	493	20
	♦ *Park County / Keith Frick / Keith Frick / 1972*									
181 4/8	36	36 2/8	15 1/8	15 1/8	11 1/8	11 1/8	23	21	507	21
	♦ *Dubois / Jack Adams / Jack Adams / 1959*									
181 2/8	42	41 4/8	14	14	8 5/8	8 2/8	24 6/8	24 6/8	538	22
	♦ *Teton Basin / Michael Huppuch / Philip Schlegel / 1901*									
180 7/8	38 3/8	39 2/8	14	14	10 3/8	10 1/8	19 6/8	18	558	23
	♦ *Park County / Picked Up / Jay Thomas / 1979*									
180 6/8	37	37 6/8	14 7/8	15	10 1/8	10	22 7/8	18 6/8	563	24
	♦ *Park County / Dwight Lyman / Dwight Lyman / 1982*									
180 5/8	39 4/8	39 5/8	13 6/8	13 5/8	10 7/8	11	22	17 6/8	574	25
	♦ *Wind River Mts. / Alfred Hume / Alfred Hume / 1960*									
180 4/8	38 6/8	39 2/8	13 6/8	13 6/8	10 3/8	10 5/8	20 6/8	20 6/8	583	26
	♦ *Park County / Picked Up / Sam L. Beasom / 1974*									
180 3/8	36 1/8	37 2/8	15 4/8	15 2/8	9 6/8	10	22	19 4/8	596	27
	♦ *Jakey's Fork / Eugene Schilling / Eugene Schilling / 1962*									
180 3/8	37 5/8	38 6/8	14 6/8	14 4/8	9 4/8	10 1/8	22 6/8	19	596	27
	♦ *Sheep Creek / Picked Up / Loren L. Lutz / 1962*									
180 3/8	37	37 7/8	15 1/8	15 2/8	9 5/8	9 5/8	23	19	596	27
	♦ *Park County / Robert G. Curtis / Robert G. Curtis / 1984*									
180 1/8	36 5/8	37 2/8	15 4/8	15 3/8	9 1/8	9 1/8	23 3/8	20 5/8	631	30
	♦ *Green River / John N. Leonard / John N. Leonard / 1953*									
180 1/8	37 2/8	34 5/8	15 4/8	15 3/8	10 4/8	9 6/8	22 1/8	16 5/8	631	30
	♦ *Gannet Peak / Wilbur Rickett / Wilbur Rickett / 1964*									
179 4/8	38 5/8	38 1/8	14 7/8	14 6/8	9	9	21 1/8	19	670	32
	♦ *Park County / Robert M. Anderson / Robert M. Anderson / 1983*									
179 4/8	38 3/8	38 3/8	15 2/8	15 3/8	8 4/8	8 2/8	20 4/8	12 3/8	670	32
	♦ *Park County / Michael S. Messenger / Michael S. Messenger / 1986*									
177 5/8	39 1/8	36 6/8	14 4/8	14 6/8	9	8 7/8	22 6/8	20	686	34
	♦ *Park County / William B. Hickman III / William B. Hickman III / 1987*									
176 6/8	36 5/8	36 1/8	15 4/8	15 6/8	8 5/8	8 2/8	22 5/8	21 4/8	692	35
	♦ *Carbon County / Jack A. Berger / Jack A. Berger / 1993*									

Charles W. Hanawalt with the bighorn ram he took with a bow on Bard Peak in Clear Creek County, Colorado, in 1990. It scores 180-1/8 points.

ALBERTA PROVINCE RECORD
WORLD'S RECORD
BIGHORN SHEEP
SCORE: 208⅛

Locality: Blind Canyon   Date: 1911
Hunter: Fred Weiller
Owner: Clarence Baird

ALBERTA

BIGHORN SHEEP

Score	Length of Horn		Circumference of Base		Circumference at Third Quarter		Greatest Spread	Tip-to-Tip Spread	All-Time Rank	State Rank
	R	L	R	L	R	L				
	◆ Locality / Hunter / Owner / Date Killed									
208 1/8	44 7/8	45	16 5/8	16 5/8	11 2/8	11 7/8	22 6/8	19 3/8	1	1
	◆ Blind Canyon / Fred Weiller / Clarence Baird / 1911									
207 2/8	45	45 2/8	15 6/8	16	11 6/8	11 7/8	23 1/8	19 3/8	2	2
	◆ Oyster Creek / Martin Bovey / Martin Bovey / 1924									
206 3/8	44 4/8	44 3/8	15 7/8	15 7/8	12 1/8	12 1/8	21 4/8	21 4/8	3	3
	◆ Burnt Timber Creek / Picked Up / Gordon L. Magnussen / 1955									
203 4/8	43 1/8	42 5/8	16 4/8	16 4/8	11 3/8	11 1/8	25 4/8	19 4/8	7	4
	◆ Sheep River / Katherine A. Pyra / Katherine A. Pyra / 1992									
202 2/8	46 7/8	44 5/8	15 5/8	15 2/8	11	10 6/8	23 2/8	23 2/8	9	5
	◆ Panther River / Tom Kerquits / Unknown / 1918									
202	46 5/8	45 1/8	15 2/8	15 3/8	10 4/8	10 4/8	22 6/8	22 5/8	10	6
	◆ Canmore / Picked Up / Alberta Fish & Wildl. Div. / 1987									
201 1/8	44	43 7/8	15 5/8	15 5/8	11 3/8	11 4/8	25	25	11	7
	◆ Jasper / Picked Up / A.H. Hilbert / 1932									
200 1/8	44 3/8	44	15 1/8	15 2/8	11 6/8	11 3/8	23	23	16	8
	◆ Brazeau River / Unknown / Norman Lougheed / 1937									
200 1/8	40 4/8	41 3/8	16 3/8	16 3/8	11 3/8	11 3/8	22 2/8	18 5/8	16	8
	◆ Alberta / Picked Up / Otis Chandler / 1955									
198 6/8	43 4/8	43 6/8	15 4/8	15 4/8	10 7/8	11 3/8	24 6/8	24 6/8	23	10
	◆ Alberta / Bill Foster / Foster's Bighorn Rest. / PR 1947									
198 1/8	42 4/8	41 3/8	15 6/8	15 6/8	12	11 3/8	23 3/8	23 3/8	24	11
	◆ Sask. Lake / Herb Klein / Herb Klein / 1965									
197 3/8	44 7/8	43 4/8	14 6/8	14 6/8	10 6/8	11 1/8	23 4/8	18 3/8	28	12
	◆ Alberta / Bill Foster / Foster's Bighorn Rest. / PR 1947									
196 7/8	41 1/8	40 4/8	17 4/8	17 3/8	10	9 7/8	23 2/8	18 1/8	33	13
	◆ Yarrow Creek / George W. Biron / George W. Biron / 1968									
196 5/8	41 5/8	42	16 2/8	16 1/8	10 6/8	10 7/8	22 2/8	20	37	14
	◆ Brazeau River / Donald S. Hopkins / Donald S. Hopkins / 1924									
196 5/8	39 5/8	41 6/8	16	16	10 5/8	11 4/8	21 2/8	19 1/8	37	14
	◆ Alberta / Bill Foster / Foster's Bighorn Rest. / 1938									
196 2/8	42 4/8	42 4/8	16 2/8	16 2/8	10	9 5/8	21 6/8	16 5/8	42	16
	◆ Highwood / Joseph F. Kubasek / Joseph F. Kubasek / 1953									
196	44 7/8	44 3/8	15	15	10 3/8	10 1/8	24 5/8	24 5/8	44	17
	◆ Cadomin / Al Leary / Al Leary / 1962									
195 5/8	41 5/8	40 2/8	16 3/8	16 5/8	11 3/8	10 4/8	22 2/8	18 6/8	47	18
	◆ Castle River / R.E. Woodward / R.E. Woodward / 1965									

Score	Length of Horn		Circumference of Base		Circumference at Third Quarter		Greatest Spread	Tip-to-Tip Spread	All-Time Rank	State Rank
	R	L	R	L	R	L				
◆ Locality / Hunter / Owner / Date Killed										
195 4/8	43	43 6/8	14 5/8	14 7/8	11 1/8	11	23	19 4/8	48	19
◆ Bow River / Indian / N.K. Luxton / 1890										
195 3/8	42 3/8	42 4/8	15 7/8	15 6/8	10 1/8	10 4/8	22 2/8	20 7/8	49	20
◆ West Sundre / Jim Neeser / Jim Neeser / 1961										
194 7/8	42 4/8	42 5/8	15 4/8	15	11 1/8	11 2/8	23 6/8	19 6/8	53	21
◆ Ram River / G.M. De Witt / G.M. De Witt / 1944										
194 6/8	42	41 6/8	15 1/8	15 3/8	10 5/8	10 7/8	20 3/8	20	55	22
◆ Storm Mt. / Bryan M. Watts / Bryan M. Watts / 1957										
194 3/8	40 4/8	41 3/8	15 7/8	15 7/8	10 6/8	10 4/8	22 2/8	17 4/8	56	23
◆ Sheep River / Picked Up / Harry McElroy / 1966										
194 2/8	45 2/8	44	15	14 7/8	9 7/8	9 4/8	21 4/8	21 4/8	58	24
◆ Panther River / Picked Up / N.K. Luxton / 1930										
194 2/8	42 7/8	43 1/8	15 5/8	15 7/8	10 2/8	10 2/8	20 7/8	18 7/8	58	24
◆ Cadomin / Al D. Kuffner / Al D. Kuffner / 1994										
194	44	42 6/8	14 4/8	14 4/8	10 6/8	10 6/8	22 3/8	21 2/8	60	26
◆ Alberta / Bill Foster / Foster's Bighorn Rest. / PR 1947										
193 6/8	39 4/8	42 4/8	16 2/8	16 3/8	9 3/8	9 4/8	22 1/8	16 7/8	61	27
◆ Yarrow Creek / F.H. Riggall / F.H. Riggall / 1906										
193 5/8	43 1/8	41 2/8	15 2/8	15 4/8	10 4/8	10 4/8	22 4/8	19 4/8	66	28
◆ Sheep River / Gary H. Cain / Gary H. Cain / 1990										
193 3/8	42 1/8	40 4/8	15 5/8	15 7/8	10 2/8	10	22 3/8	17 1/8	69	29
◆ Coleman / George Hagglund / George Hagglund / 1952										
193 2/8	42 2/8	42 6/8	16	16	9	8 7/8	23 2/8	20	70	30
◆ Luscar Mt. / Marion McLean / Marion McLean / 1994										
192 6/8	44 6/8	43 2/8	14 2/8	14 2/8	10 7/8	11 1/8	22 1/8	22 1/8	78	31
◆ Clearwater / Edward L. Fuchs / Edward L. Fuchs / 1943										
192 5/8	39 5/8	40 2/8	15 4/8	15 6/8	11 4/8	11 4/8	21 2/8	17 4/8	79	32
◆ Clearwater River / James Allan / James Allan / 1977										
192 3/8	40 7/8	40 2/8	15 6/8	15 4/8	10 5/8	11 3/8	22 7/8	18 4/8	81	33
◆ Alberta / Henry Graves, Jr. / Unknown / PR 1931										
192	41 6/8	42 4/8	15 1/8	15	10	10 3/8	21 5/8	20 1/8	87	34
◆ Narrow Creek / Henry Mitchell / Henry Mitchell / 1910										
191 7/8	41 6/8	42 3/8	15 3/8	15 3/8	9 6/8	10 2/8	22 4/8	22	89	35
◆ Alberta / Clarence Hardy / Russel Vanslett / PR 1961										
191 6/8	40	42 2/8	15 6/8	15 5/8	9 7/8	10 3/8	23 3/8	22 6/8	94	36
◆ Smoky River / Picked Up / Carl M. Borgh / 1944										
191 3/8	39 6/8	38 1/8	16 1/8	16 1/8	11 1/8	10 6/8	20	18 3/8	100	37
◆ Cadomin / Tony Oney / Tony Oney / 1966										

ALBERTA BIGHORN SHEEP *(continued)*

Score	Length of Horn R	Length of Horn L	Circumference of Base R	Circumference of Base L	Circumference at Third Quarter R	Circumference at Third Quarter L	Greatest Spread	Tip-to-Tip Spread	All-Time Rank	State Rank
	♦ *Locality / Hunter / Owner / Date Killed*									
191 2/8	41 5/8	42 1/8	15 3/8	15 3/8	10 5/8	10 5/8	22	20 5/8	104	38
	♦ *Brazeau River / Donald S. Hopkins / Donald S. Hopkins / 1937*									
191 2/8	42	41	14 5/8	14 4/8	10 6/8	10 4/8	22 1/8	19 4/8	104	38
	♦ *Leyland Mt. / Rick J. Tymchuk / Rick J. Tymchuk / 1982*									
191 1/8	40 1/8	42	15 2/8	15 3/8	10	9 6/8	19 6/8	19 6/8	108	40
	♦ *Cadomin / Frank Nuspel / Frank Nuspel / 1962*									
191 1/8	39 3/8	39 2/8	15 1/8	15 4/8	11 1/8	10 7/8	22	18 3/8	108	40
	♦ *Castle River / Picked Up / E.B. Cunningham / PR 1967*									
191 1/8	43 2/8	43 3/8	16	15 7/8	8 1/8	8 2/8	25 1/8	25 1/8	108	40
	♦ *Wolverine Creek / James R. Gaines / James R. Gaines / 1990*									
191 1/8	44	40 1/8	15 6/8	15 4/8	9	9	21 6/8	21 6/8	108	40
	♦ *Sheep River / Harvey Pyra / Harvey Pyra / 1991*									
191	40 4/8	39	15 3/8	15 4/8	11	11	22 5/8	18	112	44
	♦ *Kvass Creek / Joseph W. Dent / Joseph W. Dent / 1962*									
190 5/8	41 5/8	39 4/8	17	16 7/8	8 6/8	9	23 4/8	16 7/8	121	45
	♦ *Brazeau River / Julio Estrada / Julio Estrada / 1936*									
190 3/8	46 3/8	40	15 1/8	15 1/8	8 4/8	8 3/8	22 6/8	22 6/8	124	46
	♦ *Highwood / Nick Sekella / Nick Sekella / 1953*									
190	40	39 6/8	15 4/8	15 4/8	10 5/8	10 5/8	22 1/8	14	129	47
	♦ *Alberta / Stony Indian / Acad. Nat. Sci., Phil. / 1901*									
190	40 7/8	39 7/8	15 1/8	15 2/8	10 2/8	10 3/8	19 4/8	19 4/8	129	47
	♦ *Brazeau River / Donald S. Hopkins / Acad. Nat. Sci., Phil. / 1927*									
189 7/8	40 4/8	39 1/8	16	16 2/8	9 7/8	10 3/8	21 5/8	21 5/8	132	49
	♦ *Clearwater Forest / George Bugbee / Sally Bugbee / 1928*									
189 7/8	40 5/8	41 4/8	15 4/8	15 6/8	9	9 1/8	21 3/8	17 1/8	132	49
	♦ *Ribbon Lake / Ovar Uggen / Ovar Uggen / 1957*									
189 6/8	41	40 4/8	15 2/8	15 4/8	9 5/8	9 3/8	23 4/8	20 1/8	134	51
	♦ *Highwood Range / Unknown / Earl Johnson / 1928*									
189 5/8	38 6/8	40 1/8	16	16	9 4/8	9 3/8	23	20 2/8	136	52
	♦ *Yarrow Creek / Allan Foster / Allan Foster / 1963*									
189 4/8	41 2/8	39 2/8	15 7/8	16	9 7/8	9 6/8	19 6/8	19 3/8	138	53
	♦ *Nikanassin Range / Colleen Bodenchuk / Colleen Bodenchuk / 1976*									
189 3/8	40 3/8	41 2/8	14 4/8	14 4/8	11 3/8	11 4/8	18 6/8	17 2/8	140	54
	♦ *Panther River / Picked Up / George Browne / 1928*									
189 1/8	40 5/8	42	14 7/8	14 5/8	10 5/8	10 5/8	21 3/8	17 4/8	146	55
	♦ *Alberta / Bill Foster / Foster's Bighorn Rest. / PR 1947*									
189 1/8	37 3/8	38	15 7/8	15 6/8	11	11 1/8	19	20 7/8	146	55
	♦ *Sheep River / Patrick J. Downey / Patrick J. Downey / 1986*									

Score	Length of Horn		Circumference of Base		Circumference at Third Quarter		Greatest Spread	Tip-to-Tip Spread	All-Time Rank	State Rank
	R	L	R	L	R	L				
♦ Locality / Hunter / Owner / Date Killed										
189	39	41	15⁴⁄₈	15⁴⁄₈	9⁷⁄₈	9⁴⁄₈	19⁵⁄₈	17	149	57
♦ Highwood River / Hanson Bearspaw / W.S. Armstrong / 1917										
188⁷⁄₈	41	40¹⁄₈	14⁶⁄₈	14⁵⁄₈	10⁴⁄₈	11¹⁄₈	21³⁄₈	18	151	58
♦ Ram Creek / William N. Beach / William N. Beach / 1928										
188⁷⁄₈	43¹⁄₈	41⁴⁄₈	14⁶⁄₈	15¹⁄₈	9⁶⁄₈	9⁷⁄₈	25⁶⁄₈	25⁶⁄₈	151	58
♦ Bow Valley / Picked Up / Joseph Kovach / PR 1952										
188⁶⁄₈	40¹⁄₈	38¹⁄₈	17¹⁄₈	17¹⁄₈	8³⁄₈	8⁴⁄₈	24⁷⁄₈	20⁵⁄₈	157	60
♦ Highwood / Steve Kubasek / Steve Kubasek / 1953										
188⁶⁄₈	40	40	15¹⁄₈	15¹⁄₈	11	10⁷⁄₈	20⁴⁄₈	16⁴⁄₈	157	60
♦ Onion Lake / Martin M. Reddy / Martin M. Reddy / 1985										
188⁵⁄₈	40⁴⁄₈	41¹⁄₈	15⁵⁄₈	15⁵⁄₈	9⁴⁄₈	9⁵⁄₈	23¹⁄₈	21³⁄₈	160	62
♦ Alberta / Bill Foster / Foster's Bighorn Rest. / PR 1947										
188⁵⁄₈	43¹⁄₈	41	15¹⁄₈	15¹⁄₈	9¹⁄₈	9³⁄₈	19²⁄₈	17³⁄₈	160	62
♦ Burnt Timber Creek / Robert P. Erickson / Robert P. Erickson / 1993										
188⁴⁄₈	41	45⁴⁄₈	14⁶⁄₈	14⁵⁄₈	11	9¹⁄₈	27	27	165	64
♦ Clearwater / Unknown / Norman Lougheed / 1936										
188⁴⁄₈	40²⁄₈	40	16²⁄₈	16¹⁄₈	8⁵⁄₈	8⁶⁄₈	21¹⁄₈	19⁴⁄₈	165	64
♦ Opal Range / Robert Zebedee / Robert Zebedee / 1977										
188³⁄₈	42¹⁄₈	38	16	16	9⁴⁄₈	9²⁄₈	20⁶⁄₈	20⁶⁄₈	169	66
♦ Alberta / Arthur Smith / Arthur Smith / 1959										
188³⁄₈	39¹⁄₈	39⁶⁄₈	15⁶⁄₈	15⁶⁄₈	9⁵⁄₈	9⁷⁄₈	21⁶⁄₈	15⁴⁄₈	169	66
♦ Burnt Timber Creek / Walter O. Ford, Jr. / Walter O. Ford, Jr. / 1966										
188³⁄₈	39³⁄₈	39⁶⁄₈	15³⁄₈	15³⁄₈	11	10⁴⁄₈	22¹⁄₈	14	169	66
♦ Gibraltar Mt. / Leslie Kish / Leslie Kish / 1981										
188³⁄₈	40	39⁷⁄₈	16	16	9	8⁷⁄₈	25¹⁄₈	20¹⁄₈	169	66
♦ Sheep River / Katherine A. Pyra / Katherine A. Pyra / 1991										
188²⁄₈	45⁴⁄₈	44²⁄₈	13⁶⁄₈	13⁶⁄₈	9⁴⁄₈	9⁷⁄₈	23⁴⁄₈	22⁷⁄₈	177	70
♦ Panther River / Unknown / Harvey A. Trimble / 1932										
188²⁄₈	38⁵⁄₈	37⁷⁄₈	15⁶⁄₈	15⁷⁄₈	10⁷⁄₈	10⁴⁄₈	21²⁄₈	15	177	70
♦ Kananaskis / Terry Webber / Terry Webber / 1961										
188	41⁶⁄₈	40⁶⁄₈	14⁶⁄₈	14⁷⁄₈	10	10²⁄₈	21²⁄₈	16⁶⁄₈	188	72
♦ Kananaskis River / C. Allenhof / C. Allenhof / 1958										
188	39⁷⁄₈	39¹⁄₈	15⁴⁄₈	15³⁄₈	10⁶⁄₈	10	23⁷⁄₈	13⁴⁄₈	188	72
♦ Kananaskis Summit / Ted Howell / Ted Howell / 1963										
188	41¹⁄₈	39⁵⁄₈	15	15	10⁴⁄₈	10⁵⁄₈	20⁵⁄₈	16⁴⁄₈	188	72
♦ Cardinal River / Lawrence N. Baraniuk / Lawrence N. Baraniuk / 1986										
187⁶⁄₈	44	43²⁄₈	15¹⁄₈	15²⁄₈	8⁴⁄₈	7⁶⁄₈	24³⁄₈	24³⁄₈	191	75
♦ Ram River / George W. Parker / George W. Parker / 1961										

ALBERTA BIGHORN SHEEP *(continued)*

Score	Length of Horn		Circumference of Base		Circumference at Third Quarter		Greatest Spread	Tip-to-Tip Spread	All-Time Rank	State Rank
	R	L	R	L	R	L				
♦ *Locality / Hunter / Owner / Date Killed*										
187⁶⁄₈	39³⁄₈	38⁷⁄₈	14⁵⁄₈	14⁷⁄₈	11³⁄₈	11³⁄₈	22³⁄₈	15	191	75
♦ *Wildhay River / Jim Papst / Jim Papst / 1967*										
187⁶⁄₈	40¹⁄₈	39⁷⁄₈	16	16	9⁶⁄₈	8⁴⁄₈	21	12	191	75
♦ *Ghost River / Gerald Molnar / Gerald Molnar / 1988*										
187⁵⁄₈	40⁵⁄₈	43⁶⁄₈	14⁴⁄₈	14⁴⁄₈	10³⁄₈	10²⁄₈	22¹⁄₈	22	197	78
♦ *Butcher Creek / Vince Bruder / Vince Bruder / 1958*										
187⁴⁄₈	40⁵⁄₈	39⁷⁄₈	15³⁄₈	15³⁄₈	9⁴⁄₈	9³⁄₈	20⁴⁄₈	19²⁄₈	202	79
♦ *Ram Range / John F. Snyder / John F. Snyder / 1978*										
187³⁄₈	39²⁄₈	39³⁄₈	15⁴⁄₈	15⁴⁄₈	9⁶⁄₈	9⁷⁄₈	21⁴⁄₈	20	205	80
♦ *Sundre / Stan Burrell / Stan Burrell / 1953*										
187³⁄₈	40⁴⁄₈	40³⁄₈	16²⁄₈	16¹⁄₈	8³⁄₈	8⁴⁄₈	22⁷⁄₈	22⁷⁄₈	205	80
♦ *Elbow River / Sam R. Sloan / Sam R. Sloan / 1962*										
187²⁄₈	40³⁄₈	43¹⁄₈	14⁷⁄₈	15¹⁄₈	9¹⁄₈	9³⁄₈	22⁴⁄₈	19⁷⁄₈	208	82
♦ *McDonald Creek / Ernest F. Greenwood / Ernest F. Greenwood / 1965*										
187²⁄₈	38⁴⁄₈	39⁴⁄₈	15⁶⁄₈	15⁶⁄₈	10	10³⁄₈	22²⁄₈	17³⁄₈	208	82
♦ *Plateau Mt. / Randy Jackson / Randy Jackson / 1984*										
187²⁄₈	36³⁄₈	37¹⁄₈	16⁵⁄₈	16⁵⁄₈	9⁷⁄₈	9⁷⁄₈	22⁴⁄₈	20	208	82
♦ *Thornton Creek / John Gehan / John Gehan / 1988*										
187¹⁄₈	41⁵⁄₈	43⁴⁄₈	15	15	9¹⁄₈	8⁵⁄₈	23⁴⁄₈	23	215	85
♦ *Fallen Timber Creek / Picked Up / Joe Blakemore / 1968*										
187¹⁄₈	41	38⁵⁄₈	15⁶⁄₈	15⁷⁄₈	9	9³⁄₈	22⁶⁄₈	15²⁄₈	215	85
♦ *Red Deer River / Richard B. Smith / Richard B. Smith / 1984*										
187	40⁴⁄₈	38⁶⁄₈	16	15⁷⁄₈	9⁴⁄₈	8⁶⁄₈	15	22⁷⁄₈	219	87
♦ *Elbow River / Ralph Cervo / Ralph Cervo / 1981*										
187	39⁶⁄₈	38	16⁷⁄₈	17	8¹⁄₈	8¹⁄₈	20	21⁷⁄₈	219	87
♦ *Highwood Range / Sten B. Lundberg / Sten B. Lundberg / 1984*										
186⁷⁄₈	34³⁄₈	40²⁄₈	15⁶⁄₈	15⁶⁄₈	10⁵⁄₈	10⁵⁄₈	22⁴⁄₈	18⁶⁄₈	231	89
♦ *Burnt Timber / C.J. McElroy / C.J. McElroy / 1965*										
186⁷⁄₈	40¹⁄₈	38⁴⁄₈	16¹⁄₈	16	9	9	24³⁄₈	19	231	89
♦ *Ghost River / D. James Turner / D. James Turner / 1990*										
186⁶⁄₈	39¹⁄₈	39⁷⁄₈	15¹⁄₈	15²⁄₈	10²⁄₈	10⁴⁄₈	22	17⁴⁄₈	234	91
♦ *Whitehorse Creek / Philip H. R. Stepney / Prov. Mus. Alta. / 1978*										
186⁶⁄₈	38⁶⁄₈	38²⁄₈	16³⁄₈	16³⁄₈	8⁷⁄₈	8⁷⁄₈	23³⁄₈	18⁵⁄₈	234	91
♦ *Highwood River / Ross Nikonchuk / Ross Nikonchuk / 1984*										
186⁶⁄₈	39⁴⁄₈	40	15³⁄₈	15⁴⁄₈	10¹⁄₈	9¹⁄₈	20⁴⁄₈	15	234	91
♦ *Sheep River / Percy Pyra / Percy Pyra / 1991*										
186⁵⁄₈	42⁴⁄₈	41³⁄₈	14⁵⁄₈	14⁶⁄₈	9⁴⁄₈	9⁴⁄₈	24⁴⁄₈	21⁶⁄₈	242	94
♦ *Panther River / Picked Up / Belmore Browne / 1936*										

Score	Length of Horn		Circumference of Base		Circumference at Third Quarter		Greatest Spread	Tip-to-Tip Spread	All-Time Rank	State Rank
	R	L	R	L	R	L				
♦ *Locality / Hunter / Owner / Date Killed*										
186 5/8	38 6/8	38 3/8	15 3/8	15 3/8	10 1/8	10	22	17 7/8	242	94
♦ *Blind Canyon / Picked Up / Alberta Fish & Wildlife / 1983*										
186 4/8	38	38 4/8	17 3/8	17 3/8	8 1/8	8 4/8	20 2/8	17 2/8	247	96
♦ *Rocky Mt. House / Robert B. Johnson / Robert B. Johnson / 1960*										
186 3/8	41 7/8	40 4/8	14 1/8	14 1/8	10 4/8	10 4/8	20	18	250	97
♦ *Tyrrell Creek / Picked Up / John H. Batten / 1949*										
186 3/8	38 1/8	36	16	16 1/8	10	10	22 4/8	18 2/8	250	97
♦ *Castle River / Ed Burton / Ed Burton / 1954*										
186 2/8	41 7/8	42 1/8	14	14	9 7/8	9 7/8	22 4/8	21 4/8	257	99
♦ *Cadomin / R.A. Craig / R.A. Craig / 1936*										
186 2/8	42 3/8	41 3/8	14 5/8	14 6/8	9 4/8	9 4/8	24 2/8	20 6/8	257	99
♦ *Clearwater River / Picked Up / John H. Batten / 1954*										
186 2/8	40 3/8	40 1/8	15 1/8	15 3/8	9 7/8	9 5/8	21 4/8	19 5/8	257	99
♦ *Sheep Creek / G.A. Reiche / G.A. Reiche / 1960*										
186 2/8	37	38 4/8	15 7/8	15 7/8	10	9 4/8	20 1/8	17	257	99
♦ *Junction Mt. / Robert R. Willis / Robert R. Willis / 1978*										
186 2/8	39 6/8	39 4/8	16 1/8	16 1/8	8 5/8	8 4/8	23 3/8	17 4/8	257	99
♦ *Little Elbow River / John Liefso / John Liefso / 1982*										
186 1/8	39 4/8	38 3/8	15 2/8	15 3/8	10 4/8	10	22 3/8	15 6/8	264	104
♦ *Highwood / Terry J. Webber / Terry J. Webber / 1959*										
186 1/8	39 5/8	40 2/8	15 6/8	15 4/8	8 3/8	8 2/8	22	17 4/8	264	104
♦ *Waterton Natl. Park / Picked Up / Robert Thompson / PR 1966*										
186 1/8	39 5/8	38	15 5/8	15 3/8	9 6/8	10 2/8	20 4/8	20 4/8	264	104
♦ *Cougar Mt. / Alan E. Schroeder / Alan E. Schroeder / 1989*										
186	40 4/8	39	16	16	8 4/8	8 7/8	19 5/8	19 5/8	270	107
♦ *Clear Water / Herb Hamilton / Herb Hamilton / 1964*										
185 7/8	40 3/8	40 4/8	15	15	9 5/8	9 6/8	21	17 3/8	274	108
♦ *Panther River / J.F. Blakemore / J.F. Blakemore / 1961*										
185 7/8	41 2/8	41 3/8	14	14 2/8	10 3/8	10 6/8	22 5/8	17 3/8	274	108
♦ *Mystery Lake / Jim Baballa / Jim Baballa / 1962*										
185 7/8	38 7/8	38 2/8	15 6/8	15 5/8	10	10	21 5/8	17 1/8	274	108
♦ *Burnt Timber Creek / John T. Blackwell / John T. Blackwell / 1967*										
185 6/8	40 2/8	40 2/8	15	14 7/8	9 6/8	10 1/8	21	21	279	111
♦ *Ghost River / William D. Cox / William D. Cox / 1959*										
185 5/8	39 1/8	39 4/8	14 7/8	14 6/8	10 1/8	10 5/8	22 4/8	18	282	112
♦ *Black Diamond / Picked Up / Gordon Lait / 1962*										
185 4/8	40 6/8	40	14 5/8	14 6/8	10 1/8	10	22 4/8	20	284	113
♦ *Sask. River / Herb Klein / Herb Klein / 1963*										

Score	Length of Horn		Circumference of Base		Circumference at Third Quarter		Greatest Spread	Tip-to-Tip Spread	All-Time Rank	State Rank
	R	L	R	L	R	L				
◆ Locality / Hunter / Owner / Date Killed										
185 4/8	38 5/8	40 5/8	15 4/8	15 4/8	8 5/8	10	24	19 4/8	284	113
◆ Highwood River / W. Erdman / M.R. Wagner / 1964										
185 4/8	40 2/8	40 2/8	14 4/8	14 4/8	10 1/8	10 1/8	22	20 4/8	284	113
◆ Canyon Creek / Edith J. Nagy / Edith J. Nagy / 1981										
185 4/8	38 4/8	40 4/8	15	14 7/8	10 4/8	10 4/8	21	18 4/8	284	113
◆ Barrier Mt. / Ronald K. Smith / Ronald K. Smith / 1988										
185 3/8	39 3/8	40 2/8	15 4/8	15 6/8	10 1/8	10 6/8	21 4/8	15 6/8	293	117
◆ Banff / Unknown / E. Kent. Univ. / PR 1974										
185 1/8	40 2/8	37 5/8	15 7/8	15 7/8	9 4/8	9	23 2/8	18 2/8	305	118
◆ Big Horn River / Chris Klineburger / Chris Klineburger / 1962										
185	40 1/8	39 5/8	16 2/8	16 2/8	8 4/8	8 2/8	22	19 4/8	311	119
◆ Alberta / Gift of Lynford Biddle / Acad. Nat. Sci., Phil. / 1901										
185	40 4/8	39 4/8	15 1/8	15 1/8	9 3/8	8 6/8	20 2/8	17 2/8	311	119
◆ Cadomin / Rita Oney / Rita Oney / 1966										
184 6/8	40 1/8	40 1/8	15 2/8	15 2/8	9 7/8	9 6/8	21 5/8	19 3/8	318	121
◆ Brazeau River / Grancel Fitz / Mrs. Grancel Fitz / 1931										
184 6/8	39 4/8	39 2/8	16 3/8	16 3/8	7 6/8	8 1/8	21 1/8	17 3/8	318	121
◆ Little Elbow River / Alex Cornett / Alex Cornett / 1976										
184 5/8	39 2/8	41 1/8	14 7/8	15 1/8	9 6/8	9 6/8	20 2/8	17 6/8	324	123
◆ Clearwater / G.C. Matthews / G.C. Matthews / 1942										
184 5/8	41 6/8	42 3/8	14 2/8	14 1/8	9 7/8	9 6/8	22 1/8	22 1/8	324	123
◆ Burnt Timber Creek / Berry B. Brooks / Berry B. Brooks / 1960										
184 5/8	39 2/8	39 1/8	14 7/8	14 7/8	10 6/8	10 4/8	22 1/8	18 3/8	324	123
◆ Rock Lake / Bill Bodenchuk / Clifford Wolfe / 1960										
184 5/8	38 2/8	40 1/8	15 4/8	15 3/8	9 3/8	9 3/8	22 5/8	21 4/8	324	123
◆ Ruby Lake / Picked Up / John G. Stelfox / 1965										
184 5/8	39	40 5/8	15	15 1/8	10	10	22	18 2/8	324	123
◆ Luscar Creek / Doug W. Whiteside / Doug W. Whiteside / 1976										
184 4/8	39 2/8	39 2/8	16	16	8 4/8	8 1/8	22 3/8	17 4/8	331	128
◆ Smoky River / W.C. Barthman / W.C. Barthman / 1946										
184 4/8	39 3/8	39 3/8	15 6/8	16 3/8	8 6/8	8 7/8	21 2/8	18 1/8	331	128
◆ Exshaw Creek / Kenneth F. Bills / Kenneth F. Bills / 1993										
184 3/8	37 3/8	41 2/8	15 6/8	15 2/8	8 7/8	9	22 1/8	17 6/8	337	130
◆ Cadomin / John H. Marcum / John H. Marcum / 1969										
184 3/8	41	41 7/8	14 2/8	14 3/8	10	10	21 4/8	18 2/8	337	130
◆ Burnt Timber Creek / Terrance S. Marcum / Terrance S. Marcum / 1988										
184 2/8	38 7/8	40 3/8	15	15	10 7/8	9 4/8	20 1/8	18 4/8	342	132
◆ Drinnan Creek / John H. Epstein / John H. Epstein / 1963										

ALBERTA BIGHORN SHEEP *(continued)*

Score	Length of Horn R	Length of Horn L	Circumference of Base R	Circumference of Base L	Circumference at Third Quarter R	Circumference at Third Quarter L	Greatest Spread	Tip-to-Tip Spread	All-Time Rank	State Rank
	♦ *Locality / Hunter / Owner / Date Killed*									
184 1/8	39 5/8	42	15 2/8	15 1/8	8 5/8	8 1/8	22 5/8	22 5/8	344	133
	♦ *Alberta / Bob Wood / N. Am. Wildl. Mus. / 1964*									
184 1/8	38 7/8	39	17	17	7 7/8	7 6/8	23 1/8	23 1/8	344	133
	♦ *Castle River / E.B. Cunningham / E.B. Cunningham / 1965*									
184 1/8	39 7/8	39 4/8	15 2/8	15 4/8	9 1/8	9 3/8	24	21 7/8	344	133
	♦ *Panther River / Picked Up / Paul Ujfalusi / 1966*									
184	41 1/8	41 1/8	14 2/8	14 1/8	10	10	20 5/8	19	349	136
	♦ *Ghost River / W.D. Norwood / W.D. Norwood / 1955*									
184	35	36 4/8	16 2/8	16 1/8	10 6/8	11	21	20	349	136
	♦ *Cardston / August Glander / August Glander / 1969*									
183 7/8	41 1/8	40	14 4/8	14 4/8	9 6/8	9 4/8	23	20 5/8	356	138
	♦ *Sask. River / Basil C. Bradbury / Basil C. Bradbury / 1968*									
183 6/8	40 1/8	39 5/8	14 3/8	14 4/8	10 2/8	10 2/8	19 5/8	18 1/8	363	139
	♦ *Castle River / George Hagglund / George Hagglund / 1959*									
183 6/8	37 2/8	38	15 4/8	15 4/8	10	10	21 4/8	18 2/8	363	139
	♦ *Highwood Range / K. Fred Coleman / K. Fred Coleman / 1977*									
183 5/8	37 4/8	37 3/8	16 2/8	16 3/8	9 2/8	9 3/8	21 6/8	17 2/8	374	141
	♦ *Mystery Lake / Paul J. Inzanti / Paul J. Inzanti / 1960*									
183 5/8	37 7/8	39	15 2/8	15 3/8	9 5/8	10 1/8	22	16 1/8	374	141
	♦ *Burnt Timber Area / Jay H. Giese / Jay H. Giese / 1966*									
183 4/8	42	36 6/8	14 5/8	14 7/8	9 7/8	9 4/8	21 2/8	21 1/8	379	143
	♦ *Mystery Lake / Armando Tomasso / Armando Tomasso / 1967*									
183 4/8	39 2/8	38 6/8	16 1/8	16 1/8	8	8	21 2/8	21 2/8	379	143
	♦ *Galatea Creek / Karlo Miklic / Karlo Miklic / 1990*									
183 3/8	37 3/8	38 4/8	15 3/8	15 3/8	10 1/8	10 7/8	22	16 2/8	386	145
	♦ *Clearwater River / C.J. McElroy / C.J. McElroy / 1969*									
183 3/8	38 3/8	37 2/8	16 4/8	16 4/8	8	7 7/8	20 5/8	18 4/8	386	145
	♦ *Mt. Sparrowhawk / Gregory Kondro / Gregory Kondro / 1989*									
183 2/8	39 4/8	39 2/8	14 2/8	14 3/8	11 1/8	11 5/8	20	17 6/8	393	147
	♦ *Snake-Indian River / O. Fowler & J. Brewster / Fred Brewster / 1919*									
183 2/8	39 4/8	38	15 7/8	15 7/8	9 4/8	9 7/8	19 6/8	19 6/8	393	147
	♦ *Smoky River / Frank C. Hibben / Frank C. Hibben / 1957*									
183 2/8	39 6/8	40 4/8	14 6/8	15 1/8	9	8 6/8	23 1/8	18 2/8	393	147
	♦ *Clearwater River / Joseph C. Sellitti / Joseph C. Sellitti / 1981*									
183 2/8	38 2/8	38 6/8	15 6/8	16	8 5/8	8 6/8	20 5/8	20 5/8	393	147
	♦ *Bow River / Guy R. Woods / Guy R. Woods / 1985*									
183 2/8	39	39	15 2/8	15 2/8	9 3/8	9 4/8	21 4/8	18 6/8	393	147
	♦ *Prospect Creek / Bruce E. Williams / Bruce E. Williams / 1989*									

Score	Length of Horn		Circumference of Base		Circumference at Third Quarter		Greatest Spread	Tip-to-Tip Spread	All-Time Rank	State Rank
	R	L	R	L	R	L				
	♦ *Locality / Hunter / Owner / Date Killed*									
183 2/8	37 5/8	37 1/8	16 1/8	16 1/8	9 1/8	9 2/8	20 4/8	17 7/8	393	147
	♦ *Grizzly Creek / William J. Herchuk / William J. Herchuk / 1993*									
183 1/8	36 2/8	36 1/8	16 1/8	16 2/8	9 5/8	9 4/8	21 1/8	16 3/8	406	153
	♦ *Mt. Sparrowhawk / Randy Ward / Randy Ward / 1984*									
183	37 5/8	39 1/8	15 1/8	15 5/8	10 3/8	10 5/8	19 4/8	15 6/8	414	154
	♦ *Clearwater River / John H. Batten / John H. Batten / 1931*									
183	39 2/8	40	15 5/8	15 4/8	8 3/8	8 5/8	21 5/8	21 5/8	414	154
	♦ *Cadomin / Otis Chandler / Otis Chandler / 1969*									
183	38	38 6/8	15 1/8	15 1/8	9	9 2/8	21 1/8	21 1/8	414	154
	♦ *Solomon Creek / Picked Up / William Gosney / 1977*									
183	40 5/8	40 7/8	13 7/8	14 1/8	10 5/8	10 4/8	20 2/8	19 4/8	414	154
	♦ *Ram River / Robert G. Morgan / Robert G. Morgan / 1980*									
182 7/8	40 5/8	38 6/8	15	15 1/8	9 4/8	9 4/8	22	17 4/8	419	158
	♦ *Alberta / G.L. Gibbons / G.L. Gibbons / 1963*									
182 6/8	37 5/8	37 5/8	15 2/8	15 2/8	10	9 7/8	23 7/8	20 4/8	421	159
	♦ *Lake Louise / Picked Up / Howard Bronsdon / 1952*									
182 6/8	38 4/8	37 4/8	14 6/8	15	10 5/8	10 3/8	21 7/8	15 5/8	421	159
	♦ *Burnt Timber / Mrs. W.E. Anderson / Mrs. W.E. Anderson / 1964*									
182 6/8	39 2/8	39	15	15	9 7/8	9 4/8	22	18 6/8	421	159
	♦ *Wildhay River / Jim Papst / Jim Papst / 1968*									
182 5/8	44 1/8	42 4/8	13 7/8	14	9 3/8	8 4/8	23 1/8	23 1/8	429	162
	♦ *Alberta / John D. Hazen / Unknown / 1918*									
182 5/8	37 7/8	38 6/8	16 6/8	16 6/8	8 2/8	7 3/8	19 4/8	16	429	162
	♦ *Brazeau Forest / H.A. Yocum / H.A. Yocum / 1941*									
182 5/8	39 1/8	36 4/8	15 5/8	15 4/8	9 4/8	9 4/8	21 4/8	20 6/8	429	162
	♦ *Narraway River / John C. Seidensticker / John C. Seidensticker / 1959*									
182 5/8	38 1/8	38 4/8	15	14 7/8	9 6/8	10 2/8	21 2/8	15 6/8	429	162
	♦ *Storm Mt. / W. Glaser / W. Glaser / 1961*									
182 5/8	38 4/8	37 3/8	16	16	9 2/8	8 7/8	19 2/8	13 1/8	429	162
	♦ *Junction Creek / Robert F. Brooks / Robert F. Brooks / 1978*									
182 4/8	36 7/8	37 7/8	16 1/8	16 3/8	8 5/8	8 7/8	23 5/8	17 6/8	436	167
	♦ *S. Castle River / Leon Atwood / Leon Atwood / 1962*									
182 4/8	38 4/8	39 2/8	15 5/8	15 5/8	8 4/8	8 2/8	22 1/8	19 1/8	436	167
	♦ *Kananaskis Summit / Ted Howell / Ted Howell / 1964*									
182 4/8	35 7/8	36 3/8	16 2/8	16 2/8	9 7/8	9 7/8	22 4/8	19	436	167
	♦ *Blind Canyon / Alan W. Foster / Alan W. Foster / 1981*									
182 3/8	38 3/8	37 4/8	14 5/8	14 6/8	10 2/8	10 4/8	22	16 2/8	447	170
	♦ *Banff / Gift of Madison Grant to NCHH / Unknown / PR 1951*									

Score	Length of Horn		Circumference of Base		Circumference at Third Quarter		Greatest Spread	Tip-to-Tip Spread	All-Time Rank	State Rank
	R	L	R	L	R	L				
◆ Locality / Hunter / Owner / Date Killed										
182³⁄₈	38⁶⁄₈	37¹⁄₈	16	16	8³⁄₈	8⁷⁄₈	23⁷⁄₈	18⁶⁄₈	447	170
◆ West Sulphur River / Robert Highberg / Robert Highberg / 1980										
182³⁄₈	38⁷⁄₈	39²⁄₈	15⁶⁄₈	15⁶⁄₈	9⁴⁄₈	8⁷⁄₈	20⁶⁄₈	20¹⁄₈	447	170
◆ Pigeon Mt. / Len Guldman / Len Guldman / 1990										
182²⁄₈	39⁵⁄₈	39⁷⁄₈	15	15²⁄₈	9¹⁄₈	9⁴⁄₈	21⁴⁄₈	17⁴⁄₈	452	173
◆ Ram River / Louise McConnell / Louise McConnell / 1961										
182²⁄₈	36	36⁶⁄₈	15⁴⁄₈	15⁴⁄₈	10	10	21³⁄₈	16	452	173
◆ Sulphur River / Unknown / Roy Everest / 1963										
182²⁄₈	40¹⁄₈	39⁷⁄₈	15	14⁵⁄₈	9⁴⁄₈	10²⁄₈	21²⁄₈	21²⁄₈	452	173
◆ Wildhay River / James H. Duke, Jr. / James H. Duke, Jr. / 1967										
182²⁄₈	36⁴⁄₈	35⁶⁄₈	16¹⁄₈	16²⁄₈	9¹⁄₈	9¹⁄₈	23³⁄₈	18⁷⁄₈	452	173
◆ Rocky Creek / Randy A. Desabrais / Randy A. Desabrais / 1982										
182¹⁄₈	38³⁄₈	37⁴⁄₈	15²⁄₈	15¹⁄₈	9⁴⁄₈	9⁴⁄₈	22¹⁄₈	17³⁄₈	461	177
◆ Panther River / W.H. Slikker / W.H. Slikker / 1966										
182¹⁄₈	37⁷⁄₈	37⁴⁄₈	16	16²⁄₈	8⁵⁄₈	8⁵⁄₈	20¹⁄₈	18²⁄₈	461	177
◆ Crowsnest Lake / John Truant / John Truant / 1970										
182	37⁵⁄₈	36⁷⁄₈	15⁶⁄₈	15⁷⁄₈	9⁷⁄₈	10	21	16⁴⁄₈	466	179
◆ Pincher Creek / Delton Smith / Delton Smith / 1958										
182	37⁴⁄₈	39²⁄₈	15³⁄₈	15³⁄₈	8⁶⁄₈	8⁷⁄₈	20³⁄₈	17¹⁄₈	466	179
◆ Mt. Kidd / Dwayne W. Oneski / Dwayne W. Oneski / 1982										
182	38⁶⁄₈	38⁴⁄₈	14⁴⁄₈	14³⁄₈	10³⁄₈	10⁴⁄₈	19	17⁴⁄₈	466	179
◆ Mt. Kidd / Picked Up / Dirk Kieft / 1982										
181⁷⁄₈	39²⁄₈	39¹⁄₈	14³⁄₈	14²⁄₈	10⁵⁄₈	10¹⁄₈	20⁷⁄₈	20⁴⁄₈	479	182
◆ Coal Branch / John Caputo / John Caputo / 1962										
181⁷⁄₈	38³⁄₈	39	15²⁄₈	15¹⁄₈	9⁴⁄₈	9⁴⁄₈	21¹⁄₈	19	479	182
◆ Hinton / Darla J. Smith / Ben Morris / 1980										
181⁷⁄₈	39⁵⁄₈	40⁶⁄₈	15¹⁄₈	14⁷⁄₈	8⁴⁄₈	8⁶⁄₈	21¹⁄₈	21¹⁄₈	479	182
◆ Sundre / Dennis G. Overguard / Dennis G. Overguard / 1980										
181⁷⁄₈	39¹⁄₈	38⁴⁄₈	15¹⁄₈	15¹⁄₈	9	9¹⁄₈	20	19	479	182
◆ Kakwa River / Donald C. Fobert / Donald C. Fobert / 1983										
181⁷⁄₈	38	38⁷⁄₈	15⁷⁄₈	15⁵⁄₈	8³⁄₈	8⁶⁄₈	23²⁄₈	22⁷⁄₈	479	182
◆ Cataract Creek / Michael J. Hogan / Michael J. Hogan / 1984										
181⁶⁄₈	37	37²⁄₈	15⁴⁄₈	15²⁄₈	9⁵⁄₈	9⁵⁄₈	18	14⁴⁄₈	488	187
◆ Ghost River / L.C. Nowlin / L.C. Nowlin / PR 1940										
181⁶⁄₈	38¹⁄₈	38⁵⁄₈	15	15¹⁄₈	9⁶⁄₈	10	20⁶⁄₈	16¹⁄₈	488	187
◆ Prospect Creek / Wayne Tarnasky / Wayne Tarnasky / 1983										
181⁵⁄₈	42	40¹⁄₈	15²⁄₈	15¹⁄₈	8	7⁶⁄₈	21	20²⁄₈	493	189
◆ Ghost River / J.S. Parker / J.S. Parker / 1954										

Score	Length of Horn		Circumference of Base		Circumference at Third Quarter		Greatest Spread	Tip-to-Tip Spread	All-Time Rank	State Rank
	R	L	R	L	R	L				
◆ *Locality / Hunter / Owner / Date Killed*										
181 5/8	36 7/8	39 2/8	15 4/8	15 3/8	9	8 7/8	23 4/8	23 4/8	493	189
◆ *Elbow River / Ernest F. Dill / Ernest F. Dill / 1961*										
181 5/8	41 5/8	37 6/8	14 2/8	14 4/8	10	10 2/8	21 4/8	20 4/8	493	189
◆ *Burnt Timber Creek / George H. Glass / George H. Glass / 1967*										
181 5/8	39 3/8	37	16 4/8	16 3/8	7 3/8	7 5/8	20	15 4/8	493	189
◆ *Fisher Range / Reginald Zebedee / Reginald Zebedee / 1982*										
181 5/8	39 6/8	39 5/8	15 4/8	15 4/8	8 1/8	8 1/8	21 4/8	17 4/8	493	189
◆ *Goat Range / Christian D. Pagenkopf / Christian D. Pagenkopf / 1984*										
181 5/8	38 1/8	34 4/8	16 2/8	16 2/8	9 4/8	9 2/8	23	18	493	189
◆ *Pigeon Mt. / Paul S. Inzanti, Jr. / Paul S. Inzanti, Jr. / 1984*										
181 4/8	40	40 5/8	15 1/8	15 2/8	8 2/8	8 4/8	22	21 1/8	507	195
◆ *Sulphur River / John E. Hammett / John E. Hammett / 1938*										
181 4/8	38 6/8	41 2/8	14 6/8	14 4/8	8 5/8	8 5/8	22 2/8	22 2/8	507	195
◆ *Castle River / Cliff Johnson / Cliff Johnson / 1957*										
181 4/8	38 5/8	39 1/8	15 1/8	15 3/8	8 6/8	9	23 1/8	19 6/8	507	195
◆ *Cadomin / John Caputo / John Caputo / 1961*										
181 4/8	39	37 6/8	15 1/8	15 1/8	9	9 1/8	22	18 6/8	507	195
◆ *Spray Lake / George R. Willows / George R. Willows / 1974*										
181 4/8	38 6/8	36 4/8	16 6/8	16 5/8	7 5/8	7 3/8	19 4/8	11 7/8	507	195
◆ *Mt. Evans-Thomas / William E. MacDougall / William E. MacDougall / 1988*										
181 4/8	38 3/8	38 7/8	15 5/8	15 6/8	7 7/8	8 2/8	21 4/8	13 6/8	507	195
◆ *Burnt Timber Creek / Lambert VanDongen / Lambert VanDongen / 1991*										
181 3/8	39 3/8	39 6/8	15 1/8	14 6/8	9 4/8	9 1/8	25	21	525	201
◆ *Clearwater River / Phil Temple / Phil Temple / 1951*										
181 3/8	38 2/8	39 3/8	15 1/8	15 2/8	9 2/8	9 4/8	20 4/8	14 4/8	525	201
◆ *Big Horn Creek / Earl Foss / Earl Foss / 1960*										
181 3/8	38 6/8	37 7/8	14 7/8	14 7/8	9 3/8	9 3/8	20 4/8	19 6/8	525	201
◆ *Clearwater River / Joseph T. Pelton / Joseph T. Pelton / 1966*										
181 3/8	37 5/8	37 4/8	15	15	10 5/8	10 5/8	19	15 3/8	525	201
◆ *Cardinal River / Randy Babala / Randy Babala / 1980*										
181 3/8	37 3/8	39 2/8	15	15 1/8	9 7/8	9 5/8	20 2/8	16 4/8	525	201
◆ *Fairholme Range / Eldon Hoff / Eldon Hoff / 1989*										
181 2/8	41 1/8	40 5/8	14	13 7/8	10 1/8	9 5/8	21 2/8	19 6/8	538	206
◆ *Highwood River / Ralph Rink / George Beach / 1946*										
181 2/8	39 2/8	40 2/8	14 1/8	14	10	10 2/8	20 5/8	16 4/8	538	206
◆ *Timber Creek / Jason G. Hindes / Jason G. Hindes / 1985*										
181 2/8	40	40 6/8	15 1/8	15	7 6/8	7 6/8	21 4/8	21	538	206
◆ *Ghost River / Mike Michalezki / Mike Michalezki / 1991*										

Score	Length of Horn		Circumference of Base		Circumference at Third Quarter		Greatest Spread	Tip-to-Tip Spread	All-Time Rank	State Rank
	R	L	R	L	R	L				
\u25C6 Locality / Hunter / Owner / Date Killed										
$181\frac{1}{8}$	$38\frac{7}{8}$	35	$15\frac{5}{8}$	$15\frac{5}{8}$	$9\frac{1}{8}$	9	$20\frac{4}{8}$	15	546	209
\u25C6 Spray Lakes Reservoir / G. Robert Willows / G. Robert Willows / 1977										
$181\frac{1}{8}$	$38\frac{2}{8}$	$40\frac{3}{8}$	15	$15\frac{2}{8}$	$8\frac{5}{8}$	$8\frac{3}{8}$	$17\frac{3}{8}$	21	546	209
\u25C6 Scalp Creek / James Mills / James Mills / 1984										
$181\frac{1}{8}$	39	$38\frac{5}{8}$	$15\frac{4}{8}$	$15\frac{3}{8}$	$8\frac{5}{8}$	$8\frac{3}{8}$	$20\frac{6}{8}$	$17\frac{4}{8}$	546	209
\u25C6 Mt. Inflexible / Carl Gallant / Carl Gallant / 1987										
181	$39\frac{2}{8}$	$39\frac{2}{8}$	$15\frac{2}{8}$	$15\frac{2}{8}$	$8\frac{6}{8}$	$8\frac{6}{8}$	21	17	552	212
\u25C6 Brule / Picked Up / G.W. Warner / 1963										
181	$37\frac{6}{8}$	37	$15\frac{5}{8}$	$15\frac{5}{8}$	9	9	23	15	552	212
\u25C6 Mystery Lake / Peter Lazio / Peter Lazio / 1967										
$180\frac{7}{8}$	$39\frac{2}{8}$	$38\frac{1}{8}$	$14\frac{5}{8}$	$14\frac{6}{8}$	$9\frac{3}{8}$	$9\frac{4}{8}$	$22\frac{6}{8}$	$22\frac{2}{8}$	558	214
\u25C6 Clearwater River / Kevin Peters / Kevin Peters / 1989										
$180\frac{6}{8}$	$38\frac{2}{8}$	42	15	15	$8\frac{1}{8}$	$8\frac{3}{8}$	$22\frac{7}{8}$	$22\frac{1}{8}$	563	215
\u25C6 Seebe / Ted Trueblood / Ted Trueblood / 1956										
$180\frac{6}{8}$	$37\frac{4}{8}$	$35\frac{6}{8}$	$16\frac{2}{8}$	16	$8\frac{6}{8}$	$8\frac{4}{8}$	21	$15\frac{3}{8}$	563	215
\u25C6 Flat Creek / G.I. Franklin / G.I. Franklin / 1964										
$180\frac{6}{8}$	$37\frac{5}{8}$	$38\frac{3}{8}$	$15\frac{1}{8}$	15	$9\frac{6}{8}$	$9\frac{7}{8}$	$21\frac{3}{8}$	$16\frac{4}{8}$	563	215
\u25C6 Panther Creek / C.D. Sharp / C.D. Sharp / 1966										
$180\frac{6}{8}$	$37\frac{2}{8}$	$36\frac{4}{8}$	16	16	$9\frac{2}{8}$	$8\frac{7}{8}$	21	$17\frac{2}{8}$	563	215
\u25C6 Junction Creek / Spencer T. Nichols / Spencer T. Nichols / 1981										
$180\frac{6}{8}$	$37\frac{1}{8}$	$37\frac{7}{8}$	$15\frac{7}{8}$	$15\frac{7}{8}$	$8\frac{4}{8}$	$8\frac{7}{8}$	$21\frac{4}{8}$	$17\frac{5}{8}$	563	215
\u25C6 Forbidden Creek / Dennis H. Russell / Dennis H. Russell / 1984										
$180\frac{5}{8}$	$37\frac{3}{8}$	36	$15\frac{3}{8}$	$15\frac{3}{8}$	$9\frac{5}{8}$	$9\frac{6}{8}$	$22\frac{1}{8}$	$16\frac{2}{8}$	574	220
\u25C6 Ghost River / Robert W. Hodge / Robert W. Hodge / 1985										
$180\frac{4}{8}$	39	$41\frac{4}{8}$	$14\frac{5}{8}$	$14\frac{5}{8}$	8	$8\frac{2}{8}$	$22\frac{5}{8}$	22	583	221
\u25C6 Smoky River / H.P. Brandenburg / H.P. Brandenburg / 1924										
$180\frac{4}{8}$	$35\frac{6}{8}$	$38\frac{2}{8}$	$15\frac{2}{8}$	15	$10\frac{7}{8}$	$9\frac{3}{8}$	22	17	583	221
\u25C6 Lake Louise / Unknown / Martin Bonack / PR 1951										
$180\frac{4}{8}$	38	39	$14\frac{2}{8}$	$14\frac{2}{8}$	$10\frac{6}{8}$	$10\frac{6}{8}$	$22\frac{3}{8}$	$18\frac{2}{8}$	583	221
\u25C6 Coal Branch / R.G.F. Brown / R.G.F. Brown / 1962										
$180\frac{4}{8}$	38	$38\frac{4}{8}$	15	15	$8\frac{7}{8}$	9	$19\frac{7}{8}$	$18\frac{6}{8}$	583	221
\u25C6 Moosehorn Lake / Maynard Mathews / Maynard Mathews / 1964										
$180\frac{4}{8}$	$34\frac{7}{8}$	$35\frac{5}{8}$	$15\frac{4}{8}$	$15\frac{5}{8}$	$10\frac{1}{8}$	$10\frac{2}{8}$	$21\frac{2}{8}$	$13\frac{1}{8}$	583	221
\u25C6 Thistle Creek / Paul H. Chance / Paul H. Chance / 1975										
$180\frac{4}{8}$	$40\frac{1}{8}$	$40\frac{1}{8}$	$15\frac{4}{8}$	$15\frac{4}{8}$	$7\frac{6}{8}$	$7\frac{5}{8}$	$22\frac{6}{8}$	$20\frac{2}{8}$	583	221
\u25C6 Luscar Mt. / Jerry L. Christian / Jerry L. Christian / 1979										
$180\frac{4}{8}$	$39\frac{4}{8}$	$39\frac{2}{8}$	14	14	10	$10\frac{2}{8}$	20	$17\frac{2}{8}$	583	221
\u25C6 Skeleton Creek / James W. Campbell / James W. Campbell / 1991										

ALBERTA BIGHORN SHEEP *(continued)*

Score	Length of Horn R	Length of Horn L	Circumference of Base R	Circumference of Base L	Circumference at Third Quarter R	Circumference at Third Quarter L	Greatest Spread	Tip-to-Tip Spread	All-Time Rank	State Rank
♦ *Locality / Hunter / Owner / Date Killed*										
180 3/8	38 6/8	40 1/8	15 1/8	15 1/8	8 6/8	9 3/8	20 1/8	19	596	228
♦ *Bow Lake / Robert D. Layton / Robert D. Layton / 1942*										
180 3/8	39 6/8	39 7/8	16 2/8	16	7 1/8	7 1/8	22 1/8	22 1/8	596	228
♦ *Sulphur River / W.D. Parker / W.D. Parker / 1955*										
180 3/8	41	36 7/8	15 4/8	15 5/8	8	8 1/8	19 7/8	19 7/8	596	228
♦ *Ghost River / Art Brewster / Art Brewster / 1960*										
180 3/8	38 1/8	39 4/8	15	14 7/8	9 4/8	9	21 4/8	17	596	228
♦ *Ghost River / J.E. Edwards / J.E. Edwards / 1964*										
180 3/8	38 3/8	37 4/8	15 4/8	15 6/8	8 6/8	8 3/8	22 1/8	15 4/8	596	228
♦ *Sheep Creek / Barry Gramlich / Barry Gramlich / 1992*										
180 2/8	38 6/8	37 2/8	14 6/8	14 6/8	10 3/8	9 6/8	21 1/8	15	619	233
♦ *Burnt Timber Creek / Ruth Mahoney / Ruth Mahoney / 1963*										
180 2/8	35 3/8	35 7/8	15 5/8	15 6/8	9 7/8	10	21 1/8	14 2/8	619	233
♦ *Warden Rock / Brian N. Holthe / Brian N. Holthe / 1990*										
180 2/8	39 2/8	39 4/8	15 3/8	15 1/8	7 7/8	8	19	18 5/8	619	233
♦ *Rocky Creek / Donald R. Smith / Donald R. Smith / 1991*										
180 1/8	37 3/8	37 6/8	14 4/8	14 6/8	10	10	22 4/8	19 1/8	631	236
♦ *Ghost River / Lloyd E. Zeman / Lloyd E. Zeman / 1968*										
180 1/8	36 4/8	34 3/8	15 6/8	15 7/8	9 7/8	9 5/8	22 5/8	18 2/8	631	236
♦ *Castle River / Don W. Caldwell / Don W. Caldwell / 1969*										
180 1/8	37 4/8	35 3/8	15 4/8	15 5/8	9 7/8	9 7/8	19 4/8	16	631	236
♦ *Coral Creek / Leonard W. King / Leonard W. King / 1983*										
180 1/8	37 6/8	37 7/8	16	16	7 7/8	8	21 4/8	14 6/8	631	236
♦ *Cougar Mt. / Norman Howg / Norman Howg / 1984*										
180 1/8	37 2/8	35 3/8	16	16 1/8	8 4/8	8 4/8	21	19 3/8	631	236
♦ *Drinnan Mt. / Everitt N. Davis / Everitt N. Davis / 1992*										
180	37 1/8	38 7/8	15	15	9 4/8	10	22	18 2/8	651	241
♦ *Seebe / Anson Brooks / Anson Brooks / 1956*										
180	39 1/8	37 1/8	15	15 2/8	9 4/8	9 6/8	21	19 4/8	651	241
♦ *Forbidden Creek / James Haugland / James Haugland / 1958*										
180	37 6/8	37 2/8	14 4/8	14 4/8	10 4/8	10 4/8	22 3/8	22 3/8	651	241
♦ *Panther Creek / Walter R. Schubert / Walter R. Schubert / 1966*										
180	38 5/8	37 3/8	15 4/8	15 4/8	9	8 4/8	20 4/8	16 3/8	651	241
♦ *Whitehorse Creek / Philip H. R. Stepney / Prov. Mus. Alta. / 1978*										
179 3/8	38 4/8	35 5/8	14 7/8	14 7/8	9 7/8	9 5/8	22 7/8	19	672	245
♦ *Drummond Mt. / Dallas Maloney / Dallas Maloney / 1992*										
178 7/8	37 5/8	38 4/8	15 6/8	16 3/8	7 5/8	7 7/8	23 2/8	23 5/8	677	246
♦ *Leyland Mt. / Walter E. Hartman / Walter E. Hartman / 1984*										

Score	Length of Horn		Circumference of Base		Circumference at Third Quarter		Greatest Spread	Tip-to-Tip Spread	All-Time Rank	State Rank
	R	L	R	L	R	L				
◆ *Locality / Hunter / Owner / Date Killed*										
178 2/8	35 4/8	36 4/8	16 6/8	16 7/8	7 4/8	7 6/8	21 5/8	17 4/8	682	247
◆ *Mt. Tecumseh / Edward Friel / Edward Friel / 1992*										
178	38	37 6/8	14 2/8	14 3/8	9 5/8	10	20 7/8	17 1/8	684	248
◆ *Highwood River / William B. McClelland / William B. McClelland / 1953*										
177 5/8	37 7/8	37 6/8	14 4/8	14 5/8	8 7/8	9 3/8	21 2/8	18 4/8	686	249
◆ *Clearwater River / Don W. Noah / Don W. Noah / 1993*										
177 1/8	37 2/8	37 3/8	16	16	7 3/8	7 3/8	21 4/8	20	689	250
◆ *Pincher Creek / Stephen Taylor / Stephen Taylor / 1977*										
176 7/8	38 6/8	37 5/8	13 7/8	13 5/8	10 3/8	10 3/8	19 5/8	16 2/8	691	251
◆ *Prospect Creek / Ronald K. Penner / Ronald K. Penner / 1993*										
175 4/8	35 6/8	35 2/8	15 2/8	15 2/8	8 3/8	8 3/8	23 3/8	18 4/8	699	252
◆ *Blind Canyon / Picked Up / Allan R. Beazer / 1993*										
175 2/8	35 1/8	36 1/8	15 1/8	15 1/8	8 6/8	8 5/8	20 2/8	16 4/8	700	253
◆ *Prospect Creek / Grant M. St. Germaine / Grant M. St. Germaine / 1992*										

Nez Perce County, Idaho, yielded this impressive bighorn ram, scoring 180-3/8 points, to Don L. Scoles in 1994.

Photograph by Grancel Fitz

BRITISH COLUMBIA PROVINCE RECORD
BIGHORN SHEEP
SCORE: 204
Locality: Sheep Creek   Date: 1920
Hunter: James Simpson
Owner: American Museum of Natural History

BRITISH COLUMBIA

BIGHORN SHEEP

Score	Length of Horn R	Length of Horn L	Circumference of Base R	Circumference of Base L	Circumference at Third Quarter R	Circumference at Third Quarter L	Greatest Spread	Tip-to-Tip Spread	All-Time Rank	State Rank
	♦ *Locality / Hunter / Owner / Date Killed*									
204	49 4/8	48 2/8	15 2/8	15 3/8	10 5/8	10 2/8	23 7/8	23 7/8	5	1
	♦ *Sheep Creek / James Simpson / Am. Mus. Nat. Hist. / 1920*									
201 1/8	49 2/8	44 5/8	15 2/8	15 1/8	9 4/8	9 2/8	26 2/8	25 6/8	11	2
	♦ *Cross River / David L. Onerheim / David L. Onerheim / 1987*									
200 7/8	43 6/8	43 3/8	16 5/8	16 7/8	9	9 2/8	22 5/8	20 3/8	13	3
	♦ *Fernie / H.J. Johnson / Royal Ontario Mus. / 1902*									
199	45	45 4/8	15 1/8	15	10 3/8	10 6/8	22 5/8	22 5/8	22	4
	♦ *Spence's Bridge / Picked Up / Parliament Bldg., B.C. / 1969*									
197 2/8	39 1/8	42 3/8	17	17	9 5/8	9 6/8	23 4/8	20	29	5
	♦ *E. Kootenay / Picked Up / Victoria Fish & Game Assn. / PR 1930*									
196 6/8	45 2/8	44 2/8	16 1/8	15 7/8	9 3/8	8 7/8	23	23	35	6
	♦ *Wardner / Jim Buss / Jim Buss / 1961*									
193 6/8	40 5/8	40 5/8	15 4/8	15 4/8	10 6/8	10 6/8	22 1/8	17 4/8	61	7
	♦ *Tornado Pass / John Stuber / John Stuber / 1956*									
193 1/8	44 5/8	42 4/8	15 1/8	15 2/8	9 7/8	10 1/8	21 7/8	21 7/8	72	8
	♦ *Spence's Bridge / M. Da Rosa / M. Da Rosa / 1961*									
193 1/8	40 1/8	39 2/8	16 3/8	16 4/8	10 3/8	10 3/8	19 7/8	15	72	8
	♦ *Ewin Creek / Gary N. Goode / Gary N. Goode / 1989*									
193	43 1/8	43 5/8	14 6/8	14 6/8	10 1/8	9 7/8	22 1/8	22 1/8	75	10
	♦ *Spence's Bridge / Norman Holland / Norman Holland / 1971*									
191 3/8	42 3/8	40	14 6/8	14 7/8	10 4/8	10 7/8	21 4/8	15 2/8	100	11
	♦ *Natal / John A. Morais / John A. Morais / 1960*									
191 2/8	45 6/8	44 2/8	15 2/8	15 2/8	7 7/8	8 4/8	24 5/8	24 5/8	104	12
	♦ *Grassmere / Donald F. Letcher / Donald F. Letcher / 1965*									
191 2/8	39 6/8	41 4/8	15 6/8	15 6/8	9 7/8	10	23	17 4/8	104	12
	♦ *Fording River / Ryan D. Jones / Ryan D. Jones / 1993*									
190 6/8	42 4/8	44 4/8	14 7/8	15	9 1/8	9 2/8	23 3/8	23 3/8	116	14
	♦ *Fernie / J.J. Osman / J.J. Osman / 1950*									
190 6/8	37 1/8	37 5/8	16 7/8	16 7/8	11 1/8	11	22	15 4/8	116	14
	♦ *Elko / Charles Weikert / Charles Weikert / 1970*									
189 6/8	40 6/8	40 6/8	15 6/8	15 5/8	9 1/8	9 4/8	21 6/8	14 1/8	134	16
	♦ *Swan Lake / Billy Stork / A.C. Gilbert / 1936*									
189 3/8	43 7/8	43	14 2/8	14 4/8	10 1/8	9 4/8	22 3/8	22 3/8	140	17
	♦ *Spence's Bridge / Bert Walkem / Bert Walkem / 1964*									
189 2/8	41	39	15 6/8	15 5/8	9 7/8	9 7/8	24	20 2/8	144	18
	♦ *Canal Flat / Robert Lemaster / Robert Lemaster / 1962*									

BRITISH COLUMBIA BIGHORN SHEEP *(continued)*

Score	Length of Horn R	Length of Horn L	Circumference of Base R	Circumference of Base L	Circumference at Third Quarter R	Circumference at Third Quarter L	Greatest Spread	Tip-to-Tip Spread	All-Time Rank	State Rank
	♦ *Locality / Hunter / Owner / Date Killed*									
189 1/8	39 3/8	39 6/8	16 4/8	16 4/8	9	9 1/8	21 6/8	18	146	19
	♦ *Lost Creek / Les J. Husband / Les J. Husband / 1992*									
188 5/8	41	38 7/8	15 3/8	15 6/8	10 5/8	10 6/8	20 3/8	19	160	20
	♦ *Simpson River / Patrick Deuling / Patrick Deuling / 1985*									
188 3/8	40 6/8	39 7/8	16 1/8	16 1/8	9	9	25 2/8	21	169	21
	♦ *White Swan Lake / A.C. Gilbert / James V. Bosco / 1940*									
188 3/8	40 6/8	40 5/8	15 4/8	15 4/8	9	9	21 6/8	17 2/8	169	21
	♦ *Surprise Lake / Herb Klein / Herb Klein / 1950*									
188 2/8	42 5/8	42 5/8	15 6/8	15 6/8	8 3/8	8 4/8	25 7/8	25 7/8	177	23
	♦ *Spences Bridge / Romeo Leduc / Romeo Leduc / 1982*									
187 6/8	42 1/8	42 3/8	14 5/8	15	9 2/8	9 2/8	21 4/8	21 4/8	191	24
	♦ *Chase / L. McNary & J. Langer / Lloyd McNary / 1956*									
187 5/8	45 7/8	42	14 7/8	14 4/8	8 6/8	8 7/8	23	22 2/8	197	25
	♦ *Spence's Bridge / J. David Smith / J. David Smith / 1969*									
187 3/8	42	41 7/8	15 3/8	15 4/8	8 4/8	8 4/8	21 4/8	21 4/8	205	26
	♦ *Lytton / R.G. Jones & P.B. Wilmot / R. George Jones / 1973*									
187 1/8	41 3/8	41 4/8	15 5/8	15 4/8	9 1/8	9 1/8	21	21	215	27
	♦ *White Swan Lake / Lucius A. Chase / Lucius A. Chase / 1961*									
186 6/8	39 4/8	38 4/8	16 2/8	16 3/8	10	9 2/8	23 6/8	18 7/8	234	28
	♦ *E. Kootenay / Jerry Mortimer / Jerry Mortimer / 1959*									
186 6/8	41 2/8	40 2/8	15	15	9 6/8	9 6/8	22 5/8	18 7/8	234	28
	♦ *Tornado Creek / Clive J. Endicott / Clive J. Endicott / 1988*									
186 4/8	40 5/8	39 1/8	15 6/8	15 7/8	9 3/8	8 7/8	19	22 6/8	247	30
	♦ *Fording River / M.C. Baher / M.C. Baher / 1942*									
186 4/8	40 1/8	39 7/8	16 3/8	16 2/8	8 6/8	8 4/8	21 7/8	20 4/8	247	30
	♦ *Mt. Assiniboine / Shirley A. Malbery / Shirley A. Malbery / 1990*									
186 3/8	42	41 1/8	15 3/8	15 3/8	8 6/8	8 3/8	21 6/8	16 6/8	250	32
	♦ *Fernie / Thomas Krall / Thomas Krall / 1963*									
186 3/8	41	42 3/8	15 1/8	15 1/8	8 2/8	8 7/8	20 1/8	20 1/8	250	32
	♦ *Simpson River / James A. Walls / James A. Walls / 1981*									
186 2/8	40	41 4/8	16	16	8	8 3/8	22 2/8	22 2/8	257	34
	♦ *Rabbit Creek / Lanny E. Kniert / Lanny E. Kniert / 1982*									
186 2/8	40	41	16 1/8	16 1/8	8 5/8	8 1/8	20 7/8	13	257	34
	♦ *Riverside Mt. / Paul A. Templin / Paul A. Templin / 1983*									
186	40 2/8	40 2/8	15 2/8	15	9 7/8	9 3/8	22	18 6/8	270	36
	♦ *Sparwood / Unknown / H. Bruce Freeman / PR 1910*									
186	40 6/8	40 2/8	15 4/8	15 3/8	9 7/8	9	22	20 4/8	270	36
	♦ *Line Creek / Sam W. Stephenson / Sam W. Stephenson / 1991*									

Score	Length of Horn		Circumference of Base		Circumference at Third Quarter		Greatest Spread	Tip-to-Tip Spread	All-Time Rank	State Rank
	R	L	R	L	R	L				
◆ *Locality / Hunter / Owner / Date Killed*										
185 7/8	40 3/8	41	15 6/8	15 6/8	8 4/8	8 5/8	21 5/8	21	274	38
◆ *Botanie Creek / William J. Pincock / William J. Pincock / 1988*										
185 3/8	39 6/8	39 5/8	16 3/8	16 3/8	8	8 1/8	21 5/8	13 4/8	293	39
◆ *Natal / H. Beard / Myles Travis / 1921*										
185 3/8	40 3/8	39 6/8	14 6/8	14 7/8	10 1/8	9 5/8	23 4/8	19 4/8	293	39
◆ *Lillooet / Glen E. Park / Glen E. Park / 1964*										
185 2/8	40 6/8	41	15 3/8	15 3/8	8 7/8	8 6/8	23 2/8	20 1/8	299	41
◆ *Spence's Bridge / J.C. Atkinson / J.C. Atkinson / 1965*										
185 1/8	40 1/8	38 6/8	15 3/8	15 3/8	9 2/8	8 7/8	23	15 2/8	305	42
◆ *Tornado Mt. / Vincent Kehm / Vincent Kehm / 1958*										
185	38 6/8	41 2/8	15 1/8	15 2/8	9 2/8	9 4/8	18 4/8	17 7/8	311	43
◆ *Mitchell River / Mr. & Mrs. N.A. Meckstroth / Mr. & Mrs. N.A. Meckstroth / 1963*										
184 4/8	38 6/8	38 4/8	15 5/8	15 5/8	9 6/8	9 5/8	22 7/8	17 4/8	331	44
◆ *Kindersley Creek / James C. Johnson / James C. Johnson / 1993*										
184 1/8	40 2/8	38 1/8	15 2/8	15 3/8	9 6/8	8 6/8	23	22	344	45
◆ *Vaseux Lake / Bob McDowell / Bob McDowell / 1960*										
183 6/8	37 2/8	37 2/8	15 5/8	15 5/8	9 2/8	9 6/8	20 4/8	17 4/8	363	46
◆ *Fernie / Unknown / Fred Braatz / 1930*										
183 6/8	39 7/8	39 3/8	14 6/8	14 6/8	9 7/8	10	21 4/8	15 7/8	363	46
◆ *Natal / Mrs. A.L. Musser / A.L. Musser / 1947*										
183 4/8	39 1/8	37 5/8	16	16 4/8	8 1/8	7 6/8	22 6/8	14 2/8	379	48
◆ *Chauncey Creek / Stewart Cockshutt / Stewart Cockshutt / 1990*										
183 2/8	39 4/8	39 6/8	15 3/8	15 4/8	8 6/8	9 1/8	20 2/8	18 2/8	393	49
◆ *Simpson River / Robert T. White / Robert T. White / 1988*										
183 1/8	38 4/8	38 5/8	15 5/8	15 5/8	9	9 1/8	22 2/8	16 7/8	406	50
◆ *Kootenay River / W. Vernon Walsh / W. Vernon Walsh / 1962*										
183 1/8	36 7/8	37 2/8	15 3/8	15 3/8	10 3/8	10	22	18 4/8	406	50
◆ *Fraser River / Karl P. Willms / Karl P. Willms / 1977*										
182 7/8	37 6/8	38 5/8	16 4/8	16 6/8	7 6/8	8 1/8	22 1/8	17	419	52
◆ *Line Creek / Kevin J. Galla / Kevin J. Galla / 1989*										
182 5/8	40 3/8	39 4/8	15	15 2/8	8 6/8	8 4/8	22 7/8	13 4/8	429	53
◆ *Bull River / Ralph W. Stearns / Ralph W. Stearns / 1950*										
182 4/8	41 1/8	40 5/8	15	15	8 1/8	8 2/8	22	18 4/8	436	54
◆ *Edgewater / William N. Ward / William N. Ward / 1969*										
182 4/8	40 2/8	40	15 3/8	15 3/8	8 2/8	8 1/8	23 1/8	20	436	54
◆ *Spence's Bridge / Don Ticehurst / Don Ticehurst / 1973*										
182 4/8	38 4/8	41 2/8	15 4/8	15 2/8	8 2/8	9	22 5/8	17 2/8	436	54
◆ *Mary Ann Creek / Jack Bridgewater / Jack Bridgewater / 1981*										

Score	Length of Horn		Circumference of Base		Circumference at Third Quarter		Greatest Spread	Tip-to-Tip Spread	All-Time Rank	State Rank
	R	L	R	L	R	L				
◆ Locality / Hunter / Owner / Date Killed										
182	41	$37\frac{6}{8}$	15	$14\frac{7}{8}$	$9\frac{2}{8}$	$9\frac{1}{8}$	$21\frac{5}{8}$	$17\frac{4}{8}$	466	57
◆ Canal Flat / Allen Cudworth / Allen Cudworth / 1958										
182	$39\frac{7}{8}$	$40\frac{1}{8}$	$15\frac{2}{8}$	$15\frac{4}{8}$	8	$8\frac{1}{8}$	$20\frac{4}{8}$	$20\frac{4}{8}$	466	57
◆ Murray Creek / Nancy J. Koopman / Nancy J. Koopman / 1986										
182	$37\frac{5}{8}$	$37\frac{5}{8}$	$16\frac{2}{8}$	$16\frac{2}{8}$	$8\frac{2}{8}$	$8\frac{2}{8}$	$22\frac{4}{8}$	$18\frac{4}{8}$	466	57
◆ Wigwam River / Grant W. Markoski / Grant W. Markoski / 1990										
$181\frac{7}{8}$	$36\frac{5}{8}$	$36\frac{2}{8}$	$16\frac{5}{8}$	$16\frac{4}{8}$	$8\frac{4}{8}$	$8\frac{5}{8}$	$20\frac{7}{8}$	20	479	60
◆ Elko / Percy McGregor / Percy McGregor / 1974										
$181\frac{5}{8}$	39	$37\frac{7}{8}$	$15\frac{7}{8}$	16	9	$8\frac{3}{8}$	$19\frac{5}{8}$	$13\frac{4}{8}$	493	61
◆ Kootenay River / Arthur V. Parsons / Arthur V. Parsons / 1986										
$181\frac{4}{8}$	$40\frac{1}{8}$	$39\frac{5}{8}$	$15\frac{6}{8}$	$15\frac{6}{8}$	$7\frac{6}{8}$	$7\frac{4}{8}$	$21\frac{3}{8}$	$17\frac{6}{8}$	507	62
◆ Wildhorse Creek / Dan VanZanten / Dan VanZanten / 1994										
$181\frac{2}{8}$	$40\frac{3}{8}$	$40\frac{7}{8}$	$15\frac{4}{8}$	$15\frac{4}{8}$	$7\frac{2}{8}$	$7\frac{5}{8}$	$22\frac{4}{8}$	$22\frac{4}{8}$	538	63
◆ McBride / Alfred Saulnier / Alfred Saulnier / 1966										
181	$40\frac{5}{8}$	$45\frac{7}{8}$	$14\frac{1}{8}$	$13\frac{7}{8}$	$7\frac{6}{8}$	$7\frac{7}{8}$	$26\frac{1}{8}$	$26\frac{1}{8}$	552	64
◆ Kootenay / A.E. Matthew / A.E. Matthew / 1950										
181	$38\frac{7}{8}$	$37\frac{5}{8}$	$14\frac{2}{8}$	$14\frac{3}{8}$	$11\frac{1}{8}$	11	$19\frac{1}{8}$	$19\frac{1}{8}$	552	64
◆ Simpson Creek / Walt Failor / Walt Failor / 1968										
181	$39\frac{1}{8}$	$41\frac{1}{8}$	15	15	$7\frac{7}{8}$	$8\frac{1}{8}$	$22\frac{4}{8}$	$22\frac{4}{8}$	552	64
◆ Kindersley Creek / Karl Dorr / Karl Dorr / 1989										
$180\frac{7}{8}$	$38\frac{7}{8}$	$39\frac{4}{8}$	15	15	$9\frac{2}{8}$	$9\frac{1}{8}$	$19\frac{4}{8}$	$15\frac{4}{8}$	558	67
◆ Line Creek / Kevin J. Galla / Kevin J. Galla / 1991										
$180\frac{6}{8}$	37	$38\frac{4}{8}$	$15\frac{7}{8}$	$15\frac{7}{8}$	$8\frac{5}{8}$	$8\frac{5}{8}$	$22\frac{5}{8}$	15	563	68
◆ Bull River / Walter J. Ruehle / Walter J. Ruehle / 1962										
$180\frac{6}{8}$	$36\frac{2}{8}$	39	$16\frac{2}{8}$	$16\frac{2}{8}$	$7\frac{6}{8}$	8	$21\frac{1}{8}$	$18\frac{7}{8}$	563	68
◆ Ewin Pass / Sam W. Stephenson / Sam W. Stephenson / 1992										
$180\frac{5}{8}$	$37\frac{1}{8}$	35	$15\frac{4}{8}$	$15\frac{5}{8}$	$9\frac{4}{8}$	$9\frac{4}{8}$	$22\frac{4}{8}$	$15\frac{4}{8}$	574	70
◆ Waterton Lake / Victor T. Zarnock, Jr. / Victor T. Zarnock, Jr. / 1972										
$180\frac{4}{8}$	$40\frac{2}{8}$	$38\frac{2}{8}$	$15\frac{5}{8}$	$15\frac{4}{8}$	$8\frac{3}{8}$	8	$21\frac{2}{8}$	20	583	71
◆ White Swan Lake / John Barton / John Barton / 1936										
$180\frac{4}{8}$	41	39	14	14	$10\frac{1}{8}$	$9\frac{6}{8}$	$21\frac{4}{8}$	$18\frac{3}{8}$	583	71
◆ Simpson River / Picked Up / Sharon Buck / 1967										
$180\frac{2}{8}$	38	$39\frac{2}{8}$	$14\frac{4}{8}$	$14\frac{4}{8}$	$10\frac{2}{8}$	$10\frac{4}{8}$	21	14	619	73
◆ British Columbia / James T. Wilson / Kevin D. O'Connell / 1928										
$180\frac{2}{8}$	$36\frac{4}{8}$	$38\frac{6}{8}$	15	$15\frac{1}{8}$	9	9	$20\frac{4}{8}$	$20\frac{4}{8}$	619	73
◆ Cecelia Lake / Dan Auld / Dan Auld / 1950										
$180\frac{2}{8}$	$39\frac{5}{8}$	$39\frac{5}{8}$	$15\frac{3}{8}$	$15\frac{4}{8}$	$7\frac{7}{8}$	$7\frac{6}{8}$	$21\frac{1}{8}$	$19\frac{1}{8}$	619	73
◆ Invermere / Lyle O. Fett / Lyle O. Fett / 1982										

BRITISH COLUMBIA BIGHORN SHEEP *(continued)*

Score	Length of Horn		Circumference of Base		Circumference at Third Quarter		Greatest Spread	Tip-to-Tip Spread	All-Time Rank	State Rank
	R	L	R	L	R	L				
◆ *Locality / Hunter / Owner / Date Killed*										
$180\frac{2}{8}$	$37\frac{6}{8}$	$37\frac{4}{8}$	15	15	$10\frac{1}{8}$	$9\frac{5}{8}$	$20\frac{1}{8}$	$12\frac{7}{8}$	619	73
◆ *Ewin Creek / Bob Hildebrandt / Bob Hildebrandt / 1988*										
$180\frac{2}{8}$	$38\frac{2}{8}$	$38\frac{2}{8}$	$15\frac{2}{8}$	$15\frac{3}{8}$	$8\frac{5}{8}$	$8\frac{6}{8}$	$19\frac{5}{8}$	$16\frac{3}{8}$	619	73
◆ *Cross River / Daryl Stech / Daryl Stech / 1988*										
$180\frac{1}{8}$	$39\frac{6}{8}$	$39\frac{7}{8}$	14	$14\frac{1}{8}$	$9\frac{4}{8}$	$9\frac{4}{8}$	$22\frac{7}{8}$	$17\frac{4}{8}$	631	78
◆ *Kootenay Mts. / Picked Up / Gary E. Brown / 1963*										
180	$38\frac{1}{8}$	$38\frac{3}{8}$	$15\frac{2}{8}$	$15\frac{2}{8}$	9	9	$21\frac{5}{8}$	$18\frac{2}{8}$	651	79
◆ *Kootenay / Walter L. Bjorkman / Walter L. Bjorkman / 1963*										
$179\frac{2}{8}$	$39\frac{2}{8}$	$39\frac{2}{8}$	16	16	$7\frac{3}{8}$	$7\frac{2}{8}$	$20\frac{4}{8}$	19	673	80
◆ *Cross River / Warren K. Winkler / Warren K. Winkler / 1991*										
$178\frac{5}{8}$	40	$38\frac{5}{8}$	$15\frac{1}{8}$	$15\frac{2}{8}$	$8\frac{2}{8}$	$7\frac{7}{8}$	$22\frac{1}{8}$	21	679	81
◆ *Taseko Lakes / George F. Dennis, Jr. / George F. Dennis, Jr. / 1990*										
$178\frac{5}{8}$	$38\frac{7}{8}$	39	16	16	$7\frac{2}{8}$	$7\frac{2}{8}$	$22\frac{4}{8}$	$21\frac{7}{8}$	679	81
◆ *Elk River / John R. Isaacs / John R. Isaacs / 1992*										
177	$36\frac{4}{8}$	$36\frac{6}{8}$	$15\frac{4}{8}$	$15\frac{4}{8}$	$8\frac{3}{8}$	$8\frac{4}{8}$	$17\frac{3}{8}$	$16\frac{3}{8}$	690	83
◆ *Simpson River / Frank J. Blaha, Jr. / Frank J. Blaha, Jr. / 1990*										
$176\frac{6}{8}$	$39\frac{4}{8}$	$37\frac{2}{8}$	$15\frac{7}{8}$	$15\frac{5}{8}$	$7\frac{3}{8}$	$7\frac{6}{8}$	$21\frac{5}{8}$	$17\frac{6}{8}$	692	84
◆ *Simpson River / Frank J. Blaha, Jr. / Frank J. Blaha, Jr. / 1991*										

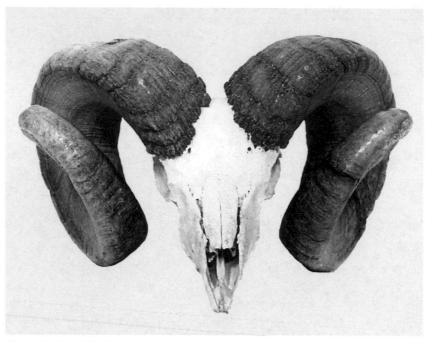

Photograph by Wm. H. Nesbitt

ARIZONA STATE RECORD
DESERT SHEEP
SCORE: 201⅜
Locality: Pima Co.   Date: Picked Up 1982
Owner: Greg Koons

ARIZONA

DESERT SHEEP

Score	Length of Horn		Circumference of Base		Circumference at Third Quarter		Greatest Spread	Tip-to-Tip Spread	All-Time Rank	State Rank
	R	L	R	L	R	L				
Locality / Hunter / Owner / Date Killed										
201 3/8	45 5/8	46 2/8	15 5/8	15 5/8	11 2/8	11 5/8	20 4/8	20	2	1
Pima County / Picked Up / Greg Koons / 1982										
197 1/8	42 3/8	41 6/8	16 1/8	16 1/8	10 5/8	11	26	26	4	2
Graham County / Arthur R. Dubs / Arthur R. Dubs / 1988										
190 3/8	41	43 7/8	15 3/8	15 5/8	9 1/8	9 1/8	23 7/8	23 7/8	10	3
Arizona / Unknown / Bruce R. Kemp, Sr. / 1903										
187 7/8	39 6/8	39 5/8	15 6/8	15 7/8	9 4/8	9 4/8	21 4/8	16 6/8	14	4
Pima County / Carl A. Mattias, Sr. / Carl A. Mattias, Sr. / 1982										
187	40 4/8	40 2/8	15 4/8	15 2/8	9 6/8	10	26	26	19	5
Kofa Mts. / Louis R. Dees / Louis R. Dees / 1965										
186 3/8	41 1/8	39	15 7/8	16	9 3/8	9 4/8	24	22 3/8	22	6
Gila County / Steven E. Wright / Steven E. Wright / 1990										
186 2/8	40 5/8	38 3/8	16	16	9	9 1/8	21 1/8	20 7/8	23	7
Maricopa County / Ralph Grossman / Ralph Grossman / 1961										
186	37	36	15 7/8	16	11 7/8	11 7/8	21 4/8	19	25	8
Arizona / Unknown / J. Michael Conoyer / 1960										
186	38 2/8	38 4/8	15 4/8	15 5/8	10 6/8	10 6/8	22 3/8	19 5/8	25	8
Yuma County / Gerry W. Nikolaus / Gerry W. Nikolaus / 1979										
185 2/8	41	40 2/8	15 7/8	15 6/8	8 2/8	9	21 1/8	20 3/8	29	10
Graham County / John W. Harris / John W. Harris / 1982										
184 6/8	42	40 6/8	14 6/8	15	9 4/8	9 2/8	29 4/8	29 4/8	34	11
Kofa Mts. / W.A. Rudd / W.A. Rudd / 1965										
184 4/8	43 1/8	45 3/8	13 7/8	13 5/8	8 6/8	8 6/8	26 4/8	26 4/8	38	12
Santa Teresa Mts. / Picked Up / Ariz. Game & Fish Dept. / 1967										
184 2/8	40 4/8	37 2/8	15 4/8	15 4/8	9 2/8	9 2/8	22 1/8	22 1/8	41	13
Pinal County / Everett A. Hodge / Everett A. Hodge / 1988										
184 1/8	38 5/8	40	15 2/8	15 2/8	9 3/8	9 4/8	22	20 1/8	42	14
Papago Indian Res. / Ralph J. Murrietta / Ollie O. Barney, Jr. / 1965										
183 3/8	40	40 3/8	14	13 7/8	10 4/8	9 6/8	24 7/8	24 1/8	46	15
Pinkley / Picked Up / Organ Pipe Cactus Natl. Mon. / 1957										
183 2/8	37 6/8	37	14 7/8	14 7/8	10 7/8	11 1/8	14 2/8	14 2/8	47	16
Pima County / Picked Up / LeRoy Van Buggenum / 1987										
182 6/8	39 2/8	37 6/8	14 6/8	14 4/8	11	10 7/8	22	20 6/8	50	17
Colo. River / Picked Up / John E. Luster / 1956										
182 5/8	36	35 5/8	16 4/8	16 3/8	9 4/8	9 6/8	22 2/8	19 5/8	52	18
Pima County / Charles W. Fisher / Charles W. Fisher / 1972										

Score	Length of Horn		Circumference of Base		Circumference at Third Quarter		Greatest Spread	Tip-to-Tip Spread	All-Time Rank	State Rank
	R	L	R	L	R	L				
◆ Locality / Hunter / Owner / Date Killed										
182 2/8	39 3/8	39 5/8	15 3/8	15 3/8	9 3/8	9	22 3/8	21 5/8	58	19
◆ Graham County / Beverly M. Nuessle / Beverly M. Nuessle / 1986										
182 1/8	40 7/8	39 6/8	15 4/8	15 4/8	8 4/8	7 3/8	22 2/8	22 2/8	59	20
◆ Graham County / James W. Ferguson / James W. Ferguson / 1984										
180 6/8	38 6/8	39	14 7/8	14 7/8	10 2/8	10	26	26	68	21
◆ Mohave County / Larry F. Snead / Larry F. Snead / 1993										
180 4/8	35 7/8	37 3/8	16 1/8	16 3/8	9	8 6/8	19 1/8	18 4/8	69	22
◆ Dragon Teeth Mt. / Raymond White / Raymond White / 1966										
180 4/8	36 7/8	37 5/8	16 2/8	16 2/8	9 4/8	9 5/8	21 5/8	17 3/8	69	22
◆ Yuma County / Weldon A. Rogers / Weldon A. Rogers / 1990										
180 3/8	38	37 5/8	14 7/8	15	10 2/8	9 4/8	21 7/8	17	71	24
◆ Yuma County / James K. McCasland / James K. McCasland / 1978										
180 2/8	38 6/8	37 6/8	14 4/8	14 5/8	10 2/8	10	21 5/8	17 1/8	75	25
◆ La Paz County / Bruce Liddy / Bruce Liddy / 1992										
180 1/8	37 4/8	39 1/8	14 3/8	14 2/8	9 3/8	9 6/8	22 5/8	22 2/8	78	26
◆ Tank Mts. / Picked Up / Calvin C. Wallerich / 1960										
180 1/8	36 5/8	35 4/8	16 5/8	16 5/8	9 1/8	8 5/8	22 4/8	21 5/8	78	26
◆ Pima County / Robert A. Christy / Robert A. Christy / 1986										
180	36 1/8	36 1/8	15 6/8	15 6/8	9 4/8	10 1/8	21 3/8	17 3/8	80	28
◆ Pima County / Clifford W. Saylor / Clifford W. Saylor / 1976										
178 7/8	36 7/8	37	15 3/8	15 4/8	9 7/8	10 1/8	23	22 6/8	95	29
◆ Sauceda Mts. / Picked Up / Edward Hunt / 1962										
178 7/8	35 2/8	36 3/8	15 2/8	15 2/8	9 7/8	10 2/8	29 5/8	29 5/8	95	29
◆ Mohave County / Earle H. Smith / Earle H. Smith / 1981										
178 5/8	37 1/8	37 2/8	15 3/8	15 3/8	8 7/8	8 7/8	21 2/8	20 2/8	101	31
◆ La Paz County / Wayne B. Smith / Wayne B. Smith / 1993										
178 4/8	38 3/8	35 3/8	15 5/8	15 5/8	9 5/8	9 1/8	22 3/8	20	103	32
◆ Pima County / Ken Broyles / Ken Broyles / 1971										
178 1/8	34	40 1/8	15	14 6/8	9 5/8	10 2/8	19 7/8	18	107	33
◆ Maricopa County / Michael Holt / Michael Holt / 1970										
177 7/8	37	37 7/8	14 7/8	15	9 5/8	9 5/8	21	19 5/8	112	34
◆ Mohave County / William C. Duffy, Jr. / William C. Duffy, Jr. / 1981										
177 7/8	36 5/8	36	15 4/8	15 6/8	9 3/8	9 5/8	22 7/8	20 5/8	112	34
◆ Yuma County / J. Dorsey Smith / J. Dorsey Smith / 1983										
177 7/8	34 2/8	38 1/8	16 2/8	16 1/8	8 3/8	8 4/8	24	23 3/8	112	34
◆ Graham County / William N. Willis / William N. Willis / 1989										
177 4/8	36 5/8	35 5/8	15 2/8	15 2/8	9 3/8	9 5/8	20 3/8	20 3/8	117	37
◆ Pima County / Mark D. Morris / Mark D. Morris / 1990										

Score	Length of Horn		Circumference of Base		Circumference at Third Quarter		Greatest Spread	Tip-to-Tip Spread	All-Time Rank	State Rank
	R	L	R	L	R	L				
◆ *Locality / Hunter / Owner / Date Killed*										
177 3/8	36 6/8	37 5/8	14 3/8	14 5/8	9 6/8	9 6/8	22 6/8	22	121	38
◆ *Yuma County / George I. Parker / George I. Parker / 1968*										
177 2/8	37	36	15 2/8	15 3/8	9 1/8	9 1/8	23	20 6/8	126	39
◆ *Yuma County / Robert Fritzinger / Robert Fritzinger / 1976*										
177 2/8	36 4/8	36 4/8	15 4/8	15 5/8	9	8 6/8	21 7/8	21 2/8	126	39
◆ *Yuma County / Julian W. Chancellor / Julian W. Chancellor / 1992*										
177 1/8	36 1/8	36 2/8	15 6/8	15 6/8	8 6/8	8 6/8	21 4/8	20 6/8	130	41
◆ *Pima County / Michael A. Jensen / Michael A. Jensen / 1978*										
176 6/8	38	39 2/8	14 6/8	14 6/8	8 6/8	7 6/8	21 3/8	20 2/8	136	42
◆ *Kofa Range / Picked Up / D.B. Sanford / 1957*										
176 6/8	37 4/8	38 2/8	15 5/8	15 6/8	8 2/8	8 2/8	23 2/8	21 6/8	136	42
◆ *Pinal County / Travis R. Holder / Travis R. Holder / 1984*										
176 4/8	36 7/8	38 3/8	16	16	7 7/8	7 7/8	20 6/8	18 4/8	143	44
◆ *Pinal County / Robbie A. Brown / Robert L. Brown / 1985*										
176 4/8	35 2/8	36 2/8	15 1/8	15	9 6/8	10 2/8	19 2/8	21 2/8	143	44
◆ *Yuma County / Gail Ferguson / Gail Ferguson / 1988*										
176 2/8	38 1/8	37 5/8	15	15 1/8	8 4/8	8 4/8	21 5/8	21 5/8	151	46
◆ *Yuma County / Vicki L. Clark / Vicki L. Clark / 1980*										
176 2/8	38 6/8	37 4/8	14 4/8	14 4/8	8 7/8	9	21	21	151	46
◆ *Pinal County / D. Mark Exline / D. Mark Exline / 1982*										
176 1/8	36 5/8	36 4/8	14 6/8	14 6/8	9 3/8	9 4/8	21 6/8	20	156	48
◆ *Pinal County / Warren A. Adams / Warren A. Adams / 1985*										
176 1/8	37	34 7/8	15 6/8	16	8 4/8	8 4/8	22 4/8	22 4/8	156	48
◆ *Pima County / Don Petersen / Don Petersen / 1988*										
176	37 2/8	38 2/8	14 4/8	15	9	9 4/8	25	25	160	50
◆ *Black Mts. / Picked Up / R.A. Wagner / 1954*										
176	37 4/8	34 2/8	15 4/8	15 5/8	9 2/8	9 2/8	21 4/8	18 4/8	160	50
◆ *Kofa Mts. / Robin Underdown / Robin Underdown / 1966*										
175 7/8	35 7/8	35 4/8	15	15 1/8	9 7/8	9 3/8	22 4/8	22	166	52
◆ *Yuma County / J. Don McGaffee / J. Don McGaffee / 1978*										
175 7/8	39 5/8	38 6/8	14	14	8 6/8	9 2/8	22 5/8	22 5/8	166	52
◆ *Yuma County / Fred W. Jerome / Fred W. Jerome / 1979*										
175 7/8	36 7/8	37	15 2/8	15 1/8	9 4/8	9 6/8	22 4/8	19	166	52
◆ *Pinal County / Tracy L. Contreras / Tracy L. Contreras / 1980*										
175 6/8	33 3/8	35 5/8	16	16	9 4/8	9 1/8	22	20 6/8	169	55
◆ *Pima County / Robert F. Lebo / Robert F. Lebo / 1977*										
175 4/8	36	36 4/8	15 4/8	15 4/8	8 4/8	8 4/8	20 6/8	19 3/8	174	56
◆ *Yuma / Picked Up / Tom D. Moore / 1956*										

Score	Length of Horn R	L	Circumference of Base R	L	Circumference at Third Quarter R	L	Greatest Spread	Tip-to-Tip Spread	All-Time Rank	State Rank

♦ *Locality / Hunter / Owner / Date Killed*

| 175⁴⁄₈ | 37²⁄₈ | 36 | 15 | 14⁴⁄₈ | 9⁴⁄₈ | 10 | 21⁴⁄₈ | 21⁴⁄₈ | 174 | 56 |

♦ *Maricopa County / Picked Up / Robert B. Thompson / 1963*

| 175⁴⁄₈ | 36⁴⁄₈ | 37⁴⁄₈ | 14⁷⁄₈ | 14⁷⁄₈ | 8⁷⁄₈ | 9⁷⁄₈ | 22³⁄₈ | 21⁶⁄₈ | 174 | 56 |

♦ *Plomosa Mts. / J. James Froelich / J. James Froelich / 1969*

| 175⁴⁄₈ | 36³⁄₈ | 36¹⁄₈ | 14³⁄₈ | 14²⁄₈ | 10¹⁄₈ | 10¹⁄₈ | 21⁶⁄₈ | 18⁴⁄₈ | 174 | 56 |

♦ *Yuma County / Anton E. Rimsza / Anton E. Rimsza / 1982*

| 175⁴⁄₈ | 37²⁄₈ | 36⁶⁄₈ | 15⁴⁄₈ | 15 | 8⁵⁄₈ | 8⁶⁄₈ | 20⁷⁄₈ | 17⁵⁄₈ | 174 | 56 |

♦ *Pima County / David R. Howell / David R. Howell / 1991*

| 175³⁄₈ | 35⁶⁄₈ | 35³⁄₈ | 15⁴⁄₈ | 15³⁄₈ | 9⁴⁄₈ | 9²⁄₈ | 21⁶⁄₈ | 18⁴⁄₈ | 180 | 61 |

♦ *Plomosa Mts. / M.S. MacCollum / M.S. MacCollum / 1968*

| 175³⁄₈ | 38²⁄₈ | 38³⁄₈ | 14⁵⁄₈ | 14⁵⁄₈ | 8⁵⁄₈ | 8⁵⁄₈ | 22 | 19⁴⁄₈ | 180 | 61 |

♦ *Yuma County / Patrick E. Hurley / Patrick E. Hurley / 1981*

| 175 | 37⁴⁄₈ | 33⁶⁄₈ | 15⁵⁄₈ | 15³⁄₈ | 8⁴⁄₈ | 8⁷⁄₈ | 20⁴⁄₈ | 18⁴⁄₈ | 194 | 63 |

♦ *Yuma County / Harry B. Cook / Harry B. Cook / 1982*

| 174⁷⁄₈ | 37 | 35¹⁄₈ | 15 | 15 | 9³⁄₈ | 8⁶⁄₈ | 20³⁄₈ | 19⁶⁄₈ | 198 | 64 |

♦ *Pima / Picked Up / Robert J. Kirkpatrick / PR 1968*

| 174⁷⁄₈ | 37¹⁄₈ | 38⁴⁄₈ | 13⁵⁄₈ | 13⁵⁄₈ | 9³⁄₈ | 9⁴⁄₈ | 23³⁄₈ | 21 | 198 | 64 |

♦ *Arizona / Picked Up / Nathan Frisby / 1974*

| 174⁶⁄₈ | 37⁴⁄₈ | 35⁴⁄₈ | 15⁶⁄₈ | 15⁶⁄₈ | 8⁶⁄₈ | 8⁶⁄₈ | 21⁴⁄₈ | 17 | 203 | 66 |

♦ *Pima County / Collins L. Cochran / Collins L. Cochran / 1992*

| 174⁴⁄₈ | 36⁴⁄₈ | 36 | 14 | 14²⁄₈ | 9⁶⁄₈ | 9⁴⁄₈ | 19⁴⁄₈ | 19⁴⁄₈ | 208 | 67 |

♦ *Maricopa County / Picked Up / Robert B. Thompson / 1963*

| 174²⁄₈ | 35³⁄₈ | 36¹⁄₈ | 14⁷⁄₈ | 14⁷⁄₈ | 9⁷⁄₈ | 10 | 25⁵⁄₈ | 25⁵⁄₈ | 213 | 68 |

♦ *Mohave County / Susan C. Nelson / Susan C. Nelson / 1979*

| 174²⁄₈ | 35⁶⁄₈ | 40⁴⁄₈ | 14⁴⁄₈ | 14⁵⁄₈ | 8¹⁄₈ | 8³⁄₈ | 30³⁄₈ | 30¹⁄₈ | 213 | 68 |

♦ *Mohave County / Howard Grounds / Howard Grounds / 1984*

| 174²⁄₈ | 34²⁄₈ | 33⁴⁄₈ | 15⁴⁄₈ | 15⁵⁄₈ | 9⁴⁄₈ | 9³⁄₈ | 24⁴⁄₈ | 21⁶⁄₈ | 213 | 68 |

♦ *Maricopa County / Debi L. Adair / Debi L. Adair / 1987*

| 174 | 36⁴⁄₈ | 37⁴⁄₈ | 15⁴⁄₈ | 15³⁄₈ | 9 | 8 | 21⁵⁄₈ | 21 | 219 | 71 |

♦ *Yuma / Wynn Robestal / U.S. Fish & Wild. Serv. / 1913*

| 174 | 31⁶⁄₈ | 34⁴⁄₈ | 15⁶⁄₈ | 15⁶⁄₈ | 9⁵⁄₈ | 9⁵⁄₈ | 22 | 20 | 219 | 71 |

♦ *Pima County / George Martin / George Martin / 1978*

| 174 | 35⁵⁄₈ | 35⁵⁄₈ | 14³⁄₈ | 14³⁄₈ | 10¹⁄₈ | 10¹⁄₈ | 22¹⁄₈ | 18 | 219 | 71 |

♦ *La Paz County / Craig R. Johnson / Craig R. Johnson / 1993*

| 173⁷⁄₈ | 37²⁄₈ | 37¹⁄₈ | 14³⁄₈ | 14⁵⁄₈ | 8⁴⁄₈ | 8⁷⁄₈ | 24⁵⁄₈ | 24⁵⁄₈ | 227 | 74 |

♦ *Kofa Mts. / William L. Snider / William L. Snider / 1965*

| 173⁷⁄₈ | 37 | 37⁵⁄₈ | 15 | 14⁶⁄₈ | 8⁶⁄₈ | 9³⁄₈ | 20 | 21⁴⁄₈ | 227 | 74 |

♦ *Yuma County / John C. Marsalla / John C. Marsalla / 1982*

Score	Length of Horn		Circumference of Base		Circumference at Third Quarter		Greatest Spread	Tip-to-Tip Spread	All-Time Rank	State Rank
	R	L	R	L	R	L				
◆ Locality / Hunter / Owner / Date Killed										
173 6/8	34 6/8	34 4/8	14 2/8	14 4/8	9 6/8	10 2/8	22 4/8	21 6/8	231	76
◆ Yuma County / Picked Up / Bob Housholder / 1953										
173 6/8	36 2/8	35 6/8	15 6/8	15 7/8	8	7 5/8	22 4/8	23	231	76
◆ Mohave County / Steve Clonts / Steve Clonts / 1991										
173 5/8	36 6/8	34 5/8	15 2/8	15 1/8	9 3/8	8 7/8	24 4/8	19 7/8	234	78
◆ Yuma County / David C. Root / David C. Root / 1983										
173 4/8	34	33 4/8	15 4/8	15 4/8	9 4/8	9 4/8	25 7/8	25 4/8	242	79
◆ Mohave County / Gordon M. Osborn / Gordon M. Osborn / 1989										
173 3/8	36	36 3/8	15 3/8	15 3/8	8 2/8	8 3/8	21 6/8	19 1/8	248	80
◆ Mohave County / Donald E. Franklin / Donald E. Franklin / 1982										
173 3/8	36 4/8	35 1/8	14 6/8	14 7/8	8 7/8	9	23 4/8	22 5/8	248	80
◆ Maricopa County / James D. Thorne / James D. Thorne / 1989										
173 2/8	34 7/8	35 3/8	15 4/8	15 4/8	8 6/8	8 5/8	25 3/8	25 3/8	255	82
◆ Little Horn Mts. / Joseph J. Sobotka / Joseph J. Sobotka / 1969										
173 1/8	37 1/8	35 2/8	14 1/8	14 5/8	9 4/8	9	21	21	259	83
◆ Little Horn Mts. / Picked Up / Duane J. Hall / 1960										
173	36	35 2/8	14 3/8	14 3/8	9 4/8	9	21 6/8	16 6/8	265	84
◆ Aguila Mts. / Picked Up / C.G. Clare / 1961										
173	37 1/8	37 1/8	13 6/8	14	10 3/8	10 5/8	20	17 5/8	265	84
◆ Maricopa County / Stephen K. Weisser / Stephen K. Weisser / 1973										
173	35 4/8	35 6/8	14 7/8	14 6/8	9 4/8	9 4/8	21 3/8	21 2/8	265	84
◆ Maricopa County / Jim L. Boyer / Jim L. Boyer / 1993										
172 7/8	34 6/8	34 1/8	15	15	9 5/8	9 7/8	22 1/8	18 2/8	274	87
◆ Gila County / Picked Up / Michael T. Miller / 1990										
172 6/8	36 3/8	36 3/8	14 3/8	14 3/8	8 4/8	8 5/8	20 3/8	19	277	88
◆ Yuma County / Norman F. Mathews / Norman F. Mathews / 1977										
172 6/8	36	36 4/8	15 5/8	15 3/8	8 2/8	8 5/8	19 1/8	18 3/8	277	88
◆ Pima County / Paul H. Harrison / Paul H. Harrison / 1981										
172 6/8	36 5/8	36 5/8	14	13 7/8	10 1/8	9 6/8	19 6/8	19 6/8	277	88
◆ Yuma County / Larry J. Landes / Larry J. Landes / 1981										
172 6/8	41 4/8	37 2/8	14 2/8	14 3/8	9 4/8	8 2/8	24 5/8	24 3/8	277	88
◆ Gila County / Byron Wiley / Byron Wiley / 1986										
172 6/8	36 4/8	35	15 2/8	15 3/8	8 7/8	8 4/8	19 1/8	22	277	88
◆ Gila County / Richard P. Carlsberg / Richard P. Carlsberg / 1989										
172 4/8	36 2/8	34 6/8	15 3/8	15 5/8	8 3/8	8 2/8	22 1/8	19 6/8	289	93
◆ Yuma County / Margaret Wood / Margaret Wood / 1958										
172 4/8	36	34 4/8	15	15	8 4/8	8 4/8	23	23	289	93
◆ Yuma County / Picked Up / Donald Ogan / 1964										

Score	Length of Horn		Circumference of Base		Circumference at Third Quarter		Greatest Spread	Tip-to-Tip Spread	All-Time Rank	State Rank
	R	L	R	L	R	L				
◆ *Locality / Hunter / Owner / Date Killed*										
172⁴⁄₈	37²⁄₈	35²⁄₈	15⁴⁄₈	15⁴⁄₈	8	8	25⁵⁄₈	23	289	93
◆ *Yuma County / William J. Paul / William J. Paul / 1987*										
172⁴⁄₈	36⁴⁄₈	37⁶⁄₈	14⁴⁄₈	14¹⁄₈	8⁶⁄₈	9³⁄₈	29⁵⁄₈	28⁴⁄₈	289	93
◆ *Mohave County / Densel M. Strang / Densel M. Strang / 1989*										
172⁴⁄₈	36²⁄₈	36²⁄₈	14³⁄₈	14⁴⁄₈	8⁷⁄₈	9	23⁶⁄₈	21²⁄₈	289	93
◆ *Coconino County / Frank J. Tucek / Frank J. Tucek / 1993*										
172³⁄₈	34⁶⁄₈	32⁵⁄₈	15	15¹⁄₈	9⁶⁄₈	9²⁄₈	21⁵⁄₈	21¹⁄₈	297	98
◆ *Sauceda Mts. / Wayne Grippin / Wayne Grippin / 1962*										
172³⁄₈	33⁵⁄₈	34	16¹⁄₈	16¹⁄₈	8⁶⁄₈	9	20²⁄₈	16²⁄₈	297	98
◆ *Pima County / Loren G. Pederson, Jr. / Loren G. Pederson, Jr. / 1985*										
172¹⁄₈	36	35⁷⁄₈	15	15²⁄₈	8⁴⁄₈	8⁴⁄₈	23	14	309	100
◆ *Kofa Range / Picked Up / Ariz. Game & Fish Dept. / 1953*										
171⁷⁄₈	35³⁄₈	36²⁄₈	15	15	9	9¹⁄₈	20²⁄₈	18²⁄₈	319	101
◆ *Graham County / Roger J. Stolp / Roger J. Stolp / 1985*										
171⁷⁄₈	34⁷⁄₈	33²⁄₈	15⁶⁄₈	15⁴⁄₈	8⁷⁄₈	9⁴⁄₈	21⁵⁄₈	18⁴⁄₈	319	101
◆ *La Paz County / Robert M.H. Gray / Robert M.H. Gray / 1987*										
171⁷⁄₈	36⁴⁄₈	35³⁄₈	15¹⁄₈	15²⁄₈	8¹⁄₈	8²⁄₈	21⁵⁄₈	21⁵⁄₈	319	101
◆ *Yuma County / John F. Heskett / John F. Heskett / 1990*										
171⁶⁄₈	37²⁄₈	36⁴⁄₈	14	13⁴⁄₈	9⁵⁄₈	9⁴⁄₈	20¹⁄₈	20¹⁄₈	325	104
◆ *Kofa Range / Harvey Davison / Harvey Davison / 1953*										
171⁵⁄₈	34⁶⁄₈	34⁷⁄₈	14⁷⁄₈	15	9	8⁴⁄₈	22³⁄₈	18	328	105
◆ *Yuma County / Miles R. Brown / Miles R. Brown / 1989*										
171⁴⁄₈	33⁶⁄₈	35	15	15¹⁄₈	8⁶⁄₈	9²⁄₈	21⁴⁄₈	20²⁄₈	338	106
◆ *Maricopa County / Unknown / Clarence House / PR 1979*										
171³⁄₈	36⁷⁄₈	36⁴⁄₈	14³⁄₈	14³⁄₈	8⁵⁄₈	8⁴⁄₈	22²⁄₈	22²⁄₈	342	107
◆ *Anvil Mt. / George Stewart, Jr. / George Stewart, Jr. / 1961*										
171³⁄₈	34²⁄₈	34³⁄₈	15⁵⁄₈	15⁶⁄₈	8²⁄₈	8⁵⁄₈	19⁷⁄₈	16¹⁄₈	342	107
◆ *Crater Mts. / Raymond I. Skipper, Jr. / Raymond I. Skipper, Jr. / 1971*										
171³⁄₈	35³⁄₈	35²⁄₈	14¹⁄₈	13⁷⁄₈	9¹⁄₈	9⁵⁄₈	23⁵⁄₈	24²⁄₈	342	107
◆ *Mojave County / Picked Up / Dan Priest / 1985*										
171²⁄₈	35²⁄₈	35⁶⁄₈	14²⁄₈	14³⁄₈	8⁶⁄₈	9²⁄₈	21²⁄₈	18³⁄₈	347	110
◆ *Growler Mts. / David E. Brown / David E. Brown / 1967*										
171²⁄₈	38	38²⁄₈	14⁶⁄₈	14³⁄₈	9³⁄₈	9⁴⁄₈	21⁶⁄₈	21⁴⁄₈	347	110
◆ *Yuma County / Lauren W. Hogan / Lauren W. Hogan / 1984*										
171²⁄₈	34⁶⁄₈	34⁶⁄₈	15⁴⁄₈	15⁴⁄₈	8³⁄₈	8¹⁄₈	21¹⁄₈	20⁴⁄₈	347	110
◆ *Coconino County / Merlynn K. Jones / Merlynn K. Jones / 1994*										
171¹⁄₈	35⁴⁄₈	35¹⁄₈	16⁴⁄₈	16⁴⁄₈	7⁶⁄₈	7²⁄₈	19¹⁄₈	19¹⁄₈	353	113
◆ *Yuma County / Elizabeth Barganski / Elizabeth Barganski / 1959*										

Score	Length of Horn		Circumference of Base		Circumference at Third Quarter		Greatest Spread	Tip-to-Tip Spread	All-Time Rank	State Rank
	R	L	R	L	R	L				
♦ Locality / Hunter / Owner / Date Killed										
$171\frac{1}{8}$	$36\frac{4}{8}$	$36\frac{7}{8}$	$14\frac{3}{8}$	$14\frac{4}{8}$	$8\frac{2}{8}$	$8\frac{3}{8}$	$22\frac{2}{8}$	$19\frac{7}{8}$	353	113
♦ Palomas Mts. / James F. Pierce / James F. Pierce / 1967										
$171\frac{1}{8}$	$35\frac{5}{8}$	$36\frac{6}{8}$	$14\frac{7}{8}$	$14\frac{6}{8}$	$8\frac{2}{8}$	$8\frac{3}{8}$	22	$21\frac{4}{8}$	353	113
♦ Yuma County / Robert J. Cordes III / Robert J. Cordes III / 1988										
$171\frac{1}{8}$	$37\frac{4}{8}$	$33\frac{3}{8}$	15	$14\frac{6}{8}$	$8\frac{1}{8}$	$8\frac{1}{8}$	$23\frac{1}{8}$	$22\frac{6}{8}$	353	113
♦ Mohave County / Gary C. Bateman / Gary C. Bateman / 1991										
$171\frac{1}{8}$	$36\frac{2}{8}$	$35\frac{1}{8}$	$14\frac{5}{8}$	$14\frac{6}{8}$	$8\frac{7}{8}$	$8\frac{6}{8}$	21	18	353	113
♦ Yuma County / Robert J. Zent / Robert J. Zent / 1991										
171	36	$36\frac{2}{8}$	$14\frac{3}{8}$	$14\frac{4}{8}$	$8\frac{4}{8}$	$8\frac{7}{8}$	$20\frac{3}{8}$	$19\frac{4}{8}$	359	118
♦ Sauceda Mts. / Kelly S. Neal, Jr. / Kelly S. Neal, Jr. / 1969										
171	$35\frac{5}{8}$	$36\frac{1}{8}$	$14\frac{7}{8}$	$14\frac{7}{8}$	$8\frac{5}{8}$	$8\frac{5}{8}$	$18\frac{3}{8}$	17	359	118
♦ Pima County / Don J. Parks, Jr. / Don J. Parks, Jr. / 1986										
171	$36\frac{1}{8}$	$35\frac{5}{8}$	$14\frac{7}{8}$	$14\frac{7}{8}$	$8\frac{2}{8}$	$8\frac{2}{8}$	$26\frac{5}{8}$	26	359	118
♦ Mohave County / Michael L. Gwaltney / Michael L. Gwaltney / 1990										
$170\frac{7}{8}$	33	$35\frac{7}{8}$	$15\frac{3}{8}$	$15\frac{3}{8}$	8	$8\frac{7}{8}$	$21\frac{4}{8}$	$18\frac{7}{8}$	365	121
♦ Pima County / Barbara J. Ridgeway / Barbara J. Ridgeway / 1984										
$170\frac{7}{8}$	37	$36\frac{1}{8}$	$15\frac{2}{8}$	$14\frac{6}{8}$	$8\frac{1}{8}$	$8\frac{2}{8}$	$24\frac{1}{8}$	$23\frac{1}{8}$	365	121
♦ Mohave County / Dale A. Kelling / Dale A. Kelling / 1987										
$170\frac{7}{8}$	$34\frac{1}{8}$	$35\frac{4}{8}$	$15\frac{4}{8}$	$15\frac{4}{8}$	$8\frac{4}{8}$	$8\frac{7}{8}$	$22\frac{6}{8}$	$19\frac{3}{8}$	365	121
♦ Yuma County / Gary L. Major / Gary L. Major / 1989										
$170\frac{6}{8}$	$36\frac{7}{8}$	$36\frac{3}{8}$	$15\frac{6}{8}$	$15\frac{3}{8}$	$7\frac{6}{8}$	$7\frac{5}{8}$	$21\frac{6}{8}$	$20\frac{7}{8}$	373	124
♦ Little Horn Mts. / Dale Wagner / Dale Wagner / 1963										
$170\frac{6}{8}$	$34\frac{1}{8}$	$36\frac{7}{8}$	15	$15\frac{1}{8}$	$8\frac{1}{8}$	$8\frac{2}{8}$	$19\frac{4}{8}$	$17\frac{4}{8}$	373	124
♦ Yuma County / Bryan L. Rogers / Bryan L. Rogers / 1986										
$170\frac{6}{8}$	$35\frac{6}{8}$	$35\frac{6}{8}$	$15\frac{1}{8}$	$15\frac{1}{8}$	8	$8\frac{4}{8}$	22	$20\frac{4}{8}$	373	124
♦ Pima County / Andrew D. Langmade / Andrew D. Langmade / 1991										
$170\frac{6}{8}$	$36\frac{3}{8}$	$36\frac{3}{8}$	$14\frac{4}{8}$	$14\frac{4}{8}$	$8\frac{2}{8}$	$8\frac{1}{8}$	$20\frac{3}{8}$	$21\frac{4}{8}$	373	124
♦ Graham County / William A. Keebler / William A. Keebler / 1993										
$170\frac{5}{8}$	$32\frac{6}{8}$	$35\frac{7}{8}$	$16\frac{1}{8}$	$16\frac{1}{8}$	$8\frac{6}{8}$	$8\frac{6}{8}$	$23\frac{1}{8}$	$23\frac{1}{8}$	383	128
♦ Pima County / David Chavez / David Chavez / 1972										
$170\frac{4}{8}$	$34\frac{7}{8}$	$34\frac{7}{8}$	$15\frac{2}{8}$	$15\frac{1}{8}$	9	9	$19\frac{3}{8}$	$19\frac{3}{8}$	387	129
♦ Mohave County / John H. Houzenga, Jr. / John H. Houzenga, Jr. / 1961										
$170\frac{4}{8}$	$33\frac{4}{8}$	35	$14\frac{6}{8}$	$14\frac{6}{8}$	$9\frac{2}{8}$	10	$19\frac{4}{8}$	$17\frac{4}{8}$	387	129
♦ La Paz County / Oscar B. Oland / Oscar B. Oland / 1992										
$170\frac{3}{8}$	$35\frac{3}{8}$	$36\frac{2}{8}$	15	15	$7\frac{5}{8}$	$7\frac{7}{8}$	$19\frac{7}{8}$	18	394	131
♦ Chemehuevi Mts. / James B. Lingo / James B. Lingo / 1970										
$170\frac{3}{8}$	$35\frac{5}{8}$	$35\frac{6}{8}$	$14\frac{4}{8}$	$14\frac{1}{8}$	$8\frac{4}{8}$	9	$23\frac{6}{8}$	23	394	131
♦ Yuma County / Gary V. Harmon / Gary V. Harmon / 1979										

Score	Length of Horn		Circumference of Base		Circumference at Third Quarter		Greatest Spread	Tip-to-Tip Spread	All-Time Rank	State Rank
	R	L	R	L	R	L				

Locality / Hunter / Owner / Date Killed

Score	R	L	R	L	R	L	Greatest Spread	Tip-to-Tip Spread	All-Time Rank	State Rank
170 3/8	36 2/8	36 1/8	14	14	9 2/8	9 2/8	20 6/8	18	394	131

La Paz County / Rick P. Palmer / Rick P. Palmer / 1989

| 170 2/8 | 34 2/8 | 35 | 14 4/8 | 14 5/8 | 9 4/8 | 10 | 21 6/8 | 19 5/8 | 401 | 134 |

Yuma County / Lance K. Parks / Lance K. Parks / 1987

| 170 2/8 | 33 | 33 | 14 7/8 | 14 7/8 | 10 1/8 | 10 1/8 | 21 | 18 7/8 | 401 | 134 |

Yuma County / Valentino J. Pugnea / Valentino J. Pugnea / 1987

| 170 2/8 | 34 1/8 | 34 5/8 | 14 4/8 | 14 5/8 | 9 2/8 | 9 5/8 | 24 | 22 6/8 | 401 | 134 |

Mohave County / Wily S. Addis / Wily S. Addis / 1992

| 170 | 33 | 33 | 15 5/8 | 15 3/8 | 9 1/8 | 9 1/8 | 21 4/8 | 19 5/8 | 417 | 137 |

Little Horn Mts. / Ivan L. Shiflet / Ivan L. Shiflet / 1966

| 170 | 36 2/8 | 36 | 15 | 14 7/8 | 9 6/8 | 9 6/8 | 22 3/8 | 21 4/8 | 417 | 137 |

Yuma County / Cheryl Machac / Cheryl Machac / 1988

| 170 | 36 | 33 4/8 | 15 | 14 5/8 | 9 1/8 | 9 2/8 | 24 2/8 | 23 4/8 | 417 | 137 |

Mohave County / Ross F. Adams / Ross F. Adams / 1993

| 169 6/8 | 33 5/8 | 34 1/8 | 14 | 14 2/8 | 10 | 10 2/8 | 22 | 20 5/8 | 426 | 140 |

Yuma County / Gary S. Sitton / Gary S. Sitton / 1986

| 169 5/8 | 34 | 33 7/8 | 15 1/8 | 15 1/8 | 8 7/8 | 8 6/8 | 20 7/8 | 18 4/8 | 431 | 141 |

Yuma County / Brad J. Ullery / Brad J. Ullery / 1981

| 169 5/8 | 33 | 34 5/8 | 15 2/8 | 15 1/8 | 8 4/8 | 8 5/8 | 18 6/8 | 18 4/8 | 431 | 141 |

Coconino County / Terrance S. Marcum / Terrance S. Marcum / 1990

| 169 4/8 | 34 4/8 | 34 6/8 | 14 1/8 | 14 3/8 | 9 6/8 | 10 5/8 | 21 | 18 5/8 | 438 | 143 |

Hart Tank / Picked Up / Greg Diley / PR 1970

| 169 4/8 | 33 6/8 | 36 | 14 6/8 | 14 7/8 | 9 2/8 | 8 5/8 | 22 7/8 | 22 5/8 | 438 | 143 |

Quartzite / Maurice D. Mathews / Maurice D. Mathews / 1975

| 169 4/8 | 32 2/8 | 34 4/8 | 15 3/8 | 15 4/8 | 10 | 9 2/8 | 21 2/8 | 20 | 438 | 143 |

Coconino County / Warren K. Winkler / Warren K. Winkler / 1990

| 169 4/8 | 36 6/8 | 33 6/8 | 14 3/8 | 14 3/8 | 8 5/8 | 8 4/8 | 21 3/8 | 18 4/8 | 438 | 143 |

Maricopa County / David T. Demaree / David T. Demaree / 1993

| 169 3/8 | 33 3/8 | 38 2/8 | 15 | 15 | 8 | 8 | 23 | 22 | 447 | 147 |

Pima County / Don L. Mattausch / Don L. Mattausch / 1979

| 169 2/8 | 33 4/8 | 34 4/8 | 15 1/8 | 15 2/8 | 8 7/8 | 8 6/8 | 21 3/8 | 21 | 449 | 148 |

La Paz County / Jim F. Phelps / Jim F. Phelps / 1988

| 169 2/8 | 35 3/8 | 34 3/8 | 14 2/8 | 14 2/8 | 10 | 9 1/8 | 23 7/8 | 23 4/8 | 449 | 148 |

Mohave County / William A. Doty / William A. Doty / 1991

| 169 1/8 | 35 | 34 1/8 | 14 2/8 | 14 2/8 | 9 1/8 | 9 | 22 4/8 | 22 4/8 | 455 | 150 |

Chocolate Mts. / Dan Oliver / Dan Oliver / 1966

| 169 | 37 | 36 | 13 4/8 | 14 | 8 | 8 4/8 | 27 | 27 | 460 | 151 |

Yuma County / Picked Up / Dean Bowdoin / 1964

Score	Length of Horn		Circumference of Base		Circumference at Third Quarter		Greatest Spread	Tip-to-Tip Spread	All-Time Rank	State Rank
	R	L	R	L	R	L				
◆ Locality / Hunter / Owner / Date Killed										
169	35⁴⁄₈	34	15	15	8⁵⁄₈	8²⁄₈	22¹⁄₈	16¹⁄₈	460	151
◆ Maricopa County / C. Ames Thompson / C. Ames Thompson / 1988										
168⁷⁄₈	34¹⁄₈	35	14⁶⁄₈	14⁴⁄₈	8⁶⁄₈	8⁶⁄₈	22²⁄₈	16³⁄₈	466	153
◆ Aquila Mts. / John Carr / John Carr / 1969										
168⁶⁄₈	36⁴⁄₈	36²⁄₈	14²⁄₈	14³⁄₈	7⁷⁄₈	7⁶⁄₈	22⁵⁄₈	21⁷⁄₈	471	154
◆ Little Horn Mts. / Dean Bowdoin / Dean Bowdoin / 1966										
168⁶⁄₈	36⁴⁄₈	37⁴⁄₈	13⁵⁄₈	13⁵⁄₈	8⁶⁄₈	9²⁄₈	21²⁄₈	22²⁄₈	471	154
◆ Yuma County / Frances B. Boggess / Frances B. Boggess / 1980										
168⁵⁄₈	36⁵⁄₈	34⁴⁄₈	13⁶⁄₈	13⁷⁄₈	9¹⁄₈	9⁴⁄₈	23⁶⁄₈	23⁶⁄₈	476	156
◆ Arizona / Picked Up / Don McBride / PR 1961										
168⁵⁄₈	36¹⁄₈	33⁶⁄₈	14	14	9³⁄₈	10	20⁷⁄₈	18	476	156
◆ Castle Dome Peak / Tommy G. Moore / Tommy G. Moore / 1966										
168⁵⁄₈	34⁷⁄₈	34⁴⁄₈	14⁵⁄₈	14⁵⁄₈	8⁷⁄₈	8⁴⁄₈	21¹⁄₈	17³⁄₈	476	156
◆ Aquila Mts. / David C. Thornburg / David C. Thornburg / 1969										
168⁴⁄₈	32³⁄₈	35³⁄₈	15	15	9¹⁄₈	8⁴⁄₈	25⁴⁄₈	25	481	159
◆ Kofa Game Range / Judy Franks / Judy Franks / 1965										
168⁴⁄₈	35	35⁴⁄₈	16³⁄₈	16³⁄₈	7²⁄₈	7	21²⁄₈	20³⁄₈	481	159
◆ Pima County / Jerald S. Wagner / Jerald S. Wagner / 1977										
168⁴⁄₈	34⁷⁄₈	35⁵⁄₈	14⁶⁄₈	14⁷⁄₈	8³⁄₈	8⁵⁄₈	25²⁄₈	24⁴⁄₈	481	159
◆ Mohave County / Louise B. Ellison / Louise B. Ellison / 1984										
168³⁄₈	34⁵⁄₈	34²⁄₈	15⁵⁄₈	15⁵⁄₈	8	7⁶⁄₈	17⁶⁄₈	17⁴⁄₈	490	162
◆ Sand Tank Mts. / Homer Coppinger / Homer Coppinger / 1960										
168³⁄₈	35	34³⁄₈	14	14⁵⁄₈	9⁶⁄₈	9²⁄₈	19¹⁄₈	17⁶⁄₈	490	162
◆ Yuma County / Leanna G. Mendenhall / Leanna G. Mendenhall / 1975										
168³⁄₈	34⁶⁄₈	34³⁄₈	15¹⁄₈	15	9	8⁴⁄₈	21⁶⁄₈	20¹⁄₈	490	162
◆ Maricopa County / Peter C. Knagge / Peter C. Knagge / 1985										
168²⁄₈	34¹⁄₈	35⁵⁄₈	14⁷⁄₈	15¹⁄₈	8³⁄₈	8¹⁄₈	22	22	494	165
◆ Yuma County / Ervin Black / Ervin Black / 1972										
168²⁄₈	34⁶⁄₈	36	13⁵⁄₈	14	8⁷⁄₈	9¹⁄₈	24	23	494	165
◆ Yuma County / Ralph C. Stayner / Ralph C. Stayner / 1985										
168¹⁄₈	32³⁄₈	31⁶⁄₈	16¹⁄₈	16¹⁄₈	8⁶⁄₈	8⁴⁄₈	19⁴⁄₈	18⁵⁄₈	505	167
◆ Pima County / Jeff R. Snodgrass / Jeff R. Snodgrass / 1970										
168	33¹⁄₈	34³⁄₈	14⁶⁄₈	14⁶⁄₈	8⁴⁄₈	9³⁄₈	18⁴⁄₈	17⁴⁄₈	511	168
◆ Mohave County / Robert L. Fletcher / Robert L. Fletcher / 1974										
168	37²⁄₈	35²⁄₈	14⁶⁄₈	14⁶⁄₈	6⁶⁄₈	6⁵⁄₈	26³⁄₈	26³⁄₈	511	168
◆ Mohave County / Tom H. Martin / Tom H. Martin / 1980										
168	35¹⁄₈	35³⁄₈	14⁶⁄₈	14⁶⁄₈	8³⁄₈	8²⁄₈	25	24²⁄₈	511	168
◆ Mojave County / Picked Up / Dean Priest / 1984										

ARIZONA DESERT SHEEP *(continued)*

Score	Length of Horn		Circumference of Base		Circumference at Third Quarter		Greatest Spread	Tip-to-Tip Spread	All-Time Rank	State Rank
	R	L	R	L	R	L				
♦ Locality / Hunter / Owner / Date Killed										
168	34	35	14 3/8	14 3/8	9 2/8	8 7/8	21	20	511	168
♦ Mohave County / Perry H. Finger / Perry H. Finger / 1985										
168	34	34 2/8	15 5/8	15 4/8	8 1/8	8 2/8	21 6/8	18 2/8	511	168
♦ Pinal County / Peter A. Inorio / Peter A. Inorio / 1986										
168	33 4/8	32 4/8	14 6/8	14 7/8	9 2/8	9 1/8	25 3/8	24 5/8	511	168
♦ Mohave County / Joseph D. Lynch / Joseph D. Lynch / 1987										
168	36 7/8	36 3/8	14 1/8	14 2/8	8 1/8	8 1/8	20 5/8	20 1/8	511	168
♦ Yuma County / Alan D. Maynard / Alan D. Maynard / 1987										
168	34 3/8	35 1/8	14 6/8	14 6/8	9	9	20 5/8	19	511	168
♦ Yuma County / Richard M. Cordova / Richard M. Cordova / 1991										
168	32 6/8	32 6/8	14 3/8	14 5/8	9 6/8	9 4/8	19 5/8	16 5/8	511	168
♦ Yuma County / Kenneth L. Blank / Kennnth L. Blank / 1993										
166 5/8	34 5/8	34 6/8	15	15 2/8	8 1/8	8	25 2/8	25 2/8	531	177
♦ Mohave County / Michael Pellegatti / Michael Pellegatti / 1992										
165 7/8	32 6/8	31 1/8	15 3/8	15 3/8	7 6/8	7 7/8	25 6/8	25 6/8	534	178
♦ Coconino County / Robert A. Yniguez / Robert A. Yniguez / 1994										
165 3/8	32 5/8	33 2/8	15 1/8	15 4/8	10 1/8	9 4/8	27 6/8	27 4/8	536	179
♦ Mohave County / Anthony P. Stinson / Anthony P. Stinson / 1991										
189	41	40 2/8	16 6/8	16 7/8	8 7/8	8 7/8	23 2/8	23 2/8	*	*
♦ Gila County / Sam Jaksick, Jr. / Sam Jaksick, Jr. / 1988										
188 3/8	40 2/8	39 3/8	15 5/8	15 5/8	10 2/8	10 1/8	24 6/8	23 6/8	*	*
♦ Yuma County / Randy W. Smith / Randy W. Smith / 1988										
188 2/8	38 2/8	37 4/8	16 3/8	16 2/8	10 3/8	10 6/8	24 3/8	21 5/8	*	*
♦ Maricopa County / Jerry Fletcher / Jerry Fletcher / 1993										
182 6/8	36	38 2/8	16	16 1/8	9 4/8	9 3/8	22	18 2/8	*	*
♦ Pima County / Richard F. Morin / Richard F. Morin / 1987										
180 7/8	38	38 1/8	15 2/8	15 1/8	9 3/8	9 4/8	22 6/8	16 3/8	*	*
♦ Yuma County / Michael J. Pace / Michael J. Pace / 1991										

Photograph Courtesy of Robert A. Yniguez

The healthy desert sheep herds of Arizona yielded this impressive ram to Robert A. Yniguez in late September 1994. Taken in Coconino County, Arizona, it scores 165-7/8 points.

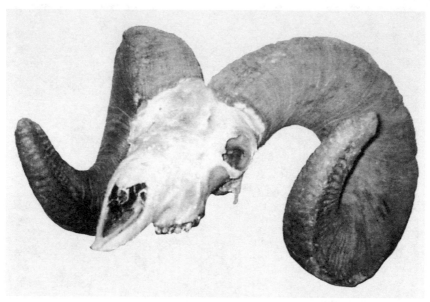

CALIFORNIA NUMBER FIVE
DESERT SHEEP
SCORE: 175⅛
Locality: Riverside Co.   Date: Picked Up 1967
Owner: George F. Stewart, Jr.

CALIFORNIA
DESERT SHEEP

Score	Length of Horn		Circumference of Base		Circumference at Third Quarter		Greatest Spread	Tip-to-Tip Spread	All-Time Rank	State Rank
	R	L	R	L	R	L				
♦ Locality / Hunter / Owner / Date Killed										
184	$40\frac{1}{8}$	$38\frac{7}{8}$	$14\frac{6}{8}$	$14\frac{6}{8}$	$10\frac{1}{8}$	$9\frac{7}{8}$	$25\frac{4}{8}$	$25\frac{4}{8}$	43	1
♦ Santa Rosa Mts. / Picked Up / Fred L. Jones / 1955										
$182\frac{4}{8}$	37	$37\frac{4}{8}$	$14\frac{7}{8}$	$15\frac{2}{8}$	10	$10\frac{2}{8}$	$22\frac{3}{8}$	$21\frac{3}{8}$	54	2
♦ Riverside County / Picked Up / Orson Morgan / 1963										
$176\frac{6}{8}$	$36\frac{3}{8}$	$36\frac{1}{8}$	$14\frac{1}{8}$	$13\frac{6}{8}$	$10\frac{5}{8}$	$10\frac{7}{8}$	$23\frac{3}{8}$	$23\frac{3}{8}$	136	3
♦ Santa Rosa Mts. / Picked Up / John C. Belcher / PR 1958										
$175\frac{6}{8}$	$35\frac{5}{8}$	$36\frac{1}{8}$	$14\frac{1}{8}$	14	$10\frac{2}{8}$	$10\frac{4}{8}$	$21\frac{2}{8}$	$17\frac{5}{8}$	169	4
♦ San Diego County / Picked Up / Anza-Borrego Desert State Park / 1951										
$175\frac{1}{8}$	$37\frac{1}{8}$	40	$13\frac{7}{8}$	$13\frac{7}{8}$	$8\frac{6}{8}$	$9\frac{3}{8}$	$20\frac{5}{8}$	$22\frac{6}{8}$	185	5
♦ Riverside County / Picked Up / George F. Stewart, Jr. / 1967										
$174\frac{6}{8}$	39	$38\frac{4}{8}$	$14\frac{6}{8}$	$15\frac{2}{8}$	$9\frac{5}{8}$	$8\frac{7}{8}$	$22\frac{1}{8}$	0	203	6
♦ Barstow / Picked Up / Thomas Hodges / 1941										
$173\frac{7}{8}$	$36\frac{5}{8}$	37	$13\frac{1}{8}$	$13\frac{4}{8}$	$10\frac{2}{8}$	$10\frac{4}{8}$	$22\frac{2}{8}$	$19\frac{3}{8}$	227	7
♦ Anza-Borrego Desert / Picked Up / Anza-Borrego Desert State Park / 1971										
$173\frac{4}{8}$	$33\frac{7}{8}$	$35\frac{7}{8}$	$14\frac{4}{8}$	$14\frac{3}{8}$	10	$10\frac{5}{8}$	$20\frac{5}{8}$	$17\frac{7}{8}$	242	8
♦ San Bernardino County / Jerry K. Chandler / Jerry K. Chandler / 1993										
$173\frac{1}{8}$	$32\frac{6}{8}$	$30\frac{7}{8}$	$15\frac{4}{8}$	$15\frac{3}{8}$	11	$11\frac{6}{8}$	$24\frac{4}{8}$	23	259	9
♦ Tulelake / Picked Up / Natl. Park Service / 1968										
$172\frac{5}{8}$	$40\frac{3}{8}$	$38\frac{6}{8}$	$13\frac{3}{8}$	$12\frac{6}{8}$	$8\frac{6}{8}$	$8\frac{2}{8}$	$26\frac{5}{8}$	$26\frac{5}{8}$	284	10
♦ White Mts. / Picked Up / Danny Lowe / 1978										
172	33	36	15	$15\frac{4}{8}$	9	$8\frac{4}{8}$	$30\frac{2}{8}$	$30\frac{2}{8}$	312	11
♦ Tulelake / Picked Up / Natl. Park Service / 1963										
$171\frac{4}{8}$	$35\frac{1}{8}$	$34\frac{7}{8}$	14	14	$10\frac{2}{8}$	10	$19\frac{4}{8}$	$19\frac{4}{8}$	338	12
♦ Bullion Mts. / Picked Up / Fred L. Jones / 1950										
$171\frac{4}{8}$	$35\frac{4}{8}$	35	$14\frac{4}{8}$	$14\frac{4}{8}$	10	10	$21\frac{4}{8}$	$20\frac{4}{8}$	338	12
♦ San Bernardino County / Leon A. Pimentel / Leon A. Pimentel / 1989										
$170\frac{6}{8}$	$33\frac{3}{8}$	$35\frac{1}{8}$	14	14	$9\frac{5}{8}$	$10\frac{2}{8}$	$23\frac{1}{8}$	$23\frac{1}{8}$	373	14
♦ San Bernadino County / Picked Up / John M. Parrish / 1960										
$170\frac{5}{8}$	34	$38\frac{5}{8}$	$13\frac{6}{8}$	$13\frac{5}{8}$	$9\frac{2}{8}$	$9\frac{1}{8}$	$24\frac{4}{8}$	$24\frac{4}{8}$	383	15
♦ Death Valley / Picked Up / Fred L. Jones / 1955										
$169\frac{6}{8}$	$37\frac{2}{8}$	37	$13\frac{6}{8}$	14	$9\frac{1}{8}$	9	$20\frac{7}{8}$	$18\frac{4}{8}$	426	16
♦ San Bernardino County / Charles E. Cook / Charles E. Cook / 1989										
$169\frac{4}{8}$	$34\frac{4}{8}$	$34\frac{2}{8}$	$14\frac{6}{8}$	$14\frac{6}{8}$	$9\frac{4}{8}$	$9\frac{1}{8}$	$23\frac{3}{8}$	$20\frac{4}{8}$	438	17
♦ San Bernardino County / Jefre R. Bugni / Jefre R. Bugni / 1989										
$169\frac{2}{8}$	$34\frac{5}{8}$	$34\frac{7}{8}$	14	$13\frac{7}{8}$	$9\frac{6}{8}$	$9\frac{7}{8}$	$21\frac{2}{8}$	$21\frac{2}{8}$	449	18
♦ White Mts. / Picked Up / Fred L. Jones / 1951										

Score	Length of Horn		Circumference of Base		Circumference at Third Quarter		Greatest Spread	Tip-to-Tip Spread	All-Time Rank	State Rank
	R	L	R	L	R	L				
◆ *Locality / Hunter / Owner / Date Killed*										
168	34⅜	34⅛	14⅜	14⁴⁄₈	9²⁄₈	9⅛	22	20⁶⁄₈	511	19
◆ *San Bernardino County / Charles L. Rensing / Charles L. Rensing / 1992*										
168	35⁶⁄₈	37²⁄₈	13⅜	13	9⅝	9⅝	22⅛	17⅜	511	19
◆ *San Bernardino County / Ron Smith / Ron Smith / 1992*										
167⅞	35²⁄₈	33⅜	14	14⅛	9⅝	9⅝	21²⁄₈	21²⁄₈	529	21
◆ *San Bernardino County / Alfred Adams / Alfred Adams / 1994*										

Photograph Courtesy of Jim L. Boyer

Jim L. Boyer and the heavy-horned ram he collected while hunting near Apache Lake in Maricopa County, Arizona, in 1993. It scores 173 points.

Photograph Courtesy of Alfred L. Raiche, Sr.

NEVADA STATE RECORD
DESERT SHEEP
SCORE: 184⅝
Locality: Nye Co.   Date: 1988
Hunter: Alfred L. Raiche, Sr.

NEVADA

DESERT SHEEP

Score	Length of Horn		Circumference of Base		Circumference at Third Quarter		Greatest Spread	Tip-to-Tip Spread	All-Time Rank	State Rank
	R	L	R	L	R	L				
◆ Locality / Hunter / Owner / Date Killed										
$184^6/_8$	$42^6/_8$	41	15	$15^1/_8$	$8^4/_8$	$8^3/_8$	$27^1/_8$	$26^6/_8$	34	1
◆ Nye County / Alfred L. Raiche, Sr. / Alfred L. Raiche, Sr. / 1988										
$183^2/_8$	$39^7/_8$	$38^1/_8$	$15^2/_8$	$15^2/_8$	$9^7/_8$	$9^6/_8$	23	23	47	2
◆ Clark County / Gerald A. Lent / Gerald A. Lent / 1976										
$181^5/_8$	$39^2/_8$	$41^3/_8$	$15^2/_8$	$15^1/_8$	$8^7/_8$	$8^7/_8$	$24^1/_8$	$24^1/_8$	63	3
◆ Sheep Mt. Range / David Ingram / David Ingram / 1962										
180	$38^2/_8$	$38^6/_8$	$15^2/_8$	$15^2/_8$	9	$9^2/_8$	22	$20^6/_8$	80	4
◆ Clark County / John V. Zenz / John V. Zenz / 1980										
$179^7/_8$	$38^7/_8$	$36^4/_8$	$15^3/_8$	$15^2/_8$	$10^2/_8$	$9^4/_8$	$25^4/_8$	$23^5/_8$	82	5
◆ Clark County / Sal Quilici / Nevada State Museum / 1978										
$179^2/_8$	$36^7/_8$	$36^7/_8$	$14^7/_8$	$14^7/_8$	$9^7/_8$	$9^6/_8$	$20^4/_8$	$20^4/_8$	88	6
◆ Clark County / Andy S. Burnett / Andy S. Burnett / 1979										
$179^2/_8$	$38^3/_8$	$40^1/_8$	$15^1/_8$	$15^2/_8$	$9^3/_8$	$9^3/_8$	$23^4/_8$	23	88	6
◆ Clark County / Tammy H. Bawcom / Tammy H. Bawcom / 1988										
$179^1/_8$	$39^5/_8$	40	$14^4/_8$	$14^4/_8$	9	9	$25^1/_8$	$24^5/_8$	92	8
◆ Clark County / Gary D. Selmi / Gary D. Selmi / 1989										
$178^6/_8$	$39^6/_8$	$39^4/_8$	$14^3/_8$	$14^4/_8$	$9^1/_8$	9	27	27	98	9
◆ Colo. River / E.A. Goldman / U.S. Natl. Mus. / 1913										
$178^5/_8$	$35^2/_8$	$36^5/_8$	$15^5/_8$	$15^5/_8$	$9^5/_8$	$9^2/_8$	$23^4/_8$	22	101	10
◆ Lincoln County / William A. Bertelson / William A. Bertelson / 1984										
$178^4/_8$	$40^4/_8$	$39^2/_8$	$14^1/_8$	$13^7/_8$	$9^6/_8$	10	$25^7/_8$	$25^7/_8$	103	11
◆ Clark County / Stephen E. Aiazzi / Stephen E. Aiazzi / 1985										
$178^2/_8$	$38^6/_8$	$36^2/_8$	$14^2/_8$	$14^2/_8$	$10^1/_8$	$10^4/_8$	$23^5/_8$	$22^4/_8$	106	12
◆ Clark County / Kenneth A. Brunk / Kenneth A. Brunk / 1989										
$178^1/_8$	$36^1/_8$	$39^4/_8$	$14^5/_8$	$14^4/_8$	$9^6/_8$	$9^5/_8$	$25^4/_8$	$25^1/_8$	107	13
◆ Lincoln County / David R. Montrose / David R. Montrose / 1993										
$177^3/_8$	$34^6/_8$	$36^3/_8$	$15^1/_8$	15	$10^4/_8$	11	19	19	121	14
◆ Clark County / Ralph W. McClintock / Ralph W. McClintock / 1980										
$177^2/_8$	$39^2/_8$	$34^4/_8$	$15^2/_8$	$15^3/_8$	$8^7/_8$	$8^4/_8$	$28^5/_8$	$28^5/_8$	126	15
◆ Clark County / Robert M. Bransford / Robert M. Bransford / 1966										
$176^6/_8$	$39^6/_8$	37	$14^6/_8$	$14^6/_8$	$9^4/_8$	9	$21^7/_8$	$22^1/_8$	136	16
◆ Clark County / Douglas E. Wendt / Douglas E. Wendt / 1989										
$176^5/_8$	39	$38^5/_8$	$14^4/_8$	$14^4/_8$	$8^6/_8$	$8^4/_8$	$28^3/_8$	$28^3/_8$	140	17
◆ Clark County / Allan R. Sundell / Kent A. Sundell / 1979										
$176^2/_8$	$35^6/_8$	$36^6/_8$	$14^3/_8$	$14^3/_8$	$9^6/_8$	10	$23^1/_8$	$22^4/_8$	151	18
◆ Clark County / F. Lorin Ronnow / F. Lorin Ronnow / 1957										

Score	Length of Horn		Circumference of Base		Circumference at Third Quarter		Greatest Spread	Tip-to-Tip Spread	All-Time Rank	State Rank
	R	L	R	L	R	L				

♦ *Locality / Hunter / Owner / Date Killed*

Score	R	L	R	L	R	L	Greatest Spread	Tip-to-Tip Spread	All-Time Rank	State Rank
$176\frac{2}{8}$	$38\frac{2}{8}$	36	$15\frac{3}{8}$	$15\frac{3}{8}$	$8\frac{4}{8}$	$8\frac{4}{8}$	$21\frac{6}{8}$	$19\frac{4}{8}$	151	18

♦ *Clark County / Christine J. Burrows / Christine J. Burrows / 1981*

$176\frac{2}{8}$	34	37	$15\frac{2}{8}$	$15\frac{2}{8}$	$9\frac{1}{8}$	$9\frac{5}{8}$	23	$21\frac{2}{8}$	151	18

♦ *Clark County / Jack Oberly / Jack Oberly / 1983*

$176\frac{1}{8}$	$37\frac{7}{8}$	$38\frac{2}{8}$	$15\frac{1}{8}$	$15\frac{4}{8}$	$8\frac{3}{8}$	8	$21\frac{5}{8}$	$21\frac{1}{8}$	156	21

♦ *Clark County / Tim L. Iverson / Tim L. Iverson / 1985*

$175\frac{6}{8}$	$36\frac{6}{8}$	$36\frac{4}{8}$	$14\frac{3}{8}$	$14\frac{3}{8}$	$9\frac{6}{8}$	$9\frac{6}{8}$	21	21	169	22

♦ *Lincoln County / Denny L. Frook / Denny L. Frook / 1977*

$175\frac{3}{8}$	37	$37\frac{3}{8}$	$14\frac{5}{8}$	$14\frac{5}{8}$	$8\frac{6}{8}$	$9\frac{2}{8}$	$21\frac{2}{8}$	$21\frac{2}{8}$	180	23

♦ *Lincoln County / Robert Fagan / Robert Fagan / 1968*

$175\frac{1}{8}$	$37\frac{2}{8}$	$38\frac{3}{8}$	$14\frac{2}{8}$	$14\frac{2}{8}$	$9\frac{2}{8}$	$8\frac{5}{8}$	$20\frac{1}{8}$	$20\frac{1}{8}$	185	24

♦ *Lamb Springs / D.B. Walkington / D.B. Walkington / 1965*

$175\frac{1}{8}$	$37\frac{1}{8}$	37	$14\frac{6}{8}$	$14\frac{6}{8}$	$9\frac{5}{8}$	$9\frac{2}{8}$	$25\frac{7}{8}$	$25\frac{7}{8}$	185	24

♦ *Clark County / Wayne C. Matley / Wayne C. Matley / 1966*

$175\frac{1}{8}$	$36\frac{4}{8}$	$37\frac{3}{8}$	$15\frac{2}{8}$	$15\frac{2}{8}$	$8\frac{4}{8}$	$8\frac{4}{8}$	$23\frac{1}{8}$	$23\frac{1}{8}$	185	24

♦ *Clark County / Lenda Z. Azcarate / Lenda Z. Azcarate / 1979*

$175\frac{1}{8}$	$36\frac{2}{8}$	$36\frac{1}{8}$	$15\frac{1}{8}$	15	9	$9\frac{5}{8}$	$23\frac{7}{8}$	$23\frac{7}{8}$	185	24

♦ *Clark County / Lloyd G. Bare / Lloyd G. Bare / 1980*

$175\frac{1}{8}$	$34\frac{4}{8}$	$36\frac{5}{8}$	15	15	10	$9\frac{6}{8}$	$23\frac{2}{8}$	22	185	24

♦ *Clark County / William J. Conner / William J. Conner / 1989*

175	$37\frac{4}{8}$	$37\frac{6}{8}$	15	15	$9\frac{2}{8}$	$9\frac{6}{8}$	$26\frac{6}{8}$	$26\frac{6}{8}$	194	29

♦ *Clark County / Timothy P. Ryan / Timothy P. Ryan / 1983*

$174\frac{7}{8}$	$35\frac{1}{8}$	35	$15\frac{7}{8}$	$15\frac{6}{8}$	$8\frac{7}{8}$	$8\frac{6}{8}$	$23\frac{5}{8}$	$23\frac{1}{8}$	198	30

♦ *Clark County / Herman H. Storey, Jr. / Herman S. Storey, Jr. / 1980*

$174\frac{7}{8}$	$35\frac{7}{8}$	$35\frac{4}{8}$	$15\frac{5}{8}$	$15\frac{6}{8}$	$8\frac{4}{8}$	$8\frac{5}{8}$	$19\frac{6}{8}$	$19\frac{6}{8}$	198	30

♦ *Clark County / Cleldon E. Nelson / Cleldon E. Nelson / 1987*

$174\frac{7}{8}$	$41\frac{4}{8}$	$41\frac{7}{8}$	$13\frac{5}{8}$	$13\frac{6}{8}$	$8\frac{1}{8}$	8	29	29	198	30

♦ *Clark County / Michael J. Ellena / Michael J. Ellena / 1993*

$174\frac{6}{8}$	$33\frac{6}{8}$	$34\frac{6}{8}$	15	$14\frac{7}{8}$	$10\frac{1}{8}$	$10\frac{1}{8}$	$25\frac{4}{8}$	$25\frac{4}{8}$	203	33

♦ *Clark County / Ron W. Biggs / Ron W. Biggs / 1980*

$174\frac{5}{8}$	$36\frac{4}{8}$	$37\frac{5}{8}$	$14\frac{6}{8}$	$14\frac{4}{8}$	$8\frac{7}{8}$	$9\frac{3}{8}$	$25\frac{1}{8}$	$25\frac{1}{8}$	206	34

♦ *Clark County / Roseanne K. Wilkinson / Roseanne K. Wilkinson / 1980*

$174\frac{4}{8}$	$36\frac{6}{8}$	$37\frac{2}{8}$	$14\frac{2}{8}$	$14\frac{2}{8}$	9	$9\frac{1}{8}$	$21\frac{4}{8}$	$18\frac{5}{8}$	208	35

♦ *Clark County / Larry G. Marshall / Larry G. Marshall / 1983*

$174\frac{4}{8}$	$37\frac{2}{8}$	$37\frac{4}{8}$	$15\frac{5}{8}$	$15\frac{5}{8}$	$7\frac{6}{8}$	$7\frac{5}{8}$	$25\frac{7}{8}$	$26\frac{2}{8}$	208	35

♦ *Clark County / Stanley R. Galvin, Jr. / Stanley R. Galvin, Jr. / 1983*

$174\frac{3}{8}$	$38\frac{1}{8}$	$38\frac{4}{8}$	$14\frac{4}{8}$	$14\frac{4}{8}$	8	$7\frac{6}{8}$	$24\frac{4}{8}$	$23\frac{5}{8}$	212	37

♦ *Clark County / Kathy E. Seaberg / K.E. & G. Seaberg / 1981*

NEVADA DESERT SHEEP *(continued)*

Score	Length of Horn		Circumference of Base		Circumference at Third Quarter		Greatest Spread	Tip-to-Tip Spread	All-Time Rank	State Rank
	R	L	R	L	R	L				
◆ *Locality / Hunter / Owner / Date Killed*										
174²⁄₈	37	38²⁄₈	14	14¹⁄₈	10¹⁄₈	10¹⁄₈	21⁷⁄₈	21⁷⁄₈	213	38
◆ *Las Vegas / Thos. R. McElhenney / Thos. R. McElhenney / 1969*										
174²⁄₈	34⁴⁄₈	35⁶⁄₈	15³⁄₈	15²⁄₈	9	9⁷⁄₈	26	26	213	38
◆ *Lincoln County / Larry M. Evans / Larry M. Evans / 1982*										
174	36⁶⁄₈	37⁴⁄₈	13⁴⁄₈	13⁵⁄₈	10	10	24⁴⁄₈	24⁴⁄₈	219	40
◆ *McCullough Mts. / Picked Up / William H. Pogue / PR 1958*										
174	37²⁄₈	38²⁄₈	14³⁄₈	14²⁄₈	8⁷⁄₈	8⁷⁄₈	22	17⁵⁄₈	219	40
◆ *Clark County / H. James Tonkin, Jr. / H. James Tonkin, Jr. / 1990*										
173⁵⁄₈	37¹⁄₈	36⁶⁄₈	15¹⁄₈	15	8⁶⁄₈	8⁶⁄₈	23⁴⁄₈	23⁴⁄₈	234	42
◆ *Clark County / Buddy H. Fujii / Buddy H. Fujii / 1980*										
173⁵⁄₈	37⁵⁄₈	36⁶⁄₈	14⁶⁄₈	14⁵⁄₈	8²⁄₈	8³⁄₈	21⁶⁄₈	20	234	42
◆ *Clark County / Dale O. Millerin / Dale O. Millerin / 1987*										
173⁴⁄₈	35	33⁴⁄₈	16	16	8⁴⁄₈	8²⁄₈	23¹⁄₈	23¹⁄₈	242	44
◆ *Clark County / Ira H. Kent / Ira H. Kent / 1978*										
173²⁄₈	35⁴⁄₈	35⁶⁄₈	15¹⁄₈	15¹⁄₈	8⁶⁄₈	9¹⁄₈	26¹⁄₈	25⁴⁄₈	255	45
◆ *Lincoln County / Ken G. Gerg / Ken G. Gerg / 1990*										
173¹⁄₈	37⁵⁄₈	32⁶⁄₈	14⁶⁄₈	14⁶⁄₈	9	11	25⁴⁄₈	25⁴⁄₈	259	46
◆ *Lincoln County / Picked Up / Billy D. Stoddard / 1965*										
173¹⁄₈	37¹⁄₈	37	14³⁄₈	14⁴⁄₈	9¹⁄₈	8³⁄₈	27⁵⁄₈	27⁵⁄₈	259	46
◆ *Clark County / Chris Hurtado / Chris Hurtado / 1975*										
173¹⁄₈	36⁵⁄₈	36	14⁷⁄₈	14⁷⁄₈	9⁵⁄₈	9⁵⁄₈	24	24	259	46
◆ *Lincoln County / Michael D. Rowe / Michael D. Rowe / 1988*										
173	36¹⁄₈	38³⁄₈	14⁶⁄₈	14⁶⁄₈	8⁴⁄₈	9¹⁄₈	19¹⁄₈	19¹⁄₈	265	49
◆ *Sheep Mt. Range / Gilbert A. Helsel / Gilbert A. Helsel / 1960*										
172⁷⁄₈	35⁶⁄₈	35¹⁄₈	14⁴⁄₈	14⁴⁄₈	10	10	22	19⁶⁄₈	274	50
◆ *Clark County / William R. Slattery / William R. Slattery / 1992*										
172⁵⁄₈	32³⁄₈	35⁴⁄₈	15²⁄₈	15⁴⁄₈	8³⁄₈	9	19²⁄₈	18⁶⁄₈	284	51
◆ *Clark County / Charles W. Knittle / Charles W. Knittle / 1976*										
172⁴⁄₈	40	36	14⁴⁄₈	14⁵⁄₈	8	7⁷⁄₈	25	25	289	52
◆ *Clark County / Scott D. Oxborrow / Scott D. Oxborrow / 1983*										
172⁴⁄₈	35⁶⁄₈	35⁴⁄₈	14⁷⁄₈	14⁷⁄₈	9⁶⁄₈	9⁵⁄₈	20³⁄₈	17⁶⁄₈	289	52
◆ *Lincoln County / Craig S. Boyack / Craig S. Boyack / 1990*										
172³⁄₈	35¹⁄₈	34⁶⁄₈	15²⁄₈	15¹⁄₈	9	9	23¹⁄₈	23¹⁄₈	297	54
◆ *Clark County / Ronald L. Giovanetti / Ronald L. Giovanetti / 1980*										
172³⁄₈	35³⁄₈	36	14⁷⁄₈	14⁷⁄₈	8⁴⁄₈	9⁵⁄₈	21²⁄₈	21²⁄₈	297	54
◆ *Clark County / John F. Lohse / John F. Lohse / 1982*										
172²⁄₈	37³⁄₈	37¹⁄₈	14²⁄₈	14⁴⁄₈	8⁵⁄₈	8⁴⁄₈	22²⁄₈	19⁶⁄₈	302	56
◆ *Clark County / Verner J. Fisher, Jr. / Verner J. Fisher, Jr. / 1988*										

Score	Length of Horn		Circumference of Base		Circumference at Third Quarter		Greatest Spread	Tip-to-Tip Spread	All-Time Rank	State Rank
	R	L	R	L	R	L				
	Locality / Hunter / Owner / Date Killed									
172²/₈	36⁴/₈	36⁴/₈	14	13⁷/₈	10	10¹/₈	19⁶/₈	21¹/₈	302	56
	Clark County / Nicholas J. Coussoulis / Nicholas J. Coussoulis / 1990									
172¹/₈	35³/₈	36⁶/₈	14⁵/₈	14³/₈	9²/₈	9³/₈	22⁶/₈	21⁴/₈	309	58
	Clark County / Robert F. Sievert / Robert F. Sievert / 1985									
172	36⁴/₈	36	14²/₈	14³/₈	9³/₈	9²/₈	22⁴/₈	22⁴/₈	312	59
	Clark County / Mike W. Steele / Mike W. Steele / 1986									
172	34	36⁴/₈	14⁶/₈	14⁴/₈	9⁴/₈	9³/₈	23³/₈	22⁵/₈	312	59
	Clark County / Jerry J. Long / Jerry J. Long / 1987									
172	36⁷/₈	37³/₈	15¹/₈	14⁷/₈	8⁵/₈	8⁶/₈	25⁷/₈	25⁷/₈	312	59
	Clark County / Dan Pocapalia / Dan Pocapalia / 1988									
172	35	35	15⁴/₈	15³/₈	8²/₈	8²/₈	22¹/₈	24⁶/₈	312	59
	Lincoln County / Gary R. Quarisa / Gary R. Quarisa / 1993									
171⁷/₈	36⁶/₈	36³/₈	14	14³/₈	9²/₈	9³/₈	22⁷/₈	21⁵/₈	319	63
	Clark County / John R. Chase / John R. Chase / 1990									
171⁶/₈	35⁶/₈	35²/₈	14	14	10	10¹/₈	23	20⁷/₈	325	64
	Lincoln County / William A. Molini / William A. Molini / 1977									
171⁵/₈	35³/₈	35⁴/₈	14⁵/₈	14⁶/₈	9³/₈	9	20⁵/₈	20⁵/₈	328	65
	Clark County / George Hueftle / George Hueftle / 1977									
171⁵/₈	34³/₈	32²/₈	15³/₈	15⁴/₈	9³/₈	9⁶/₈	21⁷/₈	20⁴/₈	328	65
	Clark County / Edward M. Evans / Edward M. Evans / 1977									
171⁵/₈	33²/₈	33³/₈	15¹/₈	15²/₈	9⁶/₈	10²/₈	22	23⁶/₈	328	65
	Lincoln County / James D. Buonamici / James D. Buonamici / 1989									
171⁴/₈	37⁴/₈	37⁶/₈	13⁶/₈	13⁶/₈	8³/₈	8³/₈	23	22⁶/₈	338	68
	Clark County / Jerry P. Devin / Jerry P. Devin / 1976									
171³/₈	38¹/₈	37	14	14²/₈	9³/₈	8⁶/₈	24	23⁵/₈	342	69
	Clark County / Daniel T. Magee / Daniel T. Magee / 1980									
171³/₈	37⁶/₈	38¹/₈	14¹/₈	14²/₈	9	9²/₈	26	25	342	69
	Lincoln County / Roy F. Lerg / Roy D. Lerg / 1984									
171²/₈	35¹/₈	36⁷/₈	14⁴/₈	14⁴/₈	8⁶/₈	8⁵/₈	20²/₈	20²/₈	347	71
	Clark County / Bill R. Balsi, Jr. / Bill R. Balsi, Jr. / 1979									
171¹/₈	35²/₈	35³/₈	15	14⁷/₈	9²/₈	8⁶/₈	25²/₈	25²/₈	353	72
	Clark County / Ray W. Diehl / Ray W. Diehl / 1979									
171	36⁴/₈	35²/₈	14⁵/₈	14⁶/₈	9⁷/₈	9³/₈	23¹/₈	21⁴/₈	359	73
	Clark County / Richard A. Bell / Richard A. Bell / 1986									
171	37⁵/₈	37¹/₈	14⁵/₈	14²/₈	7⁷/₈	8¹/₈	24⁴/₈	24⁴/₈	359	73
	Clark County / Toni M. Venturacci / Toni M. Venturacci / 1986									
170⁷/₈	34³/₈	36²/₈	14⁴/₈	14²/₈	9⁴/₈	9⁵/₈	24²/₈	24²/₈	365	75
	Clark County / Picked Up / John V. Zenz / 1991									

Score	Length of Horn		Circumference of Base		Circumference at Third Quarter		Greatest Spread	Tip-to-Tip Spread	All-Time Rank	State Rank
	R	L	R	L	R	L				
♦ Locality / Hunter / Owner / Date Killed										
170 6/8	39 4/8	37 4/8	13 1/8	13 7/8	9 4/8	8 4/8	22 6/8	22 6/8	373	76
♦ Clark County / Roy Gamblin / Roy Gamblin / 1977										
170 6/8	36 4/8	35 4/8	14 2/8	14 2/8	9 2/8	9 4/8	25	24	373	76
♦ Nye County / Donald A. Leveille / Donald A. Leveille / 1986										
170 6/8	36 3/8	37 7/8	13 6/8	14	8 4/8	8 6/8	24	24	373	76
♦ Clark County / Picked Up / Lacel Bland / 1991										
170 5/8	34 7/8	32 2/8	15	14 7/8	9 4/8	9 5/8	22 6/8	22 6/8	383	79
♦ Clark County / George W. Wilkinson, Jr. / George W. Wilkinson, Jr. / 1976										
170 4/8	36	35	14 1/8	14 3/8	10 1/8	9 1/8	20 2/8	20 2/8	387	80
♦ Clark County / Robert E. Coons / Robert E. Coons / 1971										
170 4/8	34 5/8	32 1/8	15 2/8	15 3/8	8 6/8	8 5/8	23 6/8	23	387	80
♦ Lincoln County / Robert Del Porto / Robert Del Porto / 1989										
170 3/8	35	35 7/8	14 2/8	14 2/8	9 6/8	9 6/8	23 3/8	23 3/8	394	82
♦ Lincoln County / Robert S. Mastronardi / Robert S. Mastronardi / 1982										
170 3/8	35 1/8	35 6/8	13 6/8	14 4/8	9 5/8	9 5/8	23 4/8	19 3/8	394	82
♦ Clark County / Tracy L. Wilkinson / Tracy L. Wilkinson / 1982										
170 2/8	37 7/8	34 7/8	14 7/8	14 4/8	8 2/8	8 4/8	24 1/8	24 1/8	401	84
♦ Clark County / Landon D. Mack / Landon D. Mack / 1977										
170 2/8	37 6/8	37 2/8	15 3/8	15 2/8	7	7 4/8	24 7/8	24 7/8	401	84
♦ Clark County / Raymond B. Graber II / Raymond B. Graber II / 1987										
170 1/8	40 3/8	34 2/8	13 6/8	13 6/8	8 5/8	8 3/8	25 4/8	25 4/8	411	86
♦ Mineral County / Picked Up / Nev. Dept. of Wildl. / 1969										
170 1/8	34 4/8	35 3/8	15 4/8	15 3/8	8 4/8	8 4/8	20 4/8	18 4/8	411	86
♦ Clark County / William F. Zenz, Jr. / William F. Zenz, Jr. / 1980										
170	33	34 6/8	14 2/8	14 2/8	9 6/8	10 2/8	20 7/8	18 5/8	417	88
♦ Clark County / Lee R. Williamson / Lee R. Williamson / 1972										
170	34 7/8	34 1/8	14 5/8	14 4/8	10 1/8	9 5/8	21 2/8	21 2/8	417	88
♦ Clark County / Jim Lathrop, Jr. / Jim Lathrop, Jr. / 1976										
170	35 6/8	35 2/8	14 2/8	14	9 2/8	9	20 1/8	19 4/8	417	88
♦ Clark County / Roy A. Walker / Roy A. Walker / 1985										
169 6/8	38 2/8	36	13 3/8	13 5/8	9 3/8	9 3/8	23	21 7/8	426	91
♦ Clark County / Harold D. Humes / Harold D. Humes / 1990										
169 5/8	34 5/8	36 4/8	14 3/8	14 4/8	9 1/8	9 1/8	23	19	431	92
♦ Muddy Mts. / Peter Dietrick / Peter Dietrick / 1962										
169 2/8	36 2/8	34 6/8	14 6/8	14 6/8	8 4/8	8 1/8	23 4/8	23 4/8	449	93
♦ Clark County / Richard M. McDrew / Richard M. McDrew / 1986										
169 1/8	34 4/8	35 5/8	14	14	10	10 1/8	21 6/8	21 6/8	455	94
♦ Clark County / Lee M. Smith, Jr. / Lee M. Smith, Jr. / 1979										

Score	Length of Horn R	Length of Horn L	Circumference of Base R	Circumference of Base L	Circumference at Third Quarter R	Circumference at Third Quarter L	Greatest Spread	Tip-to-Tip Spread	All-Time Rank	State Rank
♦ *Locality / Hunter / Owner / Date Killed*										
169 1/8	36	36 7/8	14 7/8	15	7	7 1/8	23 6/8	23 5/8	455	94
♦ *Clark County / Vernon C. Tays / Vernon C. Tays / 1987*										
169	36 4/8	35 2/8	15 2/8	15 2/8	7 6/8	7 6/8	25 6/8	25 6/8	460	96
♦ *Clark County / Charles E. Sibley / Charles E. Sibley / 1986*										
168 7/8	36 5/8	33 2/8	14 6/8	14 7/8	8 2/8	8 7/8	22	22	466	97
♦ *Clark County / Robert Darakjy / Robert Darakjy / 1978*										
168 7/8	33 4/8	33 7/8	14 7/8	14 7/8	9 3/8	9 2/8	20 6/8	20 6/8	466	97
♦ *Lincoln County / Melvin J. Lowe / Melvin J. Lowe / 1981*										
168 6/8	35 2/8	36 6/8	13 5/8	13 3/8	9	9 2/8	22 4/8	22 4/8	471	99
♦ *Lincoln County / Von A. Mitton / Von A. Mitton / 1966*										
168 5/8	35 5/8	34 4/8	15	15	8	8	24 1/8	22 1/8	476	100
♦ *Clark County / Joseph Machac / Joseph Machac / 1989*										
168 4/8	35 5/8	35 5/8	15 3/8	15 3/8	7 3/8	7 5/8	23 5/8	23 5/8	481	101
♦ *Clark County / James M. Machac / James M. Machac / 1987*										
168 4/8	33 6/8	35	14 6/8	14 5/8	9	8 7/8	22 6/8	22 6/8	481	101
♦ *Nye County / David E. Underwood / David E. Underwood / 1992*										
168 3/8	35 4/8	37 1/8	13 6/8	13 5/8	9 3/8	9 4/8	24 2/8	24	490	103
♦ *Clark County / Leonard L. Lerg / Leonard L. Lerg / 1985*										
168 2/8	34 1/8	34 7/8	14 4/8	14 4/8	9	8 5/8	21 4/8	19 7/8	494	104
♦ *Clark County / Marie F. Reuter / Marie F. Reuter / 1969*										
168 2/8	33 6/8	33 6/8	15 3/8	15 3/8	8 1/8	8 5/8	22 2/8	19 3/8	494	104
♦ *Clark County / Charles J. Lindberg / Charles J. Lindberg / 1971*										
168 2/8	33 5/8	34 5/8	14	14	9 2/8	9 5/8	23 3/8	23 3/8	494	104
♦ *Lincoln County / Dale Deming / Dale Deming / 1977*										
168 2/8	37	36	13 6/8	13 6/8	10 2/8	9 3/8	20	19 4/8	494	104
♦ *Lincoln County / Lee A. Raine / Lee A. Raine / 1982*										
168 2/8	35 7/8	37 1/8	14 3/8	14 4/8	7 7/8	8 2/8	25 3/8	25 3/8	494	104
♦ *Clark County / Ronald E. Brown / Ronald E. Brown / 1983*										
168 1/8	35 6/8	36 5/8	14 6/8	14 6/8	7 1/8	7 3/8	23	21 1/8	505	109
♦ *Clark County / Richard L. Deane / Richard L. Deane / 1988*										
168	35	35	14	14	10	9	25	25	511	110
♦ *Lamb Springs / Leslie H. Farr / Leslie H. Farr / 1966*										
168	34 4/8	34 4/8	15	14 6/8	8 3/8	8 6/8	21 4/8	21	511	110
♦ *Clark County / Edward Friel / Edward Friel / 1969*										
168	35	35 4/8	14 2/8	14 3/8	9 1/8	9	23	23	511	110
♦ *Clark County / Leonard M. Faike / Leonard M. Faike / 1973*										
168	36 4/8	35 6/8	14 2/8	14 4/8	8 4/8	8 1/8	23 5/8	22 2/8	511	110
♦ *Clark County / Dennis K. Evans / Dennis K. Evans / 1981*										

NEVADA DESERT SHEEP *(continued)*

Score	Length of Horn		Circumference of Base		Circumference at Third Quarter		Greatest Spread	Tip-to-Tip Spread	All-Time Rank	State Rank
	R	L	R	L	R	L				

$166\frac{5}{8}$ $34\frac{4}{8}$ $34\frac{1}{8}$ $14\frac{2}{8}$ $14\frac{2}{8}$ $8\frac{6}{8}$ $9\frac{1}{8}$ $21\frac{1}{8}$ $20\frac{4}{8}$ 531 114
♦ *Clark County / Andrew A. Koski / Andrew A. Koski / 1993*

$166\frac{3}{8}$ $35\frac{1}{8}$ $35\frac{6}{8}$ $13\frac{6}{8}$ $13\frac{6}{8}$ $8\frac{4}{8}$ $8\frac{4}{8}$ $21\frac{5}{8}$ $21\frac{2}{8}$ 533 115
♦ *Clark County / Kirk R. Ostrom / Kirk R. Ostrom / 1983*

$165\frac{5}{8}$ $32\frac{4}{8}$ $36\frac{5}{8}$ $14\frac{2}{8}$ $14\frac{2}{8}$ $9\frac{4}{8}$ $9\frac{4}{8}$ $23\frac{4}{8}$ $23\frac{4}{8}$ 535 116
♦ *Lincoln County / Hilding Lund / Hilding Lund / 1985*

$183\frac{2}{8}$ $40\frac{5}{8}$ $41\frac{5}{8}$ $15\frac{2}{8}$ $15\frac{2}{8}$ $8\frac{3}{8}$ $8\frac{6}{8}$ $27\frac{2}{8}$ $27\frac{2}{8}$ * *
♦ *Clark County / Alan G. Means / Alan G. Means / 1988*

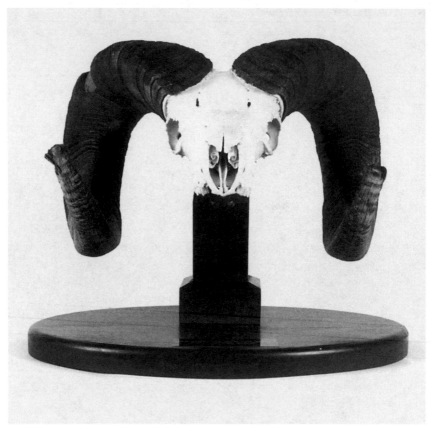

Photograph by Mike Biggs

**NEW MEXICO STATE RECORD
DESERT SHEEP
SCORE: 188⁴⁄₈**
Locality: Grant Co.   Date: Picked Up 1992
Owner: New Mexico Department of Game & Fish

NEW MEXICO

DESERT SHEEP

Score	Length of Horn		Circumference of Base		Circumference at Third Quarter		Greatest Spread	Tip-to-Tip Spread	All-Time Rank	State Rank
	R	L	R	L	R	L				
♦ Locality / Hunter / Owner / Date Killed										
188⁴⁄₈	40²⁄₈	40²⁄₈	15⁴⁄₈	15⁶⁄₈	10²⁄₈	10¹⁄₈	21⁵⁄₈	19	12	1
♦ Grant County / Picked Up / NM Dept. of Game & Fish / 1992										
178⁷⁄₈	39¹⁄₈	36	16²⁄₈	16²⁄₈	8	7⁵⁄₈	20⁵⁄₈	20	95	2
♦ Hidalgo County / L.P. McKinney / Frank McKinney / 1921										

Photograph Courtesy of Ben Hollingsworth, Jr.

TEXAS STATE RECORD
DESERT SHEEP
SCORE: 168⅔
Locality: Culberson Co.   Date: 1993
Hunter: Ben Hollingsworth, Jr.

TEXAS

DESERT SHEEP

Score	Length of Horn		Circumference of Base		Circumference at Third Quarter		Greatest Spread	Tip-to-Tip Spread	All-Time Rank	State Rank
	R	L	R	L	R	L				
♦ Locality / Hunter / Owner / Date Killed										
168 ^{2}/$_8$	34 ^{4}/$_8$	35 ^{4}/$_8$	14 ^{3}/$_8$	14 ^{3}/$_8$	8 ^{4}/$_8$	9	20 ^{7}/$_8$	19 ^{1}/$_8$	494	1
♦ Culberson County / Ben Hollingsworth, Jr. / Ben Hollingsworth, Jr. / 1993										
167	32 ^{6}/$_8$	32 ^{2}/$_8$	15	15	8 ^{4}/$_8$	8 ^{3}/$_8$	20 ^{6}/$_8$	20 ^{6}/$_8$	530	2
♦ Culberson County / S. Carl Miller, Jr. / S. Carl Miller, Jr. / 1991										

Photograph by Arlene Hanson

MEXICO RECORD
WORLD'S RECORD
DESERT SHEEP
SCORE: 205⅛
Locality: Lower Calif.   Date: 1940
Hunter: Indian
Owner: Carl M. Scrivens
Loaned to the B&C National Collection, Cody, Wyoming

MEXICO
DESERT SHEEP

Score	Length of Horn		Circumference of Base		Circumference at Third Quarter		Greatest Spread	Tip-to-Tip Spread	All-Time Rank	State Rank
	R	L	R	L	R	L				
◆ Locality / Hunter / Owner / Date Killed										
205 1/8	43 5/8	43 6/8	16 6/8	17	10 5/8	10 6/8	25 5/8	25 5/8	1	1
◆ Lower Calif. / Indian / Loaned to B&C Natl. Coll. / 1940										
197 4/8	44	43 4/8	15 7/8	15 7/8	10 5/8	10	23 7/8	23 7/8	3	2
◆ Lower Calif. / Gift of H. M. Beck / Acad. Nat. Sci., Phil. / 1892										
192 5/8	41 6/8	42 3/8	15	15 1/8	10 6/8	10 4/8	25 4/8	25	5	3
◆ Baja Calif. / Javier Lopez del Bosque / Javier Lopez del Bosque / 1979										
191 6/8	42	43 4/8	15 4/8	15 3/8	9 6/8	9 3/8	23 4/8	23 4/8	6	4
◆ Baja Calif. / Lit Ng / Lit Ng / 1968										
191 3/8	40	41 3/8	16 5/8	16 5/8	9 1/8	9 5/8	24 1/8	24 1/8	7	5
◆ Mexico / Picked Up / Snow Museum / PR 1952										
191 2/8	38 4/8	40 4/8	16 2/8	16 2/8	10 3/8	10 7/8	21 6/8	17 2/8	8	6
◆ Baja Calif. / Claude Bourguignon / Claude Bourguignon / 1982										
191 1/8	39 3/8	39 2/8	16 3/8	16 4/8	10	10	19 3/8	19 2/8	9	7
◆ Baja Calif. / Bruno Scherrer / Bruno Scherrer / 1981										
189 3/8	39 5/8	39 4/8	15 4/8	15 4/8	10 3/8	11	21 3/8	21 3/8	11	8
◆ Lower Calif. / M.B. Silva / M.B. Silva / 1939										
188 2/8	43	43	14 4/8	14 5/8	9 5/8	9 4/8	27 3/8	27 3/8	13	9
◆ Baja Calif. / A. Cal Rossi, Jr. / A. Cal Rossi, Jr. / 1974										
187 6/8	42	40	15 2/8	15 2/8	10 1/8	10 1/8	23 5/8	23 5/8	15	10
◆ Baja Calif. / Ed Stedman, Jr. / Ed Stedman, Jr. / 1976										
187 5/8	38 4/8	40 5/8	16 2/8	16 2/8	9	9 4/8	21 4/8	20 6/8	16	11
◆ Baja Calif. / Romulo Sanchez Mireles / Romulo Sanchez Mireles / 1969										
187 3/8	39 2/8	39 7/8	15 1/8	15 2/8	10 2/8	10 5/8	21	21	17	12
◆ Sonora / Herb Klein / Herb Klein / 1952										
187 3/8	39 1/8	39 2/8	16	16	10 2/8	10 3/8	17 6/8	17 6/8	17	12
◆ Sonora / Oscar J. Brooks / Oscar J. Brooks / 1955										
187	39 1/8	39 5/8	16	16	9 3/8	9 5/8	24 5/8	24 5/8	19	14
◆ Lower Calif. / Unknown / Snow Museum / PR 1952										
186 5/8	38 3/8	38 4/8	14 7/8	14 7/8	11 3/8	11 3/8	22	20 1/8	21	15
◆ Sonora / F.B. Heider / O.M. Corbett / 1927										
186 2/8	40 6/8	40 2/8	14 6/8	14 7/8	10	10	20 2/8	23	23	16
◆ Baja Calif. / Robert P. Miller / Robert P. Miller / 1981										
185 3/8	39 5/8	40	16	16	10 2/8	9 2/8	22 3/8	19 7/8	27	17
◆ Baja Calif. / Graciano Guichard / Graciano Guichard / 1970										
185 3/8	38 3/8	39 4/8	16 1/8	16 1/8	8 7/8	9	23 2/8	19 6/8	27	17
◆ Baja Calif. / Robert L. Williamson / Robert L. Williamson / 1987										

Score	Length of Horn R	L	Circumference of Base R	L	Circumference at Third Quarter R	L	Greatest Spread	Tip-to-Tip Spread	All-Time Rank	State Rank
$185\frac{2}{8}$	$39\frac{7}{8}$	$38\frac{7}{8}$	$15\frac{5}{8}$	$15\frac{6}{8}$	9	$9\frac{3}{8}$	$19\frac{4}{8}$	$16\frac{3}{8}$	29	19

♦ *Baja Calif. / Wilmer C. Hansen / Wilmer C. Hansen / 1972*

$185\frac{2}{8}$	$39\frac{2}{8}$	$39\frac{2}{8}$	$15\frac{3}{8}$	$15\frac{4}{8}$	$10\frac{4}{8}$	$9\frac{7}{8}$	$25\frac{2}{8}$	$25\frac{2}{8}$	29	19

♦ *Baja Calif. / Albert Pellizzari / Albert Pellizzari / 1978*

185	$39\frac{4}{8}$	$39\frac{2}{8}$	$15\frac{7}{8}$	$15\frac{7}{8}$	$8\frac{7}{8}$	9	$20\frac{3}{8}$	$18\frac{6}{8}$	32	21

♦ *San Borja Mts. / Alice J. Landreth / Alice J. Landreth / 1969*

185	$38\frac{6}{8}$	$37\frac{2}{8}$	$16\frac{4}{8}$	$16\frac{4}{8}$	9	$8\frac{7}{8}$	$24\frac{5}{8}$	21	32	21

♦ *Baja Calif. / Miguel Zaldivar De Valasco / Miguel Zaldivar De Valasco / 1979*

$184\frac{6}{8}$	$39\frac{4}{8}$	$38\frac{4}{8}$	$16\frac{2}{8}$	$16\frac{3}{8}$	$8\frac{5}{8}$	$8\frac{7}{8}$	$22\frac{5}{8}$	$21\frac{1}{8}$	34	23

♦ *Baja Calif. / Burton L. Smith, Sr. / Burton L. Smith, Sr. / 1973*

$184\frac{5}{8}$	$40\frac{1}{8}$	$37\frac{4}{8}$	$15\frac{1}{8}$	$15\frac{1}{8}$	10	$10\frac{3}{8}$	$22\frac{4}{8}$	$21\frac{2}{8}$	37	24

♦ *Baja Calif. / Steven L. Rose / Steven L. Rose / 1967*

$184\frac{4}{8}$	$38\frac{6}{8}$	39	$15\frac{5}{8}$	16	$9\frac{2}{8}$	$9\frac{4}{8}$	$20\frac{6}{8}$	21	38	25

♦ *Baja Calif. / H. Clayton Poole / H. Clayton Poole / 1966*

$184\frac{4}{8}$	$40\frac{4}{8}$	40	$15\frac{2}{8}$	$15\frac{2}{8}$	$9\frac{2}{8}$	9	22	22	38	25

♦ *Baja Calif. / Clint Heiber / Clint Heiber / 1978*

184	$41\frac{6}{8}$	$40\frac{4}{8}$	$15\frac{4}{8}$	$15\frac{4}{8}$	$8\frac{3}{8}$	$8\frac{7}{8}$	$25\frac{6}{8}$	$25\frac{6}{8}$	43	27

♦ *Baja Calif. / Thomas J. Brimhall / Thomas J. Brimhall / 1981*

$183\frac{7}{8}$	$39\frac{3}{8}$	$38\frac{4}{8}$	16	16	$9\frac{5}{8}$	$9\frac{3}{8}$	$23\frac{5}{8}$	$23\frac{5}{8}$	45	28

♦ *Gonzaga / Glenn Napierskie / Glenn Napierskie / 1970*

$183\frac{2}{8}$	$39\frac{4}{8}$	$41\frac{6}{8}$	$15\frac{2}{8}$	$15\frac{2}{8}$	9	9	$25\frac{3}{8}$	$25\frac{3}{8}$	47	29

♦ *Lower Calif. / George H. Gould / Unknown / 1894*

$182\frac{6}{8}$	$41\frac{6}{8}$	$38\frac{6}{8}$	$15\frac{4}{8}$	$15\frac{4}{8}$	$8\frac{2}{8}$	$8\frac{4}{8}$	$23\frac{4}{8}$	$23\frac{4}{8}$	50	30

♦ *Baja Calif. / Rita Oney / Rita Oney / 1976*

$182\frac{5}{8}$	39	$39\frac{1}{8}$	$15\frac{5}{8}$	$15\frac{6}{8}$	$8\frac{6}{8}$	$9\frac{2}{8}$	$22\frac{6}{8}$	$22\frac{6}{8}$	52	31

♦ *Baja Calif. / Duane H. Loomis / Duane H. Loomis / 1972*

$182\frac{4}{8}$	$39\frac{7}{8}$	$39\frac{3}{8}$	$14\frac{6}{8}$	$14\frac{5}{8}$	$9\frac{6}{8}$	$9\frac{7}{8}$	$21\frac{1}{8}$	$21\frac{1}{8}$	54	32

♦ *Lower Calif. / Picked Up / C.G. Clare / 1958*

$182\frac{3}{8}$	$38\frac{5}{8}$	$37\frac{6}{8}$	$14\frac{6}{8}$	15	$10\frac{5}{8}$	$10\frac{1}{8}$	$22\frac{1}{8}$	$22\frac{1}{8}$	56	33

♦ *Lower Calif. / Elgin T. Gates / Elgin T. Gates / 1940*

$182\frac{3}{8}$	$39\frac{3}{8}$	40	$14\frac{7}{8}$	15	$9\frac{3}{8}$	$9\frac{5}{8}$	22	22	56	33

♦ *Baja Calif. / Robert Zachrich / Robert Zachrich / 1978*

$182\frac{1}{8}$	$37\frac{7}{8}$	37	$14\frac{7}{8}$	$14\frac{7}{8}$	$10\frac{2}{8}$	$10\frac{1}{8}$	$23\frac{6}{8}$	$19\frac{3}{8}$	59	35

♦ *Baja Calif. / Jesus H. Garza-Villarreal / Jesus H. Garza-Villarreal / 1984*

182	38	$36\frac{6}{8}$	$15\frac{6}{8}$	$15\frac{6}{8}$	$9\frac{2}{8}$	$9\frac{2}{8}$	$22\frac{1}{8}$	$19\frac{4}{8}$	61	36

♦ *Baja Calif. / John M. Griffith, Jr. / John M. Griffith, Jr. / 1974*

$181\frac{6}{8}$	$42\frac{2}{8}$	40	$14\frac{3}{8}$	$14\frac{6}{8}$	$8\frac{5}{8}$	9	24	24	62	37

♦ *Sonora / George W. Parker / George W. Parker / 1939*

Score	Length of Horn		Circumference of Base		Circumference at Third Quarter		Greatest Spread	Tip-to-Tip Spread	All-Time Rank	State Rank
	R	L	R	L	R	L				
◆ Locality / Hunter / Owner / Date Killed										
181 5/8	36 2/8	36 3/8	16 1/8	16 1/8	10 3/8	10 3/8	22	20 1/8	63	38
◆ Baja Calif. / Elvin Hawkins / Elvin Hawkins / 1978										
181 2/8	37	37	15	15	10 3/8	10 6/8	21 7/8	21 1/8	65	39
◆ Sonora / Ira C. Green / Ira C. Green / 1939										
180 7/8	40	38 1/8	15 4/8	15 4/8	8 7/8	9 1/8	22 5/8	22 5/8	66	40
◆ Baja Calif. / Geo. H. Landreth / Geo. H. Landreth / 1969										
180 7/8	37 7/8	34 4/8	15 6/8	15 6/8	9 6/8	9 6/8	20 6/8	20 6/8	66	40
◆ Baja Calif. / Jack Atcheson, Jr. / Jack Atcheson, Jr. / 1978										
180 3/8	38 1/8	40 2/8	15 1/8	15 1/8	9	9 1/8	20 3/8	20 3/8	71	42
◆ Baja Calif. / Arthur R. Dubs / Arthur R. Dubs / 1966										
180 3/8	39 2/8	39 5/8	14 5/8	14 6/8	9 3/8	9 6/8	22 4/8	22 4/8	71	42
◆ Baja Calif. / Fritz A. Nachant / Fritz A. Nachant / 1970										
180 3/8	37 2/8	38 5/8	15 2/8	15 1/8	9 4/8	9 3/8	21 6/8	19 1/8	71	42
◆ Baja Calif. / Emory C. Thompson / Emory C. Thompson / 1985										
180 2/8	36 2/8	36 4/8	15 5/8	15 4/8	9 7/8	10 1/8	22 4/8	21 1/8	75	45
◆ Baja Calif. / Hector Aguilar Parada / Hector Aguilar Parada / 1988										
180 2/8	41 2/8	39 6/8	14 4/8	14 4/8	8 7/8	9 7/8	22 6/8	22 2/8	75	45
◆ Baja Calif. / Bernard Sippin / Bernard Sippin / 1988										
179 7/8	37 5/8	37 2/8	15 2/8	15 2/8	8 7/8	9 2/8	19 5/8	0	82	47
◆ Baja Calif. / George W. Vogt / George W. Vogt / 1978										
179 7/8	37 6/8	37 5/8	16	16 1/8	8 4/8	9	24 3/8	24 3/8	82	47
◆ Baja Calif. / Paul E. Robey / Paul E. Robey / 1979										
179 6/8	39 1/8	39 1/8	16	16	7 5/8	7 4/8	24	24	85	49
◆ Baja Calif. / Don L. Corley / Don L. Corley / 1978										
179 4/8	38 1/8	37 3/8	15 3/8	15 4/8	9 4/8	9 7/8	21	19 6/8	86	50
◆ Baja Calif. / Mrs. Carroll Pistell / Mrs. Carroll Pistell / 1969										
179 4/8	38 1/8	37 7/8	15 5/8	15 6/8	8 7/8	8 5/8	26 6/8	26 6/8	86	50
◆ Baja Calif. / Ronald J. Wade / Ronald J. Wade / 1987										
179 2/8	36 5/8	35 7/8	16 2/8	16 2/8	9 1/8	9 1/8	20 5/8	19 3/8	88	52
◆ Baja Calif. / Jim Buss / Jim Buss / 1966										
179 2/8	38 2/8	37	15 2/8	15 2/8	9 6/8	9 4/8	21 2/8	21 2/8	88	52
◆ Baja Calif. / Francisco Salido / Francisco Salido / 1968										
179 1/8	36 1/8	38 2/8	15 4/8	15 5/8	8 4/8	8 6/8	21 4/8	18 4/8	92	54
◆ Baja Calif. / W.J. Boynton, Jr. / W.J. Boynton, Jr. / 1974										
179	37 3/8	36 1/8	16 2/8	16 1/8	8 5/8	8 6/8	19 4/8	18 7/8	94	55
◆ Baja Calif. / Graciano G. Michel / Graciano G. Michel / 1970										
178 6/8	37 2/8	37	14 6/8	14 6/8	10 2/8	10 2/8	22 3/8	18 5/8	98	56
◆ Sonora / Oscar J. Brooks / Oscar J. Brooks / 1950										

Score	Length of Horn		Circumference of Base		Circumference at Third Quarter		Greatest Spread	Tip-to-Tip Spread	All-Time Rank	State Rank
	R	L	R	L	R	L				
♦ Locality / Hunter / Owner / Date Killed										
178⁶⁄₈	37²⁄₈	36⁶⁄₈	15⁷⁄₈	15⁷⁄₈	8⁴⁄₈	8³⁄₈	21⁴⁄₈	21⁴⁄₈	98	56
♦ Baja Calif. / Hobson L. Sanderson, Jr. / Hobson L. Sanderson, Jr. / 1981										
178⁴⁄₈	36⁴⁄₈	36²⁄₈	15⁶⁄₈	15⁶⁄₈	9	9²⁄₈	20⁴⁄₈	19²⁄₈	103	58
♦ Baja Calif. / Henry Culp / Henry Culp / 1978										
178	36	37	16	16	8⁶⁄₈	9	22	22	109	59
♦ Sonora / Aaron Saenz, Jr. / Aaron Saenz, Jr. / 1969										
178	38³⁄₈	37³⁄₈	15	14⁶⁄₈	9³⁄₈	9⁶⁄₈	21⁴⁄₈	19⁴⁄₈	109	59
♦ Baja Calif. / Basil C. Bradbury / Basil C. Bradbury / 1969										
178	35⁴⁄₈	38²⁄₈	16	16	8²⁄₈	8²⁄₈	24	24	109	59
♦ Baja Calif. / James G. Lagiss / James G. Lagiss / 1980										
177⁷⁄₈	39⁷⁄₈	38⁶⁄₈	15¹⁄₈	15³⁄₈	8³⁄₈	8	26⁵⁄₈	26⁵⁄₈	112	62
♦ San Boros Mts. / Jerald T. Waite / Jerald T. Waite / 1972										
177⁷⁄₈	38¹⁄₈	37⁴⁄₈	15	15¹⁄₈	9²⁄₈	9²⁄₈	20⁵⁄₈	19²⁄₈	112	62
♦ Baja Calif. / Richard C. Hansen / Richard C. Hansen / 1973										
177⁴⁄₈	38	42	14⁴⁄₈	14⁴⁄₈	8¹⁄₈	8³⁄₈	27⁶⁄₈	27⁶⁄₈	117	64
♦ Lower Calif. / Earl A. Garrettson / William Foster / 1912										
177⁴⁄₈	38	37	14⁵⁄₈	14⁶⁄₈	9⁴⁄₈	9³⁄₈	25⁵⁄₈	24	117	64
♦ Baja Calif. / Herb Klein / Herb Klein / 1966										
177⁴⁄₈	36⁷⁄₈	35⁷⁄₈	14⁷⁄₈	15¹⁄₈	9⁴⁄₈	9⁵⁄₈	15⁷⁄₈	18⁷⁄₈	117	64
♦ Baja Calif. / Joe Osterbauer / Joe Osterbauer / 1978										
177³⁄₈	38⁴⁄₈	38³⁄₈	14³⁄₈	14²⁄₈	10⁴⁄₈	9⁵⁄₈	21	21	121	67
♦ Lower Calif. / F. Stephens / U.S. Natl. Mus. / 1902										
177³⁄₈	37³⁄₈	38	15⁴⁄₈	15²⁄₈	8⁷⁄₈	8⁷⁄₈	21⁷⁄₈	21⁷⁄₈	121	67
♦ Baja Calif. / Arthur W. Carlsberg / Arthur W. Carlsberg / 1970										
177³⁄₈	37	37⁵⁄₈	16	16²⁄₈	8⁴⁄₈	8	19⁴⁄₈	16	121	67
♦ Baja Calif. / Don McBride / Don McBride / 1980										
177²⁄₈	37¹⁄₈	37¹⁄₈	15³⁄₈	15³⁄₈	9	9³⁄₈	20²⁄₈	20²⁄₈	126	70
♦ San Borjas Mts. / Lloyd Zeman / Lloyd Zeman / 1970										
177¹⁄₈	37⁶⁄₈	38⁵⁄₈	15²⁄₈	15²⁄₈	8⁶⁄₈	8²⁄₈	22⁵⁄₈	22⁵⁄₈	130	71
♦ Baja Calif. / G. Dale Monson / G. Dale Monson / 1982										
177	36⁴⁄₈	36²⁄₈	15³⁄₈	15⁴⁄₈	9	9²⁄₈	19	18	132	72
♦ Baja Calif. / Alain Ferraris / Alain Ferraris / 1966										
177	36⁴⁄₈	37	15¹⁄₈	14⁶⁄₈	9¹⁄₈	9²⁄₈	21³⁄₈	20	132	72
♦ Sonora Desert / Herb Klein / Herb Klein / 1969										
177	35⁴⁄₈	36⁶⁄₈	15⁷⁄₈	15⁷⁄₈	9²⁄₈	9¹⁄₈	19⁶⁄₈	17³⁄₈	132	72
♦ Baja Calif. / Roy A. Woodward / Roy A. Woodward / 1969										
176⁷⁄₈	38¹⁄₈	42	14²⁄₈	14²⁄₈	8²⁄₈	8³⁄₈	27⁶⁄₈	27⁶⁄₈	135	75
♦ Mexico / Bill Foster / Foster's Bighorn Rest. / PR 1967										

Score	Length of Horn		Circumference of Base		Circumference at Third Quarter		Greatest Spread	Tip-to-Tip Spread	All-Time Rank	State Rank
	R	L	R	L	R	L				

♦ *Locality / Hunter / Owner / Date Killed*

Score	L R	L	Base R	Base L	3Q R	3Q L	Greatest Spread	Tip-to-Tip	All-Time	State
176⅝	36⅜	38	15⁶⁄₈	15⁶⁄₈	8⁴⁄₈	8⅞	20	20	140	76

♦ *Baja Calif. / Fernando Garcia / Fernando Garcia / 1968*

176⅝	35⅞	36⁴⁄₈	15⁶⁄₈	15⁶⁄₈	9⅛	9⅛	19⅝	14⅝	140	76

♦ *Baja Calif. / Douglas J. Dollhopf / Douglas J. Dollhopf / 1983*

176⁴⁄₈	38⁶⁄₈	37²⁄₈	15²⁄₈	15⅛	8⅜	8⁴⁄₈	23²⁄₈	23²⁄₈	143	78

♦ *Lower Calif. / E.W. Funcke / U.S. Natl. Mus. / 1905*

176⁴⁄₈	38	38²⁄₈	13⁶⁄₈	14	10⅛	9⅞	21⁶⁄₈	21⁶⁄₈	143	78

♦ *Baja Calif. / Picked Up / Leland Brand / 1973*

176⅜	34⅝	34⁶⁄₈	16⁴⁄₈	16⅝	8⅝	9	19⅞	18⅛	147	80

♦ *Baja Calif. / William L. Baker, Jr. / William L. Baker, Jr. / 1974*

176⅜	35²⁄₈	37⅛	15⅜	16	9	9²⁄₈	21⅛	15⁶⁄₈	147	80

♦ *Baja Calif. / Joe E. Coleman / Joe E. Coleman / 1976*

176⅜	36⅝	36⁶⁄₈	15⅞	15⅞	8⁴⁄₈	8⁴⁄₈	19⅞	14⅞	147	80

♦ *Baja Calif. / Richard Wehling / Richard Wehling / 1978*

176⅜	37⅝	36	15⅜	15²⁄₈	8²⁄₈	8⅝	29⅛	29⅛	147	80

♦ *Baja Calif. / C.J. McElroy / C.J. McElroy / 1978*

176⅛	37²⁄₈	36⅝	15	15⅛	9²⁄₈	9²⁄₈	25⅜	25⅜	156	84

♦ *Baja Calif. / N.J. Segal, Jr. / N.J. Segal, Jr. / 1972*

176	38⅜	39⅞	15⅛	15⅛	7⁴⁄₈	8⅛	22⅛	20⅝	160	85

♦ *Sonora / Fritz Katz / Fritz Katz / 1941*

176	34⁶⁄₈	34²⁄₈	17⅛	17⅛	8⅜	8⅜	19⁶⁄₈	17	160	85

♦ *Sonora / Ollie O. Barney / Ollie O. Barney / 1968*

176	36	36	15⁴⁄₈	15⁴⁄₈	9	9⅛	18²⁄₈	18²⁄₈	160	85

♦ *Baja Calif. / Paul J. Inzanti / Paul J. Inzanti / 1982*

176	36²⁄₈	35⁶⁄₈	14⁶⁄₈	14⁶⁄₈	10²⁄₈	10	19⅛	16⁴⁄₈	160	85

♦ *Baja Calif. / Pedro S. Montano / Pedro S. Montano / 1986*

175⁶⁄₈	35⅜	35⅜	16⅛	16⅜	8⅝	8⅜	18⁶⁄₈	18⁶⁄₈	169	89

♦ *Baja Calif. / Jack Leeds / Jack Leeds / 1976*

175⁶⁄₈	35²⁄₈	35²⁄₈	16	16	8⅞	9⅛	20	17⁴⁄₈	169	89

♦ *Baja Calif. / William C. Cloyd / William C. Cloyd / 1984*

175⁴⁄₈	37⅜	36⅝	14⁴⁄₈	14⁶⁄₈	9⅜	9⁴⁄₈	21⁶⁄₈	19	174	91

♦ *Baja Calif. / Tony Oney / Tony Oney / 1968*

175⅜	37⅝	39⁴⁄₈	13⅞	14	9²⁄₈	9⁴⁄₈	19⅛	17⅞	180	92

♦ *Baja Calif. / Isidro Lopez-Del Bosque / Isidro Lopez-Del Bosque / 1984*

175²⁄₈	37⁴⁄₈	37⁴⁄₈	14²⁄₈	14⅜	9⅛	9⅛	21⅝	21⅜	184	93

♦ *Baja Calif. / K.C. Brown / K.C. Brown / 1966*

175⅛	36⁴⁄₈	37⅜	15²⁄₈	15⅛	8²⁄₈	8⅝	19⅜	19⅜	185	94

♦ *Mexico / Bill Foster / Foster's Bighorn Rest. / 1950*

Score	Length of Horn		Circumference of Base		Circumference at Third Quarter		Greatest Spread	Tip-to-Tip Spread	All-Time Rank	State Rank
	R	L	R	L	R	L				

◆ *Locality / Hunter / Owner / Date Killed*

Score	L-R	L-L	CB-R	CB-L	C3-R	C3-L	Greatest Spread	Tip-to-Tip Spread	All-Time Rank	State Rank
175 1/8	36 5/8	37 2/8	14 7/8	15	9 4/8	8 7/8	19 4/8	17 4/8	185	94

◆ *Sonora / Unknown / Paul W. Hughes / 1952*

| 175 1/8 | 36 6/8 | 35 5/8 | 15 2/8 | 15 2/8 | 8 7/8 | 8 7/8 | 31 1/8 | 18 6/8 | 185 | 94 |

◆ *Baja Calif. / C.J. Wimer / C.J. Wimer / 1977*

| 175 | 35 | 36 | 15 | 15 2/8 | 10 | 9 2/8 | 22 4/8 | 22 4/8 | 194 | 97 |

◆ *Sonora / Juan A. Saenz, Jr. / Juan A. Saenz, Jr. / 1969*

| 175 | 35 6/8 | 36 4/8 | 14 6/8 | 14 6/8 | 9 5/8 | 9 5/8 | 20 6/8 | 20 2/8 | 194 | 97 |

◆ *Baja Calif. / Craig Leerberg / Craig Leerberg / 1990*

| 174 5/8 | 34 7/8 | 34 6/8 | 15 7/8 | 15 5/8 | 9 1/8 | 9 2/8 | 18 7/8 | 16 4/8 | 206 | 99 |

◆ *Baja Calif. / Stanley S. Gray / Stanley S. Gray / 1972*

| 174 4/8 | 37 | 36 6/8 | 15 1/8 | 15 2/8 | 8 2/8 | 8 3/8 | 20 6/8 | 20 6/8 | 208 | 100 |

◆ *Baja Calif. / Jack Walters / Jack Walters / 1966*

| 174 2/8 | 37 | 36 | 15 7/8 | 15 7/8 | 7 7/8 | 7 5/8 | 20 4/8 | 18 3/8 | 213 | 101 |

◆ *Baja Calif. / Basil C. Bradbury / Basil C. Bradbury / 1968*

| 174 | 40 | 38 4/8 | 15 2/8 | 15 4/8 | 7 4/8 | 7 6/8 | 25 2/8 | 25 2/8 | 219 | 102 |

◆ *Lower Calif. / E.W. Funcke / Harvard Univ. Mus. / 1911*

| 174 | 37 2/8 | 36 2/8 | 14 4/8 | 14 4/8 | 9 2/8 | 9 | 19 4/8 | 18 | 219 | 102 |

◆ *Sonora / Frank C. Hibben / Frank C. Hibben / 1940*

| 174 | 36 3/8 | 35 1/8 | 15 2/8 | 15 1/8 | 9 1/8 | 8 6/8 | 23 | 23 | 219 | 102 |

◆ *Baja Calif. / James W. Owens / James W. Owens / 1983*

| 173 7/8 | 34 6/8 | 34 7/8 | 15 6/8 | 15 4/8 | 9 1/8 | 9 1/8 | 22 5/8 | 22 2/8 | 227 | 105 |

◆ *Baja Calif. / Erwin Dykstra / Erwin Dykstra / 1978*

| 173 6/8 | 35 7/8 | 36 1/8 | 16 2/8 | 16 2/8 | 8 4/8 | 8 | 20 5/8 | 20 5/8 | 231 | 106 |

◆ *Baja Calif. / Fritz A. Nachant / Fritz A. Nachant / 1969*

| 173 5/8 | 37 | 37 1/8 | 15 1/8 | 15 3/8 | 8 4/8 | 8 6/8 | 20 7/8 | 20 4/8 | 234 | 107 |

◆ *Baja Calif. / James H. Duke, Jr. / James H. Duke, Jr. / 1969*

| 173 5/8 | 35 4/8 | 34 5/8 | 15 1/8 | 15 1/8 | 9 | 8 7/8 | 22 2/8 | 22 2/8 | 234 | 107 |

◆ *Baja Calif. / John H. Batten / John H. Batten / 1975*

| 173 5/8 | 37 1/8 | 34 2/8 | 15 2/8 | 15 | 9 | 9 | 19 2/8 | 15 1/8 | 234 | 107 |

◆ *Sonora / Douglas G. Williams / Douglas G. Williams / 1983*

| 173 5/8 | 37 3/8 | 36 2/8 | 14 4/8 | 14 4/8 | 8 3/8 | 8 3/8 | 22 | 21 3/8 | 234 | 107 |

◆ *Baja Calif. / Patrick C. Allen / Patrick C. Allen / 1987*

| 173 5/8 | 35 4/8 | 36 3/8 | 15 6/8 | 15 4/8 | 8 2/8 | 8 7/8 | 21 | 20 4/8 | 234 | 107 |

◆ *Baja Calif. / John P. Reilly / John P. Reilly / 1989*

| 173 4/8 | 35 6/8 | 36 6/8 | 15 5/8 | 15 6/8 | 8 1/8 | 8 | 21 3/8 | 21 3/8 | 242 | 112 |

◆ *Muleje Baja / Victor M. Ruiza / Victor M. Ruiza / 1966*

| 173 4/8 | 34 6/8 | 33 6/8 | 16 2/8 | 16 2/8 | 8 2/8 | 9 | 19 7/8 | 15 | 242 | 112 |

◆ *Sonora / Walter Snoke / Walter Snoke / 1978*

Score	Length of Horn		Circumference of Base		Circumference at Third Quarter		Greatest Spread	Tip-to-Tip Spread	All-Time Rank	State Rank
	R	L	R	L	R	L				
$173\frac{4}{8}$	$33\frac{5}{8}$	$33\frac{7}{8}$	$16\frac{2}{8}$	$16\frac{3}{8}$	$8\frac{7}{8}$	9	$20\frac{3}{8}$	20	242	112
♦ *Sonora / Robert E. Manger / Robert E. Manger / 1993*										
$173\frac{3}{8}$	$36\frac{6}{8}$	$36\frac{1}{8}$	$14\frac{5}{8}$	$14\frac{5}{8}$	$8\frac{6}{8}$	$8\frac{5}{8}$	$21\frac{1}{8}$	$17\frac{7}{8}$	248	115
♦ *Baja Calif. / M. Alessio Robles / M. Alessio Robles / 1956*										
$173\frac{3}{8}$	$36\frac{2}{8}$	$36\frac{3}{8}$	$15\frac{5}{8}$	$15\frac{5}{8}$	$8\frac{1}{8}$	$8\frac{2}{8}$	$21\frac{3}{8}$	$20\frac{3}{8}$	248	115
♦ *Sonora / Gaston Cano / Gaston Cano / 1968*										
$173\frac{3}{8}$	$36\frac{6}{8}$	$37\frac{3}{8}$	$14\frac{6}{8}$	$14\frac{7}{8}$	$8\frac{6}{8}$	$8\frac{4}{8}$	$22\frac{3}{8}$	$22\frac{3}{8}$	248	115
♦ *Baja Calif. / Roy A. Schultz / Roy A. Schultz / 1971*										
$173\frac{3}{8}$	37	$37\frac{7}{8}$	15	$15\frac{1}{8}$	$8\frac{4}{8}$	$8\frac{6}{8}$	22	22	248	115
♦ *Baja Calif. / Dale R. Leonard / Dale R. Leonard / 1972*										
$173\frac{3}{8}$	$40\frac{5}{8}$	38	$13\frac{7}{8}$	$14\frac{6}{8}$	$8\frac{2}{8}$	$8\frac{1}{8}$	0	0	248	115
♦ *Baja Calif. / Tim C. Boyd / Tim C. Boyd / 1981*										
$173\frac{2}{8}$	$36\frac{3}{8}$	$36\frac{1}{8}$	$15\frac{5}{8}$	$15\frac{2}{8}$	$8\frac{4}{8}$	$8\frac{2}{8}$	$21\frac{4}{8}$	$19\frac{6}{8}$	255	120
♦ *Baja Calif. / Ernest Righetti / Ernest Righetti / 1974*										
$173\frac{2}{8}$	$35\frac{2}{8}$	$34\frac{6}{8}$	$15\frac{4}{8}$	$15\frac{3}{8}$	$8\frac{6}{8}$	$8\frac{6}{8}$	$21\frac{5}{8}$	$21\frac{5}{8}$	255	120
♦ *Baja Calif. / Marion H. Scott / Marion H. Scott / 1978*										
$173\frac{1}{8}$	$37\frac{4}{8}$	$40\frac{1}{8}$	14	$13\frac{1}{8}$	$7\frac{7}{8}$	$9\frac{7}{8}$	$21\frac{3}{8}$	18	259	122
♦ *Sonora Desert / Picked Up / Herb Klein / 1969*										
173	36	38	15	15	$8\frac{2}{8}$	$8\frac{4}{8}$	$24\frac{4}{8}$	$21\frac{4}{8}$	265	123
♦ *Lower Calif. / Henry H. Blagden / Henry H. Blagden / 1914*										
173	$35\frac{6}{8}$	$35\frac{6}{8}$	$15\frac{1}{8}$	$15\frac{4}{8}$	$8\frac{7}{8}$	$8\frac{3}{8}$	$20\frac{7}{8}$	$20\frac{1}{8}$	265	123
♦ *Baja Calif. / James H. Russell / James H. Russell / 1970*										
173	39	35	15	15	$8\frac{3}{8}$	$8\frac{3}{8}$	24	24	265	123
♦ *Baja Calif. / Charles Oyer / Charles Oyer / 1975*										
173	$34\frac{4}{8}$	35	$15\frac{5}{8}$	$15\frac{6}{8}$	$8\frac{2}{8}$	$8\frac{6}{8}$	$20\frac{4}{8}$	$17\frac{2}{8}$	265	123
♦ *Baja Calif. / P. Franklin Bays, Jr. / P. Franklin Bays, Jr. / 1976*										
173	$35\frac{1}{8}$	$35\frac{3}{8}$	16	$16\frac{1}{8}$	$8\frac{1}{8}$	$8\frac{1}{8}$	$20\frac{2}{8}$	$19\frac{4}{8}$	265	123
♦ *Baja Calif. / Tom W. Housh / Tom W. Housh / 1988*										
$172\frac{7}{8}$	34	$34\frac{1}{8}$	$15\frac{2}{8}$	$15\frac{2}{8}$	$9\frac{3}{8}$	$9\frac{3}{8}$	$20\frac{5}{8}$	$19\frac{4}{8}$	274	128
♦ *Baja Calif. / Mahlon T. White / Mahlon T. White / 1969*										
$172\frac{6}{8}$	$37\frac{1}{8}$	$38\frac{5}{8}$	$13\frac{4}{8}$	$13\frac{5}{8}$	9	9	$23\frac{7}{8}$	$23\frac{7}{8}$	277	129
♦ *Baja Calif. / Otis Chandler / Otis Chandler / 1966*										
$172\frac{6}{8}$	$37\frac{2}{8}$	$35\frac{4}{8}$	$15\frac{7}{8}$	$15\frac{5}{8}$	$8\frac{7}{8}$	$8\frac{4}{8}$	$21\frac{2}{8}$	$21\frac{2}{8}$	277	129
♦ *Baja Calif. / Graciano Guichard / Graciano Guichard / 1969*										
$172\frac{5}{8}$	$34\frac{1}{8}$	$36\frac{4}{8}$	$15\frac{3}{8}$	$15\frac{3}{8}$	$8\frac{1}{8}$	$9\frac{2}{8}$	$20\frac{6}{8}$	$18\frac{2}{8}$	284	131
♦ *Sonora / Lloyd O. Barrow / Lloyd O. Barrow / 1969*										
$172\frac{5}{8}$	$35\frac{7}{8}$	$35\frac{2}{8}$	$14\frac{4}{8}$	$14\frac{1}{8}$	$9\frac{6}{8}$	10	$19\frac{6}{8}$	$19\frac{6}{8}$	284	131
♦ *Baja Calif. / G. David Edwards / G. David Edwards / 1973*										

Score	Length of Horn		Circumference of Base		Circumference at Third Quarter		Greatest Spread	Tip-to-Tip Spread	All-Time Rank	State Rank
	R	L	R	L	R	L				
◆ Locality / Hunter / Owner / Date Killed										
$172\frac{5}{8}$	$37\frac{3}{8}$	36	$15\frac{5}{8}$	$15\frac{4}{8}$	8	8	$21\frac{3}{8}$	$21\frac{3}{8}$	284	131
◆ Baja Calif. / Daniel Smith / Daniel Smith / 1975										
$172\frac{4}{8}$	$33\frac{4}{8}$	$33\frac{4}{8}$	$15\frac{1}{8}$	$15\frac{3}{8}$	$9\frac{3}{8}$	$9\frac{2}{8}$	$21\frac{4}{8}$	21	289	134
◆ Baja Calif. / Hector Aguilar Parada / Hector Aguilar Parada / 1985										
$172\frac{3}{8}$	$36\frac{3}{8}$	$35\frac{2}{8}$	$14\frac{5}{8}$	$14\frac{3}{8}$	$9\frac{4}{8}$	$9\frac{4}{8}$	$20\frac{1}{8}$	$19\frac{1}{8}$	297	135
◆ Baja Calif. / H. Varley Grantham / H. Varley Grantham / 1980										
$172\frac{2}{8}$	38	$37\frac{4}{8}$	15	$15\frac{4}{8}$	$7\frac{3}{8}$	$7\frac{4}{8}$	$27\frac{1}{8}$	$27\frac{1}{8}$	302	136
◆ Baja Calif. / W.E. Humphrey / Wash. State Mus. / 1909										
$172\frac{2}{8}$	$36\frac{5}{8}$	$35\frac{3}{8}$	$15\frac{1}{8}$	$15\frac{1}{8}$	$8\frac{5}{8}$	$8\frac{4}{8}$	$20\frac{2}{8}$	$20\frac{2}{8}$	302	136
◆ Baja Calif. / Herb Klein / Herb Klein / 1966										
$172\frac{2}{8}$	$35\frac{2}{8}$	$35\frac{2}{8}$	$15\frac{6}{8}$	$15\frac{4}{8}$	9	$8\frac{6}{8}$	$19\frac{1}{8}$	$16\frac{6}{8}$	302	136
◆ Baja Calif. / Armando de la Parra / Armando de la Parra / 1966										
$172\frac{2}{8}$	35	$35\frac{6}{8}$	$15\frac{3}{8}$	$15\frac{3}{8}$	$8\frac{6}{8}$	$8\frac{6}{8}$	$22\frac{6}{8}$	$18\frac{5}{8}$	302	136
◆ Baja Calif. / Ralph A. Shoberg / Ralph A. Shoberg / 1986										
$172\frac{2}{8}$	$35\frac{3}{8}$	$34\frac{3}{8}$	$15\frac{3}{8}$	$15\frac{1}{8}$	9	$8\frac{7}{8}$	$22\frac{2}{8}$	$22\frac{2}{8}$	302	136
◆ Baja Calif. / Fred Fortier / Fred Fortier / 1989										
$172\frac{1}{8}$	$35\frac{5}{8}$	$35\frac{6}{8}$	$14\frac{7}{8}$	15	$9\frac{2}{8}$	$8\frac{6}{8}$	$20\frac{7}{8}$	$20\frac{4}{8}$	309	141
◆ Baja Calif. / Greg A. Strait / Greg A. Strait / 1989										
172	$34\frac{6}{8}$	35	15	15	$8\frac{7}{8}$	$8\frac{7}{8}$	$20\frac{6}{8}$	$20\frac{6}{8}$	312	142
◆ Baja Calif. / Robert O. Cromwell / Robert O. Cromwell / 1974										
172	$34\frac{5}{8}$	$34\frac{5}{8}$	$16\frac{4}{8}$	$16\frac{1}{8}$	$8\frac{3}{8}$	$8\frac{5}{8}$	$21\frac{3}{8}$	$20\frac{3}{8}$	312	142
◆ Baja Calif. / Bill Silveira / Bill Silveira / 1974										
$171\frac{7}{8}$	$33\frac{1}{8}$	$32\frac{6}{8}$	$16\frac{1}{8}$	$15\frac{7}{8}$	$8\frac{6}{8}$	$8\frac{6}{8}$	$19\frac{7}{8}$	$17\frac{7}{8}$	319	144
◆ Baja Calif. / Joan Leeds / Joan Leeds / 1976										
$171\frac{7}{8}$	$33\frac{7}{8}$	$35\frac{2}{8}$	$15\frac{2}{8}$	$15\frac{4}{8}$	$9\frac{7}{8}$	$9\frac{7}{8}$	$22\frac{1}{8}$	$21\frac{4}{8}$	319	144
◆ Baja Calif. / Don L. Corley / Don L. Corley / 1978										
$171\frac{6}{8}$	$36\frac{4}{8}$	36	$15\frac{6}{8}$	$15\frac{6}{8}$	$7\frac{6}{8}$	$8\frac{3}{8}$	21	$18\frac{2}{8}$	325	146
◆ Baja Calif. / Earl H. Harris / Earl H. Harris / 1968										
$171\frac{5}{8}$	$38\frac{6}{8}$	$38\frac{1}{8}$	$15\frac{5}{8}$	$15\frac{4}{8}$	7	7	23	23	328	147
◆ Sonora / Julio Estrada / Julio Estrada / 1931										
$171\frac{5}{8}$	$33\frac{3}{8}$	35	$15\frac{4}{8}$	$15\frac{5}{8}$	$8\frac{6}{8}$	$8\frac{7}{8}$	20	$18\frac{4}{8}$	328	147
◆ Baja Calif. / Dan L. Quen / Dan L. Quen / 1968										
$171\frac{5}{8}$	$35\frac{3}{8}$	$35\frac{4}{8}$	$15\frac{2}{8}$	$15\frac{4}{8}$	$8\frac{7}{8}$	$8\frac{7}{8}$	$21\frac{4}{8}$	20	328	147
◆ Baja Calif. / Roberto M. del Campo / Roberto M. del Campo / 1969										
$171\frac{5}{8}$	$35\frac{6}{8}$	$35\frac{3}{8}$	$14\frac{7}{8}$	15	$9\frac{1}{8}$	$8\frac{7}{8}$	$19\frac{3}{8}$	$19\frac{3}{8}$	328	147
◆ Baja Calif. / C.J. McElroy / C.J. McElroy / 1969										
$171\frac{5}{8}$	$36\frac{4}{8}$	$36\frac{3}{8}$	$14\frac{3}{8}$	$14\frac{5}{8}$	$8\frac{7}{8}$	$8\frac{5}{8}$	$21\frac{4}{8}$	$21\frac{4}{8}$	328	147
◆ Sonora / Picked Up / Bob C. Jones / 1970										

Score	Length of Horn		Circumference of Base		Circumference at Third Quarter		Greatest Spread	Tip-to-Tip Spread	All-Time Rank	State Rank
	R	L	R	L	R	L				

◆ *Locality / Hunter / Owner / Date Killed*

Score	R	L	R	L	R	L	Greatest Spread	Tip-to-Tip Spread	All-Time Rank	State Rank
171 5/8	36 7/8	34 2/8	16 2/8	16 2/8	7 6/8	7 5/8	20 5/8	19 7/8	328	147
171 2/8	34 4/8	35	15 4/8	15 4/8	8 2/8	8 4/8	24	24	347	153
171 2/8	35 2/8	35 6/8	15	14 7/8	9 3/8	9 1/8	21	17 3/8	347	153
171	36 4/8	35 4/8	14 4/8	14 4/8	8 7/8	8 6/8	22 1/8	22 1/8	359	155
170 7/8	35 5/8	35 4/8	16	16	8	8 1/8	22 5/8	22 5/8	365	156
170 7/8	38 1/8	37 4/8	14	14 2/8	9 3/8	8 2/8	21 5/8	21 5/8	365	156
170 7/8	32 7/8	36 4/8	14 4/8	14 4/8	9 7/8	9 5/8	19 2/8	17 6/8	365	156
170 7/8	36 5/8	37	15	15	8 2/8	8 2/8	21 4/8	21	365	156
170 6/8	35 2/8	34 6/8	15 6/8	15 6/8	7 7/8	7 7/8	20 5/8	20 5/8	373	160
170 6/8	36 1/8	36 7/8	16 3/8	16 3/8	7 2/8	7 3/8	21 4/8	21 4/8	373	160
170 5/8	34 2/8	35 3/8	15	15 2/8	8 4/8	8 2/8	19 3/8	17 6/8	383	162
170 4/8	36	34 6/8	15 7/8	16	7 5/8	7 6/8	18 7/8	18 7/8	387	163
170 4/8	32 6/8	34 2/8	16 2/8	16 2/8	8	8 3/8	24	24	387	163
170 4/8	34 7/8	35 7/8	15 1/8	15	8 7/8	8 3/8	18 7/8	19 4/8	387	163
170 3/8	32	34 3/8	16 2/8	16 2/8	7 6/8	8 7/8	19 2/8	19 2/8	394	166
170 3/8	32 5/8	32 4/8	16	16	9 1/8	9 3/8	20 2/8	15 5/8	394	166
170 2/8	35 2/8	36 4/8	15	15 2/8	8	8 4/8	20 1/8	20 1/8	401	168
170 2/8	37 2/8	35	15 4/8	15 4/8	8	7 5/8	21 3/8	20 4/8	401	168
170 2/8	34 4/8	34 2/8	15	15	9 5/8	9 4/8	18 1/8	18	401	168

◆ *Baja Calif. / Marshall J. Collins, Jr. / Marshall J. Collins, Jr. / 1994*

◆ *Baja Calif. / David L. Harshbarger / David L. Harshbarger / 1983*

◆ *Baja Calif. / L. Irvin Barnhart / L. Irvin Barnhart / 1992*

◆ *Baja Calif. / George S. Gayle III / George S. Gayle III / 1975*

◆ *Sonora Desert / Herb Klein / Herb Klein / 1962*

◆ *Baja Calif. / Michaux Nash, Jr. / Michaux Nash, Jr. / 1964*

◆ *Baja Calif. / John T. Blackwell / John T. Blackwell / 1966*

◆ *Baja Calif. / Daniel B. Moore / Daniel B. Moore / 1979*

◆ *Baja Calif. / Enrique Cervera Cicero / Enrique Cervera Cicero / 1968*

◆ *Baja Calif. / Gino Perfetto / Gino Perfetto / 1968*

◆ *Baja Calif. / Bill Lewis / Bill Lewis / 1969*

◆ *Baja Calif. / Don Turner / Don Turner / 1980*

◆ *Baja Calif. / Stephen P. Connell / Stephen P. Connell / 1986*

◆ *Baja Calif. / Edward J. Huxen / Edward J. Huxen / 1988*

◆ *Sonora / Frank C. Hibben / Frank C. Hibben / 1935*

◆ *Hermosillo / Michael Follett / Michael Follett / 1979*

◆ *Baja Calif. / Richard Buffington / Richard Buffington / 1966*

◆ *Baja Calif. / James W. Owens / James W. Owens / 1978*

◆ *Baja Calif. / A. Verne Crowell / A. Verne Crowell / 1979*

Score	Length of Horn		Circumference of Base		Circumference at Third Quarter		Greatest Spread	Tip-to-Tip Spread	All-Time Rank	State Rank
	R	L	R	L	R	L				
	♦ *Locality / Hunter / Owner / Date Killed*									
170 2/8	36	35 2/8	15 1/8	15 1/8	8 1/8	8 2/8	21 7/8	21 7/8	401	168
	♦ *Baja Calif. / David C. Southard, Jr. / David C. Southard, Jr. / 1982*									
170 2/8	34 5/8	33 7/8	14 6/8	14 6/8	9 2/8	9 1/8	21 2/8	16	401	168
	♦ *Sonora / Leonard E. Brewster / Leonard E. Brewster / 1982*									
170 1/8	34 6/8	34 7/8	14 6/8	15	8 6/8	9	19 1/8	18 2/8	411	173
	♦ *Baja Calif. / Fred T. LaBean / Fred T. LaBean / 1969*									
170 1/8	37 1/8	37	15 3/8	15 5/8	7 1/8	7 1/8	22 4/8	22 4/8	411	173
	♦ *Baja Calif. / Arthur E. Davis / Arthur E. Davis / 1972*									
170 1/8	36	36 3/8	15 3/8	15 3/8	7 7/8	7 7/8	19 2/8	16 5/8	411	173
	♦ *Baja Calif. / Edward V. Wilson / Edward V. Wilson / 1974*									
170 1/8	35 5/8	35 4/8	14 2/8	14 2/8	8 7/8	9 1/8	20 1/8	19 5/8	411	173
	♦ *Baja Calif. / Alfred Barone / Alfred Barone / 1984*									
170	37 4/8	33 4/8	15 2/8	15 1/8	7 7/8	7 6/8	22 2/8	21 7/8	417	177
	♦ *Baja Calif. / Warren K. Parker / Warren K. Parker / 1970*									
170	35 2/8	35 2/8	14 5/8	14 6/8	8 5/8	8 6/8	19 5/8	19 5/8	417	177
	♦ *Baja Calif. / Rudolf Sand / Rudolf Sand / 1973*									
169 7/8	35 3/8	35 2/8	14 6/8	14 6/8	8 3/8	8 4/8	20 4/8	19 5/8	425	179
	♦ *Baja Calif. / Harold Hallick / Harold Hallick / 1971*									
169 6/8	35 2/8	35 6/8	14 1/8	14	9 3/8	9 5/8	21 2/8	21 2/8	426	180
	♦ *Baja Calif. / William M. Wheless III / William M. Wheless III / 1974*									
169 6/8	36 4/8	36 6/8	15 3/8	15	7 4/8	7 3/8	21	20 1/8	426	180
	♦ *Baja Calif. / Richard L. Larson / Richard L. Larson / 1985*									
169 5/8	35 1/8	36 2/8	15	15	8	8 1/8	20	18 7/8	431	182
	♦ *Baja Calif. / Leonard W. Gilman / Leonard W. Gilman / 1969*									
169 5/8	35 3/8	34	15 4/8	15 4/8	8 2/8	8 2/8	20 4/8	20 4/8	431	182
	♦ *San Borjas Mts. / John T. Blackwell / John T. Blackwell / 1970*									
169 5/8	35 5/8	34	15	15	9	8 7/8	18 2/8	16 3/8	431	182
	♦ *Baja Calif. / Gunter M. Paefgen / Gunter M. Paefgen / 1975*									
169 5/8	33 6/8	34 5/8	15 7/8	16	7 6/8	8 3/8	21 6/8	21 6/8	431	182
	♦ *Baja Calif. / Emerson Hall / Emerson Hall / 1978*									
169 4/8	33	36	15 4/8	15 4/8	8 4/8	8 4/8	25 4/8	25 4/8	438	186
	♦ *Lower Calif. / Henry H. Blagden / Henry H. Blagden / 1914*									
169 4/8	35 6/8	35 6/8	14 5/8	14 4/8	8 4/8	8 5/8	18	18	438	186
	♦ *Baja Calif. / Lowell C. Hansen II / Lowell C. Hansen II / 1974*									
169 4/8	39	37 2/8	15 2/8	15	6 6/8	6 7/8	19 4/8	19 4/8	438	186
	♦ *Baja Calif. / James A. Bush, Jr. / James A. Bush, Jr. / 1981*									
169 4/8	35	35 2/8	15 1/8	15 1/8	8 1/8	8 5/8	22 5/8	21 5/8	438	186
	♦ *Baja Calif. / Steven D. Bacon / Steven D. Bacon / 1990*									

Score	Length of Horn		Circumference of Base		Circumference at Third Quarter		Greatest Spread	Tip-to-Tip Spread	All-Time Rank	State Rank
	R	L	R	L	R	L				
	♦ *Locality / Hunter / Owner / Date Killed*									
$169\frac{3}{8}$	$35\frac{3}{8}$	35	$15\frac{7}{8}$	16	$7\frac{2}{8}$	$7\frac{2}{8}$	$20\frac{4}{8}$	$20\frac{4}{8}$	447	190
	♦ *Sonora / Unknown / Unknown / PR 1939*									
$169\frac{2}{8}$	$33\frac{7}{8}$	$34\frac{7}{8}$	$15\frac{2}{8}$	$15\frac{2}{8}$	$8\frac{4}{8}$	$9\frac{1}{8}$	$18\frac{3}{8}$	$18\frac{3}{8}$	449	191
	♦ *Baja Calif. / Joe Osterbauer / Joe Osterbauer / 1977*									
$169\frac{2}{8}$	$35\frac{3}{8}$	$36\frac{1}{8}$	$15\frac{5}{8}$	$15\frac{4}{8}$	$7\frac{5}{8}$	$7\frac{5}{8}$	$20\frac{4}{8}$	$18\frac{4}{8}$	449	191
	♦ *Baja Calif. / Steve F. Reiter / Steve F. Reiter / 1984*									
$169\frac{1}{8}$	$33\frac{4}{8}$	$33\frac{7}{8}$	$14\frac{4}{8}$	$14\frac{4}{8}$	10	10	$20\frac{6}{8}$	$15\frac{5}{8}$	455	193
	♦ *Lower Calif. / Picked Up / William W. Renfrew / 1953*									
$169\frac{1}{8}$	$35\frac{6}{8}$	$38\frac{7}{8}$	15	15	$7\frac{1}{8}$	$7\frac{3}{8}$	$25\frac{4}{8}$	$25\frac{4}{8}$	455	193
	♦ *Baja Calif. / James W. Owens / James W. Owens / 1977*									
169	$36\frac{1}{8}$	$36\frac{3}{8}$	$15\frac{6}{8}$	$15\frac{4}{8}$	$6\frac{4}{8}$	$6\frac{5}{8}$	$22\frac{3}{8}$	$22\frac{2}{8}$	460	195
	♦ *Baja Calif. / W.E. Humphrey / Wash. State Mus. / 1909*									
169	$34\frac{3}{8}$	$35\frac{3}{8}$	$15\frac{3}{8}$	$15\frac{1}{8}$	$7\frac{7}{8}$	8	$14\frac{2}{8}$	21	460	195
	♦ *Baja Calif. / Gordon L. Shuster / Gordon L. Shuster / 1980*									
169	$35\frac{2}{8}$	$35\frac{2}{8}$	$13\frac{6}{8}$	$13\frac{6}{8}$	10	10	$20\frac{5}{8}$	$18\frac{2}{8}$	460	195
	♦ *Baja Calif. / Arthur L. Wehner / Arthur L. Wehner / 1980*									
$168\frac{7}{8}$	35	$33\frac{7}{8}$	16	16	$8\frac{1}{8}$	$7\frac{7}{8}$	$21\frac{4}{8}$	$21\frac{4}{8}$	466	198
	♦ *Baja Calif. / Larry R. Price / Larry R. Price / 1973*									
$168\frac{7}{8}$	$36\frac{2}{8}$	$36\frac{7}{8}$	$14\frac{6}{8}$	$14\frac{7}{8}$	$7\frac{5}{8}$	$7\frac{6}{8}$	$20\frac{1}{8}$	$18\frac{4}{8}$	466	198
	♦ *Baja Calif. / Gary Davis / Gary Davis / 1975*									
$168\frac{6}{8}$	$35\frac{2}{8}$	$33\frac{4}{8}$	14	$14\frac{2}{8}$	$10\frac{1}{8}$	$9\frac{6}{8}$	$19\frac{7}{8}$	$16\frac{4}{8}$	471	200
	♦ *Sonora / Jack O'Connor / Jack O'Connor / 1946*									
$168\frac{6}{8}$	$34\frac{6}{8}$	$35\frac{2}{8}$	$15\frac{2}{8}$	$15\frac{2}{8}$	$7\frac{6}{8}$	$8\frac{2}{8}$	19	$16\frac{3}{8}$	471	200
	♦ *Sierra De Jaraguay / Jack A. Shane, Sr. / Jack A. Shane, Sr. / 1972*									
$168\frac{5}{8}$	$35\frac{5}{8}$	$34\frac{6}{8}$	$14\frac{3}{8}$	$14\frac{3}{8}$	$8\frac{7}{8}$	9	$18\frac{3}{8}$	$18\frac{2}{8}$	476	202
	♦ *Sonora / Lionel Heinrich / Lionel Heinrich / 1982*									
$168\frac{4}{8}$	$34\frac{4}{8}$	$33\frac{6}{8}$	$15\frac{4}{8}$	$15\frac{4}{8}$	$8\frac{4}{8}$	$8\frac{7}{8}$	$18\frac{5}{8}$	$17\frac{4}{8}$	481	203
	♦ *Baja Calif. / Russell C. Cutter / Russell C. Cutter / 1964*									
$168\frac{4}{8}$	$35\frac{5}{8}$	$36\frac{3}{8}$	$13\frac{6}{8}$	$13\frac{5}{8}$	9	$9\frac{4}{8}$	$18\frac{5}{8}$	$18\frac{5}{8}$	481	203
	♦ *Baja Calif. / W.T. Yoshimoto / W.T. Yoshimoto / 1978*									
$168\frac{4}{8}$	$37\frac{2}{8}$	37	$15\frac{2}{8}$	$15\frac{1}{8}$	$7\frac{2}{8}$	$7\frac{1}{8}$	$23\frac{4}{8}$	$23\frac{4}{8}$	481	203
	♦ *Baja Calif. / Dan L. Duncan / Dan L. Duncan / 1979*									
$168\frac{4}{8}$	36	$35\frac{4}{8}$	$14\frac{2}{8}$	$14\frac{5}{8}$	$8\frac{2}{8}$	$7\frac{7}{8}$	$18\frac{7}{8}$	$18\frac{7}{8}$	481	203
	♦ *Baja Calif. / John Whitcombe / John Whitcombe / 1983*									
$168\frac{2}{8}$	$34\frac{4}{8}$	$35\frac{2}{8}$	$14\frac{7}{8}$	$14\frac{6}{8}$	8	$8\frac{4}{8}$	$21\frac{6}{8}$	$21\frac{6}{8}$	494	207
	♦ *Baja Calif. / George H. Glass / George H. Glass / 1964*									
$168\frac{2}{8}$	$34\frac{7}{8}$	$34\frac{1}{8}$	$15\frac{5}{8}$	$15\frac{6}{8}$	$7\frac{4}{8}$	$7\frac{5}{8}$	$20\frac{7}{8}$	14	494	207
	♦ *Sonora / Sergio Rios Aguilera / Sergio Rios Aguilera / 1968*									

Score	Length of Horn		Circumference of Base		Circumference at Third Quarter		Greatest Spread	Tip-to-Tip Spread	All-Time Rank	State Rank
	R	L	R	L	R	L				
			◆ *Locality / Hunter / Owner / Date Killed*							
168 2/8	35 1/8	33 1/8	15 1/8	15 1/8	8 4/8	8 3/8	19 6/8	19	494	207
			◆ *Baja Calif. / Roger R. Card / Roger R. Card / 1985*							
168 1/8	34 3/8	37 6/8	15	15	8	7 7/8	24 4/8	24 4/8	505	210
			◆ *Lower Calif. / G.L. Harrison / Acad. Nat. Sci., Phil. / 1903*							
168 1/8	34 4/8	34 5/8	14 1/8	14	8 6/8	9 2/8	20 7/8	18 3/8	505	210
			◆ *Baja Calif. / James C. Nystrom / James C. Nystrom / 1969*							
168 1/8	34 6/8	35 3/8	14 6/8	14 4/8	8 5/8	8 7/8	22 2/8	22 2/8	505	210
			◆ *Baja Calif. / C.R. Palmer / C.R. Palmer / 1979*							
168 1/8	32 2/8	34 3/8	15 2/8	15 2/8	8 5/8	9	20	15 4/8	505	210
			◆ *Sonora / David V. Collis / David V. Collis / 1985*							
168	34 4/8	35 6/8	15 1/8	15 1/8	8	8 3/8	21 1/8	21 1/8	511	214
			◆ *Baja Calif. / Lee Frudden / Lee Frudden / 1972*							
168	35 4/8	35	15 4/8	15 4/8	7 7/8	7 7/8	20	19 4/8	511	214
			◆ *Baja Calif. / Carl E. Jacobson / Carl E. Jacobson / 1985*							
168	35 2/8	35 2/8	14 1/8	14 2/8	8 7/8	8 7/8	19 6/8	17 3/8	511	214
			◆ *Baja Calif. / Mclean Bowman / Mclean Bowman / 1989*							
186 6/8	42 3/8	38 7/8	16 2/8	16 1/8	8 5/8	8 4/8	24 2/8	23 2/8	*	*
			◆ *Baja Calif. / James N. McHolme / James N. McHolme / 1981*							
180 4/8	36 4/8	36 4/8	15 7/8	15 7/8	9 4/8	9 6/8	19 1/8	18 3/8	*	*
			◆ *Baja Calif. / John B. Brelsford / John B. Brelsford / 1993*							

Photograph Courtesy of Miles R. Brown

Miles R. Brown hunted desert sheep for 10 days in 1989 in the Tule Mountains of Yuma County, Arizona, before he settled the cross hairs of his .264 Winchester Magnum on this ram that scores 171-5/8 points.

Photograph by Alex Rota

ALASKA STATE RECORD
WORLD'S RECORD
DALL'S SHEEP
SCORE: 189⅝
Locality: Wrangell Mountains Date: 1961
Hunter: Harry L. Swank, Jr.

ALASKA

DALL'S SHEEP

Score	Length of Horn		Circumference of Base		Circumference at Third Quarter		Greatest Spread	Tip-to-Tip Spread	All-Time Rank	State Rank
	R	L	R	L	R	L				
◆ Locality / Hunter / Owner / Date Killed										
189⁶⁄₈	48⁵⁄₈	47⁷⁄₈	14⁵⁄₈	14⁶⁄₈	6⁵⁄₈	6⁷⁄₈	34³⁄₈	34³⁄₈	1	1
◆ Wrangell Mts. / Harry L. Swank, Jr. / Harry L. Swank, Jr. / 1961										
185⁶⁄₈	49⁴⁄₈	44²⁄₈	14	13⁷⁄₈	6⁶⁄₈	7³⁄₈	24³⁄₈	24³⁄₈	2	2
◆ Chugach Mts. / Frank Cook / Frank Cook / 1956										
185⁴⁄₈	43⁶⁄₈	40⁴⁄₈	14⁷⁄₈	14⁷⁄₈	9⁴⁄₈	9³⁄₈	20⁷⁄₈	20⁷⁄₈	3	3
◆ Chugach Mts. / Jack W. Lentfer / Jack W. Lentfer / 1964										
184⁴⁄₈	43⁶⁄₈	46	14¹⁄₈	14³⁄₈	9	7⁶⁄₈	21⁶⁄₈	21⁶⁄₈	4	4
◆ Wrangell Mts. / B.L. Burkholder / B.L. Burkholder / 1958										
184	44⁶⁄₈	44⁴⁄₈	14²⁄₈	14²⁄₈	7¹⁄₈	7²⁄₈	24⁵⁄₈	24⁵⁄₈	5	5
◆ Chugach Mts. / Thomas C. Sheets / Thomas C. Sheets / 1962										
183⁷⁄₈	46⁵⁄₈	47⁴⁄₈	13⁶⁄₈	13⁶⁄₈	6⁴⁄₈	6⁴⁄₈	31	31	6	6
◆ Wrangell Mts. / Tony Oney / Tony Oney / 1963										
183⁶⁄₈	48	47⁴⁄₈	14	13⁶⁄₈	6²⁄₈	6⁵⁄₈	33⁴⁄₈	33⁴⁄₈	7	7
◆ Alaska Range / Jonathan T. Summar, Jr. / Jonathan T. Summar, Jr. / 1965										
183	42³⁄₈	39³⁄₈	14⁶⁄₈	14⁶⁄₈	9⁵⁄₈	9⁵⁄₈	22⁵⁄₈	19⁴⁄₈	9	8
◆ Wrangell Mts. / Gene M. Effler / Gene M. Effler / 1959										
182	38⁶⁄₈	39	15²⁄₈	15²⁄₈	10¹⁄₈	10¹⁄₈	0	0	11	9
◆ Kenai Pen. / Picked Up / C.E. Lyons / PR 1969										
181⁶⁄₈	44⁴⁄₈	44⁴⁄₈	14⁵⁄₈	14⁵⁄₈	6⁴⁄₈	6⁶⁄₈	27²⁄₈	27²⁄₈	12	10
◆ Knik River / Matthew Lahti / Unknown / 1930										
181⁵⁄₈	46²⁄₈	46⁵⁄₈	14	14¹⁄₈	6	6²⁄₈	32⁶⁄₈	32⁶⁄₈	14	11
◆ McCarthy / Bud Nelson / Bud Nelson / 1953										
181³⁄₈	42⁶⁄₈	42⁵⁄₈	15²⁄₈	15¹⁄₈	7⁴⁄₈	7⁶⁄₈	24²⁄₈	24²⁄₈	15	12
◆ Wrangell Mts. / James K. Harrower / James K. Harrower / 1961										
181³⁄₈	46⁶⁄₈	45⁵⁄₈	13	13	6⁵⁄₈	6⁵⁄₈	28³⁄₈	28³⁄₈	15	12
◆ Hartman River / Carl E. Jacobsen / Carl E. Jacobsen / 1989										
180⁷⁄₈	44²⁄₈	44¹⁄₈	14⁷⁄₈	14⁵⁄₈	6⁴⁄₈	6⁴⁄₈	30¹⁄₈	30¹⁄₈	18	14
◆ Wrangell Mts. / Robert W. Engstrom / Robert W. Engstrom / 1973										
180³⁄₈	45⁷⁄₈	46²⁄₈	13⁴⁄₈	13⁵⁄₈	6⁶⁄₈	6⁵⁄₈	29¹⁄₈	29¹⁄₈	21	15
◆ Johnson River / P.A. Johnson & J.N. Brennan / P.A. Johnson & J.N. Brennan / 1950										
180¹⁄₈	39²⁄₈	46¹⁄₈	14⁶⁄₈	15²⁄₈	7²⁄₈	7	27	27	22	16
◆ Wrangell Mts. / Harry H. Wilson / Harry H. Wilson / 1961										
180	39²⁄₈	40⁶⁄₈	14⁶⁄₈	14⁴⁄₈	8²⁄₈	8¹⁄₈	23	21	23	17
◆ Grand View / Nellie Neal / Nellie Neal / 1917										
179⁷⁄₈	45⁶⁄₈	45⁵⁄₈	13	13	6⁴⁄₈	7⁴⁄₈	27²⁄₈	27²⁄₈	24	18
◆ Kenai Pen. / A.B. Learned / A.B. Learned / 1936										

ALASKA DALL'S SHEEP (continued)

Score	Length of Horn R	L	Circumference of Base R	L	Circumference at Third Quarter R	L	Greatest Spread	Tip-to-Tip Spread	All-Time Rank	State Rank
♦ Locality / Hunter / Owner / Date Killed										
179 $^6/_8$	41 $^5/_8$	41 $^5/_8$	14 $^6/_8$	14 $^6/_8$	7	7	28 $^3/_8$	28 $^3/_8$	25	19
♦ Chugach Mts. / J.H. Esslinger / J.H. Esslinger / 1959										
179 $^1/_8$	44 $^5/_8$	44 $^2/_8$	14 $^2/_8$	14 $^2/_8$	6 $^5/_8$	6 $^4/_8$	27	27	27	20
♦ Chugach Mts. / Boyd Howard / Boyd Howard / 1957										
178 $^7/_8$	40 $^7/_8$	40 $^4/_8$	14 $^6/_8$	14 $^7/_8$	7 $^5/_8$	7 $^3/_8$	24	23 $^7/_8$	28	21
♦ Chugach Mts. / Daniel A. Story / Daniel A. Story / 1954										
178 $^6/_8$	42 $^4/_8$	42 $^2/_8$	13 $^6/_8$	13 $^2/_8$	8 $^5/_8$	8 $^2/_8$	25 $^5/_8$	25 $^5/_8$	29	22
♦ Knik River / V.A. Morgan / V.A. Morgan / 1934										
178 $^3/_8$	43 $^2/_8$	42 $^5/_8$	13 $^7/_8$	14	6 $^7/_8$	6 $^6/_8$	27 $^1/_8$	27 $^1/_8$	31	23
♦ Chugach Mts. / Sam Jaksick, Jr. / Sam Jaksick, Jr. / 1966										
178 $^2/_8$	45 $^4/_8$	42 $^2/_8$	14 $^6/_8$	14 $^6/_8$	6 $^3/_8$	6	31 $^5/_8$	31 $^5/_8$	33	24
♦ Wrangell Mts. / Wilbur Ternyik / Wilbur Ternyik / 1958										
178 $^1/_8$	45 $^7/_8$	43 $^6/_8$	13 $^4/_8$	13 $^5/_8$	7 $^1/_8$	6 $^2/_8$	23 $^6/_8$	23 $^6/_8$	35	25
♦ Wrangell Mts. / Unknown / Jeff Sievers / PR 1950										
178 $^1/_8$	45 $^7/_8$	44	14	13 $^7/_8$	7 $^4/_8$	7 $^3/_8$	28	28	35	25
♦ Chugach Mts. / J.S. Lichtenfels / J.S. Lichtenfels / 1956										
178	43 $^4/_8$	43	15	15	6 $^4/_8$	6 $^4/_8$	30 $^2/_8$	30 $^2/_8$	37	27
♦ Chitina River / Frank C. Hibben / Frank C. Hibben / 1963										
177 $^7/_8$	44 $^5/_8$	45	14 $^3/_8$	14	6 $^3/_8$	6 $^2/_8$	28 $^3/_8$	28 $^3/_8$	38	28
♦ Chugach Mts. / William R. Champlain / William R. Champlain / 1965										
177 $^6/_8$	43 $^3/_8$	44 $^3/_8$	14 $^4/_8$	14 $^2/_8$	6 $^2/_8$	6 $^1/_8$	27 $^4/_8$	27 $^4/_8$	39	29
♦ Chugach Mts. / Chris Klineburger / Chris Klineburger / 1957										
177 $^5/_8$	41 $^7/_8$	43 $^2/_8$	13 $^2/_8$	13 $^2/_8$	8 $^7/_8$	9 $^1/_8$	22	22	40	30
♦ Rainy Pass / F. Edmond Blanc / F. Edmond Blanc / 1937										
177 $^5/_8$	44	43 $^5/_8$	14 $^4/_8$	14 $^4/_8$	6	6	27 $^6/_8$	27 $^6/_8$	40	30
♦ Kenai Pen. / John Swiss / John Swiss / 1959										
177 $^5/_8$	44 $^1/_8$	44 $^4/_8$	14 $^1/_8$	14	6 $^4/_8$	6 $^6/_8$	26 $^5/_8$	26 $^5/_8$	40	30
♦ Wrangell Mts. / Elgin T. Gates / Elgin T. Gates / 1961										
177 $^4/_8$	44	43 $^6/_8$	14 $^3/_8$	14 $^2/_8$	6 $^2/_8$	6 $^2/_8$	28 $^7/_8$	28 $^7/_8$	43	33
♦ Wrangell Mts. / Rita Oney / Rita Oney / 1963										
177 $^4/_8$	45 $^4/_8$	44 $^4/_8$	13 $^6/_8$	14	6 $^1/_8$	6	28 $^5/_8$	28 $^3/_8$	43	33
♦ Chugach Mts. / Robert Kraai / Robert Kraai / 1977										
177 $^2/_8$	42 $^4/_8$	43 $^4/_8$	13 $^6/_8$	13 $^6/_8$	7	7	23 $^6/_8$	23 $^6/_8$	46	35
♦ Kenai Pen. / Luke Elwell / Luke Elwell / 1936										
177 $^2/_8$	38	40 $^6/_8$	15 $^2/_8$	15 $^2/_8$	7 $^3/_8$	7 $^2/_8$	22 $^7/_8$	20 $^1/_8$	46	35
♦ Chugach Mts. / Harry H. Wilson / Harry H. Wilson / 1960										
177 $^1/_8$	43 $^4/_8$	43 $^3/_8$	14	13 $^6/_8$	6 $^6/_8$	6 $^6/_8$	27 $^2/_8$	27 $^2/_8$	48	37
♦ Kenai Pen. / C.R. Cross, Jr. / Harvard Club of Boston / 1907										

ALASKA DALL'S SHEEP *(continued)*

Score	Length of Horn R	Length of Horn L	Circumference of Base R	Circumference of Base L	Circumference at Third Quarter R	Circumference at Third Quarter L	Greatest Spread	Tip-to-Tip Spread	All-Time Rank	State Rank
♦ *Locality / Hunter / Owner / Date Killed*										
177 1/8	43 7/8	44	13	13 1/8	7	7 1/8	22 1/8	22 1/8	48	37
♦ *Ship Creek / Oliver Tovsen / Oliver Tovsen / 1940*										
177 1/8	45 3/8	44 6/8	14	14	6	5 7/8	30 7/8	30 7/8	48	37
♦ *Chugach Mts. / Jim Milito / Jim Milito / 1971*										
177	44 6/8	44 6/8	13 7/8	13 6/8	6	6	27 1/8	27 1/8	52	40
♦ *Chugach Mts. / Paul E. Huling / Paul E. Huling / 1959*										
176 7/8	41 3/8	42	14 7/8	14 7/8	6 4/8	6 6/8	28	28	53	41
♦ *Wrangell Mts. / Vic S. Sears / Vic S. Sears / 1960*										
176 6/8	43	43	15	15	6 2/8	5 7/8	23 3/8	23 3/8	55	42
♦ *Wrangell Mts. / Ed Bilderback / Ed Bilderback / 1959*										
176 6/8	43 1/8	43 1/8	14 3/8	14 6/8	6 4/8	6 4/8	27	27	55	42
♦ *Chugach Mts. / Charles H. Rohrer / Charles H. Rohrer / 1982*										
176 4/8	46 2/8	40 6/8	13 7/8	13 6/8	6 4/8	6 4/8	22 7/8	22 7/8	58	44
♦ *Knik River / Philip English / Philip English / 1954*										
176 3/8	41 2/8	41 7/8	14	14	8	7 6/8	24 2/8	24 2/8	61	45
♦ *Chugach Mts. / Lloyd Ronning / Lloyd Ronning / 1953*										
176 2/8	41 6/8	42	14 4/8	14 3/8	7	7 1/8	27 5/8	27 5/8	62	46
♦ *Chugach Mts. / Donald P. Chase / Donald P. Chase / 1978*										
176	40 4/8	42	14 2/8	14 2/8	7	7	23	22	65	47
♦ *Knik River / John S. Lahti / John S. Lahti / 1930*										
176	42	43	14 3/8	14 3/8	6 4/8	6 4/8	22 6/8	22 6/8	65	47
♦ *Alaska / Picked Up / T.H. Rowe / PR 1960*										
176	42	41 6/8	14 7/8	15	6 5/8	6 4/8	28 7/8	28 7/8	65	47
♦ *Chugach Mts. / William D. Backman, Jr. / William D. Backman, Jr. / 1960*										
176	39	38 4/8	14 7/8	15	9 6/8	7 6/8	26	26	65	47
♦ *Tonsina Lake / Horace E. Groff / Horace E. Groff / 1960*										
176	46 4/8	45 4/8	13 2/8	13 2/8	6	6	31 4/8	31 4/8	65	47
♦ *Wrangell Mts. / Harold Meeker / Harold Meeker / 1965*										
176	41 2/8	41 4/8	15	15	6	6	25	25	65	47
♦ *Wrangell Mts. / Paul D. Weingart / Paul D. Weingart / 1974*										
175 6/8	43 7/8	43 7/8	13 5/8	13 5/8	6 4/8	6 4/8	30 3/8	30 3/8	71	53
♦ *Wrangell Mts. / Ben C. Boynton / Ben C. Boynton / 1971*										
175 5/8	41 4/8	42 3/8	13 4/8	13 4/8	7 4/8	7 5/8	24	24	74	54
♦ *Chugach Mts. / Harry Anderson / Harry Anderson / 1955*										
175 4/8	42	42	14	14	7	6 7/8	28 6/8	28 6/8	75	55
♦ *Wrangell Mts. / Swen Honkola / Swen Honkola / 1958*										
175 3/8	37 6/8	40 3/8	14 4/8	14 4/8	8 2/8	8 3/8	23 5/8	23 5/8	76	56
♦ *Wrangell Mts. / Burt Ahlstrom / Burt Ahlstrom / 1959*										

Score	Length of Horn		Circumference of Base		Circumference at Third Quarter		Greatest Spread	Tip-to-Tip Spread	All-Time Rank	State Rank
	R	L	R	L	R	L				
♦ *Locality / Hunter / Owner / Date Killed*										
175 2/8	40 4/8	46 6/8	14 6/8	14 4/8	6 2/8	6 3/8	26 4/8	26 4/8	77	57
♦ *Chitina River / Henry Boyden / Am. Mus. Nat. Hist. / 1936*										
175 2/8	41 4/8	42	14 3/8	14 5/8	6 4/8	6 6/8	26 2/8	26 2/8	77	57
♦ *Wrangell Mts. / Grant Smith / Grant Smith / 1963*										
175 2/8	41 7/8	43 3/8	14 2/8	14 4/8	6 7/8	6 6/8	30 3/8	30 3/8	77	57
♦ *Chugach Mts. / Miles Hajny / Miles Hajny / 1969*										
175 1/8	42 3/8	44 2/8	14 2/8	14	6 4/8	6 4/8	29	29	80	60
♦ *Talkeetna Mts. / Dale Caldwell / Dale Caldwell / 1957*										
175 1/8	42 1/8	37	14 3/8	14 2/8	8	8 2/8	20 2/8	19 2/8	80	60
♦ *Wrangell Mts. / Herman F. Wyman / Herman F. Wyman / 1964*										
175 1/8	41	40 7/8	14 3/8	14 3/8	6 7/8	6 7/8	23	23	80	60
♦ *Chugach Mts. / Edward A. Champlain / Edward A. Champlain / 1965*										
175 1/8	41 3/8	39	15	15	7 4/8	6 4/8	26 6/8	26	80	60
♦ *Wrangell Mts. / John M. Griffith, Jr. / John M. Griffith, Jr. / 1976*										
175	42 4/8	42 2/8	14 2/8	14 2/8	6 4/8	6 3/8	23 2/8	23 2/8	84	64
♦ *Kenai Pen. / Russel Gainer / Russel Gainer / 1959*										
175	42 7/8	42 7/8	13 7/8	14	6 6/8	6 4/8	23 4/8	23 4/8	84	64
♦ *Chugach Mts. / Arthur R. Dubs / Arthur R. Dubs / 1961*										
174 7/8	41 3/8	40 4/8	13 7/8	13 7/8	8 2/8	8	19 7/8	19 7/8	86	66
♦ *Chugach Mts. / Leroy Holen / Leroy Holen / 1957*										
174 7/8	43 1/8	43	13 5/8	13 7/8	6 6/8	6 6/8	29	29	86	66
♦ *Wrangell Mts. / R.W. Ulman / R.W. Ulman / 1962*										
174 7/8	44 6/8	42 1/8	13 6/8	13 4/8	7	6 5/8	29	29	86	66
♦ *Chitina River / Ray B. Nienhaus / Ray B. Nienhaus / 1966*										
174 6/8	45 2/8	45	13 1/8	13 1/8	9 4/8	6 2/8	28 5/8	28 5/8	91	69
♦ *Wrangell Mts. / Warren W. Wilbur / Warren W. Wilbur / 1952*										
174 6/8	40 5/8	40 3/8	14 4/8	14 3/8	6 6/8	6 7/8	26 3/8	26 3/8	91	69
♦ *Wrangell Mts. / Peter W. Bading / Peter W. Bading / 1963*										
174 6/8	42	42 4/8	14	13 6/8	6 7/8	7	23 7/8	24 1/8	91	69
♦ *Chugach Mts. / Bill Silveira / Bill Silveira / 1969*										
174 6/8	40 1/8	40 7/8	15 3/8	15 4/8	6 4/8	6 4/8	20 4/8	20 4/8	91	69
♦ *Mt. Wrangell / Tod Reichert / Tod Reichert / 1976*										
174 6/8	41 2/8	41 2/8	14	14	6 7/8	7 3/8	27 3/8	27 2/8	91	69
♦ *Wrangell Mts. / Don L. Corley / Don L. Corley / 1978*										
174 5/8	40 4/8	43 5/8	14 2/8	14 2/8	6 4/8	6 4/8	22 3/8	22 3/8	99	74
♦ *Kenai Mts. / C.A. Brauch / C.A. Brauch / 1959*										
174 4/8	41	41 4/8	13 5/8	13 6/8	8 1/8	8 5/8	22	21 3/8	102	75
♦ *Wrangell Mts. / Lloyd Walker / Lloyd Walker / 1959*										

Score	Length of Horn		Circumference of Base		Circumference at Third Quarter		Greatest Spread	Tip-to-Tip Spread	All-Time Rank	State Rank
	R	L	R	L	R	L				
♦ Locality / Hunter / Owner / Date Killed										
174 4/8	42 2/8	41 6/8	13 7/8	13 7/8	8	7 4/8	20 1/8	20 1/8	102	75
♦ Wrangell Mts. / Robert L. Jenkins / Robert L. Jenkins / 1963										
174 4/8	40 3/8	40 5/8	15 1/8	14 7/8	6 4/8	6 7/8	23 7/8	23 5/8	102	75
♦ Chugach Mts. / Lawrence T. Keenan / Lawrence T. Keenan / 1976										
174 3/8	43 2/8	43 1/8	14 3/8	14 3/8	6 2/8	6 2/8	24	24	105	78
♦ Wrangell Mts. / John J. Liska / John J. Liska / 1963										
174 2/8	41 5/8	41 5/8	14 2/8	14 2/8	6 4/8	6 3/8	26 4/8	26 4/8	107	79
♦ Talkeetna Mts. / William J. Konesky / William J. Konesky / 1958										
174 2/8	40 7/8	41 5/8	14 4/8	14 4/8	7 4/8	7	22	22	107	79
♦ Wrangell Mts. / Jerry L. Beason / Jerry L. Beason / 1961										
174 1/8	43 6/8	43 3/8	14 1/8	14 1/8	5 7/8	6	30 7/8	30 7/8	110	81
♦ Wrangell Mts. / Sven Johanson / Sven Johanson / 1960										
174	40 7/8	42 3/8	13 5/8	13 7/8	7 4/8	7 6/8	21 7/8	21 7/8	112	82
♦ Kenai Pen. / Basil C. Bradbury / Basil C. Bradbury / 1960										
174	42 4/8	45	14	14	6 1/8	6 1/8	27	27	112	82
♦ Wrangell Mts. / Howard Gilmore, Jr. / Howard Gilmore, Jr. / 1969										
174	43 3/8	44 7/8	14	14	5 5/8	5 7/8	32 1/8	31 6/8	112	82
♦ Wrangell Mts. / Dan Parker / Dan Parker / 1972										
174	43 5/8	42 1/8	14 3/8	14 4/8	5 7/8	5 4/8	29	29 2/8	112	82
♦ Alaska Range / Harry R. Hannon / Harry R. Hannon / 1976										
173 6/8	42 6/8	43 2/8	14 2/8	14 5/8	6 1/8	6 4/8	29 3/8	29 3/8	117	86
♦ Talkeetna Mts. / Frank Cook / Frank Cook / 1961										
173 6/8	36 2/8	41 6/8	15 1/8	15	7 2/8	7 2/8	24 6/8	24 6/8	117	86
♦ Wrangell Mts. / Gene Effler / Gene Effler / 1964										
173 5/8	45 2/8	45 1/8	13 1/8	13 2/8	5 7/8	5 6/8	30 6/8	30 7/8	120	88
♦ Chitina / Dene Leonard, Jr. / Dene Leonard, Jr. / 1959										
173 5/8	38 5/8	38 2/8	13 7/8	13 7/8	9 3/8	9 3/8	21 1/8	19 6/8	120	88
♦ Wrangell Mts. / B.L. Burkholder / B.L. Burkholder / 1960										
173 5/8	42 1/8	42 6/8	14 3/8	14 6/8	5 4/8	5 4/8	28	28	120	88
♦ Chugach Mts. / Richard T. Kopsack / Richard T. Kopsack / 1961										
173 5/8	41 4/8	41 7/8	14 2/8	14 2/8	6 7/8	6 7/8	24 2/8	24 2/8	120	88
♦ Lake Clark / Melvin C. Paxton / Melvin C. Paxton / 1968										
173 4/8	42	44 4/8	13 7/8	13 7/8	6 3/8	6 4/8	29 7/8	29 7/8	126	92
♦ Wrangell Mts. / James Harrower / James Harrower / 1963										
173 4/8	41 1/8	40 7/8	14 6/8	14 7/8	6 4/8	6 4/8	31 1/8	30 6/8	126	92
♦ Chitina Glacier / Robert W. Kubick / Robert W. Kubick / 1967										
173 4/8	41 7/8	41 5/8	13 6/8	14	6 6/8	6 6/8	26 4/8	26 4/8	126	92
♦ Troublesome Creek / David G. Urban / David G. Urban / 1991										

Score	Length of Horn		Circumference of Base		Circumference at Third Quarter		Greatest Spread	Tip-to-Tip Spread	All-Time Rank	State Rank
	R	L	R	L	R	L				
♦ Locality / Hunter / Owner / Date Killed										
173 3/8	43 5/8	43	13 5/8	13 5/8	6 5/8	6 4/8	28 4/8	28 4/8	130	95
♦ Tonseno Lake / James St. Amour / James St. Amour / 1957										
173 3/8	44 6/8	44 7/8	13 3/8	13 3/8	5 6/8	5 6/8	28 6/8	28 6/8	130	95
♦ Chugach Mts. / Howard Haney / Howard Haney / 1961										
173 3/8	42 2/8	43 3/8	13 2/8	13 1/8	6 2/8	6 4/8	19 4/8	19 4/8	130	95
♦ Kenai Pen. / Spud Dillon / Spud Dillon / 1966										
173 3/8	39 7/8	44 4/8	13 7/8	13 5/8	6 4/8	6 2/8	25 3/8	24 4/8	130	95
♦ Wrangell Mts. / Basil C. Bradbury / Basil C. Bradbury / 1968										
173 3/8	42	42 7/8	13 3/8	13 4/8	7	7 4/8	22 3/8	22 3/8	130	95
♦ Alaska Range / Arthur L. Spicer / Arthur L. Spicer / 1970										
173 2/8	35 2/8	45	14 3/8	14 4/8	6 2/8	6 7/8	25 2/8	23 3/8	136	100
♦ Wrangell Mts. / J.H. Shelton / J.H. Shelton / 1958										
173 1/8	46 4/8	41 5/8	13 3/8	13 2/8	6	6	20 1/8	26 7/8	137	101
♦ Kenai Pen. / W.R. Shellhorn / D. Shellhorn / 1936										
173	42	42 4/8	13 4/8	13 5/8	6 4/8	6 4/8	28 1/8	28 1/8	139	102
♦ Wrangell Mts. / Ken Knudson / Ken Knudson / 1961										
173	45 6/8	45 2/8	13 3/8	13 4/8	5 5/8	5 4/8	33	33	139	102
♦ Wrangell Mts. / Bob Merz / Bob Merz / 1966										
173	40 5/8	41 5/8	13 5/8	13 3/8	7 2/8	7 2/8	20 5/8	20 5/8	139	102
♦ Chugach Mts. / J.C. Hemming / J.C. Hemming / 1970										
173	40 6/8	43	14 7/8	14 5/8	5 7/8	5 7/8	28 3/8	27 7/8	139	102
♦ Wrangell Mts. / Charles A. Pohland / Charles A. Pohland / 1971										
173	43 6/8	44	13 5/8	13 5/8	6	6	28	28	139	102
♦ Chugach Mts. / Thomas Clark / Thomas Clark / 1975										
173	40 4/8	40 6/8	13 7/8	14	6 7/8	6 6/8	24 3/8	24 1/8	139	102
♦ Chugach Mts. / Daniel G. Montgomery / Daniel G. Montgomery / 1991										
172 7/8	40 1/8	40 4/8	14 2/8	14 4/8	6 2/8	6 3/8	25 1/8	25 1/8	146	108
♦ Chugach Mts. / Peter W. Bading / Peter W. Bading / 1961										
172 7/8	39 1/8	39	14 2/8	14 2/8	7 7/8	7 5/8	25 1/8	25 1/8	146	108
♦ Wrangell Mts. / Ralph Cox / Ralph Cox / 1971										
172 7/8	43 7/8	42 6/8	14 4/8	14 4/8	6 1/8	5 7/8	24 2/8	24	146	108
♦ Alaska Range / George Faerber / George Faerber / 1976										
172 6/8	38 7/8	43 5/8	14 2/8	14 2/8	8	6 4/8	27 7/8	27 7/8	149	111
♦ Nabesna River / J.C. Phillips / J.C. Phillips / 1956										
172 6/8	41 2/8	41 2/8	13 5/8	13 5/8	6 6/8	6 6/8	25 6/8	25 6/8	149	111
♦ Chugach Mts. / Ruby Wyatt / Ruby Wyatt / 1960										
172 6/8	43 5/8	43 3/8	13 5/8	13 5/8	6 4/8	6 4/8	33	33	149	111
♦ Chugach Mts. / Richard Kopsack / Richard Kopsack / 1963										

Score	Length of Horn		Circumference of Base		Circumference at Third Quarter		Greatest Spread	Tip-to-Tip Spread	All-Time Rank	State Rank
	R	L	R	L	R	L				

Locality / Hunter / Owner / Date Killed

Score	Length of Horn R	L	Circ. Base R	L	Circ. Third Qtr R	L	Greatest Spread	Tip-to-Tip Spread	All-Time Rank	State Rank
172 6/8	41 2/8	42 2/8	14 2/8	14 1/8	6 4/8	6 3/8	28 5/8	28 5/8	149	111
172 6/8	40	40 4/8	14 4/8	15	7	6 5/8	30 3/8	30 3/8	149	111
172 6/8	43 2/8	43	13 6/8	13 5/8	5 7/8	6 1/8	28 5/8	28 5/8	149	111
172 6/8	43 1/8	43 7/8	14	14	5 5/8	5 6/8	30 3/8	30 1/8	149	111
172 5/8	43 4/8	42 3/8	12 7/8	13 2/8	7	7	29 4/8	29 4/8	159	118
172 5/8	42	41 3/8	14 5/8	14 6/8	5 7/8	5 6/8	32	32	159	118
172 5/8	41 1/8	41 6/8	14 1/8	14 1/8	6 3/8	6 3/8	29 7/8	29 7/8	159	118
172 4/8	42 4/8	41 4/8	14 2/8	14 2/8	6 4/8	6 6/8	26 1/8	26 1/8	166	121
172 4/8	43 4/8	42 6/8	13 1/8	13 1/8	7 2/8	6 7/8	24 3/8	24 3/8	166	121
172 4/8	39 5/8	45 1/8	14 1/8	14	5 6/8	5 6/8	27 5/8	27 5/8	166	121
172 3/8	41 5/8	41 2/8	13 5/8	13 6/8	6 6/8	6 6/8	25 1/8	25	171	124
172 3/8	45	41 3/8	14	13 7/8	5 5/8	5 6/8	27 2/8	27 2/8	171	124
172 2/8	45 7/8	44 7/8	13 2/8	13 2/8	5 5/8	6	32	32	175	126
172 2/8	43 1/8	43 3/8	13 5/8	13 4/8	6 2/8	6 3/8	26 6/8	26 4/8	175	126
172 1/8	40	39 7/8	14 2/8	14 2/8	6 4/8	6 6/8	24 3/8	24 3/8	177	128
172 1/8	39 7/8	39	15 4/8	15 3/8	7	6 5/8	26	26	177	128
172 1/8	38 5/8	42	14 1/8	14 1/8	7	7	21 7/8	21 3/8	177	128
172 1/8	42	41 7/8	14 5/8	14 6/8	6	6 2/8	25 6/8	25 6/8	177	128
172 1/8	43	38 7/8	14 4/8	14 4/8	5 7/8	5 7/8	29 2/8	29 2/8	177	128

◆ Wrangell Mts. / Alvin W. Huba, Jr. / Alvin W. Huba, Jr. / 1968
◆ Gerstle River / John A. Shilling / John A. Shilling / 1968
◆ Chandalar River / Robert M. Welch / Robert M. Welch / 1974
◆ Wrangell Mts. / Robert J. Wykel / Robert J. Wykel / 1976
◆ Knik Glacier / Picked Up / Howard G. Romig / 1932
◆ Wrangell Mts. / William T. Ellis / William T. Ellis / 1960
◆ Knik River / Miles G. France / Miles G. France / 1969
◆ Wrangell Mts. / W.A. Bailey, Jr. / W.A. Bailey, Jr. / 1959
◆ Wrangell Mts. / H.E. Eldred / H.E. Eldred / 1960
◆ Chugach Mts. / Raymond Capossela / Raymond Capossela / 1963
◆ Chugach Mts. / Chuck Moe / Chuck Moe / 1979
◆ Alaska Range / Joseph C. LoMonaco / Joseph C. LoMonaco / 1992
◆ Copper River / C.J. McElroy / C.J. McElroy / 1977
◆ Chugach Mts. / Michael L. Kasterin / Michael L. Kasterin / 1986
◆ Wrangell Mts. / Kirk Gay / Kirk Gay / 1958
◆ Wrangell Mts. / Horace Groff / Horace Groff / 1961
◆ Chugach Mts. / E.F. Craig / E.F. Craig / 1963
◆ Wrangell Mts. / Walter E. Cox / Walter E. Cox / 1966
◆ Kuskokwim River / Ken M. Wilson / Ken M. Wilson / 1973

Score	Length of Horn		Circumference of Base		Circumference at Third Quarter		Greatest Spread	Tip-to-Tip Spread	All-Time Rank	State Rank
	R	L	R	L	R	L				
◆ Locality / Hunter / Owner / Date Killed										
172	41 3/8	41 7/8	14 5/8	14 6/8	6 2/8	5 7/8	26 2/8	26 2/8	182	133
◆ Wrangell Mts. / Carroll W. Gibbs / Carroll W. Gibbs / 1957										
172	43 6/8	44 6/8	13 6/8	13 6/8	5 6/8	6	26 1/8	26 1/8	182	133
◆ Chugach Mts. / M.L. Magnusson / M.L. Magnusson / 1957										
172	36	39	15	15 1/8	8	8	22 6/8	20	182	133
◆ Chugach Mts. / Ward Gay, Jr. / Ward Gay, Jr. / 1962										
171 7/8	45 2/8	42 7/8	13 1/8	13 1/8	6	6 7/8	27 6/8	27 6/8	187	136
◆ McCarthy / Eugene E. Saxton / Eugene E. Saxton / 1953										
171 7/8	43 2/8	41 3/8	13 5/8	13 4/8	6 2/8	6 1/8	25 4/8	25 4/8	187	136
◆ Talkeetna Mts. / Paul S. Lawrence / Paul S. Lawrence / 1960										
171 7/8	39 5/8	38	15 6/8	15 7/8	6	6 2/8	25 6/8	25 6/8	187	136
◆ Wrangell Mts. / Kenneth Knudson / Kenneth Knudson / 1963										
171 7/8	41 4/8	40 1/8	13 3/8	13 3/8	7 6/8	7 3/8	24 4/8	24 4/8	187	136
◆ Chugach Mts. / Herb Klein / Herb Klein / 1964										
171 7/8	41 5/8	40 2/8	14 6/8	14 4/8	6 1/8	6 3/8	22 6/8	22 2/8	187	136
◆ Chugach Mts. / Frank Cook / Frank Cook / 1965										
171 7/8	40 4/8	40 5/8	14 1/8	14 2/8	6 3/8	6 3/8	28 2/8	28 2/8	187	136
◆ Wrangell Mts. / Brent R. Hanks / Brent R. Hanks / 1983										
171 7/8	42 7/8	43	13 1/8	13 1/8	6 7/8	6 6/8	25 1/8	25 1/8	187	136
◆ Robertson River / David C. Sharp / David C. Sharp / 1987										
171 6/8	38 7/8	42 5/8	14	13 7/8	6 5/8	6 4/8	28 4/8	28 4/8	194	143
◆ Wrangell Mts. / Charles C. Parsons / Charles C. Parsons / 1955										
171 6/8	42 7/8	42 3/8	13 7/8	14	6 3/8	6 2/8	30 7/8	30 7/8	194	143
◆ Wrangell Mts. / Ross Jardine / Ross Jardine / 1960										
171 6/8	35 4/8	42	14 7/8	14 7/8	6 5/8	6 7/8	24 3/8	24 3/8	194	143
◆ Chugach Mts. / C.J. McElroy / C.J. McElroy / 1969										
171 6/8	44 2/8	40 2/8	13 7/8	13 7/8	6 2/8	6 3/8	30 3/8	30 3/8	194	143
◆ Ivishak River / Charles W. Troutman / Charles W. Troutman / 1987										
171 6/8	41 5/8	42 1/8	14 6/8	14 7/8	5 6/8	5 6/8	23 5/8	23 5/8	194	143
◆ Chugach Mts. / Mark D. Truax / Mark D. Truax / 1992										
171 5/8	41 7/8	41 6/8	14 3/8	14 1/8	5 7/8	6 1/8	26 5/8	26 5/8	200	148
◆ Chugach Mts. / Justin L. Smith / Justin L. Smith / 1963										
171 5/8	40 3/8	41	14 4/8	14 4/8	6 5/8	6 7/8	22 1/8	22 1/8	200	148
◆ Nabesna Glacier / John F. Saltz / John F. Saltz / 1983										
171 4/8	40 5/8	40 5/8	13 6/8	13 6/8	6 7/8	6 7/8	23 4/8	23 4/8	202	150
◆ Kenai Pen. / C.R. Wright / C.R. Wright / 1936										
171 4/8	41 5/8	42 5/8	13 5/8	13 5/8	6 3/8	6 6/8	26	26	202	150
◆ Wrangell Mts. / Robert V. Walker / Robert V. Walker / 1971										

Score	Length of Horn		Circumference of Base		Circumference at Third Quarter		Greatest Spread	Tip-to-Tip Spread	All-Time Rank	State Rank
	R	L	R	L	R	L				
◆ *Locality / Hunter / Owner / Date Killed*										
171 3/8	44 3/8	45 2/8	12 7/8	13	6 7/8	5 6/8	34 2/8	34 2/8	205	152
◆ *Wood River / R.R.M. Carpenter / Acad. Nat. Sci., Phil. / 1940*										
171 3/8	39 4/8	40 1/8	13 5/8	13 6/8	7 5/8	7 7/8	27 2/8	27 2/8	205	152
◆ *Coal Creek / W.W. Fultz / W.W. Fultz / 1955*										
171 3/8	41 1/8	41 2/8	14	14	6 3/8	6 2/8	30 3/8	30 3/8	205	152
◆ *Chugach Mts. / Perley Colbeth / Perley Colbeth / 1958*										
171 3/8	42	42 3/8	13 3/8	13 3/8	7 2/8	7 3/8	29 2/8	29 2/8	205	152
◆ *Wrangell Mts. / Arthur R. Dubs / Arthur R. Dubs / 1962*										
171 3/8	36 3/8	44	14 6/8	14 5/8	6 3/8	6 7/8	26 4/8	25 6/8	205	152
◆ *Wrangell Mts. / Doug McRae, Sr. / Doug McRae, Sr. / 1972*										
171 3/8	41 1/8	42 2/8	14	14	6	6 7/8	26 6/8	26 4/8	205	152
◆ *Chugach Mts. / Michael J. Ebner / Michael J. Ebner / 1977*										
171 3/8	42 1/8	42 4/8	14	13 6/8	5 4/8	5 6/8	22 2/8	22 2/8	205	152
◆ *Chugach Mts. / Anthony R. Russ / Anthony R. Russ / 1988*										
171 2/8	36 3/8	38 1/8	14 7/8	14 7/8	7 6/8	7 6/8	24 3/8	24 1/8	213	159
◆ *Wrangell Mts. / Gordon Madole / Gordon Madole / 1956*										
171 2/8	39 6/8	41 2/8	14 7/8	14 6/8	6 5/8	6	24 1/8	23 7/8	213	159
◆ *Wrangell Mts. / Rudolpho Valladolid / Rudolpho Valladolid / 1974*										
171 1/8	45	44 1/8	12 1/8	12 1/8	6 2/8	6 2/8	26 4/8	26 4/8	217	161
◆ *Wrangell Mts. / Picked Up / Dick Gunlogson / 1968*										
171 1/8	40 7/8	40 6/8	13 6/8	14	6 5/8	6 5/8	22 2/8	22 2/8	217	161
◆ *Robertson River / Beuron A. McKenzie / Beuron A. McKenzie / 1971*										
171 1/8	43 2/8	42 7/8	13 2/8	13 1/8	6	6	26 4/8	26 2/8	217	161
◆ *Chugach Mts. / Emil V. Nelson / Emil V. Nelson / 1988*										
171	36 7/8	39 3/8	14	14	8	8 3/8	20 6/8	19 3/8	221	164
◆ *Chugach Mts. / Raymond Capossela / Raymond Capossela / 1961*										
171	40 6/8	40 6/8	14 2/8	14 2/8	6 1/8	6 2/8	29	29	221	164
◆ *Greyling Creek / Michael M. Stitzel / Michael M. Stitzel / 1986*										
171	43	42 6/8	13 4/8	13 3/8	6	6 4/8	28 6/8	28 6/8	221	164
◆ *Little Tok River / Kenneth L. House / Kenneth L. House / 1992*										
170 7/8	41 5/8	41 4/8	14 6/8	14 6/8	5 3/8	5 4/8	26 3/8	26 3/8	227	167
◆ *Kenai Pen. / David Jones / David Jones / 1963*										
170 7/8	35 3/8	39 6/8	15 2/8	15 2/8	7 1/8	7 2/8	25 7/8	25 7/8	227	167
◆ *Wrangell Mts. / Richard Stingley / Richard Stingley / 1965*										
170 7/8	42	41 5/8	14 1/8	14 4/8	6 5/8	6 3/8	29 5/8	29 5/8	227	167
◆ *Wrangell Mts. / Thomas Sperstad / Thomas Sperstad / 1969*										
170 7/8	36	36 5/8	14	14 2/8	9 1/8	9 1/8	25 4/8	24 5/8	227	167
◆ *Chugach Mts. / Gerald L. Warnock / Gerald L. Warnock / 1970*										

Score	Length of Horn		Circumference of Base		Circumference at Third Quarter		Greatest Spread	Tip-to-Tip Spread	All-Time Rank	State Rank
	R	L	R	L	R	L				
◆ Locality / Hunter / Owner / Date Killed										

170⅞ 41⁶⁄₈ 41⁵⁄₈ 14⅛ 14 6⅛ 6 29 29 227 167
◆ *Wrangell Mts. / Unknown / J. Michael Conoyer / 1980*

170⅞ 41⅛ 40⁶⁄₈ 13⁵⁄₈ 13⁴⁄₈ 6⁴⁄₈ 6⁴⁄₈ 25³⁄₈ 24⁶⁄₈ 227 167
◆ *Chugach Mts. / Kenneth P. Meinzer / Kenneth P. Meinzer / 1992*

170⁶⁄₈ 41⁵⁄₈ 41⅞ 14⅛ 14⅛ 5⁶⁄₈ 5⁶⁄₈ 26⁴⁄₈ 26⁴⁄₈ 234 173
◆ *Wrangell Mts. / Joseph A. Tedesco / Joseph A. Tedesco / 1959*

170⁶⁄₈ 39²⁄₈ 39²⁄₈ 14⁶⁄₈ 14⅞ 6⁶⁄₈ 6⁶⁄₈ 28²⁄₈ 28²⁄₈ 234 173
◆ *Wrangell Mts. / George Stelious / George Stelious / 1962*

170⁶⁄₈ 42²⁄₈ 42⁴⁄₈ 13⁶⁄₈ 13⁶⁄₈ 6 6⅛ 26⁴⁄₈ 26⁴⁄₈ 234 173
◆ *Wrangell Mts. / Robert V. Broadbent / Robert V. Broadbent / 1965*

170⁵⁄₈ 41⁴⁄₈ 41⅞ 14 14 6²⁄₈ 6²⁄₈ 30⅛ 30⅛ 238 176
◆ *Nabesna River / J.S. Rutherford / J.S. Rutherford / 1956*

170⁵⁄₈ 42⅛ 40⁶⁄₈ 12⅞ 12⅞ 7⁴⁄₈ 7⁶⁄₈ 21³⁄₈ 21³⁄₈ 238 176
◆ *Wrangell Mts. / W.A. Fisher / W.A. Fisher / 1959*

170⁵⁄₈ 41³⁄₈ 42²⁄₈ 13⅞ 13⅞ 6³⁄₈ 6⁴⁄₈ 25⅛ 25⅛ 238 176
◆ *Wrangell Mts. / Gene Sperstad / Gene Sperstad / 1961*

170⁵⁄₈ 43²⁄₈ 40⅞ 14⅛ 14⅛ 5⁵⁄₈ 5⁶⁄₈ 25⁶⁄₈ 25⁶⁄₈ 238 176
◆ *Nutzotin Mts. / Dorothy Andersen / Larry Folger / 1965*

170⁵⁄₈ 41²⁄₈ 42⅛ 15 14⁶⁄₈ 5²⁄₈ 5³⁄₈ 28 28 238 176
◆ *Chugach Mts. / Harry C. Heckendorn / Harry C. Heckendorn / 1972*

170⁴⁄₈ 44²⁄₈ 38 13⁵⁄₈ 13⁶⁄₈ 6⁴⁄₈ 6⁴⁄₈ 29³⁄₈ 29³⁄₈ 244 181
◆ *Wrangell Mts. / Harry L. Swank, Jr. / Harry L. Swank, Jr. / 1962*

170⁴⁄₈ 41²⁄₈ 41²⁄₈ 14²⁄₈ 14²⁄₈ 6³⁄₈ 6⁴⁄₈ 23⁶⁄₈ 23⁶⁄₈ 244 181
◆ *Brooks Range / Donald E. Harrell / Donald E. Harrell / 1979*

170⁴⁄₈ 43⅛ 43⅞ 13²⁄₈ 13²⁄₈ 6 6³⁄₈ 25⅞ 25⁶⁄₈ 244 181
◆ *Eklutna River / Robert L. Lynch / Robert L. Lynch / 1994*

170³⁄₈ 40 40³⁄₈ 14²⁄₈ 14²⁄₈ 6²⁄₈ 6²⁄₈ 22 22 249 184
◆ *Kenai Pen. / Vance Corrigan / Vance Corrigan / 1957*

170³⁄₈ 39⅞ 43 14²⁄₈ 14²⁄₈ 6²⁄₈ 6²⁄₈ 28 28 249 184
◆ *Wrangell Mts. / J.A. Tadesco / J.A. Tadesco / 1960*

170³⁄₈ 41⁵⁄₈ 42⁴⁄₈ 14²⁄₈ 14²⁄₈ 5⁶⁄₈ 5⅞ 27⅞ 27⅞ 249 184
◆ *Wrangell Mts. / Willie Bogner, Sr. / Willie Bogner, Sr. / 1961*

170³⁄₈ 42⁴⁄₈ 43⁵⁄₈ 13²⁄₈ 13²⁄₈ 5⅞ 6⁴⁄₈ 31²⁄₈ 31²⁄₈ 249 184
◆ *Chugach Mts. / William H. Smith / William H. Smith / 1961*

170³⁄₈ 40⁶⁄₈ 40³⁄₈ 13⅞ 13⅞ 6⅞ 6⁶⁄₈ 23⅞ 23⅞ 249 184
◆ *Alaska Range / James W. Thompson / James W. Thompson / 1986*

170²⁄₈ 40⁵⁄₈ 41³⁄₈ 14⅛ 14²⁄₈ 5⁶⁄₈ 6⅛ 22²⁄₈ 22²⁄₈ 254 189
◆ *Kenai Pen. / C.R. Wright / C.R. Wright / 1935*

Score	Length of Horn		Circumference of Base		Circumference at Third Quarter		Greatest Spread	Tip-to-Tip Spread	All-Time Rank	State Rank
	R	L	R	L	R	L				
♦ Locality / Hunter / Owner / Date Killed										
$170\frac{2}{8}$	$39\frac{5}{8}$	$41\frac{7}{8}$	$15\frac{3}{8}$	$15\frac{3}{8}$	$5\frac{6}{8}$	$5\frac{6}{8}$	$23\frac{3}{8}$	$23\frac{3}{8}$	254	189
♦ Tonsina River / R.J. Uhl / R.J. Uhl / 1959										
$170\frac{2}{8}$	$38\frac{7}{8}$	$39\frac{7}{8}$	$13\frac{6}{8}$	$13\frac{6}{8}$	$7\frac{6}{8}$	$7\frac{6}{8}$	$19\frac{6}{8}$	$19\frac{6}{8}$	254	189
♦ Chugach Mts. / Donald Stroble / Donald Stroble / 1961										
$170\frac{2}{8}$	$37\frac{2}{8}$	38	$14\frac{7}{8}$	$14\frac{7}{8}$	7	$6\frac{7}{8}$	$20\frac{6}{8}$	$19\frac{4}{8}$	254	189
♦ Kenai Pen. / Lee Miller / Lee Miller / 1963										
$170\frac{2}{8}$	$40\frac{3}{8}$	$40\frac{3}{8}$	$14\frac{6}{8}$	$14\frac{7}{8}$	$6\frac{2}{8}$	$6\frac{2}{8}$	$27\frac{2}{8}$	$27\frac{2}{8}$	254	189
♦ Wrangell Mts. / C. Driskell / C. Driskell / 1965										
$170\frac{2}{8}$	41	40	$14\frac{5}{8}$	$14\frac{5}{8}$	$6\frac{5}{8}$	$5\frac{7}{8}$	$28\frac{3}{8}$	$28\frac{3}{8}$	254	189
♦ Wrangell Mts. / Jim Baballa / Jim Baballa / 1967										
$170\frac{2}{8}$	$38\frac{2}{8}$	$37\frac{6}{8}$	$13\frac{6}{8}$	$13\frac{7}{8}$	$8\frac{2}{8}$	$9\frac{2}{8}$	21	$20\frac{5}{8}$	254	189
♦ Robertson River / John W. Redmond / John W. Redmond / 1970										
$170\frac{2}{8}$	$41\frac{2}{8}$	$41\frac{4}{8}$	$13\frac{6}{8}$	$13\frac{7}{8}$	$6\frac{4}{8}$	$6\frac{4}{8}$	$25\frac{7}{8}$	$25\frac{7}{8}$	254	189
♦ Talkeetna Mts. / H. Albertas Hall / H. Albertas Hall / 1971										
$170\frac{2}{8}$	40	40	$14\frac{4}{8}$	$14\frac{4}{8}$	$6\frac{4}{8}$	7	$26\frac{6}{8}$	$23\frac{6}{8}$	254	189
♦ Wrangell Mts. / Bernard J. Meinerz / Bernard J. Meinerz / 1972										
$170\frac{2}{8}$	$39\frac{6}{8}$	39	$14\frac{3}{8}$	$14\frac{2}{8}$	$6\frac{4}{8}$	$6\frac{2}{8}$	$29\frac{2}{8}$	29	254	189
♦ Hunter Creek / James C. Becker / James C. Becker / 1993										
$170\frac{1}{8}$	$40\frac{2}{8}$	$40\frac{3}{8}$	$13\frac{2}{8}$	$13\frac{4}{8}$	$7\frac{6}{8}$	$7\frac{5}{8}$	22	22	267	199
♦ Wrangell Mts. / Chester Beer / Chester Beer / 1959										
$170\frac{1}{8}$	$41\frac{4}{8}$	$41\frac{1}{8}$	14	14	$5\frac{5}{8}$	$5\frac{5}{8}$	$24\frac{5}{8}$	$24\frac{5}{8}$	267	199
♦ Chugach Mts. / James A. Kirsch / James A. Kirsch / 1961										
$170\frac{1}{8}$	38	$37\frac{3}{8}$	14	$14\frac{2}{8}$	$8\frac{3}{8}$	$8\frac{2}{8}$	$20\frac{3}{8}$	$20\frac{3}{8}$	267	199
♦ Wrangell Mts. / W.T. Yoshimoto / W.T. Yoshimoto / 1967										
170	42	$42\frac{2}{8}$	$13\frac{1}{8}$	$13\frac{1}{8}$	$6\frac{1}{8}$	$6\frac{2}{8}$	$30\frac{1}{8}$	$30\frac{1}{8}$	272	202
♦ Wrangell Mts. / Ralph Morava, Jr. / Ralph Morava, Jr. / 1954										
170	$40\frac{6}{8}$	$42\frac{2}{8}$	$14\frac{3}{8}$	$14\frac{1}{8}$	$6\frac{1}{8}$	$6\frac{1}{8}$	$27\frac{3}{8}$	$27\frac{3}{8}$	272	202
♦ Nabesna River / Raymond A. Talbott / Raymond A. Talbott / 1958										
170	$41\frac{5}{8}$	$42\frac{5}{8}$	$13\frac{5}{8}$	$13\frac{6}{8}$	$6\frac{1}{8}$	6	$23\frac{4}{8}$	$23\frac{4}{8}$	272	202
♦ Wrangell Mts. / Mrs. Melvin Soder / Mrs. Melvin Soder / 1961										
170	$41\frac{6}{8}$	42	$13\frac{3}{8}$	$13\frac{3}{8}$	$6\frac{4}{8}$	$6\frac{5}{8}$	$23\frac{5}{8}$	$23\frac{5}{8}$	272	202
♦ Farewell Lake / Frank G. Merz / Frank G. Merz / 1983										
170	$41\frac{7}{8}$	$42\frac{7}{8}$	$13\frac{7}{8}$	14	$5\frac{7}{8}$	$5\frac{6}{8}$	$24\frac{4}{8}$	$24\frac{4}{8}$	272	202
♦ Haley Creek / Larry C. Munn / Larry C. Munn / 1985										
170	$40\frac{5}{8}$	$37\frac{7}{8}$	14	$13\frac{6}{8}$	$7\frac{2}{8}$	$7\frac{2}{8}$	$22\frac{1}{8}$	$22\frac{1}{8}$	272	202
♦ Chugach Mts. / Russell Scribner / Russell Scribner / 1988										
170	$39\frac{5}{8}$	$37\frac{1}{8}$	14	14	$7\frac{4}{8}$	$7\frac{4}{8}$	$21\frac{6}{8}$	$19\frac{2}{8}$	272	202
♦ Ptarmigan Creek / Mark W. Bills / Mark W. Bills / 1993										

Score	Length of Horn		Circumference of Base		Circumference at Third Quarter		Greatest Spread	Tip-to-Tip Spread	All-Time Rank	State Rank
	R	L	R	L	R	L				
◆ Locality / Hunter / Owner / Date Killed										
168 6/8	42 2/8	43 6/8	13 2/8	13 3/8	5 3/8	5 3/8	25 1/8	25 1/8	283	209
◆ Iron Creek / Robert M. Pepper, Jr. / Robert M. Pepper, Jr. / 1985										
168 6/8	40	40 4/8	13 7/8	13 7/8	5 7/8	6 1/8	25 2/8	24 5/8	283	209
◆ Talkeetna Mts. / Jeffrey D. Wallis / Jeffrey D. Wallis / 1988										
168 1/8	40 3/8	40	12 5/8	12 7/8	8	7 5/8	24 1/8	24 1/8	287	211
◆ Big River / Floyd R. Lunde / Floyd R. Lunde / 1986										
168	43 2/8	43	13 2/8	13 2/8	5 3/8	5 3/8	30 4/8	30 3/8	288	212
◆ Robertson River / John D. Graham / John D. Graham / 1993										
167 7/8	44 3/8	42	14	14	5 4/8	5	32 1/8	32 1/8	289	213
◆ Stony River / Thomas J. Harrison / Thomas J. Harrison / 1993										
167 5/8	40 3/8	41 6/8	14 3/8	14	6	6	28 4/8	28 4/8	291	214
◆ Brooks Range / James B. Leet / James B. Leet / 1989										
167 2/8	42 2/8	41 4/8	14	14	6 2/8	5 4/8	26 7/8	26 7/8	292	215
◆ Hulahula River / Robert D. Boutang / Robert D. Boutang / 1989										
167 1/8	45 4/8	43 3/8	12 2/8	12 3/8	5 6/8	6	29 4/8	29 2/8	293	216
◆ Alaska Range / Robert W. Cassell / Robert W. Cassell / 1985										
167	36	37 4/8	13 4/8	13 4/8	8 5/8	8 4/8	21	21	294	217
◆ Brooks Range / G. Todd Ralstin / G. Todd Ralstin / 1989										
166 1/8	39 1/8	39 2/8	14 2/8	14 2/8	6 2/8	6	28	28	296	218
◆ Rocky Mt. / Edward B. Crain III / Edward B. Crain III / 1992										
165 7/8	41 2/8	41 5/8	13 3/8	13 1/8	5 5/8	5 5/8	25 2/8	25	297	219
◆ Chugach Mts. / Daniel G. Montgomery / Daniel G. Montgomery / 1992										
165 1/8	40 7/8	40	13 2/8	13 2/8	5 4/8	5 5/8	26 3/8	26 3/8	301	220
◆ Chandalar River / Charles E. White / Charles E. White / 1988										
165	40	40	12 5/8	12 7/8	7 2/8	7 2/8	21	21	303	221
◆ Alaska Range / Donald W. Bunselmeier / Donald W. Bunselmeier / 1988										
165	36	43	14 2/8	14 3/8	5 5/8	6 2/8	25 1/8	25 1/8	303	221
◆ White Mts. / Edward B. Crain II / Edward B. Crain II / 1989										
164 3/8	36 6/8	41 1/8	13 5/8	13 6/8	6 2/8	6 2/8	22 2/8	21 3/8	309	223
◆ Brooks Range / Dwain Spray / Dwain Spray / 1991										
163 6/8	41 3/8	37 7/8	14	13 7/8	5 2/8	5 4/8	23 4/8	20 6/8	310	224
◆ Kuskokwim River / Basil T. Moore, Jr. / Basil T. Moore, Jr. / 1990										
163 4/8	41 3/8	41 5/8	12 7/8	12 7/8	5 5/8	5 4/8	25	25	311	225
◆ Chugach Mts. / Gary L. Godfrey / Gary L. Godfrey / 1991										
162 6/8	38 2/8	38	13 5/8	13 5/8	6 2/8	6 2/8	20 1/8	20	316	226
◆ Crescent Lake / Gary E. Martin / Gary E. Martin / 1994										
161 6/8	38 3/8	38 1/8	13 1/8	13 4/8	6 4/8	6 3/8	27 1/8	27 1/8	317	227
◆ Alaska Range / James L. Kedrowski / James L. Kedrowski / 1987										

Score	Length of Horn		Circumference of Base		Circumference at Third Quarter		Greatest Spread	Tip-to-Tip Spread	All-Time Rank	State Rank
	R	L	R	L	R	L				
◆ Locality / Hunter / Owner / Date Killed										
161³⁄₈	37⁵⁄₈	38⁶⁄₈	14	14	5⁴⁄₈	5⁵⁄₈	25¹⁄₈	24⁶⁄₈	318	228
◆ Tazlina Glacier / Vincent A. Pisani / Vincent A. Pisani / 1994										
161²⁄₈	40²⁄₈	35⁶⁄₈	14¹⁄₈	13⁷⁄₈	5⁴⁄₈	5⁶⁄₈	24¹⁄₈	24¹⁄₈	319	229
◆ Robertson River / Douglas J. Miller / Douglas J. Miller / 1989										
160³⁄₈	35¹⁄₈	41	13¹⁄₈	13¹⁄₈	6²⁄₈	6²⁄₈	26	26	321	230
◆ Brooks Range / Stan J. Neitling, Jr. / Stan J. Neitling, Jr. / 1989										
187¹⁄₈	45¹⁄₈	47²⁄₈	14³⁄₈	14²⁄₈	7³⁄₈	7⁴⁄₈	25⁵⁄₈	25⁵⁄₈	*	*
◆ Jacksina Creek / Sherwin N. Scott / Sherwin N. Scott / 1984										
184⁷⁄₈	43⁷⁄₈	43²⁄₈	14⁶⁄₈	15	7³⁄₈	7³⁄₈	26¹⁄₈	26¹⁄₈	*	*
◆ Brooks Range / Paul S. Zaczkowski / Paul S. Zaczkowski / 1990										
183⁴⁄₈	45⁵⁄₈	46¹⁄₈	13⁴⁄₈	13⁴⁄₈	8²⁄₈	8¹⁄₈	23	22³⁄₈	*	*
◆ Brooks Range / Terry M. Webb / Terry M. Webb / 1990										
178⁴⁄₈	42⁴⁄₈	43²⁄₈	14⁴⁄₈	14⁴⁄₈	6⁶⁄₈	7²⁄₈	27⁶⁄₈	27⁶⁄₈	*	*
◆ Nabesna Glacier / Floyd Saltz, Jr. / Floyd Saltz, Jr. / 1982										
176¹⁄₈	41	40¹⁄₈	14⁴⁄₈	14⁴⁄₈	8	7¹⁄₈	25⁵⁄₈	25²⁄₈	*	*
◆ Swift River / Guy J. Turner / Guy J. Turner / 1989										
176	41⁴⁄₈	41⁶⁄₈	14⁷⁄₈	14⁷⁄₈	6²⁄₈	6³⁄₈	24²⁄₈	24²⁄₈	*	*
◆ Nabesna Glacier / Sandra T. Saltz / Sandra T. Saltz / 1982										
175²⁄₈	39	39⁴⁄₈	15	15	7³⁄₈	7³⁄₈	26³⁄₈	26³⁄₈	*	*
◆ Wrangell Mts. / Russell A. Reed / Russell A. Reed / 1983										
174⁴⁄₈	42¹⁄₈	41³⁄₈	15¹⁄₈	15	6³⁄₈	6⁴⁄₈	27⁵⁄₈	27³⁄₈	*	*
◆ Snowcap Mt. / Brenton J. Whaley / Brenton J. Whaley / 1992										
173⁶⁄₈	43⁶⁄₈	43⁶⁄₈	13⁷⁄₈	13⁷⁄₈	5⁶⁄₈	5⁶⁄₈	28¹⁄₈	28¹⁄₈	*	*
◆ Robertson River / Thomas A. Berg / Thomas A. Berg / 1992										
173⁵⁄₈	40²⁄₈	40⁵⁄₈	14⁵⁄₈	14⁵⁄₈	6³⁄₈	6⁵⁄₈	25⁶⁄₈	25⁶⁄₈	*	*
◆ Chugach Mts. / Keith A. Douglas / Keith A. Douglas / 1993										
172²⁄₈	42³⁄₈	41³⁄₈	13⁴⁄₈	13⁵⁄₈	6⁵⁄₈	6⁵⁄₈	23	22⁷⁄₈	*	*
◆ Chugach Mts. / Ethan Williams / Ethan Williams / 1988										

Photograph Courtesy of Robert & Connie Landis

BRITISH COLUMBIA PROVINCE RECORD
DALL'S SHEEP
SCORE: 181⁶/₈
Locality: Atlin   Date: 1969
Hunter: Robert Landis

BRITISH COLUMBIA
DALL'S SHEEP

Score	Length of Horn		Circumference of Base		Circumference at Third Quarter		Greatest Spread	Tip-to-Tip Spread	All-Time Rank	State Rank
	R	L	R	L	R	L				
◆ Locality / Hunter / Owner / Date Killed										
181⁶⁄₈	47³⁄₈	47⁵⁄₈	14⁶⁄₈	14⁴⁄₈	5⁷⁄₈	6²⁄₈	28⁷⁄₈	28⁷⁄₈	12	1
◆ Atlin / Robert Landis / Robert Landis / 1969										
172⁶⁄₈	41⁷⁄₈	41⁷⁄₈	14¹⁄₈	14¹⁄₈	6³⁄₈	6²⁄₈	29	29	149	2
◆ Radelet Creek / Norman W. Dougan / Norman W. Dougan / 1972										
170⁶⁄₈	44	44	13⁴⁄₈	13³⁄₈	5⁷⁄₈	5⁵⁄₈	30⁶⁄₈	30⁶⁄₈	234	3
◆ Teepee Mt. / Steve Snider / Jon K. Mahoney / 1983										

Photograph Courtesy of Joseph Scott

NORTHWEST TERRITORIES PROVINCE RECORD
DALL'S SHEEP
SCORE: 177⅛
Locality: Mackenzie River   Date: 1973
Hunter: Joseph Scott

NORTHWEST TERRITORIES

DALL'S SHEEP

Score	Length of Horn		Circumference of Base		Circumference at Third Quarter		Greatest Spread	Tip-to-Tip Spread	All-Time Rank	State Rank
	R	L	R	L	R	L				
♦ Locality / Hunter / Owner / Date Killed										
177 1/8	44 3/8	45 4/8	13 5/8	13 5/8	6 2/8	6 1/8	25 3/8	25 3/8	48	1
♦ Mackenzie River / Joseph Scott / Joseph Scott / 1973										
176 4/8	43 5/8	43 5/8	14	14	6 7/8	6 6/8	25 6/8	25 6/8	58	2
♦ Mt. River / Daniel E. Yaeger / Daniel E. Yaeger / 1973										
174 3/8	42 1/8	42 4/8	14 1/8	14 2/8	6 4/8	6 5/8	25 6/8	25 6/8	105	3
♦ Nahannie Range / Nick Trenke / Nick Trenke / 1979										
173 7/8	44 1/8	42 4/8	13 7/8	13 7/8	6 2/8	6 5/8	26	26	116	4
♦ Twitya River / Lewis W. Lindemer / Lewis W. Lindemer / 1970										
173 6/8	40 2/8	40 2/8	14 7/8	14 6/8	5 4/8	5 4/8	30 4/8	30 4/8	117	5
♦ Keele River / John M. Azevedo / John M. Azevedo / 1975										
172 6/8	40 2/8	41 2/8	15	15	5 7/8	6 2/8	29	28 5/8	149	6
♦ Mountain River / Edmond D. Henley / Edmond D. Henley / 1983										
172 4/8	40 6/8	42	14 6/8	15	6 4/8	6 3/8	26 6/8	26 6/8	166	7
♦ Mackenzie Mts. / Leslie C. Finger / Leslie C. Finger / 1985										
172 3/8	41 4/8	41 7/8	14 1/8	14 2/8	6 4/8	6 6/8	23	22 7/8	171	8
♦ Mackenzie Mts. / Dan L. Johnerson / Dan L. Johnerson / 1989										
172	41 4/8	41 4/8	14 4/8	14 2/8	6 2/8	6 2/8	22 3/8	22 3/8	182	9
♦ Sekwi Mt. / J.D. Martin, Jr. / J.D. Martin, Jr. / 1978										
171 3/8	42 2/8	42 3/8	14	14	5 6/8	5 7/8	32 2/8	32 2/8	205	10
♦ Carcajou River / Colin J. Kure / Colin J. Kure / 1980										
170 7/8	40 6/8	40 7/8	14 2/8	14 2/8	6	6	25 7/8	25 7/8	227	11
♦ Trench Lake / Wayne G. Myers / Wayne G. Myers / 1974										
170 5/8	39 4/8	41 3/8	14	14	7	6 4/8	19 2/8	18 6/8	238	12
♦ S. Nahanni River / Lionel G. Heinrich / Lionel G. Heinrich / 1987										
170 2/8	41 1/8	41 1/8	14	13 7/8	6 5/8	6 6/8	21 4/8	21 2/8	254	13
♦ Mackenzie Mts. / Alan Means / Alan Means / 1991										
170	41 1/8	40 1/8	13 7/8	13 7/8	6 7/8	6 6/8	28 2/8	28 2/8	272	14
♦ Arctic Red River / Philipp Heuchert / Philipp Heuchert / 1991										
168 7/8	45	42 5/8	13	13	5 4/8	5 3/8	31 2/8	31 2/8	282	15
♦ Mackenzie Mts. / Lyle Foster / Lyle Foster / 1990										
168 6/8	42 2/8	41 6/8	13 4/8	13 4/8	5 7/8	5 7/8	26 3/8	26 3/8	283	16
♦ Mackenzie Mts. / J. Wesley Jones / J. Wesley Jones / 1990										
168 5/8	40 2/8	39 1/8	15 2/8	15 1/8	5 7/8	5 7/8	27 2/8	27 1/8	286	17
♦ Redstone / Murray Jones / Murray Jones / 1991										
166 4/8	43 2/8	42 6/8	13 2/8	13 3/8	5 3/8	5 5/8	27 7/8	27 7/8	295	18
♦ Godlin River / John R. Connelly / John R. Connelly / 1990										

Score	Length of Horn R	L	Circumference of Base R	L	Circumference at Third Quarter R	L	Greatest Spread	Tip-to-Tip Spread	All-Time Rank	State Rank
$165\frac{7}{8}$	$38\frac{6}{8}$	$38\frac{3}{8}$	$14\frac{1}{8}$	$14\frac{1}{8}$	$6\frac{2}{8}$	$6\frac{3}{8}$	$24\frac{4}{8}$	$23\frac{4}{8}$	297	19
♦ Mackenzie Mts. / Lynn B. Jackson / Lynn B. Jackson / 1986										
$165\frac{4}{8}$	$40\frac{7}{8}$	$38\frac{3}{8}$	$13\frac{3}{8}$	$13\frac{3}{8}$	$6\frac{2}{8}$	$6\frac{1}{8}$	$22\frac{3}{8}$	$22\frac{3}{8}$	299	20
♦ Mackenzie Mts. / Frank Moryle / W. & V. St. Germaine / 1946										
165	$40\frac{4}{8}$	$41\frac{4}{8}$	$13\frac{6}{8}$	$13\frac{6}{8}$	$5\frac{5}{8}$	$5\frac{6}{8}$	$28\frac{4}{8}$	$28\frac{4}{8}$	303	21
♦ Nahanni Butte / Gary T. Laya / Gary T. Laya / 1986										
165	$39\frac{3}{8}$	$40\frac{5}{8}$	$13\frac{7}{8}$	$13\frac{6}{8}$	$6\frac{2}{8}$	$5\frac{7}{8}$	$24\frac{1}{8}$	24	303	21
♦ Mackenzie Mts. / Vicki St. Germaine / Vicki St. Germaine / 1987										
$164\frac{6}{8}$	41	$39\frac{4}{8}$	$13\frac{7}{8}$	$13\frac{6}{8}$	$5\frac{5}{8}$	$5\frac{4}{8}$	$25\frac{5}{8}$	$25\frac{6}{8}$	307	23
♦ Divide Lake / James R. Cook / James R. Cook / 1988										
$164\frac{5}{8}$	41	$40\frac{5}{8}$	$13\frac{4}{8}$	$13\frac{4}{8}$	$5\frac{6}{8}$	$5\frac{5}{8}$	$28\frac{2}{8}$	$28\frac{2}{8}$	308	24
♦ Divide Lake / Mark C. Cook / Mark C. Cook / 1988										
$163\frac{3}{8}$	$38\frac{1}{8}$	41	14	$14\frac{1}{8}$	$5\frac{6}{8}$	$5\frac{6}{8}$	$32\frac{1}{8}$	32	313	25
♦ Carcajou River / Lee M. Wahlund / Lee M. Wahlund / 1986										
$163\frac{3}{8}$	$41\frac{7}{8}$	$41\frac{6}{8}$	$13\frac{1}{8}$	$13\frac{1}{8}$	$5\frac{6}{8}$	$5\frac{2}{8}$	$24\frac{5}{8}$	$24\frac{5}{8}$	313	25
♦ Mackenzie Mts. / Ralph Fleegle / Ralph Fleegle / 1991										
$173\frac{3}{8}$	44	$43\frac{7}{8}$	$14\frac{4}{8}$	$14\frac{4}{8}$	$5\frac{3}{8}$	$5\frac{3}{8}$	$30\frac{2}{8}$	$30\frac{2}{8}$	*	*
♦ Cache Lake / Lester Behrns / Lester Behrns / 1980										
173	$41\frac{6}{8}$	$41\frac{6}{8}$	$14\frac{1}{8}$	$14\frac{2}{8}$	$6\frac{6}{8}$	$6\frac{4}{8}$	28	28	*	*
♦ Mackenzie Mts. / F. Michael Parkowski / F. Michael Parkowski / 1991										

George F. Dennis proudly poses with the full-curled Dall's sheep he took
near Aishihik Lake, Yukon Territory, during the 1993 hunting season.

Photograph Courtesy of Earl J. Thee

YUKON TERRITORY NUMBER TWO
DALL'S SHEEP
SCORE: 182²⁄₈
Localty: Champagne   Date: 1948
Hunter: Earl J. Thee

YUKON TERRITORY

DALL'S SHEEP

Score	Length of Horn R	Length of Horn L	Circumference of Base R	Circumference of Base L	Circumference at Third Quarter R	Circumference at Third Quarter L	Greatest Spread	Tip-to-Tip Spread	All-Time Rank	State Rank
♦ *Locality / Hunter / Owner / Date Killed*										
183 4/8	45 7/8	45 1/8	13 7/8	14	7 1/8	7 6/8	27 7/8	27 7/8	8	1
♦ *Whitehorse / W. Newhall / Robert E. Barnes / 1924*										
182 2/8	44 4/8	43 6/8	14 1/8	14 5/8	7 2/8	7 1/8	23 4/8	23 4/8	10	2
♦ *Champagne / Earl J. Thee / Earl J. Thee / 1948*										
181	46 3/8	46 7/8	13 4/8	13 6/8	6 2/8	6 2/8	28 7/8	28 7/8	17	3
♦ *Mt. Selous / George C. Morris, Sr. / George C. Morris, Sr. / 1962*										
180 6/8	43 1/8	43 7/8	14 1/8	14 1/8	7 2/8	7 2/8	27	25 3/8	19	4
♦ *Kluane Lake / Indian / Joe Jacquot / 1953*										
180 6/8	42 4/8	44 2/8	15	15	6 2/8	7	26 5/8	26 5/8	19	4
♦ *Yukon / Billy Jack / Yukon Government / 1966*										
179 5/8	40 7/8	41 4/8	14 5/8	14 4/8	8	8	26 2/8	26 2/8	26	6
♦ *Kluane Lake / George E. Thompson / George E. Thompson / 1956*										
178 6/8	40 2/8	40 4/8	15 6/8	15 6/8	7	7	30 2/8	30 2/8	29	7
♦ *Champagne / B.V. Seigel / B.V. Seigel / 1964*										
178 3/8	45 3/8	43 6/8	13 5/8	13 4/8	7	6 4/8	23 6/8	23 6/8	31	8
♦ *Alaska Hwy. / William H. Miller / William H. Miller / 1947*										
178 2/8	45 6/8	46 4/8	13	13	6 5/8	6 3/8	26 3/8	26 3/8	33	9
♦ *Pelly Mts. / Eric W. French / Eric W. French / 1958*										
177 4/8	43 2/8	44	14 2/8	14 1/8	6 3/8	6 4/8	25 6/8	25 6/8	43	10
♦ *Aishihik Lake / Eleanor O'Connor / Loaned to B&C Natl. Coll. / 1963*										
176 7/8	43 5/8	42 2/8	14 6/8	14 7/8	6 3/8	6 1/8	23 4/8	23 4/8	53	11
♦ *Sifton Range / Jack O'Connor / Jack O'Connor / 1950*										
176 5/8	44 4/8	44 7/8	13 1/8	13 1/8	6 5/8	6 6/8	26 1/8	26 1/8	57	12
♦ *Mayo / C.L. Bestoule / C.L. Bestoule / 1960*										
176 4/8	45	45 6/8	13	13 3/8	7 2/8	7	32	32	58	13
♦ *Donjek / Olof Erickson / Mrs. Jacquot / 1933*										
176 2/8	40 4/8	42 2/8	14 4/8	14 4/8	6 4/8	7	24	24	62	14
♦ *Champagne / H.W. Meisch / H.W. Meisch / 1957*										
176 2/8	40 7/8	41 3/8	13 4/8	13 4/8	8 4/8	8 2/8	21 2/8	18 2/8	62	14
♦ *Ruby Range / J. Martin Benchoff / J. Martin Benchoff / 1963*										
175 6/8	40 4/8	46 6/8	13 4/8	13 4/8	6 6/8	6 7/8	23 4/8	23 4/8	71	16
♦ *Ruby Range / John K. Hansen / John K. Hansen / 1960*										
175 6/8	42 3/8	42 7/8	15	14 7/8	6 2/8	6 2/8	23 5/8	22 7/8	71	16
♦ *Yukon / William E. Portman / William E. Portman / 1966*										
174 7/8	44 5/8	44	13 3/8	13 3/8	6 6/8	6 5/8	26 5/8	26 5/8	86	18
♦ *Lake Arkell / J.J. Elliott / J.J. Elliott / 1924*										

Score	Length of Horn		Circumference of Base		Circumference at Third Quarter		Greatest Spread	Tip-to-Tip Spread	All-Time Rank	State Rank
	R	L	R	L	R	L				
◆ *Locality / Hunter / Owner / Date Killed*										
174⅞	42²⁄₈	40³⁄₈	13⅞	14	7⁴⁄₈	7⅞	28²⁄₈	28²⁄₈	86	18
◆ *Aishihik Lake / Abe Goldberg / Abe Goldberg / 1962*										
174⁶⁄₈	47⁴⁄₈	47	13	12⁶⁄₈	5⁶⁄₈	5⁶⁄₈	26	26	91	20
◆ *Carcross / Billy Smith / Acad. Nat. Sci., Phil. / 1927*										
174⁶⁄₈	46⁶⁄₈	43	13	13	7⅛	6⅛	25⁴⁄₈	25⁴⁄₈	91	20
◆ *Sifton Mt. Range / Herb Klein / Herb Klein / 1950*										
174⁶⁄₈	41³⁄₈	43⅝	14⁴⁄₈	14⅝	6⁴⁄₈	6⅛	28²⁄₈	28²⁄₈	91	20
◆ *Wheaton / Herbert Carlson / Herbert Carlson / 1963*										
174⅝	40⅝	42²⁄₈	14⅝	14⅝	7²⁄₈	6⁴⁄₈	27⅛	27⅛	99	23
◆ *Raft Creek / Marvin Wood / Marvin Wood / 1961*										
174⅝	43⁴⁄₈	42³⁄₈	13⅞	14⅛	6⅝	6⁶⁄₈	26⅛	26⅛	99	23
◆ *Kusawa Lake / Lawrence J. Kolar / Lawrence J. Kolar / 1973*										
174²⁄₈	41⁴⁄₈	43⁴⁄₈	13⅞	14	6³⁄₈	6³⁄₈	31⅛	31⅛	107	25
◆ *Coast Mts. / Clarence Hinkle / Clarence Hinkle / 1963*										
174⅛	40	42⅞	14⅝	14⁴⁄₈	6⁴⁄₈	6⁴⁄₈	25	25	110	26
◆ *Ruby Range / Lawrence S. Kellogg / T.A. Alujevic / 1958*										
173⅝	41⁶⁄₈	45³⁄₈	12⅞	13	7	6⅞	24⁶⁄₈	24⁶⁄₈	120	27
◆ *Ruby Range / John E. Hammett / John E. Hammett / 1949*										
173⅝	43⁴⁄₈	41³⁄₈	13²⁄₈	13⁴⁄₈	7²⁄₈	7²⁄₈	23³⁄₈	22²⁄₈	120	27
◆ *Champagne / Edmund D. Patterson, Jr. / Edmund D. Patterson, Jr. / 1963*										
173⁴⁄₈	43⅝	43⅝	13⁶⁄₈	14	5⅞	5⅞	29⅞	29⅞	126	29
◆ *Primrose River / W.R. Collier / W.R. Collier / 1962*										
173³⁄₈	40⅛	40⁴⁄₈	15	15	6⅛	6²⁄₈	27⅝	27⅝	130	30
◆ *Whitehorse / Francis Bouchard / Francis Bouchard / 1961*										
173⅛	41²⁄₈	39⅞	14³⁄₈	14²⁄₈	7⁴⁄₈	7³⁄₈	18⁴⁄₈	21⅞	137	31
◆ *Dawson Mts. / Bill Goosman / Bill Goosman / 1972*										
173	40³⁄₈	40³⁄₈	15	15	6³⁄₈	6⁴⁄₈	28⁶⁄₈	28⁶⁄₈	139	32
◆ *Whitehorse / Earl DuBois / Earl DuBois / 1961*										
172⁶⁄₈	40³⁄₈	40³⁄₈	13⁴⁄₈	13⁴⁄₈	7⅞	7⁶⁄₈	22	20⁶⁄₈	149	33
◆ *Kusawa Lake / John I. Moore / John I. Moore / 1955*										
172⅝	42⅛	42⁴⁄₈	13⁴⁄₈	13⁶⁄₈	6⁶⁄₈	6⁴⁄₈	26³⁄₈	26³⁄₈	159	34
◆ *Mt. Arkell / Stuart Hall / Stuart Hall / 1957*										
172⅝	38⅞	39²⁄₈	14⅞	15³⁄₈	6⅝	6⅞	33⅞	33⅛	159	34
◆ *Caribou Creek / Harold J. Lund / Harold J. Lund / 1963*										
172⅝	41⅝	42	14⁴⁄₈	14²⁄₈	8⁶⁄₈	6²⁄₈	27⅛	27⅛	159	34
◆ *Yukon / S.P. Viezner / S.P. Viezner / 1964*										
172⅝	42	41³⁄₈	13	13	7⁶⁄₈	7³⁄₈	21⁶⁄₈	21⁶⁄₈	159	34
◆ *Talbot Creek / Lloyd E. Zeman / Lloyd E. Zeman / 1969*										

Score	Length of Horn		Circumference of Base		Circumference at Third Quarter		Greatest Spread	Tip-to-Tip Spread	All-Time Rank	State Rank
	R	L	R	L	R	L				
◆ Locality / Hunter / Owner / Date Killed										
172 4/8	41 1/8	42 1/8	14 2/8	14 2/8	6 1/8	6	31 3/8	31 3/8	166	38
◆ Primrose Lake / Walter Sutton / Walter Sutton / 1968										
172 3/8	42 7/8	41 6/8	14 2/8	14 2/8	6 5/8	6 1/8	21 1/8	21 1/8	171	39
◆ Granite Lake / William E. Medley II / William E. Medley II / 1980										
172	41 6/8	42	13 5/8	13 6/8	6 4/8	7	25 3/8	25 3/8	182	40
◆ Sheep Mt. / Ray Hoffman III / Ray Hoffman III / 1961										
171 6/8	42	41	14 5/8	14 5/8	5 5/8	5 4/8	24 3/8	24 2/8	194	41
◆ Canyon Creek / George F. Dennis, Jr. / George F. Dennis, Jr. / 1993										
171 4/8	40 6/8	39 4/8	14 6/8	15	6 2/8	5 7/8	28	28	202	42
◆ Whitehorse / Howard Creason / Howard Creason / 1969										
171 2/8	39 4/8	40	12 4/8	12 3/8	9 3/8	9 4/8	21 6/8	21 6/8	213	43
◆ Ruby Range / Picked Up / William J. Joslin / 1960										
171 2/8	39	39 6/8	14 3/8	14 3/8	7	7 1/8	19 6/8	19 6/8	213	43
◆ Kluane River / Phil Temple / Phil Temple / 1972										
171 1/8	42	42 5/8	13 7/8	14	6 1/8	6 6/8	24	24	217	45
◆ Kusawa Lake / Maurice G. Katz / Maurice G. Katz / 1970										
171	42 7/8	43 1/8	13 5/8	13 5/8	5 6/8	5 7/8	30 4/8	30 4/8	221	46
◆ Carcross / Henry Brockhouse / Henry Brockhouse / 1955										
171	42 1/8	41 1/8	14	13 7/8	6 1/8	6 2/8	26 7/8	26 7/8	221	46
◆ Alligator Lake / D. Graham / D. Graham / 1968										
171	40 6/8	41 2/8	13 6/8	14	6 4/8	6 3/8	26 3/8	26 3/8	221	46
◆ Ruby Range / Harry T. Scharfenberg / Harry T. Scharfenberg / 1977										
170 4/8	40 2/8	40 6/8	14 4/8	14 4/8	6 2/8	6 4/8	21 3/8	21 3/8	244	49
◆ Ruby Range / Harold C. Casey / Harold C. Casey / 1964										
170 4/8	41 3/8	41 3/8	13 5/8	13 5/8	6 7/8	6 7/8	26 3/8	26 3/8	244	49
◆ Ogilvie River / Charles L. Baldridge / Charles L. Baldridge / 1987										
170 2/8	39 7/8	39 7/8	14 5/8	14 5/8	6 2/8	6 4/8	25 3/8	25 3/8	254	51
◆ Champagne / Walter Butcher / Walter Butcher / 1956										
170 2/8	42 7/8	42 7/8	13 4/8	13 4/8	5 7/8	6	29 2/8	29 2/8	254	51
◆ Snake River / Norman M. Thachuk / Norman M. Thachuk / 1982										
170 1/8	42	42 7/8	13 5/8	13 5/8	6 5/8	6 7/8	28	28	267	53
◆ Donjek / Unknown / Acad. Nat. Sci., Phil. / 1921										
170 1/8	40 1/8	41	14 5/8	14 5/8	6 3/8	6 2/8	25 4/8	25 4/8	267	53
◆ Mt. Arkell / Ed Steiner / Ed Steiner / 1955										
170	40 2/8	39 4/8	13 4/8	13 1/8	7 5/8	8 2/8	23 3/8	23 3/8	272	55
◆ Kluane Lake / Herb Graham / Herb Graham / 1959										
170	38 7/8	40 7/8	14	14 1/8	6 6/8	6 5/8	24	24	272	55
◆ Snake River / Clark Johnson / Clark Johnson / 1988										

Score	Length of Horn		Circumference of Base		Circumference at Third Quarter		Greatest Spread	Tip-to-Tip Spread	All-Time Rank	State Rank
	R	L	R	L	R	L				
◆ *Locality / Hunter / Owner / Date Killed*										
167⅞	40	40⅛	14	14⅛	6	6	28⁶⁄₈	28⁶⁄₈	289	57
◆ *Kusawa Lake / Wendell E. Gordon / Wendell E. Gordon / 1992*										
165³⁄₈	38²⁄₈	40⁵⁄₈	13⁶⁄₈	13⁶⁄₈	6⅛	6⅛	22⅞	22⁴⁄₈	300	58
◆ *Nisling River / Joe W. Carroll / Joe W. Carroll / 1980*										
165⅛	39⁶⁄₈	39⁵⁄₈	13⁶⁄₈	13⁴⁄₈	6³⁄₈	6⁵⁄₈	25	24⅞	301	59
◆ *Ruby Range / George L. Tickell / George L. Tickell / 1989*										
163⁴⁄₈	40²⁄₈	39⁶⁄₈	13²⁄₈	13²⁄₈	6	6	24⁴⁄₈	24²⁄₈	311	60
◆ *Ruby Range / Theodore E. Dugey, Jr. / Theodore E. Dugey, Jr. / 1982*										
162⅞	39⅛	40⁶⁄₈	13	13	5⅞	6²⁄₈	27⁶⁄₈	27⁴⁄₈	315	61
◆ *Mackintosh Creek / John R. Fowler / John R. Fowler / 1990*										
160⁴⁄₈	39⁴⁄₈	39	12⅞	12⅞	6³⁄₈	6⅛	24⁶⁄₈	24⁴⁄₈	320	62
◆ *Sanpete Creek / Mark Farnam / Mark Farnam / 1988*										
185³⁄₈	46	45⅞	15²⁄₈	15²⁄₈	6³⁄₈	6⁴⁄₈	29³⁄₈	29³⁄₈	*	*
◆ *Coast Mts. / David W. Young / David W. Young / 1972*										
175⁶⁄₈	42	43²⁄₈	15²⁄₈	15	6	6	27³⁄₈	27³⁄₈	*	*
◆ *Mt. Ingram / Steve Zimmerman / Steve Zimmerman / 1979*										

Photograph Courtesy of Larry C. Fisher

In 1991 Larry C. Fisher (right) hunted with his partner, Brian Postill in the Cassiar Mountains, British Columbia, where he connected with this magnificent Stone's sheep that scores 177-2/8 points.

Photograph by Wm. H. Nesbitt

BRITISH COLUMBIA PROVINCE RECORD
WORLD'S RECORD
STONE'S SHEEP
SCORE: 196⅝
Locality: Muskwa River   Date: 1936
Hunter: L.S. Chadwick
Owner: B&C National Collection, Cody, Wyoming

BRITISH COLUMBIA
STONE'S SHEEP

Score	Length of Horn		Circumference of Base		Circumference at Third Quarter		Greatest Spread	Tip-to-Tip Spread	All-Time Rank	State Rank
	R	L	R	L	R	L				
♦ Locality / Hunter / Owner / Date Killed										
$196\frac{6}{8}$	$50\frac{1}{8}$	$51\frac{5}{8}$	$14\frac{6}{8}$	$14\frac{6}{8}$	$6\frac{6}{8}$	7	31	31	1	1
♦ *Muskwa River / L.S. Chadwick / B&C National Collection / 1936*										
190	$46\frac{6}{8}$	$46\frac{6}{8}$	$15\frac{2}{8}$	$15\frac{1}{8}$	$6\frac{5}{8}$	$6\frac{6}{8}$	$30\frac{6}{8}$	$30\frac{6}{8}$	2	2
♦ *Sikanni River / Norman Blank / Norman Blank / 1962*										
$189\frac{6}{8}$	$48\frac{2}{8}$	$46\frac{2}{8}$	$14\frac{7}{8}$	$14\frac{7}{8}$	$7\frac{2}{8}$	$7\frac{4}{8}$	28	28	3	3
♦ *Blue Sheep Lake / G.C.F. Dalziel / G.C.F. Dalziel / 1965*										
$187\frac{4}{8}$	43	44	$14\frac{6}{8}$	$14\frac{6}{8}$	$8\frac{4}{8}$	$8\frac{4}{8}$	22	22	4	4
♦ *Ospika River / Paul D. Weingart / Paul D. Weingart / 1970*										
$186\frac{3}{8}$	$44\frac{1}{8}$	44	16	$16\frac{1}{8}$	$6\frac{1}{8}$	$6\frac{2}{8}$	$26\frac{3}{8}$	$26\frac{3}{8}$	5	5
♦ *Watson Lake / / Keith Brown / 1971*										
$184\frac{6}{8}$	43	$43\frac{4}{8}$	$15\frac{6}{8}$	$15\frac{6}{8}$	7	$7\frac{1}{8}$	$28\frac{4}{8}$	$28\frac{4}{8}$	6	6
♦ *Prophet River / Joseph H. Shirk / Mrs. C. Barnaby / 1948*										
$184\frac{4}{8}$	$44\frac{4}{8}$	45	$15\frac{4}{8}$	$15\frac{3}{8}$	$6\frac{3}{8}$	$6\frac{4}{8}$	$26\frac{3}{8}$	$26\frac{3}{8}$	7	7
♦ *Hudson Hope / John W. Pitney / Am. Mus. Nat. Hist. / 1936*										
$184\frac{3}{8}$	$44\frac{3}{8}$	46	$14\frac{1}{8}$	$14\frac{2}{8}$	8	7	$28\frac{6}{8}$	$28\frac{6}{8}$	8	8
♦ *Colt Lake / Lloyd E. Hall / Lloyd E. Hall / 1963*										
$184\frac{2}{8}$	$42\frac{1}{8}$	$42\frac{3}{8}$	$16\frac{2}{8}$	$16\frac{2}{8}$	$7\frac{1}{8}$	$7\frac{1}{8}$	$24\frac{4}{8}$	$24\frac{4}{8}$	9	9
♦ *Blue Sheep Lake / G.C.F. Dalziel / G.C.F. Dalziel / 1964*										
$184\frac{2}{8}$	$47\frac{5}{8}$	$45\frac{3}{8}$	$14\frac{2}{8}$	$14\frac{4}{8}$	$6\frac{6}{8}$	$6\frac{3}{8}$	$31\frac{3}{8}$	$31\frac{3}{8}$	9	9
♦ *Colt Lake / Herb Klein / Herb Klein / 1965*										
$184\frac{2}{8}$	$45\frac{7}{8}$	$42\frac{7}{8}$	$14\frac{7}{8}$	15	$7\frac{3}{8}$	$7\frac{3}{8}$	$22\frac{5}{8}$	$22\frac{3}{8}$	9	9
♦ *Kechika Range / Arthur R. Dubs / Arthur R. Dubs / 1966*										
$183\frac{7}{8}$	$44\frac{4}{8}$	$45\frac{5}{8}$	$13\frac{7}{8}$	$13\frac{7}{8}$	7	$7\frac{5}{8}$	$23\frac{7}{8}$	$23\frac{7}{8}$	12	12
♦ *Hudson Hope / Picked Up / Bill Beattie / 1961*										
$183\frac{6}{8}$	$44\frac{3}{8}$	$44\frac{5}{8}$	$14\frac{6}{8}$	$14\frac{6}{8}$	7	$6\frac{7}{8}$	$20\frac{5}{8}$	19	13	13
♦ *Dease Lake / Otis Chandler / Otis Chandler / 1966*										
$183\frac{5}{8}$	$43\frac{3}{8}$	$43\frac{2}{8}$	$14\frac{7}{8}$	$14\frac{7}{8}$	$7\frac{1}{8}$	7	$25\frac{7}{8}$	$25\frac{7}{8}$	14	14
♦ *Sikanni Chief River / Picked Up / Bob & Don Beattie / 1962*										
$183\frac{5}{8}$	$43\frac{3}{8}$	44	$14\frac{4}{8}$	$14\frac{4}{8}$	$8\frac{1}{8}$	8	$20\frac{1}{8}$	$22\frac{6}{8}$	14	14
♦ *Muncho Lake / Jeff Browne / Jeff Browne / 1990*										
$183\frac{3}{8}$	$44\frac{6}{8}$	$44\frac{1}{8}$	15	15	$6\frac{6}{8}$	$6\frac{4}{8}$	$26\frac{3}{8}$	$26\frac{1}{8}$	16	16
♦ *Kechika Range / John Caputo, Jr. / John Caputo, Jr. / 1961*										
$183\frac{3}{8}$	$49\frac{2}{8}$	$44\frac{7}{8}$	$13\frac{4}{8}$	$13\frac{4}{8}$	$6\frac{6}{8}$	$6\frac{5}{8}$	25	25	16	16
♦ *Terminus Mt. / Picked Up / Herb Klein / 1969*										
$183\frac{1}{8}$	$44\frac{7}{8}$	$46\frac{4}{8}$	$14\frac{1}{8}$	$14\frac{1}{8}$	$6\frac{7}{8}$	7	$29\frac{6}{8}$	$29\frac{5}{8}$	18	18
♦ *Cassiar Mts. / Robert S. Jackson / Robert S. Jackson / 1968*										

Score	Length of Horn		Circumference of Base		Circumference at Third Quarter		Greatest Spread	Tip-to-Tip Spread	All-Time Rank	State Rank
	R	L	R	L	R	L				
◆ *Locality / Hunter / Owner / Date Killed*										
183	45⁴⁄₈	44⁴⁄₈	14	14	7⁶⁄₈	7⁶⁄₈	25³⁄₈	25³⁄₈	19	19
◆ *Muskwa River / T.E. Shillingburg / T.E. Shillingburg / 1937*										
183	44	44⁶⁄₈	14⁵⁄₈	14⁵⁄₈	7	7³⁄₈	25⁷⁄₈	25⁷⁄₈	19	19
◆ *Kechika Range / John Caputo, Sr. / John Caputo, Sr. / 1966*										
183	45⁶⁄₈	44⁶⁄₈	14⁶⁄₈	14⁶⁄₈	6⁵⁄₈	6⁴⁄₈	27⁶⁄₈	27⁶⁄₈	19	19
◆ *Cassiar Mts. / Gordon Studer / Gordon Studer / 1967*										
182⁶⁄₈	46¹⁄₈	45⁷⁄₈	14⁴⁄₈	14²⁄₈	6⁶⁄₈	6⁵⁄₈	26³⁄₈	26²⁄₈	22	22
◆ *Cassiar Mts. / Alex Cox / Alex Cox / 1959*										
182⁶⁄₈	43	42²⁄₈	15¹⁄₈	15¹⁄₈	7¹⁄₈	7³⁄₈	24⁷⁄₈	24⁷⁄₈	22	22
◆ *Redfern Lake / James P. Winters / James P. Winters / 1970*										
182⁴⁄₈	42⁵⁄₈	41⁷⁄₈	14⁶⁄₈	14⁴⁄₈	7⁷⁄₈	7⁷⁄₈	24	24	24	24
◆ *Chlotapecta Creek / Gary F. Bogner / Gary F. Bogner / 1987*										
182³⁄₈	45¹⁄₈	45⁶⁄₈	14⁵⁄₈	14⁶⁄₈	6³⁄₈	6⁴⁄₈	31⁴⁄₈	31²⁄₈	25	25
◆ *Telegraph Creek / Mrs. John Crowe / Mrs. John Crowe / 1967*										
182³⁄₈	43	44⁷⁄₈	14⁵⁄₈	14⁶⁄₈	7	7	26⁶⁄₈	26⁶⁄₈	25	25
◆ *Kechika Range / Hallett Ward, Jr. / Hallett Ward, Jr. / 1967*										
182	41	42	15⁴⁄₈	15⁴⁄₈	8	8²⁄₈	27	27	27	27
◆ *Prophet River / John E. Hammett, Jr. / John E. Hammett, Jr. / 1944*										
182	45⁶⁄₈	45⁴⁄₈	14²⁄₈	14²⁄₈	6⁷⁄₈	7¹⁄₈	26⁴⁄₈	26⁴⁄₈	27	27
◆ *Sand Pile Lake / Al Robbins / Al Robbins / 1963*										
182	45¹⁄₈	44⁵⁄₈	14³⁄₈	14⁴⁄₈	6⁵⁄₈	6⁵⁄₈	26	26	27	27
◆ *Gataga River / Gary Moore / Gary Moore / 1965*										
181⁷⁄₈	43³⁄₈	43⁴⁄₈	15	15¹⁄₈	6⁴⁄₈	6⁵⁄₈	26⁵⁄₈	26⁵⁄₈	30	30
◆ *Cassiar Mts. / Norman Lougheed / Norman Lougheed / 1965*										
181⁴⁄₈	39	45²⁄₈	14³⁄₈	14⁴⁄₈	7⁶⁄₈	7⁶⁄₈	23⁶⁄₈	23⁶⁄₈	31	31
◆ *Burnt Rose Lake / Lloyd Zeman / Lloyd Zeman / 1970*										
181³⁄₈	44³⁄₈	44⁶⁄₈	15	14⁷⁄₈	6⁴⁄₈	6⁶⁄₈	27²⁄₈	27²⁄₈	32	32
◆ *Toad River / Jerry E. Dahl / Jerry E. Dahl / 1971*										
181	44³⁄₈	44⁷⁄₈	14³⁄₈	14⁴⁄₈	6²⁄₈	6³⁄₈	30⁵⁄₈	30⁵⁄₈	33	33
◆ *Watson Lake / C.W. Houle / C.W. Houle / 1967*										
180⁷⁄₈	41⁴⁄₈	42³⁄₈	15	14⁷⁄₈	7²⁄₈	7³⁄₈	26⁶⁄₈	26⁶⁄₈	34	34
◆ *Hudson Hope / Don Beattie / Don Beattie / 1945*										
180⁷⁄₈	44	43¹⁄₈	14⁷⁄₈	14⁶⁄₈	6⁶⁄₈	6⁷⁄₈	26²⁄₈	26²⁄₈	34	34
◆ *Sand Pile Lake / David S. Loos / David S. Loos / 1967*										
180⁵⁄₈	40⁵⁄₈	43	14¹⁄₈	14²⁄₈	7⁷⁄₈	8	22⁴⁄₈	22²⁄₈	36	36
◆ *Hudson Hope / David Slutker / David Slutker / 1966*										
180⁵⁄₈	38⁶⁄₈	38⁵⁄₈	15¹⁄₈	15²⁄₈	9¹⁄₈	9²⁄₈	23²⁄₈	19	36	36
◆ *Prophet River / Joseph Madonia / Joseph Madonia / 1970*										

Score	Length of Horn		Circumference of Base		Circumference at Third Quarter		Greatest Spread	Tip-to-Tip Spread	All-Time Rank	State Rank
	R	L	R	L	R	L				
◆ Locality / Hunter / Owner / Date Killed										
180 4/8	44 4/8	44 4/8	14 2/8	14 3/8	6 6/8	6 6/8	23 6/8	23 6/8	38	38
◆ Kechika Range / Tucker Davis / Tucker Davis / 1965										
180 3/8	45 6/8	44 5/8	14 2/8	14 3/8	6	6 3/8	29	29	39	39
◆ Telegraph Creek / John B. Winsor / John B. Winsor / 1966										
180 2/8	44 4/8	44	14 2/8	14 2/8	7	6 5/8	26 3/8	26 3/8	40	40
◆ Burnt Rose Lake / E.L. Cook / E.L. Cook / 1970										
179 7/8	42 7/8	42 2/8	14 5/8	14 4/8	8	7 7/8	24 7/8	24 7/8	41	41
◆ Prophet River / Bill Thomas / Bill Thomas / 1963										
179 7/8	44	43 3/8	14 2/8	14 1/8	7 1/8	7 5/8	0	28	41	41
◆ Ice Mt. / J.E. Mason / J.E. Mason / 1966										
179 5/8	39 4/8	44 5/8	13 6/8	13 7/8	9	8 6/8	21 3/8	21 3/8	43	43
◆ Cassiar Mts. / Ralph W. Hull / Ralph W. Hull / 1963										
179 3/8	43 2/8	39 3/8	14 6/8	14 5/8	7 3/8	7 5/8	21 3/8	21 3/8	44	44
◆ Pink Mt. / Gerald E. Howe / Gerald E. Howe / 1970										
179 3/8	45 4/8	44 7/8	14 3/8	14 2/8	6 5/8	6 3/8	24	24	44	44
◆ Gathto Creek / Gary J. Powell / Gary J. Powell / 1970										
179 2/8	43 3/8	44 5/8	13 7/8	13 6/8	7 2/8	6 6/8	26 3/8	26 3/8	46	46
◆ Toad River / Dennis Callison / Dennis Callison / 1957										
179 1/8	40 2/8	40 5/8	14 5/8	14 6/8	8 2/8	8 4/8	22 6/8	19 2/8	47	47
◆ Eydee Creek / Jack McNeill / Jack McNeill / 1967										
179 1/8	41 7/8	42 2/8	15	15 1/8	7	6 5/8	26 6/8	26	47	47
◆ Muskwa River / Cliff C. Cory / Cliff C. Cory / 1987										
178 7/8	44 4/8	45 5/8	13 6/8	14	6 7/8	6 4/8	28 3/8	28 3/8	49	49
◆ Kechika River / W.C. Waldron / W.C. Waldron / 1967										
178 3/8	39 3/8	48	13 6/8	13 6/8	7	7 3/8	26	24 2/8	50	50
◆ Moody Lake / J. Martin Benchoff / J. Martin Benchoff / 1966										
178 2/8	43 4/8	42 4/8	14 4/8	14 4/8	6 3/8	6 4/8	27 6/8	27 6/8	51	51
◆ Muskwa River / Don S. Hopkins / Don S. Hopkins / 1948										
178 2/8	43 6/8	44 2/8	14 2/8	14 2/8	6 5/8	6 4/8	24 2/8	24 2/8	51	51
◆ Tuchodi Lakes / Ross Peck / Ross Peck / 1963										
178 2/8	40 7/8	41 1/8	14 6/8	14 7/8	7 4/8	7 4/8	24	24	51	51
◆ Moody Lake / Raymond G. Speer / Raymond G. Speer / 1966										
178 1/8	43 3/8	45	13 7/8	14	6 6/8	6 7/8	26 6/8	26 4/8	54	54
◆ Gataga Mts. / Dan Auld / Dan Auld / 1960										
178 1/8	42 4/8	43 7/8	14 4/8	14 2/8	7 1/8	7	27 4/8	27 4/8	54	54
◆ Watson Lake / James C. Maly / James C. Maly / 1963										
177 7/8	41 5/8	40 2/8	14 2/8	14 3/8	8 5/8	8 7/8	24 3/8	24 3/8	56	56
◆ Frog River / Don Palmer / Don Palmer / 1968										

Score	Length of Horn R	L	Circumference of Base R	L	Circumference at Third Quarter R	L	Greatest Spread	Tip-to-Tip Spread	All-Time Rank	State Rank
	◆ *Locality / Hunter / Owner / Date Killed*									
177⁶⁄₈	43¹⁄₈	44⁷⁄₈	13⁶⁄₈	14	6⁶⁄₈	6⁶⁄₈	27⁵⁄₈	27³⁄₈	58	57
	◆ *Kechika Range / John Caputo, Sr. / John Caputo, Sr. / 1961*									
177⁶⁄₈	44⁴⁄₈	44	13⁷⁄₈	13⁶⁄₈	6³⁄₈	6³⁄₈	28⁴⁄₈	28²⁄₈	58	57
	◆ *Sikanni Chief River / Steven L. Rose / Steven L. Rose / 1961*									
177⁶⁄₈	39¹⁄₈	39³⁄₈	14⁵⁄₈	14⁵⁄₈	9	9	22⁷⁄₈	22²⁄₈	58	57
	◆ *Turnagain River / Byron Dalziel / Byron Dalziel / 1970*									
177⁵⁄₈	43¹⁄₈	44	14³⁄₈	14²⁄₈	6²⁄₈	6⁷⁄₈	26²⁄₈	26²⁄₈	61	60
	◆ *Telegraph Creek / Paul O'Hollaren / Paul O'Hollaren / 1967*									
177⁵⁄₈	45²⁄₈	44³⁄₈	13²⁄₈	13	7	6⁶⁄₈	27⁶⁄₈	27⁶⁄₈	61	60
	◆ *Toad River / Dewey Rawlings / Dewey Rawlings / 1969*									
177³⁄₈	42¹⁄₈	42	13⁴⁄₈	13⁵⁄₈	8	8¹⁄₈	23⁴⁄₈	23⁴⁄₈	64	62
	◆ *Toad River / John Huml / John Huml / 1969*									
177²⁄₈	42²⁄₈	42	14⁴⁄₈	13⁷⁄₈	7²⁄₈	7⁵⁄₈	22⁴⁄₈	22⁴⁄₈	65	63
	◆ *Racing River / Robert H. Kunzli / Robert H. Kunzli / 1959*									
177²⁄₈	44⁵⁄₈	44³⁄₈	13⁶⁄₈	13⁶⁄₈	6⁴⁄₈	6²⁄₈	24⁶⁄₈	24⁶⁄₈	65	63
	◆ *Atlin / Delmar Aldrich / Delmar Aldrich / 1964*									
177²⁄₈	40⁴⁄₈	42⁴⁄₈	15¹⁄₈	15¹⁄₈	6⁵⁄₈	6⁶⁄₈	29²⁄₈	29²⁄₈	65	63
	◆ *Ft. St. John / Ted T. Dabrowski / Ted T. Dabrowski / 1967*									
177²⁄₈	43¹⁄₈	42³⁄₈	14⁵⁄₈	14⁶⁄₈	6¹⁄₈	6¹⁄₈	29⁴⁄₈	29⁴⁄₈	65	63
	◆ *Cassiar Mts. / H.H. Kissinger / H.H. Kissinger / 1970*									
177¹⁄₈	44	42³⁄₈	14⁶⁄₈	15	6¹⁄₈	6	27⁷⁄₈	27⁷⁄₈	70	67
	◆ *Redfern Lake / W.H. Kirk / Unknown / 1923*									
177¹⁄₈	40⁷⁄₈	40⁶⁄₈	14²⁄₈	14²⁄₈	7¹⁄₈	7²⁄₈	23⁵⁄₈	23⁵⁄₈	70	67
	◆ *Mt. Lady Laurier / Chet Gifford / Chet Gifford / 1963*									
177	42¹⁄₈	40³⁄₈	14⁴⁄₈	14⁵⁄₈	6⁶⁄₈	6⁶⁄₈	25⁶⁄₈	25⁴⁄₈	72	69
	◆ *Prophet River / Wade Martin / Wade Martin / 1960*									
176⁷⁄₈	44⁵⁄₈	45⁴⁄₈	13¹⁄₈	13³⁄₈	6⁶⁄₈	6⁶⁄₈	29	29	73	70
	◆ *Dease Lake / Thomas M. Dye / Thomas M. Dye / 1966*									
176⁷⁄₈	41⁶⁄₈	39¹⁄₈	15²⁄₈	15	7¹⁄₈	7	25³⁄₈	25³⁄₈	73	70
	◆ *Rabbit River / George H. Rhoads / George H. Rhoads / 1971*									
176⁶⁄₈	44²⁄₈	43⁴⁄₈	14	14	6	6	24³⁄₈	24³⁄₈	75	72
	◆ *Cassiar Mts. / Donald J. Robb / Donald J. Robb / 1969*									
176⁵⁄₈	40	43⁷⁄₈	14⁶⁄₈	14⁴⁄₈	6⁷⁄₈	7⁴⁄₈	23	23	76	73
	◆ *Muskwa River / T.E. Shillingburg / T.E. Shillingburg / 1947*									
176⁴⁄₈	42⁷⁄₈	39⁷⁄₈	13⁶⁄₈	13²⁄₈	8³⁄₈	8⁴⁄₈	21⁵⁄₈	21	77	74
	◆ *Prophet River / Jim Caves / Jim Caves / 1959*									
176⁴⁄₈	45³⁄₈	44⁵⁄₈	14³⁄₈	14³⁄₈	5⁵⁄₈	5⁴⁄₈	28¹⁄₈	28¹⁄₈	77	74
	◆ *Gataga River / David C. Coleman / David C. Coleman / 1980*									

Score	Length of Horn		Circumference of Base		Circumference at Third Quarter		Greatest Spread	Tip-to-Tip Spread	All-Time Rank	State Rank
	R	L	R	L	R	L				
♦ *Locality / Hunter / Owner / Date Killed*										
176 4/8	41 2/8	41	14 5/8	14 6/8	7	6 6/8	24	23 6/8	77	74
♦ *Tuchodi River / James M. Peek / James M. Peek / 1993*										
176 3/8	40 7/8	40 2/8	15 4/8	15 4/8	6 7/8	6 4/8	23 6/8	23 6/8	80	77
♦ *Prophet River / O.B. Kahn / O.B. Kahn / 1965*										
176 3/8	44	44 7/8	14 2/8	14 2/8	6 3/8	6 3/8	28 3/8	28 3/8	80	77
♦ *Cassiar Mts. / Gene Klineburger / Gene Klineburger / 1965*										
176 3/8	42 7/8	43 4/8	15	15	5 6/8	5 5/8	29 4/8	29 2/8	80	77
♦ *Nabesche River / Kenneth W. Kleiman / Kenneth W. Kleiman / 1973*										
176 2/8	41 6/8	44	14 4/8	14 4/8	6 1/8	6 1/8	26 7/8	26 7/8	83	80
♦ *Prophet River / W.A. Newmiller / W.A. Newmiller / 1958*										
176 1/8	36 3/8	39 2/8	15	15	8 7/8	7 7/8	22 6/8	18 6/8	84	81
♦ *Richard Creek / James Milito / James Milito / 1967*										
176 1/8	40 7/8	36	15	15	7 4/8	7 6/8	21 7/8	19 7/8	84	81
♦ *Pink Mt. / Roland Schroeder / Roland Schroeder / 1968*										
176 1/8	43 3/8	43 2/8	14 1/8	14 1/8	6 5/8	6 5/8	25 4/8	25 4/8	84	81
♦ *Watson Lake / Elgin T. Gates / Elgin T. Gates / 1969*										
176	45 7/8	41 1/8	13 7/8	13 6/8	6 6/8	7	25 4/8	25 4/8	87	84
♦ *Cassiar Mts. / Walter O. Ford, Jr. / Walter O. Ford, Jr. / 1967*										
176	39	41 2/8	15 2/8	15 2/8	6 5/8	6 4/8	23 6/8	23 6/8	87	84
♦ *Tetsa River / Ron Sedor / Ron Sedor / 1988*										
176	41 2/8	40 2/8	14 2/8	14 4/8	8 1/8	8 1/8	21 6/8	21 6/8	87	84
♦ *Tuchodi Lakes / Terry Filas / Terry Filas / 1989*										
175 6/8	41 4/8	39 6/8	14 7/8	14 7/8	7 2/8	7 2/8	22 4/8	22 4/8	90	87
♦ *Prophet River / Jack O'Connor / Jack O'Connor / 1946*										
175 6/8	40 4/8	40 6/8	13 3/8	13 3/8	8 7/8	9	23 1/8	23 1/8	90	87
♦ *Terminus Mt. / Irvin Hart / Irvin Hart / 1964*										
175 6/8	42 1/8	37 1/8	15 5/8	15 5/8	7	7 1/8	21 1/8	20 7/8	90	87
♦ *Turnagain River / Lester C. Brewick / Lester C. Brewick / 1967*										
175 6/8	43 2/8	43 4/8	14 1/8	13 7/8	6 6/8	6 7/8	29 2/8	29 2/8	90	87
♦ *Blue Sheep Lake / John M. Griffith, Jr. / John M. Griffith, Jr. / 1971*										
175 5/8	42 4/8	41 5/8	14	14	6 6/8	6 7/8	21 6/8	21 6/8	94	91
♦ *Top Lake / Richard Buffington / Richard Buffington / 1964*										
175 5/8	46 3/8	43 4/8	13 5/8	13 5/8	5 5/8	5 4/8	28	27 7/8	94	91
♦ *Hudson Hope / Jim Papst / Jim Papst / 1966*										
175 4/8	46 6/8	48	12 6/8	12 5/8	5 5/8	5 5/8	30 6/8	30 6/8	97	93
♦ *Kiniskan Lake / Richard Stough / Richard Stough / 1961*										
175 4/8	41 2/8	41 2/8	14	14 2/8	7 3/8	7 5/8	23 6/8	23 6/8	97	93
♦ *Frog River / Robert McMurray / Robert McMurray / 1968*										

Score	Length of Horn		Circumference of Base		Circumference at Third Quarter		Greatest Spread	Tip-to-Tip Spread	All-Time Rank	State Rank
	R	L	R	L	R	L				
♦ Locality / Hunter / Owner / Date Killed										
175⁴⁄₈	42²⁄₈	42	14⁷⁄₈	14⁶⁄₈	6³⁄₈	6²⁄₈	28¹⁄₈	28¹⁄₈	97	93
♦ Colt Lake / Marsh Dear / Marsh Dear / 1970										
175⁴⁄₈	40¹⁄₈	36³⁄₈	14⁴⁄₈	14⁴⁄₈	8	7⁷⁄₈	22²⁄₈	19⁴⁄₈	97	93
♦ Prophet River / Sam C. Arnett III / Sam C. Arnett III / 1972										
175⁴⁄₈	38²⁄₈	38	15	15	8	8	23⁷⁄₈	21¹⁄₈	97	93
♦ Muskwa River / Robert M. Case / Robert M. Case / 1980										
175²⁄₈	41³⁄₈	42³⁄₈	12⁷⁄₈	12⁷⁄₈	8⁷⁄₈	9²⁄₈	22	21⁶⁄₈	103	98
♦ Tetsa River / Stanley Walchuk, Jr. / Stanley Walchuk, Jr. / 1992										
175	42²⁄₈	41⁶⁄₈	14²⁄₈	14²⁄₈	6⁵⁄₈	6⁵⁄₈	26⁵⁄₈	26⁵⁄₈	104	99
♦ Hudson Hope / Harry M. Haywood / Harry M. Haywood / 1949										
175	40⁵⁄₈	41³⁄₈	14¹⁄₈	14²⁄₈	7	7¹⁄₈	22	21⁵⁄₈	104	99
♦ Cassiar / John Sochor / John Sochor / 1962										
175	42⁶⁄₈	42⁶⁄₈	13⁷⁄₈	13⁷⁄₈	6³⁄₈	6⁵⁄₈	28⁵⁄₈	28⁵⁄₈	104	99
♦ Cold Fish Lake / Chris Reynolds / Chris Reynolds / 1963										
175	42⁴⁄₈	43²⁄₈	14²⁄₈	14²⁄₈	6¹⁄₈	6²⁄₈	24	24	104	99
♦ Colt Lake / Warren Page / Warren Page / 1965										
175	40⁴⁄₈	42	14	14¹⁄₈	8²⁄₈	7⁶⁄₈	22⁵⁄₈	20¹⁄₈	104	99
♦ Toad River / William E. Butler / William E. Butler / 1975										
174⁷⁄₈	41⁶⁄₈	42³⁄₈	14⁶⁄₈	14⁵⁄₈	6⁷⁄₈	6⁴⁄₈	21⁷⁄₈	21⁷⁄₈	109	104
♦ Cassiar / John W. Hull / John W. Hull / 1962										
174⁷⁄₈	38²⁄₈	38³⁄₈	13⁷⁄₈	14	9³⁄₈	9¹⁄₈	19⁶⁄₈	17	109	104
♦ Summit Lake / John D. Chalk III / John D. Chalk III / 1989										
174⁶⁄₈	38⁶⁄₈	38²⁄₈	14⁵⁄₈	14⁵⁄₈	7⁷⁄₈	8	21⁴⁄₈	19⁷⁄₈	111	106
♦ Watson Lake / Philip English / Philip English / 1965										
174⁵⁄₈	42¹⁄₈	41⁴⁄₈	14⁶⁄₈	14⁴⁄₈	6¹⁄₈	6	30²⁄₈	30²⁄₈	112	107
♦ Stikine River / Hugh J. O'Dower / Hugh J. O'Dower / 1952										
174⁵⁄₈	41⁴⁄₈	41⁵⁄₈	14¹⁄₈	14¹⁄₈	7³⁄₈	6⁵⁄₈	24⁷⁄₈	24⁷⁄₈	112	107
♦ Sikanni Chief River / Joseph W. Quarto / Joseph W. Quarto / 1965										
174⁵⁄₈	36⁷⁄₈	39	14⁶⁄₈	14⁶⁄₈	8³⁄₈	8⁴⁄₈	20⁷⁄₈	20²⁄₈	112	107
♦ Prophet River / Craig R. Johnson / Craig R. Johnson / 1989										
174⁴⁄₈	40⁶⁄₈	41²⁄₈	15	14⁶⁄₈	8	8²⁄₈	27⁴⁄₈	27⁴⁄₈	115	110
♦ Dease Lake / Alice J. Landreth / Alice J. Landreth / 1964										
174⁴⁄₈	42⁶⁄₈	42	14⁵⁄₈	14⁶⁄₈	5⁵⁄₈	6	24⁶⁄₈	24⁶⁄₈	115	110
♦ Ram Lake / Walter Smetaniuk / Walter Smetaniuk / 1966										
174⁴⁄₈	40	40²⁄₈	15	15	6⁷⁄₈	6⁷⁄₈	22⁶⁄₈	21	115	110
♦ Dall Lake / Darrell Orth / Darrell Orth / 1990										
174³⁄₈	41²⁄₈	40¹⁄₈	13⁴⁄₈	13⁵⁄₈	7⁵⁄₈	8	20⁵⁄₈	20⁵⁄₈	118	113
♦ Racing River / Lash Callison / Lash Callison / 1959										

BRITISH COLUMBIA STONE'S SHEEP *(continued)*

Score	Length of Horn		Circumference of Base		Circumference at Third Quarter		Greatest Spread	Tip-to-Tip Spread	All-Time Rank	State Rank
	R	L	R	L	R	L				
	Locality / Hunter / Owner / Date Killed									
174³⁄₈	39⁴⁄₈	41⁵⁄₈	14⁶⁄₈	14⁶⁄₈	7³⁄₈	6⁴⁄₈	21⁶⁄₈	21⁶⁄₈	118	113
Top Lake / W.E. Fisher / W.E. Fisher / 1964										
174³⁄₈	37	38⁵⁄₈	14⁴⁄₈	14³⁄₈	8⁷⁄₈	8⁶⁄₈	21⁶⁄₈	21	118	113
Cassiar Mts. / Gordon Studer / Gordon Studer / 1966										
174³⁄₈	40³⁄₈	40⁶⁄₈	15	15¹⁄₈	6¹⁄₈	6⁴⁄₈	24	24	118	113
Tuchodi Lakes / Lydell Johnson / Lydell Johnson / 1993										
174²⁄₈	46⁴⁄₈	46²⁄₈	13³⁄₈	13³⁄₈	5⁴⁄₈	5³⁄₈	33	33	122	117
Watson Lake / G.C.F. Dalziel / G.C.F. Dalziel / 1962										
174²⁄₈	42²⁄₈	46²⁄₈	12⁵⁄₈	12⁴⁄₈	6⁵⁄₈	6⁵⁄₈	26³⁄₈	26³⁄₈	122	117
W. Toad River / Unknown / N.B. Sorenson / PR 1969										
174²⁄₈	39⁷⁄₈	39¹⁄₈	15¹⁄₈	15¹⁄₈	6⁷⁄₈	6⁶⁄₈	22⁵⁄₈	22⁵⁄₈	122	117
Toad River / Bill Hicks, Jr. / Bill Hicks, Jr. / 1990										
174²⁄₈	38²⁄₈	39²⁄₈	15⁴⁄₈	15⁶⁄₈	6⁷⁄₈	6⁶⁄₈	26⁶⁄₈	26⁴⁄₈	122	117
Redfern Lake / Wilf Klingsat / Wilf Klingsat / 1990										
174¹⁄₈	42²⁄₈	40⁷⁄₈	14	14	7	7⁶⁄₈	23	23	126	121
Cold Fish Lake / Roberto De La Garza / Roberto De La Garza / 1961										
174¹⁄₈	42²⁄₈	41³⁄₈	14⁷⁄₈	15²⁄₈	5²⁄₈	5²⁄₈	25	25	126	121
Gold Bar / Henry O. Carlson / Henry O. Carlson / 1962										
174¹⁄₈	39²⁄₈	43³⁄₈	14⁴⁄₈	14⁴⁄₈	6⁴⁄₈	6²⁄₈	25³⁄₈	25³⁄₈	126	121
Mt. Winston / Norman A. Hill / Norman A. Hill / 1967										
174¹⁄₈	41¹⁄₈	41⁴⁄₈	14¹⁄₈	14³⁄₈	6⁵⁄₈	6⁷⁄₈	23⁵⁄₈	23⁵⁄₈	126	121
Muskwa River / Gary Powell / Gary Powell / 1974										
174	44⁶⁄₈	41	14	13⁶⁄₈	6²⁄₈	6⁷⁄₈	22⁷⁄₈	22⁷⁄₈	130	125
Muskwa River / Wade Martin / Wade Martin / 1961										
174	44⁶⁄₈	40	14¹⁄₈	14¹⁄₈	6⁴⁄₈	6⁴⁄₈	27	27	130	125
Cassiar Mts. / Russell Castner / Russell Castner / 1966										
174	41⁶⁄₈	38⁴⁄₈	14¹⁄₈	14¹⁄₈	6⁶⁄₈	6⁷⁄₈	26³⁄₈	26³⁄₈	130	125
Cassiar Mts. / George H. Glass / George H. Glass / 1966										
174	40	41	14⁵⁄₈	14⁶⁄₈	6⁵⁄₈	6⁶⁄₈	20³⁄₈	19⁴⁄₈	130	125
Muskwa Area / W.R. Collie / W.R. Collie / 1972										
173⁷⁄₈	44²⁄₈	43⁵⁄₈	13⁴⁄₈	13⁴⁄₈	7	6²⁄₈	27²⁄₈	27²⁄₈	134	129
Stikine River / Vernon D. E. Smith / Vernon D. E. Smith / 1960										
173⁷⁄₈	44³⁄₈	44²⁄₈	13²⁄₈	13³⁄₈	5⁷⁄₈	6	29⁷⁄₈	29⁷⁄₈	134	129
Cassiar / Fred F. Wells / Fred F. Wells / 1961										
173⁷⁄₈	39⁶⁄₈	38¹⁄₈	14⁴⁄₈	14³⁄₈	8⁷⁄₈	9	25	25	134	129
Gataga River / H.L. Hale / H.L. Hale / 1968										
173⁷⁄₈	40¹⁄₈	38⁴⁄₈	13⁴⁄₈	13⁶⁄₈	8³⁄₈	8³⁄₈	20²⁄₈	16	134	129
Tetsa River / Eugene P. LaSota / Eugene P. LaSota / 1973										

BRITISH COLUMBIA STONE'S SHEEP *(continued)*

Score	Length of Horn R	Length of Horn L	Circumference of Base R	Circumference of Base L	Circumference at Third Quarter R	Circumference at Third Quarter L	Greatest Spread	Tip-to-Tip Spread	All-Time Rank	State Rank
	♦ *Locality / Hunter / Owner / Date Killed*									
173 7/8	41 5/8	41 4/8	15	14 5/8	6 6/8	6 6/8	21 5/8	21 5/8	134	129
	♦ *Rabbit River / Terry J. Ridley / Terry J. Ridley / 1994*									
173 6/8	47 3/8	43 1/8	13 4/8	13 4/8	6 4/8	5 3/8	25 2/8	25 2/8	139	134
	♦ *Halfway River / Lynn Ross / Lynn Ross / 1957*									
173 6/8	43 4/8	43 4/8	13 5/8	14	6 2/8	6 2/8	28 2/8	28 2/8	139	134
	♦ *Terminus Mt. / Chester A. Crago / Chester A. Crago / 1962*									
173 6/8	41 4/8	43	14	14	6 3/8	6 4/8	30 4/8	30 4/8	139	134
	♦ *Kechika Range / Russell C. Cutter / Russell C. Cutter / 1965*									
173 6/8	41 5/8	40 7/8	14 4/8	14 4/8	6 5/8	7 2/8	25 6/8	25 6/8	139	134
	♦ *Muskwa River / W. Michalsky / W. Michalsky / 1965*									
173 6/8	41 4/8	40 6/8	14 1/8	14 2/8	6 5/8	6 5/8	22 6/8	22 6/8	139	134
	♦ *Toad River / Peter C. Swenson / Peter C. Swenson / 1993*									
173 5/8	45 4/8	40 1/8	13 4/8	13 4/8	6 5/8	6 5/8	26 2/8	26 2/8	144	139
	♦ *Peace River / Melvin Shearer / Unknown / 1933*									
173 5/8	42 5/8	42	14 3/8	14 3/8	6 3/8	5 7/8	23 2/8	23 2/8	144	139
	♦ *Hudson Hope / G.F. Moore / G.F. Moore / 1963*									
173 4/8	40 2/8	41 2/8	13 4/8	13 3/8	8 1/8	7 7/8	20 4/8	20 4/8	147	141
	♦ *Cassiar / Charles F. Haas / Charles F. Haas / 1960*									
173 4/8	41 6/8	41 6/8	14 1/8	14 1/8	6 2/8	6 2/8	28 5/8	28 5/8	147	141
	♦ *Telegraph Creek / L. Iverson / L. Iverson / 1961*									
173 4/8	39	42	15	15	7 4/8	6 4/8	22 4/8	22 4/8	147	141
	♦ *Dease Lake / George I. Parker / George I. Parker / 1963*									
173 4/8	41	41 6/8	14	14	9 4/8	9	27	27	147	141
	♦ *Dease Lake / John T. Blackwell / John T. Blackwell / 1964*									
173 4/8	41 3/8	41 5/8	14 4/8	14 2/8	6 2/8	6 2/8	26 4/8	26 4/8	147	141
	♦ *Coldfish Lake / Roger Britton / Roger Britton / 1986*									
173 4/8	39 6/8	40 2/8	15 4/8	15 3/8	6 2/8	6 1/8	24 7/8	24 6/8	147	141
	♦ *Schooler Creek / Wade Nielsen / Wade Nielsen / 1992*									
173 3/8	43 3/8	44	13 4/8	13 4/8	6	6 6/8	28	28	154	147
	♦ *Toad River / H.L. Vidricksen / H.L. Vidricksen / 1960*									
173 3/8	38 3/8	38 4/8	14 4/8	14 6/8	8 3/8	8	20 6/8	19 3/8	154	147
	♦ *Tuchodi Lakes / George S. Gayle III / George S. Gayle III / 1972*									
173 3/8	41 5/8	42 6/8	14 3/8	14 4/8	5 5/8	5 5/8	26 4/8	26 4/8	154	147
	♦ *Racing River / Dick Sullivan / Dick Sullivan / 1982*									
173 3/8	39 3/8	38 6/8	15 3/8	15 4/8	6 3/8	6 6/8	21 6/8	20 6/8	154	147
	♦ *Sikanni Chief River / Ray M. Fabri / Ray M. Fabri / 1992*									
173 2/8	41 6/8	41 2/8	14 4/8	14 3/8	6 4/8	6 2/8	24 6/8	24 6/8	158	151
	♦ *Cassiar Mts. / John Caputo / John Caputo / 1962*									

Score	Length of Horn		Circumference of Base		Circumference at Third Quarter		Greatest Spread	Tip-to-Tip Spread	All-Time Rank	State Rank
	R	L	R	L	R	L				
◆ Locality / Hunter / Owner / Date Killed										
$173\frac{2}{8}$	$44\frac{4}{8}$	45	$13\frac{2}{8}$	$13\frac{2}{8}$	$5\frac{5}{8}$	$5\frac{7}{8}$	$26\frac{5}{8}$	$26\frac{5}{8}$	158	151
◆ Cassiar Mts. / William Warrick / William Warrick / 1963										
$173\frac{1}{8}$	$40\frac{1}{8}$	$41\frac{2}{8}$	14	14	7	$6\frac{7}{8}$	$24\frac{5}{8}$	$24\frac{5}{8}$	160	153
◆ Halfway River / Frank H. Rogers / Frank H. Rogers / 1962										
$173\frac{1}{8}$	$40\frac{4}{8}$	$41\frac{3}{8}$	$14\frac{7}{8}$	$14\frac{7}{8}$	6	$6\frac{3}{8}$	$27\frac{4}{8}$	$27\frac{4}{8}$	160	153
◆ Cassiar Mts. / Charles F. Nadler / Charles F. Nadler / 1967										
$173\frac{1}{8}$	$41\frac{3}{8}$	40	$14\frac{1}{8}$	$14\frac{2}{8}$	$7\frac{2}{8}$	$7\frac{2}{8}$	$21\frac{6}{8}$	$21\frac{6}{8}$	160	153
◆ Summit Lake / Henry L. Baddley / Henry L. Baddley / 1979										
173	$39\frac{4}{8}$	38	$14\frac{4}{8}$	$14\frac{4}{8}$	8	8	26	26	163	156
◆ Muskwa River / Elmer Keith / Elmer Keith / 1937										
173	34	45	15	15	$7\frac{4}{8}$	$7\frac{1}{8}$	$24\frac{2}{8}$	$24\frac{2}{8}$	163	156
◆ Gataga River / Wilson Southwell / Wilson Southwell / 1958										
173	$40\frac{3}{8}$	$41\frac{3}{8}$	$13\frac{6}{8}$	$13\frac{7}{8}$	$7\frac{2}{8}$	$7\frac{5}{8}$	$23\frac{4}{8}$	$21\frac{4}{8}$	163	156
◆ Prophet River / Merrimen M. Watkins / Merrimen M. Watkins / 1965										
173	42	$42\frac{2}{8}$	$13\frac{6}{8}$	14	$6\frac{6}{8}$	$6\frac{5}{8}$	$23\frac{2}{8}$	$23\frac{2}{8}$	163	156
◆ Prophet River / Robert E. Hammond / Robert E. Hammond / 1969										
173	$42\frac{5}{8}$	$42\frac{3}{8}$	14	14	$5\frac{6}{8}$	$5\frac{6}{8}$	$27\frac{1}{8}$	$27\frac{1}{8}$	163	156
◆ Cold Fish Lake / A.H. Clise / A.H. Clise / 1970										
173	$41\frac{5}{8}$	$42\frac{5}{8}$	$14\frac{1}{8}$	$13\frac{7}{8}$	$5\frac{5}{8}$	$5\frac{7}{8}$	$24\frac{3}{8}$	$24\frac{3}{8}$	163	156
◆ Mile 422 / Garland N. Teich / Garland N. Teich / 1971										
$172\frac{7}{8}$	$40\frac{4}{8}$	$39\frac{5}{8}$	$14\frac{3}{8}$	$14\frac{4}{8}$	$6\frac{6}{8}$	$6\frac{6}{8}$	$24\frac{1}{8}$	$24\frac{1}{8}$	170	162
◆ Prophet River / Harry M. Haywood / Harry M. Haywood / 1956										
$172\frac{7}{8}$	$40\frac{7}{8}$	$42\frac{4}{8}$	$14\frac{7}{8}$	$14\frac{7}{8}$	$5\frac{4}{8}$	6	$25\frac{3}{8}$	$25\frac{3}{8}$	170	162
◆ Summit Lake / A. Tony Mathisen / A. Tony Mathisen / 1958										
$172\frac{7}{8}$	$42\frac{7}{8}$	$42\frac{2}{8}$	$13\frac{7}{8}$	$13\frac{7}{8}$	$6\frac{4}{8}$	$6\frac{3}{8}$	$25\frac{1}{8}$	$25\frac{1}{8}$	170	162
◆ Cassiar Mts. / Wayne C. Eubank / Wayne C. Eubank / 1963										
$172\frac{7}{8}$	$46\frac{3}{8}$	35	14	14	$6\frac{4}{8}$	$6\frac{4}{8}$	$21\frac{2}{8}$	$21\frac{2}{8}$	170	162
◆ Cassiar Mts. / Orval H. Ause / Orval H. Ause / 1968										
$172\frac{7}{8}$	$37\frac{7}{8}$	37	15	$14\frac{6}{8}$	$7\frac{5}{8}$	$7\frac{7}{8}$	23	20	170	162
◆ Cassiar Mts. / Greg Williams / Greg Williams / 1976										
$172\frac{6}{8}$	$36\frac{4}{8}$	37	$14\frac{6}{8}$	15	$8\frac{3}{8}$	$8\frac{4}{8}$	$19\frac{1}{8}$	$19\frac{1}{8}$	175	167
◆ Sikanni Chief River / Mrs. Maitland Armstrong / Mrs. Maitland Armstrong / 1962										
$172\frac{6}{8}$	$40\frac{2}{8}$	$41\frac{6}{8}$	$14\frac{2}{8}$	$14\frac{3}{8}$	$6\frac{5}{8}$	7	22	22	175	167
◆ Gataga River / Basil C. Bradbury / Basil C. Bradbury / 1968										
$172\frac{6}{8}$	$36\frac{4}{8}$	$36\frac{2}{8}$	$14\frac{6}{8}$	15	$8\frac{6}{8}$	$8\frac{4}{8}$	$21\frac{3}{8}$	$15\frac{3}{8}$	175	167
◆ Muskwa River / Andrew A. Samuels, Jr. / Andrew A. Samuels, Jr. / 1969										
$172\frac{6}{8}$	42	$41\frac{6}{8}$	$14\frac{5}{8}$	$14\frac{4}{8}$	$6\frac{2}{8}$	$6\frac{1}{8}$	$27\frac{5}{8}$	$27\frac{5}{8}$	175	167
◆ Dall Lake / Robert J. Rood / Robert J. Rood / 1971										

BRITISH COLUMBIA STONE'S SHEEP *(continued)*

Score	Length of Horn R	Length of Horn L	Circumference of Base R	Circumference of Base L	Circumference at Third Quarter R	Circumference at Third Quarter L	Greatest Spread	Tip-to-Tip Spread	All-Time Rank	State Rank
♦ *Locality / Hunter / Owner / Date Killed*										
172 5/8	40 3/8	40 4/8	14 2/8	14 2/8	7 2/8	7 1/8	24 5/8	24 5/8	179	171
♦ *Liard River / Jack N. Allen / Jack N. Allen / 1959*										
172 5/8	38 7/8	40	14 7/8	14 7/8	6 6/8	6 6/8	24 6/8	23	179	171
♦ *Blue Sheep Lake / John Deromedi / John Deromedi / 1989*										
172 5/8	43 2/8	42 5/8	14 1/8	14 1/8	5 7/8	5 4/8	26 1/8	26 1/8	179	171
♦ *Kechika River / William B. McClelland / William B. McClelland / 1991*										
172 4/8	42 2/8	42	13 7/8	13 5/8	6 1/8	5 7/8	29 4/8	29 4/8	182	174
♦ *Halfway River / Cecil V. Mumbert / Cecil V. Mumbert / 1958*										
172 4/8	40 4/8	41 6/8	14 4/8	14 2/8	6 4/8	6 2/8	25	25	182	174
♦ *Dease Lake / John T. Blackwell / John T. Blackwell / 1963*										
172 4/8	37 2/8	38	15 2/8	15 5/8	6 6/8	6 6/8	27 5/8	27 5/8	182	174
♦ *Prophet River / William A. Miller / William A. Miller / 1969*										
172 4/8	39 6/8	42	14 1/8	14 2/8	6 6/8	7	25 3/8	25 3/8	182	174
♦ *Watson Lake / Julian Gutierrez / Julian Gutierrez / 1970*										
172 4/8	37 3/8	41 7/8	14 4/8	14 3/8	6 4/8	7	23 3/8	23 1/8	182	174
♦ *Muskwa River / L.A. Denson / L.A. Denson / 1971*										
172 4/8	41 1/8	41 1/8	15 1/8	15 1/8	6	6 1/8	28 2/8	28 2/8	182	174
♦ *Mile Creek / H.D. Miller / H.D. Miller / 1980*										
172 3/8	37 1/8	38 4/8	14 2/8	14 2/8	8 4/8	8 3/8	23 1/8	17 2/8	188	180
♦ *Sandbar Creek / John La Rocca / John La Rocca / 1957*										
172 3/8	45 1/8	45 2/8	13	13	5 5/8	5 7/8	28	28	188	180
♦ *Cold Fish Lake / Juan Brittingham / Juan Brittingham / 1961*										
172 3/8	39 3/8	39 6/8	15 5/8	15 5/8	6 6/8	6	20 2/8	20 2/8	188	180
♦ *Ospika Drainage / Mark Swenson / Mark Swenson / 1964*										
172 3/8	41 5/8	41 4/8	14 5/8	14 5/8	6 2/8	6 1/8	23 4/8	23 4/8	188	180
♦ *Dall Lake / Paul M. Rothermel, Jr. / Paul M. Rothermel, Jr. / 1965*										
172 3/8	38 6/8	38 7/8	15 1/8	15 2/8	6 5/8	6 5/8	25 1/8	25 1/8	188	180
♦ *Muskwa River / Ken W. Scheer / Ken W. Scheer / 1985*										
172 2/8	41 1/8	41 1/8	14 2/8	14 1/8	6 5/8	6	21 4/8	21 3/8	194	185
♦ *Prophet River / George F. Crain / George F. Crain / 1961*										
172 2/8	40 4/8	38 2/8	14 3/8	14 4/8	6 7/8	7	21 4/8	20	194	185
♦ *Muskwa River / Arvid F. Benson / Arvid F. Benson / 1963*										
172 2/8	41 6/8	36 6/8	14 2/8	14 4/8	7 4/8	8	23 1/8	23 1/8	194	185
♦ *Sikanni Chief River / John B. Collier IV / John B. Collier IV / 1967*										
172 2/8	39 6/8	42 2/8	14	14 2/8	7 7/8	6 6/8	26 4/8	26 4/8	194	185
♦ *Cassiar Mts. / Michaux Nash, Jr. / Michaux Nash, Jr. / 1967*										
172 2/8	42 4/8	42 2/8	14 4/8	14 4/8	5 6/8	5 4/8	29	29	194	185
♦ *Prophet River / S.E. Burrell / S.E. Burrell / 1967*										

Score	Length of Horn		Circumference of Base		Circumference at Third Quarter		Greatest Spread	Tip-to-Tip Spread	All-Time Rank	State Rank
	R	L	R	L	R	L				
♦ *Locality / Hunter / Owner / Date Killed*										
172²⁄₈	41⁶⁄₈	41²⁄₈	14⁴⁄₈	14⁵⁄₈	6	6¹⁄₈	28⁴⁄₈	28⁴⁄₈	194	185
♦ *Akie River / O.J. Baggenstoss / O.J. Baggenstoss / 1968*										
172²⁄₈	39	38⁴⁄₈	14⁴⁄₈	14⁴⁄₈	7⁴⁄₈	7³⁄₈	20²⁄₈	18²⁄₈	194	185
♦ *Prophet River / Larry Ciejka / Larry Ciejka / 1977*										
172²⁄₈	40⁶⁄₈	41⁶⁄₈	14⁴⁄₈	14⁴⁄₈	6²⁄₈	6³⁄₈	22¹⁄₈	22¹⁄₈	194	185
♦ *Chlotapeeta Creek / Merle Freyborg / Merle Freyborg / 1992*										
172¹⁄₈	41⁵⁄₈	41	13	13	9²⁄₈	9²⁄₈	30	30	202	193
♦ *Dease Lake / W.M. Rudd / W.M. Rudd / 1964*										
172¹⁄₈	37⁶⁄₈	34⁵⁄₈	14	14²⁄₈	9¹⁄₈	9¹⁄₈	23²⁄₈	19	202	193
♦ *Cassiar Mts. / Keith M. Kissinger / Keith M. Kissinger / 1968*										
172¹⁄₈	39	40⁵⁄₈	14⁴⁄₈	14²⁄₈	7¹⁄₈	6⁷⁄₈	23²⁄₈	23²⁄₈	202	193
♦ *Alaska Hwy. / Robert Murdock / Robert Murdock / 1968*										
172¹⁄₈	40²⁄₈	38¹⁄₈	14²⁄₈	14²⁄₈	7³⁄₈	7²⁄₈	23²⁄₈	21²⁄₈	202	193
♦ *Burnt Rose Lake / John K. De Broux / John K. De Broux / 1970*										
172¹⁄₈	40³⁄₈	41	14³⁄₈	14²⁄₈	6³⁄₈	6⁴⁄₈	20⁵⁄₈	20²⁄₈	202	193
♦ *Muskwa River / Greg L. Stires / Greg L. Stires / 1984*										
172	39²⁄₈	40²⁄₈	15	15	6⁵⁄₈	6⁴⁄₈	23²⁄₈	23²⁄₈	207	198
♦ *Hudson Hope / Don Stewart / Don Stewart / 1961*										
172	45⁵⁄₈	43³⁄₈	12⁷⁄₈	13	6²⁄₈	6²⁄₈	25⁷⁄₈	25⁷⁄₈	207	198
♦ *Atlin / Thomas E. Francis / Thomas E. Francis / 1964*										
172	40²⁄₈	41⁶⁄₈	14²⁄₈	14²⁄₈	6¹⁄₈	6	25²⁄₈	25²⁄₈	207	198
♦ *Pelly Creek / Robert A. Lubeck / Robert A. Lubeck / 1968*										
172	41²⁄₈	41⁴⁄₈	14³⁄₈	14²⁄₈	6²⁄₈	6¹⁄₈	26⁶⁄₈	26⁶⁄₈	207	198
♦ *Denetiah Lake / Michael G. Meeker / Michael G. Meeker / 1969*										
172	40²⁄₈	40	14⁵⁄₈	14⁵⁄₈	6²⁄₈	6¹⁄₈	29	29	207	198
♦ *Prairie River / C.J. McElroy / C.J. McElroy / 1969*										
172	42¹⁄₈	42¹⁄₈	14	14	6²⁄₈	6²⁄₈	25¹⁄₈	25¹⁄₈	207	198
♦ *Toad River / David G. Kidder / David G. Kidder / 1975*										
172	41²⁄₈	40⁶⁄₈	13⁴⁄₈	13⁴⁄₈	6⁷⁄₈	6⁵⁄₈	23	23	207	198
♦ *Toad River / Steve Best / Steve Best / 1988*										
171⁷⁄₈	38⁶⁄₈	38¹⁄₈	14²⁄₈	14¹⁄₈	7³⁄₈	7⁵⁄₈	23⁶⁄₈	20²⁄₈	214	205
♦ *Akie River / Henry K. Leworthy / Henry K. Leworthy / 1966*										
171⁷⁄₈	38³⁄₈	39	13⁷⁄₈	13⁷⁄₈	8⁵⁄₈	8⁷⁄₈	20⁴⁄₈	20⁴⁄₈	214	205
♦ *Island Lake / Martin F. Wood / Martin F. Wood / 1970*										
171⁷⁄₈	43²⁄₈	41³⁄₈	14¹⁄₈	14¹⁄₈	5⁶⁄₈	5⁶⁄₈	30²⁄₈	30²⁄₈	214	205
♦ *Cache Creek / Kenneth A. Jeronimus / Kenneth A. Jeronimus / 1974*										
171⁷⁄₈	42³⁄₈	39⁶⁄₈	14¹⁄₈	14²⁄₈	6²⁄₈	6³⁄₈	23⁵⁄₈	23⁵⁄₈	214	205
♦ *Toad River / Larry Jenkins / Larry Jenkins / 1988*										

Score	Length of Horn		Circumference of Base		Circumference at Third Quarter		Greatest Spread	Tip-to-Tip Spread	All-Time Rank	State Rank
	R	L	R	L	R	L				

♦ *Locality / Hunter / Owner / Date Killed*

$171\frac{6}{8}$	$39\frac{2}{8}$	41	$13\frac{4}{8}$	$13\frac{4}{8}$	8	8	$27\frac{4}{8}$	$27\frac{4}{8}$	218	209

♦ *Gataga River / Dan Auld / Dan Auld / 1958*

$171\frac{6}{8}$	$43\frac{2}{8}$	43	$14\frac{4}{8}$	$14\frac{2}{8}$	$5\frac{3}{8}$	$5\frac{4}{8}$	$27\frac{1}{8}$	$27\frac{1}{8}$	218	209

♦ *Cassiar Mts. / John Caputo, Sr. / John Caputo, Sr. / 1960*

$171\frac{6}{8}$	$40\frac{4}{8}$	$42\frac{6}{8}$	14	$14\frac{1}{8}$	$6\frac{4}{8}$	$7\frac{2}{8}$	$24\frac{6}{8}$	$24\frac{6}{8}$	218	209

♦ *Trimble Lake / Roy E. Stare / Roy E. Stare / 1962*

$171\frac{6}{8}$	$36\frac{2}{8}$	37	$14\frac{4}{8}$	$14\frac{5}{8}$	$10\frac{2}{8}$	$8\frac{3}{8}$	$21\frac{6}{8}$	$13\frac{4}{8}$	218	209

♦ *Muskwa River / W.I. Spencer / W.I. Spencer / 1963*

$171\frac{6}{8}$	$39\frac{2}{8}$	$41\frac{2}{8}$	$14\frac{7}{8}$	$14\frac{7}{8}$	6	$6\frac{4}{8}$	$23\frac{5}{8}$	$23\frac{5}{8}$	218	209

♦ *Dease Lake / Michaux Nash, Jr. / Michaux Nash, Jr. / 1965*

$171\frac{6}{8}$	$37\frac{6}{8}$	$39\frac{6}{8}$	16	16	$6\frac{7}{8}$	$6\frac{3}{8}$	$21\frac{3}{8}$	$21\frac{3}{8}$	218	209

♦ *Gataga River / D.R. Seabaugh / D.R. Seabaugh / 1971*

$171\frac{6}{8}$	$38\frac{4}{8}$	$38\frac{4}{8}$	$15\frac{5}{8}$	$15\frac{5}{8}$	$6\frac{3}{8}$	$6\frac{7}{8}$	$23\frac{5}{8}$	$24\frac{2}{8}$	218	209

♦ *Prophet River / Don Haemmerlein / Don Haemmerlein / 1977*

$171\frac{6}{8}$	$42\frac{4}{8}$	$42\frac{6}{8}$	14	$14\frac{2}{8}$	$6\frac{3}{8}$	6	$24\frac{7}{8}$	$24\frac{7}{8}$	218	209

♦ *Rock Island Lake / William K. Mortlock / William K. Mortlock / 1988*

$171\frac{5}{8}$	$37\frac{2}{8}$	$37\frac{1}{8}$	14	14	$8\frac{6}{8}$	$8\frac{6}{8}$	$20\frac{3}{8}$	$20\frac{3}{8}$	226	217

♦ *Tuchodi Lakes / Win Condict / Win Condict / 1951*

$171\frac{5}{8}$	$42\frac{4}{8}$	$42\frac{3}{8}$	$13\frac{4}{8}$	$13\frac{4}{8}$	$6\frac{1}{8}$	$6\frac{2}{8}$	$26\frac{1}{8}$	26	226	217

♦ *Dease Lake / C.E. Krieger / C.E. Krieger / 1962*

$171\frac{5}{8}$	$44\frac{1}{8}$	40	$13\frac{5}{8}$	$13\frac{4}{8}$	$6\frac{3}{8}$	$6\frac{2}{8}$	$25\frac{6}{8}$	$25\frac{6}{8}$	226	217

♦ *Muncho Lake / H.W. Julien / H.W. Julien / 1966*

$171\frac{5}{8}$	$38\frac{6}{8}$	$36\frac{3}{8}$	$14\frac{2}{8}$	$14\frac{2}{8}$	$8\frac{5}{8}$	$8\frac{5}{8}$	$20\frac{1}{8}$	$20\frac{1}{8}$	226	217

♦ *Toad River / H.W. Julien / H.W. Julien / 1969*

$171\frac{5}{8}$	$37\frac{2}{8}$	$45\frac{3}{8}$	$14\frac{1}{8}$	$14\frac{1}{8}$	6	$6\frac{1}{8}$	24	$21\frac{2}{8}$	226	217

♦ *Prophet River / John Whitcombe / John Whitcombe / 1981*

$171\frac{4}{8}$	$40\frac{4}{8}$	$40\frac{4}{8}$	$14\frac{2}{8}$	$14\frac{2}{8}$	$6\frac{2}{8}$	$6\frac{2}{8}$	$23\frac{3}{8}$	$23\frac{3}{8}$	231	222

♦ *Prophet River / L.A. Denson / L.A. Denson / 1963*

$171\frac{4}{8}$	37	$38\frac{4}{8}$	$14\frac{4}{8}$	$14\frac{4}{8}$	$7\frac{4}{8}$	$7\frac{6}{8}$	$22\frac{2}{8}$	17	231	222

♦ *Trutch / Charles F. Waterman / Charles F. Waterman / 1964*

$171\frac{4}{8}$	39	$38\frac{4}{8}$	$14\frac{6}{8}$	$14\frac{6}{8}$	7	7	23	23	231	222

♦ *Cassiar Mts. / Robert R. Bridges / Robert R. Bridges / 1966*

$171\frac{4}{8}$	$45\frac{4}{8}$	45	$13\frac{5}{8}$	$13\frac{6}{8}$	$5\frac{6}{8}$	$5\frac{4}{8}$	$29\frac{7}{8}$	$29\frac{7}{8}$	231	222

♦ *Turnagain River / George H. Landreth / George H. Landreth / 1966*

$171\frac{4}{8}$	$42\frac{5}{8}$	$43\frac{5}{8}$	$13\frac{6}{8}$	$13\frac{6}{8}$	$5\frac{7}{8}$	$6\frac{1}{8}$	$29\frac{7}{8}$	$29\frac{7}{8}$	231	222

♦ *Turnagain River / Lewis M. Mull / Lewis M. Mull / 1966*

$171\frac{4}{8}$	45	$43\frac{6}{8}$	$13\frac{2}{8}$	$13\frac{1}{8}$	$5\frac{4}{8}$	$5\frac{4}{8}$	$28\frac{4}{8}$	$28\frac{4}{8}$	231	222

♦ *Cassiar Mts. / William A. Kelly / William A. Kelly / 1969*

Score	Length of Horn R	L	Circumference of Base R	L	Circumference at Third Quarter R	L	Greatest Spread	Tip-to-Tip Spread	All-Time Rank	State Rank
◆ Locality / Hunter / Owner / Date Killed										

171 4/8	39	34 4/8	15 6/8	15 5/8	7	7 2/8	25 6/8	23	231	222

◆ *Lower Besa River / Peter Hochleitner / Peter Hochleitner / 1977*

171 3/8	43	42 7/8	13 6/8	14	6	6	30 4/8	30 4/8	238	229

◆ *Kechika Range / H.I.H. Prince Abdorreza Pahlavi / H.I.H. Prince Abdorreza Pahlavi / 1960*

171 3/8	39 2/8	38 5/8	14 1/8	14	7 4/8	7 3/8	22 4/8	22 4/8	238	229

◆ *Besa River / Dale Webber / Dale Webber / 1984*

171 2/8	42 5/8	42 5/8	13 5/8	13 6/8	6 4/8	6 6/8	24 3/8	24 3/8	241	231

◆ *Muskwa River / Bernard J. Brown / Bernard J. Brown / 1953*

171 2/8	41 6/8	43	13 6/8	13 6/8	5 7/8	6 2/8	27 2/8	27 2/8	241	231

◆ *Cold Fish Lake / Robert Brittingham / Robert Brittingham / 1961*

171 2/8	44 1/8	43 1/8	12 7/8	12 7/8	5 7/8	5 6/8	27 3/8	27 3/8	241	231

◆ *Pelly Lake / Robert M. Mallett / Robert M. Mallett / 1966*

171 2/8	41	39 6/8	14 3/8	14 4/8	6 7/8	6 6/8	21 6/8	20 6/8	241	231

◆ *Cassiar Mts. / G.A. Treschow / G.A. Treschow / 1966*

171 2/8	38	45 4/8	13	13 3/8	6 2/8	7 2/8	20 4/8	20 4/8	241	231

◆ *Telegraph Creek / Picked Up / John Crowe / PR 1967*

171 2/8	39 1/8	40 3/8	15 2/8	15 3/8	5 7/8	6	25 1/8	25 1/8	241	231

◆ *Colt Lake / Roscoe Hurd / Roscoe Hurd / 1967*

171 2/8	42	42 2/8	13 5/8	13 5/8	6 3/8	6	26 3/8	26 3/8	241	231

◆ *Cassiar / Herb Parsons / Herb Parsons / 1969*

171	41	42	14	14 2/8	6	6	30	30	249	238

◆ *Cassiar / Wilson Potter / Harvard Univ. Mus. / 1906*

171	40 3/8	39 7/8	15	15	5 5/8	5 5/8	28 7/8	28 7/8	249	238

◆ *Sandbar Creek / John La Rocca / John La Rocca / 1958*

171	40	40	14 2/8	14 2/8	6 4/8	6 4/8	25 5/8	25 5/8	249	238

◆ *Halfway River / S.J. Seidensticker / S.J. Seidensticker / 1962*

171	41 7/8	41 3/8	14	14 2/8	5 7/8	5 7/8	24 7/8	24 7/8	249	238

◆ *Cassiar Mts. / Sam Jaksick, Jr. / Sam Jaksick, Jr. / 1967*

171	35 6/8	40 6/8	14 4/8	14 4/8	6 7/8	6 7/8	22 3/8	22 3/8	249	238

◆ *Wrede Creek / Jack Feightner / Jack Feightner / 1972*

171	41	44 4/8	13 4/8	13 5/8	5 7/8	6	27 1/8	27 1/8	249	238

◆ *Cassiar Mts. / Ed Stedman, Jr. / Ed Stedman, Jr. / 1974*

171	38 5/8	38 7/8	14 7/8	15	6 1/8	6 1/8	24 5/8	24 5/8	249	238

◆ *Ice Mt. / David P. Jacobson / David P. Jacobson / 1974*

171	39 5/8	40 1/8	14 7/8	14 7/8	6 2/8	6 4/8	21 3/8	18 6/8	249	238

◆ *Burnt Rose Lake / John Drift / John Drift / 1977*

170 7/8	41 2/8	41 5/8	13 3/8	13 3/8	7	7 1/8	26 5/8	26 5/8	258	246

◆ *Watson Lake / Ed Ball / Ed Ball / 1960*

Score	Length of Horn		Circumference of Base		Circumference at Third Quarter		Greatest Spread	Tip-to-Tip Spread	All-Time Rank	State Rank
	R	L	R	L	R	L				
$170\frac{7}{8}$	$39\frac{6}{8}$	$39\frac{5}{8}$	$14\frac{4}{8}$	15	$6\frac{3}{8}$	$6\frac{1}{8}$	$19\frac{6}{8}$	$19\frac{6}{8}$	258	246
♦ Prophet River / John J. Lo Monaco / John J. Lo Monaco / 1963										
$170\frac{7}{8}$	38	$38\frac{1}{8}$	$14\frac{2}{8}$	14	$7\frac{7}{8}$	8	$19\frac{7}{8}$	19	258	246
♦ Prophet River / Ted Howell / Ted Howell / 1964										
$170\frac{7}{8}$	$37\frac{5}{8}$	$38\frac{4}{8}$	$14\frac{5}{8}$	$14\frac{5}{8}$	$7\frac{3}{8}$	$7\frac{4}{8}$	$24\frac{6}{8}$	$18\frac{1}{8}$	258	246
♦ Tuchodi Lakes / Robert C. Ries / Robert C. Ries / 1965										
$170\frac{7}{8}$	$39\frac{2}{8}$	$41\frac{1}{8}$	$14\frac{4}{8}$	$14\frac{4}{8}$	$6\frac{3}{8}$	$6\frac{2}{8}$	$28\frac{1}{8}$	$28\frac{1}{8}$	258	246
♦ Telegraph Creek / R.B. England / R.B. England / 1966										
$170\frac{7}{8}$	$37\frac{3}{8}$	$38\frac{6}{8}$	$14\frac{6}{8}$	$14\frac{6}{8}$	$7\frac{2}{8}$	$7\frac{2}{8}$	23	$22\frac{3}{8}$	258	246
♦ Cassiar Mts. / W.G. Rathmann / W.G. Rathmann / 1971										
$170\frac{6}{8}$	$42\frac{2}{8}$	$42\frac{4}{8}$	$13\frac{7}{8}$	$13\frac{6}{8}$	$6\frac{4}{8}$	$6\frac{2}{8}$	32	32	265	252
♦ Pink Mt. / Unknown / J. Michael Conoyer / 1960										
$170\frac{6}{8}$	42	41	$13\frac{7}{8}$	14	$6\frac{5}{8}$	$6\frac{3}{8}$	$24\frac{4}{8}$	$24\frac{4}{8}$	265	252
♦ Peace River / C.A. Freese / C.A. Freese / 1960										
$170\frac{6}{8}$	41	41	14	14	6	6	$27\frac{4}{8}$	$27\frac{4}{8}$	265	252
♦ Gataga River / Herb Klein / Herb Klein / 1963										
$170\frac{6}{8}$	43	$42\frac{2}{8}$	$13\frac{4}{8}$	$13\frac{5}{8}$	$5\frac{6}{8}$	$5\frac{7}{8}$	$22\frac{2}{8}$	$22\frac{2}{8}$	265	252
♦ Pelly Creek / Jon A. Jourdonnais / Jon A. Jourdonnais / 1968										
$170\frac{6}{8}$	$40\frac{6}{8}$	41	$14\frac{1}{8}$	$14\frac{2}{8}$	$6\frac{3}{8}$	$6\frac{3}{8}$	$25\frac{3}{8}$	$25\frac{3}{8}$	265	252
♦ Kechika Range / Ferdinand Stemann / Ferdinand Stemann / 1970										
$170\frac{6}{8}$	$41\frac{6}{8}$	$37\frac{6}{8}$	14	$14\frac{1}{8}$	$6\frac{6}{8}$	7	$25\frac{5}{8}$	$25\frac{5}{8}$	265	252
♦ Tuchodi Lakes / Larry Tooze / Larry Tooze / 1986										
$170\frac{5}{8}$	$43\frac{2}{8}$	$43\frac{3}{8}$	$13\frac{5}{8}$	$13\frac{4}{8}$	$5\frac{5}{8}$	$6\frac{1}{8}$	$29\frac{6}{8}$	$29\frac{6}{8}$	271	258
♦ Cassiar / John W. Beban / John W. Beban / 1956										
$170\frac{5}{8}$	$40\frac{4}{8}$	$40\frac{1}{8}$	$14\frac{4}{8}$	$14\frac{4}{8}$	6	6	$29\frac{5}{8}$	$29\frac{5}{8}$	271	258
♦ Prophet River / E.R. Wells / E.R. Wells / 1967										
$170\frac{5}{8}$	$41\frac{3}{8}$	39	14	$14\frac{2}{8}$	$6\frac{4}{8}$	$6\frac{7}{8}$	$21\frac{2}{8}$	$21\frac{2}{8}$	271	258
♦ Toad River / Jay Stewart / Jay Stewart / 1969										
$170\frac{5}{8}$	$40\frac{7}{8}$	$40\frac{6}{8}$	14	14	$6\frac{2}{8}$	$6\frac{4}{8}$	$24\frac{3}{8}$	$24\frac{3}{8}$	271	258
♦ Prophet River / Robert E. Speegle / Robert E. Speegle / 1983										
$170\frac{5}{8}$	$41\frac{1}{8}$	$42\frac{2}{8}$	$14\frac{1}{8}$	$14\frac{1}{8}$	$6\frac{1}{8}$	$6\frac{4}{8}$	$25\frac{4}{8}$	$25\frac{4}{8}$	271	258
♦ Sharktooth Mt. / Steven J. DeRicco / Steven J. DeRicco / 1990										
$170\frac{4}{8}$	42	42	$13\frac{4}{8}$	$13\frac{4}{8}$	$6\frac{1}{8}$	$6\frac{1}{8}$	$26\frac{4}{8}$	$26\frac{4}{8}$	276	263
♦ Telegraph Creek / Joseph T. Pelton / Joseph T. Pelton / 1963										
$170\frac{4}{8}$	$39\frac{4}{8}$	40	14	14	7	$6\frac{4}{8}$	22	$20\frac{4}{8}$	276	263
♦ Toad River / Fred Sothmann / Fred Sothmann / 1963										
$170\frac{4}{8}$	$40\frac{7}{8}$	$39\frac{3}{8}$	$14\frac{2}{8}$	$14\frac{2}{8}$	$6\frac{7}{8}$	$6\frac{3}{8}$	$21\frac{6}{8}$	$21\frac{6}{8}$	276	263
♦ Dease Lake / Melvin A. Hetland / Melvin A. Hetland / 1965										

Score	Length of Horn		Circumference of Base		Circumference at Third Quarter		Greatest Spread	Tip-to-Tip Spread	All-Time Rank	State Rank
	R	L	R	L	R	L				
♦ Locality / Hunter / Owner / Date Killed										
170 4/8	40	40 4/8	14 2/8	14 3/8	6 7/8	6 4/8	21 2/8	22 4/8	276	263
♦ Watson Lake / W. Brandon Macomber / W. Brandon Macomber / 1966										
170 4/8	41 2/8	40	14 4/8	14 4/8	6 2/8	6 2/8	26 1/8	26 1/8	276	263
♦ Pink Mt. / Rita Oney / Rita Oney / 1966										
170 4/8	32	41 4/8	14 4/8	14 6/8	8	8 4/8	22	24	276	263
♦ Muskwa River / Donald P. Eickhoff / E.C. Eickhoff / 1968										
170 4/8	42 2/8	40 2/8	13 4/8	13 5/8	6 4/8	6 4/8	25 4/8	25 2/8	276	263
♦ Mt. Ediza / William J. Pollard / William J. Pollard / 1974										
170 3/8	41 3/8	40 2/8	13 7/8	13 7/8	6 2/8	6 2/8	22 3/8	22 3/8	284	270
♦ Sikanni / W.A.K. Seale / W.A.K. Seale / 1961										
170 3/8	39 6/8	40 7/8	14	14 2/8	6 1/8	6 3/8	28	28	284	270
♦ Kechika Range / Basil C. Bradbury / Basil C. Bradbury / 1965										
170 3/8	37 5/8	38 2/8	14 6/8	14 6/8	6 5/8	6 5/8	22 4/8	22 4/8	284	270
♦ Ospika Area / Ray E. Bigler / Ray E. Bigler / 1972										
170 2/8	40	43 2/8	13 3/8	13 4/8	6 4/8	6 5/8	25 4/8	25 6/8	287	273
♦ Beale Lake / John Forester / John Forester / 1963										
170 2/8	35	35 2/8	14 6/8	14 5/8	8	8 2/8	21 6/8	19 2/8	287	273
♦ Richards Creek / Herbert A. Leupold / Herbert A. Leupold / 1965										
170 2/8	38 4/8	39	15	14 7/8	6 7/8	6 5/8	22 6/8	22 6/8	287	273
♦ Halfway River / Steven L. Rose / Steven L. Rose / 1967										
170 2/8	41	41	14 2/8	14 2/8	6 1/8	6 2/8	26	26	287	273
♦ Keohka River / Fritz A. Nachant / Fritz A. Nachant / 1970										
170 2/8	39 4/8	39 6/8	14 6/8	14 7/8	6 1/8	6	21 7/8	21 2/8	287	273
♦ Muskwa River / James S. Griffin / James S. Griffin / 1972										
170 2/8	38 4/8	43 2/8	14 1/8	14 1/8	6 3/8	6 3/8	23 6/8	23 6/8	287	273
♦ Turnagain River / Jerald T. Waite / Jerald T. Waite / 1976										
170 2/8	36 2/8	37	14 2/8	14 2/8	8 2/8	8	20 7/8	19 4/8	287	273
♦ Townsley Creek / Robert L. Williamson / Robert L. Williamson / 1981										
170 2/8	41	39 2/8	14 5/8	14 3/8	6 1/8	6 1/8	24 2/8	24 2/8	287	273
♦ Racing River / Bill Stevenson / Bill Stevenson / 1983										
170 2/8	40 4/8	39 2/8	14 5/8	14 5/8	6 1/8	6 1/8	25 3/8	25 3/8	287	273
♦ Prophet River / Steve J. Polich / Steve J. Polich / 1984										
170 2/8	39 5/8	40 7/8	14 2/8	14 2/8	6 4/8	6 6/8	27 1/8	27 1/8	287	273
♦ Cutbank Creek / Brett M. Moore / Brett M. Moore / 1987										
170 1/8	43 1/8	42 6/8	13 3/8	13 3/8	6	6 2/8	30 7/8	30 7/8	297	283
♦ Rabbit River / George W. Young / George W. Young / 1965										
170 1/8	39 4/8	38 1/8	14 7/8	14 7/8	6	6 2/8	24 6/8	24 6/8	297	283
♦ Ram Creek / Kim Cox / Kim Cox / 1966										

Score	Length of Horn R	Length of Horn L	Circumference of Base R	Circumference of Base L	Circumference at Third Quarter R	Circumference at Third Quarter L	Greatest Spread	Tip-to-Tip Spread	All-Time Rank	State Rank
	♦ *Locality / Hunter / Owner / Date Killed*									
170 1/8	39 2/8	43 7/8	13 4/8	13 4/8	6	6 1/8	21 5/8	21 5/8	297	283
	♦ *Needham Creek / Roy Fukunaga / Roy Fukunaga / 1974*									
170 1/8	43 2/8	42 3/8	12 5/8	12 5/8	6 4/8	6 2/8	27 5/8	27 5/8	297	283
	♦ *Cassiar Mts. / James H. Duke, Jr. / James H. Duke, Jr. / 1976*									
170 1/8	40	40 1/8	14 1/8	14 1/8	6 4/8	6 4/8	24 7/8	24 7/8	297	283
	♦ *Rabbit River / Frank F. Azcarate / Frank F. Azcarate / 1985*									
170	42 4/8	38 6/8	14 1/8	14 2/8	6	6	24 3/8	24 3/8	302	288
	♦ *Prophet River / Walter B. McClurkan / Walter B. McClurkan / 1945*									
170	39 2/8	43 4/8	13 7/8	13 5/8	6 3/8	6	25	25	302	288
	♦ *Cold Fish Lake / Howard Boazman / Howard Boazman / 1962*									
170	42	37	14 1/8	14 1/8	6 4/8	6 5/8	22 4/8	22 4/8	302	288
	♦ *Alaska Hwy. / Arthur Gordon / Arthur Gordon / 1965*									
170	39 4/8	39 2/8	14 5/8	14 6/8	6 4/8	6 3/8	27 3/8	27 3/8	302	288
	♦ *Cassiar Mts. / Neil Castner / Neil Castner / 1966*									
170	39 5/8	40 1/8	14 2/8	14 4/8	6 4/8	6 4/8	21 5/8	16 5/8	302	288
	♦ *Cassiar Mts. / Glen E. Park / Glen E. Park / 1967*									
170	38 4/8	39 4/8	13 6/8	13 7/8	7 2/8	7 3/8	21	17 5/8	302	288
	♦ *Tetsa River / Owen R. Walker / Owen R. Walker / 1967*									
170	41	41	14	14	6 2/8	6 4/8	20 6/8	20 6/8	302	288
	♦ *Prophet River / Jim Nystrom / Jim Nystrom / 1968*									
170	42 3/8	43 7/8	13 2/8	13 2/8	6	6 1/8	29 2/8	29 2/8	302	288
	♦ *Gataga River / Paul L.C. Snider / Paul L.C. Snider / 1970*									
170	40	39 2/8	15 4/8	15 4/8	5 2/8	5 2/8	22 6/8	22 6/8	302	288
	♦ *Muskwa River / W.J. Boynton III / W.J. Boynton III / 1970*									
170	37	37 6/8	14 6/8	14 6/8	7 2/8	7 4/8	22 2/8	18 1/8	302	288
	♦ *Prophet River / Doug Heinrich / Doug Heinrich / 1992*									
170	35 4/8	37	14 1/8	14 1/8	8 4/8	8 5/8	19 6/8	17 1/8	302	288
	♦ *Toad River / Rick Davis / Rick Davis / 1993*									
169 5/8	40 5/8	41 4/8	13 7/8	41 1/8	6 3/8	6 5/8	24 2/8	24 2/8	313	299
	♦ *Gataga River / Donald P. Travis / Donald P. Travis / 1993*									
169 3/8	40 4/8	41 5/8	13 4/8	13 4/8	6 3/8	6 3/8	25	25	314	300
	♦ *Cullivan Creek / Russell LeSage / Russell LeSage / 1991*									
169 2/8	40 1/8	40 7/8	15 5/8	15 3/8	5 5/8	5 5/8	27 6/8	27 6/8	315	301
	♦ *Richards Creek / Dan E. McBride / Dan E. McBride / 1986*									
168 4/8	43 1/8	40 7/8	14 1/8	14 1/8	5 6/8	6	31 5/8	31 5/8	316	302
	♦ *Prophet River / Loyal H. Loveness / Loyal H. Loveness / 1962*									
166 7/8	41 1/8	42 2/8	13 3/8	13 4/8	5 4/8	6	27 6/8	27 4/8	318	303
	♦ *Toad River / Anna M. Blattgerste / Anna M. Blattgerste / 1990*									

Score	Length of Horn		Circumference of Base		Circumference at Third Quarter		Greatest Spread	Tip-to-Tip Spread	All-Time Rank	State Rank
	R	L	R	L	R	L				
◆ Locality / Hunter / Owner / Date Killed										
166⁴⁄₈	42¹⁄₈	35⁷⁄₈	14²⁄₈	14²⁄₈	6¹⁄₈	5⁷⁄₈	27²⁄₈	27³⁄₈	320	304
◆ Richards Creek / S. Randy Archibald / S. Randy Archibald / 1987										
166⁴⁄₈	38⁵⁄₈	37⁷⁄₈	14¹⁄₈	14²⁄₈	6⁵⁄₈	7¹⁄₈	21²⁄₈	21²⁄₈	320	304
◆ Prophet River / Keith Martin / Keith Martin / 1988										
166²⁄₈	38⁴⁄₈	39⁴⁄₈	15	15⁴⁄₈	6	6¹⁄₈	24¹⁄₈	24¹⁄₈	322	306
◆ Graham River / David V. Collis / David V. Collis / 1982										
165¹⁄₈	36³⁄₈	37⁴⁄₈	13⁶⁄₈	13⁵⁄₈	7	7	22⁴⁄₈	22	323	307
◆ Tentsi Creek / John R. Fowler / John R. Fowler / 1991										
165¹⁄₈	41²⁄₈	42⁷⁄₈	13³⁄₈	13	5⁴⁄₈	6¹⁄₈	26⁵⁄₈	26⁵⁄₈	323	307
◆ Cassiar Mts. / John F. Connolly / John F. Connolly / 1994										
165	40⁴⁄₈	40²⁄₈	13⁴⁄₈	13⁶⁄₈	5⁷⁄₈	5⁷⁄₈	22⁵⁄₈	22⁵⁄₈	325	309
◆ West Toad River / Dennis C. Campbell / Dennis C. Campbell / 1982										
185⁵⁄₈	47⁵⁄₈	49²⁄₈	13⁴⁄₈	13³⁄₈	6⁴⁄₈	7⁴⁄₈	29	29	*	*
◆ Ice Mt. / Picked Up / Bruce Creyke / 1977										
185³⁄₈	45⁶⁄₈	44³⁄₈	15⁷⁄₈	15⁷⁄₈	6¹⁄₈	5⁷⁄₈	29³⁄₈	29³⁄₈	*	*
◆ Prophet River / Felipe Palau / Felipe Palau / 1970										
181⁵⁄₈	40³⁄₈	41²⁄₈	14²⁄₈	14²⁄₈	9	8⁷⁄₈	24⁷⁄₈	24⁷⁄₈	*	*
◆ Tuchodi Lakes / Romeo Leduc / Romeo Leduc / 1981										
177⁴⁄₈	41⁵⁄₈	42¹⁄₈	14⁴⁄₈	14³⁄₈	7²⁄₈	7³⁄₈	25	24⁶⁄₈	*	*
◆ Racing River / Floyd W. Ternier / F.W. & C. Ternier / 1994										
177²⁄₈	43³⁄₈	42³⁄₈	14⁶⁄₈	14⁶⁄₈	6⁵⁄₈	6⁶⁄₈	26⁵⁄₈	26²⁄₈	*	*
◆ Cassiar Mts. / Larry C. Fisher / Larry C. Fisher / 1991										
177¹⁄₈	42¹⁄₈	41⁶⁄₈	15³⁄₈	15⁴⁄₈	6⁴⁄₈	6	27²⁄₈	27	*	*
◆ Muskwa River / Gerald A. Paille / Gerald A. Paille / 1986										
177¹⁄₈	44⁷⁄₈	45²⁄₈	14	14	5⁶⁄₈	6	31	31	*	*
◆ Muskwa River / Kevin H. Olmstead / Kevin H. Olmstead / 1993										
177	36	40⁴⁄₈	15¹⁄₈	15	8²⁄₈	8¹⁄₈	21⁶⁄₈	18⁶⁄₈	*	*
◆ Sikanni Chief River / Don R. Hughes / Don R. Hughes / 1988										
176³⁄₈	45	38⁷⁄₈	14⁴⁄₈	14⁴⁄₈	7²⁄₈	6⁵⁄₈	23	23	*	*
◆ Wokkpash Creek / H. Robert Grounds / H. Robert Grounds / 1987										
175⁶⁄₈	39²⁄₈	39²⁄₈	14¹⁄₈	14¹⁄₈	8⁴⁄₈	8⁴⁄₈	20⁴⁄₈	20	*	*
◆ Tuchodi River / Roy D. Brown / Roy D. Brown / 1992										
174	40¹⁄₈	40¹⁄₈	15²⁄₈	15³⁄₈	6³⁄₈	6⁴⁄₈	25¹⁄₈	24⁷⁄₈	*	*
◆ Muskwa River / R.L. Gearhart / R.L. Gearhart / 1983										
173	41⁴⁄₈	42⁴⁄₈	13⁶⁄₈	13⁵⁄₈	6⁶⁄₈	7	24	23⁵⁄₈	*	*
◆ Rapid River / Bill Silveira / Bill Silveira / 1983										

Photograph Courtesy of Ira H. Kent

YUKON TERRITORY PROVINCE RECORD
STONE'S SHEEP
SCORE: 177⅞
Locality: Skookum Mountain   Date: 1968
Hunter: Ira H. Kent

YUKON TERRITORY
STONE'S SHEEP

Score	Length of Horn		Circumference of Base		Circumference at Third Quarter		Greatest Spread	Tip-to-Tip Spread	All-Time Rank	State Rank
	R	L	R	L	R	L				
Locality / Hunter / Owner / Date Killed										
177⁷⁄₈	44³⁄₈	43²⁄₈	15	15	5⁷⁄₈	6	31	31	56	1
◆ *Skookum Mt. / Ira H. Kent / Ira H. Kent / 1968*										
177⁴⁄₈	44²⁄₈	42²⁄₈	14⁴⁄₈	14⁵⁄₈	6⁵⁄₈	6³⁄₈	24²⁄₈	24²⁄₈	63	2
◆ *Watson Lake / Edgar A. Robertson / Edgar A. Robertson / 1968*										
177²⁄₈	38¹⁄₈	38¹⁄₈	14⁵⁄₈	14⁵⁄₈	9	8⁷⁄₈	20⁷⁄₈	20⁷⁄₈	65	3
◆ *Watson Lake / Keith Thompson / Keith Thompson / 1969*										
175⁵⁄₈	42⁵⁄₈	42⁶⁄₈	14⁴⁄₈	14²⁄₈	6²⁄₈	6³⁄₈	22	22	94	4
◆ *Pelly Mts. / John Caputo / John Caputo / 1953*										
175³⁄₈	43	42⁵⁄₈	14²⁄₈	14⁴⁄₈	6⁴⁄₈	6⁴⁄₈	26	26	102	5
◆ *Pelly Mts. / Pat S. McInturff / Pat S. McInturff / 1962*										
173⁵⁄₈	42³⁄₈	42	14³⁄₈	14²⁄₈	6²⁄₈	6²⁄₈	22⁴⁄₈	22⁴⁄₈	144	6
◆ *Rose Mt. / Karl Fritzsche / Karl Fritzsche / 1972*										
173⁴⁄₈	39⁴⁄₈	41	14	14²⁄₈	8¹⁄₈	8	23	23	147	7
◆ *Watson Lake / Harry S. Rinker / Harry S. Rinker / 1964*										
173	42	42²⁄₈	14²⁄₈	14³⁄₈	5⁶⁄₈	5⁶⁄₈	22⁵⁄₈	22⁵⁄₈	163	8
◆ *Watson Lake / E.P. Gray / E.P. Gray / 1968*										
172³⁄₈	41⁶⁄₈	42³⁄₈	14³⁄₈	14⁴⁄₈	5⁷⁄₈	5⁷⁄₈	27⁶⁄₈	27⁶⁄₈	188	9
◆ *Pelly Mts. / Walter R. Michael / Walter R. Michael / 1960*										
171³⁄₈	37⁷⁄₈	37	14	14¹⁄₈	8⁴⁄₈	8⁷⁄₈	21⁷⁄₈	18³⁄₈	238	10
◆ *Horseshoe Lake / Jack G. Giannola / Jack G. Giannola / 1973*										
171²⁄₈	41²⁄₈	41	13⁷⁄₈	13⁷⁄₈	6³⁄₈	6	26²⁄₈	26²⁄₈	241	11
◆ *Pelly Mts. / Jack Tillotson / Jack Tillotson / 1955*										
171	40²⁄₈	39⁶⁄₈	14⁶⁄₈	14⁵⁄₈	6	5⁷⁄₈	20⁶⁄₈	20⁵⁄₈	249	12
◆ *Ice Lake / Terrance S. Marcum / Terrance S. Marcum / 1992*										
170⁷⁄₈	44⁵⁄₈	41⁴⁄₈	13²⁄₈	13³⁄₈	6¹⁄₈	6¹⁄₈	28	28	258	13
◆ *Watson Lake / Richard G. Peters / Richard G. Peters / 1962*										
170⁴⁄₈	42⁷⁄₈	42⁵⁄₈	13⁴⁄₈	13⁴⁄₈	6	5⁷⁄₈	33¹⁄₈	33¹⁄₈	276	14
◆ *Pelly Mts. / William Fisher / William Fisher / 1957*										
168⁴⁄₈	42	41⁴⁄₈	14³⁄₈	14³⁄₈	5⁴⁄₈	5⁵⁄₈	25⁷⁄₈	25⁷⁄₈	316	15
◆ *McNeil Lake / John M. Torok / John M. Torok / 1993*										
166⁵⁄₈	40⁴⁄₈	41⁵⁄₈	14	14²⁄₈	5⁵⁄₈	5⁵⁄₈	25²⁄₈	25²⁄₈	319	16
◆ *Fox Mt. / George F. Dennis, Jr. / George F. Dennis, Jr. / 1990*										
178	44⁷⁄₈	44⁷⁄₈	13⁵⁄₈	13⁵⁄₈	6⁶⁄₈	6⁶⁄₈	29⁴⁄₈	29⁴⁄₈	*	*
◆ *Rose Mt. / William P. Williamson / William P. Williamson / 1987*										
170⁶⁄₈	43⁵⁄₈	45¹⁄₈	12⁶⁄₈	12⁶⁄₈	6³⁄₈	6²⁄₈	26³⁄₈	26³⁄₈	*	*
◆ *Anvil Range / John A. Capdeville / John A. Capdeville / 1991*										

TOP 5 ROCKY MOUNTAIN GOAT LISTINGS INDEX

Tabulations of Recorded Rocky Mountain Goat

The trophy data shown on the following pages are taken from score charts in the records archives of the Boone and Crockett Club.

Rocky Mountain goats historically occur in the mountains of Alaska, Idaho, Montana, Washington, and Wyoming, as well as the provinces of Alberta, British Columbia, Northwest Territories, and Yukon Territory. They were introduced into the states of Colorado, Oregon, South Dakota, Utah, and Nevada.

The scores and ranks shown are final, except for the trophies shown with an asterisk (*). The asterisk identifies entry scores subject to final certification by an Awards Panel of Judges. The asterisk can be removed (except in the case of a potential World's Record) by the submission of two additional, independent scorings by Official Measurers of the Boone and Crockett Club. The Records Committee of the Club will review the three scorings available (original plus two additional) and determine which, if any, will be accepted in lieu of the Judges' Panel measurement. When the score has been accepted as final by the Records Committee, the asterisk will be removed in future editions of this book and the all-time records book, *Records of North American Big Game*. In the case of a potential World's Record, the trophy must come before a Judges' Panel at the end of an entry period. Only a Judges' Panel can certify a World's Record and finalize its score. Asterisked trophies are unranked at the end of their category.

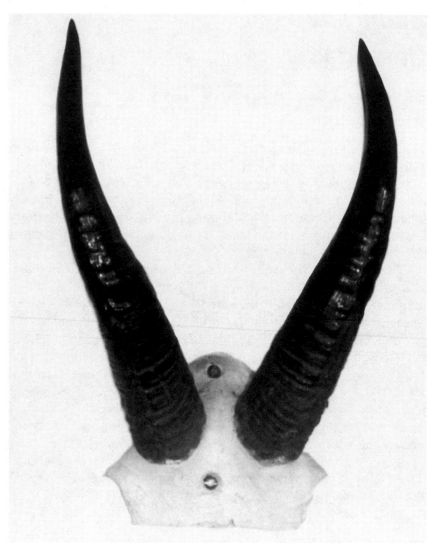

Photograph by Jack Reneau

**ALASKA STATE RECORD
ROCKY MOUNTAIN GOAT
SCORE: 56²⁄₈**
Locality: Helm Bay   Date: 1933
Hunter: W. H. Jackson
Owner: B&C National Collection

ALASKA

ROCKY MOUNTAIN GOAT

Score	Length of Horn		Circumference of Base		Circumference at Third Quarter		Greatest Spread	Tip-to-Tip Spread	All-Time Rank	State Rank
	R	L	R	L	R	L				
◆ Locality / Hunter / Owner / Date Killed										
56²⁄₈	11⁵⁄₈	11⁵⁄₈	5⁶⁄₈	5⁵⁄₈	2⅛	2⅛	7²⁄₈	6⁴⁄₈	2	1
◆ Helm Bay / W.H. Jackson / B&C National Collection / 1933										
56	10⁴⁄₈	10⁶⁄₈	6⅛	6	2⁵⁄₈	2⁶⁄₈	6⁷⁄₈	6⁴⁄₈	4	2
◆ Kenai Pen. / Peter W. Bading / Peter W. Bading / 1963										
55	11⁷⁄₈	11⁷⁄₈	5⁴⁄₈	5³⁄₈	2	2	8³⁄₈	6⁴⁄₈	6	3
◆ Cleveland Pen. / Elmer W. Copstead / Jonas Bros. of Seattle / 1939										
55	12⅛	12⅛	5²⁄₈	5⅛	2	2²⁄₈	7⁷⁄₈	5⁶⁄₈	6	3
◆ Alex. Archipelago / James Wilson / James Wilson / 1969										
54⁶⁄₈	11³⁄₈	11³⁄₈	5⁶⁄₈	5⁵⁄₈	2	2	7⁶⁄₈	5⁵⁄₈	8	5
◆ Reflection Lake / Lue Wilson, Jr. / Lue Wilson, Jr. / 1979										
54²⁄₈	11⁶⁄₈	12	5⁴⁄₈	5⁴⁄₈	1⁷⁄₈	1⁷⁄₈	7²⁄₈	5²⁄₈	12	6
◆ Yes Bay / Wally L. Grover / Wally L. Grover / 1991										
53²⁄₈	10⁶⁄₈	11	5⁷⁄₈	5⁷⁄₈	2	2	6⁶⁄₈	5⁶⁄₈	33	7
◆ Ketchikan / Charles E. Slajer / Charles E. Slajer / 1966										
53²⁄₈	11²⁄₈	11⁵⁄₈	5⁴⁄₈	5⁴⁄₈	1⁷⁄₈	2	7	6⅛	33	7
◆ Halfmoon Lake / Robert A. Hewitt / Robert A. Hewitt / 1980										
53	10⅛	10	5⁶⁄₈	5⁵⁄₈	2⅛	2	8⁴⁄₈	8	38	9
◆ Skagway / Charles R. Heath / Charles R. Heath / 1965										
53	11²⁄₈	10⁵⁄₈	6	6⅛	2	2	6⁵⁄₈	4⁷⁄₈	38	9
◆ Aaron Mt. / John Sturgeon / John Sturgeon / 1973										
53	10⁴⁄₈	10⁴⁄₈	6	6	2	2	8²⁄₈	8⅛	38	9
◆ Homer / Robert W. Hertz, Jr. / Robert W. Hertz, Jr. / 1974										
52⁶⁄₈	10⁴⁄₈	10⁴⁄₈	5⁵⁄₈	5⁵⁄₈	2⅛	2⅛	7⅛	6⁴⁄₈	49	12
◆ Reflection Lake / Timothy F. McGinn / Timothy F. McGinn / 1985										
52⁴⁄₈	10⁶⁄₈	10⁷⁄₈	5³⁄₈	5³⁄₈	2	2⅛	7³⁄₈	6⁶⁄₈	61	13
◆ Granite Basin Lake / Scott D. Hansen / Scott D. Hansen / 1988										
52²⁄₈	10⁴⁄₈	10²⁄₈	5⁷⁄₈	5⁷⁄₈	2	2	8²⁄₈	7⁶⁄₈	73	14
◆ Copper River / Fritz Maier / Fritz Maier / 1964										
52²⁄₈	10⁷⁄₈	10⁷⁄₈	5²⁄₈	5²⁄₈	1⁷⁄₈	1⁷⁄₈	8	7⁵⁄₈	73	14
◆ Boca De Quadra / Dan Hook / Dan Hook / 1968										
52²⁄₈	11	10⁷⁄₈	5⁴⁄₈	5⁵⁄₈	2	1⁷⁄₈	7⁶⁄₈	7⅛	73	14
◆ Boca De Quadra / Doug Vann / Doug Vann / 1968										
52²⁄₈	10⁵⁄₈	10⁵⁄₈	5⁷⁄₈	5⁷⁄₈	2	2	8²⁄₈	7⁷⁄₈	73	14
◆ Seward / Donald R. Platt, Sr. / Donald R. Platt, Sr. / 1969										
52²⁄₈	10⁶⁄₈	10²⁄₈	5⁷⁄₈	5⁷⁄₈	2	2	7⁵⁄₈	7⅛	73	14
◆ Bradfield Canal / C. Wayne Treadway / C. Wayne Treadway / 1988										

Score	Length of Horn		Circumference of Base		Circumference at Third Quarter		Greatest Spread	Tip-to-Tip Spread	All-Time Rank	State Rank
	R	L	R	L	R	L				
	◆ *Locality / Hunter / Owner / Date Killed*									
$52\frac{2}{8}$	$10\frac{2}{8}$	$10\frac{3}{8}$	$5\frac{7}{8}$	$5\frac{7}{8}$	$1\frac{7}{8}$	$1\frac{7}{8}$	$7\frac{7}{8}$	$6\frac{6}{8}$	73	14
	◆ *Lynn Canal / Charles F. Roy / Charles F. Roy / 1990*									
52	$10\frac{7}{8}$	11	$5\frac{4}{8}$	$5\frac{4}{8}$	$1\frac{7}{8}$	$1\frac{7}{8}$	$7\frac{4}{8}$	$6\frac{7}{8}$	99	20
	◆ *Watson Peak / Harold M. Wright / Harold M. Wright / 1957*									
52	10	10	6	6	2	2	$7\frac{3}{8}$	7	99	20
	◆ *Sundial Lake / Arnold W. Johnson / Arnold W. Johnson / 1962*									
52	$11\frac{4}{8}$	$11\frac{3}{8}$	$5\frac{3}{8}$	$5\frac{3}{8}$	2	2	7	$4\frac{5}{8}$	99	20
	◆ *Boca De Quadra / James Todahl / James Todahl / 1962*									
52	$10\frac{7}{8}$	$10\frac{2}{8}$	$5\frac{4}{8}$	$5\frac{4}{8}$	$1\frac{7}{8}$	$1\frac{7}{8}$	$9\frac{6}{8}$	$9\frac{2}{8}$	99	20
	◆ *Auke Bay / Kenneth L. Klawunder / Kenneth L. Klawunder / 1968*									
52	$10\frac{4}{8}$	$10\frac{6}{8}$	$6\frac{2}{8}$	$6\frac{2}{8}$	$1\frac{6}{8}$	$1\frac{7}{8}$	$6\frac{3}{8}$	$5\frac{7}{8}$	99	20
	◆ *Mt. Saint Elias / Terry L. Friske / Terry L. Friske / 1980*									
52	$12\frac{1}{8}$	$11\frac{6}{8}$	$5\frac{3}{8}$	$5\frac{3}{8}$	$1\frac{7}{8}$	$1\frac{7}{8}$	$8\frac{1}{8}$	$7\frac{5}{8}$	99	20
	◆ *Horn Cliffs / Jack W. McKernan / Jack W. McKernan / 1981*									
52	$9\frac{7}{8}$	$9\frac{4}{8}$	$5\frac{6}{8}$	$5\frac{6}{8}$	$2\frac{2}{8}$	$2\frac{2}{8}$	$5\frac{3}{8}$	$5\frac{2}{8}$	99	20
	◆ *Yes Bay / Roddy Shelton / Roddy Shelton / 1987*									
$51\frac{6}{8}$	$10\frac{6}{8}$	$10\frac{6}{8}$	$5\frac{4}{8}$	$5\frac{5}{8}$	$1\frac{7}{8}$	2	$7\frac{5}{8}$	$7\frac{4}{8}$	131	27
	◆ *Mile 402 / E.J. Blumenshine / E.J. Blumenshine / 1948*									
$51\frac{6}{8}$	$10\frac{1}{8}$	$10\frac{2}{8}$	$5\frac{7}{8}$	$5\frac{6}{8}$	$1\frac{7}{8}$	$1\frac{7}{8}$	$8\frac{4}{8}$	$8\frac{4}{8}$	131	27
	◆ *Wrangell Mts. / Basil C. Bradbury / Basil C. Bradbury / 1968*									
$51\frac{6}{8}$	$10\frac{6}{8}$	$10\frac{7}{8}$	$5\frac{5}{8}$	$5\frac{5}{8}$	$1\frac{7}{8}$	$1\frac{7}{8}$	$6\frac{3}{8}$	5	131	27
	◆ *Tongass Natl. For. / Roderick Martin / Roderick Martin / 1970*									
$51\frac{6}{8}$	10	10	$5\frac{7}{8}$	$5\frac{7}{8}$	2	2	$6\frac{6}{8}$	$5\frac{1}{8}$	131	27
	◆ *Bradfield River / James M. Remza / James M. Remza / 1970*									
$51\frac{6}{8}$	$10\frac{7}{8}$	$10\frac{6}{8}$	$5\frac{5}{8}$	$5\frac{5}{8}$	2	$1\frac{7}{8}$	$7\frac{2}{8}$	$6\frac{3}{8}$	131	27
	◆ *Cleveland Pen. / H.D. Costello / H.D. Costello / 1973*									
$51\frac{6}{8}$	11	$10\frac{6}{8}$	$5\frac{6}{8}$	$5\frac{6}{8}$	2	$1\frac{7}{8}$	$7\frac{3}{8}$	7	131	27
	◆ *Ketchikan / Donald K. Oldenburg / Donald K. Oldenburg / 1977*									
$51\frac{6}{8}$	$10\frac{2}{8}$	$10\frac{1}{8}$	6	$5\frac{7}{8}$	2	2	$7\frac{7}{8}$	$7\frac{2}{8}$	131	27
	◆ *Behm Canal / Michael L. Ward / Michael L. Ward / 1980*									
$51\frac{6}{8}$	$10\frac{2}{8}$	$10\frac{2}{8}$	$5\frac{5}{8}$	$5\frac{5}{8}$	$2\frac{1}{8}$	$2\frac{1}{8}$	$6\frac{5}{8}$	6	131	27
	◆ *Tyee Lake / Daniel G. Bowden / Daniel G. Bowden / 1982*									
$51\frac{6}{8}$	$10\frac{6}{8}$	$10\frac{5}{8}$	$5\frac{3}{8}$	$5\frac{3}{8}$	2	2	$7\frac{1}{8}$	6	131	27
	◆ *Leduc Lake / Steve Lepschat / Steve Lepschat / 1982*									
$51\frac{6}{8}$	$10\frac{2}{8}$	$10\frac{4}{8}$	$5\frac{6}{8}$	$5\frac{5}{8}$	2	$2\frac{1}{8}$	$6\frac{3}{8}$	$5\frac{1}{8}$	131	27
	◆ *Lake Rowena / George T. Law / George T. Law / 1983*									
$51\frac{6}{8}$	$9\frac{6}{8}$	$9\frac{6}{8}$	$5\frac{6}{8}$	$5\frac{5}{8}$	2	2	6	$4\frac{4}{8}$	131	27
	◆ *Cleveland Pen. / Michael L. Ward / Michael L. Ward / 1983*									

Score	Length of Horn		Circumference of Base		Circumference at Third Quarter		Greatest Spread	Tip-to-Tip Spread	All-Time Rank	State Rank
	R	L	R	L	R	L				
♦ Locality / Hunter / Owner / Date Killed										
51 4/8	10 3/8	10 3/8	5 6/8	5 6/8	2	1 7/8	6 3/8	5 7/8	171	38
♦ Cleveland Pen. / Allen E. Linn / Allen E. Linn / 1961										
51 4/8	10 2/8	10 2/8	5 5/8	5 4/8	1 7/8	1 7/8	6 6/8	6	171	38
♦ Boca De Quadra / Charles E. Simmons / Charles E. Simmons / 1961										
51 4/8	10 5/8	10 7/8	5 6/8	5 6/8	1 6/8	1 7/8	7 1/8	6 6/8	171	38
♦ Kenai Pen. / Alan Olson / Alan Olson / 1962										
51 4/8	9 5/8	9 5/8	5 6/8	5 6/8	1 6/8	1 6/8	7 4/8	6 7/8	171	38
♦ Chugach Mts. / Donald A. Turcke / Donald A. Turcke / 1964										
51 4/8	11 1/8	11 3/8	5 3/8	5 3/8	1 7/8	1 7/8	6 3/8	4 1/8	171	38
♦ Boca De Quadra / Arthur N. Wilson, Jr. / Arthur N. Wilson, Jr. / 1965										
51 4/8	10 3/8	10 3/8	5 6/8	5 6/8	2	2	8	7 4/8	171	38
♦ Bowen Lake / Ted A. Dedmon / Ted A. Dedmon / 1971										
51 4/8	10 4/8	10 2/8	5 7/8	5 7/8	1 7/8	1 7/8	7 2/8	6 4/8	171	38
♦ Ketchikan / Kevin Downey / Kevin Downey / 1973										
51 4/8	11	10 3/8	5 6/8	5 6/8	1 7/8	1 7/8	6 2/8	5 5/8	171	38
♦ Stikine River / Donald E. Fossen / Donald E. Fossen / 1973										
51 4/8	10 4/8	10 4/8	5 4/8	5 6/8	1 6/8	1 6/8	8 6/8	8 6/8	171	38
♦ Kodiak Island / Ron Eller / Ron Eller / 1978										
51 4/8	10 1/8	10 1/8	5 7/8	5 6/8	1 7/8	1 7/8	7 4/8	6 5/8	171	38
♦ Halfmoon Lake / Kurt W. Kuehl / Kurt W. Kuehl / 1982										
51 4/8	10	10 1/8	6	6	1 7/8	1 7/8	7 7/8	7 7/8	171	38
♦ Bradley Lake / Paul H. Ross / Paul H. Ross / 1989										
51 2/8	10 1/8	10 1/8	5 4/8	5 4/8	2	2	8 1/8	8 1/8	212	49
♦ Katalla / John Goeres / John Goeres / 1943										
51 2/8	9 3/8	9 2/8	6 1/8	6 1/8	2 2/8	2 1/8	7 7/8	7 5/8	212	49
♦ Anchorage / Wade Charles / Wade Charles / 1966										
51 2/8	10 1/8	10 4/8	5 3/8	5 2/8	2 2/8	2 1/8	8 2/8	7 6/8	212	49
♦ Wrangell Mts. / John E. Meyers / John E. Meyers / 1971										
51 2/8	10 6/8	10 7/8	5 6/8	5 5/8	1 6/8	1 6/8	7 3/8	6 5/8	212	49
♦ Chilkat Mt. / Terry L. Friske / Terry L. Friske / 1980										
51 2/8	10	10 2/8	5 5/8	5 5/8	2 1/8	2 1/8	5 7/8	5	212	49
♦ Tyee Lake / David L. Bowden / David L. Bowden / 1982										
51 2/8	10 4/8	10	5 5/8	5 5/8	2	1 7/8	8 3/8	7 6/8	212	49
♦ Glenallen / Kirk Z. Smith / Kirk Z. Smith / 1982										
51 2/8	10 1/8	10 1/8	5 6/8	5 6/8	1 7/8	1 7/8	6 7/8	6 6/8	212	49
♦ Crown Mt. / Robert L. Hales / Robert L. Hales / 1986										
51 2/8	10 2/8	10 4/8	6	6	1 6/8	1 7/8	8 1/8	7 2/8	212	49
♦ Moose Creek / Michael R. Morava / Michael R. Morava / 1993										

Score	Length of Horn		Circumference of Base		Circumference at Third Quarter		Greatest Spread	Tip-to-Tip Spread	All-Time Rank	State Rank
	R	L	R	L	R	L				

♦ *Locality / Hunter / Owner / Date Killed*

51	9 6/8	9 5/8	5 7/8	5 6/8	2 2/8	2 1/8	6 6/8	6 1/8	249	57

♦ *Resurrection Bay / Peter W. Bading / Peter W. Bading / 1961*

51	10 6/8	10 4/8	5 6/8	5 3/8	1 7/8	1 7/8	7 1/8	5 5/8	249	57

♦ *Alaska Panhandle / Donald W. Moody / Donald W. Moody / 1966*

51	10 4/8	10 4/8	5 5/8	5 5/8	1 6/8	1 6/8	7 3/8	7 3/8	249	57

♦ *Nuka Bay / Curt Henning / Curt Henning / 1968*

51	10	9 6/8	5 6/8	5 5/8	2	2 1/8	6 6/8	6	249	57

♦ *Yakutat / Robert Sinko / Robert Sinko / 1971*

51	9 7/8	9 5/8	5 7/8	5 7/8	1 7/8	1 7/8	6	4 6/8	249	57

♦ *Granite Basin / Gerry D. Downey / Gerry D. Downey / 1983*

51	10 4/8	10 4/8	5 6/8	5 6/8	1 6/8	1 6/8	8 3/8	8 2/8	249	57

♦ *Skilak Glacier / Mark A. Gaede / Mark A. Gaede / 1988*

51	10 4/8	10 7/8	5 4/8	5 4/8	1 7/8	2	6 2/8	5 5/8	249	57

♦ *Cleveland Pen. / Lynn K. Herbert / Lynn K. Herbert / 1989*

51	10 2/8	10 3/8	5 5/8	5 6/8	1 7/8	2	6 1/8	5	249	57

♦ *Wrangell / Kerry Kammer / Kerry Kammer / 1992*

50 6/8	10 2/8	10 2/8	5 5/8	5 6/8	1 7/8	1 7/8	6 7/8	6 1/8	285	65

♦ *Cordova / Ralph E. Renner / Ralph E. Renner / 1950*

50 6/8	9 5/8	10 1/8	5 7/8	5 7/8	2 1/8	1 7/8	8	7 3/8	285	65

♦ *Knik River / C.M. Van Meter / C.M. Van Meter / 1956*

50 6/8	10 1/8	10 2/8	5 6/8	5 6/8	2	2	7 1/8	5 7/8	285	65

♦ *Boca De Quadra Inlet / Lyman Reynoldson / Lyman Reynoldson / 1957*

50 6/8	10 4/8	10 3/8	5 6/8	5 6/8	2	2	8 2/8	7 5/8	285	65

♦ *Kenai Pen. / Elgin T. Gates / Elgin T. Gates / 1961*

50 6/8	9 7/8	9 7/8	5 7/8	5 7/8	2	2	7 7/8	7 1/8	285	65

♦ *Kenai Mts. / Stephen D. LaBelle / Stephen D. LaBelle / 1971*

50 6/8	10 1/8	10	5 7/8	5 7/8	1 7/8	1 7/8	7 7/8	7 2/8	285	65

♦ *Kenai Pen. / Jack Allen / Jack Allen / 1974*

50 6/8	10 3/8	10 3/8	5 5/8	5 5/8	1 6/8	1 7/8	9 5/8	9 5/8	285	65

♦ *Day Harbor / Steen Henriksen / Steen Henriksen / 1984*

50 4/8	11 1/8	11 1/8	5	5	2	2	7	5 2/8	340	72

♦ *Stikine River / W.F. Littleton / W.F. Littleton / 1953*

50 4/8	10 2/8	10 4/8	5 1/8	5 1/8	1 7/8	1 7/8	0	0	340	72

♦ *Seward / Picked Up / A.D. Stenger / PR 1957*

50 4/8	9 6/8	9 6/8	5 6/8	5 6/8	1 7/8	1 7/8	8 1/8	7 5/8	340	72

♦ *Chugach Mts. / Elmer A. Patson / Elmer A. Patson / 1958*

50 4/8	10	10 2/8	5 6/8	5 6/8	1 7/8	1 7/8	8 1/8	7 6/8	340	72

♦ *Kenai Pen. / G. Best & R. Reed / Gordon Best / 1962*

ALASKA ROCKY MOUNTAIN GOAT *(continued)*

Score	Length of Horn		Circumference of Base		Circumference at Third Quarter		Greatest Spread	Tip-to-Tip Spread	All-Time Rank	State Rank
	R	L	R	L	R	L				
	♦ Locality / Hunter / Owner / Date Killed									
50⁴⁄₈	10⅝	10⁶⁄₈	5⁴⁄₈	5⁴⁄₈	1⁶⁄₈	1⁶⁄₈	7²⁄₈	6⅞	340	72
	♦ Cape Yakataga / Lynn M. Castle / Lynn M. Castle / 1964									
50⁴⁄₈	10	10	5⅞	5⅞	1⁶⁄₈	1⅝	7⅛	5⁴⁄₈	340	72
	♦ Wrangell Mts. / Charles S. Moses / Charles S. Moses / 1965									
50⁴⁄₈	10⅝	10⅜	5⁴⁄₈	5⅜	1⅞	1⅞	7⅜	5⁴⁄₈	340	72
	♦ Winstanley Lakes / James R. Simms / James R. Simms / 1966									
50⁴⁄₈	10⁴⁄₈	10⅜	5⅝	5⅝	1⅞	1⁶⁄₈	7⅜	7⅞	340	72
	♦ Seward / Frank W. Pinkerton / Frank W. Pinkerton / 1966									
50⁴⁄₈	11	11	5⁴⁄₈	5⅝	1⅞	1⁶⁄₈	7⅛	5⅛	340	72
	♦ Stikine River / Donald E. Fossen / Donald E. Fossen / 1973									
50⁴⁄₈	9⅞	9⁶⁄₈	5⁶⁄₈	5⁶⁄₈	1⅞	1⅞	7	6⁴⁄₈	340	72
	♦ Wrangell Mts. / Leonard O. Farlow / Leonard O. Farlow / 1978									
50⁴⁄₈	10⁶⁄₈	10⅞	5⅜	5⅜	1⅞	1⅞	7⁴⁄₈	6⁴⁄₈	340	72
	♦ Leduc Lake / James M. Judd / James M. Judd / 1985									
50⁴⁄₈	10⁶⁄₈	10⁶⁄₈	5⅜	5⅜	1⅞	1⅞	8	7⅝	340	72
	♦ Icy Bay / David W. Dillard / David W. Dillard / 1985									
50⁴⁄₈	10⁴⁄₈	10⅜	5⅝	5⁴⁄₈	1⅞	1⅞	7⁶⁄₈	7⅜	340	72
	♦ Puget Bay / Ross Darst / Ross Darst / 1992									
50²⁄₈	10²⁄₈	10²⁄₈	5⅝	5⁶⁄₈	1⁶⁄₈	1⁶⁄₈	7²⁄₈	6	395	85
	♦ Sheridan Glacier / Leslie B. Maxwell / Leslie B. Maxwell / 1959									
50²⁄₈	10⅛	10⅛	5⅜	5⁴⁄₈	2	2	7⅝	7⅝	395	85
	♦ Lynn Canal / Jacques M. Norvell, Sr. / Jacques M. Norvell, Sr. / 1968									
50²⁄₈	9⅞	9⅝	5⅝	5⅝	2	2	6⅞	6²⁄₈	395	85
	♦ Juneau / Jerry Kressin / Jerry Kressin / 1971									
50²⁄₈	10²⁄₈	10²⁄₈	5⁴⁄₈	5⁶⁄₈	1⅞	1⅞	6⅝	5⁴⁄₈	395	85
	♦ Eagle Lake / Dale E. Gibbons / Dale E. Gibbons / 1982									
50²⁄₈	10	9⅞	5⁶⁄₈	5⁶⁄₈	1⅞	1⅞	7⅝	7⅜	395	85
	♦ Kenai Pen. / David W. Doner / David W. Doner / 1992									
50	10⅛	10	5⁶⁄₈	5⅞	1⁶⁄₈	1⅝	4⅝	6⁴⁄₈	444	90
	♦ Rudyerd Bay / Joseph H. Keeney / Joseph H. Keeney / 1946									
50	9⅜	9⁴⁄₈	6	6	2	1⅞	7⅜	6⁴⁄₈	444	90
	♦ Kenai Pen. / Coke Elms / Coke Elms / 1956									
50	9⅜	10	5⅞	5⅞	1⅞	2	7⅛	6⁴⁄₈	444	90
	♦ Cape Yakataga / Edward I. Worst / Edward I. Worst / 1960									
50	9⅞	9⁴⁄₈	5⁶⁄₈	5⁶⁄₈	1⅞	1⅞	7⅝	7⅜	444	90
	♦ Girdwood / Franklin Maus / Franklin Maus / 1961									
50	10⅛	10	5⁶⁄₈	5⁶⁄₈	1⁶⁄₈	1⁶⁄₈	8²⁄₈	8	444	90
	♦ Chilkat Range / Jacques M. Norvell / Jacques M. Norvell / 1965									

ALASKA ROCKY MOUNTAIN GOAT *(continued)*

Score	Length of Horn R	Length of Horn L	Circumference of Base R	Circumference of Base L	Circumference at Third Quarter R	Circumference at Third Quarter L	Greatest Spread	Tip-to-Tip Spread	All-Time Rank	State Rank
	◆ *Locality / Hunter / Owner / Date Killed*									
50	10 1/8	10 1/8	5 6/8	5 7/8	1 6/8	1 7/8	8 3/8	8 3/8	444	90
	◆ *Seward / John Lee / John Lee / 1966*									
50	11 2/8	11 2/8	5	5	1 6/8	1 7/8	8 1/8	7 6/8	444	90
	◆ *Petersburg / James Briggs / James Briggs / 1966*									
50	10 3/8	10 3/8	5 4/8	5 4/8	1 6/8	1 7/8	7 5/8	7 4/8	444	90
	◆ *Kenai Pen. / A.P. Funk / A.P. Funk / 1967*									
50	9 6/8	9 6/8	5 5/8	5 5/8	1 7/8	1 7/8	7 6/8	7 6/8	444	90
	◆ *Whittier / Myron D. Cowell / Myron D. Cowell / 1968*									
50	10 2/8	10 2/8	5 4/8	5 4/8	1 6/8	1 6/8	7 1/8	6 2/8	444	90
	◆ *Skagway / Don Sather / Don Sather / 1968*									
50	10 2/8	10 3/8	5 2/8	5 3/8	2	2	8 6/8	8 6/8	444	90
	◆ *Port Dick / Neil Smith / Neil Smith / 1972*									
50	9 6/8	9 7/8	5 6/8	5 5/8	1 7/8	1 7/8	6 4/8	6	444	90
	◆ *Rudyerd Bay / Gerry D. Downey / Gerry D. Downey / 1975*									
50	10 2/8	10 1/8	5 3/8	5 2/8	1 7/8	1 7/8	8 2/8	7 4/8	444	90
	◆ *Prince William Sound / Ernest H. Youngs / Ernest H. Youngs / 1978*									
50	9 7/8	10	5 6/8	5 7/8	1 6/8	1 6/8	7 1/8	7	444	90
	◆ *Kodiak Island / Terry R. Stockman / Terry R. Stockman / 1986*									
50	10 2/8	10 5/8	5 6/8	5 6/8	1 6/8	1 7/8	6 3/8	5	444	90
	◆ *Bradfield Canal / James L. Beskin / James L. Beskin / 1989*									
50	10 2/8	10	5 7/8	5 7/8	1 7/8	1 7/8	7 1/8	6 5/8	444	90
	◆ *Bradley Lake / John L. Hendrix / John L. Hendrix / 1992*									
50	9 3/8	9 3/8	5 7/8	5 7/8	2	2	6 4/8	5 3/8	444	90
	◆ *Checats Lake / Mark W. Agnew / Mark W. Agnew / 1992*									
50	9 6/8	9 6/8	5 4/8	5 4/8	1 6/8	1 6/8	6 7/8	6	444	90
	◆ *Kenai Pen. / Les Rainey / Les Rainey / 1993*									
49 6/8	10	10	5 5/8	5 5/8	1 6/8	1 6/8	7 2/8	6 4/8	518	108
	◆ *Johnstone Bay / Stephen K. Karcz / Stephen K. Karcz / 1988*									
49 6/8	9 4/8	9 4/8	5 6/8	5 6/8	2	1 7/8	7 3/8	7 3/8	518	108
	◆ *Bradley Lake / Michael L. Ross / Michael L. Ross / 1989*									
49 6/8	10 1/8	10 2/8	5 2/8	5 2/8	1 7/8	1 7/8	6 3/8	5 2/8	518	108
	◆ *Sumdum Mountain / Duncan Gilchrist / Duncan Gilchrist / 1992*									
49 4/8	10 3/8	10 2/8	5 3/8	5 3/8	1 7/8	1 7/8	6 7/8	6 4/8	523	111
	◆ *Tyee Lake / Craig Trulock / Craig Trulock / 1993*									
48 6/8	9 2/8	9 2/8	5 3/8	5 2/8	2	2	8 2/8	7 6/8	534	112
	◆ *Kenai Mts. / Daniel G. Detert / Daniel G. Detert / 1978*									
48 6/8	10	10	5 4/8	5 4/8	1 6/8	1 7/8	8	7 7/8	534	112
	◆ *Sheep Creek / Miles Collier / Miles Collier / 1988*									

Score	Length of Horn R	Length of Horn L	Circumference of Base R	Circumference of Base L	Circumference at Third Quarter R	Circumference at Third Quarter L	Greatest Spread	Tip-to-Tip Spread	All-Time Rank	State Rank
♦ *Locality / Hunter / Owner / Date Killed*										
48 6/8	9 6/8	9 6/8	5 5/8	5 4/8	1 6/8	1 7/8	6 1/8	4 5/8	534	112
♦ *Endicott Arm / Thomas H. Pitts / Lorraine K. Harrison / 1988*										
48 6/8	9 4/8	9 4/8	5 6/8	5 6/8	1 6/8	1 6/8	7 6/8	7 5/8	534	112
♦ *Knik Glacier / Sandro Crivelli / Sandro Crivelli / 1990*										
48 6/8	10 2/8	10 2/8	5 4/8	5 4/8	1 6/8	1 6/8	7 7/8	7 6/8	534	112
♦ *Brown Mt. / David A. Baril / David A. Baril / 1992*										
48 4/8	10 2/8	10 3/8	5 3/8	5 3/8	1 5/8	1 6/8	6 5/8	5 7/8	540	117
♦ *Miles Glacier / Robert L. Pagel / Robert L. Pagel / 1974*										
48 4/8	9 7/8	9 5/8	5 4/8	5 5/8	1 6/8	1 6/8	8 3/8	8 2/8	540	117
♦ *Bradley Lake / Jeffrey B. Green / Jeffrey B. Green / 1992*										
48 2/8	9 7/8	10 1/8	5 2/8	5 3/8	1 6/8	1 6/8	7 2/8	6 7/8	549	119
♦ *Day Harbor / Danny W. Pankoski / Danny W. Pankoski / 1987*										
48 2/8	9 2/8	9 7/8	5 6/8	5 6/8	1 6/8	1 6/8	7 7/8	7 4/8	549	119
♦ *Kenai Peninsula / Cecil R. Jones / Cecil R. Jones / 1988*										
48 2/8	10 1/8	10	5	5 1/8	1 7/8	1 7/8	7 5/8	7 2/8	549	119
♦ *Endicott Arm / Loren M. Grosskopf / Loren M. Grosskopf / 1993*										
48 2/8	10 2/8	9 6/8	5 4/8	5 4/8	1 6/8	2	7 4/8	6 6/8	549	119
♦ *Dawes Glacier / David E. Parker / David E. Parker / 1993*										
48	9 7/8	9 7/8	5 4/8	5 3/8	1 6/8	1 6/8	7 4/8	7 4/8	557	123
♦ *Wild Creek / Charles H. Rohrer / Charles H. Rohrer / 1984*										
47 6/8	9 4/8	9 7/8	5 1/8	5 1/8	1 6/8	1 7/8	6 4/8	5 4/8	564	124
♦ *Allison Creek / Ron W. Biggs / Ron W. Biggs / 1987*										
47 6/8	9 4/8	9 6/8	5 4/8	5 5/8	1 6/8	1 6/8	7 7/8	7 5/8	564	124
♦ *Kenai Pen. / R. Lynn Highland / R. Lynn Highland / 1991*										
47 4/8	10 5/8	10 2/8	5 1/8	5 1/8	1 6/8	1 5/8	6 6/8	5 3/8	571	126
♦ *Horn Cliffs / Brent R. Akers / Brent R. Akers / 1989*										
47 4/8	9	9	5 5/8	5 4/8	1 6/8	1 6/8	6 1/8	5 7/8	571	126
♦ *Terror Lake / Patricia A. Stewart / Patricia A. Stewart / 1989*										
47 4/8	9 1/8	9 2/8	5 3/8	5 3/8	1 7/8	1 7/8	7 2/8	7 1/8	571	126
♦ *Kenai Pen. / James P. Cofske / James P. Cofske / 1993*										
47 2/8	10	10	5	5	1 6/8	1 7/8	7	5 5/8	575	129
♦ *Chugach Mts. / William J. Swartz, Jr. / William J. Swartz, Jr. / 1982*										
47	10 1/8	10 3/8	5	5 2/8	1 5/8	1 6/8	6 2/8	5 3/8	583	130
♦ *Chaix Hills / Richard O. Burns, Jr. / Richard O. Burns, Jr. / 1984*										
47	9	9 5/8	5 6/8	5 7/8	1 5/8	1 5/8	7	6 1/8	583	130
♦ *Takhin River / John E. Clark / John E. Clark / 1985*										
54 6/8	10 4/8	10	6 1/8	6 1/8	2 2/8	2 2/8	6 6/8	5 7/8	*	*
♦ *Cleveland Pen. / Lana L. DeLong / Roger DeLong / 1979*										

ALASKA ROCKY MOUNTAIN GOAT *(continued)*

Score	Length of Horn R	Length of Horn L	Circumference of Base R	Circumference of Base L	Circumference at Third Quarter R	Circumference at Third Quarter L	Greatest Spread	Tip-to-Tip Spread	All-Time Rank	State Rank
♦ *Locality / Hunter / Owner / Date Killed*										
54 4/8	10 3/8	10 4/8	5 4/8	5 4/8	2 3/8	2 3/8	8	8 1/8	*	*
♦ *McCarthy Creek / George A. Morelock / George A. Morelock / 1981*										
54 4/8	11	10 7/8	6	6	2	2 1/8	7	6 2/8	*	*
♦ *Stikine River / Patrick Flanary / Patrick Flanary / 1986*										
54	11 4/8	11 5/8	5 5/8	5 5/8	1 7/8	1 7/8	8 4/8	7 5/8	*	*
♦ *Cleveland Pen. / Chris Guggenbrickler / C. & T. Guggenbrickler / 1987*										
53 4/8	11 3/8	11 3/8	5 5/8	5 5/8	2	2	8 2/8	7 7/8	*	*
♦ *Yakataga Cape / William F. Sherman / Thomas M. Bradley / 1990*										

This nearly symmetrical Rocky Mountain goat, scoring 47-6/8 points, was shot by K. James Malady III in 1989 near Maria Creek, British Columbia.

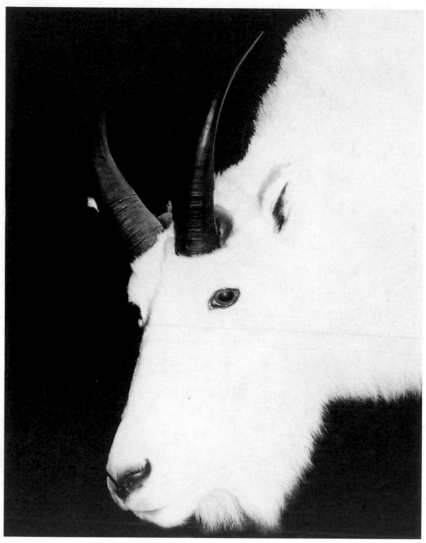

Photograph Courtesy of Lyle K. Willmarth

**COLORADO STATE RECORD
ROCKY MOUNTAIN GOAT
SCORE: 52⅝**
Locality: Park Co.   Date: 1988
Hunter: Lyle K. Willmarth

COLORADO
ROCKY MOUNTAIN GOAT

Score	Length of Horn		Circumference of Base		Circumference at Third Quarter		Greatest Spread	Tip-to-Tip Spread	All-Time Rank	State Rank
	R	L	R	L	R	L				
◆ Locality / Hunter / Owner / Date Killed										
52⁶⁄₈	11³⁄₈	11²⁄₈	5⁷⁄₈	5⁷⁄₈	1⁷⁄₈	1⁶⁄₈	8²⁄₈	7³⁄₈	49	1
◆ Park County / Lyle K. Willmarth / Lyle K. Willmarth / 1988										
51	10³⁄₈	10³⁄₈	5⁵⁄₈	5⁵⁄₈	2	1⁷⁄₈	7	6⁴⁄₈	249	2
◆ Clear Creek County / Janice L. Hemingson / Janice L. Hemingson / 1988										
50⁶⁄₈	10²⁄₈	10³⁄₈	6¹⁄₈	6¹⁄₈	1⁵⁄₈	1⁵⁄₈	6	5⁷⁄₈	285	3
◆ Mt. Antero / Leroy C. Wood / Leroy C. Wood / 1965										

Photograph Courtesy of Charlie T. Knox

IDAHO NUMBER TWO
ROCKY MOUNTAIN GOAT
SCORE: 52
Locality: Idaho Co.   Date: 1959
Hunter: Charlie T. Knox

IDAHO

ROCKY MOUNTAIN GOAT

Score	Length of Horn		Circumference of Base		Circumference at Third Quarter		Greatest Spread	Tip-to-Tip Spread	All-Time Rank	State Rank
	R	L	R	L	R	L				
◆ Locality / Hunter / Owner / Date Killed										
52⁶⁄₈	11⁴⁄₈	11⁴⁄₈	5⅝	5⅝	1⅞	1⅞	7⁴⁄₈	7⅜	49	1
◆ Idaho County / Farrell M. Trenary / Farrell M. Trenary / 1933										
52	10⁶⁄₈	10³⁄₈	5⁶⁄₈	5⁶⁄₈	2	2	6⅞	6²⁄₈	99	2
◆ Idaho County / Charlie T. Knox / Charlie T. Knox / 1959										
51⁶⁄₈	10⅛	10³⁄₈	6	6	1⅝	1⁶⁄₈	7⅞	7⁴⁄₈	131	3
◆ Bonneville County / K. Rands Wiley / K. Rands Wiley / 1983										
51²⁄₈	10⁴⁄₈	10³⁄₈	5⅝	5⅝	1⅞	1⅞	7²⁄₈	6⁴⁄₈	212	4
◆ Idaho County / Lorraine Ravary / Lorraine Ravary / 1978										
50⁴⁄₈	10	10⅛	5⅝	5⅝	1⅞	1⅞	6⅞	6⅞	340	5
◆ Bonneville County / William D. Stoddard / William D. Stoddard / 1986										
50²⁄₈	10⅛	10²⁄₈	5⅝	5⅝	1⅞	1⁶⁄₈	7⁶⁄₈	7	395	6
◆ Bonneville County / Arnae R. Hillam / Arnae R. Hillam / 1993										
50	10⅞	10⁶⁄₈	5⅝	5⁶⁄₈	1⁶⁄₈	1⅝	6⅝	5⁶⁄₈	444	7
◆ Squaw Creek / William A. Callaway / William H. Lockhart / 1959										
50	10	10	5⁶⁄₈	5⁶⁄₈	1⁶⁄₈	1⁶⁄₈	6²⁄₈	5⁴⁄₈	444	7
◆ Bear Point / Aaron U. Jones / Aaron U. Jones / 1961										
50	9²⁄₈	9²⁄₈	5²⁄₈	5²⁄₈	1⅞	1⅞	7⅛	7⅛	444	7
◆ Bonneville County / Charles E. Wood / Charles E. Wood / 1983										
48⁴⁄₈	10	9⅞	5³⁄₈	5³⁄₈	1⅞	1⁶⁄₈	7⅝	7	540	10
◆ Custer County / Gerald L. Walters / Gerald L. Walters / 1993										
48⁴⁄₈	9⁶⁄₈	9⁴⁄₈	5⁴⁄₈	5⁴⁄₈	1⅞	2	7⅞	7	540	10
◆ Bonneville County / David G. Paullin / David G. Paullin / 1994										
48²⁄₈	9⅝	9⁶⁄₈	5⁴⁄₈	5⅝	1⁶⁄₈	1⁶⁄₈	7⅞	7⁶⁄₈	549	12
◆ Clark County / Larry D. Orchard / Larry D. Orchard / 1993										
48	9⁴⁄₈	9⁴⁄₈	5⁴⁄₈	5⁴⁄₈	1⁶⁄₈	1⅝	6³⁄₈	6⅛	557	13
◆ Bonneville County / Thomas F. Call / Thomas F. Call / 1993										
47²⁄₈	9⁴⁄₈	9⅝	5³⁄₈	5³⁄₈	1⅝	1⅝	6⅞	6²⁄₈	575	14
◆ Bonneville County / Stephen W. Deiro / Stephen W. Deiro / 1985										

Photograph Courtesy of Charles N. Johns

MONTANA STATE RECORD
ROCKY MOUNTAIN GOAT
SCORE: 52⅔
Locality: Lewis & Clark Co.   Date: 1981
Hunter: Charles N. Johns

MONTANA
ROCKY MOUNTAIN GOAT

Score	Length of Horn		Circumference of Base		Circumference at Third Quarter		Greatest Spread	Tip-to-Tip Spread	All-Time Rank	State Rank
	R	L	R	L	R	L				
52 2/8	10 4/8	10 4/8	5 6/8	5 6/8	2	2	7 3/8	7	73	1
◆ Lewis & Clark County / Charles N. Johns / Charles N. Johns / 1981										
51 6/8	10 3/8	10 2/8	6 1/8	6 1/8	1 7/8	1 7/8	6 3/8	6 2/8	131	2
◆ Lake County / Glenn Conklin / Glenn Conklin / 1958										
51 6/8	10 4/8	10 4/8	5 6/8	5 6/8	2	2	8 4/8	8 2/8	131	2
◆ Wolf Creek / Jim B. Beard / Jim B. Beard / 1963										
51 6/8	11 2/8	11	5 6/8	5 6/8	1 6/8	1 6/8	7 4/8	6 7/8	131	2
◆ Flathead County / John J. Allmaras / John J. Allmaras / 1965										
51 6/8	11	10 7/8	5 4/8	5 5/8	1 7/8	1 7/8	7 2/8	6 3/8	131	2
◆ Gallatin County / Todd E. Barry / Todd E. Barry / 1994										
51 4/8	10 2/8	10 4/8	6 1/8	6 1/8	1 7/8	1 7/8	8 1/8	7 5/8	171	6
◆ Montana / Unknown / James Fredrick / PR 1981										
51 4/8	10 3/8	10 3/8	5 6/8	5 6/8	1 7/8	1 7/8	6 7/8	6 2/8	171	6
◆ Chouteau County / Larry W. Lander / Larry W. Lander / 1983										
51 4/8	10 1/8	10 1/8	5 7/8	5 7/8	1 7/8	1 7/8	7 7/8	7 4/8	171	6
◆ Gallatin County / Jack D. Yadon / Jack D. Yadon / 1986										
51 4/8	9 7/8	10	6	6	2	2	6 7/8	6 3/8	171	6
◆ Beaverhead County / Shawn M. Probst / Shawn M. Probst / 1990										
51	10 3/8	10 5/8	5 2/8	5 2/8	1 6/8	1 6/8	7 2/8	6 2/8	249	10
◆ Flathead County / Johnny Powell / Johnny Powell / 1965										
51	10 3/8	10 6/8	5 7/8	6	1 6/8	1 7/8	0	0	249	10
◆ Ravalli County / John K. Frederikson / John K. Frederikson / 1979										
51	10 7/8	10 7/8	5 3/8	5 4/8	1 6/8	1 7/8	6 4/8	5 6/8	249	10
◆ Gallatin County / Ronald K. Lewis / Ronald K. Lewis / 1984										
50 6/8	11	11 1/8	5 4/8	5 4/8	1 6/8	1 6/8	5 4/8	4 3/8	285	13
◆ Flathead County / Picked Up / Charlie Shaw / 1936										
50 6/8	10 2/8	10 3/8	5 5/8	5 5/8	1 7/8	1 7/8	6 5/8	6 1/8	285	13
◆ Chouteau County / Craig L. Nowak / Craig L. Nowak / 1990										
50 4/8	10 3/8	10 4/8	5 6/8	6	1 6/8	1 6/8	7 7/8	7 7/8	340	15
◆ Lewis & Clark County / Robert F. Thelen / Donald C. Thelen / 1974										
50 4/8	10 1/8	10 1/8	5 6/8	5 6/8	1 4/8	1 5/8	6 4/8	5 6/8	340	15
◆ Missoula County / Bill R. Tillerson / Bill R. Tillerson / 1985										
50 4/8	9 7/8	10	5 6/8	5 6/8	1 6/8	1 6/8	6 2/8	5 5/8	340	15
◆ Lewis & Clark County / Don St. Clair / Don St. Clair / 1986										
50 4/8	10	10 1/8	5 6/8	5 6/8	1 7/8	1 7/8	5 6/8	5	340	15
◆ Madison County / Corey M. Halvorson / Corey M. Halvorson / 1986										

Score	Length of Horn		Circumference of Base		Circumference at Third Quarter		Greatest Spread	Tip-to-Tip Spread	All-Time Rank	State Rank
	R	L	R	L	R	L				
◆ *Locality / Hunter / Owner / Date Killed*										
50 2/8	10 4/8	10 3/8	5 4/8	5 5/8	1 6/8	1 6/8	6 6/8	6 6/8	395	19
◆ *Pentagon Mt. / Guy Brash / Guy Brash / 1957*										
50 2/8	10 4/8	10 3/8	5 5/8	5 6/8	1 6/8	1 6/8	8	7 2/8	395	19
◆ *Ravalli County / Mark J. Jakobson / Mark J. Jakobson / 1965*										
50 2/8	10 3/8	10 2/8	5 6/8	5 6/8	1 6/8	1 6/8	7 4/8	6 7/8	395	19
◆ *Chouteau County / Robert E. Young / Robert E. Young / 1983*										
50	10 4/8	10 2/8	5 4/8	5 4/8	2	1 6/8	7 2/8	6 6/8	444	22
◆ *Flathead River / Gene Biddle / Gene Biddle / 1957*										
50	10 1/8	10 1/8	5 4/8	5 4/8	2	2	6 7/8	6 1/8	444	22
◆ *Lincoln / James A. Gunn III / James A. Gunn III / 1963*										
50	10 7/8	10 7/8	5 4/8	5 4/8	1 5/8	1 5/8	7	6	444	22
◆ *Missoula County / Charles Barry / Charles Barry / 1965*										
50	10 3/8	10 6/8	5 5/8	5 5/8	1 6/8	1 6/8	6 7/8	6 1/8	444	22
◆ *Lincoln County / Wayne Hill / Wayne Hill / 1988*										
49 6/8	10	9 7/8	5 6/8	5 5/8	1 6/8	1 5/8	7	6 5/8	518	26
◆ *Chouteau County / Rosita Moe / Rosita Moe / 1991*										
49 4/8	10 3/8	9 7/8	5 6/8	5 5/8	1 6/8	1 7/8	7 4/8	7	523	27
◆ *Gallatin County / Doug Columbik / Doug Columbik / 1990*										
49	10 2/8	10 1/8	5 6/8	5 6/8	1 5/8	1 5/8	6 3/8	5 6/8	532	28
◆ *Powell County / Daniel T. Morgan / Daniel T. Morgan / 1990*										
48 4/8	10	10 1/8	5 4/8	5 4/8	1 6/8	1 5/8	6 6/8	5 7/8	540	29
◆ *Gallatin County / Dale L. Martin / Dale L. Martin / 1990*										
48 4/8	9 2/8	9 1/8	5 4/8	5 5/8	1 5/8	1 5/8	7 4/8	7 3/8	540	29
◆ *Sweet Grass County / Douglas W. Schimmel / Douglas W. Schimmel / 1992*										
47 4/8	9 6/8	9 6/8	5 3/8	5 2/8	1 6/8	1 6/8	7 2/8	6 7/8	571	31
◆ *Gallatin County / Shiela G. Sinclair / Shiela G. Sinclair / 1991*										
47 2/8	10 1/8	10 2/8	5 2/8	5 3/8	1 5/8	1 5/8	6 6/8	6 2/8	575	32
◆ *Saunders County / Byron E. Wates, Jr. / Byron E. Wates, Jr. / 1987*										
47 2/8	10 2/8	9 7/8	5 2/8	5 3/8	1 5/8	1 5/8	8	7 6/8	575	32
◆ *Madison County / Timothy A. Olson / Timothy A. Olson / 1993*										
47	9 6/8	9 7/8	5	5	1 5/8	1 5/8	6 7/8	6 4/8	583	34
◆ *Chouteau County / Jerry E. Copenhaver / Jerry E. Copenhaver / 1987*										

Montana has produced 34 records book goats, including this billy taken in Powell County by Daniel T. Morgan in 1990. It scores 49 points.

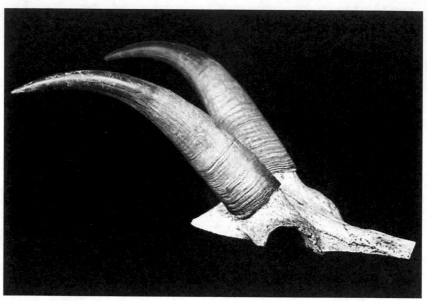

**NEVADA STATE RECORD
ROCKY MOUNTAIN GOAT
SCORE: 53⅝**
Locality: Elko Co.   Date: 1978
Hunter: Robert D. Kennedy

NEVADA

ROCKY MOUNTAIN GOAT

Score	Length of Horn R	Length of Horn L	Circumference of Base R	Circumference of Base L	Circumference at Third Quarter R	Circumference at Third Quarter L	Greatest Spread	Tip-to-Tip Spread	All-Time Rank	State Rank
♦ *Locality / Hunter / Owner / Date Killed*										
53 6/8	10 3/8	10 3/8	5 7/8	6	2 1/8	2 1/8	7 7/8	7 5/8	21	1
♦ *Elko County / Robert D. Kennedy / Robert D. Kennedy / 1978*										
52 2/8	10 2/8	10 2/8	5 7/8	5 7/8	1 7/8	1 7/8	6 4/8	6 2/8	73	2
♦ *Elko County / Daniel E. Warren / Daniel E. Warren / 1994*										
52	10 1/8	10 1/8	5 6/8	5 6/8	2 1/8	2	7	6 3/8	99	3
♦ *Elko County / Les Boni / Les Boni / 1978*										
50	9 6/8	9 6/8	5 7/8	5 6/8	1 6/8	1 6/8	7 3/8	7	444	4
♦ *Elko County / Tammy H. Bawcom / Tammy H. Bawcom / 1993*										

Photograph Courtesy of Lloyd Weaver

SOUTH DAKOTA STATE RECORD
ROCKY MOUNTAIN GOAT
SCORE: 50⅝
Locality: Black Hills   Date: 1967
Hunter: Lloyd Weaver

SOUTH DAKOTA

ROCKY MOUNTAIN GOAT

Score	Length of Horn		Circumference of Base		Circumference at Third Quarter		Greatest Spread	Tip-to-Tip Spread	All-Time Rank	State Rank
	R	L	R	L	R	L				
♦ Locality / Hunter / Owner / Date Killed										
50⁶⁄₈	10²⁄₈	10⁴⁄₈	5⁷⁄₈	5⁶⁄₈	1⁷⁄₈	1⁷⁄₈	6⁶⁄₈	5⁷⁄₈	285	1
♦ Black Hills / Lloyd Weaver / Lloyd Weaver / 1967										
50⁴⁄₈	10⁵⁄₈	10⁵⁄₈	5³⁄₈	5³⁄₈	1⁶⁄₈	1⁶⁄₈	7²⁄₈	6³⁄₈	340	2
♦ Black Hills / Robert M. Aalseth / Robert M. Aalseth / 1967										
50⁴⁄₈	10	10	5⁷⁄₈	5⁷⁄₈	1⁷⁄₈	1⁷⁄₈	7¹⁄₈	6⁶⁄₈	340	2
♦ Pennington County / Floyd J. Campbell / Floyd J. Campbell / 1978										

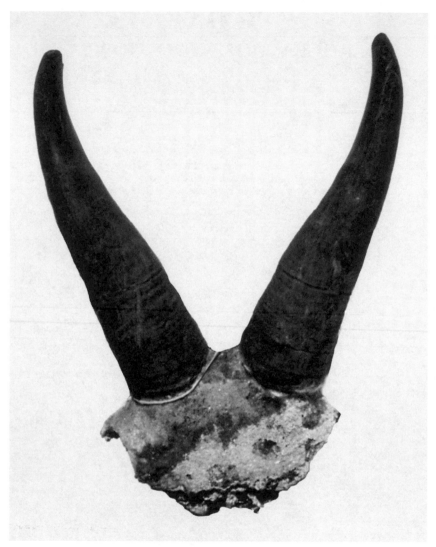

Photograph Courtesy of Andrea L. Shaffer

UTAH STATE RECORD
ROCKY MOUNTAIN GOAT
SCORE: 51
Locality: Salt Lake Co.   Date: 1987
Hunter: Andrea L. Shaffer

UTAH

ROCKY MOUNTAIN GOAT

Score	Length of Horn		Circumference of Base		Circumference at Third Quarter		Greatest Spread	Tip-to-Tip Spread	All-Time Rank	State Rank
	R	L	R	L	R	L				
	◆ Locality / Hunter / Owner / Date Killed									
51	8⁴⁄₈	8⁶⁄₈	6	5⁷⁄₈	2²⁄₈	2³⁄₈	7⁵⁄₈	7²⁄₈	249	1
	◆ Salt Lake County / Andrea L. Shaffer / Andrea L. Shaffer / 1987									
50⁶⁄₈	9⁶⁄₈	9⁷⁄₈	5⁷⁄₈	6	1⁶⁄₈	1⁷⁄₈	5⁷⁄₈	5⁴⁄₈	285	2
	◆ Salt Lake County / Picked Up / Utah Div. of Wildl. Resc. / 1985									
50⁶⁄₈	9⁵⁄₈	9⁵⁄₈	5⁶⁄₈	5⁶⁄₈	1⁷⁄₈	1⁷⁄₈	6⁶⁄₈	6²⁄₈	285	2
	◆ Salt Lake County / Macie J. Manire / Macie J. Manire / 1988									
50	9⁴⁄₈	9⁴⁄₈	5⁶⁄₈	5⁶⁄₈	1⁷⁄₈	1⁷⁄₈	6⁶⁄₈	6²⁄₈	444	4
	◆ Utah County / Ned W. Walker / Ned W. Walker / 1994									

Photograph Courtesy of Arie Vander Hoek, Jr.

WASHINGTON STATE RECORD
ROCKY MOUNTAIN GOAT
SCORE: 52⅝
Locality: Whatcom Co.   Date: 1966
Hunter: Arie Vander Hoek, Jr.

WASHINGTON

ROCKY MOUNTAIN GOAT

Score	Length of Horn		Circumference of Base		Circumference at Third Quarter		Greatest Spread	Tip-to-Tip Spread	All-Time Rank	State Rank
	R	L	R	L	R	L				
◆ Locality / Hunter / Owner / Date Killed										
52 6/8	11 4/8	11 4/8	5 1/8	5 1/8	1 6/8	1 6/8	7 5/8	7 4/8	49	1
◆ Whatcom County / Arie Vanderhoek, Jr. / Arie Vanderhoek, Jr. / 1966										
52 4/8	10 4/8	10 2/8	5 7/8	5 7/8	2	2	7 6/8	7 2/8	61	2
◆ Okanogan County / Richard Shatto / Richard Shatto / 1962										
52 4/8	11 1/8	11 3/8	5 5/8	5 4/8	1 7/8	1 7/8	7 1/8	6	61	2
◆ Whatcom County / John W. Bullene / John W. Bullene / 1965										
52 4/8	10 1/8	10	6	6	2	2	7 6/8	7 2/8	61	2
◆ Sheep Creek / R.C. Dukart / R.C. Dukart / 1967										
52 2/8	10 6/8	10 6/8	5 6/8	5 6/8	2	1 7/8	8 5/8	8	73	5
◆ Whatcom County / Al Hershey / Al Hershey / 1969										
52 2/8	10 6/8	10 5/8	5 6/8	5 6/8	1 7/8	1 7/8	8 2/8	7 5/8	73	5
◆ Chelan County / John W. Lane / John W. Lane / 1973										
52 2/8	10 1/8	10 1/8	5 6/8	5 6/8	2	2	6 7/8	6 4/8	73	5
◆ Chelan County / Thomas A. Lovas / Thomas A. Lovas / 1976										
52 2/8	10 2/8	10 4/8	6	6 1/8	1 6/8	1 7/8	7	6 2/8	73	5
◆ Chelan County / Nat Steele / Nat Steele / 1980										
52	10 3/8	10 3/8	5 4/8	5 5/8	2	2 1/8	6 7/8	4 5/8	99	9
◆ Jumbo Mt. / Clyde Lewis / Clyde Lewis / 1948										
52	10 2/8	10 1/8	6 1/8	6 1/8	2	2	6 1/8	5 3/8	99	9
◆ Okanogan County / E.W. Butler / E.W. Butler / 1967										
52	9 7/8	9 6/8	5 6/8	5 6/8	2	2	7 5/8	7	99	9
◆ Skagit County / John C. Casebeer / John C. Casebeer / 1970										
52	10 1/8	10 2/8	6	6 1/8	1 7/8	2	7	6 3/8	99	9
◆ Chelan County / Robert A. Beckton / Robert A. Beckton / 1971										
52	10 2/8	10 1/8	6	6	2 1/8	2	7	5 3/8	99	9
◆ Whatcom County / George W. Bowen / George W. Bowen / 1978										
52	10 2/8	10 6/8	5 6/8	5 7/8	2	2	7 4/8	6 4/8	99	9
◆ Whatcom County / Gary W. Cunningham / Gary W. Cunningham / 1991										
51 6/8	10 5/8	10 6/8	5 4/8	5 7/8	1 7/8	2	6	5 2/8	131	15
◆ Snohomish County / Des F. Hinds / Des F. Hinds / 1974										
51 6/8	9 7/8	10 5/8	5 4/8	5 4/8	2 1/8	2 2/8	6 4/8	5 5/8	131	15
◆ Snohomish County / Michael J. Simon / John M. Mitchell / 1981										
51 6/8	10 5/8	10 4/8	5 5/8	5 5/8	1 7/8	1 7/8	7 1/8	6 1/8	131	15
◆ Snohomish County / Edward M. Beitner / Edward M. Beitner / 1984										
51 6/8	10	9 6/8	5 4/8	5 4/8	2 1/8	2	6 6/8	6 2/8	131	15
◆ Snohomish County / Terry L. Wagner / Terry L. Wagner / 1990										

Score	Length of Horn R	L	Circumference of Base R	L	Circumference at Third Quarter R	L	Greatest Spread	Tip-to-Tip Spread	All-Time Rank	State Rank

♦ Locality / Hunter / Owner / Date Killed

51⁴⁄₈	10²⁄₈	10¹⁄₈	5⁴⁄₈	5⁴⁄₈	1⁷⁄₈	1⁷⁄₈	6⁷⁄₈	5⁵⁄₈	171	19

♦ *Chelan County / Virgil N. Carpenter / Virgil N. Carpenter / 1973*

51⁴⁄₈	10⁷⁄₈	10⁴⁄₈	5⁴⁄₈	5⁴⁄₈	1⁷⁄₈	1⁷⁄₈	7²⁄₈	7¹⁄₈	171	19

♦ *Snohomish County / Theodore H. Kiser / Theodore H. Kiser / 1985*

51²⁄₈	10⁴⁄₈	10²⁄₈	6	5⁷⁄₈	2	1⁷⁄₈	6⁴⁄₈	5³⁄₈	212	21

♦ *Pend Oreille County / William R. Stevens / William R. Stevens / 1975*

51²⁄₈	10⁶⁄₈	10⁶⁄₈	5⁴⁄₈	5³⁄₈	2	2	8³⁄₈	7⁷⁄₈	212	21

♦ *Kittitas County / Michael W. Duby / Michael W. Duby / 1980*

51²⁄₈	10¹⁄₈	10¹⁄₈	5⁶⁄₈	5⁶⁄₈	1⁷⁄₈	1⁷⁄₈	6⁶⁄₈	6²⁄₈	212	21

♦ *Okanogan County / Richard D. Grant / Richard D. Grant / 1982*

51	10²⁄₈	10²⁄₈	5²⁄₈	5²⁄₈	2	2	6⁶⁄₈	5⁷⁄₈	249	24

♦ *Snohomish County / David T. Lewis / David T. Lewis / 1972*

51	10⁴⁄₈	10⁵⁄₈	5⁵⁄₈	5⁵⁄₈	1⁷⁄₈	1⁷⁄₈	7³⁄₈	6⁶⁄₈	249	24

♦ *Snohomish County / John W. Lane / John W. Lane / 1982*

51	9³⁄₈	9⁶⁄₈	5⁶⁄₈	5⁶⁄₈	1⁷⁄₈	1⁷⁄₈	6⁴⁄₈	5⁷⁄₈	249	24

♦ *Yakima County / Stephanie L. Peyser / Stephanie L. Peyser / 1992*

50⁶⁄₈	10⁴⁄₈	10⁴⁄₈	5⁵⁄₈	5⁶⁄₈	1⁶⁄₈	1⁶⁄₈	8⁴⁄₈	8¹⁄₈	285	27

♦ *Chelan County / Raymond J. Hammer / Raymond J. Hammer / 1973*

50⁶⁄₈	10	10	5⁷⁄₈	5⁷⁄₈	1⁷⁄₈	1⁷⁄₈	7⁵⁄₈	7²⁄₈	285	27

♦ *Okanogan County / Jerrel R. Harmon / Jerrel R. Harmon / 1984*

50⁶⁄₈	10	10	5⁶⁄₈	5⁷⁄₈	1⁶⁄₈	1⁷⁄₈	6⁵⁄₈	6³⁄₈	285	27

♦ *Okanogan County / Susan M. Fletcher / Susan M. Fletcher / 1985*

50⁶⁄₈	10⁵⁄₈	10⁵⁄₈	5⁶⁄₈	5⁶⁄₈	1⁶⁄₈	1⁷⁄₈	6⁷⁄₈	6⁵⁄₈	285	27

♦ *Chelan County / David L. Metzler / David L. Metzler / 1986*

50⁶⁄₈	10¹⁄₈	9⁷⁄₈	5⁴⁄₈	5⁴⁄₈	1⁷⁄₈	1⁷⁄₈	8²⁄₈	7⁷⁄₈	285	27

♦ *Okanogan County / Monica M. Knight / Monica M. Knight / 1987*

50⁶⁄₈	11²⁄₈	10¹⁄₈	5⁵⁄₈	5⁵⁄₈	2	2	8	7¹⁄₈	285	27

♦ *Whatcom County / James C. Zevely / James C. Zevely / 1993*

50⁴⁄₈	10	10	5⁶⁄₈	5⁶⁄₈	1⁷⁄₈	1⁶⁄₈	6⁵⁄₈	6⁴⁄₈	340	33

♦ *Okanogan Mts. / Neil Castner / Neil Castner / 1956*

50⁴⁄₈	10³⁄₈	10²⁄₈	5⁶⁄₈	5⁶⁄₈	2	2	6⁶⁄₈	5¹⁄₈	340	33

♦ *Okanogan / Bob Hazelbrook / Bob Hazelbrook / 1960*

50²⁄₈	10	10	5⁶⁄₈	5⁶⁄₈	1⁶⁄₈	1⁷⁄₈	7	6⁴⁄₈	395	35

♦ *Blue Goat Mt. / Picked Up / Charles F. Martinsen / 1956*

50²⁄₈	10	10¹⁄₈	5⁶⁄₈	5⁵⁄₈	2	1⁷⁄₈	8	7⁶⁄₈	395	35

♦ *Okanogan County / Victor E. Moss / Victor E. Moss / 1957*

50²⁄₈	10	10	5⁷⁄₈	5⁵⁄₈	1⁶⁄₈	1⁶⁄₈	7⁴⁄₈	6⁵⁄₈	395	35

♦ *Chelan County / Ned Shiflett / Ned Shiflett / 1966*

WASHINGTON ROCKY MOUNTAIN GOAT *(continued)*

Score	Length of Horn		Circumference of Base		Circumference at Third Quarter		Greatest Spread	Tip-to-Tip Spread	All-Time Rank	State Rank
	R	L	R	L	R	L				
◆ *Locality / Hunter / Owner / Date Killed*										
50 2/8	10	9 6/8	6	5 7/8	1 7/8	1 7/8	6 4/8	6	395	35
◆ *Lake Chelan / Gary L. Aichlmayr / Gary L. Aichlmayr / 1969*										
50 2/8	9 3/8	9 1/8	5 7/8	5 7/8	1 7/8	1 7/8	6 7/8	6 3/8	395	35
◆ *Okanogan County / Richard J. Wristen / Richard J. Wristen / 1982*										
50 2/8	9 4/8	9 5/8	5 6/8	5 6/8	1 7/8	2	7	6 5/8	395	35
◆ *Snohomish County / Wayne E. Ritter / Wayne E. Ritter / 1985*										
50 2/8	10 4/8	10 6/8	5 4/8	5 5/8	1 6/8	1 6/8	6 7/8	6 4/8	395	35
◆ *Whatcom County / Darrel Van Kekerix / Darrel Van Kekerix / 1992*										
50	10 1/8	10 1/8	5 4/8	5 4/8	2	1 7/8	7 6/8	7 7/8	444	42
◆ *Okanogan County / John Hutchinson / Ralph Hutchinson / 1950*										
50	9 3/8	9 7/8	6	6	2	2	6 7/8	6 6/8	444	42
◆ *Lake Chelan / Ed Pariseu / Ed Pariseu / 1962*										
50	10	10 2/8	5 7/8	5 7/8	1 6/8	1 6/8	7	6 4/8	444	42
◆ *Oroville / G. Pickering / G. Pickering / 1963*										
50	9 3/8	9 6/8	6	5 7/8	1 6/8	1 7/8	6 2/8	5 2/8	444	42
◆ *Lake Chelan / Don Francis / Don Francis / 1966*										
50	10 2/8	10 2/8	5 5/8	5 4/8	1 7/8	1 7/8	6	4 6/8	444	42
◆ *Chelan County / Carl Lewis / Carl Lewis / 1968*										
50	9 7/8	9 7/8	5 6/8	5 7/8	1 6/8	1 7/8	5	4 3/8	444	42
◆ *Chelan County / John F. Hooper / William R. Hooper / 1970*										
50	10 1/8	9 7/8	5 2/8	5 2/8	2	2	7 4/8	6 3/8	444	42
◆ *Snobomish County / Jeffrey J. Nelson / Jeffrey J. Nelson / 1989*										
50	10 4/8	10 2/8	5 5/8	5 4/8	1 7/8	1 6/8	6 2/8	5 7/8	444	42
◆ *King County / Spencer C. Davis / Spencer C. Davis / 1990*										
49 4/8	9 3/8	10 7/8	5 5/8	5 6/8	1 7/8	1 7/8	5 2/8	4 2/8	523	50
◆ *Chelan County / Dennis K. Rudolph / Dennis K. Rudolph / 1992*										
49	9 4/8	9 2/8	5 7/8	5 6/8	2	2	5 7/8	5	532	51
◆ *Snohomish County / Colin F. MacRae / Colin F. MacRae / 1991*										
48 4/8	9 4/8	9 4/8	5 2/8	5 2/8	1 7/8	1 7/8	5 6/8	5	540	52
◆ *King County / Donald L. Williams, Jr. / Donald L. Williams, Jr. / 1993*										
48 2/8	9 5/8	9 6/8	5 3/8	5 3/8	1 7/8	1 7/8	5 4/8	4 4/8	549	53
◆ *Whatcom County / Greg J. Bullene / Greg J. Bullene / 1986*										
48 2/8	9 2/8	9 2/8	5 6/8	5 7/8	1 6/8	1 6/8	6 7/8	6 2/8	549	53
◆ *Yakima County / Benjamin M. Jergens / Benjamin M. Jergens / 1991*										
47 6/8	10	9 7/8	5 2/8	5 2/8	1 7/8	1 6/8	7 4/8	6 7/8	564	55
◆ *Okanogan County / Mark Cook / Mark Cook / 1987*										
47	8 7/8	8 7/8	5 6/8	5 5/8	1 6/8	1 6/8	6 2/8	5 2/8	583	56
◆ *Yakima County / Lee M. Shetler / Lee M. Shetler / 1989*										

Photograph Courtesy of Paul L. Scott, Jr.

WYOMING STATE RECORD
ROCKY MOUNTAIN GOAT
SCORE: 47
Locality: Park Co.   Date: 1989
Hunter: Paul L. Scott, Jr.

WYOMING

ROCKY MOUNTAIN GOAT

Score	Length of Horn R	Length of Horn L	Circumference of Base R	Circumference of Base L	Circumference at Third Quarter R	Circumference at Third Quarter L	Greatest Spread	Tip-to-Tip Spread	All-Time Rank	State Rank
♦ *Locality / Hunter / Owner / Date Killed*										
47	9⅞	9⅜	5⁴⁄₈	5⅝	1⅝	1⅝	7⅜	6⁶⁄₈	583	1
♦ *Park County / Paul L. Scott, Jr. / Paul L. Scott, Jr. / 1989*										

Photograph Courtesy of N.K. Luxton

ALBERTA PROVINCE RECORD
ROCKY MOUNTAIN GOAT
SCORE: 54
Locality: Bow Summit   Date: 1907
Hunter: Indian
Owner: N.K. Luxton

ALBERTA

ROCKY MOUNTAIN GOAT

Score	Length of Horn		Circumference of Base		Circumference at Third Quarter		Greatest Spread	Tip-to-Tip Spread	All-Time Rank	State Rank
	R	L	R	L	R	L				
◆ Locality / Hunter / Owner / Date Killed										
54	11²⁄₈	11 ⅛	6²⁄₈	6²⁄₈	2	2	9²⁄₈	9²⁄₈	18	1
◆ Bow Summit / Indian / N.K. Luxton / 1907										
51⁴⁄₈	10⅛	9⅞	5⅞	6⅛	1⅞	1⅞	7⁴⁄₈	7²⁄₈	171	2
◆ Sheep Creek / Russell A. Fischer / Russell A. Fischer / 1967										
51²⁄₈	10²⁄₈	10⁴⁄₈	6⅛	6⅛	1⁶⁄₈	1⁶⁄₈	7⅞	7⅝	212	3
◆ Hard Scrabble Pass / Justus von Lengerke / Justus von Lengerke / 1937										
50⁴⁄₈	10²⁄₈	10⁴⁄₈	5²⁄₈	5⅜	2	2	7	5⅝	340	4
◆ Brazeau River / Walter B. McClurkan / Walter B. McClurkan / 1942										
50⁴⁄₈	9⁴⁄₈	9⁴⁄₈	5⁶⁄₈	5⁶⁄₈	2⅛	2⅛	8	8	340	4
◆ Smoky River / Terry Thrift, Jr. / Terry Thrift, Jr. / 1965										

Photograph from Boone & Crockett Club Archives

BRITISH COLUMBIA PROVINCE RECORD
WORLD'S RECORD
ROCKY MOUNTAIN GOAT
SCORE: 56⁶⁄₈
Locality: Babine Mountains   Date: 1949
Hunter: E.C. Haase
Owner: B&C National Collection, Cody, Wyoming

BRITISH COLUMBIA
ROCKY MOUNTAIN GOAT

Score	Length of Horn		Circumference of Base		Circumference at Third Quarter		Greatest Spread	Tip-to-Tip Spread	All-Time Rank	State Rank
	R	L	R	L	R	L				
♦ Locality / Hunter / Owner / Date Killed										
56 6/8	12	12	6 4/8	6 4/8	2	2	9 2/8	9	1	1
♦ Babine Mts. / E.C. Haase / B&C National Collection / 1949										
56 2/8	11 3/8	11 3/8	6 3/8	6 4/8	2 1/8	2	8 6/8	8 3/8	2	2
♦ Hedley / Picked Up / Robert Kitto / 1969										
55 2/8	10 6/8	11	6 2/8	6 3/8	2	2 1/8	7 6/8	7 2/8	5	3
♦ Oliver Creek / Patrick P. Moleski / Patrick P. Moleski / 1994										
54 6/8	10 5/8	11 3/8	6 2/8	6 2/8	2	1 7/8	8 3/8	7 5/8	8	4
♦ Coquihalla Mts. / Fred D. Fouty / Fred D. Fouty / 1959										
54 6/8	10 7/8	11 2/8	6	6	2 3/8	2 3/8	7 5/8	6 5/8	8	4
♦ Telkwa Mts. / Mrs. V. Goudie / Mrs. V. Goudie / 1964										
54 6/8	11 3/8	11 2/8	5 7/8	6	2	2	8 1/8	7 7/8	8	4
♦ Chupaka Mts. / Dennis F. Gaines / Dennis F. Gaines / 1991										
54 2/8	11	11	6 3/8	6 3/8	1 6/8	1 7/8	10 1/8	10	12	7
♦ Fairmont Range / Ira McLemore / Ira McLemore / 1947										
54 2/8	11 2/8	11 4/8	6	5 7/8	1 7/8	1 7/8	10	9 3/8	12	7
♦ Hastings Arm / Rupert Maier / Rupert Maier / 1963										
54 2/8	10 3/8	10 4/8	6	5 7/8	2 2/8	2 2/8	8 2/8	7 4/8	12	7
♦ Cassiar Mts. / Richard J. Wristen / Richard J. Wristen / 1978										
54 2/8	11	10 6/8	6 2/8	6 2/8	2	2	9 6/8	9 4/8	12	7
♦ Cassiar Mts. / Raymond M. Stenger / Raymond M. Stenger / 1979										
54 2/8	10 5/8	10 5/8	6 2/8	6 2/8	2 1/8	2	7 5/8	6 7/8	12	7
♦ Mt. Meehaus / Denis J. Chagnon / Denis J. Chagnon / 1989										
54	11	11	6 1/8	6 1/8	2	2	8 1/8	8 1/8	18	12
♦ Terminus Mt. / Herb Klein / Herb Klein / 1965										
54	10 7/8	10 6/8	6	6 1/8	2	2 1/8	9 1/8	8 5/8	18	12
♦ Sicintine Range / Thomas R. VanEvery / Thomas R. VanEvery / 1994										
53 6/8	11 1/8	11 2/8	5 7/8	5 7/8	2	1 7/8	9 4/8	8 4/8	21	14
♦ Telegraph Creek / V.D.E. Smith / V.D.E. Smith / 1954										
53 6/8	10 7/8	10 7/8	6	6	1 7/8	1 7/8	7 6/8	6 6/8	21	14
♦ Tumeka Lake / Robert H. Edwards / Robert H. Edwards / 1972										
53 6/8	10 6/8	10 6/8	5 7/8	6	2	2	8 6/8	8	21	14
♦ Sheslay River / Dan Stobbe / Dan Stobbe / 1987										
53 6/8	10 6/8	10 5/8	6	6	2	2	8 3/8	8 2/8	21	14
♦ Telegraph Creek / Steven M. Gross / Steven M. Gross / 1991										
53 4/8	11 4/8	11 2/8	5 7/8	5 7/8	2	2	7 4/8	6 7/8	26	18
♦ Stikine River / John Creyke / John Creyke / 1926										

Score	Length of Horn		Circumference of Base		Circumference at Third Quarter		Greatest Spread	Tip-to-Tip Spread	All-Time Rank	State Rank
	R	L	R	L	R	L				
	♦ *Locality / Hunter / Owner / Date Killed*									
53⁴⁄₈	10⁶⁄₈	11	6	6	1⅞	1⅞	9²⁄₈	8⅞	26	18
	♦ *Coldstream Creek / R.J. Pop / Herb Klein / 1952*									
53⁴⁄₈	11⁴⁄₈	11⁴⁄₈	5⁶⁄₈	5⅞	1⅞	1⅞	8⅛	7⁴⁄₈	26	18
	♦ *Kitimat / Fred Hahn / Fred Hahn / 1966*									
53⁴⁄₈	10⅞	9⅝	6⅝	6⁶⁄₈	2	2³⁄₈	7	6	26	18
	♦ *Bella Coola / Darryl Hodson / Darryl Hodson / 1966*									
53⁴⁄₈	11⁴⁄₈	11³⁄₈	5⅝	5⅝	2	2	9²⁄₈	8⅞	26	18
	♦ *Cassiar Mts. / William Rohlfs / William Rohlfs / 1971*									
53⁴⁄₈	10⁶⁄₈	10³⁄₈	6²⁄₈	6²⁄₈	2	2	7	5²⁄₈	26	18
	♦ *Mt. Horetzky / Jackie O. Arnold / Jackie O. Arnold / 1980*									
53⁴⁄₈	10⁴⁄₈	10⁶⁄₈	6²⁄₈	6⅛	2	2	8⅝	8⅛	26	18
	♦ *Beggerlay Creek / Joe Hamelink / Joe Hamelink / 1986*									
53²⁄₈	11⅛	11⅛	5⁶⁄₈	5⁶⁄₈	2	2	8⅞	7⅞	33	25
	♦ *Cassiar Mts. / W. Reuen Fisher / W. Reuen Fisher / 1945*									
53²⁄₈	10⅞	11⅛	6³⁄₈	6³⁄₈	1⁶⁄₈	1⅞	7⅞	7²⁄₈	33	25
	♦ *Mt. Findlay / Glenn Welsh / Glenn Welsh / 1971*									
53²⁄₈	10³⁄₈	10³⁄₈	5⅞	6	2⅛	2⅛	7⁶⁄₈	7²⁄₈	33	25
	♦ *Skeena River / Robin B. Freeman / Robin B. Freeman / 1985*									
53	10⅞	11	5⅞	6	1⅞	1⅞	6⅝	6²⁄₈	38	28
	♦ *Skeena-Copper Rivers / John A. Paetkau / John W. Kroeker / 1967*									
53	9⅞	10	6²⁄₈	6²⁄₈	2	2	8⅞	8⅞	38	28
	♦ *Cassiar Mts. / Jack Thorndike / Jack Thorndike / 1970*									
53	11	10⅞	5⅞	5⁶⁄₈	2	1⅞	10⅛	9³⁄₈	38	28
	♦ *Sheslay Mt. / Wallace E. Sills / Wallace E. Sills / 1985*									
53	10⁴⁄₈	10⁴⁄₈	5⁴⁄₈	5⁴⁄₈	2	2	9⁶⁄₈	9³⁄₈	38	28
	♦ *Tagish Lake / Larry W. White / Larry W. White / 1987*									
53	10⅞	10⅞	5⅞	6	1⅞	2	8⁶⁄₈	8⅝	38	28
	♦ *Toms Creek / Tommy B. Lee, Jr. / Tommy B. Lee, Jr. / 1988*									
53	11	11²⁄₈	5⅝	5⁶⁄₈	2	2	8⅛	7⅝	38	28
	♦ *Morice River / Elizabeth D. Saunders / Rob Saunders / 1989*									
53	10⅞	10⁶⁄₈	6	6	1⅞	1⅞	7⅛	6²⁄₈	38	28
	♦ *Skeena River / Russil Tanner / Russil Tanner / 1990*									
53	11	10⅞	6	6	1⅞	1⅞	8	7⁴⁄₈	38	28
	♦ *Nahlin River / James T. Kruger / James T. Kruger / 1992*									
52⁶⁄₈	11	11	5⅞	5⅞	1⅞	1⅞	8⅝	8²⁄₈	49	36
	♦ *Kootenay / A.C. Gilbert / Jules V. Lane / 1935*									
52⁶⁄₈	10⅛	10⅛	6	5⅞	2³⁄₈	2³⁄₈	6⅝	5⁶⁄₈	49	36
	♦ *Cold Fish Lake / Stanley W. Glasscock / Stanley W. Glasscock / 1967*									

Score	Length of Horn		Circumference of Base		Circumference at Third Quarter		Greatest Spread	Tip-to-Tip Spread	All-Time Rank	State Rank
	R	L	R	L	R	L				
♦ Locality / Hunter / Owner / Date Killed										
$52^6/_8$	$10^2/_8$	$10^5/_8$	$5^7/_8$	6	$2^1/_8$	$2^1/_8$	$8^3/_8$	$8^1/_8$	49	36
♦ Ashnola Valley / Brian Chipperfield / Brian Chipperfield / 1968										
$52^6/_8$	$11^1/_8$	$11^1/_8$	$5^6/_8$	$5^6/_8$	2	2	$6^3/_8$	$5^5/_8$	49	36
♦ Vernon / Robert B. Procter / Robert B. Procter / 1968										
$52^6/_8$	$10^3/_8$	$10^3/_8$	6	6	2	2	$7^5/_8$	7	49	36
♦ Terrace / R.P. Kolterman / R.P. Kolterman / 1971										
$52^6/_8$	$10^4/_8$	$10^2/_8$	$5^6/_8$	$5^7/_8$	2	2	$8^2/_8$	$7^4/_8$	49	36
♦ Cassiar Mts. / H. Scott Whyel / H. Scott Whyel / 1981										
$52^6/_8$	$10^5/_8$	$10^5/_8$	6	6	$1^7/_8$	$1^7/_8$	$7^6/_8$	6	49	36
♦ Foch Lake / A.S. Griffin, Jr. / A.S. Griffin, Jr. / 1985										
$52^6/_8$	$10^5/_8$	$10^5/_8$	$5^6/_8$	$5^6/_8$	2	2	$7^5/_8$	$6^7/_8$	49	36
♦ Inklin River / Anthony C. Ruggeri / Anthony C. Ruggeri / 1993										
$52^4/_8$	$10^1/_8$	$10^1/_8$	$5^7/_8$	$5^7/_8$	2	2	$6^1/_8$	$6^6/_8$	61	44
♦ Colt Lake / George P. Jackson, Jr. / George P. Jackson, Jr. / 1965										
$52^4/_8$	$10^6/_8$	11	6	$5^7/_8$	$1^7/_8$	$1^6/_8$	$9^1/_8$	$8^6/_8$	61	44
♦ Terminus Mt. / Herb Klein / Herb Klein / 1965										
$52^4/_8$	$10^7/_8$	$10^7/_8$	$5^5/_8$	$5^6/_8$	2	2	$10^2/_8$	10	61	44
♦ Cassiar / Otto Machek / Otto Machek / 1968										
$52^4/_8$	$10^1/_8$	$10^4/_8$	$5^7/_8$	$5^7/_8$	$2^1/_8$	$2^1/_8$	$7^7/_8$	$7^7/_8$	61	44
♦ Spectrum Range / Kelly Good / Kelly Good / 1973										
$52^4/_8$	$10^1/_8$	$10^2/_8$	6	6	2	2	$8^2/_8$	$7^3/_8$	61	44
♦ Rock Island Lake / Joe E. Coleman / Joe E. Coleman / 1976										
$52^4/_8$	10	$10^6/_8$	$5^7/_8$	$5^6/_8$	$2^1/_8$	$2^1/_8$	$8^2/_8$	$7^3/_8$	61	44
♦ Skeena Mts. / Hardy Murr / Hardy Murr / 1977										
$52^4/_8$	$9^6/_8$	$9^7/_8$	6	$5^7/_8$	$2^1/_8$	2	$8^1/_8$	$7^5/_8$	61	44
♦ Taku River / Fritz Stork / Fritz Stork / 1985										
$52^4/_8$	11	$11^3/_8$	6	6	$1^6/_8$	$1^7/_8$	$10^1/_8$	10	61	44
♦ Sicintine Lake / Albert C. Nassan / Albert C. Nassan / 1992										
$52^2/_8$	11	$11^1/_8$	$5^6/_8$	$5^6/_8$	$1^7/_8$	2	$8^3/_8$	8	73	52
♦ Swan Lake / A.C. Gilbert / James V. Bosco, Jr. / 1938										
$52^2/_8$	$10^3/_8$	$10^3/_8$	6	6	2	2	$7^1/_8$	6	73	52
♦ Cassiar / Frank H. Schramm / Frank H. Schramm / 1947										
$52^2/_8$	$10^1/_8$	$10^1/_8$	$5^6/_8$	$5^6/_8$	2	2	$7^3/_8$	$6^6/_8$	73	52
♦ Hastings Arm / Ernest Dietschi / Ernest Dietschi / 1963										
$52^2/_8$	$10^3/_8$	$10^3/_8$	$5^7/_8$	$5^7/_8$	$1^7/_8$	$1^7/_8$	$6^5/_8$	$5^3/_8$	73	52
♦ Bella Bella / William B. Chivers / William B. Chivers / 1965										
$52^2/_8$	11	$11^1/_8$	$6^1/_8$	6	$1^6/_8$	$1^6/_8$	$9^3/_8$	$8^3/_8$	73	52
♦ Cassiar Mts. / Peter Fenchak / Peter Fenchak / 1970										

Score	Length of Horn		Circumference of Base		Circumference at Third Quarter		Greatest Spread	Tip-to-Tip Spread	All-Time Rank	State Rank
	R	L	R	L	R	L				
	◆ *Locality / Hunter / Owner / Date Killed*									
52 2/8	10 6/8	10 4/8	6 1/8	6	1 7/8	1 6/8	6 7/8	5 2/8	73	52
	◆ *Mt. Cronin / Vinko Strgar / Vinko Strgar / 1972*									
52 2/8	10	10	5 7/8	6	1 7/8	1 7/8	9 4/8	8 6/8	73	52
	◆ *Cold Fish Lake / Larry Bonetti / Larry Bonetti / 1975*									
52 2/8	10 1/8	10 2/8	5 4/8	5 4/8	1 5/8	1 6/8	8 4/8	8 3/8	73	52
	◆ *Kutcho Creek / J.C. Page / J.C. Page / 1975*									
52 2/8	10 2/8	10	6 2/8	6 1/8	2	2	7 5/8	7 1/8	73	52
	◆ *Sheslay River / Frank L. Stukel / Frank L. Stukel / 1984*									
52 2/8	11 1/8	11 1/8	5 5/8	5 5/8	1 7/8	1 7/8	6 7/8	6	73	52
	◆ *Mt. Meehaus / George A. Angello, Jr. / George A. Angello, Jr. / 1988*									
52 2/8	11	10 5/8	5 4/8	5 4/8	1 7/8	1 7/8	9 5/8	9 3/8	73	52
	◆ *Little Oliver Creek / James K. Hansen / James K. Hansen / 1988*									
52 2/8	10 5/8	10 6/8	5 6/8	5 6/8	2	2	10	9 7/8	73	52
	◆ *Sheslay River / Steve Parks / Steve Parks / 1988*									
52 2/8	10 2/8	10 2/8	5 4/8	5 4/8	2 1/8	2 1/8	6 7/8	6 2/8	73	52
	◆ *Cassiar Mts. / Debbie S. Sanowski / Debbie S. Sanowski / 1989*									
52 2/8	10 4/8	10 4/8	6 1/8	6 1/8	1 6/8	1 6/8	6 5/8	5 7/8	73	52
	◆ *Fife Creek / George M. Klein / George M. Klein / 1991*									
52	10 1/8	10 4/8	6 1/8	6 1/8	2	2	8 6/8	8 4/8	99	66
	◆ *Cassiar / Walter R. Peterson / Walter R. Peterson / 1937*									
52	10 4/8	10	5 6/8	5 6/8	2	2	9	9	99	66
	◆ *Tweedsmuir Park / Chester G. Moore / Chester G. Moore / 1946*									
52	10 2/8	10 3/8	5 7/8	6	2	1 7/8	7 6/8	7 5/8	99	66
	◆ *Mission Ridge / B. Naimark / B. Naimark / 1960*									
52	10 4/8	11	5 7/8	6	2 1/8	2 1/8	8 7/8	8 2/8	99	66
	◆ *Bulkley Range / Ingvar Wickstrom / Ingvar Wickstrom / 1960*									
52	10 1/8	10 2/8	5 7/8	5 7/8	1 7/8	1 7/8	7 2/8	6 1/8	99	66
	◆ *Kootenay River / Howard Paish / Howard Paish / 1961*									
52	10 3/8	10 2/8	5 7/8	5 7/8	2 1/8	2	7 4/8	7 1/8	99	66
	◆ *Coquihalla / Fred D. Fouty / Fred D. Fouty / 1962*									
52	10 1/8	10 2/8	5 7/8	5 7/8	2	2	9 1/8	7 6/8	99	66
	◆ *Skeena River / R.H. Simonds / R.H. Simonds / 1963*									
52	9 7/8	10	5 6/8	5 6/8	2 1/8	2 1/8	8	7 5/8	99	66
	◆ *Hart Mt. / Donna Loewenstein / Donna Loewenstein / 1965*									
52	10 5/8	10 6/8	6	6 1/8	1 7/8	1 7/8	7 2/8	6	99	66
	◆ *Kitsumgallum Lake / Manfred Beier / Manfred Beier / 1965*									
52	10 1/8	10 2/8	5 5/8	5 4/8	2	2	6 3/8	5 4/8	99	66
	◆ *Southgate River / R.T. Ostby / R.T. Ostby / 1966*									

BRITISH COLUMBIA ROCKY MOUNTAIN GOAT *(continued)*

Score	Length of Horn R	Length of Horn L	Circumference of Base R	Circumference of Base L	Circumference at Third Quarter R	Circumference at Third Quarter L	Greatest Spread	Tip-to-Tip Spread	All-Time Rank	State Rank
	♦ *Locality / Hunter / Owner / Date Killed*									
52	10 1/8	10 3/8	5 6/8	5 6/8	2 2/8	2 2/8	8 5/8	8	99	66
	♦ *Camp Island Lake / C.N. Hoffman / C.N. Hoffman / 1971*									
52	9 4/8	9 5/8	5 7/8	5 7/8	2 1/8	2 2/8	7	5 7/8	99	66
	♦ *Skeena Mts. / William F. Jury / William F. Jury / 1971*									
52	11	10 6/8	6 1/8	6	1 6/8	1 6/8	8 4/8	7 7/8	99	66
	♦ *Kispiox Range / John W. Allen / John W. Allen / 1974*									
52	10 2/8	10 2/8	5 6/8	5 7/8	2	2	8 1/8	7 4/8	99	66
	♦ *Burnie Lake / Paul R. Levan / Paul R. Levan / 1983*									
52	10 6/8	10 5/8	5 6/8	5 7/8	1 7/8	1 7/8	7	6 3/8	99	66
	♦ *Telegraph Creek / Britt W. Wilson / Britt W. Wilson / 1986*									
52	10 5/8	10 4/8	5 7/8	5 7/8	2	2	7 4/8	7 4/8	99	66
	♦ *Old Tom Creek / Dusty R. Cooper / Dusty R. Cooper / 1986*									
52	10	10 1/8	5 7/8	5 7/8	2 1/8	2 1/8	8	7	99	66
	♦ *Shemes River / Russil Tanner / Russil Tanner / 1990*									
51 6/8	10 3/8	10 3/8	5 5/8	5 5/8	2	2	8 7/8	8 3/8	131	83
	♦ *Telegraph Creek / John S. McCormick, Jr. / John S. McCormick, Jr. / 1936*									
51 6/8	10 2/8	10	5 7/8	5 7/8	2	2	7 7/8	7	131	83
	♦ *Telegraph Creek / John Caputo, Sr. / John Caputo, Sr. / 1965*									
51 6/8	10 6/8	10 5/8	5 6/8	5 7/8	1 7/8	1 7/8	9 3/8	9 1/8	131	83
	♦ *Atlin / Bill Slikker / Bill Slikker / 1965*									
51 6/8	11 5/8	12	5 1/8	5 1/8	1 6/8	1 6/8	13	13	131	83
	♦ *Cassiar Mts. / Bruce N. Spencer / Bruce N. Spencer / 1966*									
51 6/8	10 4/8	10 4/8	5 6/8	5 6/8	1 7/8	2	7 5/8	7 1/8	131	83
	♦ *Kildala River / Lorne Hallman / Lorne Hallman / 1966*									
51 6/8	10 1/8	10	5 7/8	5 7/8	2	2	6 6/8	5 7/8	131	83
	♦ *Ecstall River / W.A. Kristmanson / W.A. Kristmanson / 1967*									
51 6/8	10 4/8	10 3/8	5 6/8	5 6/8	1 7/8	1 7/8	7 4/8	5 7/8	131	83
	♦ *Copper-Skeena Rivers / Henry Dyck / Henry Dyck / 1967*									
51 6/8	10 5/8	10 4/8	5 4/8	5 4/8	1 7/8	1 7/8	7 7/8	7 5/8	131	83
	♦ *Skeena-Exstew Rivers / Frans Fait / Frans Fait / 1968*									
51 6/8	10 3/8	10 4/8	6 1/8	6 1/8	1 6/8	1 7/8	9 2/8	8 7/8	131	83
	♦ *Hobo Creek / Roy K. Pysher / Roy K. Pysher / 1968*									
51 6/8	10 5/8	10 7/8	5 5/8	5 5/8	2	2	6 2/8	5 1/8	131	83
	♦ *The Pinnacles Mt. / Michael Bigford / Michael Bigford / 1968*									
51 6/8	10 2/8	10 3/8	5 6/8	5 6/8	1 6/8	1 6/8	7	6 2/8	131	83
	♦ *Turnagain River / John R. Braun / John R. Braun / 1968*									
51 6/8	11 2/8	11 3/8	5 6/8	5 6/8	1 5/8	1 5/8	10	9 7/8	131	83
	♦ *Clearwater Creek / Stephen W. Cook / Stephen W. Cook / 1968*									

Score	Length of Horn		Circumference of Base		Circumference at Third Quarter		Greatest Spread	Tip-to-Tip Spread	All-Time Rank	State Rank
	R	L	R	L	R	L				

♦ *Locality / Hunter / Owner / Date Killed*

Score	R	L	R	L	R	L	Greatest Spread	Tip-to-Tip Spread	All-Time Rank	State Rank
51⁶⁄₈	10³⁄₈	10²⁄₈	6	6	2	2	7⁶⁄₈	7⅛	131	83
♦ *Burns Lake / Ellis D. Skidmore / Ellis D. Skidmore / 1969*										
51⁶⁄₈	10²⁄₈	10³⁄₈	6	6	1⁷⁄₈	2	6	4⁵⁄₈	131	83
♦ *Mt. Allard / David Brousseau / David Brousseau / 1975*										
51⁶⁄₈	10⁵⁄₈	10³⁄₈	5⁴⁄₈	5⁶⁄₈	1⁷⁄₈	1⁷⁄₈	8⁶⁄₈	7⁶⁄₈	131	83
♦ *Zymoetz River / William E. Bond / William E. Bond / 1978*										
51⁶⁄₈	10³⁄₈	10⁴⁄₈	5⁶⁄₈	5⁷⁄₈	2	2	6⁶⁄₈	5⁴⁄₈	131	83
♦ *Mt. Carthew / Harry McCowan / Harry McCowan / 1980*										
51⁶⁄₈	10³⁄₈	10³⁄₈	5⁷⁄₈	5⁶⁄₈	1⁶⁄₈	1⁶⁄₈	6⁵⁄₈	5⁴⁄₈	131	83
♦ *Kaza Lake / J.C. Priebe & W.A. Bolles / J.C. Priebe & W.A. Bolles / 1980*										
51⁶⁄₈	10³⁄₈	10²⁄₈	5⁷⁄₈	5⁷⁄₈	1⁷⁄₈	1⁷⁄₈	7³⁄₈	7⅛	131	83
♦ *Spatsizi Plateau / Gary R. Schneider / Gary R. Schneider / 1986*										
51⁶⁄₈	10²⁄₈	10⁴⁄₈	5⁷⁄₈	6	1⁷⁄₈	2	8	6⁶⁄₈	131	83
♦ *McGavin Creek / Charles H. Menzer / Charles H. Menzer / 1987*										
51⁶⁄₈	10⅛	10⅛	5⁶⁄₈	5⁶⁄₈	2	2	7	6³⁄₈	131	83
♦ *Chita Creek / Anthony D. Tindall / 1Anthony D. Tindall / 1989*										
51⁴⁄₈	11	11²⁄₈	5⁶⁄₈	5⁶⁄₈	1⁶⁄₈	1⁶⁄₈	8⁴⁄₈	7⁶⁄₈	171	103
♦ *Kootenay / Herb Klein / Herb Klein / 1946*										
51⁴⁄₈	11³⁄₈	11⁵⁄₈	5⁴⁄₈	5⁵⁄₈	1⁶⁄₈	1⁶⁄₈	7⁴⁄₈	7³⁄₈	171	103
♦ *Ella River / Lee G. Smith / Walter Ozorowski / 1950*										
51⁴⁄₈	10²⁄₈	10⅛	5⁶⁄₈	5⁶⁄₈	2	2	6⁶⁄₈	5⁷⁄₈	171	103
♦ *Cold Fish Lake / George W. Hooker / George W. Hooker / 1956*										
51⁴⁄₈	10	10	5⁶⁄₈	5⁶⁄₈	1⁷⁄₈	1⁷⁄₈	0	6⁷⁄₈	171	103
♦ *Jarvis Lake / G.F. Juhl / G.F. Juhl / 1960*										
51⁴⁄₈	10	10	5⁷⁄₈	5⁷⁄₈	2	2	7	6²⁄₈	171	103
♦ *Cassiar / Adolf Doerre / Adolf Doerre / 1961*										
51⁴⁄₈	10⁴⁄₈	10³⁄₈	5⁶⁄₈	5⁶⁄₈	1⁷⁄₈	1⁶⁄₈	9³⁄₈	9³⁄₈	171	103
♦ *Cold Fish Lake / Dan Edwards / Dan Edwards / 1961*										
51⁴⁄₈	10⁶⁄₈	10⁷⁄₈	5⁴⁄₈	5⁴⁄₈	1⁶⁄₈	1⁷⁄₈	8⅛	7⁶⁄₈	171	103
♦ *Kechika Range / W.C. Dabney, Jr. / W.C. Dabney, Jr. / 1965*										
51⁴⁄₈	10⅛	10²⁄₈	6	6	2	1⁷⁄₈	7⁴⁄₈	6⁵⁄₈	171	103
♦ *Coast Range / S. Lantenhammer / S. Lantenhammer / 1967*										
51⁴⁄₈	10⁶⁄₈	10⁵⁄₈	5⁷⁄₈	5⁷⁄₈	1⁶⁄₈	1⁶⁄₈	6⁶⁄₈	5⁴⁄₈	171	103
♦ *Clearwater Creek / Richard H. Leedy / Richard H. Leedy / 1967*										
51⁴⁄₈	9⁵⁄₈	9⁶⁄₈	6	6	2	2	7⅛	6²⁄₈	171	103
♦ *Toad River / Bill Goosman / Bill Goosman / 1970*										
51⁴⁄₈	10²⁄₈	10⁴⁄₈	5⁷⁄₈	5⁶⁄₈	1⁷⁄₈	2	8⁴⁄₈	8	171	103
♦ *Terrace / George A. Shaw / George A. Shaw / 1972*										

Score	Length of Horn		Circumference of Base		Circumference at Third Quarter		Greatest Spread	Tip-to-Tip Spread	All-Time Rank	State Rank
	R	L	R	L	R	L				
	◆ Locality / Hunter / Owner / Date Killed									
$51\frac{4}{8}$	$10\frac{2}{8}$	$10\frac{3}{8}$	$5\frac{7}{8}$	6	2	$2\frac{1}{8}$	$7\frac{4}{8}$	$7\frac{1}{8}$	171	103
	◆ Stikine Range / L.A. Candelaria / L.A. Candelaria / 1974									
$51\frac{4}{8}$	$10\frac{4}{8}$	$10\frac{5}{8}$	$5\frac{6}{8}$	$5\frac{6}{8}$	$1\frac{7}{8}$	2	$8\frac{5}{8}$	$8\frac{1}{8}$	171	103
	◆ Mt. Edziza / A. Coe Frankhauser / A. Coe Frankhauser / 1974									
$51\frac{4}{8}$	$9\frac{4}{8}$	$9\frac{7}{8}$	$5\frac{7}{8}$	$5\frac{7}{8}$	$1\frac{7}{8}$	$1\frac{7}{8}$	$9\frac{3}{8}$	$8\frac{6}{8}$	171	103
	◆ Pine Lake / Charles H. Duke, Jr. / Charles H. Duke, Jr. / 1975									
$51\frac{4}{8}$	$10\frac{2}{8}$	$10\frac{5}{8}$	$5\frac{6}{8}$	$5\frac{5}{8}$	$2\frac{1}{8}$	$2\frac{1}{8}$	$8\frac{1}{8}$	$7\frac{4}{8}$	171	103
	◆ Bulkley Mts. / Gordon Hannas / Gordon Hannas / 1976									
$51\frac{4}{8}$	$9\frac{7}{8}$	$9\frac{7}{8}$	6	6	2	2	$8\frac{5}{8}$	$8\frac{1}{8}$	171	103
	◆ Telegraph Creek / Casey G. Terry / Casey G. Terry / 1979									
$51\frac{4}{8}$	$9\frac{7}{8}$	$9\frac{7}{8}$	$5\frac{7}{8}$	$5\frac{6}{8}$	2	2	$5\frac{1}{8}$	$5\frac{1}{8}$	171	103
	◆ Big Wideen River / Steven D. Skipper / Steven D. Skipper / 1980									
$51\frac{4}{8}$	$10\frac{1}{8}$	$10\frac{1}{8}$	$5\frac{4}{8}$	$5\frac{4}{8}$	$2\frac{1}{8}$	$2\frac{1}{8}$	$7\frac{7}{8}$	$7\frac{5}{8}$	171	103
	◆ Little Oliver Creek / JoAnn F. Flemming / JoAnn F. Flemming / 1985									
$51\frac{4}{8}$	$10\frac{3}{8}$	$10\frac{3}{8}$	$5\frac{6}{8}$	$5\frac{6}{8}$	$1\frac{7}{8}$	$1\frac{7}{8}$	$8\frac{1}{8}$	$7\frac{5}{8}$	171	103
	◆ Taku River / Bernard Sippin / Bernard Sippin / 1987									
$51\frac{4}{8}$	11	$10\frac{6}{8}$	$5\frac{6}{8}$	$5\frac{6}{8}$	$1\frac{7}{8}$	2	7	$6\frac{3}{8}$	171	103
	◆ Nass River / Scott McDonald / Scott McDonald / 1988									
$51\frac{4}{8}$	10	10	$5\frac{7}{8}$	$5\frac{7}{8}$	$1\frac{7}{8}$	$1\frac{7}{8}$	$8\frac{7}{8}$	$8\frac{7}{8}$	171	103
	◆ Tahltan River / Wayne H. Kingsley / Wayne H. Kingsley / 1988									
$51\frac{4}{8}$	$11\frac{1}{8}$	11	$5\frac{4}{8}$	$5\frac{4}{8}$	$1\frac{6}{8}$	$1\frac{7}{8}$	$7\frac{4}{8}$	$7\frac{4}{8}$	171	103
	◆ Maiyuk Creek / John P. Katrichak / John P. Katrichak / 1988									
$51\frac{4}{8}$	$9\frac{5}{8}$	$9\frac{5}{8}$	6	6	$2\frac{1}{8}$	2	$7\frac{4}{8}$	7	171	103
	◆ Sheslay River / Daniel E. Gorecki / Daniel E. Gorecki / 1989									
$51\frac{2}{8}$	$10\frac{7}{8}$	$10\frac{7}{8}$	$5\frac{6}{8}$	6	$1\frac{6}{8}$	$1\frac{6}{8}$	$8\frac{1}{8}$	$7\frac{7}{8}$	212	126
	◆ Kootenay / Teddy MacLachlan / W.K. Porter / 1925									
$51\frac{2}{8}$	10	10	$6\frac{1}{8}$	$6\frac{1}{8}$	2	2	$6\frac{6}{8}$	6	212	126
	◆ Mt. Robson / E.T. Reilly / E.T. Reilly / 1948									
$51\frac{2}{8}$	$10\frac{6}{8}$	$10\frac{6}{8}$	$5\frac{6}{8}$	$5\frac{6}{8}$	$1\frac{5}{8}$	$1\frac{6}{8}$	$8\frac{7}{8}$	$8\frac{5}{8}$	212	126
	◆ Cassiar / Elmer E. Rasmuson / Elmer E. Rasmuson / 1952									
$51\frac{2}{8}$	$10\frac{4}{8}$	$10\frac{6}{8}$	$5\frac{5}{8}$	$5\frac{6}{8}$	$1\frac{6}{8}$	$1\frac{7}{8}$	$7\frac{2}{8}$	$6\frac{7}{8}$	212	126
	◆ Bulkley Range / Mrs. Billie Gardiner / Mrs. Billie Gardiner / 1959									
$51\frac{2}{8}$	10	$10\frac{4}{8}$	6	6	$1\frac{7}{8}$	$2\frac{1}{8}$	$7\frac{7}{8}$	$7\frac{5}{8}$	212	126
	◆ Kechika Range / Paul A. Bagalio / Paul A. Bagalio / 1965									
$51\frac{2}{8}$	$9\frac{6}{8}$	$9\frac{6}{8}$	$5\frac{7}{8}$	$5\frac{7}{8}$	2	$2\frac{1}{8}$	$7\frac{5}{8}$	7	212	126
	◆ Gataga River / Robert C. McAtee / Robert C. McAtee / 1965									
$51\frac{2}{8}$	$10\frac{3}{8}$	$10\frac{3}{8}$	$5\frac{6}{8}$	$5\frac{5}{8}$	2	2	$8\frac{4}{8}$	$7\frac{5}{8}$	212	126
	◆ Atlin / Nolan Martins / Nolan Martins / 1967									

Score	Length of Horn		Circumference of Base		Circumference at Third Quarter		Greatest Spread	Tip-to-Tip Spread	All-Time Rank	State Rank
	R	L	R	L	R	L				
◆ *Locality / Hunter / Owner / Date Killed*										
51²⁄₈	9⁶⁄₈	10	5⁶⁄₈	5⁶⁄₈	2	2	7⁴⁄₈	6⁷⁄₈	212	126
◆ *Atlin Lake / Walter O. Johnston / Walter O. Johnston / 1968*										
51²⁄₈	10³⁄₈	10³⁄₈	5⁶⁄₈	5⁷⁄₈	1⁷⁄₈	1⁷⁄₈	7⁴⁄₈	6⁶⁄₈	212	126
◆ *Vetter Peak / Tracy Skead / Tracy Skead / 1969*										
51²⁄₈	10¹⁄₈	10¹⁄₈	5⁶⁄₈	5⁶⁄₈	2	2	6⁴⁄₈	5⁶⁄₈	212	126
◆ *Kechika Range / W.A. McKay / W.A. McKay / 1970*										
51²⁄₈	10⁵⁄₈	10⁷⁄₈	5⁶⁄₈	5⁶⁄₈	1⁷⁄₈	1⁷⁄₈	8⁴⁄₈	8²⁄₈	212	126
◆ *Skeena Mts. / Michael A. Wright / Michael A. Wright / 1972*										
51²⁄₈	10³⁄₈	10³⁄₈	5⁶⁄₈	5⁵⁄₈	1⁷⁄₈	1⁷⁄₈	7³⁄₈	6³⁄₈	212	126
◆ *Tsetia Creek / Douglas V. Turner / Douglas V. Turner / 1973*										
51²⁄₈	10²⁄₈	10	5⁷⁄₈	5⁷⁄₈	2	2	7²⁄₈	6³⁄₈	212	126
◆ *Morice Lake / G. Fitchett & L. Austin / George Fitchett / 1978*										
51²⁄₈	9⁶⁄₈	9⁶⁄₈	6¹⁄₈	6¹⁄₈	1⁶⁄₈	1⁶⁄₈	8²⁄₈	7⁵⁄₈	212	126
◆ *Swan Lake / John Dobish / John Dobish / 1981*										
51²⁄₈	10⁴⁄₈	10²⁄₈	5⁵⁄₈	5⁵⁄₈	2	2	7	8¹⁄₈	212	126
◆ *Duti Lake / T.J. Tucker / T.J. Tucker / 1981*										
51²⁄₈	10⁵⁄₈	10⁵⁄₈	6	5⁷⁄₈	1⁷⁄₈	1⁷⁄₈	7⁴⁄₈	6⁷⁄₈	212	126
◆ *Kaustua Creek / Duane Pankratz / Duane Pankratz / 1982*										
51²⁄₈	10⁶⁄₈	10³⁄₈	5⁴⁄₈	5⁴⁄₈	2	2¹⁄₈	8⁴⁄₈	8²⁄₈	212	126
◆ *Nass River / Larry Zilinski / Larry Zilinski / 1982*										
51²⁄₈	9¹⁄₈	9¹⁄₈	5⁵⁄₈	5⁵⁄₈	2⁴⁄₈	2⁴⁄₈	7⁴⁄₈	6⁶⁄₈	212	126
◆ *Taku River / Charles W. Schmidt / Charles W. Schmidt / 1985*										
51²⁄₈	10²⁄₈	10²⁄₈	5⁴⁄₈	5⁴⁄₈	2	2	7	6²⁄₈	212	126
◆ *Mt. Guanton / Charles R. McKinley / Charles R. McKinley / 1986*										
51²⁄₈	9⁷⁄₈	9⁷⁄₈	5⁵⁄₈	5⁶⁄₈	2	2	6²⁄₈	5³⁄₈	212	126
◆ *Snehumption Creek / Raymond C. Croissant / Raymond C. Croissant / 1989*										
51²⁄₈	10⁶⁄₈	10⁷⁄₈	5⁵⁄₈	5⁶⁄₈	1⁷⁄₈	1⁷⁄₈	7²⁄₈	6²⁄₈	212	126
◆ *Cassiar Mts. / Robert A. Lenzini / Robert A. Lenzini / 1991*										
51²⁄₈	10⁶⁄₈	11	5⁶⁄₈	5⁵⁄₈	1⁷⁄₈	1⁷⁄₈	8	7²⁄₈	212	126
◆ *Taku River / John H. Garnett, Sr. / John H. Garnett, Sr. / 1992*										
51²⁄₈	10⁶⁄₈	10⁵⁄₈	5⁵⁄₈	5⁶⁄₈	1⁷⁄₈	1⁷⁄₈	7⁷⁄₈	7²⁄₈	212	126
◆ *Hugh Creek / Gerhard Volz / Gerhard Volz / 1993*										
51	9⁶⁄₈	10	5⁷⁄₈	5⁷⁄₈	2	2	8²⁄₈	7⁷⁄₈	249	149
◆ *Morice River / Warren Bodeker / Warren Bodeker / 1958*										
51	9⁴⁄₈	9⁴⁄₈	5⁵⁄₈	5⁶⁄₈	2¹⁄₈	2¹⁄₈	5⁶⁄₈	4⁴⁄₈	249	149
◆ *Terrace / Gerald Prosser / Gerald Prosser / 1962*										
51	11	10⁶⁄₈	5⁷⁄₈	5⁷⁄₈	1⁷⁄₈	1⁶⁄₈	7²⁄₈	6⁴⁄₈	249	149
◆ *Smithers / John Strban / John Strban / 1962*										

Score	Length of Horn		Circumference of Base		Circumference at Third Quarter		Greatest Spread	Tip-to-Tip Spread	All-Time Rank	State Rank
	R	L	R	L	R	L				
	Locality / Hunter / Owner / Date Killed									
51	$10\frac{7}{8}$	11	$5\frac{7}{8}$	$5\frac{7}{8}$	$1\frac{6}{8}$	$1\frac{6}{8}$	$7\frac{1}{8}$	$6\frac{6}{8}$	249	149
	Kootenay Range / Norbert M. Welch / Norbert M. Welch / 1963									
51	$10\frac{2}{8}$	$10\frac{6}{8}$	$5\frac{4}{8}$	$5\frac{4}{8}$	2	2	$7\frac{5}{8}$	$6\frac{1}{8}$	249	149
	Butte Inlet / Reuben C. Carlson / Reuben C. Carlson / 1963									
51	10	10	$5\frac{6}{8}$	$5\frac{6}{8}$	2	2	$7\frac{6}{8}$	7	249	149
	Dease Lake / W.M. Rudd / W.M. Rudd / 1964									
51	$10\frac{2}{8}$	$10\frac{2}{8}$	$5\frac{5}{8}$	$5\frac{5}{8}$	$1\frac{7}{8}$	$1\frac{7}{8}$	$7\frac{4}{8}$	$7\frac{3}{8}$	249	149
	Telegraph Creek / John Caputo, Jr. / John Caputo, Jr. / 1965									
51	$10\frac{2}{8}$	$10\frac{2}{8}$	$5\frac{5}{8}$	$5\frac{5}{8}$	2	2	$8\frac{3}{8}$	$7\frac{7}{8}$	249	149
	Okanagan / Earl Dawson / Earl Dawson / 1967									
51	$10\frac{1}{8}$	$10\frac{6}{8}$	6	6	$1\frac{7}{8}$	$1\frac{7}{8}$	$7\frac{3}{8}$	$6\frac{6}{8}$	249	149
	Tete Jaune / George Hanschen / George Hanschen / 1967									
51	$10\frac{2}{8}$	$10\frac{2}{8}$	$5\frac{5}{8}$	$5\frac{5}{8}$	2	$1\frac{7}{8}$	8	$7\frac{3}{8}$	249	149
	Telegraph Creek / George McCullough / George McCullough / 1967									
51	$10\frac{6}{8}$	$10\frac{1}{8}$	$5\frac{6}{8}$	$5\frac{5}{8}$	2	2	$9\frac{2}{8}$	9	249	149
	Terrace / Gary Townsend / Gary Townsend / 1967									
51	$9\frac{6}{8}$	$9\frac{6}{8}$	$5\frac{6}{8}$	$5\frac{7}{8}$	2	2	$7\frac{3}{8}$	$7\frac{2}{8}$	249	149
	Hart Mt. / Marvin F. Lawrence / Marvin F. Lawrence / 1967									
51	$9\frac{4}{8}$	$9\frac{5}{8}$	$5\frac{7}{8}$	$5\frac{7}{8}$	$1\frac{7}{8}$	$1\frac{7}{8}$	$5\frac{6}{8}$	$5\frac{5}{8}$	249	149
	McBride / Ervin Voelk / Ervin Voelk / 1968									
51	$10\frac{5}{8}$	$10\frac{5}{8}$	$5\frac{5}{8}$	$5\frac{6}{8}$	$1\frac{6}{8}$	$1\frac{7}{8}$	$8\frac{3}{8}$	$7\frac{6}{8}$	249	149
	Lillooet / Helmut Krieger / Helmut Krieger / 1969									
51	$10\frac{3}{8}$	$10\frac{3}{8}$	$5\frac{7}{8}$	$5\frac{7}{8}$	$1\frac{7}{8}$	$1\frac{7}{8}$	8	$7\frac{5}{8}$	249	149
	Findlay Creek / Sharon Robey / Sharon Robey / 1978									
51	$10\frac{4}{8}$	$10\frac{4}{8}$	$5\frac{6}{8}$	$5\frac{6}{8}$	$1\frac{7}{8}$	$1\frac{7}{8}$	$7\frac{2}{8}$	$5\frac{7}{8}$	249	149
	Tahtsa Lake / Vernon J. Boose / Vernon J. Boose / 1981									
51	$10\frac{4}{8}$	$10\frac{3}{8}$	$5\frac{6}{8}$	$5\frac{6}{8}$	$1\frac{7}{8}$	$1\frac{7}{8}$	$7\frac{3}{8}$	$6\frac{7}{8}$	249	149
	Sheslay River / Steven M. Sullivan / Steven M. Sullivan / 1985									
51	$10\frac{1}{8}$	10	6	6	$1\frac{7}{8}$	$1\frac{7}{8}$	0	$7\frac{1}{8}$	249	149
	Serrated Peak / Philip E. Blacher, Jr. / Philip E. Blacher, Jr. / 1989									
51	$10\frac{2}{8}$	$10\frac{1}{8}$	$6\frac{1}{8}$	$6\frac{2}{8}$	$1\frac{7}{8}$	$1\frac{6}{8}$	7	$6\frac{3}{8}$	249	149
	Nanika Lake / Gary Eby / Gary Eby / 1993									
51	$10\frac{2}{8}$	$10\frac{2}{8}$	$5\frac{5}{8}$	$5\frac{5}{8}$	2	$1\frac{6}{8}$	$7\frac{1}{8}$	$6\frac{7}{8}$	249	149
	Similkameen River / Charles H. Veasey / Charles H. Veasey / 1993									
$50\frac{6}{8}$	$10\frac{1}{8}$	$10\frac{3}{8}$	$5\frac{6}{8}$	$5\frac{7}{8}$	$1\frac{7}{8}$	2	$7\frac{1}{8}$	$6\frac{4}{8}$	285	169
	Cassiar / W.N. Beach / W.N. Beach / 1918									
$50\frac{6}{8}$	$10\frac{4}{8}$	$11\frac{1}{8}$	$5\frac{4}{8}$	$5\frac{4}{8}$	$1\frac{5}{8}$	$1\frac{5}{8}$	9	$8\frac{5}{8}$	285	169
	Cassiar / Clement B. Newbold / Clement B. Newbold / 1926									

Score	Length of Horn		Circumference of Base		Circumference at Third Quarter		Greatest Spread	Tip-to-Tip Spread	All-Time Rank	State Rank
	R	L	R	L	R	L				
◆ Locality / Hunter / Owner / Date Killed										
50 6/8	9 4/8	9 4/8	5 7/8	5 7/8	2 1/8	2 1/8	7 7/8	7 6/8	285	169
◆ Similkameen / Peter Braun / John D. Rempel / 1939										
50 6/8	10 4/8	10 2/8	5 5/8	5 4/8	2	2	8 3/8	7 6/8	285	169
◆ Cassiar / Peter Schramm / Peter Schramm / 1950										
50 6/8	10 7/8	11 2/8	5 5/8	5 5/8	1 6/8	1 7/8	9 1/8	8	285	169
◆ Telegraph Creek / Wayne C. Eubank / Wayne C. Eubank / 1953										
50 6/8	9 5/8	9 6/8	5 6/8	5 7/8	1 7/8	2	7 4/8	7 2/8	285	169
◆ Telegraph Creek / A.J. Duany / A.J. Duany / 1954										
50 6/8	9 6/8	9 6/8	6	6	2	2	7 1/8	5 6/8	285	169
◆ Maxan Lake / K.J. Nysven / K.J. Nysven / 1961										
50 6/8	10 2/8	10	6	6	2	1 7/8	7 4/8	6 6/8	285	169
◆ Cold Fish Lake / Howard Boazman / Howard Boazman / 1962										
50 6/8	10 4/8	10 5/8	5 6/8	5 5/8	1 7/8	1 7/8	9 4/8	8 3/8	285	169
◆ Gataga River / Herb Klein / Herb Klein / 1963										
50 6/8	9 6/8	9 6/8	5 7/8	6	1 6/8	2	6 1/8	5 5/8	285	169
◆ Keremeos / Bill Postill / Bill Postill / 1963										
50 6/8	10	9 4/8	6	6	2 1/8	2 1/8	9 2/8	8 6/8	285	169
◆ Atlin / G. Vernon Boggs / G. Vernon Boggs / 1964										
50 6/8	10 3/8	10 3/8	5 3/8	5 2/8	2 1/8	2 1/8	8	7 5/8	285	169
◆ Cold Fish Lake / Armin Baltensweiler / Armin Baltensweiler / 1965										
50 6/8	10 1/8	10 1/8	5 6/8	5 6/8	1 7/8	2	7 7/8	7 4/8	285	169
◆ Cassiar Mts. / Ernest Granum / Ernest Granum / 1965										
50 6/8	9 7/8	9 6/8	5 7/8	5 7/8	1 7/8	1 7/8	8 1/8	8 1/8	285	169
◆ Klappan Range / Larry P. Miller / Larry P. Miller / 1965										
50 6/8	9 2/8	9 5/8	6 1/8	6 1/8	1 7/8	2	6 7/8	6 3/8	285	169
◆ Hedley / Donald J. Robb / Donald J. Robb / 1965										
50 6/8	9 3/8	9 3/8	5 7/8	5 7/8	1 7/8	1 7/8	6 2/8	6	285	169
◆ Kechika Range / Basil C. Bradbury / Basil C. Bradbury / 1965										
50 6/8	10 1/8	10 1/8	5 3/8	5 3/8	1 7/8	1 7/8	7 5/8	7 3/8	285	169
◆ Ashnola River / Robert C. Bateson / Robert C. Bateson / 1966										
50 6/8	9 7/8	9 6/8	5 6/8	5 7/8	2 1/8	2 1/8	8 3/8	8 2/8	285	169
◆ Toad River / Walt Paulk / Walt Paulk / 1966										
50 6/8	10 5/8	10 5/8	5 5/8	5 5/8	1 7/8	1 7/8	6 6/8	5 6/8	285	169
◆ Skeena River / G. Best / G. Best / 1966										
50 6/8	10 1/8	10 7/8	5 6/8	5 6/8	1 7/8	2	8 3/8	6 5/8	285	169
◆ Horsethief Creek / Bill Pitt / Bill Pitt / 1966										
50 6/8	9 6/8	9 4/8	5 5/8	5 6/8	2 2/8	2 2/8	7 3/8	7 1/8	285	169
◆ Dease Lake / John H. Epp / John H. Epp / 1972										

Score	Length of Horn R	Length of Horn L	Circumference of Base R	Circumference of Base L	Circumference at Third Quarter R	Circumference at Third Quarter L	Greatest Spread	Tip-to-Tip Spread	All-Time Rank	State Rank
	♦ *Locality / Hunter / Owner / Date Killed*									
50 6/8	10 1/8	9 7/8	5 5/8	5 7/8	2	2	8 5/8	8 3/8	285	169
	♦ *Kechika River / Dennis Laabs / Dennis Laabs / 1973*									
50 6/8	10	8 7/8	6 1/8	6	2 1/8	2 1/8	7 2/8	6 5/8	285	169
	♦ *Cassiar Mts. / Kenneth E. Bishop / Kenneth E. Bishop / 1979*									
50 6/8	10 3/8	10 2/8	5 5/8	5 6/8	1 7/8	1 7/8	7 6/8	7 2/8	285	169
	♦ *Johnston Lake / Brian A. Halina / Brian A. Halina / 1979*									
50 6/8	9 5/8	9 5/8	5 6/8	5 6/8	2	2	8	7 5/8	285	169
	♦ *Klastline River / Glenn E. Hisey / Glenn E. Hisey / 1979*									
50 6/8	10 3/8	10 5/8	5 5/8	5 7/8	1 6/8	1 6/8	7 1/8	6 1/8	285	169
	♦ *Dutch Creek / Tom Housh / Tom Housh / 1982*									
50 6/8	10 4/8	10 4/8	5 5/8	5 4/8	2	2	7 4/8	7	285	169
	♦ *Stewart / Harry J. McCowan / Harry J. McCowan / 1983*									
50 6/8	11 2/8	11 7/8	5 5/8	5 5/8	1 5/8	1 5/8	7 7/8	7	285	169
	♦ *Beaverfoot Range / Kelley Knight / Kelley Knight / 1984*									
50 6/8	11	10 5/8	6	5 7/8	2	1 6/8	7 3/8	6 2/8	285	169
	♦ *Little Oliver Creek / David J. Flemming / David J. Flemming / 1985*									
50 6/8	10 1/8	10 1/8	5 6/8	5 6/8	1 7/8	1 7/8	6 2/8	5 6/8	285	169
	♦ *Williams Lake / Norwood N. Kern / Norwood N. Kern / 1988*									
50 6/8	9 7/8	9 7/8	5 7/8	5 7/8	1 7/8	1 6/8	7 6/8	7 6/8	285	169
	♦ *Belcourt Creek / Cameron Todd / Cameron Todd / 1988*									
50 6/8	10 5/8	10 5/8	5 6/8	5 6/8	1 6/8	1 6/8	7 2/8	7 1/8	285	169
	♦ *Kootenay Mt. / Ted A. Trout / Ted A. Trout / 1988*									
50 6/8	10 2/8	10 2/8	5 4/8	5 5/8	1 7/8	2	8 1/8	7 7/8	285	169
	♦ *Chopaka Mts. / John D. Chalk III / John D. Chalk III / 1991*									
50 6/8	10	10	5 6/8	5 7/8	1 7/8	1 7/8	5 3/8	3 5/8	285	169
	♦ *Coldstream Creek / Richard P. Price / Richard P. Price / 1991*									
50 6/8	10 2/8	10 5/8	5 5/8	5 5/8	1 6/8	1 7/8	9	8 6/8	285	169
	♦ *Atlin Lake / John R. Busby / John R. Busby / 1992*									
50 6/8	10 2/8	10 3/8	6	6	1 6/8	1 6/8	6	5 2/8	285	169
	♦ *Lardeau River / Rod Smaldon / Rod Smaldon / 1993*									
50 4/8	12 1/8	12 4/8	4 6/8	4 6/8	1 6/8	1 7/8	7 1/8	6 4/8	340	205
	♦ *Cassiar / A. Bryan Williams / Mrs. N.S. Gooch / PR 1916*									
50 4/8	10 2/8	10 3/8	5 4/8	5 4/8	2	2	7 4/8	7	340	205
	♦ *Cassiar / George E. Burghard / George E. Burghard / 1925*									
50 4/8	10 1/8	10 2/8	5 5/8	5 5/8	1 7/8	1 7/8	7 2/8	6 5/8	340	205
	♦ *Telegraph Creek / John S. McCormick, Jr. / John S. McCormick, Jr. / 1936*									
50 4/8	10 4/8	10 5/8	5 6/8	5 5/8	2	1 7/8	7 1/8	6	340	205
	♦ *Bull River / Albert Markstein / Albert Markstein / 1954*									

BRITISH COLUMBIA ROCKY MOUNTAIN GOAT *(continued)*

Score	Length of Horn R	Length of Horn L	Circumference of Base R	Circumference of Base L	Circumference at Third Quarter R	Circumference at Third Quarter L	Greatest Spread	Tip-to-Tip Spread	All-Time Rank	State Rank
	♦ *Locality / Hunter / Owner / Date Killed*									
50 4/8	10 1/8	9 7/8	5 4/8	5 4/8	1 7/8	2 1/8	8 2/8	7 1/8	340	205
	♦ *Cold Fish Lake / Joseph Smith / Joseph Smith / 1955*									
50 4/8	10 1/8	10	5 5/8	5 6/8	1 6/8	1 6/8	8	7 1/8	340	205
	♦ *Cold Fish Lake / Patrick Britell / Patrick Britell / 1957*									
50 4/8	10 4/8	10 4/8	5 4/8	5 4/8	2	2	7 4/8	6 7/8	340	205
	♦ *Cold Fish Lake / L.A. Wunsch / L.A. Wunsch / 1958*									
50 4/8	10 1/8	10 2/8	5 6/8	5 6/8	1 6/8	1 6/8	7 7/8	6 7/8	340	205
	♦ *Smithers / A.S. Langan / A.S. Langan / 1960*									
50 4/8	10 2/8	10 3/8	5 1/8	5 1/8	2 1/8	2	7	7	340	205
	♦ *Chilco Lake / C. Marc Miller / C. Marc Miller / 1960*									
50 4/8	10 1/8	9 7/8	5 6/8	5 6/8	1 7/8	2	7	6 2/8	340	205
	♦ *White Sales Mt. / Robert McDonald / Robert McDonald / 1962*									
50 4/8	10	10 1/8	5 4/8	5 4/8	2	2	7 5/8	7	340	205
	♦ *Atlin Lake / Wendell Bever / Wendell Bever / 1962*									
50 4/8	9 3/8	9 3/8	5 5/8	5 5/8	2 1/8	2 1/8	6 3/8	5 4/8	340	205
	♦ *Mt. Stoyoma / Frank S.T. Bradley / Frank S.T. Bradley / 1962*									
50 4/8	9 7/8	10	5 7/8	5 7/8	1 7/8	2	7 2/8	7 2/8	340	205
	♦ *Kechika Range / G.W. Hawkins / G.W. Hawkins / 1963*									
50 4/8	10 3/8	10 4/8	5 5/8	5 5/8	1 7/8	1 7/8	7 6/8	6 6/8	340	205
	♦ *Lake Kinniskan / Michel Boel / Michel Boel / 1965*									
50 4/8	10 2/8	10 3/8	5 4/8	5 4/8	1 7/8	1 7/8	6	5 1/8	340	205
	♦ *Revelstoke / Picked Up / George Lines / 1966*									
50 4/8	9 6/8	9 4/8	5 5/8	5 6/8	2	2	8 1/8	7 6/8	340	205
	♦ *Atlin / Raymond Bartram / Raymond Bartram / 1966*									
50 4/8	10 1/8	10 2/8	5 4/8	5 6/8	2	1 7/8	7 3/8	6 2/8	340	205
	♦ *McDonald Lake / Henry P. Foradora / Henry P. Foradora / 1966*									
50 4/8	9 6/8	9 7/8	5 5/8	5 6/8	2	2	8	7 5/8	340	205
	♦ *Sloko Lake / John Haefeli / John Haefeli / 1966*									
50 4/8	10 1/8	10 1/8	5 6/8	5 6/8	1 7/8	1 7/8	9 2/8	9 2/8	340	205
	♦ *Cassiar Mts. / Donovan N. Branch / Donovan N. Branch / 1967*									
50 4/8	10 2/8	10 2/8	5 4/8	5 4/8	1 7/8	1 7/8	8 4/8	7 6/8	340	205
	♦ *Telegraph Creek / T.T. Stroup / T.T. Stroup / 1968*									
50 4/8	10 1/8	9 7/8	5 7/8	6	2	1 7/8	6 5/8	5 4/8	340	205
	♦ *Turnagain River / Howard S. Duffield / Howard S. Duffield / 1969*									
50 4/8	10	10 2/8	5 6/8	5 6/8	1 7/8	2	7 7/8	7 5/8	340	205
	♦ *Dease Lake / James T. Knutson / James T. Knutson / 1975*									
50 4/8	10 4/8	10 4/8	5 5/8	5 5/8	1 6/8	1 6/8	6 7/8	5 7/8	340	205
	♦ *Bingay Creek / C.P. Podrasky / C.P. Podrasky / 1981*									

Score	Length of Horn		Circumference of Base		Circumference at Third Quarter		Greatest Spread	Tip-to-Tip Spread	All-Time Rank	State Rank
	R	L	R	L	R	L				
♦ Locality / Hunter / Owner / Date Killed										
50⁴⁄₈	10	9⁷⁄₈	5⁶⁄₈	5⁵⁄₈	2	2	9⅛	9	340	205
♦ Stikine Canyon / Reuben F. Gerecke / Reuben F. Gerecke / 1982										
50⁴⁄₈	10⁴⁄₈	10³⁄₈	5⁷⁄₈	5⁷⁄₈	1⁶⁄₈	1⁶⁄₈	7⁷⁄₈	7³⁄₈	340	205
♦ Mt. Cummins / Rod Aune / Rod Aune / 1984										
50⁴⁄₈	11	11	5⁵⁄₈	5⁴⁄₈	1⁶⁄₈	1⁶⁄₈	5⁶⁄₈	4⁴⁄₈	340	205
♦ Beaver Lake / Richard G. Henke / Richard G. Henke / 1986										
50⁴⁄₈	9⁷⁄₈	10²⁄₈	5⁶⁄₈	5⁶⁄₈	1⁷⁄₈	2⅛	8²⁄₈	7⁵⁄₈	340	205
♦ Cassiar Mts. / Charles Reichenau / Charles Reichenau / 1991										
50⁴⁄₈	9⁷⁄₈	10	5⁵⁄₈	5⁵⁄₈	1⁷⁄₈	1⁷⁄₈	7	6⅛	340	205
♦ Jug Lake / Larry W. Steeley / Larry W. Steeley / 1991										
50⁴⁄₈	9⁴⁄₈	9⁵⁄₈	5⁶⁄₈	5⁶⁄₈	2⅛	2⅛	7⁶⁄₈	7⁴⁄₈	340	205
♦ Palliser River / Ernie F. Knight / Ernie F. Knight / 1992										
50⁴⁄₈	10	10	5⁵⁄₈	5⁶⁄₈	2	2	8³⁄₈	7⁷⁄₈	340	205
♦ Eagle Nest Mt. / Paul Green / Paul Green / 1993										
50²⁄₈	10⁴⁄₈	10⁴⁄₈	5⁶⁄₈	5⁶⁄₈	1⁶⁄₈	1⁶⁄₈	8⁵⁄₈	8⁴⁄₈	395	235
♦ Swan Lake / A.C. Gilbert / A.C. Gilbert / 1938										
50²⁄₈	9⁵⁄₈	9⁷⁄₈	5⁶⁄₈	5⁶⁄₈	2	2	7⁴⁄₈	6⁷⁄₈	395	235
♦ Taseko Lake / L.W. Howell / L.W. Howell / 1952										
50²⁄₈	10	10	5⁵⁄₈	5⁵⁄₈	2	2	7⁴⁄₈	7⁴⁄₈	395	235
♦ Cold Fish Lake / T.A. Walker / Univ. of B.C. / 1952										
50²⁄₈	10⁴⁄₈	10³⁄₈	5⁴⁄₈	5⁴⁄₈	1⁶⁄₈	1⁶⁄₈	7²⁄₈	7²⁄₈	395	235
♦ Turnagain River / John La Rocca / John La Rocca / 1957										
50²⁄₈	10⅛	10³⁄₈	5⁵⁄₈	5⁶⁄₈	1⁷⁄₈	1⁷⁄₈	8	7⁴⁄₈	395	235
♦ Shuswap Creek / Nolan Rad / Nolan Rad / 1958										
50²⁄₈	10²⁄₈	10²⁄₈	5⁵⁄₈	5⁵⁄₈	1⁷⁄₈	1⁶⁄₈	6³⁄₈	5²⁄₈	395	235
♦ Smithers / William Stallone / William Stallone / 1960										
50²⁄₈	9⁴⁄₈	9⅛	5⁶⁄₈	5⁶⁄₈	2⅛	2	7⁴⁄₈	7²⁄₈	395	235
♦ Ft. St. John / Billy Ross / Billy Ross / 1962										
50²⁄₈	10²⁄₈	10⅛	5⁶⁄₈	5⁶⁄₈	1⁶⁄₈	1⁶⁄₈	8⁴⁄₈	8²⁄₈	395	235
♦ Sukunka River / Robert C. Sutton / Robert C. Sutton / 1962										
50²⁄₈	10⁵⁄₈	9⁵⁄₈	6	6	2	1⁷⁄₈	7³⁄₈	7³⁄₈	395	235
♦ Cassiar / James E. Kelley / James E. Kelley / 1963										
50²⁄₈	11²⁄₈	10⁶⁄₈	5⁵⁄₈	5⁴⁄₈	1⁶⁄₈	1⁶⁄₈	8⁴⁄₈	7⁷⁄₈	395	235
♦ Elk Valley / Emile Gele / Emile Gele / 1964										
50²⁄₈	10⁵⁄₈	10³⁄₈	5⁴⁄₈	5⁴⁄₈	1⁶⁄₈	1⁶⁄₈	6⁶⁄₈	5²⁄₈	395	235
♦ Invermere / Laszlo Molnar / Laszlo Molnar / 1965										
50²⁄₈	10⁷⁄₈	11	5⁴⁄₈	5³⁄₈	1⁷⁄₈	1⁷⁄₈	8⁴⁄₈	8⅛	395	235
♦ Atlin / Walter F. Ramage / Walter F. Ramage / 1965										

Score	Length of Horn R	L	Circumference of Base R	L	Circumference at Third Quarter R	L	Greatest Spread	Tip-to-Tip Spread	All-Time Rank	State Rank
50 2/8	10 2/8	10 2/8	5 6/8	5 6/8	1 6/8	1 6/8	7 5/8	7 3/8	395	235
♦ Koch Creek / Pat Archibald / Pat Archibald / 1965										
50 2/8	10 2/8	10 1/8	5 4/8	5 4/8	1 7/8	1 7/8	6 4/8	5 5/8	395	235
♦ Chehalis Lake / Fred E. Harper / Fred E. Harper / 1965										
50 2/8	10 6/8	10 7/8	5 5/8	5 4/8	1 6/8	1 6/8	6 5/8	5 6/8	395	235
♦ Skeena River / Jack E. Monet / Jack E. Monet / 1966										
50 2/8	10 2/8	10 3/8	5 6/8	5 6/8	1 4/8	1 5/8	6 3/8	5 1/8	395	235
♦ Telkwa / A.W. Phillips / A.W. Phillips / 1967										
50 2/8	9 4/8	9 4/8	5 6/8	5 6/8	2	2	7 4/8	7	395	235
♦ Cassiar / John A. Mueller / John A. Mueller / 1968										
50 2/8	10 5/8	10 2/8	5 3/8	5 4/8	1 7/8	2	6 5/8	5	395	235
♦ Ecstall River / Thomas J. Perry / Thomas J. Perry / 1970										
50 2/8	10 1/8	10 2/8	5 6/8	5 6/8	1 7/8	1 7/8	7 1/8	6 2/8	395	235
♦ Tumeka Lake / Dan M. Edwards, Jr. / Dan M. Edwards, Jr. / 1972										
50 2/8	10 1/8	10 1/8	5 3/8	5 3/8	1 7/8	1 7/8	7 7/8	7 5/8	395	235
♦ Dease Lake / Carl K. Beaudry / Carl K. Beaudry / 1975										
50 2/8	10 6/8	10 6/8	5 4/8	5 5/8	1 6/8	1 7/8	8 7/8	8 2/8	395	235
♦ Stikine River / R.H. Weaver / R.H. Weaver / 1976										
50 2/8	9 7/8	9 7/8	5 6/8	5 6/8	1 7/8	1 7/8	7 3/8	6 4/8	395	235
♦ Cassiar Mts. / Ron Ragan / Ron Ragan / 1978										
50 2/8	9 7/8	9 6/8	5 7/8	5 7/8	2	1 7/8	7 5/8	7 5/8	395	235
♦ Ice Mt. / J.S. Van Alsburg / J.S. Van Alsburg / 1978										
50 2/8	10 1/8	10	5 6/8	5 6/8	1 7/8	1 7/8	6 6/8	5 5/8	395	235
♦ Pemberton / Weldon Talbot / Weldon Talbot / 1982										
50 2/8	10 7/8	10 5/8	5 5/8	5 4/8	1 6/8	1 6/8	8	7 2/8	395	235
♦ Skeena / Clarence J. Fields / Clarence J. Fields / 1983										
50 2/8	10 1/8	10 1/8	5 5/8	5 4/8	2	2	8 1/8	7 3/8	395	235
♦ Kildala River / Philip Perrone / Philip Perrone / 1983										
50 2/8	10 3/8	10 3/8	5 5/8	5 5/8	1 6/8	1 6/8	7 6/8	7 4/8	395	235
♦ Mt. Stockdale / James C. King / James C. King / 1983										
50 2/8	10 5/8	10 5/8	5 4/8	5 4/8	1 6/8	1 6/8	6 7/8	6 3/8	395	235
♦ Bleasdell Creek / Daniel Fediuk / Daniel Fediuk / 1984										
50 2/8	9 7/8	9 5/8	5 6/8	5 6/8	1 7/8	1 7/8	7	6 4/8	395	235
♦ Kudwat Creek / William R. Orth / William R. Orth / 1986										
50 2/8	9 2/8	9 2/8	5 7/8	5 7/8	1 7/8	1 7/8	7 1/8	6 6/8	395	235
♦ Sicintine Range / Roger L. Pock / Roger L. Pock / 1988										
50 2/8	9 6/8	10	5 6/8	5 6/8	1 7/8	1 7/8	8 1/8	7 5/8	395	235
♦ Kitimat / Steven M. Cooper / Steven M. Cooper / 1990										

Score	Length of Horn R	L	Circumference of Base R	L	Circumference at Third Quarter R	L	Greatest Spread	Tip-to-Tip Spread	All-Time Rank	State Rank
	◆ *Locality / Hunter / Owner / Date Killed*									
50²⁄₈	10¹⁄₈	9⁵⁄₈	5⁶⁄₈	5⁶⁄₈	2	2	9⁴⁄₈	9	395	235
	◆ *Gataga River / Wilson S. Stout / Wilson S. Stout / 1993*									
50²⁄₈	10	10²⁄₈	5⁵⁄₈	5⁵⁄₈	1⁷⁄₈	1⁶⁄₈	7²⁄₈	6²⁄₈	395	235
	◆ *Flameau Creek / Robert Reisert / Robert Reisert / 1994*									
50	10²⁄₈	10⁶⁄₈	5⁵⁄₈	5⁵⁄₈	1⁷⁄₈	1⁶⁄₈	7³⁄₈	7	444	268
	◆ *Klinaklini River / Powhatan Robinson / Camp Fire Club / 1916*									
50	10¹⁄₈	9⁶⁄₈	5⁶⁄₈	5⁶⁄₈	2	2	7⁷⁄₈	7¹⁄₈	444	268
	◆ *Cassiar Mts. / James King / James King / 1947*									
50	10¹⁄₈	10¹⁄₈	5⁶⁄₈	5⁶⁄₈	1⁷⁄₈	2¹⁄₈	7⁶⁄₈	6⁷⁄₈	444	268
	◆ *Prophet River / Frand C. Hibben / Frank C. Hibben / 1956*									
50	9⁶⁄₈	10	5⁶⁄₈	5⁶⁄₈	2	1⁷⁄₈	6	5⁵⁄₈	444	268
	◆ *Keremeos Mt. / Robert Quaedvlieg / Robert Quaedvlieg / 1956*									
50	9⁶⁄₈	9⁴⁄₈	5⁷⁄₈	5⁷⁄₈	1⁷⁄₈	1⁷⁄₈	5²⁄₈	6	444	268
	◆ *K-Mountain / Fred D. Fouty / Fred D. Fouty / 1961*									
50	9⁶⁄₈	10²⁄₈	6	6	1⁶⁄₈	1⁶⁄₈	7	6⁶⁄₈	444	268
	◆ *Grand Forks / Norman Dawson, Jr. / Norman Dawson, Jr. / 1962*									
50	9⁶⁄₈	9⁴⁄₈	5⁵⁄₈	5⁶⁄₈	2²⁄₈	2¹⁄₈	6⁷⁄₈	6⁷⁄₈	444	268
	◆ *Telegraph Creek / Anthony Bechik / Anthony Bechik / 1963*									
50	10³⁄₈	10²⁄₈	5³⁄₈	5³⁄₈	1⁶⁄₈	1⁷⁄₈	9²⁄₈	8²⁄₈	444	268
	◆ *Gataga River / Herb Klein / Herb Klein / 1963*									
50	10³⁄₈	10²⁄₈	5⁴⁄₈	5⁴⁄₈	1⁷⁄₈	1⁷⁄₈	6⁷⁄₈	6⁴⁄₈	444	268
	◆ *Spatsizi / William L. Searle / William L. Searle / 1963*									
50	9⁴⁄₈	9⁴⁄₈	5⁴⁄₈	5⁴⁄₈	2¹⁄₈	2²⁄₈	7⁵⁄₈	7⁵⁄₈	444	268
	◆ *Halfway River / Victor Tullis / Victor Tullis / 1963*									
50	9⁶⁄₈	9⁵⁄₈	5⁶⁄₈	5⁷⁄₈	1⁷⁄₈	1⁷⁄₈	6	5¹⁄₈	444	268
	◆ *Blue Sheep Lake / O.A. McClintock / O.A. McClintock / 1964*									
50	10³⁄₈	10³⁄₈	5⁵⁄₈	5⁵⁄₈	1⁶⁄₈	1⁶⁄₈	7⁶⁄₈	6⁶⁄₈	444	268
	◆ *Smithers / John Rienhart / John Rienhart / 1964*									
50	9⁶⁄₈	9⁶⁄₈	5⁴⁄₈	5⁴⁄₈	2	2	6	6⁷⁄₈	444	268
	◆ *Keremeos / Picked Up / Bob Kitto / 1965*									
50	9⁷⁄₈	10¹⁄₈	5⁴⁄₈	5⁵⁄₈	2	2¹⁄₈	7⁷⁄₈	6²⁄₈	444	268
	◆ *Heart Peaks / Bob Loewenstein / Bob Loewenstein / 1965*									
50	10	10¹⁄₈	5⁵⁄₈	5⁶⁄₈	2	2	7²⁄₈	7²⁄₈	444	268
	◆ *Morice River / Dennis A. Sperling / Dennis A. Sperling / 1965*									
50	10⁴⁄₈	10⁶⁄₈	5³⁄₈	5³⁄₈	1⁶⁄₈	1⁷⁄₈	6⁵⁄₈	5⁶⁄₈	444	268
	◆ *Hope / Peter Konrad / Peter Konrad / 1965*									
50	9⁷⁄₈	9⁶⁄₈	5⁶⁄₈	5⁶⁄₈	1⁷⁄₈	1⁷⁄₈	6³⁄₈	5⁶⁄₈	444	268
	◆ *Nass River / Vernon Rydde / Vernon Rydde / 1966*									

Score	Length of Horn R	L	Circumference of Base R	L	Circumference at Third Quarter R	L	Greatest Spread	Tip-to-Tip Spread	All-Time Rank	State Rank
	◆ Locality / Hunter / Owner / Date Killed									
50	10	10	5⁴⁄₈	5⁴⁄₈	2	2	8⁶⁄₈	8⁶⁄₈	444	268
	◆ Cassiar Mts. / E. David Slye / E. David Slye / 1967									
50	9⁶⁄₈	9⁷⁄₈	5⁶⁄₈	5⁶⁄₈	1⁷⁄₈	1⁷⁄₈	6⁶⁄₈	5⁴⁄₈	444	268
	◆ Tatla Lake / Jack Close / Jack Close / 1967									
50	10²⁄₈	10²⁄₈	5⁴⁄₈	5⁴⁄₈	1⁶⁄₈	1⁶⁄₈	7³⁄₈	6⁷⁄₈	444	268
	◆ Cassiar Mts. / Arthur M. Scully, Jr. / Arthur M. Scully, Jr. / 1967									
50	9⁷⁄₈	9⁶⁄₈	5⁴⁄₈	5⁴⁄₈	2	2	7⁵⁄₈	7³⁄₈	444	268
	◆ Nass River / D.E. O'Shea / D.E. O'Shea / 1967									
50	9⁷⁄₈	10²⁄₈	5²⁄₈	5²⁄₈	2	2	7⁴⁄₈	6⁵⁄₈	444	268
	◆ Hastings Arm / Walter J. Eisele / Walter J. Eisele / 1968									
50	10⁵⁄₈	10⁶⁄₈	5⁵⁄₈	5⁵⁄₈	1⁵⁄₈	1⁵⁄₈	6⁶⁄₈	6	444	268
	◆ St. Mary's River / Frederick Brahniuk / Frederick Brahniuk / 1969									
50	9⁶⁄₈	9⁶⁄₈	5⁵⁄₈	5⁵⁄₈	2	2	6⁶⁄₈	5⁷⁄₈	444	268
	◆ Lake Kitchener / Aubrey W. Minshall / Aubrey W. Minshall / 1971									
50	9⁶⁄₈	9⁶⁄₈	5⁵⁄₈	5⁵⁄₈	1⁷⁄₈	1⁷⁄₈	6⁵⁄₈	6	444	268
	◆ Hendon River / R.A. Wiseman / R.A. Wiseman / 1973									
50	10³⁄₈	10³⁄₈	5⁶⁄₈	5⁶⁄₈	1⁷⁄₈	1⁷⁄₈	8³⁄₈	8	444	268
	◆ Goodwin Lake / Bill Moomey / Bill Moomey / 1974									
50	10¹⁄₈	10¹⁄₈	5⁴⁄₈	5³⁄₈	2	1⁷⁄₈	7³⁄₈	6⁵⁄₈	444	268
	◆ Gataga River / Jerald T. Waite / Jerald T. Waite / 1975									
50	9⁷⁄₈	9⁷⁄₈	5⁴⁄₈	5⁴⁄₈	1⁷⁄₈	1⁷⁄₈	8²⁄₈	7⁷⁄₈	444	268
	◆ Cassiar Mts. / Gordon A. Read / Gordon A. Read / 1976									
50	10²⁄₈	10²⁄₈	5⁵⁄₈	5⁶⁄₈	1⁷⁄₈	1⁷⁄₈	7⁵⁄₈	7⁵⁄₈	444	268
	◆ Terrace / Joe Zucchiatti / Joe Zucchiatti / 1976									
50	10³⁄₈	10⁵⁄₈	5⁶⁄₈	5⁵⁄₈	1⁶⁄₈	1⁶⁄₈	8²⁄₈	7⁵⁄₈	444	268
	◆ Cassiar Mts. / Murray B. Wilson / Murray B. Wilson / 1977									
50	10¹⁄₈	10²⁄₈	5⁵⁄₈	5⁶⁄₈	1⁶⁄₈	1⁷⁄₈	7⁴⁄₈	6⁶⁄₈	444	268
	◆ Skeena Mts. / Dee J. Burnett / Dee J. Burnett / 1982									
50	10³⁄₈	10²⁄₈	5⁵⁄₈	5⁵⁄₈	1⁷⁄₈	2	8²⁄₈	7	444	268
	◆ Yeth Creek / Michael Follett / Michael Follett / 1983									
50	10¹⁄₈	10¹⁄₈	5⁴⁄₈	5⁵⁄₈	1⁷⁄₈	1⁷⁄₈	7⁴⁄₈	8	444	268
	◆ Inklin River / John V. Macaluso / John V. Macaluso / 1984									
50	9⁵⁄₈	9⁷⁄₈	5⁷⁄₈	5⁷⁄₈	1⁷⁄₈	1⁶⁄₈	6⁷⁄₈	6¹⁄₈	444	268
	◆ Yohetta Creek / Terry R. Wagner / Terry R. Wagner / 1986									
50	10²⁄₈	10²⁄₈	5⁵⁄₈	5⁶⁄₈	2	2	8¹⁄₈	7⁴⁄₈	444	268
	◆ Rapid River / Michael D. Rowe / Michael D. Rowe / 1988									
50	9⁷⁄₈	9⁷⁄₈	5⁵⁄₈	5⁵⁄₈	1⁷⁄₈	1⁷⁄₈	7⁷⁄₈	7⁷⁄₈	444	268
	◆ Nass River / Murray McDonald / Murray McDonald / 1988									

Score	Length of Horn		Circumference of Base		Circumference at Third Quarter		Greatest Spread	Tip-to-Tip Spread	All-Time Rank	State Rank
	R	L	R	L	R	L				
♦ *Locality / Hunter / Owner / Date Killed*										
50	$10\frac{3}{8}$	$10\frac{2}{8}$	$5\frac{5}{8}$	$5\frac{5}{8}$	$1\frac{7}{8}$	$1\frac{7}{8}$	$7\frac{7}{8}$	$7\frac{3}{8}$	444	268
♦ *Palliser River / Louis B. Wood, Jr. / Louis B. Wood, Jr. / 1989*										
50	$9\frac{1}{8}$	$9\frac{3}{8}$	$5\frac{6}{8}$	$5\frac{6}{8}$	2	2	$7\frac{3}{8}$	$7\frac{1}{8}$	444	268
♦ *Thunder Mt. / Jimmy E. Dixon / Jimmy E. Dixon / 1990*										
50	$9\frac{6}{8}$	$10\frac{2}{8}$	$5\frac{6}{8}$	$5\frac{6}{8}$	$1\frac{7}{8}$	$1\frac{7}{8}$	$7\frac{1}{8}$	$6\frac{2}{8}$	444	268
♦ *Elk River / Santo Rocca / Santo Rocca / 1993*										
$49\frac{6}{8}$	$10\frac{4}{8}$	$10\frac{6}{8}$	$5\frac{5}{8}$	$5\frac{4}{8}$	$1\frac{6}{8}$	$1\frac{7}{8}$	$6\frac{5}{8}$	6	518	307
♦ *Quash Creek / Anthony Gioffre / Anthony Gioffre / 1985*										
$49\frac{4}{8}$	$10\frac{2}{8}$	$10\frac{2}{8}$	$5\frac{3}{8}$	$5\frac{4}{8}$	$1\frac{6}{8}$	$1\frac{7}{8}$	$8\frac{1}{8}$	$7\frac{1}{8}$	523	308
♦ *Fredrickson Lake / Robert W. Dager / Robert W. Dager / 1990*										
$49\frac{4}{8}$	$10\frac{1}{8}$	$10\frac{4}{8}$	$5\frac{5}{8}$	$5\frac{4}{8}$	$1\frac{6}{8}$	$1\frac{6}{8}$	$8\frac{7}{8}$	$8\frac{4}{8}$	523	308
♦ *Dawson Creek / Charles H. Eddy / Charles H. Eddy / 1991*										
$49\frac{4}{8}$	$10\frac{3}{8}$	$10\frac{2}{8}$	$5\frac{6}{8}$	$5\frac{6}{8}$	$1\frac{6}{8}$	$1\frac{6}{8}$	$6\frac{6}{8}$	$5\frac{6}{8}$	523	308
♦ *Boss Mt. / David Petrella / David Petrella / 1991*										
$49\frac{4}{8}$	$10\frac{2}{8}$	$10\frac{2}{8}$	$5\frac{4}{8}$	$5\frac{4}{8}$	$1\frac{6}{8}$	$1\frac{6}{8}$	$7\frac{4}{8}$	$6\frac{7}{8}$	523	308
♦ *Goat Mt. / Jim Evans / Jim Evans / 1993*										
$49\frac{2}{8}$	$10\frac{3}{8}$	$10\frac{4}{8}$	$5\frac{2}{8}$	$5\frac{2}{8}$	$1\frac{6}{8}$	$1\frac{6}{8}$	$5\frac{6}{8}$	$5\frac{3}{8}$	530	312
♦ *Purcell Mts. / Robert G. Helming / Robert G. Helming / 1986*										
$49\frac{2}{8}$	10	$10\frac{2}{8}$	$5\frac{4}{8}$	$5\frac{1}{8}$	$1\frac{7}{8}$	$1\frac{7}{8}$	$6\frac{2}{8}$	5	530	312
♦ *Mt. Meehaus / John L. Hutchins / John L. Hutchins / 1992*										
$48\frac{6}{8}$	$10\frac{1}{8}$	$9\frac{5}{8}$	$5\frac{4}{8}$	$5\frac{4}{8}$	$1\frac{7}{8}$	$1\frac{7}{8}$	$6\frac{7}{8}$	$5\frac{7}{8}$	534	314
♦ *Zaggodetchino Mt. / Wyatt W. Dawson, Jr. / Wyatt W. Dawson, Jr. / 1985*										
$48\frac{4}{8}$	$9\frac{4}{8}$	$9\frac{4}{8}$	$5\frac{5}{8}$	$5\frac{5}{8}$	$1\frac{6}{8}$	$1\frac{6}{8}$	$7\frac{3}{8}$	$6\frac{7}{8}$	540	315
♦ *Spatsizi Plateau / William G. Farley / William G. Farley / 1989*										
$48\frac{4}{8}$	$10\frac{4}{8}$	$9\frac{7}{8}$	$5\frac{2}{8}$	$5\frac{4}{8}$	$1\frac{7}{8}$	2	$7\frac{1}{8}$	$6\frac{6}{8}$	540	315
♦ *Kinskuch Lake / Randy L. Dietrich / Randy L. Dietrich / 1990*										
$48\frac{2}{8}$	10	$9\frac{6}{8}$	$5\frac{4}{8}$	$5\frac{4}{8}$	$1\frac{6}{8}$	$1\frac{6}{8}$	$6\frac{3}{8}$	$5\frac{4}{8}$	549	317
♦ *Pelly Lake / Russ L. Martin / Russ L. Martin / 1989*										
48	$9\frac{4}{8}$	$9\frac{4}{8}$	$5\frac{4}{8}$	$5\frac{3}{8}$	$1\frac{6}{8}$	$1\frac{7}{8}$	$7\frac{3}{8}$	$7\frac{1}{8}$	557	318
♦ *Inklin River / William H. Moyer / William H. Moyer / 1990*										
48	$9\frac{5}{8}$	$9\frac{3}{8}$	$5\frac{6}{8}$	$5\frac{6}{8}$	$1\frac{6}{8}$	$1\frac{6}{8}$	$6\frac{5}{8}$	$6\frac{1}{8}$	557	318
♦ *Sawyer Creek / John C. Shifflett / John C. Shifflett / 1991*										
48	10	10	$5\frac{3}{8}$	$5\frac{3}{8}$	$1\frac{6}{8}$	$1\frac{6}{8}$	$7\frac{3}{8}$	7	557	318
♦ *Tipperary Lake / P.J. Wright, Jr. / P.J. Wright, Jr. / 1992*										
48	$9\frac{3}{8}$	$9\frac{3}{8}$	$5\frac{2}{8}$	$5\frac{2}{8}$	$1\frac{7}{8}$	$1\frac{7}{8}$	$7\frac{1}{8}$	$6\frac{4}{8}$	557	318
♦ *Sediments Creek / Joseph F. Dalton / Joseph F. Dalton / 1993*										
48	$9\frac{3}{8}$	$9\frac{3}{8}$	$5\frac{4}{8}$	$5\frac{3}{8}$	$1\frac{6}{8}$	$1\frac{6}{8}$	$6\frac{4}{8}$	$6\frac{1}{8}$	557	318
♦ *Chilko Lake / K. Marc Barre, Jr. / K. Marc Barre, Jr. / 1994*										

Score	Length of Horn R	L	Circumference of Base R	L	Circumference at Third Quarter R	L	Greatest Spread	Tip-to-Tip Spread	All-Time Rank	State Rank

♦ *Locality / Hunter / Owner / Date Killed*

Score	Length of Horn R	L	Circumference of Base R	L	Circumference at Third Quarter R	L	Greatest Spread	Tip-to-Tip Spread	All-Time Rank	State Rank
47 6/8	9 4/8	9 4/8	5 4/8	5 4/8	1 6/8	1 6/8	0	7 1/8	564	323
47 6/8	9	9	5 4/8	5 3/8	1 7/8	1 7/8	6 5/8	6 3/8	564	323
47 6/8	9 5/8	9 6/8	5 2/8	5 2/8	1 7/8	1 7/8	7	6 4/8	564	323
47 6/8	8 7/8	8 7/8	5 4/8	5 5/8	1 7/8	1 7/8	7	6 3/8	564	323
47 2/8	9 2/8	9 1/8	5 4/8	5 4/8	1 7/8	1 7/8	8 1/8	8	575	327
47 2/8	9 7/8	9 7/8	5 1/8	5 1/8	1 6/8	1 6/8	6 1/8	5 4/8	575	327
47 2/8	9 6/8	9 6/8	5 3/8	5 3/8	1 4/8	1 4/8	5 7/8	5 6/8	575	327
47 2/8	9 3/8	9 4/8	5 3/8	5 4/8	1 6/8	1 6/8	6 2/8	5 4/8	575	327
47	9 7/8	10	5 2/8	5 2/8	1 6/8	1 6/8	7 2/8	7	583	331
47	9 4/8	9 4/8	5 3/8	5 3/8	1 6/8	1 6/8	7 5/8	7 2/8	583	331
47	9 4/8	9 5/8	5 3/8	5 4/8	1 5/8	1 6/8	6	5 3/8	583	331
55 6/8	10 5/8	10 4/8	6 1/8	6 1/8	2 2/8	2 2/8	7 6/8	6 3/8	*	*
55 6/8	10 6/8	11	6 1/8	6 2/8	2	2 1/8	8 5/8	8 5/8	*	*
54 6/8	11 3/8	11 2/8	6 2/8	6 1/8	1 7/8	1 7/8	7 6/8	6 3/8	*	*
53 6/8	10 2/8	10 2/8	6	6	2 1/8	2	7 2/8	7	*	*
52 6/8	10 6/8	10 6/8	6	6 1/8	1 7/8	2	9	8 7/8	*	*
52 6/8	10 1/8	9 7/8	6	6	2 1/8	2 1/8	7 7/8	7 1/8	*	*

♦ *Maria Creek / K. James Malady III / K. James Malady III / 1989*

♦ *Carmen Mt. / Stanley W. Janusiewicz / Stanley W. Janusiewicz / 1990*

♦ *Driftpile Creek / David J. Craite / David J. Craite / 1990*

♦ *Chilko Lake / Kenneth M. Barre, Sr. / Kenneth M. Barre, Sr. / 1994*

♦ *Ice Mt. / Jerald E. Mason / Jerald E. Mason / 1966*

♦ *Squaw Creek / Salvatore Cetrulo / Salvatore Cetrulo / 1992*

♦ *Osilinka River / Brad K. Smith / Brad K. Smith / 1993*

♦ *Nakina River / Bruce Cepicky / Bruce Cepicky / 1994*

♦ *Poutang Creek / Reg R. Smith / Reg R. Smith / 1977*

♦ *Bear Creek / William A. Brooks, Sr. / William A. Brooks, Sr. / 1989*

♦ *Lake Revelstoke / George R. Skaggs / George R. Skaggs / 1992*

♦ *Blunt Mt. / Picked Up / Jack Adams / 1970*

♦ *Skeena Mts. / William E. Gourlie / William E. Gourlie / 1985*

♦ *Bowser Lake / Perley E. Holmes / Perley E. Holmes / 1993*

♦ *Shoemaker Creek / Brian D. Shepherd / Brian D. Shepherd / 1991*

♦ *Similkameen River / Doug & Judy Crossley / Doug & Judy Crossley / 1983*

♦ *Nimbus Mt. / J.D. Souza / J.D. Souza / 1985*

This British Columbia billy received the first place award at Boone and Crockett Club's 22nd Awards Program and Banquet held in Dallas, Texas, in 1995. It was taken by Patrick P. Moleski on Oliver Creek in 1994 and scores 55-2/8 points.

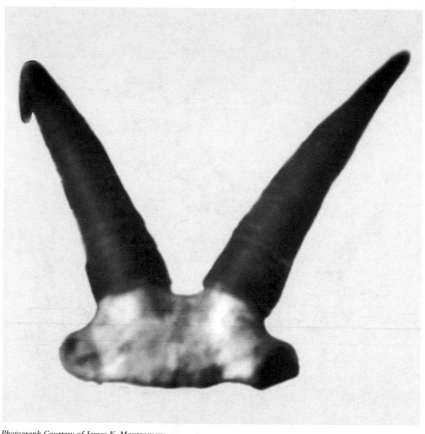

Photograph Courtesy of James K. Montgomery

YUKON TERRITORY PROVINCE RECORD
ROCKY MOUNTAIN GOAT
SCORE: 51⅔
Locality: Marker Lake   Date: 1978
Hunter: James K. Montgomery

YUKON TERRITORY

ROCKY MOUNTAIN GOAT

Score	Length of Horn		Circumference of Base		Circumference at Third Quarter		Greatest Spread	Tip-to-Tip Spread	All-Time Rank	State Rank
	R	L	R	L	R	L				
◆ *Locality / Hunter / Owner / Date Killed*										
51²⁄₈	10⁵⁄₈	10⁶⁄₈	5⁴⁄₈	5⁵⁄₈	1⁷⁄₈	1⁷⁄₈	10⁴⁄₈	10³⁄₈	212	1
◆ *Marker Lake / James K. Montgomery / James K. Montgomery / 1978*										
50⁴⁄₈	10²⁄₈	10¹⁄₈	5⁵⁄₈	5⁵⁄₈	2	2	7²⁄₈	6³⁄₈	340	2
◆ *Lake Bennet / H. Kennedy / H. Kennedy / 1958*										

TOP 5 PRONGHORN LISTINGS INDEX

Tabulations of Recorded Pronghorn

The trophy data shown on the following pages are taken from score charts in the records archives of the Boone and Crockett Club.

Pronghorn are found over most of the western one-third of the United States; southern Saskatchewan and southeastern Alberta; and northern Mexico.

The scores and ranks shown are final, except for the trophies shown with an asterisk (*). The asterisk identifies entry scores subject to final certification by an Awards Panel of Judges. The asterisk can be removed (except in the case of a potential World's Record) by the submission of two additional, independent scorings by Official Measurers of the Boone and Crockett Club. The Records Committee of the Club will review the three scorings available (original plus two additional) and determine which, if any, will be accepted in lieu of the Judges' Panel measurement. When the score has been accepted as final by the Records Committee, the asterisk will be removed in future editions of this book and the all-time records book, *Records of North American Big Game*. In the case of a potential World's Record, the trophy must come before a Judges' Panel at the end of an entry period. Only a Judges' Panel can certify a World's Record and finalize its score. Asterisked trophies are unranked at the end of their category.

Photograph Courtesy of Michael J. O'Haco, Jr.

ARIZONA STATE RECORD
WORLD'S RECORD
PRONGHORN
SCORE: 93⁴⁄₈
Locality: Coconino Co.   Date: 1985
Hunter: Michael J. O'Haco, Jr.

ARIZONA

PRONGHORN

Score	Length of Horn		Circumference of Base		Inside Spread	Tip-to-Tip Spread	Length of Prong		All-Time Rank	State Rank
	R	L	R	L			R	L		
◆ Locality / Hunter / Owner / Date Killed										
$93\frac{3}{8}$	$17\frac{6}{8}$	$17\frac{4}{8}$	$6\frac{7}{8}$	7	$12\frac{5}{8}$	$8\frac{1}{8}$	8	$8\frac{2}{8}$	1	1
◆ Coconino County / Michael J. O'Haco, Jr. / Michael J. O'Haco, Jr. / 1985										
93	$18\frac{1}{8}$	$18\frac{2}{8}$	$7\frac{2}{8}$	7	$10\frac{1}{8}$	$6\frac{5}{8}$	$7\frac{6}{8}$	$7\frac{2}{8}$	2	2
◆ Yavapai County / Edwin L. Wetzler / Loaned to B&C Natl. Coll. / 1975										
$92\frac{5}{8}$	$16\frac{4}{8}$	$16\frac{4}{8}$	$7\frac{2}{8}$	$7\frac{1}{8}$	$12\frac{4}{8}$	$9\frac{5}{8}$	$7\frac{3}{8}$	$7\frac{4}{8}$	3	3
◆ Coconino County / Sam Jaksick, Jr. / Sam Jaksick, Jr. / 1991										
$91\frac{6}{8}$	$17\frac{2}{8}$	$17\frac{1}{8}$	$7\frac{6}{8}$	$7\frac{6}{8}$	$13\frac{4}{8}$	9	7	$7\frac{3}{8}$	4	4
◆ Coconino County / Steven E. Hopkins / Steven E. Hopkins / 1992										
$91\frac{4}{8}$	$20\frac{1}{8}$	20	$7\frac{4}{8}$	7	12	$11\frac{3}{8}$	$4\frac{5}{8}$	$5\frac{3}{8}$	5	5
◆ Arizona / Wilson Potter / Unknown / 1899										
$90\frac{4}{8}$	$18\frac{1}{8}$	$18\frac{3}{8}$	$6\frac{5}{8}$	$6\frac{5}{8}$	$10\frac{3}{8}$	$2\frac{7}{8}$	7	$6\frac{4}{8}$	14	6
◆ Yavapai County / Joe P. Fornara / Joe P. Fornara / 1984										
$89\frac{6}{8}$	$18\frac{3}{8}$	18	$6\frac{5}{8}$	$6\frac{4}{8}$	$9\frac{4}{8}$	4	$7\frac{1}{8}$	$7\frac{3}{8}$	17	7
◆ Seligman / J.W. Johnson / J.W. Johnson / 1959										
$89\frac{6}{8}$	$18\frac{2}{8}$	18	7	$6\frac{7}{8}$	$9\frac{7}{8}$	$3\frac{3}{8}$	$6\frac{3}{8}$	$6\frac{3}{8}$	17	7
◆ Coconino County / James W. Barrett / James W. Barrett / 1987										
$89\frac{6}{8}$	$16\frac{6}{8}$	17	$7\frac{4}{8}$	$7\frac{5}{8}$	$10\frac{2}{8}$	$5\frac{1}{8}$	$6\frac{4}{8}$	$6\frac{2}{8}$	17	7
◆ Coconino County / Sam Jaksick, Jr. / Sam Jaksick, Jr. / 1993										
$89\frac{2}{8}$	$17\frac{2}{8}$	$17\frac{2}{8}$	$6\frac{7}{8}$	$6\frac{6}{8}$	$12\frac{1}{8}$	$4\frac{4}{8}$	$5\frac{7}{8}$	$5\frac{6}{8}$	28	10
◆ Cochise County / Rene J. Dube, Jr. / Rene J. Dube, Jr. / 1985										
$88\frac{6}{8}$	19	$18\frac{4}{8}$	$6\frac{2}{8}$	$6\frac{2}{8}$	$18\frac{2}{8}$	$15\frac{6}{8}$	$5\frac{6}{8}$	$5\frac{4}{8}$	41	11
◆ Yavapai County / Jerry P. Carver / Jerry P. Carver / 1993										
$88\frac{4}{8}$	$19\frac{2}{8}$	$18\frac{6}{8}$	$6\frac{5}{8}$	$6\frac{5}{8}$	$13\frac{4}{8}$	$10\frac{4}{8}$	$5\frac{4}{8}$	$5\frac{3}{8}$	51	12
◆ Coconino County / Harold R. Edgemon / Harold R. Edgemon / 1984										
$88\frac{4}{8}$	18	$17\frac{5}{8}$	$6\frac{4}{8}$	$6\frac{4}{8}$	$13\frac{2}{8}$	8	$6\frac{4}{8}$	$6\frac{7}{8}$	51	12
◆ Coconino County / Randall W. Smith / Randall W. Smith / 1985										
$88\frac{4}{8}$	$17\frac{7}{8}$	$17\frac{7}{8}$	$6\frac{6}{8}$	$6\frac{6}{8}$	$13\frac{7}{8}$	8	$5\frac{5}{8}$	$5\frac{6}{8}$	51	12
◆ Yavapai County / Arthur C. Savoini / Arthur C. Savoini / 1988										
$88\frac{4}{8}$	$18\frac{1}{8}$	$18\frac{2}{8}$	7	$7\frac{1}{8}$	10	$5\frac{7}{8}$	$5\frac{4}{8}$	$5\frac{3}{8}$	51	12
◆ Coconino County / Arthur R. Dubs / Arthur R. Dubs / 1990										
$88\frac{4}{8}$	18	18	$6\frac{6}{8}$	$6\frac{6}{8}$	$11\frac{4}{8}$	$6\frac{1}{8}$	$5\frac{4}{8}$	$5\frac{3}{8}$	51	12
◆ Cochise County / Tom R. Braun / Tom R. Braun / 1991										
$88\frac{2}{8}$	$18\frac{2}{8}$	$18\frac{2}{8}$	$6\frac{6}{8}$	$6\frac{6}{8}$	$11\frac{4}{8}$	$8\frac{4}{8}$	5	$5\frac{3}{8}$	59	17
◆ Navajo County / John M. Griffith, Jr. / John M. Griffith, Jr. / 1983										
$88\frac{2}{8}$	$16\frac{7}{8}$	$16\frac{7}{8}$	7	$6\frac{6}{8}$	$10\frac{6}{8}$	$5\frac{5}{8}$	$5\frac{3}{8}$	$5\frac{7}{8}$	59	17
◆ Yavapai County / Larry D. Saylor / Larry D. Saylor / 1984										

Score	Length of Horn R	L	Circumference of Base R	L	Inside Spread	Tip-to-Tip Spread	Length of Prong R	L	All-Time Rank	State Rank
	♦ *Locality / Hunter / Owner / Date Killed*									
88²⁄₈	17⁶⁄₈	18¹⁄₈	6⁷⁄₈	6⁷⁄₈	11³⁄₈	6⁴⁄₈	5⁴⁄₈	5²⁄₈	59	17
	♦ *Mohave County / Peter E. Mangelsdorf / Peter E. Mangelsdorf / 1989*									
88	16⁶⁄₈	17¹⁄₈	7	7	9⁴⁄₈	5¹⁄₈	5⁵⁄₈	5⁶⁄₈	66	20
	♦ *Coconino County / Richard J. Hallock / Richard J. Hallock / 1973*									
88	16⁶⁄₈	16⁷⁄₈	6⁵⁄₈	6³⁄₈	11⁶⁄₈	8⁷⁄₈	6²⁄₈	6³⁄₈	66	20
	♦ *Apache County / Richard L. Hazelwood / Richard L. Hazelwood / 1992*									
87⁶⁄₈	17²⁄₈	17⁵⁄₈	6⁶⁄₈	6⁶⁄₈	14⁴⁄₈	9⁵⁄₈	5⁶⁄₈	6	74	22
	♦ *Coconino County / Thomas R. Roberts / Thomas R. Roberts / 1986*									
87²⁄₈	17	17²⁄₈	6⁷⁄₈	7	14⁴⁄₈	8⁷⁄₈	5⁷⁄₈	5⁷⁄₈	85	23
	♦ *Yavapai County / Ervin G. Rothfuss II / Ervin G. Rothfuss II / 1991*									
87	15⁶⁄₈	16	6⁴⁄₈	6⁴⁄₈	11⁵⁄₈	5⁶⁄₈	6¹⁄₈	6²⁄₈	101	24
	♦ *Cochise County / David J. Braun / David J. Braun / 1984*									
87	16⁴⁄₈	17⁴⁄₈	6⁷⁄₈	6⁶⁄₈	10⁵⁄₈	5⁷⁄₈	6³⁄₈	6²⁄₈	101	24
	♦ *Yavapai County / Robbie A. Jochim / Robbie A. Jochim / 1989*									
86⁶⁄₈	18⁷⁄₈	18⁶⁄₈	6³⁄₈	6³⁄₈	12⁴⁄₈	7¹⁄₈	4⁶⁄₈	5	114	26
	♦ *Anderson Mesa / Gene Tolle / Gene Tolle / 1941*									
86⁶⁄₈	17⁴⁄₈	17⁵⁄₈	6³⁄₈	6³⁄₈	9⁶⁄₈	6¹⁄₈	5⁵⁄₈	5²⁄₈	114	26
	♦ *Yavapai County / Louis R. Dees / Louis R. Dees / 1963*									
86⁶⁄₈	17³⁄₈	17¹⁄₈	7	6⁶⁄₈	10²⁄₈	6⁵⁄₈	5⁴⁄₈	5²⁄₈	114	26
	♦ *Coconino County / Ralph C. Stayner / Ralph C. Stayner / 1980*									
86⁶⁄₈	17	17³⁄₈	7¹⁄₈	7	11³⁄₈	5²⁄₈	6	5⁷⁄₈	114	26
	♦ *Coconino County / Ben E. Stayner / Ben E. Stayner / 1991*									
86⁶⁄₈	17³⁄₈	18	6⁶⁄₈	6⁶⁄₈	8⁴⁄₈	4²⁄₈	6⁶⁄₈	6	114	26
	♦ *Coconino County / Norman E. Gammons / Norman E. Gammons / 1992*									
86⁶⁄₈	16	16	7¹⁄₈	7¹⁄₈	12	8¹⁄₈	6	6	114	26
	♦ *Yavapai County / James M. Machac / James M. Machac / 1993*									
86⁶⁄₈	17²⁄₈	17	7²⁄₈	7	12⁴⁄₈	9⁴⁄₈	6²⁄₈	5²⁄₈	114	26
	♦ *Coconino County / Harry L. Hussey / Harry L. Hussey / 1993*									
86⁶⁄₈	17³⁄₈	16⁷⁄₈	7¹⁄₈	7¹⁄₈	18⁴⁄₈	18²⁄₈	5⁷⁄₈	6¹⁄₈	114	26
	♦ *Coconino County / George V. Escobedo / George V. Escobedo / 1994*									
86⁴⁄₈	18	17⁵⁄₈	6⁴⁄₈	6⁴⁄₈	10⁴⁄₈	6⁴⁄₈	5³⁄₈	6	140	34
	♦ *Navajo County / John D. Higginbotham / John D. Higginbotham / 1979*									
86⁴⁄₈	16⁶⁄₈	16⁵⁄₈	7²⁄₈	7	15	14	5⁷⁄₈	5⁷⁄₈	140	34
	♦ *Coconino County / Arthur R. Dubs / Arthur R. Dubs / 1991*									
86⁴⁄₈	16⁶⁄₈	16⁵⁄₈	6⁷⁄₈	6⁷⁄₈	14	9⁵⁄₈	6	6¹⁄₈	140	34
	♦ *Coconino County / Sam Jaksick, Jr. / Sam Jaksick, Jr. / 1992*									
86²⁄₈	16	16²⁄₈	7¹⁄₈	7²⁄₈	9⁷⁄₈	5⁴⁄₈	6⁵⁄₈	6⁵⁄₈	155	37
	♦ *Coconino County / Eugene Anderson / Eugene Anderson / 1961*									

ARIZONA PRONGHORN *(continued)*

Score	Length of Horn R	Length of Horn L	Circumference of Base R	Circumference of Base L	Inside Spread	Tip-to-Tip Spread	Length of Prong R	Length of Prong L	All-Time Rank	State Rank	♦ *Locality / Hunter / Owner / Date Killed*
86 2/8	16 7/8	16 6/8	6 6/8	6 4/8	11 7/8	4 7/8	5 4/8	5	155	37	♦ *Du Gas / Rex Earl / Rex Earl / 1962*
86 2/8	17 6/8	17 6/8	6 3/8	6 3/8	10 6/8	7 4/8	5 3/8	5 3/8	155	37	♦ *Coconino County / Jon H. Bryan / Jon H. Bryan / 1970*
86 2/8	17 7/8	17 6/8	6 4/8	6 4/8	14 2/8	9 1/8	4 5/8	4 4/8	155	37	♦ *Ft. Apache Res. / Jack Pierce / Jack Pierce / 1974*
86 2/8	17 5/8	17 6/8	6 5/8	6 4/8	15 6/8	13 4/8	4 7/8	5	155	37	♦ *Coconino County / Scott J. Reger / Scott J. Reger / 1988*
86	17 3/8	18	6 6/8	6 7/8	12 6/8	8	6 4/8	6 3/8	182	42	♦ *Coconino County / Richard R. Barney / Richard R. Barney / 1969*
86	17 1/8	16 4/8	6 7/8	7	11 3/8	7 6/8	5 6/8	6 7/8	182	42	♦ *Yavapai County / Ruth McCasland / Ruth McCasland / 1975*
86	16 3/8	16 4/8	6 6/8	7 1/8	6 6/8	2 2/8	4 3/8	3 5/8	182	42	♦ *Apache County / Charles R. Sprung / Charles R. Sprung / 1984*
86	15 2/8	15	7 3/8	7 4/8	12 6/8	8 1/8	6 7/8	6 3/8	182	42	♦ *Coconino County / John S. Harrison / John S. Harrison / 1986*
86	15 5/8	15 4/8	6 5/8	6 5/8	10 2/8	7 4/8	5 7/8	6	182	42	♦ *Apache County / Jennifer C. Flaherty / Jennifer C. Flaherty / 1990*
86	17 2/8	16 1/8	6 5/8	6 7/8	13 1/8	11 2/8	5 5/8	5 5/8	182	42	♦ *Coconino County / Walter E. George / Walter E. George / 1992*
86	16	16	7 1/8	7 1/8	10 6/8	4 6/8	6	6	182	42	♦ *Coconino County / Sam Jaksick, Jr. / Sam Jaksick, Jr. / 1994*
85 7/8	16 5/8	16 3/8	6 7/8	6 6/8	17	15 3/8	6 2/8	6 1/8	210	49	♦ *Yavapai County / Vincent J. Conti / Vincent J. Conti / 1986*
85 6/8	16 4/8	16 5/8	6 4/8	6 5/8	9 6/8	4 4/8	6 4/8	6 4/8	211	50	♦ *Yavapai County / Randy Modisett / Randy Modisett / 1974*
85 6/8	15 7/8	16 1/8	7 4/8	7 4/8	12 6/8	9 3/8	6 2/8	6 2/8	211	50	♦ *Navajo County / C. Boyd Austin / C. Boyd Austin / 1987*
85 6/8	18 1/8	18	6 3/8	6 3/8	17 1/8	13	6 1/8	5 7/8	211	50	♦ *Coconino County / Gene Coon / Gene Coon / 1993*
85 6/8	16 3/8	16 5/8	6 6/8	6 4/8	12 6/8	8 1/8	6 1/8	6	211	50	♦ *Yavapai County / James W.P. Roe / James W.P. Roe / 1994*
85 4/8	18 1/8	18 4/8	6 4/8	6 4/8	17 4/8	13 5/8	5 4/8	5 5/8	238	54	♦ *Apache County / Don L. Corley / Don L. Corley / 1985*
85 4/8	16 5/8	16 5/8	6 7/8	6 7/8	9 3/8	4 1/8	5 4/8	6 1/8	238	54	♦ *Yavapai County / Steven C. Dunn / Steven C. Dunn / 1987*
85 4/8	16 4/8	16 4/8	6 6/8	6 5/8	11 2/8	5	5 7/8	5 7/8	238	54	♦ *Coconino County / Lester E. Bradley / Lester E. Bradley / 1990*

Score	Length of Horn R	Length of Horn L	Circumference of Base R	Circumference of Base L	Inside Spread	Tip-to-Tip Spread	Length of Prong R	Length of Prong L	All-Time Rank	State Rank
	♦ *Locality / Hunter / Owner / Date Killed*									
85 4/8	16 5/8	16 5/8	6 4/8	6 4/8	12 6/8	7 7/8	5 4/8	5 4/8	238	54
	♦ *Coconino County / Don W. Drew / Don R. Drew / 1990*									
85 2/8	17 4/8	17 6/8	7 2/8	7 2/8	7 2/8	2	5 4/8	5 4/8	268	58
	♦ *Yavapai County / Robert C. Bogart / Robert C. Bogart / 1963*									
85 2/8	16 7/8	16 7/8	6 6/8	6 6/8	11 6/8	6 5/8	5 1/8	5 3/8	268	58
	♦ *Coconino County / Philip S. Leiendecker / Philip S. Leiendecker / 1982*									
85 2/8	16 4/8	16 3/8	6 6/8	6 6/8	7 1/8	2 2/8	6 3/8	5 7/8	268	58
	♦ *Navajo County / Robert A. Dodson / Robert A. Dodson / 1989*									
85	19 3/8	18 7/8	6 4/8	6 2/8	14 1/8	8 5/8	5 3/8	4 7/8	301	61
	♦ *Williams / Donovan E. Smith / Donovan E. Smith / 1959*									
85	17 3/8	17 7/8	6 2/8	6 4/8	13 5/8	8 5/8	4 7/8	4 7/8	301	61
	♦ *Yavapai County / David M. Sanders / David M. Sanders / 1976*									
85	17 5/8	18 1/8	6 6/8	6 3/8	10 7/8	3 1/8	5 3/8	5 2/8	301	61
	♦ *Coconino County / John L. Neely / John L. Neely / 1989*									
85	16 6/8	17 6/8	6 5/8	6 5/8	12 3/8	8 2/8	5 4/8	5 3/8	301	61
	♦ *Yavapai County / Craig R. Johnson / Craig R. Johnson / 1993*									
84 6/8	16 5/8	16 6/8	6 7/8	6 6/8	14 6/8	11 2/8	6 7/8	5 5/8	336	65
	♦ *Anderson Mesa / Elgin T. Gates / Elgin T. Gates / 1955*									
84 6/8	16 2/8	16 3/8	6	6 1/8	8 5/8	3 5/8	7	6 7/8	336	65
	♦ *Navajo County / George M. Owen / George M. Owen / 1966*									
84 6/8	19 7/8	19 4/8	6 1/8	5 7/8	18	13 6/8	5 2/8	4 5/8	336	65
	♦ *Boquillas Ranch / Bob Dixon / Bob Dixon / 1970*									
84 6/8	15 7/8	15 6/8	6 5/8	6 5/8	13 5/8	8 6/8	5 4/8	5 2/8	336	65
	♦ *Ft. Apache Res. / Donald Smith / Donald Smith / 1972*									
84 6/8	16 4/8	16 3/8	6 5/8	6 5/8	8 4/8	3 6/8	6 4/8	6 5/8	336	65
	♦ *Cochise County / David J. Braun / David J. Braun / 1991*									
84 6/8	17 1/8	17 1/8	6 4/8	6 4/8	12 4/8	8 2/8	5 6/8	5 6/8	336	65
	♦ *Coconino County / Jerrell F. Coburn / Jerrell F. Coburn / 1991*									
84 4/8	18 4/8	18	7	7	13	8 4/8	5	3 4/8	390	71
	♦ *Seligman / Garth A. Brown / Garth A. Brown / 1964*									
84 4/8	17 5/8	17 3/8	6 2/8	6 3/8	7 5/8	4 6/8	5 7/8	6	390	71
	♦ *Yavapai County / John Jerome / John Jerome / 1983*									
84 2/8	17 1/8	16 4/8	6 4/8	6 4/8	13	6 7/8	5 4/8	5 1/8	436	73
	♦ *Anderson Mesa / Bill Gray / Bill Gray / 1960*									
84 2/8	17 7/8	17 7/8	6 1/8	6	12 1/8	7 6/8	4 6/8	4 5/8	436	73
	♦ *Ft. Apache Res. / Frank E. White / Frank E. White / 1967*									
84 2/8	16 6/8	16 7/8	6 5/8	6 6/8	8 4/8	3 7/8	5 4/8	5 3/8	436	73
	♦ *Apache County / Alaine D. Neal / Alaine D. Neal / 1973*									

Score	Length of Horn R	L	Circumference of Base R	L	Inside Spread	Tip-to-Tip Spread	Length of Prong R	L	All-Time Rank	State Rank
$84\frac{2}{8}$	17	$16\frac{6}{8}$	$6\frac{4}{8}$	$6\frac{3}{8}$	$12\frac{2}{8}$	$8\frac{4}{8}$	6	$6\frac{1}{8}$	436	73
◆ Coconino County / Michael A. Cromer / Michael A. Cromer / 1982										
$84\frac{2}{8}$	$16\frac{6}{8}$	$16\frac{7}{8}$	$6\frac{2}{8}$	$6\frac{2}{8}$	$9\frac{1}{8}$	$6\frac{6}{8}$	$5\frac{3}{8}$	$5\frac{2}{8}$	436	73
◆ Coconino County / William R. Vaughn / William R. Vaughn / 1983										
$84\frac{2}{8}$	$16\frac{4}{8}$	$18\frac{2}{8}$	$6\frac{2}{8}$	$6\frac{2}{8}$	$11\frac{1}{8}$	$6\frac{5}{8}$	$6\frac{1}{8}$	$6\frac{1}{8}$	436	73
◆ Coconino County / Kevin B. Call / Kevin B. Call / 1987										
$84\frac{2}{8}$	16	16	$6\frac{6}{8}$	$6\frac{5}{8}$	10	4	7	$6\frac{6}{8}$	436	73
◆ Yavapai County / Brian Murray / Brian Murray / 1988										
84	$16\frac{4}{8}$	$17\frac{2}{8}$	$6\frac{2}{8}$	6	$10\frac{6}{8}$	$5\frac{6}{8}$	6	$5\frac{3}{8}$	500	80
◆ Yavapai County / Walter Tibbs / Walter Tibbs / 1959										
84	$16\frac{7}{8}$	$16\frac{7}{8}$	$6\frac{5}{8}$	$6\frac{5}{8}$	$10\frac{6}{8}$	$4\frac{7}{8}$	$5\frac{4}{8}$	$5\frac{2}{8}$	500	80
◆ Coconino County / Robert F. Veazey / Robert F. Veazey / 1979										
84	$17\frac{6}{8}$	$17\frac{5}{8}$	$6\frac{1}{8}$	$6\frac{2}{8}$	$13\frac{6}{8}$	$8\frac{2}{8}$	5	$4\frac{7}{8}$	500	80
◆ Yavapai County / James O. Pierce / James O. Pierce / 1980										
84	$15\frac{5}{8}$	$15\frac{5}{8}$	$6\frac{6}{8}$	$6\frac{4}{8}$	$15\frac{1}{8}$	$11\frac{2}{8}$	$5\frac{1}{8}$	$5\frac{2}{8}$	500	80
◆ Coconino County / Fred J. Nobbe, Jr. / Fred J. Nobbe, Jr. / 1982										
84	$17\frac{4}{8}$	$16\frac{2}{8}$	$6\frac{7}{8}$	$6\frac{6}{8}$	$10\frac{3}{8}$	$4\frac{6}{8}$	$5\frac{7}{8}$	$5\frac{2}{8}$	500	80
◆ Yavapai County / Fredrick T. Lau / Fredrick T. Lau / 1985										
84	$16\frac{2}{8}$	$16\frac{7}{8}$	$6\frac{5}{8}$	$6\frac{6}{8}$	$14\frac{7}{8}$	$16\frac{6}{8}$	$5\frac{5}{8}$	$6\frac{1}{8}$	500	80
◆ Yavapai County / James K. McCasland / James K. McCasland / 1987										
84	$15\frac{6}{8}$	$15\frac{7}{8}$	$6\frac{6}{8}$	$6\frac{5}{8}$	$11\frac{3}{8}$	$6\frac{1}{8}$	$5\frac{6}{8}$	$5\frac{5}{8}$	500	80
◆ Navajo County / Alan K. Nulliner / Alan K. Nulliner / 1989										
84	$16\frac{2}{8}$	$16\frac{2}{8}$	$6\frac{4}{8}$	$6\frac{3}{8}$	$10\frac{6}{8}$	$7\frac{2}{8}$	$5\frac{2}{8}$	$5\frac{5}{8}$	500	80
◆ Coconino County / William B. Bullock / William B. Bullock / 1991										
84	17	$17\frac{4}{8}$	$6\frac{4}{8}$	$6\frac{4}{8}$	$9\frac{1}{8}$	$3\frac{7}{8}$	$5\frac{2}{8}$	$5\frac{1}{8}$	500	80
◆ Apache County / Charlinda Webster / Charlinda Webster / 1991										
84	$16\frac{6}{8}$	17	$6\frac{2}{8}$	$6\frac{2}{8}$	$14\frac{5}{8}$	$8\frac{7}{8}$	$5\frac{3}{8}$	$5\frac{3}{8}$	500	80
◆ Coconino County / Paul F. Musser / Paul F. Musser / 1993										
$83\frac{6}{8}$	$16\frac{4}{8}$	17	$6\frac{6}{8}$	$6\frac{6}{8}$	$12\frac{4}{8}$	6	$5\frac{4}{8}$	$5\frac{4}{8}$	565	90
◆ Coconino County / Marvin Redburn / Marvin Redburn / 1950										
$83\frac{6}{8}$	$16\frac{4}{8}$	$15\frac{7}{8}$	$6\frac{6}{8}$	$6\frac{6}{8}$	$12\frac{6}{8}$	$8\frac{6}{8}$	$5\frac{3}{8}$	$5\frac{1}{8}$	565	90
◆ Chino Valley / Max Durfee / Max Durfee / 1960										
$83\frac{6}{8}$	$17\frac{4}{8}$	$16\frac{6}{8}$	6	6	$10\frac{6}{8}$	$6\frac{7}{8}$	$5\frac{6}{8}$	$3\frac{6}{8}$	565	90
◆ Williams / Dave Blair / Dave Blair / 1961										
$83\frac{6}{8}$	$16\frac{5}{8}$	$16\frac{7}{8}$	$6\frac{4}{8}$	$6\frac{4}{8}$	$15\frac{6}{8}$	$10\frac{6}{8}$	$4\frac{4}{8}$	$4\frac{5}{8}$	565	90
◆ Yavapai County / C.J. Adair / C.J. Adair / 1961										
$83\frac{6}{8}$	$16\frac{6}{8}$	$16\frac{4}{8}$	$6\frac{3}{8}$	$6\frac{3}{8}$	10	$5\frac{6}{8}$	$4\frac{7}{8}$	5	565	90
◆ Black Tank / George M. Lewis / George M. Lewis / 1968										

Score	Length of Horn R	L	Circumference of Base R	L	Inside Spread	Tip-to-Tip Spread	Length of Prong R	L	All-Time Rank	State Rank
83⁶⁄₈	15⁴⁄₈	15²⁄₈	7²⁄₈	7²⁄₈	13⁴⁄₈	10	5⁵⁄₈	5⁶⁄₈	565	90

♦ *Yavapai County / Michael J. Rusing / Michael J. Rusing / 1990*

| 83⁶⁄₈ | 15⁷⁄₈ | 16 | 6³⁄₈ | 6¹⁄₈ | 11⁴⁄₈ | 6⁷⁄₈ | 5⁶⁄₈ | 6²⁄₈ | 565 | 90 |

♦ *Yavapai County / Roland J. Chooljian / Roland J. Chooljian / 1991*

| 83⁶⁄₈ | 16¹⁄₈ | 16¹⁄₈ | 6⁴⁄₈ | 6⁴⁄₈ | 13⁵⁄₈ | 13⁶⁄₈ | 5⁴⁄₈ | 5⁶⁄₈ | 565 | 90 |

♦ *Yavapai County / Jerry T. Harper / Jerry T. Harper / 1992*

| 83⁴⁄₈ | 18¹⁄₈ | 17⁶⁄₈ | 6⁴⁄₈ | 6³⁄₈ | 16 | 14²⁄₈ | 5⁶⁄₈ | 5²⁄₈ | 624 | 98 |

♦ *Arizona / O. Patton / William N. Henry / 1956*

| 83⁴⁄₈ | 17 | 17 | 6⁴⁄₈ | 6⁴⁄₈ | 10²⁄₈ | 5⁷⁄₈ | 5 | 4⁶⁄₈ | 624 | 98 |

♦ *Navajo County / Mrs. Don Lambert / Mrs. Don Lambert / 1961*

| 83⁴⁄₈ | 17 | 17¹⁄₈ | 6⁵⁄₈ | 6⁶⁄₈ | 6²⁄₈ | 1³⁄₈ | 4⁵⁄₈ | 4⁶⁄₈ | 624 | 98 |

♦ *Coconino County / Cheryl Alderman / Cheryl Alderman / 1974*

| 83⁴⁄₈ | 17²⁄₈ | 17¹⁄₈ | 6²⁄₈ | 6³⁄₈ | 14⁶⁄₈ | 9⁵⁄₈ | 5⁵⁄₈ | 5⁶⁄₈ | 624 | 98 |

♦ *Coconino County / Thomas A. Dunlap / Thomas A. Dunlap / 1974*

| 83⁴⁄₈ | 17³⁄₈ | 17⁴⁄₈ | 6⁴⁄₈ | 6⁴⁄₈ | 13³⁄₈ | 11²⁄₈ | 4⁴⁄₈ | 4⁴⁄₈ | 624 | 98 |

♦ *Coconino County / Duane D. Backhaus / Duane D. Backhaus / 1984*

| 83⁴⁄₈ | 16²⁄₈ | 16³⁄₈ | 6⁴⁄₈ | 6⁴⁄₈ | 13²⁄₈ | 8⁵⁄₈ | 5⁴⁄₈ | 5¹⁄₈ | 624 | 98 |

♦ *Yavapai County / Glenn E. Leslie, Jr. / Glenn E. Leslie, Jr. / 1984*

| 83⁴⁄₈ | 17⁵⁄₈ | 17⁵⁄₈ | 6 | 6 | 10⁷⁄₈ | 8 | 5³⁄₈ | 5 | 624 | 98 |

♦ *Coconino County / Arthur A. Smith / Arthur A. Smith / 1984*

| 83²⁄₈ | 16⁷⁄₈ | 15²⁄₈ | 6⁴⁄₈ | 6⁴⁄₈ | 12 | 7⁴⁄₈ | 6²⁄₈ | 6⁴⁄₈ | 690 | 105 |

♦ *Coconino County / Vernon E. North / Vernon E. North / 1972*

| 83²⁄₈ | 17²⁄₈ | 17¹⁄₈ | 6⁷⁄₈ | 6²⁄₈ | 9⁴⁄₈ | 6²⁄₈ | 5 | 5⁴⁄₈ | 690 | 105 |

♦ *Coconino County / Russell Fischer / Russell Fischer / 1973*

| 83²⁄₈ | 17⁵⁄₈ | 17⁴⁄₈ | 6²⁄₈ | 6³⁄₈ | 12⁶⁄₈ | 6³⁄₈ | 4¹⁄₈ | 4⁴⁄₈ | 690 | 105 |

♦ *Yavapai County / J. Mike Foley / J. Mike Foley / 1975*

| 83²⁄₈ | 16³⁄₈ | 17 | 6⁷⁄₈ | 7 | 15⁴⁄₈ | 12⁶⁄₈ | 6⁵⁄₈ | 5¹⁄₈ | 690 | 105 |

♦ *Yavapai County / Ralph Koepke / Ralph Koepke / 1975*

| 83²⁄₈ | 17 | 17 | 6²⁄₈ | 6²⁄₈ | 15 | 11³⁄₈ | 5²⁄₈ | 5⁴⁄₈ | 690 | 105 |

♦ *Coconino County / Edmond C. Morton / Edmond C. Morton / 1975*

| 83²⁄₈ | 15⁶⁄₈ | 15⁶⁄₈ | 6⁴⁄₈ | 6⁴⁄₈ | 9 | 2⁶⁄₈ | 5²⁄₈ | 5 | 690 | 105 |

♦ *Cochise County / Keith L. Miller / Keith L. Miller / 1976*

| 83²⁄₈ | 16⁴⁄₈ | 16⁵⁄₈ | 6²⁄₈ | 6 | 11⁵⁄₈ | 8¹⁄₈ | 4⁷⁄₈ | 4⁷⁄₈ | 690 | 105 |

♦ *Coconino County / Gilbert S. Garside / Gilbert S. Garside / 1982*

| 83²⁄₈ | 17³⁄₈ | 17⁴⁄₈ | 7 | 6⁶⁄₈ | 12³⁄₈ | 7 | 5¹⁄₈ | 3⁶⁄₈ | 690 | 105 |

♦ *Apache County / Robert A. Stacy / Robert A. Stacy / 1983*

| 83²⁄₈ | 17¹⁄₈ | 17³⁄₈ | 6²⁄₈ | 6³⁄₈ | 12⁴⁄₈ | 6⁶⁄₈ | 4⁵⁄₈ | 4⁶⁄₈ | 690 | 105 |

♦ *Coconino County / Delroy Western / Delroy Western / 1983*

Score	Length of Horn		Circumference of Base		Inside Spread	Tip-to-Tip Spread	Length of Prong		All-Time Rank	State Rank
	R	L	R	L			R	L		
	♦ *Locality / Hunter / Owner / Date Killed*									
$83\frac{2}{8}$	$15\frac{6}{8}$	$15\frac{7}{8}$	$6\frac{2}{8}$	$6\frac{2}{8}$	$8\frac{5}{8}$	$4\frac{5}{8}$	$4\frac{5}{8}$	$4\frac{7}{8}$	690	105
	♦ *Coconino County / Matthew Dominy / Matthew Dominy / 1984*									
$83\frac{2}{8}$	$16\frac{2}{8}$	15	$6\frac{6}{8}$	$6\frac{4}{8}$	$11\frac{4}{8}$	$7\frac{3}{8}$	$6\frac{1}{8}$	6	690	105
	♦ *Cochise County / Jim Tomlin / Jim Tomlin / 1984*									
$83\frac{2}{8}$	18	$17\frac{4}{8}$	$6\frac{4}{8}$	$6\frac{3}{8}$	$10\frac{2}{8}$	$3\frac{4}{8}$	$4\frac{2}{8}$	6	690	105
	♦ *Cochise County / Neil G. Sutherland II / Neil G. Sutherland II / 1986*									
$83\frac{2}{8}$	$17\frac{1}{8}$	$17\frac{2}{8}$	$6\frac{2}{8}$	$6\frac{2}{8}$	$10\frac{1}{8}$	$4\frac{5}{8}$	$5\frac{6}{8}$	$5\frac{2}{8}$	690	105
	♦ *Coconino County / H. Keith Neitch / H. Keith Neitch / 1988*									
$83\frac{2}{8}$	$17\frac{7}{8}$	18	6	6	$11\frac{7}{8}$	$6\frac{2}{8}$	$4\frac{5}{8}$	$4\frac{5}{8}$	690	105
	♦ *Apache County / R. Steve Bass / R. Steve Bass / 1993*									
$83\frac{2}{8}$	$16\frac{3}{8}$	$16\frac{2}{8}$	$6\frac{1}{8}$	$6\frac{1}{8}$	$11\frac{5}{8}$	$9\frac{7}{8}$	$5\frac{1}{8}$	5	690	105
	♦ *Apache County / Susanne W. Queenan / Susanne W. Queenan / 1993*									
83	$15\frac{2}{8}$	$14\frac{7}{8}$	$6\frac{5}{8}$	$6\frac{4}{8}$	$12\frac{2}{8}$	$9\frac{1}{8}$	6	$5\frac{5}{8}$	775	120
	♦ *Heber / Grady L. Beard / Grady L. Beard / 1954*									
83	$18\frac{2}{8}$	$18\frac{2}{8}$	$6\frac{2}{8}$	$6\frac{3}{8}$	$12\frac{5}{8}$	$8\frac{3}{8}$	$4\frac{4}{8}$	$4\frac{2}{8}$	775	120
	♦ *Navajo County / Joseph R. Rencher / Joseph R. Rencher / 1970*									
83	$16\frac{5}{8}$	17	$6\frac{4}{8}$	$6\frac{3}{8}$	11	$6\frac{4}{8}$	$5\frac{7}{8}$	6	775	120
	♦ *Yavapai County / Artie L. Thrower / Artie L. Thrower / 1975*									
83	$17\frac{1}{8}$	17	$6\frac{4}{8}$	$6\frac{4}{8}$	$12\frac{1}{8}$	$8\frac{6}{8}$	$3\frac{7}{8}$	$4\frac{4}{8}$	775	120
	♦ *Graham County / Marvin R. Selke / Marvin R. Selke / 1987*									
83	17	$17\frac{2}{8}$	$6\frac{2}{8}$	$6\frac{2}{8}$	$15\frac{3}{8}$	$12\frac{2}{8}$	$5\frac{5}{8}$	$5\frac{5}{8}$	775	120
	♦ *Coconino County / Billie F. Bechtel / Billie F. Bechtel / 1988*									
83	$15\frac{6}{8}$	$16\frac{3}{8}$	$6\frac{2}{8}$	$6\frac{1}{8}$	$16\frac{5}{8}$	$15\frac{2}{8}$	6	6	775	120
	♦ *Navajo County / Ray V. Pogue / Ray V. Pogue / 1989*									
83	$17\frac{4}{8}$	$17\frac{4}{8}$	$6\frac{3}{8}$	$6\frac{1}{8}$	$9\frac{3}{8}$	$8\frac{1}{8}$	$5\frac{3}{8}$	$4\frac{6}{8}$	775	120
	♦ *Greenlee County / Paul E. Palmer / Paul E. Palmer / 1990*									
83	$17\frac{4}{8}$	$17\frac{2}{8}$	$6\frac{4}{8}$	$6\frac{6}{8}$	12	$7\frac{6}{8}$	5	$4\frac{7}{8}$	775	120
	♦ *Coconino County / Gene Sewell / Gene Sewell / 1991*									
83	$16\frac{2}{8}$	$16\frac{2}{8}$	$6\frac{7}{8}$	$6\frac{7}{8}$	$8\frac{1}{8}$	6	$4\frac{5}{8}$	$4\frac{4}{8}$	775	120
	♦ *Coconino County / Michael L. Allen / Michael L. Allen / 1991*									
$82\frac{6}{8}$	$17\frac{6}{8}$	$17\frac{4}{8}$	$6\frac{4}{8}$	$6\frac{4}{8}$	$13\frac{3}{8}$	$9\frac{4}{8}$	$4\frac{7}{8}$	$5\frac{2}{8}$	868	129
	♦ *Yavapai County / Vaughan Rock / Vaughan Rock / 1959*									
$82\frac{6}{8}$	$17\frac{6}{8}$	$17\frac{4}{8}$	6	6	$14\frac{2}{8}$	$9\frac{1}{8}$	$4\frac{6}{8}$	$4\frac{7}{8}$	868	129
	♦ *Ft. Apache Res. / Robert L. Martin / Robert L. Martin / 1965*									
$82\frac{6}{8}$	$17\frac{2}{8}$	$17\frac{3}{8}$	$6\frac{5}{8}$	$6\frac{6}{8}$	$8\frac{6}{8}$	$1\frac{6}{8}$	4	$4\frac{2}{8}$	868	129
	♦ *Round Mt. / Dennis L. Fife / Dennis L. Fife / 1967*									
$82\frac{6}{8}$	$15\frac{4}{8}$	$15\frac{3}{8}$	$6\frac{6}{8}$	$6\frac{5}{8}$	$10\frac{5}{8}$	$4\frac{3}{8}$	$6\frac{4}{8}$	$7\frac{1}{8}$	868	129
	♦ *Yavapai County / Roy T. Hume / Roy T. Hume / 1985*									

Score	Length of Horn R	L	Circumference of Base R	L	Inside Spread	Tip-to-Tip Spread	Length of Prong R	L	All-Time Rank	State Rank
82⅝	15⁶⁄₈	15⅝	6⅜	6²⁄₈	15⅞	13	6⅜	6²⁄₈	948	133

♦ Yavapai County / Joseph C. Cancilliere / Joseph C. Cancilliere / 1984

82⁴⁄₈	16⅞	16⁶⁄₈	6⅛	6⅛	10	6⅞	5⁴⁄₈	5⁴⁄₈	949	134

♦ Seligman / Cleo E. Wallace / Cleo E. Wallace / 1959

82⁴⁄₈	17	17	6²⁄₈	6²⁄₈	10⁴⁄₈	6⅜	5⁴⁄₈	5	949	134

♦ Springerville / Malcolm Silvia / Malcolm Silvia / 1962

82⁴⁄₈	16⅝	16⁶⁄₈	6²⁄₈	6²⁄₈	10⅝	7⅜	5⁴⁄₈	5⁴⁄₈	949	134

♦ Seligman / Glenn Olson / Glenn Olson / 1965

82⁴⁄₈	17²⁄₈	17⅛	6⁴⁄₈	6⁴⁄₈	10²⁄₈	5	5	4⁶⁄₈	949	134

♦ Coconino County / Robert J. Hallock / Robert J. Hallock / 1973

82⁴⁄₈	17	17²⁄₈	6²⁄₈	6²⁄₈	11⁶⁄₈	7⁶⁄₈	5⅜	5	949	134

♦ Coconino County / David S. Hibbert / David S. Hibbert / 1976

82⁴⁄₈	15⅝	15⅜	6⁴⁄₈	6⁴⁄₈	8	3⁶⁄₈	6	5⁶⁄₈	949	134

♦ Navajo County / Perry H. Finger / Perry H. Finger / 1984

82⁴⁄₈	17⅛	15⁴⁄₈	6⁴⁄₈	6⁴⁄₈	8⅝	6²⁄₈	6	5⅞	949	134

♦ Yavapai County / Chris Skoczylas / Chris Skoczylas / 1988

82⁴⁄₈	15⁶⁄₈	15⁶⁄₈	6²⁄₈	6⁴⁄₈	9²⁄₈	3	5⁴⁄₈	5⅝	949	134

♦ Graham County / Daniel C. Hicks / Daniel C. Hicks / 1989

82²⁄₈	17⁴⁄₈	17⅜	6⁴⁄₈	6⅜	14⅛	10	4²⁄₈	4⁴⁄₈	1058	142

♦ Anderson Mesa / Roy Stevens / Roy Stevens / 1953

82²⁄₈	16⅝	16²⁄₈	6²⁄₈	6⅛	13²⁄₈	10⅜	5⅝	5⅝	1058	142

♦ Williams / Fred Udine / Fred Udine / 1959

82²⁄₈	16²⁄₈	16⅝	6⁴⁄₈	6⅝	13	8⅜	5⁴⁄₈	5⁴⁄₈	1058	142

♦ Coconino County / William L. Butler / William L. Butler / 1973

82²⁄₈	16²⁄₈	16²⁄₈	6⅝	6⅝	12²⁄₈	8	5⁶⁄₈	5⁶⁄₈	1058	142

♦ Apache County / Richard L. Simmons, Sr. / Richard L. Simmons, Sr. / 1978

82²⁄₈	16	16	6⅛	6⅛	10²⁄₈	6	6	6	1058	142

♦ Navajo County / Collins L. Cochran / Collins L. Cochran / 1983

82²⁄₈	16⅝	16²⁄₈	6⁶⁄₈	6⁴⁄₈	15	11	5	5⅛	1058	142

♦ Navajo County / A.T. Boultinghouse / John L. Stein / 1983

82²⁄₈	15⁶⁄₈	15⁶⁄₈	6⅜	6⅜	10⅜	4⁶⁄₈	6⅛	6²⁄₈	1058	142

♦ Mohave County / Ronald D. Wood / Ronald D. Wood / 1987

82²⁄₈	15⅛	15⅞	7⅛	7	10⁶⁄₈	8²⁄₈	5⅛	5⅜	1058	142

♦ Coconino County / Dale H. Haggard / Dale H. Haggard / 1991

82²⁄₈	16⅝	16⁴⁄₈	6	5⅞	10²⁄₈	4⅜	6²⁄₈	6	1058	142

♦ Coconino County / Charles M. Wiedmaier / Charles M. Wiedmaier / 1993

82	16²⁄₈	15⁶⁄₈	6⁴⁄₈	6⁴⁄₈	11	7²⁄₈	5	5²⁄₈	1157	151

♦ Mormon Lake / Bob Housholder / Bob Housholder / 1949

Score	Length of Horn		Circumference of Base		Inside Spread	Tip-to-Tip Spread	Length of Prong		All-Time Rank	State Rank
	R	L	R	L			R	L		
◆ Locality / Hunter / Owner / Date Killed										
82	$17\frac{7}{8}$	$17\frac{4}{8}$	$6\frac{5}{8}$	$6\frac{5}{8}$	16	$11\frac{7}{8}$	$3\frac{5}{8}$	$3\frac{4}{8}$	1157	151
◆ Williams / Paul D. Hosman / Paul D. Hosman / 1951										
82	$15\frac{4}{8}$	$15\frac{5}{8}$	$6\frac{5}{8}$	$6\frac{4}{8}$	$16\frac{3}{8}$	$14\frac{2}{8}$	$6\frac{2}{8}$	$5\frac{6}{8}$	1157	151
◆ Navajo County / Joe D. Sutton / Joe D. Sutton / 1951										
82	$16\frac{1}{8}$	$15\frac{6}{8}$	$6\frac{7}{8}$	$6\frac{7}{8}$	$11\frac{4}{8}$	5	$5\frac{2}{8}$	$4\frac{7}{8}$	1157	151
◆ Anderson Mesa / Mrs. C.C. Cooper / Mrs. C.C. Cooper / 1953										
82	$16\frac{1}{8}$	16	$6\frac{6}{8}$	$6\frac{6}{8}$	$12\frac{7}{8}$	$11\frac{4}{8}$	$5\frac{2}{8}$	$5\frac{3}{8}$	1157	151
◆ Navajo County / John Welch III / John Welch III / 1965										
82	17	$17\frac{2}{8}$	$6\frac{2}{8}$	$6\frac{1}{8}$	$11\frac{2}{8}$	$5\frac{4}{8}$	$5\frac{6}{8}$	$5\frac{7}{8}$	1157	151
◆ Coconino County / Jerry R. Killman / Jerry R. Killman / 1973										
82	$16\frac{3}{8}$	$16\frac{2}{8}$	$6\frac{3}{8}$	$6\frac{4}{8}$	$9\frac{6}{8}$	$3\frac{5}{8}$	$5\frac{5}{8}$	$5\frac{5}{8}$	1157	151
◆ Coconino County / Fred W. Fernow, Jr. / Fred W. Fernow, Jr. / 1981										
82	16	$15\frac{7}{8}$	$6\frac{2}{8}$	$6\frac{3}{8}$	$9\frac{6}{8}$	5	5	$5\frac{3}{8}$	1157	151
◆ Coconino County / Charles L. Holland / Charles L. Holland / 1984										
82	$17\frac{4}{8}$	18	$5\frac{6}{8}$	$5\frac{6}{8}$	18	$16\frac{2}{8}$	$4\frac{6}{8}$	$4\frac{5}{8}$	1157	151
◆ Graham County / James P. Kniffin / James P. Kniffin / 1987										
82	$16\frac{1}{8}$	16	$6\frac{6}{8}$	$6\frac{5}{8}$	$11\frac{6}{8}$	$7\frac{5}{8}$	6	$5\frac{3}{8}$	1157	151
◆ Apache County / Leonard J. Imperial / Leonard J. Imperial / 1987										
82	$15\frac{4}{8}$	$15\frac{6}{8}$	6	$6\frac{1}{8}$	$10\frac{2}{8}$	$4\frac{1}{8}$	6	$5\frac{4}{8}$	1157	151
◆ Mohave County / Jeff K. Gunnell / Jeff K. Gunnell / 1989										
82	$16\frac{4}{8}$	$16\frac{4}{8}$	$6\frac{5}{8}$	$6\frac{5}{8}$	7	$2\frac{3}{8}$	$4\frac{1}{8}$	$4\frac{1}{8}$	1157	151
◆ Cochise County / Brad Wedding / Brad Wedding / 1991										
82	$14\frac{6}{8}$	$14\frac{6}{8}$	$6\frac{2}{8}$	$6\frac{2}{8}$	$6\frac{3}{8}$	$1\frac{3}{8}$	$4\frac{2}{8}$	$4\frac{3}{8}$	1157	151
◆ Apache County / Shane D. Koury / Shane D. Koury / 1993										
82	$17\frac{4}{8}$	$17\frac{3}{8}$	6	$6\frac{1}{8}$	$15\frac{2}{8}$	$9\frac{2}{8}$	5	$5\frac{1}{8}$	1157	151
◆ Navajo County / Earl A. Petznick, Jr. / Earl A. Petznick, Jr. / 1994										
$81\frac{2}{8}$	$15\frac{6}{8}$	$15\frac{6}{8}$	$6\frac{1}{8}$	6	$11\frac{2}{8}$	$6\frac{5}{8}$	5	$4\frac{4}{8}$	1290	165
◆ Apache County / Lloyd L. Parker / Lloyd L. Parker / 1985										
$80\frac{6}{8}$	$17\frac{7}{8}$	$17\frac{3}{8}$	6	6	$14\frac{6}{8}$	$10\frac{3}{8}$	$4\frac{1}{8}$	$4\frac{1}{8}$	1327	166
◆ Yavapai County / Howard N. Woodruff / Howard N. Woodruff / 1992										
$80\frac{4}{8}$	$16\frac{4}{8}$	$16\frac{5}{8}$	6	$5\frac{6}{8}$	$9\frac{1}{8}$	$2\frac{5}{8}$	6	6	1345	167
◆ Mohave County / Charles A. Grimmett / Charles A. Grimmett / 1984										
$80\frac{4}{8}$	16	$15\frac{2}{8}$	$6\frac{2}{8}$	$6\frac{3}{8}$	$9\frac{4}{8}$	$5\frac{1}{8}$	$5\frac{4}{8}$	$5\frac{3}{8}$	1345	167
◆ Apache County / Paul G. Neely / Paul G. Neely / 1991										
$80\frac{4}{8}$	$16\frac{4}{8}$	$16\frac{5}{8}$	$6\frac{3}{8}$	$6\frac{3}{8}$	$10\frac{2}{8}$	$5\frac{6}{8}$	$5\frac{1}{8}$	5	1345	167
◆ Coconino County / Barbara J. Rackley / Barbara J. Rackley / 1993										
$80\frac{2}{8}$	$16\frac{5}{8}$	$16\frac{7}{8}$	$6\frac{4}{8}$	$6\frac{4}{8}$	$10\frac{4}{8}$	$5\frac{4}{8}$	$4\frac{4}{8}$	4	1360	170
◆ Coconino County / Noel S. Allen / Noel S. Allen / 1989										

ARIZONA PRONGHORN *(continued)*

Score	Length of Horn		Circumference of Base		Inside Spread	Tip-to-Tip Spread	Length of Prong		All-Time Rank	State Rank
	R	L	R	L			R	L		
	◆ *Locality / Hunter / Owner / Date Killed*									
80²⁄₈	15³⁄₈	15²⁄₈	6⁷⁄₈	6⁷⁄₈	12²⁄₈	8³⁄₈	5⁴⁄₈	4⁷⁄₈	1360	170
	◆ *Yavapai County / David A. Miller / David A. Miller / 1993*									
80	16⁴⁄₈	16⁴⁄₈	6⁴⁄₈	6³⁄₈	13¹⁄₈	10	4⁶⁄₈	4⁷⁄₈	1386	172
	◆ *Coconino County / Kenneth D. Smith / Kenneth D. Smith / 1990*									

Photograph Courtesy of Craig R. Johnson

Craig R. Johnson, past president of the Foundation for North American Wild Sheep, and the records book pronghorn he shot in Yavapai County, Arizona, in 1993. In spite of a broken horn tip that's missing one inch, this buck still scores 85 points.

Photograph Courtesy of George W. Conant

CALIFORNIA STATE RECORD
PRONGHORN
SCORE: 89
Locality: Lassen Co.   Date: Picked Up 1985
Owner: George W. Conant

CALIFORNIA

PRONGHORN

Score	Length of Horn R	Length of Horn L	Circumference of Base R	Circumference of Base L	Inside Spread	Tip-to-Tip Spread	Length of Prong R	Length of Prong L	All-Time Rank	State Rank
♦ *Locality / Hunter / Owner / Date Killed*										
89	17	16 3/8	7 2/8	7 1/8	11	5 2/8	6 5/8	6 5/8	36	1
♦ *Lassen County / Picked Up / George W. Conant / 1985*										
87 4/8	16	17 4/8	7 1/8	7	11 2/8	12	6	6 4/8	79	2
♦ *Modoc County / Lynn M. Greene / Lynn M. Greene / 1971*										
87 4/8	17 2/8	17 2/8	6 3/8	6 3/8	9 4/8	2 4/8	6 5/8	6 5/8	79	2
♦ *Modoc County / Ron L. Reasor / Ron L. Reasor / 1979*										
86	16	15 6/8	7	6 6/8	13 4/8	10 6/8	6 1/8	6 2/8	182	4
♦ *Lassen County / David A. Tye / David A. Tye / 1987*										
85 4/8	16	16	6 6/8	6 6/8	8 4/8	3 7/8	6 1/8	6	238	5
♦ *Lassen County / Jeff R. Rogers / Jeff R. Rogers / 1990*										
84 6/8	15 7/8	16 1/8	7 3/8	7 3/8	7	1	6 2/8	5 6/8	336	6
♦ *Modoc County / William A. Shaw / William A. Shaw / 1942*										
84 6/8	16 5/8	17	6 2/8	6 2/8	10 4/8	5 1/8	6 5/8	6 5/8	336	6
♦ *Modoc County / Leland C. Lehman / Leland C. Lehman / 1969*										
84 6/8	16 6/8	16 5/8	6 1/8	6 1/8	9 7/8	5	6 3/8	6 1/8	336	6
♦ *Modoc County / Earnest Anacleto / Earnest Anacleto / 1980*										
84 6/8	16 4/8	16 5/8	6 4/8	6 4/8	11 1/8	6 3/8	6 3/8	7 1/8	336	6
♦ *Lassen County / Gary Caraccioli / Gary Caraccioli / 1990*										
84 4/8	17 1/8	16 6/8	6 2/8	6 3/8	15 6/8	13 7/8	6 3/8	6 7/8	390	10
♦ *Modoc County / J. Bob Johnson / J. Bob Johnson / 1978*										
84 2/8	15 4/8	15 5/8	7 1/8	7	9	9 6/8	4 6/8	4 5/8	436	11
♦ *Modoc County / Unknown / Jess Jones / PR 1978*										
84 2/8	15 5/8	16 1/8	6 2/8	6 2/8	9 1/8	5 2/8	6 2/8	6 7/8	436	11
♦ *Modoc County / Larry A. Owens, Sr. / Larry A. Owens, Sr. / 1981*										
84 2/8	17 3/8	17	6 2/8	6 2/8	9 3/8	3 2/8	6 6/8	6 4/8	436	11
♦ *Modoc County / Don Perrien / Don Perrien / 1994*										
84	16 3/8	16 1/8	6 7/8	6 6/8	11	5 4/8	6	6	500	14
♦ *Lassen County / Al J. Accurso, Jr. / Al J. Accurso, Jr. / 1986*										
84	14 7/8	15 6/8	7	6 7/8	13 1/8	10 2/8	7 4/8	7	500	14
♦ *Lassen County / Larry R. Brower / Larry R. Brower / 1990*										
83 6/8	16 6/8	16 6/8	6 4/8	6 1/8	7 1/8	2	6 4/8	6 4/8	565	16
♦ *Modoc County / William B. Steig / William B. Steig / 1977*										
83 4/8	15 6/8	15 6/8	7 1/8	7	11 5/8	7 6/8	6 3/8	6 1/8	624	17
♦ *Lassen County / Jason W. Langslet / Jason W. Langslet / 1994*										
83 2/8	14 2/8	14 6/8	6 6/8	6 6/8	10 5/8	5 5/8	7 2/8	7	690	18
♦ *Modoc County / David T. Eveland / David T. Eveland / 1990*										

Score	Length of Horn		Circumference of Base		Inside Spread	Tip-to-Tip Spread	Length of Prong		All-Time Rank	State Rank
	R	L	R	L			R	L		
◆ Locality / Hunter / Owner / Date Killed										
83²⁄₈	15⁵⁄₈	15³⁄₈	6³⁄₈	6³⁄₈	12⅛	11⁵⁄₈	6⁶⁄₈	6⁴⁄₈	690	18
◆ Lassen County / Timothy L. Hartin / Timothy L. Hartin / 1992										
83	16⁵⁄₈	16⁶⁄₈	6⁴⁄₈	6²⁄₈	11⅞	7⅞	5²⁄₈	5	775	20
◆ Modoc County / Richard Bishop / Richard Bishop / 1986										
82⁶⁄₈	16³⁄₈	16	6²⁄₈	6²⁄₈	13	7⁴⁄₈	6	5²⁄₈	868	21
◆ Modoc County / Dennis McClelland / Dennis McClelland / 1977										
82⁶⁄₈	16	15⁷⁄₈	6⁴⁄₈	6⁴⁄₈	10⁵⁄₈	7⁶⁄₈	7	6⁵⁄₈	868	21
◆ Modoc County / Mary L. Crabtree / Mary L. Crabtree / 1992										
82⁶⁄₈	16⁶⁄₈	16⁶⁄₈	6⁵⁄₈	6⁵⁄₈	14⅛	10⁶⁄₈	5⁶⁄₈	5⁶⁄₈	868	21
◆ Modoc County / Kevin D. Fabiq / Kevin D. Fabiq / 1992										
82⁴⁄₈	17⅛	17	6⅛	6	8	3⅛	6	6	949	24
◆ California / Bill Foster / Foster's Bighorn Rest. / 1930										
82⁴⁄₈	15³⁄₈	15³⁄₈	6⁴⁄₈	6³⁄₈	13⁵⁄₈	10⁴⁄₈	6³⁄₈	7	949	24
◆ Lassen County / Brad L. Ayotte / Brad L. Ayotte / 1977										
82⁴⁄₈	15⁴⁄₈	15²⁄₈	6⁶⁄₈	6⁵⁄₈	12²⁄₈	7⅛	5⁵⁄₈	5⁶⁄₈	949	24
◆ Modoc County / Mark Hansen / Mark Hansen / 1978										
82⁴⁄₈	16²⁄₈	16³⁄₈	7	6⁷⁄₈	8⅛	6²⁄₈	5⁵⁄₈	5³⁄₈	949	24
◆ Siskiyou County / Rodney F. Royer / Rodney F. Royer / 1979										
82⁴⁄₈	16⁴⁄₈	16⁶⁄₈	6⁵⁄₈	6³⁄₈	12⅛	7	4⁷⁄₈	4⁷⁄₈	949	24
◆ Lassen County / Bob Freed / Bob Freed / 1985										
82²⁄₈	15⁶⁄₈	16	6⅛	6⅛	12⁴⁄₈	9	6⁴⁄₈	7	1058	29
◆ Lassen County / Del S. Oliver / Del S. Oliver / 1978										
82²⁄₈	17³⁄₈	16⁷⁄₈	6²⁄₈	6	11⅞	9⁴⁄₈	6²⁄₈	5⁵⁄₈	1058	29
◆ Siskiyou County / Laird E. Marshall / Laird E. Marshall / 1984										
82²⁄₈	18⅞	19⁴⁄₈	5⁶⁄₈	5⁶⁄₈	17⅞	15⁴⁄₈	4⁵⁄₈	4⁵⁄₈	1058	29
◆ Modoc County / Rod Eisenbeis / Rod Eisenbeis / 1991										
82	16⅛	16⅛	6⁵⁄₈	6⁴⁄₈	12⁶⁄₈	7³⁄₈	5⁵⁄₈	5⁵⁄₈	1157	32
◆ Lassen County / Robert D. Luna, Jr. / Robert D. Luna, Jr. / 1979										
82	15³⁄₈	15⁴⁄₈	6⁵⁄₈	6³⁄₈	12	8⅞	4⁵⁄₈	4³⁄₈	1157	32
◆ Lassen County / Tommy B. Esperance / Tommy B. Esperance / 1991										
82	15⁴⁄₈	15	7²⁄₈	7³⁄₈	10⁶⁄₈	7³⁄₈	4⁶⁄₈	4³⁄₈	1157	32
◆ Lassen County / Joseph D. Nolan / Joseph D. Nolan / 1991										

Photograph Courtesy of Jennifer C. Flaherty

Jennifer C. Flaherty scored big in Apache County, Arizona, in 1990 when she was successful in drawing one of the coveted pronghorn permits. This buck scores 86 points.

Photograph by Ray Glaser

COLORADO NUMBER THREE
PRONGHORN
SCORE: 86⅝
Locality: Bent Co.   Date: 1992
Hunter: Rodney D. Glaser

COLORADO
PRONGHORN

Score	Length of Horn		Circumference of Base		Inside Spread	Tip-to-Tip Spread	Length of Prong		All-Time Rank	State Rank
	R	L	R	L			R	L		
$91\frac{4}{8}$	$15\frac{1}{8}$	$15\frac{2}{8}$	$7\frac{7}{8}$	$7\frac{7}{8}$	$10\frac{4}{8}$	$9\frac{4}{8}$	7	7	5	1
◆ Weld County / Bob Schneidmiller / Bob Schneidmiller / 1965										
$89\frac{2}{8}$	$17\frac{1}{8}$	$17\frac{1}{8}$	7	7	$7\frac{6}{8}$	$1\frac{5}{8}$	6	6	28	2
◆ Moffat County / Gerald Scott / Gerald Scott / 1982										
$86\frac{6}{8}$	$16\frac{2}{8}$	$16\frac{4}{8}$	$7\frac{5}{8}$	$7\frac{5}{8}$	11	$7\frac{2}{8}$	6	$6\frac{4}{8}$	114	3
◆ Bent County / Rodney D. Glaser / Rodney D. Glaser / 1992										
$86\frac{4}{8}$	$16\frac{7}{8}$	$16\frac{7}{8}$	$6\frac{5}{8}$	$6\frac{5}{8}$	$10\frac{5}{8}$	$10\frac{5}{8}$	6	$5\frac{4}{8}$	140	4
◆ Moffat County / Joseph R. Maynard / Joseph R. Maynard / 1972										
$86\frac{2}{8}$	$16\frac{5}{8}$	17	$7\frac{5}{8}$	$7\frac{2}{8}$	$14\frac{3}{8}$	$8\frac{1}{8}$	$5\frac{2}{8}$	$5\frac{1}{8}$	155	5
◆ El Paso County / Maurice Cutting / Maurice Cutting / 1981										
$84\frac{6}{8}$	$16\frac{3}{8}$	$16\frac{3}{8}$	7	$7\frac{1}{8}$	11	$5\frac{1}{8}$	$5\frac{6}{8}$	$5\frac{7}{8}$	336	6
◆ Moffat County / James C. MacLachlan / James C. MacLachlan / 1975										
$84\frac{2}{8}$	$15\frac{7}{8}$	$15\frac{7}{8}$	$6\frac{7}{8}$	$6\frac{6}{8}$	$9\frac{2}{8}$	$4\frac{6}{8}$	$6\frac{5}{8}$	$7\frac{1}{8}$	436	7
◆ Weld County / M. Wayne Hoeben / M. Wayne Hoeben / 1989										
$84\frac{2}{8}$	$15\frac{6}{8}$	16	7	$6\frac{7}{8}$	$7\frac{2}{8}$	$2\frac{2}{8}$	$6\frac{3}{8}$	$6\frac{1}{8}$	436	7
◆ Jackson County / Jerrald L. Copple / Jerrald L. Copple / 1991										
84	$16\frac{4}{8}$	$16\frac{3}{8}$	$6\frac{6}{8}$	$6\frac{4}{8}$	8	3	$5\frac{3}{8}$	$5\frac{2}{8}$	500	9
◆ Washington County / Christian Heyden / Christian Heyden / 1967										
84	$16\frac{3}{8}$	$16\frac{1}{8}$	$7\frac{2}{8}$	$7\frac{2}{8}$	$9\frac{4}{8}$	$3\frac{6}{8}$	$5\frac{5}{8}$	$5\frac{5}{8}$	500	9
◆ Jackson County / Barry A. Weaver / Barry A. Weaver / 1993										
$83\frac{6}{8}$	$15\frac{6}{8}$	$15\frac{7}{8}$	$6\frac{2}{8}$	$6\frac{2}{8}$	11	$7\frac{6}{8}$	6	$6\frac{1}{8}$	565	11
◆ Jackson County / Cylestine A. Manguso / Cylestine A. Manguso / 1983										
$83\frac{4}{8}$	16	$15\frac{7}{8}$	$6\frac{4}{8}$	$6\frac{4}{8}$	$10\frac{5}{8}$	$5\frac{7}{8}$	7	$6\frac{6}{8}$	624	12
◆ Boone / Mahlon T. White / Mahlon T. White / 1966										
$83\frac{4}{8}$	$15\frac{5}{8}$	$15\frac{7}{8}$	$7\frac{2}{8}$	$7\frac{1}{8}$	$11\frac{1}{8}$	$7\frac{1}{8}$	$5\frac{2}{8}$	$5\frac{4}{8}$	624	12
◆ Craig / Albert Johnson / Albert Johnson / 1969										
$83\frac{4}{8}$	$14\frac{1}{8}$	$14\frac{2}{8}$	$6\frac{5}{8}$	$6\frac{5}{8}$	$8\frac{5}{8}$	4	$6\frac{3}{8}$	$6\frac{2}{8}$	624	12
◆ Jackson County / Cynthia L. Welle / Cynthia L. Welle / 1982										
$83\frac{4}{8}$	$15\frac{6}{8}$	$15\frac{6}{8}$	7	7	$8\frac{5}{8}$	$3\frac{2}{8}$	$5\frac{5}{8}$	$5\frac{5}{8}$	624	12
◆ Moffat County / Brad A. Winder / Brad A. Winder / 1990										
$83\frac{4}{8}$	$15\frac{2}{8}$	$14\frac{4}{8}$	$6\frac{7}{8}$	$6\frac{7}{8}$	$10\frac{4}{8}$	$9\frac{5}{8}$	5	5	624	12
◆ Weld County / Delmar C. Brewer / Delmar C. Brewer / 1993										
$83\frac{2}{8}$	$14\frac{5}{8}$	$14\frac{5}{8}$	7	$6\frac{6}{8}$	$9\frac{5}{8}$	$7\frac{1}{8}$	$5\frac{1}{8}$	$5\frac{1}{8}$	690	17
◆ Jackson County / James R. Mosman / James R. Mosman / 1975										
83	$16\frac{2}{8}$	$16\frac{5}{8}$	$6\frac{7}{8}$	$6\frac{6}{8}$	$8\frac{7}{8}$	$3\frac{7}{8}$	$5\frac{5}{8}$	$5\frac{5}{8}$	775	18
◆ Boyero / Henry H. Zietz / Henry H. Zietz / 1965										

Score	Length of Horn		Circumference of Base		Inside Spread	Tip-to-Tip Spread	Length of Prong		All-Time Rank	State Rank
	R	L	R	L			R	L		
	♦ *Locality / Hunter / Owner / Date Killed*									
83	16⁶⁄₈	17¹⁄₈	6⁵⁄₈	6⁵⁄₈	14⁴⁄₈	13⁷⁄₈	5⁴⁄₈	4³⁄₈	775	18
	♦ *Thatcher / M.A. May / M.A. May / 1965*									
83	16¹⁄₈	16²⁄₈	6⁴⁄₈	6²⁄₈	8⁷⁄₈	8	6⁴⁄₈	6⁵⁄₈	775	18
	♦ *Moffat County / Michael Coleman / Michael Coleman / 1971*									
83	16¹⁄₈	16⁴⁄₈	6⁴⁄₈	6⁴⁄₈	15	14²⁄₈	5²⁄₈	5³⁄₈	775	18
	♦ *Washington County / Gina R. Cass / Gina R. Cass / 1979*									
83	12⁶⁄₈	13	7	7	9⁶⁄₈	9³⁄₈	5⁴⁄₈	5⁷⁄₈	775	18
	♦ *Jackson County / Charles J. Cesar / Charles J. Cesar / 1985*									
83	17²⁄₈	16²⁄₈	6⁶⁄₈	6⁴⁄₈	11³⁄₈	9⁶⁄₈	5²⁄₈	5⁷⁄₈	775	18
	♦ *Moffat County / Marvin L. Shepard / Marvin L. Shepard / 1987*									
83	15⁶⁄₈	15⁶⁄₈	6⁶⁄₈	6⁷⁄₈	5⁴⁄₈	8⁴⁄₈	5⁶⁄₈	5²⁄₈	775	18
	♦ *Jackson County / Douglas A. Weimer / Douglas A. Weimer / 1988*									
83	16⁴⁄₈	16⁴⁄₈	6⁵⁄₈	6⁴⁄₈	15⁷⁄₈	15³⁄₈	5⁴⁄₈	5²⁄₈	775	18
	♦ *Moffat County / Mike Wallers / Mike Wallers / 1989*									
83	16³⁄₈	17	7⁵⁄₈	7⁵⁄₈	7⁴⁄₈	1⁶⁄₈	5¹⁄₈	4⁴⁄₈	775	18
	♦ *Weld County / Gregory A. Peters / Gregory A. Peters / 1993*									
83	16	16	6⁶⁄₈	6⁶⁄₈	8⁷⁄₈	7²⁄₈	5¹⁄₈	5	775	18
	♦ *Las Animas County / Mike R. Caldarella / Mike R. Caldarella / 1993*									
82⁶⁄₈	15¹⁄₈	15²⁄₈	6⁵⁄₈	6⁷⁄₈	10⁵⁄₈	8⁶⁄₈	6¹⁄₈	5⁶⁄₈	868	28
	♦ *Rocky Ford / Henry A. Helmke / Henry A. Helmke / 1967*									
82⁶⁄₈	15⁵⁄₈	16³⁄₈	6³⁄₈	6³⁄₈	10⁶⁄₈	5⁶⁄₈	6⁴⁄₈	6⁵⁄₈	868	28
	♦ *Weld County / Chester N. Erwin / Ronald G. Erwin / 1978*									
82⁶⁄₈	16²⁄₈	16⁴⁄₈	6⁵⁄₈	6³⁄₈	12⁴⁄₈	9³⁄₈	6¹⁄₈	5⁶⁄₈	868	28
	♦ *Larimer County / James D. Brink / James D. Brink / 1986*									
82⁴⁄₈	16³⁄₈	16⁶⁄₈	7⁵⁄₈	7⁵⁄₈	10²⁄₈	4¹⁄₈	4⁶⁄₈	5	949	31
	♦ *Park County / Mrs. Cotton Gordon / Mrs. Cotton Gordon / 1964*									
82⁴⁄₈	15³⁄₈	15²⁄₈	6⁵⁄₈	6³⁄₈	8⁷⁄₈	4⁶⁄₈	6⁴⁄₈	6²⁄₈	949	31
	♦ *Moffat County / Charles W. Klaassens / Charles W. Klaassens / 1981*									
82⁴⁄₈	15	15	6⁶⁄₈	7	13³⁄₈	10⁵⁄₈	6⁶⁄₈	6³⁄₈	949	31
	♦ *Saguache County / Michael J. Atwood, Sr. / Michael J. Atwood, Sr. / 1986*									
82⁴⁄₈	14²⁄₈	14²⁄₈	6⁶⁄₈	6⁶⁄₈	13⁵⁄₈	12⁶⁄₈	5⁴⁄₈	5⁵⁄₈	949	31
	♦ *Jackson County / Loren D. Reid / Loren D. Reid / 1989*									
82⁴⁄₈	15⁴⁄₈	15⁶⁄₈	6⁵⁄₈	6⁵⁄₈	8²⁄₈	3⁷⁄₈	6¹⁄₈	6⁴⁄₈	949	31
	♦ *Moffat County / S. Wayne Olson / S. Wayne Olson / 1991*									
82⁴⁄₈	16	16	6³⁄₈	6²⁄₈	6⁵⁄₈	1⁶⁄₈	6	6	949	31
	♦ *Moffat County / Brad A. Winder / Brad A. Winder / 1992*									
82⁴⁄₈	16	16¹⁄₈	6³⁄₈	6³⁄₈	8¹⁄₈	2⁶⁄₈	5³⁄₈	5³⁄₈	949	31
	♦ *Moffat County / Brad A. Winder / Brad A. Winder / 1994*									

Score	Length of Horn		Circumference of Base		Inside Spread	Tip-to-Tip Spread	Length of Prong		All-Time Rank	State Rank
	R	L	R	L			R	L		
◆ Locality / Hunter / Owner / Date Killed										
82²⁄₈	17²⁄₈	17²⁄₈	6²⁄₈	6²⁄₈	11³⁄₈	5⁵⁄₈	5⁴⁄₈	5⁴⁄₈	1058	38
◆ Weld County / James Gertson, Jr. / Howard E. Bates / 1955										
82²⁄₈	14⁷⁄₈	15	6⁴⁄₈	6⁵⁄₈	9¹⁄₈	5⁶⁄₈	6²⁄₈	6²⁄₈	1058	38
◆ Weld County / Mrs. Paul Goodwin / Mrs. Paul Goodwin / 1967										
82²⁄₈	16	15⁶⁄₈	6²⁄₈	6¹⁄₈	13²⁄₈	10	6	5⁴⁄₈	1058	38
◆ Morgan County / Kenneth L. Kelly / Kenneth L. Kelly / 1977										
82	15²⁄₈	15²⁄₈	7	7	14⁶⁄₈	12³⁄₈	5⁶⁄₈	5³⁄₈	1157	41
◆ Limon / Walt Paulk / Walt Paulk / 1958										
81²⁄₈	15	14⁷⁄₈	6²⁄₈	6²⁄₈	10⁴⁄₈	6⁴⁄₈	5	4⁷⁄₈	1290	42
◆ Baca County / Charles A. Grimmett / Charles A. Grimmett / 1989										
81	14⁶⁄₈	14⁶⁄₈	6⁴⁄₈	6⁴⁄₈	9³⁄₈	7	6⁴⁄₈	6¹⁄₈	1310	43
◆ Moffat County / Terry N. Oman / Terry N. Oman / 1991										
80⁴⁄₈	14¹⁄₈	14¹⁄₈	7	7	10¹⁄₈	8³⁄₈	5²⁄₈	5³⁄₈	1345	44
◆ Jackson County / Beryl J. Palmer / Beryl J. Palmer / 1991										
80⁴⁄₈	15⁴⁄₈	15⁵⁄₈	6¹⁄₈	6¹⁄₈	12⁴⁄₈	9⁵⁄₈	5³⁄₈	5⁶⁄₈	1345	44
◆ Park County / Joseph D. Malik / Joseph D. Malik / 1991										
80⁴⁄₈	17¹⁄₈	17¹⁄₈	6²⁄₈	6²⁄₈	10⁶⁄₈	7⁶⁄₈	3⁶⁄₈	3¹⁄₈	1345	44
◆ Park County / Tracy L. Downare / Tracy L. Downare / 1993										
80²⁄₈	14⁶⁄₈	14⁶⁄₈	6⁷⁄₈	6⁶⁄₈	10⁵⁄₈	8⁴⁄₈	6	5⁷⁄₈	1360	47
◆ Moffat County / Pamela S. Coburn / Pamela S. Coburn / 1993										

IDAHO STATE RECORD (TIE)
PRONGHORN
SCORE: 86⅝
Locality: Blaine Co.   Date: 1992
Hunter: Johnny Unser

IDAHO

PRONGHORN

Score	Length of Horn R	L	Circumference of Base R	L	Inside Spread	Tip-to-Tip Spread	Length of Prong R	L	All-Time Rank	State Rank
◆ Locality / Hunter / Owner / Date Killed										
86⁶⁄₈	16²⁄₈	17	7	7	8¹⁄₈	3⁴⁄₈	6⁵⁄₈	6¹⁄₈	114	1
◆ Jefferson County / Dale Nealis / Dale Nealis / 1961										
86⁶⁄₈	16⁶⁄₈	16⁶⁄₈	6⁴⁄₈	6⁴⁄₈	7⁷⁄₈	4⁴⁄₈	6²⁄₈	6¹⁄₈	114	1
◆ Blaine County / Johnny Unser / Johnny Unser / 1992										
85⁴⁄₈	17⁷⁄₈	17³⁄₈	6³⁄₈	6¹⁄₈	9¹⁄₈	4²⁄₈	6³⁄₈	5⁷⁄₈	238	3
◆ Lemhi County / Michael Wolf / Michael Wolf / 1982										
85⁴⁄₈	16⁵⁄₈	16⁵⁄₈	6⁶⁄₈	6⁶⁄₈	15¹⁄₈	11¹⁄₈	5⁶⁄₈	6	238	3
◆ Butte County / Picked Up / S. Eric Krasa / 1988										
84⁶⁄₈	17	16⁶⁄₈	6⁵⁄₈	6⁵⁄₈	17	16	5³⁄₈	5¹⁄₈	336	5
◆ Custer County / Claus Karlson / Claus Karlson / 1966										
84⁶⁄₈	17	16⁵⁄₈	6⁵⁄₈	6⁵⁄₈	8	1⁵⁄₈	6	5⁴⁄₈	336	5
◆ Lemhi County / Sherl L. Chapman / Sherl L. Chapman / 1983										
84	16	15⁶⁄₈	6³⁄₈	6³⁄₈	14²⁄₈	12⁶⁄₈	5	4⁶⁄₈	500	7
◆ Blaine County / Charles R. Hisaw / Charles R. Hisaw / 1981										
83⁴⁄₈	16⁶⁄₈	16⁶⁄₈	6⁴⁄₈	6⁴⁄₈	11⁴⁄₈	5⁶⁄₈	5⁴⁄₈	5⁴⁄₈	624	8
◆ Custer County / Wayne L. Coleman / Wayne L. Coleman / 1981										
83⁴⁄₈	16⁵⁄₈	16⁷⁄₈	5⁴⁄₈	5⁵⁄₈	9³⁄₈	4⁵⁄₈	6²⁄₈	6⁴⁄₈	624	8
◆ Custer County / Michael J. Felton / Michael J. Felton / 1991										
83⁴⁄₈	16¹⁄₈	15⁶⁄₈	6	6¹⁄₈	10²⁄₈	5¹⁄₈	4⁷⁄₈	5²⁄₈	624	8
◆ Butte County / Sandie L. Goodson / Sandie L. Goodson / 1991										
82⁶⁄₈	17³⁄₈	17	6	6	9⁵⁄₈	5¹⁄₈	5⁴⁄₈	5³⁄₈	868	11
◆ Custer County / William P. Benscoter / William P. Benscoter / 1985										
82⁶⁄₈	15⁷⁄₈	15⁵⁄₈	6²⁄₈	6²⁄₈	15³⁄₈	11⁷⁄₈	6¹⁄₈	5⁷⁄₈	868	11
◆ Lemhi County / Richard W. Feagan / Richard W. Feagan / 1988										
82⁴⁄₈	17¹⁄₈	17²⁄₈	6	6	9⁵⁄₈	7⁴⁄₈	6¹⁄₈	5⁴⁄₈	949	13
◆ Custer County / Ronald E. Pruyn / Ronald E. Pruyn / 1988										
82²⁄₈	15⁵⁄₈	15⁴⁄₈	6⁵⁄₈	6⁵⁄₈	10²⁄₈	4³⁄₈	5⁵⁄₈	5⁶⁄₈	1058	14
◆ Butte County / Jon L. Wadkins / Jon L. Wadkins / 1981										
82²⁄₈	16³⁄₈	15⁷⁄₈	6³⁄₈	6³⁄₈	10⁵⁄₈	6³⁄₈	6¹⁄₈	5⁷⁄₈	1058	14
◆ Butte County / Chris Tiller / Chris Tiller / 1983										
82	17⁴⁄₈	17⁴⁄₈	6⁴⁄₈	6²⁄₈	14⁶⁄₈	11⁶⁄₈	3⁴⁄₈	4	1157	16
◆ Pahsimeroi Valley / Elmer Keith / Elmer Keith / 1936										
82	15³⁄₈	15³⁄₈	5⁶⁄₈	5⁶⁄₈	11	9	6	5⁷⁄₈	1157	16
◆ Arco / Ernest L. Ellis, Jr. / Ernest L. Ellis, Jr. / 1965										

Photograph Courtesy of Cory Urban

KANSAS STATE RECORD
PRONGHORN
SCORE: 84⁴/₈
Locality: Logan Co.   Date: 1990
Hunter: Corey Urban

KANSAS

PRONGHORN

Score	Length of Horn R	Length of Horn L	Circumference of Base R	Circumference of Base L	Inside Spread	Tip-to-Tip Spread	Length of Prong R	Length of Prong L	All-Time Rank	State Rank
♦ *Locality / Hunter / Owner / Date Killed*										
84 4/8	14 2/8	14 1/8	6 7/8	6 7/8	8 6/8	4 4/8	6	6 1/8	390	1
♦ *Logan County / Corey Urban / Corey Urban / 1990*										
83 2/8	15 3/8	15 2/8	7 1/8	7	15 3/8	14	4 4/8	4 6/8	690	2
♦ *Thomas County / Charles M. Barnett / Charles M. Barnett / 1985*										
82	15 2/8	15 3/8	6 6/8	6 4/8	9	2 7/8	5 6/8	5 6/8	1157	3
♦ *Wallace County / Curtis R. Penner / Curtis R. Penner / 1976*										
80 6/8	14 7/8	15	6 1/8	6 1/8	6 6/8	3 3/8	6 4/8	6 1/8	1327	4
♦ *Wallace County / Jeanie Bell / Jeanie Bell / 1992*										

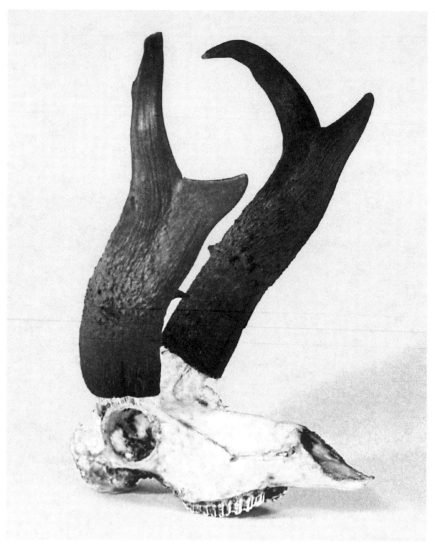

Photograph by Wm. H. Nesbitt

MONTANA STATE RECORD
PRONGHORN
SCORE: 91⁴⁄₈
Locality: Garfield Co.   Date: 1977
Hunter: Donald W. Yates

MONTANA
PRONGHORN

Score	Length of Horn		Circumference of Base		Inside Spread	Tip-to-Tip Spread	Length of Prong		All-Time Rank	State Rank
	R	L	R	L			R	L		
◆ Locality / Hunter / Owner / Date Killed										
91⁴⁄₈	17¹⁄₈	17	7³⁄₈	7¹⁄₈	13⁵⁄₈	10¹⁄₈	4⁴⁄₈	4⁷⁄₈	5	1
◆ Garfield County / Donald W. Yates / Donald W. Yates / 1977										
89⁶⁄₈	17²⁄₈	17⁴⁄₈	7	6⁷⁄₈	12⁵⁄₈	11¹⁄₈	7⁴⁄₈	7²⁄₈	17	2
◆ Rosebud County / Jim Ollom / Jim Ollom / 1973										
88¹⁄₈	17²⁄₈	17²⁄₈	7	7	17³⁄₈	14	6²⁄₈	6²⁄₈	65	3
◆ Carter County / Carl T. Clapp / Carl T. Clapp / 1955										
88	17³⁄₈	17	7⁴⁄₈	7⁶⁄₈	12⁷⁄₈	7⁵⁄₈	6	6	66	4
◆ Sweet Grass County / William S. Amos / William S. Amos / 1971										
87	16⁵⁄₈	16⁶⁄₈	6⁷⁄₈	6⁵⁄₈	9¹⁄₈	2⁶⁄₈	5²⁄₈	5³⁄₈	101	5
◆ Chouteau County / Darrell J. Woodahl / Darrell J. Woodahl / 1990										
87	16²⁄₈	15⁴⁄₈	6⁶⁄₈	6⁶⁄₈	9⁶⁄₈	5²⁄₈	8	7⁴⁄₈	101	5
◆ Rosebud County / Shane A. Siewert / Shane A. Siewert / 1991										
86	16²⁄₈	16³⁄₈	7³⁄₈	7	9⁷⁄₈	4¹⁄₈	4⁴⁄₈	4⁴⁄₈	182	7
◆ Carter County / Jamie Byrne / Jamie Byrne / 1972										
86	16⁴⁄₈	16⁴⁄₈	6⁶⁄₈	6⁵⁄₈	14³⁄₈	12⁴⁄₈	6¹⁄₈	5⁵⁄₈	182	7
◆ Valley County / Ernie Freebury / Ernie Freebury / 1981										
86	16	16⁵⁄₈	6⁵⁄₈	6⁷⁄₈	10⁴⁄₈	7²⁄₈	6⁷⁄₈	6⁶⁄₈	182	7
◆ McCone County / Danny L. Curtiss / Danny L. Curtiss / 1983										
86	16⁴⁄₈	16⁶⁄₈	6⁶⁄₈	6⁷⁄₈	9²⁄₈	4³⁄₈	5⁷⁄₈	6	182	7
◆ Wibaux County / Raymond G. Marciniak / Raymond G. Marciniak / 1984										
86	14⁶⁄₈	14²⁄₈	8¹⁄₈	8¹⁄₈	12	10	6	5²⁄₈	182	7
◆ Rosebud County / William E. Butler / William E. Butler / 1989										
86	15⁶⁄₈	15⁶⁄₈	6³⁄₈	6²⁄₈	14⁴⁄₈	12³⁄₈	5²⁄₈	5⁴⁄₈	182	7
◆ Carter County / Keith L. Folk / Keith L. Folk / 1992										
85⁶⁄₈	17²⁄₈	17²⁄₈	6⁷⁄₈	6⁷⁄₈	12¹⁄₈	10⁴⁄₈	4⁵⁄₈	4⁶⁄₈	211	13
◆ Fergus County / H.H. Applegate / H.H. Applegate / 1951										
85⁶⁄₈	16⁴⁄₈	16⁵⁄₈	6⁶⁄₈	6⁵⁄₈	9¹⁄₈	5¹⁄₈	6¹⁄₈	6	211	13
◆ Beaverhead County / Vern Hensley / Vern Hensley / 1968										
85⁴⁄₈	16	16⁶⁄₈	6⁷⁄₈	6⁷⁄₈	11¹⁄₈	10²⁄₈	6⁴⁄₈	6²⁄₈	238	15
◆ Rosebud County / Calvin F. Mayes / Calvin F. Mayes / 1973										
85⁴⁄₈	16⁵⁄₈	16⁶⁄₈	6⁷⁄₈	6⁷⁄₈	7	1¹⁄₈	6	5⁵⁄₈	238	15
◆ Rosebud County / John A. Hill / John A. Hill / 1989										
85²⁄₈	17³⁄₈	17³⁄₈	7²⁄₈	7	12	7²⁄₈	5²⁄₈	5³⁄₈	268	17
◆ Rosebud County / Dale R. Brauer / Dale R. Brauer / 1983										
85	17³⁄₈	17⁵⁄₈	6⁶⁄₈	6⁶⁄₈	17³⁄₈	14⁴⁄₈	5	5¹⁄₈	301	18
◆ Forsyth / John M. Broadwell / John M. Broadwell / 1961										

Score	Length of Horn		Circumference of Base		Inside Spread	Tip-to-Tip Spread	Length of Prong		All-Time Rank	State Rank
	R	L	R	L			R	L		
♦ *Locality / Hunter / Owner / Date Killed*										
85	$15\frac{4}{8}$	$15\frac{4}{8}$	$6\frac{6}{8}$	$6\frac{4}{8}$	10	$5\frac{4}{8}$	5	$4\frac{6}{8}$	301	18
♦ *Brusett / Unknown / Frank McKeever / PR 1962*										
85	$16\frac{1}{8}$	$15\frac{6}{8}$	$6\frac{7}{8}$	7	$10\frac{4}{8}$	$7\frac{4}{8}$	$6\frac{7}{8}$	$6\frac{2}{8}$	301	18
♦ *Garfield County / W.A. Delaney / W.A. Delaney / 1965*										
85	$16\frac{1}{8}$	16	$6\frac{6}{8}$	$6\frac{6}{8}$	$13\frac{1}{8}$	$8\frac{2}{8}$	$4\frac{4}{8}$	$4\frac{4}{8}$	301	18
♦ *Garfield County / Jeff M. Busse / Jeff M. Busse / 1988*										
85	$16\frac{6}{8}$	$16\frac{7}{8}$	$6\frac{6}{8}$	$6\frac{6}{8}$	$11\frac{4}{8}$	$8\frac{3}{8}$	5	5	301	18
♦ *Rosebud County / Daniel D. Ova / Daniel D. Ova / 1988*										
$84\frac{6}{8}$	$16\frac{2}{8}$	$16\frac{1}{8}$	$7\frac{2}{8}$	$7\frac{2}{8}$	$9\frac{3}{8}$	$3\frac{1}{8}$	$5\frac{5}{8}$	$5\frac{4}{8}$	336	23
♦ *Carter County / Daniel Goodman / Daniel Goodman / 1993*										
$84\frac{6}{8}$	$15\frac{3}{8}$	$15\frac{3}{8}$	7	7	$14\frac{6}{8}$	$11\frac{4}{8}$	$7\frac{2}{8}$	7	336	23
♦ *Petroleum County / Daniel S. Wentz / Daniel S. Wentz / 1993*										
$84\frac{4}{8}$	$16\frac{4}{8}$	$16\frac{2}{8}$	$6\frac{3}{8}$	6	9	$5\frac{1}{8}$	$7\frac{1}{8}$	7	390	25
♦ *Phillips County / Donald W. Hellhake / Donald W. Hellhake / 1984*										
$84\frac{4}{8}$	$16\frac{1}{8}$	$16\frac{5}{8}$	7	7	$7\frac{3}{8}$	$2\frac{5}{8}$	$4\frac{6}{8}$	$5\frac{1}{8}$	390	25
♦ *Prairie County / Duane R. Pisk / Duane R. Pisk / 1988*										
$84\frac{2}{8}$	$17\frac{2}{8}$	$17\frac{4}{8}$	$6\frac{3}{8}$	$6\frac{2}{8}$	$14\frac{6}{8}$	$10\frac{4}{8}$	$6\frac{1}{8}$	6	436	27
♦ *Powder River County / Sam C. Borla / Sam C. Borla / 1982*										
$84\frac{2}{8}$	16	$16\frac{2}{8}$	7	7	12	$7\frac{2}{8}$	$6\frac{2}{8}$	$6\frac{4}{8}$	436	27
♦ *Yellowstone County / Jim B. Cherpeski / Jim B. Cherpeski / 1986*										
$84\frac{2}{8}$	$14\frac{5}{8}$	$14\frac{2}{8}$	$6\frac{7}{8}$	$6\frac{7}{8}$	$7\frac{2}{8}$	$6\frac{7}{8}$	$6\frac{4}{8}$	$6\frac{4}{8}$	436	27
♦ *Carter County / Robert Cunningham / Robert Cunningham / 1986*										
$84\frac{2}{8}$	$15\frac{4}{8}$	$15\frac{6}{8}$	$7\frac{2}{8}$	$7\frac{2}{8}$	$9\frac{6}{8}$	5	6	$5\frac{7}{8}$	436	27
♦ *Carbon County / Patrick I. Kalloch / Patrick I. Kalloch / 1990*										
84	$15\frac{4}{8}$	$15\frac{4}{8}$	$6\frac{5}{8}$	$6\frac{5}{8}$	$11\frac{6}{8}$	$8\frac{7}{8}$	$7\frac{1}{8}$	$6\frac{7}{8}$	500	31
♦ *Choteau County / W.E. Cherry / W.E. Cherry / 1968*										
84	$16\frac{4}{8}$	$16\frac{3}{8}$	$6\frac{7}{8}$	$6\frac{6}{8}$	$9\frac{7}{8}$	$5\frac{1}{8}$	$5\frac{6}{8}$	$5\frac{5}{8}$	500	31
♦ *Dawson County / Jeff S. Trangmoe / Jeff S. Trangmoe / 1985*										
84	17	$16\frac{7}{8}$	$6\frac{6}{8}$	$6\frac{5}{8}$	$11\frac{7}{8}$	$8\frac{6}{8}$	$5\frac{7}{8}$	$5\frac{7}{8}$	500	31
♦ *Custer County / Don A. Bryendl / Don A. Bryendl / 1988*										
$83\frac{6}{8}$	15	$15\frac{1}{8}$	$6\frac{7}{8}$	$6\frac{6}{8}$	$10\frac{2}{8}$	$6\frac{6}{8}$	$6\frac{6}{8}$	$6\frac{2}{8}$	565	34
♦ *Big Horn County / Michael Ferri / Michael Ferri / 1982*										
$83\frac{6}{8}$	$15\frac{2}{8}$	$15\frac{2}{8}$	$6\frac{5}{8}$	$6\frac{5}{8}$	9	$5\frac{4}{8}$	6	$6\frac{5}{8}$	565	34
♦ *Rosebud County / William E. Butler / William E. Butler / 1992*										
$83\frac{4}{8}$	$16\frac{7}{8}$	17	7	7	$10\frac{4}{8}$	$6\frac{7}{8}$	$5\frac{2}{8}$	$5\frac{2}{8}$	624	36
♦ *Miles City / J. Louis Mann / J. Louis Mann / 1954*										
$83\frac{4}{8}$	$15\frac{4}{8}$	$15\frac{5}{8}$	$6\frac{6}{8}$	$6\frac{7}{8}$	13	$10\frac{1}{8}$	$5\frac{1}{8}$	$5\frac{3}{8}$	624	36
♦ *Rosebud County / James D. Cameron / James D. Cameron / 1981*										

MONTANA PRONGHORN *(continued)*

Score	Length of Horn R	Length of Horn L	Circumference of Base R	Circumference of Base L	Inside Spread	Tip-to-Tip Spread	Length of Prong R	Length of Prong L	All-Time Rank	State Rank
♦ *Locality / Hunter / Owner / Date Killed*										
83 4/8	16 4/8	16 6/8	6 4/8	6 3/8	10 1/8	2 7/8	6 4/8	6 2/8	624	36
♦ *Prairie County / L.H. Lindquist / L.H. Lindquist / 1982*										
83 4/8	14 5/8	14 7/8	7 2/8	7 2/8	6 3/8	2 3/8	5 4/8	5 4/8	624	36
♦ *Carter County / Angelo J. Feroleto / Angelo J. Feroleto / 1992*										
83 2/8	14 7/8	14 7/8	6 2/8	6 2/8	9 7/8	6	4 6/8	4 5/8	690	40
♦ *Fergus County / Steven G. Ard / Steven G. Ard / 1962*										
83 2/8	14 5/8	14 5/8	6 5/8	6 6/8	12 4/8	10	7 2/8	7 6/8	690	40
♦ *Carter County / Joseph Henderson / Joseph Henderson / 1975*										
83 2/8	15 6/8	16	6 5/8	6 6/8	9 6/8	4 4/8	6 3/8	6	690	40
♦ *Sweet Grass County / Dennis E. Moos / Dennis E. Moos / 1977*										
83 2/8	16 3/8	16 2/8	6 4/8	6 4/8	12 1/8	7 2/8	6	6 1/8	690	40
♦ *Beaverhead County / Scott Withers / Scott Withers / 1980*										
83 2/8	16 2/8	16 2/8	6 6/8	6 6/8	8 5/8	5 2/8	5 2/8	5 2/8	690	40
♦ *Musselshell County / Caroll M. Lumpkin, Jr. / Caroll M. Lumpkin, Jr. / 1980*										
83 2/8	16 2/8	16 5/8	6	6	9 1/8	3 5/8	7	6 5/8	690	40
♦ *Carter County / Martin Crane / Martin Crane / 1983*										
83 2/8	16	15	7 1/8	7	8 4/8	2 3/8	5 5/8	5 5/8	690	40
♦ *Rosebud County / Anthony J. Emmerich / Anthony J. Emmerich / 1989*										
83 2/8	17 1/8	17 2/8	6 2/8	6 3/8	12 6/8	9 2/8	6 1/8	6 2/8	690	40
♦ *Sweet Grass County / Daniel Phariss / Daniel Phariss / 1989*										
83 2/8	16 3/8	16 1/8	6 3/8	6 3/8	10 3/8	7	6 3/8	6 2/8	690	40
♦ *Rosebud County / Gary M. Van Dyke / Gary M. Van Dyke / 1989*										
83 2/8	16	16	6 6/8	6 6/8	10	6 7/8	4 7/8	4 7/8	690	40
♦ *Carter County / Donald W. Mindemann, Jr. / Donald W. Mindemann, Jr. / 1990*										
83 2/8	17 1/8	16 2/8	6 6/8	6 6/8	12 3/8	7 2/8	5 7/8	6 1/8	690	40
♦ *Custer County / Eric S. Doeden / Eric S. Doeden / 1991*										
83	16	16 1/8	6 4/8	6 4/8	11	5 1/8	5 7/8	5 7/8	775	51
♦ *Lame Deer / G.E. Badgley / G.E. Badgley / 1961*										
83	15 4/8	15 2/8	7 1/8	7 2/8	13 4/8	9 3/8	5 3/8	6 1/8	775	51
♦ *Plevna / Joseph P. Burger / Joseph P. Burger / 1963*										
83	16 2/8	16 2/8	6 3/8	6 2/8	15	12 5/8	5 2/8	5 2/8	775	51
♦ *Valley County / Timothy R. Logan / Timothy R. Logan / 1976*										
83	15 6/8	16	6 1/8	6 1/8	8 1/8	3 3/8	6 6/8	6 6/8	775	51
♦ *Chouteau County / Brad Burney / Brad Burney / 1994*										
82 6/8	16 6/8	17	6 4/8	6 4/8	14 3/8	14	5	5 1/8	868	55
♦ *Prairie County / Gordon Spears / Gordon Spears / 1954*										
82 6/8	15 3/8	15 3/8	6 6/8	6 3/8	8 5/8	5 1/8	6 1/8	6	868	55
♦ *Custer County / George E. Sanquist / George E. Sanquist / 1970*										

Score	Length of Horn		Circumference of Base		Inside Spread	Tip-to-Tip Spread	Length of Prong		All-Time Rank	State Rank
	R	L	R	L			R	L		

Locality / Hunter / Owner / Date Killed

Score										
82⁶⁄₈	15³⁄₈	15⁴⁄₈	6⁶⁄₈	6⁶⁄₈	12	9	5⁶⁄₈	6¹⁄₈	868	55

♦ Carter County / Lloyd R. Norvell / Lloyd R. Norvell / 1982

82⁶⁄₈	16³⁄₈	16⁴⁄₈	6¹⁄₈	6	13⁷⁄₈	10¹⁄₈	5²⁄₈	5²⁄₈	868	55

♦ Yellowstone County / Robert M. Labert / Robert M. Labert / 1984

82⁴⁄₈	16¹⁄₈	15⁷⁄₈	6²⁄₈	6²⁄₈	10⁴⁄₈	6⁵⁄₈	6¹⁄₈	6¹⁄₈	949	59

♦ Park County / William E. Randall / William E. Randall / 1947

82⁴⁄₈	16⁶⁄₈	16⁶⁄₈	6¹⁄₈	6²⁄₈	16¹⁄₈	11⁴⁄₈	5	5⁷⁄₈	949	59

♦ Ingomar / L.P. Treaster / L.P. Treaster / 1965

82⁴⁄₈	14⁵⁄₈	14³⁄₈	7	6⁷⁄₈	9⁵⁄₈	5⁵⁄₈	5⁵⁄₈	5⁵⁄₈	949	59

♦ Rosebud County / Norman G. Kern / Norman G. Kern / 1974

82⁴⁄₈	16	16³⁄₈	6³⁄₈	6²⁄₈	11¹⁄₈	6⁶⁄₈	5⁶⁄₈	5⁷⁄₈	949	59

♦ Custer County / Harry Zirwas / Harry Zirwas / 1974

82⁴⁄₈	14⁷⁄₈	14⁷⁄₈	7	7	11⁷⁄₈	8⁷⁄₈	5²⁄₈	5⁴⁄₈	949	59

♦ Richland County / Lloyd Holland / Lloyd Holland / 1977

82⁴⁄₈	16	16¹⁄₈	6⁶⁄₈	6⁶⁄₈	12³⁄₈	8¹⁄₈	5²⁄₈	5	949	59

♦ Carter County / James A. White / James A. White / 1977

82⁴⁄₈	16	15⁵⁄₈	6⁶⁄₈	6⁶⁄₈	9	4	5³⁄₈	5³⁄₈	949	59

♦ Rosebud County / Robert B. DeLattre / Robert B. DeLattre / 1985

82⁴⁄₈	15³⁄₈	15³⁄₈	6³⁄₈	6²⁄₈	11	6²⁄₈	5³⁄₈	5⁵⁄₈	949	59

♦ Yellowstone County / Jon J. Wilson / Jon J. Wilson / 1988

82⁴⁄₈	16	15⁷⁄₈	6³⁄₈	6⁴⁄₈	6³⁄₈	0³⁄₈	5⁵⁄₈	5⁵⁄₈	949	59

♦ Casade County / John P. Michalies / John P. Michalies / 1991

82⁴⁄₈	15⁶⁄₈	15⁴⁄₈	6⁶⁄₈	6⁷⁄₈	8⁶⁄₈	2⁶⁄₈	5⁴⁄₈	5⁴⁄₈	949	59

♦ Treasure County / David W. Shannon / David W. Shannon / 1991

82⁴⁄₈	15⁵⁄₈	15⁷⁄₈	6	6	12³⁄₈	7⁵⁄₈	5⁷⁄₈	6²⁄₈	949	59

♦ Judith Basin County / Sarah M. Brown / Sarah M. Brown / 1991

82⁴⁄₈	15⁵⁄₈	15⁵⁄₈	6³⁄₈	6⁶⁄₈	13⁴⁄₈	9⁷⁄₈	7	7	949	59

♦ Jefferson County / Tom R. Osborne / Tom R. Osborne / 1992

82⁴⁄₈	16⁵⁄₈	16⁵⁄₈	6⁵⁄₈	6⁴⁄₈	9	4	5¹⁄₈	5²⁄₈	949	59

♦ Fergus County / Scott D. Boelman / Scott D. Boelman / 1993

82²⁄₈	15⁴⁄₈	15⁴⁄₈	6⁶⁄₈	6⁵⁄₈	10¹⁄₈	5	5⁶⁄₈	6	1058	72

♦ Lewis & Clark County / Leo M. Bergthold / Leo M. Bergthold / 1963

82²⁄₈	15⁶⁄₈	16	6⁴⁄₈	6⁴⁄₈	13¹⁄₈	9	6³⁄₈	5⁷⁄₈	1058	72

♦ Lavina / W.J. Morrelle / W.J. Morrelle / 1963

82²⁄₈	15⁷⁄₈	15⁷⁄₈	6⁶⁄₈	6⁴⁄₈	9⁶⁄₈	4⁵⁄₈	6	6¹⁄₈	1058	72

♦ Powderville / Morrel W. Ivie / Morrel W. Ivie / 1969

82²⁄₈	15⁶⁄₈	15⁷⁄₈	6⁶⁄₈	6⁶⁄₈	10⁷⁄₈	4⁴⁄₈	5⁵⁄₈	5⁷⁄₈	1058	72

♦ Fergus County / Carl Aus / Carl Aus / 1971

Score	Length of Horn R	L	Circumference of Base R	L	Inside Spread	Tip-to-Tip Spread	Length of Prong R	L	All-Time Rank	State Rank
$82\frac{2}{8}$	$15\frac{5}{8}$	$15\frac{5}{8}$	$6\frac{4}{8}$	$6\frac{4}{8}$	$9\frac{6}{8}$	$5\frac{7}{8}$	$5\frac{5}{8}$	$5\frac{5}{8}$	1058	72
◆ Treasure County / Joseph A. Balmelli / Joseph A. Balmelli / 1974										
$82\frac{2}{8}$	17	$16\frac{6}{8}$	$6\frac{5}{8}$	$6\frac{4}{8}$	$8\frac{4}{8}$	$5\frac{6}{8}$	$4\frac{7}{8}$	$4\frac{7}{8}$	1058	72
◆ Valley County / David D. Rittenhouse / David D. Rittenhouse / 1982										
$82\frac{2}{8}$	$16\frac{2}{8}$	$16\frac{2}{8}$	$6\frac{4}{8}$	$6\frac{4}{8}$	$9\frac{5}{8}$	$3\frac{5}{8}$	$5\frac{4}{8}$	$5\frac{4}{8}$	1058	72
◆ Garfield County / William E. Butler / William E. Butler / 1983										
$82\frac{2}{8}$	16	$15\frac{7}{8}$	$6\frac{5}{8}$	$6\frac{4}{8}$	$11\frac{1}{8}$	$9\frac{3}{8}$	$4\frac{7}{8}$	$4\frac{4}{8}$	1058	72
◆ Fergus County / Patricia M. Dreeszen / Patricia M. Dreeszen / 1986										
$82\frac{2}{8}$	$14\frac{6}{8}$	$14\frac{7}{8}$	$6\frac{7}{8}$	$7\frac{1}{8}$	$8\frac{1}{8}$	$5\frac{3}{8}$	$5\frac{6}{8}$	$5\frac{7}{8}$	1058	72
◆ Rosebud County / Cory Nissen / Cory Nissen / 1988										
$82\frac{2}{8}$	$17\frac{5}{8}$	$17\frac{2}{8}$	$6\frac{3}{8}$	$6\frac{3}{8}$	9	$6\frac{7}{8}$	5	$5\frac{4}{8}$	1058	72
◆ Big Horn County / Valley C. Sian / Valley C. Sian / 1993										
82	$14\frac{6}{8}$	$14\frac{6}{8}$	$6\frac{4}{8}$	$6\frac{3}{8}$	$8\frac{7}{8}$	$3\frac{6}{8}$	7	6	1157	82
◆ Garfield County / Dean V. Ashton / Dean V. Ashton / 1968										
82	$14\frac{3}{8}$	14	$7\frac{4}{8}$	$7\frac{3}{8}$	13	$9\frac{4}{8}$	$6\frac{6}{8}$	7	1157	82
◆ Garfield County / Don E. Traughber / Don E. Traughber / 1973										
82	$16\frac{1}{8}$	$16\frac{4}{8}$	$6\frac{7}{8}$	$6\frac{5}{8}$	11	$7\frac{2}{8}$	$2\frac{6}{8}$	$3\frac{4}{8}$	1157	82
◆ Wolf Point / Raymond A. Gould / Raymond A. Gould / 1974										
82	$16\frac{3}{8}$	$16\frac{3}{8}$	$6\frac{6}{8}$	$6\frac{5}{8}$	$10\frac{1}{8}$	$4\frac{4}{8}$	$5\frac{5}{8}$	$5\frac{4}{8}$	1157	82
◆ Rosebud County / Denver W. Holt / Denver W. Holt / 1992										
82	15	15	$7\frac{2}{8}$	$7\frac{1}{8}$	10	$7\frac{6}{8}$	6	$5\frac{6}{8}$	1157	82
◆ Garfield County / Kip K. Karges / Kip K. Karges / 1992										
$81\frac{4}{8}$	$15\frac{1}{8}$	$14\frac{7}{8}$	$6\frac{7}{8}$	$6\frac{7}{8}$	$10\frac{3}{8}$	$5\frac{7}{8}$	$6\frac{2}{8}$	6	1283	87
◆ Lewis & Clark County / Mark A. Susag / Mark A. Susag / 1994										
$81\frac{2}{8}$	$15\frac{5}{8}$	$15\frac{5}{8}$	$6\frac{7}{8}$	$6\frac{6}{8}$	$11\frac{4}{8}$	8	$4\frac{6}{8}$	5	1290	88
◆ McCone County / Jerry D. Curtiss / Jerry D. Curtiss / 1990										
$81\frac{2}{8}$	$15\frac{3}{8}$	$15\frac{5}{8}$	$6\frac{4}{8}$	$6\frac{4}{8}$	$8\frac{1}{8}$	$4\frac{6}{8}$	6	$5\frac{4}{8}$	1290	88
◆ Valley County / John C. Burdick / John C. Burdick / 1994										
81	$15\frac{3}{8}$	15	$6\frac{6}{8}$	$6\frac{6}{8}$	$12\frac{3}{8}$	$9\frac{1}{8}$	6	6	1310	90
◆ Musselshell County / Omer Ware / Omer Ware / 1989										
81	$16\frac{7}{8}$	17	$5\frac{7}{8}$	$5\frac{6}{8}$	$11\frac{6}{8}$	$7\frac{3}{8}$	$5\frac{4}{8}$	$5\frac{3}{8}$	1310	90
◆ Valley County / Kevin L. Wieberg / Kevin L. Wieberg / 1989										
$80\frac{6}{8}$	$16\frac{3}{8}$	$16\frac{3}{8}$	$6\frac{4}{8}$	$6\frac{3}{8}$	$11\frac{4}{8}$	8	5	5	1327	92
◆ Powder River County / John J. Landa / John J. Landa / 1988										
$80\frac{4}{8}$	15	$14\frac{6}{8}$	$6\frac{4}{8}$	$6\frac{4}{8}$	$12\frac{6}{8}$	$10\frac{2}{8}$	6	$5\frac{6}{8}$	1345	93
◆ Custer County / Brandon P. Taylor / Brandon P. Taylor / 1990										
$80\frac{2}{8}$	$14\frac{6}{8}$	$14\frac{6}{8}$	$6\frac{4}{8}$	$6\frac{4}{8}$	$11\frac{2}{8}$	$7\frac{6}{8}$	$5\frac{6}{8}$	$5\frac{6}{8}$	1360	94
◆ Fergus County / Patricia M. Dreeszen / Patricia M. Dreeszen / 1988										

◆ *Locality / Hunter / Owner / Date Killed*

Score	Length of Horn		Circumference of Base		Inside Spread	Tip-to-Tip Spread	Length of Prong		All-Time Rank	State Rank
	R	L	R	L			R	L		
◆ *Locality / Hunter / Owner / Date Killed*										
80²⁄₈	15⁴⁄₈	15²⁄₈	6	6	8¹⁄₈	2⁶⁄₈	6⁴⁄₈	6¹⁄₈	1360	94
◆ *Rosebud County / Steven L. Rogers / Steven L. Rogers / 1989*										
80²⁄₈	14⁴⁄₈	14¹⁄₈	7	6⁷⁄₈	10²⁄₈	7⁷⁄₈	5⁵⁄₈	5⁴⁄₈	1360	94
◆ *Custer County / John W. Hitch / John W. Hitch / 1991*										
80²⁄₈	13⁷⁄₈	13⁶⁄₈	7¹⁄₈	7¹⁄₈	10⁵⁄₈	7⁶⁄₈	5⁵⁄₈	5⁶⁄₈	1360	94
◆ *Garfield County / Ryon K. Harriman / Ryon K. Harriman / 1993*										
80²⁄₈	15⁴⁄₈	15⁴⁄₈	6¹⁄₈	6	8	2⁶⁄₈	5⁴⁄₈	5³⁄₈	1360	94
◆ *Garfield County / Brooke Pfohl / Brooke Pfohl / 1994*										
80	16¹⁄₈	15⁷⁄₈	6²⁄₈	6²⁄₈	11³⁄₈	11	5⁴⁄₈	5⁴⁄₈	1386	99
◆ *Prairie County / Thomas G. Marallo / Thomas G. Marallo / 1984*										

Photograph Courtesy of Don Perrien

Don Perrien and the 17-inch pronghorn he took near Nelson Spring, Modoc County, California, during the 1994 hunting season. It scores 84-2/8 points.

Photograph Courtesy of Gerald R. Larson

NEBRASKA STATE RECORD
PRONGHORN
SCORE: 85⅝
Locality: Sioux Co.   Date: 1962
Hunter: Gerald R. Larson

NEBRASKA
PRONGHORN

Score	Length of Horn		Circumference of Base		Inside Spread	Tip-to-Tip Spread	Length of Prong		All-Time Rank	State Rank
	R	L	R	L			R	L		
◆ Locality / Hunter / Owner / Date Killed										
85⁶⁄₈	15	15⁴⁄₈	7⁴⁄₈	7¹⁄₈	6	2²⁄₈	6⁴⁄₈	6²⁄₈	211	1
◆ Sioux County / Gerald R. Larson / Gerald R. Larson / 1962										
85⁴⁄₈	16¹⁄₈	15⁷⁄₈	7	7¹⁄₈	10⁴⁄₈	5⁶⁄₈	7¹⁄₈	6⁷⁄₈	238	2
◆ Sioux County / John W. Hlavacek / John W. Hlavacek / 1983										
84⁶⁄₈	16	16¹⁄₈	7²⁄₈	7¹⁄₈	12¹⁄₈	6⁶⁄₈	5	4⁶⁄₈	336	3
◆ Alliance / Joseph Nelson / Joseph Nelson / 1962										
84⁶⁄₈	15⁶⁄₈	15⁵⁄₈	7¹⁄₈	7¹⁄₈	10²⁄₈	7¹⁄₈	6³⁄₈	5⁷⁄₈	336	3
◆ Garden County / Richard Mosley / Richard Mosley / 1978										
84	15¹⁄₈	14⁷⁄₈	6⁴⁄₈	6⁵⁄₈	11¹⁄₈	9⁶⁄₈	6⁶⁄₈	5⁷⁄₈	500	5
◆ Sioux County / Harvey Y. Suetsugu / Harvey Y. Suetsugu / 1977										
84	14⁶⁄₈	14⁵⁄₈	7²⁄₈	7²⁄₈	11¹⁄₈	7⁵⁄₈	6¹⁄₈	5⁵⁄₈	500	5
◆ Sheridan County / Wayne M. Kelly / Wayne M. Kelly / 1983										
84	15¹⁄₈	15	8²⁄₈	7⁶⁄₈	16⁴⁄₈	14⁴⁄₈	5²⁄₈	5⁷⁄₈	500	5
◆ Sioux County / Royce S. Schaeffer / Royce S. Schaeffer / 1993										
83⁴⁄₈	16⁴⁄₈	16⁴⁄₈	6⁶⁄₈	6⁵⁄₈	10⁴⁄₈	5³⁄₈	4⁷⁄₈	5²⁄₈	624	8
◆ Box Butte County / Derald E. Morgan / Derald E. Morgan / 1977										
83	15³⁄₈	15⁵⁄₈	7	7	9	7	5²⁄₈	5⁶⁄₈	775	9
◆ Box Butte County / Lynda G. Sydow / Lynda G. Sydow / 1984										
83	15³⁄₈	15²⁄₈	7²⁄₈	7	8	5⁴⁄₈	5⁷⁄₈	4⁷⁄₈	775	9
◆ Kimball County / Mayda M. Zimmerman / Mayda M. Zimmerman / 1992										
82⁶⁄₈	16	16²⁄₈	6⁴⁄₈	6⁴⁄₈	12¹⁄₈	11⁵⁄₈	5	5	868	11
◆ Angora / Harold C. Rusk / Neb. Game & Parks Comm. / 1954										
80⁶⁄₈	16	16¹⁄₈	6⁴⁄₈	6⁴⁄₈	11⁶⁄₈	7	5⁴⁄₈	5⁵⁄₈	1327	12
◆ Thomas County / Andrew L. Glidden / Andrew L. Glidden / 1993										

NEVADA STATE RECORD
PRONGHORN
SCORE: 91
Locality: Humboldt Co.   Date: 1990
Hunter: Steve W. Dustin

NEVADA

PRONGHORN

Score	Length of Horn R	Length of Horn L	Circumference of Base R	Circumference of Base L	Inside Spread	Tip-to-Tip Spread	Length of Prong R	Length of Prong L	All-Time Rank	State Rank
	♦ *Locality / Hunter / Owner / Date Killed*									
91	17 7/8	17 5/8	6 7/8	6 7/8	14	8 2/8	7 1/8	7 3/8	8	1
	♦ *Humboldt County / Steve W. Dustin / Steve W. Dustin / 1990*									
89 4/8	17 2/8	17 5/8	6 7/8	7	9 4/8	3 2/8	6 6/8	6 3/8	23	2
	♦ *Humboldt County / Richard Steinmetz / Richard Steinmetz / 1977*									
89 2/8	17 4/8	17 1/8	7 2/8	7 1/8	12 5/8	8 6/8	7	7 1/8	28	3
	♦ *Washoe County / Jaime L. Fuentes / Jaime L. Fuentes / 1990*									
89 2/8	15 4/8	15 4/8	6 6/8	6 6/8	10	4 4/8	8	8	28	3
	♦ *Washoe County / Marjorie A. Puryear / Marjorie A. Puryear / 1990*									
88 6/8	18	17 7/8	6 6/8	6 5/8	15 4/8	11 5/8	6 7/8	6 3/8	41	5
	♦ *Washoe County / Bruce L. Zeller / Bruce L. Zeller / 1986*									
88 6/8	16 4/8	16 6/8	7 5/8	7 4/8	8 4/8	4 7/8	5 6/8	5 5/8	41	5
	♦ *White Pine County / William W. Diekmann / William W. Diekmann / 1987*									
88 6/8	18 1/8	18	7 2/8	7 1/8	15 3/8	11 2/8	6	6 3/8	41	5
	♦ *Washoe County / Kerry E. Kilgore / Kerry E. Kilgore / 1992*									
88 6/8	16 2/8	16 5/8	7 3/8	7 3/8	11 2/8	6 7/8	6 2/8	5 6/8	41	5
	♦ *Humboldt County / Werner Estes / Werner Estes / 1994*									
88 4/8	17 7/8	17 6/8	7	7	15 6/8	11 6/8	5	5 1/8	51	9
	♦ *Humboldt County / Clifford J. Heaverne / Clifford J. Heaverne / 1983*									
87 2/8	16 2/8	16 2/8	6 7/8	6 7/8	12 2/8	10 4/8	7	6 7/8	85	10
	♦ *Humboldt County / Steve Young / Steve Young / 1975*									
87 2/8	19 1/8	18 4/8	7	7 2/8	14 3/8	8 2/8	5 1/8	5 2/8	85	10
	♦ *Humboldt County / Jared R. Nuffer / Jared R. Nuffer / 1988*									
87 2/8	16 4/8	16 5/8	7 2/8	7	11 7/8	8	7 2/8	6 4/8	85	10
	♦ *Washoe County / Pierre M. Leautier / Pierre M. Leautier / 1989*									
87 2/8	17 4/8	17 2/8	7 4/8	7 4/8	9 4/8	5 6/8	6 1/8	6	85	10
	♦ *Humboldt County / James M. Machac / James M. Machac / 1992*									
87 2/8	16 6/8	16 7/8	6 5/8	6 7/8	14 7/8	11 1/8	6 3/8	6 1/8	85	10
	♦ *Humboldt County / Gary D. Bader / Gary D. Bader / 1994*									
87 2/8	17 2/8	17	7 2/8	7 2/8	12	6 4/8	5 4/8	5 2/8	85	10
	♦ *Washoe County / Jay T. Gunter / Jay T. Gunter / 1994*									
87	16 2/8	16 1/8	6 3/8	6 3/8	10 6/8	4 7/8	6 4/8	6 5/8	101	16
	♦ *Washoe County / William E. Walker / William E. Walker / 1970*									
86 6/8	17	17 1/8	7	6 7/8	14	9 1/8	5 5/8	5 6/8	114	17
	♦ *Humboldt County / Rebecca J. Hall / Rebecca J. Hall / 1981*									
86 4/8	17 2/8	17 2/8	6 6/8	6 6/8	9 1/8	2	6 1/8	5 5/8	140	18
	♦ *Washoe County / Bruce D. Gallio / Bruce D. Gallio / 1983*									

Score	Length of Horn		Circumference of Base		Inside Spread	Tip-to-Tip Spread	Length of Prong		All-Time Rank	State Rank
	R	L	R	L			R	L		
◆ Locality / Hunter / Owner / Date Killed										
86²/₈	17²/₈	17¹/₈	6⁴/₈	6⁴/₈	11⁴/₈	7³/₈	5²/₈	5³/₈	155	19
◆ Washoe County / Daniel E. Warren / Daniel E. Warren / 1983										
86²/₈	17²/₈	17²/₈	7²/₈	7	9¹/₈	4⁴/₈	4⁶/₈	5⁵/₈	155	19
◆ Pershing County / Matthew K. Morris / Matthew K. Morris / 1994										
86²/₈	15²/₈	15	7¹/₈	7¹/₈	11	8¹/₈	5⁵/₈	5⁴/₈	155	19
◆ Humboldt County / David C. Rahn / David C. Rahn / 1994										
85⁶/₈	16	16	6⁵/₈	6⁵/₈	13¹/₈	8	6²/₈	6²/₈	211	22
◆ Humboldt County / Thomas R. Pitts / Thomas R. Pitts / 1973										
85⁴/₈	16⁶/₈	16⁶/₈	7⁶/₈	7⁴/₈	10²/₈	2²/₈	6²/₈	5⁵/₈	238	23
◆ Washoe County / Mario E. Gildone / Mario E. Gildone / 1977										
85⁴/₈	17²/₈	17¹/₈	6⁴/₈	6³/₈	15¹/₈	11¹/₈	6¹/₈	6	238	23
◆ Washoe County / Maryanne Robinson / Melbourne & Maryanne Robinson / 1981										
85⁴/₈	17²/₈	17²/₈	6⁶/₈	6⁷/₈	17²/₈	13⁴/₈	5¹/₈	5³/₈	238	23
◆ Washoe County / Peter K. Beers / Peter K. Beers / 1988										
85⁴/₈	16⁶/₈	16⁷/₈	7	7	12⁵/₈	8⁵/₈	4⁴/₈	4²/₈	238	23
◆ Washoe County / Gregg A. Menter / Gregg A. Menter / 1991										
85⁴/₈	15⁵/₈	15⁶/₈	6⁷/₈	6⁷/₈	12⁵/₈	9¹/₈	6	6¹/₈	238	23
◆ Nye County / E. William Almberg / E. William Almberg / 1993										
85	17⁵/₈	17⁴/₈	5⁵/₈	5⁵/₈	9⁷/₈	7²/₈	6²/₈	6³/₈	301	28
◆ Washoe County / Walter C. Bell / Walter C. Bell / 1949										
84⁶/₈	17¹/₈	17⁴/₈	6²/₈	6⁴/₈	10	5	5¹/₈	5²/₈	336	29
◆ Washoe County / Lloyd B. Miller / Lloyd B. Miller / 1980										
84⁴/₈	16³/₈	16⁴/₈	7²/₈	7¹/₈	13³/₈	7⁷/₈	5⁶/₈	5⁶/₈	390	30
◆ Washoe County / Frances M. Hansell / Frances M. Hansell / 1974										
84⁴/₈	17¹/₈	17¹/₈	7	7	11⁶/₈	8²/₈	4²/₈	4⁷/₈	390	30
◆ Washoe County / Tracy A. Tripp / Tracy A. Tripp / 1989										
84⁴/₈	17¹/₈	17	6¹/₈	6²/₈	12²/₈	6⁴/₈	6³/₈	6²/₈	390	30
◆ Humboldt County / Shawn R. Hall / Shawn R. Hall / 1990										
84⁴/₈	14⁴/₈	14³/₈	7²/₈	7²/₈	10²/₈	7³/₈	6⁴/₈	6²/₈	390	30
◆ Humboldt County / Rebecca L. Webley / Rebecca L. Webley / 1993										
84⁴/₈	15³/₈	15⁴/₈	6⁶/₈	7	10⁶/₈	7²/₈	5⁴/₈	5⁷/₈	390	30
◆ Humboldt County / Eric D. Olson / Eric D. Olson / 1994										
84²/₈	17⁴/₈	17⁴/₈	7²/₈	7²/₈	8⁴/₈	5⁴/₈	4¹/₈	6	436	35
◆ Humboldt County / Gerald A. Lent / Gerald A. Lent / 1970										
84²/₈	16⁴/₈	16³/₈	6⁴/₈	6³/₈	8²/₈	5¹/₈	5⁵/₈	6¹/₈	436	35
◆ Humboldt County / David Perondi / David Perondi / 1976										
84²/₈	15⁵/₈	15⁶/₈	7	6⁷/₈	6⁴/₈	2	6⁶/₈	6⁶/₈	436	35
◆ Humboldt County / James R. Puryear / James R. Puryear / 1980										

Score	Length of Horn		Circumference of Base		Inside Spread	Tip-to-Tip Spread	Length of Prong		All-Time Rank	State Rank
	R	L	R	L			R	L		
$84\frac{2}{8}$	$17\frac{2}{8}$	$17\frac{3}{8}$	$6\frac{4}{8}$	$6\frac{6}{8}$	$8\frac{5}{8}$	$2\frac{2}{8}$	$5\frac{6}{8}$	$5\frac{4}{8}$	436	35
	◆ Washoe County / Judy Taylor / Judy Taylor / 1983									
$84\frac{2}{8}$	15	15	$6\frac{7}{8}$	$6\frac{6}{8}$	$12\frac{5}{8}$	$10\frac{2}{8}$	$6\frac{2}{8}$	6	436	35
	◆ White Pine County / Paul E. Podborny / Paul E. Podborny / 1985									
$84\frac{2}{8}$	16	16	$7\frac{4}{8}$	$7\frac{3}{8}$	$13\frac{2}{8}$	12	$4\frac{6}{8}$	$4\frac{2}{8}$	436	35
	◆ Washoe County / Eugene E. Belli / Eugene E. Belli / 1986									
$84\frac{2}{8}$	$17\frac{4}{8}$	$17\frac{1}{8}$	$6\frac{3}{8}$	$6\frac{3}{8}$	$10\frac{4}{8}$	$4\frac{4}{8}$	$5\frac{3}{8}$	$5\frac{2}{8}$	436	35
	◆ Humboldt County / Gary J. Farotte / Gary J. Farotte / 1994									
84	$15\frac{6}{8}$	$16\frac{2}{8}$	$6\frac{6}{8}$	$6\frac{7}{8}$	$14\frac{2}{8}$	9	$6\frac{4}{8}$	$6\frac{5}{8}$	500	42
	◆ Washoe County / Robert L. Mallory / Robert L. Mallory / 1969									
84	$16\frac{5}{8}$	$16\frac{3}{8}$	$6\frac{7}{8}$	$6\frac{6}{8}$	$8\frac{6}{8}$	$2\frac{3}{8}$	$6\frac{1}{8}$	$6\frac{3}{8}$	500	42
	◆ Humboldt County / Gary D. Bader / Gary D. Bader / 1970									
84	$17\frac{6}{8}$	$17\frac{4}{8}$	$6\frac{2}{8}$	$6\frac{1}{8}$	6	$5\frac{3}{8}$	6	$5\frac{3}{8}$	500	42
	◆ Washoe County / Jamie L. Kent / Jamie L. Kent / 1980									
84	16	16	$6\frac{4}{8}$	$6\frac{5}{8}$	10	$7\frac{6}{8}$	$5\frac{7}{8}$	$6\frac{1}{8}$	500	42
	◆ Washoe County / Bert F. Carder / Bert F. Carder / 1984									
84	$16\frac{3}{8}$	$16\frac{3}{8}$	$6\frac{6}{8}$	$6\frac{5}{8}$	$11\frac{3}{8}$	8	$5\frac{3}{8}$	$5\frac{3}{8}$	500	42
	◆ Elko County / Larri R. Naveran / Larri R. Naveran / 1989									
84	$17\frac{2}{8}$	$17\frac{4}{8}$	$6\frac{6}{8}$	$6\frac{6}{8}$	$14\frac{6}{8}$	$8\frac{5}{8}$	5	$4\frac{6}{8}$	500	42
	◆ Washoe County / Roger D. Puccinelli / Roger D. Puccinelli / 1989									
84	$17\frac{2}{8}$	$17\frac{2}{8}$	$6\frac{4}{8}$	$6\frac{6}{8}$	7	$2\frac{3}{8}$	$6\frac{4}{8}$	$6\frac{6}{8}$	500	42
	◆ Humboldt County / Andrew M. Specht / Andrew M. Specht / 1991									
84	$15\frac{6}{8}$	$15\frac{6}{8}$	$6\frac{6}{8}$	$6\frac{6}{8}$	$8\frac{7}{8}$	$4\frac{4}{8}$	6	$5\frac{7}{8}$	500	42
	◆ Washoe County / Timothy H. Humes / Timothy H. Humes / 1993									
$83\frac{6}{8}$	$16\frac{1}{8}$	$16\frac{4}{8}$	$6\frac{7}{8}$	$6\frac{4}{8}$	$9\frac{1}{8}$	$5\frac{6}{8}$	$6\frac{1}{8}$	$6\frac{3}{8}$	565	50
	◆ Humboldt County / Harold J. Ward / Harold J. Ward / 1981									
$83\frac{6}{8}$	$14\frac{7}{8}$	$15\frac{2}{8}$	$6\frac{2}{8}$	$6\frac{3}{8}$	$6\frac{5}{8}$	$3\frac{1}{8}$	5	$4\frac{5}{8}$	565	50
	◆ Washoe County / Robert A. Colon / Robert A. Colon / 1982									
$83\frac{6}{8}$	$16\frac{1}{8}$	$16\frac{1}{8}$	$6\frac{4}{8}$	$6\frac{3}{8}$	$12\frac{7}{8}$	$9\frac{6}{8}$	$6\frac{2}{8}$	6	565	50
	◆ Washoe County / Arthur L. Biggs / Arthur L. Biggs / 1984									
$83\frac{6}{8}$	17	$17\frac{2}{8}$	$6\frac{6}{8}$	$6\frac{6}{8}$	16	$11\frac{4}{8}$	$4\frac{5}{8}$	$4\frac{1}{8}$	565	50
	◆ Washoe County / P.D. Kiser / P.D. Kiser / 1990									
$83\frac{6}{8}$	$16\frac{5}{8}$	$16\frac{7}{8}$	$6\frac{4}{8}$	$6\frac{4}{8}$	$11\frac{7}{8}$	7	$5\frac{2}{8}$	5	565	50
	◆ Humboldt County / Sam Lair / Sam Lair / 1991									
$83\frac{4}{8}$	$15\frac{3}{8}$	$15\frac{3}{8}$	$6\frac{3}{8}$	$6\frac{3}{8}$	$10\frac{3}{8}$	$6\frac{4}{8}$	6	$6\frac{1}{8}$	624	55
	◆ Washoe County / James R. Cobb / James R. Cobb / 1978									
$83\frac{4}{8}$	$16\frac{4}{8}$	$16\frac{4}{8}$	$6\frac{4}{8}$	$6\frac{4}{8}$	$11\frac{7}{8}$	$6\frac{5}{8}$	$5\frac{5}{8}$	$5\frac{4}{8}$	624	55
	◆ Elko County / Eugene E. Schain / Eugene E. Schain / 1991									

Score	Length of Horn		Circumference of Base		Inside Spread	Tip-to-Tip Spread	Length of Prong		All-Time Rank	State Rank
	R	L	R	L			R	L		
◆ *Locality / Hunter / Owner / Date Killed*										
$83\frac{4}{8}$	$17\frac{3}{8}$	$17\frac{2}{8}$	$6\frac{5}{8}$	$6\frac{4}{8}$	10	5	$5\frac{5}{8}$	$5\frac{4}{8}$	624	55
◆ *Humboldt County / William J. Swartz, Jr. / William J. Swartz, Jr. / 1991*										
$83\frac{4}{8}$	$17\frac{3}{8}$	$16\frac{7}{8}$	$6\frac{3}{8}$	$6\frac{3}{8}$	8	$4\frac{7}{8}$	$6\frac{3}{8}$	$6\frac{4}{8}$	624	55
◆ *Washoe County / Robert J. Cornelius / Robert J. Cornelius / 1992*										
$83\frac{4}{8}$	$17\frac{5}{8}$	$17\frac{2}{8}$	$6\frac{2}{8}$	$6\frac{2}{8}$	17	15	$5\frac{6}{8}$	$6\frac{1}{8}$	624	55
◆ *Washoe County / Thomas V. Guio / Thomas V. Guio / 1994*										
$83\frac{2}{8}$	$17\frac{1}{8}$	$17\frac{1}{8}$	$6\frac{5}{8}$	$6\frac{6}{8}$	8	$2\frac{4}{8}$	$5\frac{1}{8}$	5	690	60
◆ *Washoe County / David Pohl / David Pohl / 1972*										
$83\frac{2}{8}$	$17\frac{5}{8}$	$17\frac{7}{8}$	$6\frac{5}{8}$	$6\frac{4}{8}$	15	$9\frac{1}{8}$	$4\frac{2}{8}$	$4\frac{7}{8}$	690	60
◆ *Humboldt County / Robert E. Stopper / Robert E. Stopper / 1979*										
$83\frac{2}{8}$	16	$16\frac{2}{8}$	$6\frac{1}{8}$	$6\frac{1}{8}$	$9\frac{5}{8}$	$3\frac{3}{8}$	$4\frac{4}{8}$	$4\frac{3}{8}$	690	60
◆ *Lincoln County / Linda P. Allen / Linda P. Allen / 1985*										
$83\frac{2}{8}$	$16\frac{2}{8}$	$16\frac{2}{8}$	$6\frac{4}{8}$	$6\frac{4}{8}$	$9\frac{4}{8}$	4	5	$5\frac{1}{8}$	690	60
◆ *Washoe County / Steve F. Holmes / Steve F. Holmes / 1990*										
$83\frac{2}{8}$	$15\frac{7}{8}$	$15\frac{7}{8}$	$6\frac{2}{8}$	$6\frac{2}{8}$	$9\frac{6}{8}$	$6\frac{6}{8}$	$5\frac{5}{8}$	$5\frac{6}{8}$	690	60
◆ *Mineral County / Victor Trujillo / Victor Trujillo / 1991*										
83	$15\frac{7}{8}$	$15\frac{7}{8}$	$6\frac{7}{8}$	7	$8\frac{6}{8}$	$6\frac{1}{8}$	$5\frac{2}{8}$	$5\frac{4}{8}$	775	65
◆ *Washoe County / Richard J. Depaoli / Richard J. Depaoli / 1982*										
83	$15\frac{4}{8}$	$15\frac{6}{8}$	$7\frac{2}{8}$	7	$10\frac{6}{8}$	$4\frac{6}{8}$	$5\frac{5}{8}$	$5\frac{4}{8}$	775	65
◆ *Humboldt County / Thomas S. Kelley / Thomas S. Kelley / 1983*										
83	$16\frac{5}{8}$	$17\frac{1}{8}$	$7\frac{1}{8}$	$7\frac{1}{8}$	$15\frac{6}{8}$	$13\frac{6}{8}$	$4\frac{5}{8}$	$4\frac{5}{8}$	775	65
◆ *Humboldt County / Lenda Z. Azcarate / Lenda Z. Azcarate / 1986*										
83	$15\frac{1}{8}$	15	7	$7\frac{1}{8}$	$9\frac{3}{8}$	7	$5\frac{6}{8}$	$5\frac{4}{8}$	775	65
◆ *Washoe County / Christopher T. Rores / Christopher T. Rores / 1987*										
83	$15\frac{4}{8}$	$15\frac{2}{8}$	$6\frac{4}{8}$	$6\frac{4}{8}$	8	3	$5\frac{5}{8}$	5	775	65
◆ *Washoe County / Edward J. Smith / Edward J. Smith / 1987*										
83	$15\frac{1}{8}$	$15\frac{3}{8}$	$7\frac{1}{8}$	7	14	$13\frac{4}{8}$	$5\frac{5}{8}$	$5\frac{3}{8}$	775	65
◆ *Washoe County / Joseph A. Burkhamer / Joseph A. Burkhamer / 1992*										
83	$15\frac{6}{8}$	16	$6\frac{7}{8}$	$6\frac{7}{8}$	$10\frac{7}{8}$	$7\frac{4}{8}$	$5\frac{3}{8}$	$5\frac{1}{8}$	775	65
◆ *Humboldt County / Harvey J. Estes / Harvey J. Estes / 1994*										
$82\frac{6}{8}$	$17\frac{1}{8}$	$17\frac{4}{8}$	$6\frac{6}{8}$	$6\frac{5}{8}$	$11\frac{1}{8}$	$4\frac{5}{8}$	$5\frac{2}{8}$	$5\frac{3}{8}$	868	72
◆ *Washoe County / Michael J. Lange / Michael J. Lange / 1983*										
$82\frac{6}{8}$	17	$16\frac{6}{8}$	$6\frac{6}{8}$	$6\frac{4}{8}$	$9\frac{3}{8}$	2	$5\frac{6}{8}$	$5\frac{5}{8}$	868	72
◆ *Washoe County / David E. Messmann / David E. Messmann / 1988*										
$82\frac{6}{8}$	$15\frac{4}{8}$	$15\frac{5}{8}$	$7\frac{2}{8}$	$7\frac{1}{8}$	$12\frac{1}{8}$	$7\frac{2}{8}$	$6\frac{3}{8}$	$5\frac{7}{8}$	868	72
◆ *Humboldt County / Darren K. Bader / Darren K. Bader / 1989*										
$82\frac{6}{8}$	$17\frac{3}{8}$	$17\frac{5}{8}$	$6\frac{3}{8}$	$6\frac{3}{8}$	$12\frac{4}{8}$	$9\frac{1}{8}$	$4\frac{7}{8}$	$4\frac{6}{8}$	868	72
◆ *Humboldt County / Christopher C. Hornbarger / Christopher C. Hornbarger / 1989*										

Score	Length of Horn		Circumference of Base		Inside Spread	Tip-to-Tip Spread	Length of Prong		All-Time Rank	State Rank
	R	L	R	L			R	L		

♦ *Locality / Hunter / Owner / Date Killed*

Score	R	L	R	L	Inside Spread	Tip-to-Tip	Prong R	Prong L	All-Time	State
$82^4/_8$	$15^6/_8$	$15^5/_8$	$6^5/_8$	$6^5/_8$	14	$10^7/_8$	$5^3/_8$	$5^4/_8$	949	76

♦ *Washoe County / James R. Stoner, Jr. / James R. Stoner, Jr. / 1969*

$82^4/_8$	$15^6/_8$	$15^3/_8$	$6^6/_8$	$6^5/_8$	$8^7/_8$	$6^4/_8$	$5^4/_8$	$5^4/_8$	949	76

♦ *Humboldt County / Robert C. Lawson / Robert C. Lawson / 1970*

$82^4/_8$	$15^7/_8$	$16^2/_8$	$6^1/_8$	$6^3/_8$	$14^6/_8$	$9^7/_8$	$6^1/_8$	$6^2/_8$	949	76

♦ *White Pine County / Tom I. Papagna, Jr. / Tom I. Papagna, Jr. / 1980*

$82^4/_8$	$16^6/_8$	$16^1/_8$	$6^6/_8$	$6^5/_8$	$8^1/_8$	$2^6/_8$	$5^7/_8$	$5^4/_8$	949	76

♦ *Washoe County / Vernon E. Benney / Vernon E. Benney / 1983*

$82^4/_8$	$16^4/_8$	$16^4/_8$	$6^3/_8$	$6^3/_8$	$11^2/_8$	$5^6/_8$	5	$5^4/_8$	949	76

♦ *Humboldt County / Frank K. Azcarate, Jr. / Frank K. Azcarate, Jr. / 1985*

$82^4/_8$	$17^1/_8$	$16^6/_8$	$6^4/_8$	$6^2/_8$	$11^6/_8$	$6^6/_8$	$5^6/_8$	$6^2/_8$	949	76

♦ *Humboldt County / Michael K. McBeath / Michael K. McBeath / 1988*

$82^4/_8$	$16^4/_8$	$16^5/_8$	$6^6/_8$	$6^6/_8$	$11^4/_8$	$9^1/_8$	5	$5^1/_8$	949	76

♦ *Humboldt County / Richard Vanderkous / Richard Vanderkous / 1989*

$82^4/_8$	$16^2/_8$	$16^3/_8$	$6^5/_8$	$6^6/_8$	$9^7/_8$	5	$4^5/_8$	$4^7/_8$	949	76

♦ *Washoe County / Dean C. Tischler / Dean C. Tischler / 1991*

$82^4/_8$	$15^5/_8$	$16^2/_8$	$6^6/_8$	$6^4/_8$	$9^3/_8$	$7^6/_8$	6	$5^4/_8$	949	76

♦ *Washoe County / Sydney M. Smith / Sydney M. Smith / 1992*

$82^2/_8$	$16^6/_8$	$16^4/_8$	$6^4/_8$	$6^5/_8$	$11^5/_8$	$8^6/_8$	$4^7/_8$	$4^7/_8$	1058	85

♦ *Washoe County / Thomas O. Malone / Thomas O. Malone / 1982*

$82^2/_8$	$18^2/_8$	$18^7/_8$	$6^3/_8$	$6^2/_8$	$9^5/_8$	$5^5/_8$	$5^2/_8$	$4^7/_8$	1058	85

♦ *Humboldt County / David E. Boyles, Sr. / David E. Boyles, Sr. / 1984*

$82^2/_8$	$15^2/_8$	15	$7^1/_8$	$7^1/_8$	$9^4/_8$	5	$5^2/_8$	$4^7/_8$	1058	85

♦ *Humboldt County / Andrew S. Burnett / Andrew S. Burnett / 1986*

$82^2/_8$	16	$15^5/_8$	$6^6/_8$	$6^5/_8$	$14^2/_8$	$10^1/_8$	$5^4/_8$	$5^3/_8$	1058	85

♦ *Washoe County / Robert E. Hill / Robert E. Hill / 1990*

82	$15^3/_8$	15	7	7	$10^1/_8$	5	$6^2/_8$	$5^3/_8$	1157	89

♦ *Washoe County / Oliver V. Iveson / Oliver V. Iveson / 1970*

82	$16^1/_8$	16	$6^1/_8$	$6^1/_8$	14	$10^1/_8$	$6^4/_8$	$6^4/_8$	1157	89

♦ *Washoe County / Jerry L. Nelms / Jerry L. Nelms / 1981*

82	$16^2/_8$	$15^6/_8$	$6^5/_8$	$6^5/_8$	$7^2/_8$	1	$5^7/_8$	$5^7/_8$	1157	89

♦ *Washoe County / Jack D. Bothwell / Jack D. Bothwell / 1984*

82	$15^3/_8$	$15^3/_8$	$6^6/_8$	$6^5/_8$	$7^2/_8$	$3^4/_8$	$6^2/_8$	$6^2/_8$	1157	89

♦ *Elko County / Roger L. Curry / Roger L. Curry / 1988*

82	$16^2/_8$	$15^7/_8$	$6^7/_8$	$6^5/_8$	$10^6/_8$	$5^4/_8$	$5^6/_8$	$5^5/_8$	1157	89

♦ *Washoe County / James E. Puryear / James E. Puryear / 1989*

82	$17^4/_8$	$17^3/_8$	$6^2/_8$	$6^2/_8$	$8^2/_8$	$2^7/_8$	$4^7/_8$	$4^7/_8$	1157	89

♦ *Washoe County / Paul J. Jesch / Paul J. Jesch / 1990*

Score	Length of Horn		Circumference of Base		Inside Spread	Tip-to-Tip Spread	Length of Prong		All-Time Rank	State Rank
	R	L	R	L			R	L		
	♦ *Locality / Hunter / Owner / Date Killed*									
82	15 7/8	15 7/8	6 4/8	6 4/8	9 7/8	5 3/8	4 6/8	5	1157	89
	♦ *Washoe County / James D. Jones / James D. Jones / 1991*									
82	16 2/8	16 3/8	6 4/8	6 3/8	6 3/8	0 1/8	5 1/8	5 1/8	1157	89
	♦ *Washoe County / Richard T. Adams / Richard T. Adams / 1992*									
81 6/8	15 4/8	15 6/8	7 1/8	7 1/8	11 4/8	6 4/8	4 6/8	4 4/8	1276	97
	♦ *Washoe County / Roger E. Hillygus / Roger E. Hillygus / 1990*									
81	14 7/8	15 3/8	7 2/8	7 1/8	12 5/8	9 4/8	4 6/8	5	1310	98
	♦ *Elko County / Sarah R. MacDonald / Sarah R. MacDonald / 1994*									
80 4/8	14 5/8	14 7/8	6 2/8	6 4/8	9 5/8	8 4/8	6	5 6/8	1345	99
	♦ *Washoe County / Jason C. Fritz / Jason C. Fritz / 1992*									
80 2/8	15 7/8	16	6 2/8	6 1/8	10 2/8	5 5/8	5 3/8	5 1/8	1360	100
	♦ *Humboldt County / Kenneth G. Detweiler / Kenneth G. Detweiler / 1991*									
80 2/8	15 5/8	15 4/8	6 6/8	6 5/8	14 6/8	10 5/8	5 4/8	5 1/8	1360	100
	♦ *Elko County / L. William Traverso / L. William Traverso / 1991*									
80	16 6/8	16 3/8	6 5/8	6 4/8	13	7 5/8	5 6/8	4 4/8	1386	102
	♦ *Washoe County / John P. Nolan / John P. Nolan / 1991*									
80	16 2/8	16 1/8	6 7/8	6 7/8	15 7/8	12 2/8	5 3/8	5 1/8	1386	102
	♦ *Elko County / Cheryl A. Porter / Cheryl A. Porter / 1994*									

John D. Fetcho filled his 1993 pronghorn permit with this massive trophy, scoring 88-6/8 points, that he shot on the UU Bar Ranch in Mora County, New Mexico.

Photograph Courtesy of John P. Grimmett

NEW MEXICO STATE RECORD
PRONGHORN
SCORE: 90%⁄8
Locality: Catron Co.   Date: 1986
Hunter: John P. Grimmett

NEW MEXICO

PRONGHORN

Score	Length of Horn		Circumference of Base		Inside Spread	Tip-to-Tip Spread	Length of Prong		All-Time Rank	State Rank
	R	L	R	L			R	L		
◆ Locality / Hunter / Owner / Date Killed										
90⁶⁄₈	17⁵⁄₈	17⁵⁄₈	7¹⁄₈	6⁷⁄₈	9⁵⁄₈	3⁴⁄₈	5⁴⁄₈	5²⁄₈	11	1
◆ Catron County / John P. Grimmett / John P. Grimmett / 1986										
89⁶⁄₈	18⁷⁄₈	19	6¹⁄₈	6	12⁴⁄₈	8	6	5⁶⁄₈	17	2
◆ Colfax County / Hudson DeCray / Hudson DeCray / 1989										
89⁴⁄₈	16	15⁴⁄₈	7⁴⁄₈	7⁴⁄₈	12	8⁵⁄₈	6⁵⁄₈	5⁶⁄₈	23	3
◆ Sierra County / P.K. Colquitt, Jr. / Thomas V. Schrivner / 1961										
89²⁄₈	18⁶⁄₈	18⁴⁄₈	7¹⁄₈	7⁵⁄₈	11¹⁄₈	3⁶⁄₈	5¹⁄₈	5²⁄₈	28	4
◆ Grant County / Jerry Saint / N.M. Dept. Game & Fish / 1975										
89²⁄₈	17²⁄₈	17¹⁄₈	7⁴⁄₈	7⁴⁄₈	11⁷⁄₈	4⁷⁄₈	6²⁄₈	5⁷⁄₈	28	4
◆ Mora County / Michael R. Memmer / Michael R. Memmer / 1991										
89	18	18¹⁄₈	6⁷⁄₈	7	10²⁄₈	3⁵⁄₈	6²⁄₈	6	36	6
◆ Lincoln County / Arthur E. Long / Arthur E. Long / 1985										
89	16²⁄₈	16²⁄₈	6⁷⁄₈	6⁶⁄₈	10²⁄₈	4⁵⁄₈	6⁴⁄₈	6⁴⁄₈	36	6
◆ Catron County / Picked Up / Charles A. Grimmett / 1989										
88⁶⁄₈	18⁷⁄₈	18⁶⁄₈	7²⁄₈	7	11⁷⁄₈	10¹⁄₈	6²⁄₈	5¹⁄₈	41	8
◆ Socorro County / J. Lyn Perry / J. Lyn Perry / 1976										
88⁶⁄₈	16⁵⁄₈	16⁵⁄₈	6³⁄₈	6³⁄₈	15⁶⁄₈	12⁷⁄₈	5⁷⁄₈	5⁷⁄₈	41	8
◆ Catron County / Gerald Roland Gold / Gerald Roland Gold / 1990										
88⁶⁄₈	16³⁄₈	16³⁄₈	7³⁄₈	7²⁄₈	13⁶⁄₈	12²⁄₈	5⁷⁄₈	6²⁄₈	41	8
◆ Socorro County / Grant L. Perry / Grant L. Perry / 1991										
88⁶⁄₈	17⁴⁄₈	17³⁄₈	6⁶⁄₈	6⁶⁄₈	16	12⁴⁄₈	5¹⁄₈	5¹⁄₈	41	8
◆ Mora County / John D. Fetcho / John D. Fetcho / 1993										
88⁴⁄₈	16⁵⁄₈	16²⁄₈	7	6⁷⁄₈	8	2¹⁄₈	5⁶⁄₈	5⁷⁄₈	51	12
◆ Catron County / Doug W. Kasey / Doug W. Kasey / 1987										
88	17¹⁄₈	17⁴⁄₈	7¹⁄₈	7	14¹⁄₈	9	5⁷⁄₈	6¹⁄₈	66	13
◆ Chaves County / Grant L. Perry / Grant L. Perry / 1988										
88	18⁶⁄₈	18¹⁄₈	6⁵⁄₈	6⁵⁄₈	9	3¹⁄₈	5⁵⁄₈	6³⁄₈	66	13
◆ Lincoln County / Vincent C. Gunn / Vincent C. Gunn / 1994										
87⁶⁄₈	16²⁄₈	16	7¹⁄₈	7¹⁄₈	11⁵⁄₈	9²⁄₈	6²⁄₈	6¹⁄₈	74	15
◆ Socorro County / Paul A. Stewart / Paul A. Stewart / 1993										
87⁴⁄₈	16²⁄₈	16³⁄₈	7	6⁷⁄₈	8³⁄₈	4¹⁄₈	5⁴⁄₈	5⁴⁄₈	79	16
◆ Socorro County / Enoch D. Brandenburg / Enoch D. Brandenburg / 1987										
87⁴⁄₈	16⁷⁄₈	16⁵⁄₈	6⁶⁄₈	6⁶⁄₈	11⁷⁄₈	7²⁄₈	6¹⁄₈	6¹⁄₈	79	16
◆ Mora County / Anthony J. Garrett / Anthony J. Garrett / 1987										
87⁴⁄₈	16²⁄₈	16¹⁄₈	7¹⁄₈	7²⁄₈	11⁶⁄₈	7²⁄₈	5⁶⁄₈	5⁵⁄₈	79	16
◆ Socorro County / Kevin B. Oliver / Kevin B. Oliver / 1993										

Score	Length of Horn		Circumference of Base		Inside Spread	Tip-to-Tip Spread	Length of Prong		All-Time Rank	State Rank
	R	L	R	L			R	L		
◆ *Locality / Hunter / Owner / Date Killed*										
87²/₈	16⁵/₈	17	7	7	13⁶/₈	10	5⁶/₈	5⁵/₈	85	19
◆ *Chaves County / Charles A. Grimmett / Charles A. Grimmett / 1988*										
87²/₈	16⁶/₈	16⁷/₈	7⁶/₈	7⁴/₈	15⁶/₈	12⁴/₈	5¹/₈	4⁶/₈	85	19
◆ *Colfax County / Calvin H. Rabb, Jr. / Calvin H. Rabb, Jr. / 1991*										
87²/₈	17⁶/₈	18¹/₈	6⁶/₈	7¹/₈	10²/₈	3⁴/₈	5⁶/₈	6	85	19
◆ *Catron County / Roy Holdridge / Roy Holdridge / 1991*										
87²/₈	15⁶/₈	15⁶/₈	6⁴/₈	6⁴/₈	10⁵/₈	6⁵/₈	6⁶/₈	6⁷/₈	85	19
◆ *Mora County / Stephen C. LeBlanc / Stephen C. LeBlanc / 1992*										
87	17⁶/₈	17⁴/₈	6³/₈	6³/₈	15⁴/₈	10⁴/₈	5²/₈	5³/₈	101	23
◆ *Magdalena / Picked Up / John L. Stein / 1970*										
87	16²/₈	16⁶/₈	6⁷/₈	7¹/₈	12³/₈	6⁷/₈	6	6⁴/₈	101	23
◆ *Catron County / Laurie Scott / Laurie Scott / 1987*										
86⁶/₈	17¹/₈	17	7	7	12⁴/₈	11²/₈	5¹/₈	5¹/₈	114	25
◆ *Catron County / John H. Bevel / John H. Bevel / 1986*										
86⁴/₈	15⁷/₈	15⁷/₈	7²/₈	7²/₈	12⁶/₈	9	5⁴/₈	5³/₈	140	26
◆ *Catron County / H. James Tonkin, Jr. / H. James Tonkin, Jr. / 1987*										
86²/₈	15⁶/₈	15⁶/₈	6³/₈	6²/₈	11	5⁷/₈	8³/₈	8⁴/₈	155	27
◆ *Otero County / Robert B. West / Dorothy West / 1957*										
86²/₈	18	17⁴/₈	6⁵/₈	6⁴/₈	9³/₈	7	3⁴/₈	3⁶/₈	155	27
◆ *Mora County / Hub R. Grounds / Hub R. Grounds / 1992*										
86²/₈	17¹/₈	17²/₈	7¹/₈	7²/₈	11⁴/₈	6³/₈	5⁵/₈	5¹/₈	155	27
◆ *Mora County / Len H. Guldman / Len H. Guldman / 1993*										
86²/₈	16⁷/₈	16⁷/₈	7¹/₈	7	11	4⁶/₈	5	4⁶/₈	155	27
◆ *Colfax County / James D. Knight / James D. Knight / 1994*										
86	17	17¹/₈	6³/₈	6²/₈	0	7⁴/₈	6³/₈	6²/₈	182	31
◆ *De Baca County / Bennie F. Hromadka / Bennie F. Hromadka / 1985*										
86	16²/₈	16²/₈	7	6⁷/₈	11⁷/₈	7⁶/₈	6³/₈	6⁷/₈	182	31
◆ *Sierra County / Vicki L. Leonard / Vicki L. Leonard / 1987*										
86	16¹/₈	16	6⁷/₈	7	11	7⁵/₈	6³/₈	5⁴/₈	182	31
◆ *Catron County / / N.M. Game & Fish Dept. / 1990*										
86	17¹/₈	16⁵/₈	6⁷/₈	6⁵/₈	11²/₈	5	6³/₈	6⁴/₈	182	31
◆ *Catron County / Armando J. Garcia / Armando J. Garcia / 1991*										
86	17²/₈	18	6⁴/₈	6⁴/₈	9⁵/₈	3⁴/₈	5⁵/₈	5⁴/₈	182	31
◆ *Socorro County / Joseph C. Sawyers / Joseph C. Sawyers / 1991*										
86	16²/₈	16³/₈	6⁷/₈	6⁷/₈	11²/₈	3²/₈	5	4⁵/₈	182	31
◆ *Colfax County / Robert D. Jones / Robert D. Jones / 1994*										
85⁶/₈	18⁴/₈	18¹/₈	6	6¹/₈	6⁵/₈	0	6¹/₈	6	211	37
◆ *Socorro County / V.F. Tannich / V.F. Tannich / 1965*										

Score	Length of Horn R	L	Circumference of Base R	L	Inside Spread	Tip-to-Tip Spread	Length of Prong R	L	All-Time Rank	State Rank
$85\frac{6}{8}$	17	$16\frac{7}{8}$	7	$6\frac{7}{8}$	11	$4\frac{7}{8}$	$5\frac{6}{8}$	$5\frac{4}{8}$	211	37
♦ Mora County / Michael J. Loomis / Michael J. Loomis / 1990										
$85\frac{4}{8}$	$17\frac{2}{8}$	$17\frac{3}{8}$	$6\frac{6}{8}$	$6\frac{3}{8}$	$11\frac{4}{8}$	$9\frac{4}{8}$	$6\frac{7}{8}$	$6\frac{2}{8}$	238	39
♦ Mora County / Roger B. Heemeier / Roger B. Heemeier / 1982										
$85\frac{4}{8}$	$15\frac{5}{8}$	$15\frac{7}{8}$	$6\frac{4}{8}$	$6\frac{4}{8}$	$9\frac{7}{8}$	$5\frac{6}{8}$	$7\frac{3}{8}$	$6\frac{4}{8}$	238	39
♦ Torrance County / James D. Moreland / James D. Moreland / 1991										
$85\frac{4}{8}$	$17\frac{4}{8}$	$17\frac{2}{8}$	6	6	$11\frac{4}{8}$	8	$4\frac{5}{8}$	$4\frac{4}{8}$	238	39
♦ De Baca County / Samuel S. Pattillo / Samuel S. Pattillo / 1991										
$85\frac{4}{8}$	$15\frac{6}{8}$	$15\frac{6}{8}$	7	7	$12\frac{3}{8}$	$10\frac{2}{8}$	4	$4\frac{2}{8}$	238	39
♦ Catron County / Tanya M. Horwath / Tanya M. Horwath / 1992										
$85\frac{2}{8}$	$17\frac{4}{8}$	$17\frac{5}{8}$	7	7	$9\frac{4}{8}$	$6\frac{1}{8}$	$4\frac{6}{8}$	$5\frac{2}{8}$	268	43
♦ Colfax County / Rick H. Jackson / Rick H. Jackson / 1977										
$85\frac{2}{8}$	$17\frac{7}{8}$	$18\frac{1}{8}$	$6\frac{7}{8}$	$6\frac{4}{8}$	$11\frac{1}{8}$	$4\frac{7}{8}$	5	$4\frac{3}{8}$	268	43
♦ Colfax County / John D. Pearson / John D. Pearson / 1977										
$85\frac{2}{8}$	17	$17\frac{1}{8}$	$6\frac{4}{8}$	$6\frac{4}{8}$	$14\frac{1}{8}$	$13\frac{2}{8}$	$5\frac{1}{8}$	$5\frac{1}{8}$	268	43
♦ Colfax County / S.X. Callahan III / S.X. Callahan III / 1983										
$85\frac{2}{8}$	16	18	$6\frac{6}{8}$	$6\frac{6}{8}$	13	$9\frac{2}{8}$	$5\frac{7}{8}$	6	268	43
♦ Socorro County / L. Steve Waide / L. Steve Waide / 1986										
85	$15\frac{3}{8}$	$15\frac{2}{8}$	$7\frac{4}{8}$	$7\frac{4}{8}$	11	$10\frac{1}{8}$	$6\frac{4}{8}$	6	301	47
♦ Henderson / Ron Vance / Ron Vance / 1943										
85	$16\frac{3}{8}$	$16\frac{1}{8}$	$6\frac{3}{8}$	$6\frac{4}{8}$	$9\frac{2}{8}$	$3\frac{5}{8}$	$5\frac{5}{8}$	$5\frac{5}{8}$	301	47
♦ Torrance County / Stephen A. Nisbet / Stephen A. Nisbet / 1975										
85	$18\frac{2}{8}$	$18\frac{5}{8}$	$6\frac{4}{8}$	$6\frac{5}{8}$	$13\frac{1}{8}$	9	5	$5\frac{3}{8}$	301	47
♦ Sierra County / Charles R. Bowen / Charles R. Bowen / 1977										
85	17	17	7	7	$15\frac{2}{8}$	$10\frac{6}{8}$	$5\frac{3}{8}$	$5\frac{4}{8}$	301	47
♦ De Baca County / Ernie Davis / Ernie Davis / 1991										
85	$15\frac{1}{8}$	$15\frac{1}{8}$	$7\frac{2}{8}$	$7\frac{3}{8}$	12	$9\frac{7}{8}$	5	5	301	47
♦ Socorro County / Jess Jones / Jess Jones / 1992										
$84\frac{6}{8}$	$16\frac{4}{8}$	$16\frac{4}{8}$	$6\frac{2}{8}$	$6\frac{2}{8}$	$13\frac{6}{8}$	$11\frac{4}{8}$	$4\frac{4}{8}$	$4\frac{4}{8}$	336	52
♦ Lincoln County / Pat McCarty / Pat McCarty / 1980										
$84\frac{6}{8}$	$15\frac{4}{8}$	$16\frac{2}{8}$	$7\frac{2}{8}$	$7\frac{1}{8}$	$11\frac{7}{8}$	$7\frac{7}{8}$	6	$6\frac{3}{8}$	336	52
♦ Mora County / William P. Boone / William P. Boone / 1987										
$84\frac{6}{8}$	$16\frac{1}{8}$	16	$6\frac{5}{8}$	$6\frac{5}{8}$	$8\frac{5}{8}$	$2\frac{2}{8}$	$5\frac{6}{8}$	$5\frac{5}{8}$	336	52
♦ Catron County / John P. Grimmett / John P. Grimmett / 1989										
$84\frac{6}{8}$	$16\frac{1}{8}$	$15\frac{7}{8}$	$6\frac{6}{8}$	$6\frac{6}{8}$	$11\frac{1}{8}$	$7\frac{4}{8}$	$5\frac{5}{8}$	$5\frac{6}{8}$	336	52
♦ Mora County / Linda J. McBride / Linda J. McBride / 1991										
$84\frac{6}{8}$	$17\frac{4}{8}$	$17\frac{5}{8}$	$7\frac{1}{8}$	$6\frac{7}{8}$	$13\frac{4}{8}$	$11\frac{6}{8}$	$4\frac{6}{8}$	$4\frac{6}{8}$	336	52
♦ Mora County / Robert Model / Robert Model / 1991										

Score	Length of Horn		Circumference of Base		Inside Spread	Tip-to-Tip Spread	Length of Prong		All-Time Rank	State Rank
	R	L	R	L			R	L		
♦ *Locality / Hunter / Owner / Date Killed*										
84⁶⁄₈	16⁵⁄₈	16⁶⁄₈	6⁴⁄₈	6⁴⁄₈	12⁴⁄₈	6⁷⁄₈	6²⁄₈	6²⁄₈	336	52
♦ *Socorro County / Charles A. Grimmett / Charles A. Grimmett / 1991*										
84⁶⁄₈	17	16⁴⁄₈	6⁴⁄₈	6⁵⁄₈	11⁴⁄₈	6⁴⁄₈	6	5⁴⁄₈	336	52
♦ *Lincoln County / Jay B. Robert / Jay B. Robert / 1991*										
84⁶⁄₈	16³⁄₈	16²⁄₈	6²⁄₈	6²⁄₈	15²⁄₈	11⁴⁄₈	5⁷⁄₈	6	336	52
♦ *Mora County / Donald W. Martin / Donald W. Martin / 1992*										
84⁶⁄₈	16	15²⁄₈	7	6⁷⁄₈	13⁷⁄₈	12	6	6	336	52
♦ *Mora County / Walter O. Ford, Jr. / Walter O. Ford, Jr. / 1994*										
84⁴⁄₈	16⁶⁄₈	16⁶⁄₈	6⁶⁄₈	6⁶⁄₈	15	11⁶⁄₈	5	5²⁄₈	390	61
♦ *Union County / Walter R. Schreiner, Jr. / Walter R. Schreiner, Jr. / 1991*										
84⁴⁄₈	16³⁄₈	16⁵⁄₈	6⁴⁄₈	6²⁄₈	13⁴⁄₈	9⁷⁄₈	6⁴⁄₈	6²⁄₈	390	61
♦ *Mora County / Kenneth L. Ebbens / Kenneth L. Ebbens / 1991*										
84²⁄₈	17¹⁄₈	17¹⁄₈	5⁷⁄₈	5⁶⁄₈	8⁷⁄₈	1¹⁄₈	7	6⁷⁄₈	436	63
♦ *Abbott / George H. Ray III / George H. Ray III / 1974*										
84²⁄₈	16⁴⁄₈	16²⁄₈	6⁵⁄₈	6⁵⁄₈	11⁶⁄₈	7³⁄₈	5⁴⁄₈	6²⁄₈	436	63
♦ *Mora County / Scott Steinkruger / Scott Steinkruger / 1989*										
84²⁄₈	17¹⁄₈	16²⁄₈	7¹⁄₈	7¹⁄₈	12	7⁷⁄₈	6⁷⁄₈	6²⁄₈	436	63
♦ *San Miguel County / Larry R. Griffin / Larry R. Griffin / 1990*										
84²⁄₈	17²⁄₈	17²⁄₈	6⁵⁄₈	6⁴⁄₈	12⁴⁄₈	8²⁄₈	5	5	436	63
♦ *Quay County / Marvin S. Keating / Marvin S. Keating / 1991*										
84²⁄₈	17³⁄₈	17³⁄₈	6⁶⁄₈	7	11⁷⁄₈	6⁶⁄₈	5³⁄₈	5⁷⁄₈	436	63
♦ *Mora County / Ralph C. Stayner / Ralph C. Stayner / 1991*										
84	16²⁄₈	16²⁄₈	6⁴⁄₈	6⁵⁄₈	12	9⁵⁄₈	5³⁄₈	5¹⁄₈	500	68
♦ *Mora County / Roger B. Coit / Roger B. Coit / 1983*										
84	16⁷⁄₈	17²⁄₈	6⁶⁄₈	6⁷⁄₈	12⁶⁄₈	7³⁄₈	5⁴⁄₈	5²⁄₈	500	68
♦ *Sierra County / Mike W. Leonard / Mike W. Leonard / 1987*										
84	14²⁄₈	14⁵⁄₈	7	7¹⁄₈	11¹⁄₈	7³⁄₈	5⁴⁄₈	5³⁄₈	500	68
♦ *Colfax County / Ruel T. Holt / Ruel T. Holt / 1988*										
84	16²⁄₈	16⁶⁄₈	6⁶⁄₈	6⁵⁄₈	10²⁄₈	6⁴⁄₈	5⁴⁄₈	5¹⁄₈	500	68
♦ *Mora County / Joseph J. Bongiovi, Jr. / Joseph J. Bongiovi, Jr. / 1992*										
84	16³⁄₈	16⁴⁄₈	6⁴⁄₈	6⁴⁄₈	12⁵⁄₈	6⁶⁄₈	5³⁄₈	5⁶⁄₈	500	68
♦ *Mora County / Mel L. Helm / Mel L. Helm / 1992*										
83⁶⁄₈	16³⁄₈	16⁷⁄₈	6²⁄₈	6¹⁄₈	8⁵⁄₈	2	6	6⁵⁄₈	565	73
♦ *Lincoln County / James R. Doverspike / James R. Doverspike / 1982*										
83⁶⁄₈	16⁷⁄₈	17	6³⁄₈	6⁴⁄₈	10⁶⁄₈	5⁶⁄₈	5	5¹⁄₈	565	73
♦ *Colfax County / Stephen C. LeBlanc / Stephen C. LeBlanc / 1985*										
83⁶⁄₈	15⁴⁄₈	15⁴⁄₈	7³⁄₈	7⁴⁄₈	13¹⁄₈	9⁶⁄₈	6²⁄₈	5⁶⁄₈	565	73
♦ *Colfax County / LeGrand C. Kirby III / LeGrand C. Kirby III / 1986*										

Score	Length of Horn		Circumference of Base		Inside Spread	Tip-to-Tip Spread	Length of Prong		All-Time Rank	State Rank
	R	L	R	L			R	L		

♦ Locality / Hunter / Owner / Date Killed

Score	R	L	R	L	Inside	Tip-to-Tip	R	L	Rank	Rank
83⁶⁄₈	16¹⁄₈	15⁷⁄₈	6⁵⁄₈	6⁴⁄₈	15²⁄₈	11⁵⁄₈	6³⁄₈	6	565	73

♦ *Catron County / Charles A. Grimmett / Charles A. Grimmett / 1986*

83⁶⁄₈	16⁶⁄₈	16⁵⁄₈	6⁵⁄₈	6⁴⁄₈	13³⁄₈	10	5⁴⁄₈	5²⁄₈	565	73

♦ *De Baca County / Ben L. Mueller / Ben L. Mueller / 1986*

83⁶⁄₈	17¹⁄₈	17³⁄₈	6	6¹⁄₈	9⁵⁄₈	4³⁄₈	5²⁄₈	5⁴⁄₈	565	73

♦ *Socorro County / William W. Klein / William W. Klein / 1991*

83⁶⁄₈	16⁴⁄₈	16⁶⁄₈	6³⁄₈	6⁴⁄₈	13⁶⁄₈	10	5	5¹⁄₈	565	73

♦ *Mora County / Brody Bonnett / Brody Bonnett / 1992*

83⁶⁄₈	16⁶⁄₈	16⁷⁄₈	6¹⁄₈	6¹⁄₈	10⁶⁄₈	6	5⁶⁄₈	5⁵⁄₈	565	73

♦ *Mora County / Edward C. Joseph / Edward C. Joseph / 1992*

83⁶⁄₈	15⁴⁄₈	15⁴⁄₈	6⁶⁄₈	6⁶⁄₈	14²⁄₈	11⁴⁄₈	6²⁄₈	6¹⁄₈	565	73

♦ *Mora County / Richard E. Joseph / Richard E. Joseph / 1993*

83⁴⁄₈	17	17	6⁵⁄₈	6³⁄₈	10⁶⁄₈	6⁶⁄₈	5¹⁄₈	5¹⁄₈	624	82

♦ *De Baca County / Glenn C. Conner / Glenn C. Conner / 1977*

83⁴⁄₈	17⁴⁄₈	17	6⁵⁄₈	7⁴⁄₈	9⁴⁄₈	4⁶⁄₈	5	5²⁄₈	624	82

♦ *Colfax County / James H. Hoffman / James H. Hoffman / 1982*

83⁴⁄₈	17⁴⁄₈	17²⁄₈	6⁷⁄₈	6⁷⁄₈	18	14	4⁵⁄₈	4⁵⁄₈	624	82

♦ *Colfax County / David S. Dickenson / David S. Dickenson / 1984*

83⁴⁄₈	16⁴⁄₈	16⁵⁄₈	6¹⁄₈	6	12⁴⁄₈	9¹⁄₈	5²⁄₈	5²⁄₈	624	82

♦ *Mora County / Brent Arrant / Brent Arrant / 1986*

83⁴⁄₈	16⁵⁄₈	16⁷⁄₈	6⁴⁄₈	6⁵⁄₈	9	3⁶⁄₈	5¹⁄₈	5³⁄₈	624	82

♦ *Colfax County / David M. Lackie / David M. Lackie / 1989*

83⁴⁄₈	15⁵⁄₈	16	6⁵⁄₈	6⁴⁄₈	15⁵⁄₈	12⁴⁄₈	5⁷⁄₈	5²⁄₈	624	82

♦ *Colfax County / Louie Alcon / Louie Alcon / 1990*

83⁴⁄₈	15⁶⁄₈	15⁵⁄₈	6⁶⁄₈	6⁷⁄₈	15⁵⁄₈	12⁴⁄₈	6³⁄₈	6³⁄₈	624	82

♦ *Socorro County / Michael T. Miller / Michael T. Miller / 1990*

83⁴⁄₈	17²⁄₈	17³⁄₈	6	6	8⁶⁄₈	3³⁄₈	5³⁄₈	5²⁄₈	624	82

♦ *Socorro County / Randy W. Tonkin / Randy W. Tonkin / 1991*

83⁴⁄₈	15⁷⁄₈	16	6⁶⁄₈	7	14⁷⁄₈	11⁵⁄₈	6	5²⁄₈	624	82

♦ *Mora County / Jeffrey D. Warren / Jeffrey D. Warren / 1991*

83⁴⁄₈	17⁵⁄₈	17⁵⁄₈	6³⁄₈	6³⁄₈	12	6⁷⁄₈	5	4⁶⁄₈	624	82

♦ *Otero County / Harold W. Lisby / Harold W. Lisby / 1992*

83⁴⁄₈	15⁶⁄₈	16	6	5⁷⁄₈	10¹⁄₈	5³⁄₈	6¹⁄₈	6¹⁄₈	624	82

♦ *Colfax County / Mark B. Henkel / Mark B. Henkel / 1994*

83²⁄₈	16⁷⁄₈	16⁷⁄₈	6²⁄₈	6¹⁄₈	11²⁄₈	7⁶⁄₈	5⁴⁄₈	5⁴⁄₈	690	93

♦ *Capitan / Lee H. Ingalls / Lee H. Ingalls / 1969*

83²⁄₈	16³⁄₈	16¹⁄₈	7²⁄₈	6⁷⁄₈	10⁷⁄₈	4⁶⁄₈	4⁶⁄₈	4	690	93

♦ *Socorro County / Charles M. McLaughlin / Charles M. McLaughlin / 1979*

Score	Length of Horn R	L	Circumference of Base R	L	Inside Spread	Tip-to-Tip Spread	Length of Prong R	L	All-Time Rank	State Rank
	◆ *Locality / Hunter / Owner / Date Killed*									
83 2/8	17 1/8	17 2/8	6 2/8	6 2/8	16 1/8	13	4 6/8	4 7/8	690	93
	◆ *Roosevelt County / Danny L. Tivis / Danny L. Tivis / 1979*									
83 2/8	16 1/8	16 3/8	6 6/8	6 5/8	14 3/8	10 1/8	5	5 2/8	690	93
	◆ *Mora County / James E. Davenport, Jr. / James E. Davenport, Jr. / 1983*									
83 2/8	17	17	6 6/8	6 5/8	9 7/8	4 5/8	5	4 7/8	690	93
	◆ *Colfax County / Stephen C. LeBlanc / Stephen C. LeBlanc / 1984*									
83 2/8	17 2/8	17 2/8	6	6	9 6/8	6 6/8	5 3/8	5 5/8	690	93
	◆ *Mora County / Patrick F. Taylor / Patrick F. Taylor / 1988*									
83 2/8	16	15 6/8	7	7	11 2/8	9	5 1/8	5 3/8	690	93
	◆ *Socorro County / Arthur R. Dubs / Arthur R. Dubs / 1989*									
83 2/8	16 7/8	16 6/8	6 2/8	6 3/8	11 4/8	6 4/8	5 7/8	5 6/8	690	93
	◆ *Colfax County / Robert J. Seeds / Robert J. Seeds / 1991*									
83 2/8	14 2/8	14 2/8	6 7/8	7	7 6/8	3 6/8	6 6/8	6 2/8	690	93
	◆ *Mora County / Robert J. Seeds / Robert J. Seeds / 1993*									
83	16	16	6 6/8	6 6/8	13 6/8	10 4/8	5	5	775	102
	◆ *Springer / Ronald E. McKinney / Ronald E. McKinney / 1973*									
83	16 2/8	16 3/8	6 4/8	6 3/8	10 2/8	4 1/8	5 6/8	4 6/8	775	102
	◆ *Colfax County / Jim Hoots / Jim Hoots / 1975*									
83	17	16 6/8	6 1/8	6 1/8	13 5/8	9 6/8	4 6/8	5 2/8	775	102
	◆ *Wagon Mound / Dale R. Leonard / Dale R. Leonard / 1976*									
83	16 2/8	16 1/8	6 6/8	6 5/8	11 6/8	10 7/8	5 7/8	5 4/8	775	102
	◆ *Harding County / Stephen C. LeBlanc / Stephen C. LeBlanc / 1977*									
83	15 7/8	15 7/8	7 1/8	7	13 6/8	9 3/8	5 6/8	5 4/8	775	102
	◆ *Colfax County / John W. Ladd / John W. Ladd / 1983*									
83	17 2/8	17 5/8	6	6	12 6/8	9	5 7/8	5 7/8	775	102
	◆ *Catron County / Dan L. Harper / Dan L. Harper / 1987*									
83	17 4/8	17 4/8	6 1/8	6	14 4/8	10	5	4	775	102
	◆ *Sierra County / Steven A. Berry / Steven A. Berry / 1988*									
83	15 4/8	15 6/8	7	7	9 2/8	6 1/8	5	5 6/8	775	102
	◆ *Mora County / Gerald W. Pullin / Gerald W. Pullin / 1990*									
83	16 1/8	15 6/8	6 2/8	6 1/8	10 1/8	4	5 7/8	5 6/8	775	102
	◆ *Lincoln County / Robert M. Rogulic / Robert M. Rogulic / 1990*									
83	17 1/8	17	6 4/8	6 3/8	13 1/8	8 5/8	5 1/8	4 6/8	775	102
	◆ *Socorro County / David A. Berry / David A. Berry / 1990*									
83	14	14 5/8	7	7	10 4/8	7 7/8	6 6/8	6 6/8	775	102
	◆ *Lincoln County / Johnny Bliznak / Johnny Bliznak / 1991*									
83	16 5/8	16 5/8	6 1/8	6	9 5/8	5 6/8	5 5/8	5 4/8	775	102
	◆ *Colfax County / W. Douglas Appling / W. Douglas Appling / 1993*									

Score	Length of Horn R	Length of Horn L	Circumference of Base R	Circumference of Base L	Inside Spread	Tip-to-Tip Spread	Length of Prong R	Length of Prong L	All-Time Rank	State Rank
	♦ *Locality / Hunter / Owner / Date Killed*									
83	15 7/8	15 5/8	6 4/8	6 3/8	10 6/8	6 2/8	5 4/8	5 2/8	775	102
	♦ *Colfax County / Robert D. Jones / Robert D. Jones / 1993*									
83	16	16	7 2/8	7 1/8	13 4/8	8 6/8	5 2/8	5 6/8	775	102
	♦ *Mora County / Len H. Guldman / Len H. Guldman / 1994*									
82 6/8	17 3/8	17 3/8	6 2/8	6 2/8	14 6/8	10 2/8	4 2/8	4 4/8	868	116
	♦ *Mora County / R.L. Wakefield / R.L. Wakefield / 1965*									
82 6/8	16 5/8	16 4/8	6 3/8	6 4/8	15 4/8	13 2/8	5 4/8	5 1/8	868	116
	♦ *Socorro County / Lawrence D. Vigil / Lawrence D. Vigil / 1970*									
82 6/8	16 6/8	17 2/8	6 6/8	6 6/8	10 5/8	6	5 1/8	5 2/8	868	116
	♦ *Catron County / David Chavez / David Chavez / 1978*									
82 6/8	16 7/8	16 6/8	6 2/8	6 2/8	11 3/8	8 3/8	4 7/8	5	868	116
	♦ *Mora County / Donald R. Warren / Donald R. Warren / 1982*									
82 6/8	16 2/8	16 3/8	6 3/8	6 3/8	12 1/8	8 7/8	6 1/8	6 1/8	868	116
	♦ *Catron County / H. James Tonkin, Jr. / H. James Tonkin, Jr. / 1990*									
82 6/8	16 4/8	16 6/8	6 1/8	6 1/8	9 4/8	7 3/8	6 2/8	6 2/8	868	116
	♦ *Mora County / Gilbert T. Adams / Gilbert T. Adams / 1992*									
82 6/8	16 1/8	15 5/8	6 1/8	6	7 1/8	0 5/8	6 6/8	6 2/8	868	116
	♦ *Lincoln County / Michael R. Tiffany / Michael R. Tiffany / 1992*									
82 6/8	16 4/8	16 4/8	7 2/8	7	10 7/8	5 4/8	4 7/8	4 7/8	868	116
	♦ *Mora County / Linda J. McBride / Linda J. McBride / 1993*									
82 6/8	17 7/8	17 6/8	6 5/8	6 5/8	15 2/8	10 7/8	5 2/8	5 1/8	868	116
	♦ *Mora County / Ernie Davis / Ernie Davis / 1993*									
82 4/8	16 1/8	16 6/8	6 6/8	6 6/8	11 2/8	5 6/8	5 3/8	5 4/8	949	125
	♦ *Catron County / C.J. Boyd / C.J. Boyd / 1952*									
82 4/8	14 4/8	14 6/8	7 1/8	7	11	9 3/8	6	5 6/8	949	125
	♦ *Cimarron / Ronald E. McKinney / Ronald E. McKinney / 1974*									
82 4/8	15 1/8	15 1/8	6 2/8	6 2/8	10 2/8	8 2/8	6	6 1/8	949	125
	♦ *Socorro County / Clyde C. Brumley / Clyde C. Brumley / 1981*									
82 4/8	16 6/8	16 6/8	6 3/8	6 3/8	10 6/8	5 4/8	5	5 4/8	949	125
	♦ *Union County / John W. Saunders / John W. Saunders / 1982*									
82 4/8	15 3/8	15 3/8	7 1/8	7 2/8	11 5/8	7 4/8	5 2/8	4 7/8	949	125
	♦ *Colfax County / John A. Jones / John A. Jones / 1987*									
82 4/8	15 6/8	15 6/8	6 3/8	6 3/8	8 4/8	3 4/8	5 6/8	5 7/8	949	125
	♦ *Colfax County / Roy G. Jones / Roy G. Jones / 1989*									
82 4/8	17 6/8	17 6/8	5 5/8	5 4/8	9 7/8	3 3/8	5 2/8	5 2/8	949	125
	♦ *Mora County / Gilbert T. Adams / Gilbert T. Adams / 1991*									
82 4/8	17 2/8	17 6/8	6 1/8	6	10 1/8	4 7/8	6 2/8	5 6/8	949	125
	♦ *Mora County / Dan E. McBride / Dan E. McBride / 1991*									

Score	Length of Horn		Circumference of Base		Inside Spread	Tip-to-Tip Spread	Length of Prong		All-Time Rank	State Rank
	R	L	R	L			R	L		

♦ *Locality / Hunter / Owner / Date Killed*

Score	R	L	R	L	Inside Spread	Tip-to-Tip	R	L	All-Time	State
82 4/8	17	16 6/8	6 3/8	6 3/8	9	2 6/8	5 2/8	5 1/8	949	125

♦ *Mora County / Kenneth G. Planet / Kenneth G. Planet / 1991*

| 82 4/8 | 16 4/8 | 16 1/8 | 6 2/8 | 6 2/8 | 10 7/8 | 5 5/8 | 5 6/8 | 5 4/8 | 949 | 125 |

♦ *Colfax County / Robert J. Seeds / Robert J. Seeds / 1992*

| 82 2/8 | 16 7/8 | 16 7/8 | 5 7/8 | 6 | 14 5/8 | 13 4/8 | 6 2/8 | 6 3/8 | 1058 | 135 |

♦ *Chaves County / Harvey Pirtle / Glenn Marshall / 1939*

| 82 2/8 | 14 5/8 | 14 4/8 | 7 1/8 | 7 1/8 | 8 2/8 | 4 4/8 | 5 4/8 | 5 5/8 | 1058 | 135 |

♦ *Henderson / Ron Vance / Ron Vance / 1947*

| 82 2/8 | 17 2/8 | 16 6/8 | 6 | 6 | 7 2/8 | 12 6/8 | 6 2/8 | 6 3/8 | 1058 | 135 |

♦ *New Mexico / Joan V. Gordon / Joan V. Gordon / 1961*

| 82 2/8 | 16 6/8 | 16 4/8 | 6 3/8 | 6 4/8 | 15 | 11 | 6 1/8 | 6 1/8 | 1058 | 135 |

♦ *Otero County / Heber Simmons, Jr. / Heber Simmons, Jr. / 1978*

| 82 2/8 | 17 | 17 2/8 | 6 2/8 | 6 2/8 | 8 6/8 | 3 4/8 | 4 4/8 | 4 4/8 | 1058 | 135 |

♦ *Torrance County / Michael F. Killoy / Michael F. Killoy / 1987*

| 82 2/8 | 16 5/8 | 16 4/8 | 6 | 6 | 11 | 6 7/8 | 5 5/8 | 5 6/8 | 1058 | 135 |

♦ *Catron County / Harry J. Turiello / Harry J. Turiello / 1987*

| 82 2/8 | 16 4/8 | 17 | 6 2/8 | 6 3/8 | 10 4/8 | 6 1/8 | 6 3/8 | 4 6/8 | 1058 | 135 |

♦ *Catron County / Todd Garrison / Todd Garrison / 1990*

| 82 2/8 | 14 4/8 | 14 4/8 | 6 6/8 | 6 5/8 | 10 5/8 | 6 6/8 | 6 | 5 2/8 | 1058 | 135 |

♦ *Colfax County / Virgil A. Lair / Virgil A. Lair / 1990*

| 82 2/8 | 15 5/8 | 15 6/8 | 6 4/8 | 6 4/8 | 10 3/8 | 7 6/8 | 5 2/8 | 5 4/8 | 1058 | 135 |

♦ *Mora County / Allen E. Thomas / Allen E. Thomas / 1990*

| 82 2/8 | 17 2/8 | 16 7/8 | 6 3/8 | 6 4/8 | 11 1/8 | 5 | 5 1/8 | 5 | 1058 | 135 |

♦ *Sierra County / Gerald S. Janos / Gerald S. Janos / 1991*

| 82 2/8 | 16 2/8 | 16 2/8 | 6 2/8 | 6 2/8 | 10 4/8 | 5 7/8 | 4 7/8 | 5 | 1058 | 135 |

♦ *Colfax County / Cooper Moore / Cooper Moore / 1992*

| 82 2/8 | 17 1/8 | 17 | 6 | 5 7/8 | 9 1/8 | 4 5/8 | 5 6/8 | 6 | 1058 | 135 |

♦ *Quay County / Lonnie L. Ritchey / Lonnie L. Ritchey / 1992*

| 82 2/8 | 15 | 15 | 7 | 6 7/8 | 8 2/8 | 2 7/8 | 4 6/8 | 4 6/8 | 1058 | 135 |

♦ *Catron County / Sam Jaksick, Jr. / Sam Jaksick, Jr. / 1992*

| 82 2/8 | 16 1/8 | 16 1/8 | 6 3/8 | 6 2/8 | 7 7/8 | 2 6/8 | 5 3/8 | 5 2/8 | 1058 | 135 |

♦ *Mora County / Anses Joseph, Jr. / Anses Joseph, Jr. / 1993*

| 82 2/8 | 15 5/8 | 15 5/8 | 6 2/8 | 6 3/8 | 10 5/8 | 5 3/8 | 5 | 5 | 1058 | 135 |

♦ *Catron County / David Fulson / David Fulson / 1994*

| 82 2/8 | 16 6/8 | 16 3/8 | 5 6/8 | 5 6/8 | 11 5/8 | 8 5/8 | 6 7/8 | 6 6/8 | 1058 | 135 |

♦ *Socorro County / Mark A. Cadwallader / Mark A. Cadwallader / 1994*

| 82 | 15 4/8 | 15 5/8 | 6 7/8 | 6 7/8 | 12 4/8 | 6 3/8 | 5 4/8 | 5 4/8 | 1157 | 151 |

♦ *Catron County / Floyd Todd / Floyd Todd / 1947*

NEW MEXICO PRONGHORN *(continued)*

Score	Length of Horn R	L	Circumference of Base R	L	Inside Spread	Tip-to-Tip Spread	Length of Prong R	L	All-Time Rank	State Rank
	♦ *Locality / Hunter / Owner / Date Killed*									
82	17⁴⁄₈	17⁵⁄₈	6¹⁄₈	6	12³⁄₈	5⁶⁄₈	4⁵⁄₈	4⁶⁄₈	1157	151
	♦ *Santa Rosa / Frank C. Hibben / Frank C. Hibben / 1955*									
82	17	17	6²⁄₈	6¹⁄₈	12¹⁄₈	6⁴⁄₈	4³⁄₈	3²⁄₈	1157	151
	♦ *McKinley County / W.R. Phillips / W.R. Phillips / 1965*									
82	17⁷⁄₈	17⁶⁄₈	5⁵⁄₈	5⁴⁄₈	12⁷⁄₈	6⁷⁄₈	5⁴⁄₈	5³⁄₈	1157	151
	♦ *Otero County / Robert E. Anton / Robert E. Anton / 1978*									
82	16⁵⁄₈	16³⁄₈	6¹⁄₈	6⁴⁄₈	14¹⁄₈	10¹⁄₈	5⁶⁄₈	5⁶⁄₈	1157	151
	♦ *Quay County / Donald E. Fritz / Donald E. Fritz / 1984*									
82	16	15³⁄₈	6⁴⁄₈	6⁴⁄₈	11	8¹⁄₈	4⁶⁄₈	4⁶⁄₈	1157	151
	♦ *Harding County / Andrew J. Ortega / Andrew J. Ortega / 1988*									
82	16⁷⁄₈	17	6³⁄₈	6⁴⁄₈	11²⁄₈	6	4⁶⁄₈	4⁴⁄₈	1157	151
	♦ *Mora County / H.P. Wood / H.P. Wood / 1988*									
82	15⁷⁄₈	16²⁄₈	6³⁄₈	6⁴⁄₈	10³⁄₈	4⁶⁄₈	6¹⁄₈	5⁷⁄₈	1157	151
	♦ *Mora County / Todd S. Hyden / Todd S. Hyden / 1990*									
82	17	17²⁄₈	6⁶⁄₈	6⁶⁄₈	9²⁄₈	3	3⁵⁄₈	5¹⁄₈	1157	151
	♦ *Lincoln County / Steve A. Marasovich, Jr. / Steve A. Marasovich, Jr. / 1990*									
82	15⁷⁄₈	15³⁄₈	7¹⁄₈	7¹⁄₈	11⁴⁄₈	7²⁄₈	4³⁄₈	4⁴⁄₈	1157	151
	♦ *Mora County / Raymond R. Gonzales / Charlie Hooser / 1991*									
82	16²⁄₈	16¹⁄₈	6	6	13³⁄₈	8⁶⁄₈	5	5³⁄₈	1157	151
	♦ *Catron County / Spence Dupree / Spence Dupree / 1992*									
82	16¹⁄₈	16¹⁄₈	6⁴⁄₈	6⁴⁄₈	13⁶⁄₈	10²⁄₈	5⁵⁄₈	5⁵⁄₈	1157	151
	♦ *Colfax County / Kyle G. Hyden / Kyle G. Hyden / 1992*									
82	16³⁄₈	16³⁄₈	6⁵⁄₈	6⁵⁄₈	7	2⁵⁄₈	4⁷⁄₈	4⁷⁄₈	1157	151
	♦ *Mora County / Luke C. Kellogg / Luke C. Kellogg / 1992*									
82	16¹⁄₈	16	6⁴⁄₈	6⁴⁄₈	9²⁄₈	3	4⁴⁄₈	4⁶⁄₈	1157	151
	♦ *Colfax County / Maurice R. Strawn / Maurice R. Strawn / 1992*									
82	16¹⁄₈	16⁵⁄₈	7	6⁷⁄₈	12	7⁴⁄₈	4⁶⁄₈	4⁶⁄₈	1157	151
	♦ *Colfax County / James D. Verbrugge / James D. Verbrugge / 1992*									
82	16²⁄₈	16¹⁄₈	6¹⁄₈	5⁶⁄₈	10⁷⁄₈	5⁴⁄₈	6¹⁄₈	5⁶⁄₈	1157	151
	♦ *Catron County / Donald K. Lash / Donald K. Lash / 1992*									
82	17	16⁵⁄₈	6	6	15⁶⁄₈	14	6³⁄₈	5⁶⁄₈	1157	151
	♦ *Colfax County / David R. Raemisch / David R. Raemisch / 1993*									
81⁶⁄₈	16⁵⁄₈	16⁶⁄₈	6⁴⁄₈	6⁴⁄₈	14⁴⁄₈	11³⁄₈	4⁶⁄₈	5²⁄₈	1276	168
	♦ *Catron County / Shelton I. Pricer / Shelton I. Pricer / 1987*									
81⁶⁄₈	15²⁄₈	15	6¹⁄₈	6¹⁄₈	10²⁄₈	5⁷⁄₈	6¹⁄₈	6⁴⁄₈	1276	168
	♦ *Colfax County / Scott D. Fink / Scott D. Fink / 1993*									
81⁴⁄₈	14⁶⁄₈	15	6⁷⁄₈	6⁶⁄₈	8⁶⁄₈	4³⁄₈	5⁵⁄₈	5⁶⁄₈	1283	170
	♦ *Colfax County / LeGrand C. Kirby III / LeGrand C. Kirby III / 1989*									

Score	Length of Horn R	L	Circumference of Base R	L	Inside Spread	Tip-to-Tip Spread	Length of Prong R	L	All-Time Rank	State Rank
	◆ *Locality / Hunter / Owner / Date Killed*									
81⁴⁄₈	16⁶⁄₈	16³⁄₈	6¹⁄₈	6¹⁄₈	6³⁄₈	1²⁄₈	6⁴⁄₈	6⁶⁄₈	1283	170
	◆ *Mora County / Kenneth L. Ebbens / Kenneth L. Ebbens / 1990*									
81²⁄₈	16⁷⁄₈	16⁷⁄₈	6	6¹⁄₈	8²⁄₈	1⁶⁄₈	5⁵⁄₈	5⁷⁄₈	1290	172
	◆ *Mora County / S. Kim Bonnett / S. Kim Bonnett / 1990*									
81²⁄₈	15⁷⁄₈	15⁶⁄₈	6⁴⁄₈	6⁵⁄₈	9⁶⁄₈	4³⁄₈	5³⁄₈	5⁴⁄₈	1290	172
	◆ *Union County / Orville L. Harris / Orville L. Harris / 1990*									
81²⁄₈	16³⁄₈	16⁴⁄₈	6¹⁄₈	6¹⁄₈	12	9¹⁄₈	4⁷⁄₈	5²⁄₈	1290	172
	◆ *Socorro County / Stephen J. McGaughey / Stephen J. McGaughey / 1990*									
81²⁄₈	15⁷⁄₈	16³⁄₈	6²⁄₈	6⁴⁄₈	11³⁄₈	10³⁄₈	5	4⁷⁄₈	1290	172
	◆ *Union County / Keith E. Philippi / Keith E. Philippi / 1991*									
81²⁄₈	16⁵⁄₈	16⁶⁄₈	6	6	12¹⁄₈	7⁶⁄₈	5³⁄₈	5⁴⁄₈	1290	172
	◆ *Torrance County / Robin A. Rader / Robin A. Rader / 1991*									
81²⁄₈	16	15⁴⁄₈	6²⁄₈	6⁴⁄₈	12²⁄₈	8⁴⁄₈	6¹⁄₈	6	1290	172
	◆ *Harding County / Joseph Madrid / Joseph Madrid / 1992*									
81	15⁴⁄₈	15⁴⁄₈	6³⁄₈	6²⁄₈	11⁷⁄₈	7⁶⁄₈	6⁶⁄₈	6¹⁄₈	1310	178
	◆ *Socorro County / Donald Reuter / Donald Reuter / 1985*									
81	15⁶⁄₈	15⁵⁄₈	6⁵⁄₈	6⁴⁄₈	13⁴⁄₈	9	5⁵⁄₈	5	1310	178
	◆ *Colfax County / John J. Doherty / John J. Doherty / 1987*									
81	16¹⁄₈	16³⁄₈	6¹⁄₈	6²⁄₈	15⁴⁄₈	12¹⁄₈	5⁵⁄₈	5⁵⁄₈	1310	178
	◆ *Colfax County / Robert D. Jones / Robert D. Jones / 1992*									
81	16⁷⁄₈	17	6⁴⁄₈	6⁵⁄₈	8⁴⁄₈	2⁵⁄₈	4⁵⁄₈	4¹⁄₈	1310	178
	◆ *Colfax County / Kelly L. Beckstrom / Kelly L. Beckstrom / 1994*									
81	15⁷⁄₈	15⁷⁄₈	6⁴⁄₈	6⁴⁄₈	11⁵⁄₈	6⁵⁄₈	4³⁄₈	4	1310	178
	◆ *Colfax County / Scott D. Fink / Scott D. Fink / 1994*									
80⁶⁄₈	15⁴⁄₈	15⁴⁄₈	7	6⁶⁄₈	11⁷⁄₈	9⁵⁄₈	5²⁄₈	5	1327	183
	◆ *Socorro County / Mark D. Nuessle / Mark D. Nuessle / 1987*									
80⁶⁄₈	17⁴⁄₈	16⁶⁄₈	6⁴⁄₈	6⁴⁄₈	9	3	4⁴⁄₈	5	1327	183
	◆ *Colfax County / Dana C. Nelson / Dana C. Nelson / 1991*									
80⁶⁄₈	15	15	7³⁄₈	7³⁄₈	6	3³⁄₈	4²⁄₈	4²⁄₈	1327	183
	◆ *Mora County / Donald J. Greener / Donald J. Greener / 1992*									
80⁶⁄₈	15³⁄₈	15³⁄₈	6³⁄₈	6³⁄₈	14¹⁄₈	11⁵⁄₈	5⁷⁄₈	5¹⁄₈	1327	183
	◆ *Catron County / Patrick Gilligan, Jr. / Patrick Gilligan, Jr. / 1994*									
80⁴⁄₈	15	15	6²⁄₈	6²⁄₈	12¹⁄₈	8	5⁴⁄₈	5²⁄₈	1345	187
	◆ *Catron County / Charles A. Grimmett / Charles A. Grimmett / 1987*									
80²⁄₈	17	16⁶⁄₈	6¹⁄₈	6¹⁄₈	11⁶⁄₈	8¹⁄₈	5⁴⁄₈	5⁵⁄₈	1360	188
	◆ *Socorro County / James E. Smith, Jr. / James E. Smith, Jr. / 1990*									
80²⁄₈	15²⁄₈	15⁴⁄₈	6¹⁄₈	6¹⁄₈	10⁶⁄₈	8²⁄₈	5⁴⁄₈	5²⁄₈	1360	188
	◆ *Mora County / Edward J. Moxley / Edward J. Moxley / 1990*									

NEW MEXICO PRONGHORN *(continued)*

Score	Length of Horn R	Length of Horn L	Circumference of Base R	Circumference of Base L	Inside Spread	Tip-to-Tip Spread	Length of Prong R	Length of Prong L	All-Time Rank	State Rank
	♦ *Locality / Hunter / Owner / Date Killed*									
80	17 3/8	16 7/8	6 2/8	6 2/8	9 5/8	3 7/8	3 4/8	3 7/8	1386	190
	♦ *Mora County / Michael E. Bailey / Michael E. Bailey / 1987*									
80	15 5/8	15 7/8	5 6/8	6	9 1/8	4 2/8	5 5/8	5 6/8	1386	190
	♦ *Chaves County / William T. Simmons / William T. Simmons / 1987*									
80	15 4/8	15	6	5 7/8	10 5/8	6 1/8	5 4/8	5 6/8	1386	190
	♦ *Catron County / Mike Steele / Mike Steele / 1989*									
80	16 2/8	16 4/8	6 2/8	6 1/8	9 6/8	3 2/8	5 2/8	5 7/8	1386	190
	♦ *Mora County / Kerry Egan / Kerry Egan / 1991*									
80	16 1/8	16 1/8	6 1/8	6 1/8	6	2 1/8	5 2/8	5	1386	190
	♦ *Lincoln County / James K. Court / James K. Court / 1993*									

Photograph Courtesy of Archie Malm

NORTH DAKOTA NUMBER THREE
PRONGHORN
SCORE: 85
Locality: Raleigh   Date: 1958
Hunter: Archie Malm

NORTH DAKOTA
PRONGHORN

Score	Length of Horn		Circumference of Base		Inside Spread	Tip-to-Tip Spread	Length of Prong		All-Time Rank	State Rank
	R	L	R	L			R	L		
◆ Locality / Hunter / Owner / Date Killed										
86 4/8	16 6/8	16 7/8	6 4/8	6 5/8	9	2 4/8	5 5/8	5 6/8	140	1
◆ Billings County / Greg A. Ganje / Greg A. Ganje / 1990										
85 2/8	15	14 7/8	7 1/8	7 1/8	10 3/8	7 3/8	6 3/8	5 7/8	268	2
◆ McKenzie County / Michael A. Palmer / Michael A. Palmer / 1990										
85	15	15	6 6/8	6 5/8	14 1/8	10 7/8	5 7/8	6	301	3
◆ Raleigh / Archie Malm / Archie Malm / 1958										
84 4/8	15 7/8	15 6/8	7 2/8	7 4/8	10 6/8	5 5/8	5 2/8	6 3/8	390	4
◆ North Dakota / Dale Linderman / Dale Linderman / PR 1952										
83 4/8	14	14 4/8	6 7/8	6 4/8	12 5/8	10 1/8	6 4/8	6 2/8	624	5
◆ Watford City / Dean Etl / Dean Etl / 1964										
82 4/8	15 1/8	16	6 5/8	6 3/8	6 3/8	4 5/8	6 1/8	6 4/8	949	6
◆ Butte / E.J. Weigel / E.J. Weigel / 1966										
82 4/8	16 7/8	17	6 2/8	6 1/8	10 2/8	6 1/8	5 2/8	5 5/8	949	6
◆ Slope County / Marlin J. Kapp / Marlin J. Kapp / 1975										
82 4/8	15 2/8	15 2/8	6 5/8	6 5/8	9 5/8	4 7/8	5 4/8	5 3/8	949	6
◆ McKenzie County / Nathan S. Gilbertson / Nathan S. Gilbertson / 1990										
82 2/8	16 5/8	16 6/8	6 4/8	6 3/8	10 5/8	4 5/8	4 5/8	4 4/8	1058	9
◆ Hettinger / Art Score / Art Score / 1957										
82 2/8	16 6/8	16 3/8	6 5/8	6 4/8	11	11 4/8	5	5	1058	9
◆ Bowen / Lee Atkinson / Sioux Sport Goods / 1966										
82 2/8	16 6/8	16 5/8	6 2/8	6 2/8	11	7	5	5 2/8	1058	9
◆ Slope County / Marty Beard / Marty Beard / 1992										
82	15 7/8	15 7/8	6 3/8	6 3/8	14 4/8	11	5 3/8	5 4/8	1157	12
◆ Billings County / Curtis D. Decker / Curtis D. Decker / 1988										
82	16 5/8	16 7/8	6 2/8	6 1/8	16 3/8	12 3/8	5 2/8	5	1157	12
◆ Slope County / Todd M. Quinn / Todd M. Quinn / 1990										
82	16 2/8	15 4/8	6 3/8	6 3/8	11 1/8	6 3/8	5 7/8	6 3/8	1157	12
◆ Slope County / Sherry L. Niesar / Sherry L. Niesar / 1993										

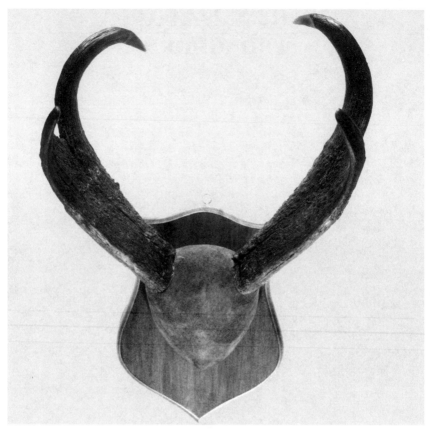

Photograph Courtesy of R.L. Williams

OKLAHOMA STATE RECORD
PRONGHORN
SCORE: 85⅝
Locality: Boise City   Date: 1966
Hunter: R.L. Williams

OKLAHOMA
PRONGHORN

Score	Length of Horn		Circumference of Base		Inside Spread	Tip-to-Tip Spread	Length of Prong		All-Time Rank	State Rank
	R	L	R	L			R	L		
	◆ *Locality / Hunter / Owner / Date Killed*									
85⁶⁄₈	16	15⁶⁄₈	7	6⁵⁄₈	10⁶⁄₈	6⅛	6³⁄₈	6⅛	211	1
	◆ *Boise City / R.L. Williams / R.L. Williams / 1966*									

Photograph Courtesy of E.C. Starr

**OREGON STATE RECORD
PRONGHORN
SCORE: 90**
Locality: Guano Creek   Date: 1942
Hunter: E.C. Starr

OREGON

PRONGHORN

Score	Length of Horn		Circumference of Base		Inside Spread	Tip-to-Tip Spread	Length of Prong		All-Time Rank	State Rank
	R	L	R	L			R	L		
◆ Locality / Hunter / Owner / Date Killed										
90	19⁴⁄₈	19⁵⁄₈	7	6⁶⁄₈	10¹⁄₈	8	4⁷⁄₈	4⁶⁄₈	16	1
◆ Guano Creek / E.C. Starr / E.C. Starr / 1942										
87²⁄₈	16⁴⁄₈	17	7	6⁷⁄₈	13³⁄₈	11⁴⁄₈	7⁴⁄₈	7²⁄₈	85	2
◆ Lake County / Ronald E. Hills / Ronald E. Hills / 1966										
87	17²⁄₈	17²⁄₈	6⁴⁄₈	6⁶⁄₈	10⁷⁄₈	6⁴⁄₈	6²⁄₈	5⁷⁄₈	101	3
◆ Lake County / JoAnn Hathaway / JoAnn Hathaway / 1976										
86⁴⁄₈	15⁷⁄₈	15⁷⁄₈	6⁵⁄₈	6⁵⁄₈	10⁴⁄₈	5²⁄₈	6⁷⁄₈	7	140	4
◆ Lake County / James W. Greer / James W. Greer / 1976										
86⁴⁄₈	17³⁄₈	17⁵⁄₈	6⁴⁄₈	6⁴⁄₈	14⁶⁄₈	13	6⁵⁄₈	7	140	4
◆ Malheur County / Nicholas J. Vidan / Nicholas J. Vidan / 1991										
86⁴⁄₈	17⁵⁄₈	17⁴⁄₈	6⁶⁄₈	6⁶⁄₈	10⁷⁄₈	4²⁄₈	5⁴⁄₈	5⁴⁄₈	140	4
◆ Harney County / Sam L. Wilkins, Jr. / Sam L. Wilkins, Jr. / 1991										
86	14²⁄₈	14⁵⁄₈	7⁴⁄₈	7⁵⁄₈	10²⁄₈	7⁵⁄₈	6⁷⁄₈	7	182	7
◆ Lake County / Frank Biggs / Frank Biggs / 1985										
85⁴⁄₈	17⁶⁄₈	17³⁄₈	7	7	14¹⁄₈	12²⁄₈	5³⁄₈	6	238	8
◆ Lake County / Edna J. Kettenburg / Edna J. Kettenburg / 1985										
85⁴⁄₈	16	16²⁄₈	7¹⁄₈	6⁵⁄₈	12⁵⁄₈	8³⁄₈	6	5⁴⁄₈	238	8
◆ Harney County / Van G. Decker / Van G. Decker / 1990										
85²⁄₈	15²⁄₈	15¹⁄₈	7⁵⁄₈	7³⁄₈	10⁶⁄₈	6³⁄₈	4	4¹⁄₈	268	10
◆ Baker County / Robert Spears / Robert Spears / 1977										
85²⁄₈	16¹⁄₈	16¹⁄₈	6⁷⁄₈	7	13⁴⁄₈	11⁷⁄₈	6⁵⁄₈	6³⁄₈	268	10
◆ Lake County / James H. Hastings / James H. Hastings / 1979										
85²⁄₈	15⁴⁄₈	15⁶⁄₈	7⁶⁄₈	7³⁄₈	8	4¹⁄₈	5⁷⁄₈	5⁶⁄₈	268	10
◆ Baker County / Eldon L. Buckner / Eldon L. Buckner / 1981										
85²⁄₈	17	16⁷⁄₈	6⁵⁄₈	6³⁄₈	12³⁄₈	7⁴⁄₈	5⁴⁄₈	6	268	10
◆ Baker County / Gordon C. Van Patten / Gordon C. Van Patten / 1990										
85²⁄₈	16⁵⁄₈	17	7¹⁄₈	7²⁄₈	12⁶⁄₈	10⁷⁄₈	5⁴⁄₈	6²⁄₈	268	10
◆ Harney County / Sharon L. Ganos / Sharon L. Ganos / 1992										
85	14⁷⁄₈	15¹⁄₈	6⁴⁄₈	6⁴⁄₈	14⁴⁄₈	12²⁄₈	5³⁄₈	5⁶⁄₈	301	15
◆ Brothers / Orlo Flock / Orlo Flock / 1955										
85	16⁵⁄₈	16⁵⁄₈	6⁶⁄₈	6⁶⁄₈	10⁶⁄₈	7²⁄₈	6	5⁷⁄₈	301	15
◆ Lake County / Frank R. Biggs / Frank R. Biggs / 1978										
84⁷⁄₈	18	18¹⁄₈	6⁵⁄₈	6⁴⁄₈	18²⁄₈	14⁴⁄₈	5¹⁄₈	5¹⁄₈	334	17
◆ Plush / Ernest E. Puddy / Ernest E. Puddy / 1949										
84⁶⁄₈	15⁴⁄₈	15⁴⁄₈	6⁴⁄₈	6⁶⁄₈	7⁴⁄₈	1⁷⁄₈	5⁴⁄₈	5⁵⁄₈	336	18
◆ Harney County / D.R. Knoll / D.R. Knoll / 1963										

Score	Length of Horn		Circumference of Base		Inside Spread	Tip-to-Tip Spread	Length of Prong		All-Time Rank	State Rank
	R	L	R	L			R	L		
♦ Locality / Hunter / Owner / Date Killed										
$84^6/8$	$16^2/8$	$16^3/8$	$6^4/8$	$6^3/8$	$11^1/8$	$8^3/8$	$6^5/8$	$6^2/8$	336	18
♦ Baker County / Martin Vavra / Martin Vavra / 1980										
$84^6/8$	$16^2/8$	$16^2/8$	$6^5/8$	$6^5/8$	$10^2/8$	$5^2/8$	7	$6^5/8$	336	18
♦ Lake County / Patrick R. McConnell / Patrick R. McConnell / 1991										
$84^4/8$	$14^5/8$	$14^7/8$	$6^7/8$	$7^1/8$	$12^6/8$	$8^6/8$	$6^1/8$	$6^5/8$	390	21
♦ Lake County / Gene Cormie / Gene Cormie / 1973										
$84^4/8$	17	$16^5/8$	$7^2/8$	$7^2/8$	$9^6/8$	$7^4/8$	6	$6^1/8$	390	21
♦ Fields / John H. Johnson / John H. Johnson / 1974										
$84^4/8$	$17^7/8$	$17^6/8$	$7^5/8$	$7^4/8$	$13^6/8$	$8^1/8$	$5^1/8$	$4^6/8$	390	21
♦ Lake County / Rodger D. Bates / Rodger D. Bates / 1980										
$84^4/8$	17	$17^4/8$	7	$6^7/8$	15	11	$5^2/8$	$5^2/8$	390	21
♦ Deschutes County / Rick Ward / Rick Ward / 1985										
$84^2/8$	$16^4/8$	$16^2/8$	$6^7/8$	$6^6/8$	$13^7/8$	$10^3/8$	6	6	436	25
♦ Malheur County / Matt J. Brundridge / Matt J. Brundridge / 1982										
$84^2/8$	$15^2/8$	$15^1/8$	$6^1/8$	6	$11^3/8$	$7^2/8$	$5^5/8$	$5^2/8$	436	25
♦ Baker County / Paul W. Schon / Paul W. Schon / 1987										
$84^2/8$	$16^7/8$	$16^6/8$	$6^5/8$	$6^3/8$	$8^5/8$	$1^3/8$	$5^6/8$	6	436	25
♦ Harney County / Douglas J. Modey / Douglas J. Modey / 1990										
$84^2/8$	16	$16^1/8$	$6^6/8$	$6^5/8$	$9^1/8$	$3^1/8$	$6^1/8$	$5^6/8$	436	25
♦ Harney County / Timothy A. Barnhart / Timothy A. Barnhart / 1992										
84	$16^4/8$	$16^2/8$	$7^2/8$	$7^2/8$	10	$6^3/8$	$5^7/8$	$5^3/8$	500	29
♦ Lake County / Del J. DeSart / Del J. DeSart / 1986										
84	$15^6/8$	$15^6/8$	$6^2/8$	$6^2/8$	$12^3/8$	$11^1/8$	$5^5/8$	$5^6/8$	500	29
♦ Harney County / James E. Baley / James E. Baley / 1988										
$83^6/8$	$15^2/8$	$15^1/8$	$6^6/8$	$6^5/8$	$11^7/8$	$6^7/8$	$6^7/8$	$7^1/8$	565	31
♦ Meridian / Dale E. Beattie / Dale E. Beattie / 1967										
$83^6/8$	$15^6/8$	$15^7/8$	$7^4/8$	$7^2/8$	$9^3/8$	$4^1/8$	$5^1/8$	$5^2/8$	565	31
♦ Lake County / Dennis E. Carter / Dennis E. Carter / 1972										
$83^6/8$	$15^6/8$	16	$7^4/8$	$7^5/8$	$15^5/8$	$11^6/8$	$5^6/8$	$6^3/8$	565	31
♦ Lake County / Barbara J. Smallwood / Barbara J. Smallwood / 1983										
$83^6/8$	$16^3/8$	$16^3/8$	$6^4/8$	$6^4/8$	$9^1/8$	$4^3/8$	$5^6/8$	$6^4/8$	565	31
♦ Harney County / Lyle W. Crawford / Lyle W. Crawford / 1990										
$83^6/8$	$16^2/8$	$16^3/8$	7	$7^1/8$	$10^2/8$	$5^3/8$	$5^3/8$	$5^4/8$	565	31
♦ Harney County / John S. Hansen / John S. Hansen / 1990										
$83^6/8$	$15^6/8$	$15^5/8$	$6^7/8$	$6^6/8$	$10^4/8$	$5^7/8$	$6^2/8$	$6^2/8$	565	31
♦ Lake County / Brian R. Hayes / Brian R. Hayes / 1992										
$83^4/8$	$16^3/8$	$16^2/8$	$7^2/8$	$7^2/8$	$9^4/8$	$3^6/8$	$8^3/8$	$4^3/8$	624	37
♦ Harney County / Craig Foster / Craig Foster / 1977										

OREGON PRONGHORN *(continued)*

Score	Length of Horn R	Length of Horn L	Circumference of Base R	Circumference of Base L	Inside Spread	Tip-to-Tip Spread	Length of Prong R	Length of Prong L	All-Time Rank	State Rank
♦ *Locality / Hunter / Owner / Date Killed*										
83 4/8	14 6/8	14 7/8	6 3/8	6 3/8	9	3 5/8	7 3/8	7 4/8	624	37
♦ *Lake County / Thomas A. Jones / Thomas A. Jones / 1980*										
83 4/8	16 7/8	17	6 4/8	6 4/8	14 1/8	10 2/8	5 4/8	5 5/8	624	37
♦ *Lake County / Donald R. Davidson / Donald R. Davidson / 1984*										
83 2/8	16 3/8	16 6/8	7 5/8	7 4/8	12 2/8	7 3/8	5 2/8	5 3/8	690	40
♦ *Harney County / Gary L. Wilfert / Gary L. Wilfert / 1981*										
83 2/8	14 6/8	14 6/8	7 3/8	7 3/8	13 5/8	11 1/8	5 2/8	5 4/8	690	40
♦ *Lake County / Clyde L. Dehlinger / Clyde L. Dehlinger / 1983*										
83 2/8	15 2/8	15 7/8	7 1/8	6 7/8	11 6/8	6 5/8	5 5/8	5 5/8	690	40
♦ *Lake County / Richard L. Smith / Richard L. Smith / 1983*										
83 2/8	17 3/8	17	6 3/8	6 4/8	14 1/8	10 3/8	5 6/8	5 5/8	690	40
♦ *Harney County / Patricia A. Kaiser / Patricia A. Kaiser / 1991*										
83	16 3/8	16 7/8	6 2/8	6 2/8	11	5 7/8	5 6/8	6 1/8	775	44
♦ *Lake County / Ken Smith / Ken Smith / 1962*										
83	16 5/8	16 4/8	6 2/8	6 2/8	11 2/8	7 1/8	6 4/8	6 3/8	775	44
♦ *Lake County / Francis G. Dalrymple / Francis G. Dalrymple / 1978*										
83	15 7/8	15 5/8	6 4/8	6 4/8	10 1/8	8 5/8	5 7/8	5 7/8	775	44
♦ *Lake County / Jerry J. Peacore / Jerry J. Peacore / 1980*										
83	15 5/8	16	7 1/8	7 2/8	13 4/8	10 7/8	4 7/8	5	775	44
♦ *Baker County / Richard R. Mason / Richard R. Mason / 1986*										
83	16 1/8	16	6 3/8	6 3/8	12 6/8	9	4 2/8	4 7/8	775	44
♦ *Lake County / Wil L. Wilson / Wil L. Wilson / 1991*										
82 6/8	16 6/8	16 4/8	6 2/8	6 2/8	11	5 7/8	5 4/8	5 7/8	868	49
♦ *Lake County / Kenneth Smith / Kenneth Smith / 1963*										
82 6/8	14 5/8	14 5/8	6 6/8	6 6/8	11 2/8	7 5/8	7 2/8	7 2/8	868	49
♦ *Grant County / A. Paul Malstrom / A. Paul Malstrom / 1978*										
82 6/8	17	17 1/8	6 3/8	6 3/8	10	4 4/8	5 6/8	5 2/8	868	49
♦ *Lake County / Steve W. Thompson / Steve W. Thompson / 1986*										
82 6/8	16 6/8	16 7/8	7	6 7/8	13 3/8	8 4/8	5 3/8	5 5/8	868	49
♦ *Lake County / Wayne W. Wingert / Wayne W. Wingert / 1986*										
82 6/8	16 2/8	16	6 3/8	6 4/8	10 7/8	8 1/8	6	6 2/8	868	49
♦ *Malheur County / Terrence L. Vaughan / Terrence L. Vaughan / 1988*										
82 6/8	16 2/8	16 2/8	7	6 7/8	13 3/8	9 6/8	5 7/8	5	868	49
♦ *Harney County / Garry L. Whitmore / Garry L. Whitmore / 1990*										
82 4/8	16 1/8	16 1/8	6 5/8	6 6/8	12 1/8	6 3/8	5 6/8	5 6/8	949	55
♦ *Lake County / Charles R. Waite / Charles R. Waite / 1969*										
82 4/8	16 7/8	16 4/8	6 2/8	6 2/8	10	8 6/8	5 5/8	5 1/8	949	55
♦ *Harney County / Terry L. Greene / Terry L. Greene / 1992*										

Score	Length of Horn		Circumference of Base		Inside Spread	Tip-to-Tip Spread	Length of Prong		All-Time Rank	State Rank
	R	L	R	L			R	L		
◆ Locality / Hunter / Owner / Date Killed										
82²⁄₈	15³⁄₈	14⁷⁄₈	6⁶⁄₈	6⁶⁄₈	13²⁄₈	9⁶⁄₈	6³⁄₈	6³⁄₈	1058	57
◆ Harney County / Dean Dunson / Dean Dunson / 1977										
82²⁄₈	15¹⁄₈	15	6⁶⁄₈	6⁷⁄₈	9⁵⁄₈	7	6⁴⁄₈	6²⁄₈	1058	57
◆ Lake County / Richard R. Delfs / Richard R. Delfs / 1981										
82	16⁵⁄₈	16³⁄₈	6¹⁄₈	6¹⁄₈	9³⁄₈	8⁴⁄₈	5⁷⁄₈	5⁶⁄₈	1157	59
◆ Lake County / Eldon Hayes / Eldon Hayes / 1966										
82	16²⁄₈	16¹⁄₈	6¹⁄₈	6	8²⁄₈	5	6	5⁶⁄₈	1157	59
◆ Lake County / Calvin M. Auvil / Calvin M. Auvil / 1976										
82	17¹⁄₈	17¹⁄₈	6²⁄₈	6²⁄₈	9⁷⁄₈	4³⁄₈	4¹⁄₈	4¹⁄₈	1157	59
◆ Harney County / Errol W. Claire / Errol W. Claire / 1994										
81⁴⁄₈	15¹⁄₈	15¹⁄₈	6⁴⁄₈	6³⁄₈	12¹⁄₈	7	6³⁄₈	6⁴⁄₈	1283	62
◆ Lake County / Ralph Buckingham / Ralph Buckingham / 1988										
81²⁄₈	15¹⁄₈	15¹⁄₈	6⁵⁄₈	6⁵⁄₈	11⁵⁄₈	6³⁄₈	6²⁄₈	6	1290	63
◆ Lake County / Steve B. Laskey / Steve B. Laskey / 1985										
81	15¹⁄₈	15³⁄₈	6⁷⁄₈	6⁵⁄₈	11¹⁄₈	8	5³⁄₈	5²⁄₈	1310	64
◆ Harney County / John E. Eckrich / John E. Eckrich / 1992										
81	15¹⁄₈	15¹⁄₈	6⁴⁄₈	6⁵⁄₈	11⁵⁄₈	8⁷⁄₈	5³⁄₈	5³⁄₈	1310	64
◆ Lake County / Alan Takemoto / Alan Takemoto / 1993										
80⁶⁄₈	16⁶⁄₈	16⁴⁄₈	6²⁄₈	6¹⁄₈	13¹⁄₈	11⁷⁄₈	3⁶⁄₈	4¹⁄₈	1327	66
◆ Lake County / Steve O. Carter / Steve O. Carter / 1991										
80⁶⁄₈	15²⁄₈	15²⁄₈	6¹⁄₈	6¹⁄₈	10	6⁵⁄₈	4⁶⁄₈	4⁴⁄₈	1327	66
◆ Baker County / Gary D. Wright / Gary D. Wright / 1993										
80²⁄₈	16¹⁄₈	16²⁄₈	6²⁄₈	6²⁄₈	10⁵⁄₈	6⁴⁄₈	3³⁄₈	3⁷⁄₈	1360	68
◆ Baker County / Patrick M. Bruce / Patrick M. Bruce / 1988										
80²⁄₈	16⁶⁄₈	16⁶⁄₈	6²⁄₈	6²⁄₈	13⁵⁄₈	9²⁄₈	5²⁄₈	5	1360	68
◆ Harney County / Betty R. Van Dyke / Betty R. Van Dyke / 1994										
80	15³⁄₈	15²⁄₈	6⁴⁄₈	6⁴⁄₈	9⁶⁄₈	5³⁄₈	5³⁄₈	5³⁄₈	1386	70
◆ Baker County / V. Kent Searles / V. Kent Searles / 1992										
80	15²⁄₈	15³⁄₈	6³⁄₈	6⁴⁄₈	10⁶⁄₈	6⁵⁄₈	5⁷⁄₈	5⁷⁄₈	1386	70
◆ Lake County / Rusty Lindberg / Rusty Lindberg / 1993										

Photograph Courtesy of Donald K. Lash

Donald K. Lash was hunting pronghorn on the Adobe Ranch in Catron County, New Mexico, in 1992 when he collected this keeper that scores 82 points.

Photograph by Wm. H. Nesbitt

SOUTH DAKOTA STATE RECORD (TIE)
PRONGHORN
SCORE: 86⁶⁄₈

Locality: South Dakota   Date: Prior to 1940
Hunter: Unknown
Owner: Daniel E. McBride

SOUTH DAKOTA

PRONGHORN

Score	Length of Horn R	Length of Horn L	Circumference of Base R	Circumference of Base L	Inside Spread	Tip-to-Tip Spread	Length of Prong R	Length of Prong L	All-Time Rank	State Rank
♦ *Locality / Hunter / Owner / Date Killed*										
86 6/8	16 6/8	17 3/8	6 7/8	6 7/8	15 3/8	9 6/8	6 6/8	6 6/8	114	1
♦ *South Dakota / Unknown / Daniel E. McBride / PR 1940*										
86 6/8	14 2/8	14 6/8	7 5/8	7 5/8	6	2 2/8	6 1/8	6 2/8	114	1
♦ *Perkins County / Scott R. Dell / Scott R. Dell / 1990*										
84 4/8	16 6/8	16 5/8	6 1/8	6 1/8	10 3/8	4 2/8	6 3/8	6 2/8	390	3
♦ *Tripp County / Roy Hazuka / Roy Hazuka / 1962*										
84 2/8	16 4/8	17 2/8	6 7/8	6 6/8	16	11 4/8	5 6/8	6	436	4
♦ *Meade County / John Hostetter / John Hostetter / 1975*										
84 2/8	15 3/8	15 4/8	6 6/8	6 6/8	9 6/8	5 3/8	6 1/8	6 1/8	436	4
♦ *Dewey County / Bernard P. Fuhrmann / Bernard P. Fuhrmann / 1993*										
84	15 5/8	15 5/8	6 7/8	6 7/8	14 7/8	12 2/8	6 4/8	6 4/8	500	6
♦ *Leola / Leonard Lahr / Leonard Lahr / 1967*										
84	17 2/8	17 2/8	6 5/8	6 4/8	9 3/8	5 4/8	4 5/8	5 7/8	500	6
♦ *Bennett County / Paul R. Nelson / Paul R. Nelson / 1983*										
83 6/8	16 1/8	16 1/8	6 7/8	7	10 2/8	8 3/8	5 7/8	6 3/8	565	8
♦ *Plainview / Bernie Wanhanen / Bernie Wanhanen / 1960*										
83 4/8	16 7/8	17	6 6/8	6 5/8	10 3/8	4 6/8	5	5 1/8	624	9
♦ *Harding County / John R. Simpson / John R. Simpson / 1981*										
83 2/8	16	16	7	6 7/8	11 6/8	7 5/8	5 5/8	6	690	10
♦ *Harding County / Kathleen Prestjohn / Kathleen Prestjohn / 1975*										
83	16 2/8	16 3/8	6 3/8	6 4/8	11 1/8	7 5/8	5 3/8	5 1/8	775	11
♦ *Custer County / Edward J. Schauer / Edward J. Schauer / 1979*										
83	16 4/8	16 5/8	6 4/8	6 2/8	11 1/8	5 6/8	6 2/8	6 6/8	775	11
♦ *Meade County / Randy A. Cammack / Randy A. Cammack / 1982*										
83	16 1/8	15 6/8	7 2/8	7 2/8	11 2/8	7	4 3/8	5 2/8	775	11
♦ *Perkins County / Dick D. Knock / Dick D. Knock / 1990*										
82 6/8	17 3/8	17 3/8	6	5 7/8	10 4/8	3 5/8	5 6/8	5 6/8	868	14
♦ *Butte County / P.T. Theodore / P.T. Theodore / 1958*										
82 6/8	15 2/8	15 2/8	7 2/8	7 1/8	11 7/8	9 1/8	5	5	868	14
♦ *Glad Valley / D.M. Davis / D.M. Davis / 1958*										
82 2/8	16 7/8	16 5/8	6	6	11 1/8	5	6	5 4/8	1058	16
♦ *Arpan / Dell Shanks / Dell Shanks / 1960*										
82 2/8	15	15 4/8	6 7/8	6 6/8	11 2/8	7 3/8	6 4/8	6 6/8	1058	16
♦ *Vivian / Larry K. Lantz / Larry K. Lantz / 1969*										
82 2/8	17	16 7/8	6 2/8	6 2/8	9	3 4/8	6 1/8	6 1/8	1058	16
♦ *Dewey County / Alan Ruhlman / Alan Ruhlman / 1991*										

Score	Length of Horn		Circumference of Base		Inside Spread	Tip-to-Tip Spread	Length of Prong		All-Time Rank	State Rank
	R	L	R	L			R	L		

♦ *Locality / Hunter / Owner / Date Killed*

Score	R	L	R	L	Inside	Tip-to-Tip	R	L	Rank	State
82²⁄₈	16⁴⁄₈	16³⁄₈	6²⁄₈	6²⁄₈	10	5²⁄₈	5⁵⁄₈	5⁵⁄₈	1058	16

♦ *Butte County / Bernerd E. Emery / Bernerd E. Emery / 1992*

81⁴⁄₈	16¹⁄₈	16³⁄₈	6⁷⁄₈	7¹⁄₈	12	9⁴⁄₈	5⁷⁄₈	5⁴⁄₈	1283	20

♦ *Butte County / Timothy B. Meland / Timothy B. Meland / 1992*

81²⁄₈	16	16	6⁷⁄₈	6⁷⁄₈	9⁶⁄₈	5²⁄₈	5⁵⁄₈	5²⁄₈	1290	21

♦ *Harding County / Lonnie G. Tschumper / Lonnie G. Tschumper / 1992*

80²⁄₈	15⁵⁄₈	15³⁄₈	6⁴⁄₈	6⁴⁄₈	15²⁄₈	10²⁄₈	5⁶⁄₈	5⁶⁄₈	1360	22

♦ *Dewey County / James H. Lohrman / James H. Lohrman / 1991*

80	14⁵⁄₈	14⁵⁄₈	7⁴⁄₈	7⁴⁄₈	10	6	6²⁄₈	6	1386	23

♦ *Perkins County / Bill M. Soyland / Bill M. Soyland / 1991*

B&C Official Measurer Rusty Lindberg tagged this Lake County, Oregon, pronghorn (80 points) during the 1993 hunting season.

Photograph by Mike Biggs

TEXAS STATE RECORD
PRONGHORN
SCORE: 90⁴/₈
Locality: Hudspeth Co.   Date: 1994
Hunter: Walter O. Ford III

TEXAS
PRONGHORN

Score	Length of Horn		Circumference of Base		Inside Spread	Tip-to-Tip Spread	Length of Prong		All-Time Rank	State Rank
	R	L	R	L			R	L		

♦ Locality / Hunter / Owner / Date Killed

Score	R	L	R	L	Inside Spread	Tip-to-Tip	R	L	Rank	State
$90\frac{4}{8}$	$18\frac{2}{8}$	$18\frac{6}{8}$	$6\frac{5}{8}$	$6\frac{6}{8}$	$10\frac{1}{8}$	4	6	6	14	1

♦ Hudspeth County / Walter O. Ford III / Walter O. Ford III / 1994

$89\frac{2}{8}$	$16\frac{3}{8}$	$16\frac{3}{8}$	7	$6\frac{7}{8}$	$9\frac{6}{8}$	$6\frac{6}{8}$	$7\frac{2}{8}$	$6\frac{7}{8}$	28	2

♦ Hudspeth County / Jack E. Beal / Jack E. Beal / 1987

$88\frac{6}{8}$	$18\frac{4}{8}$	$18\frac{4}{8}$	$7\frac{6}{8}$	$7\frac{6}{8}$	12	12	$4\frac{6}{8}$	$4\frac{6}{8}$	41	3

♦ Brewster County / John W. Houchins / John W. Houchins / 1988

88	$17\frac{1}{8}$	$16\frac{1}{8}$	$7\frac{4}{8}$	$6\frac{5}{8}$	$8\frac{7}{8}$	$6\frac{6}{8}$	$7\frac{4}{8}$	$7\frac{3}{8}$	66	4

♦ Hudspeth County / Gibson D. Lewis / Gibson D. Lewis / 1986

87	$16\frac{2}{8}$	$15\frac{6}{8}$	$7\frac{3}{8}$	$7\frac{4}{8}$	16	$12\frac{2}{8}$	$6\frac{3}{8}$	7	101	5

♦ Hudspeth County / E.R. Rinehart / E.R. Rinehart / 1959

$86\frac{6}{8}$	$16\frac{7}{8}$	$16\frac{7}{8}$	$6\frac{6}{8}$	$6\frac{7}{8}$	$8\frac{5}{8}$	$4\frac{3}{8}$	5	$5\frac{5}{8}$	114	6

♦ Hudspeth County / Peter L. Bright / Peter L. Bright / 1988

$86\frac{2}{8}$	$15\frac{2}{8}$	15	$6\frac{6}{8}$	$6\frac{4}{8}$	$9\frac{6}{8}$	$5\frac{6}{8}$	5	$4\frac{6}{8}$	155	7

♦ Hartley County / Ernie Davis / Ernie Davis / 1983

85	$16\frac{6}{8}$	$16\frac{6}{8}$	$6\frac{3}{8}$	$6\frac{3}{8}$	$10\frac{2}{8}$	$3\frac{5}{8}$	$6\frac{2}{8}$	$5\frac{5}{8}$	301	8

♦ Hudspeth County / Vernon Dodd / Vernon Dodd / 1984

85	$17\frac{4}{8}$	18	6	$5\frac{6}{8}$	17	$13\frac{6}{8}$	$5\frac{5}{8}$	$5\frac{6}{8}$	301	8

♦ Hudspeth County / Ronnie L. Hinze / Ronnie L. Hinze / 1988

85	$16\frac{2}{8}$	$16\frac{1}{8}$	$6\frac{2}{8}$	$6\frac{2}{8}$	13	$10\frac{5}{8}$	$6\frac{1}{8}$	$5\frac{7}{8}$	301	8

♦ Dallam County / Charles R. Senter / Charles R. Senter / 1992

$84\frac{7}{8}$	$15\frac{1}{8}$	$16\frac{1}{8}$	$7\frac{4}{8}$	$7\frac{4}{8}$	$18\frac{2}{8}$	$17\frac{1}{8}$	$5\frac{4}{8}$	$5\frac{4}{8}$	334	11

♦ Ochiltree County / Wayne Blue / Wayne Blue / 1988

$84\frac{6}{8}$	$16\frac{7}{8}$	$17\frac{2}{8}$	$6\frac{5}{8}$	$6\frac{3}{8}$	$16\frac{5}{8}$	$11\frac{1}{8}$	$7\frac{1}{8}$	5	336	12

♦ Hudspeth County / Ernie Davis / Ernie Davis / 1986

$84\frac{6}{8}$	16	$16\frac{1}{8}$	$6\frac{6}{8}$	$6\frac{6}{8}$	$8\frac{6}{8}$	6	$4\frac{7}{8}$	5	336	12

♦ Hudspeth County / Charles D. Tuttle / Charles D. Tuttle / 1986

$84\frac{6}{8}$	$15\frac{7}{8}$	$15\frac{4}{8}$	7	$7\frac{2}{8}$	$9\frac{3}{8}$	$6\frac{4}{8}$	$5\frac{3}{8}$	$5\frac{6}{8}$	336	12

♦ Hutchinson County / Rex A. Umbarger / Rex A. Umbarger / 1990

$84\frac{4}{8}$	$16\frac{7}{8}$	17	$6\frac{3}{8}$	$6\frac{2}{8}$	$12\frac{2}{8}$	$6\frac{4}{8}$	$6\frac{2}{8}$	$5\frac{7}{8}$	390	15

♦ Hudspeth County / Larry R. Price / Larry R. Price / 1991

$84\frac{2}{8}$	17	$16\frac{7}{8}$	$6\frac{2}{8}$	$6\frac{1}{8}$	$13\frac{1}{8}$	$7\frac{7}{8}$	$6\frac{1}{8}$	$6\frac{1}{8}$	436	16

♦ Hudspeth County / Sam H. Gann IV / Sam H. Gann IV / 1988

$84\frac{2}{8}$	$17\frac{4}{8}$	$17\frac{3}{8}$	$5\frac{7}{8}$	$5\frac{6}{8}$	$8\frac{3}{8}$	2	6	6	436	16

♦ Hartley County / Ernie Davis / Ernie Davis / 1994

84	$16\frac{3}{8}$	$16\frac{3}{8}$	$6\frac{6}{8}$	$6\frac{6}{8}$	$11\frac{6}{8}$	$8\frac{3}{8}$	$5\frac{4}{8}$	$5\frac{5}{8}$	500	18

♦ Presidio County / W. Wayne Roye / W. Wayne Roye / 1977

Score	Length of Horn R	Length of Horn L	Circumference of Base R	Circumference of Base L	Inside Spread	Tip-to-Tip Spread	Length of Prong R	Length of Prong L	All-Time Rank	State Rank
	♦ *Locality / Hunter / Owner / Date Killed*									
84	17 5/8	17 6/8	6 2/8	6 3/8	18 5/8	14 3/8	5 5/8	5 6/8	500	18
	♦ *Hudspeth County / Gibson D. Lewis / Gibson D. Lewis / 1988*									
84	16 1/8	16 3/8	6 2/8	6 2/8	16 5/8	13	6	7	500	18
	♦ *Hudspeth County / W. Wayne Spahn / W. Wayne Spahn / 1988*									
83 6/8	17 5/8	17 3/8	6 3/8	6 3/8	8 6/8	10 7/8	5 2/8	5	565	21
	♦ *Hudspeth County / Jim Perry / Jim Perry / 1963*									
83 6/8	15 6/8	15 5/8	7 2/8	7	10 3/8	6 1/8	6 2/8	6 2/8	565	21
	♦ *Hudspeth County / Basil C. Bradbury / Basil C. Bradbury / 1966*									
83 6/8	18 4/8	19 1/8	6 1/8	6 2/8	7 7/8	8 3/8	4 5/8	4 4/8	565	21
	♦ *Motley County / Ron Vandiver / Ron Vandiver / 1967*									
83 6/8	15 7/8	15 7/8	6 4/8	6 3/8	9 6/8	3 5/8	5 7/8	6	565	21
	♦ *Hudspeth County / A. Alan Griffin / A. Alan Griffin / 1988*									
83 4/8	16 4/8	16 6/8	6 2/8	6 1/8	8 7/8	3 2/8	6	6	624	25
	♦ *Hudspeth County / Carl H. Green / Carl H. Green / 1991*									
83 4/8	18 3/8	18	5 7/8	6	10 3/8	8 4/8	6	5 6/8	624	25
	♦ *Hudspeth County / Eduardo Padilla / Eduardo Padilla / 1991*									
83 4/8	16 6/8	16 1/8	6 3/8	6 2/8	9 6/8	6	6 3/8	5 4/8	624	25
	♦ *Hudspeth County / Ray O. Herzog / Ray O. Herzog / 1992*									
83 2/8	17	17	6 2/8	6 3/8	13 1/8	9 2/8	5 3/8	5 3/8	690	28
	♦ *Culberson County / Jim Smith / Jim Smith / 1972*									
83 2/8	16 3/8	16 1/8	6 4/8	6 4/8	8 7/8	3 5/8	4 6/8	4 7/8	690	28
	♦ *Brewster County / Richard T. Delgado / Richard T. Delgado / 1982*									
83 2/8	16 7/8	16 6/8	6 2/8	6 2/8	13 6/8	9 3/8	4 1/8	3 6/8	690	28
	♦ *Hartley County / Ernie Davis / Ernie Davis / 1989*									
83	15 2/8	15 3/8	6 4/8	6 2/8	11 5/8	7 2/8	5 4/8	5	775	31
	♦ *Hartley County / William G. Kendrick / William G. Kendrick / 1953*									
83	16	16 3/8	5 5/8	5 5/8	8 1/8	1 2/8	4	4 2/8	775	31
	♦ *Hudspeth County / Ernie Davis / Ernie Davis / 1980*									
83	17 2/8	17 1/8	6 1/8	6 2/8	15 2/8	6 2/8	4 4/8	4 4/8	775	31
	♦ *Hudspeth County / Larry P. Panebaker / Larry P. Panebaker / 1991*									
82 6/8	15 6/8	15 7/8	6 4/8	6 5/8	8	5 3/8	5 5/8	5 6/8	868	34
	♦ *Hudspeth County / L.A. Grelling / L.A. Grelling / 1980*									
82 6/8	17 6/8	18	6	6	13	8 6/8	5 1/8	5	868	34
	♦ *Hudspeth County / Louise G. Davis / Louise G. Davis / 1991*									
82 6/8	16	16 2/8	6 7/8	6 6/8	13 5/8	12 7/8	5 2/8	5	868	34
	♦ *Hudspeth County / Linda J. McBride / Linda J. McBride / 1994*									
82 4/8	13 6/8	13 6/8	9 2/8	9 1/8	9 4/8	6 4/8	5 1/8	5 1/8	949	37
	♦ *Pecos County / Ben H. Moore, Jr. / Ben H. Moore, Jr. / 1967*									

Score	Length of Horn		Circumference of Base		Inside Spread	Tip-to-Tip Spread	Length of Prong		All-Time Rank	State Rank
	R	L	R	L			R	L		
◆ *Locality / Hunter / Owner / Date Killed*										
82$\frac{4}{8}$	15$\frac{1}{8}$	15$\frac{3}{8}$	6$\frac{6}{8}$	6$\frac{7}{8}$	8$\frac{5}{8}$	4	3$\frac{6}{8}$	3$\frac{6}{8}$	949	37
◆ *Brewster County / Joseph W. Burkett III / Joseph W. Burkett III / 1971*										
82$\frac{4}{8}$	17$\frac{6}{8}$	17$\frac{3}{8}$	6	6	11$\frac{2}{8}$	6	5$\frac{2}{8}$	5$\frac{4}{8}$	949	37
◆ *Hudspeth County / Ray A. Acker, Sr. / Ray A. Acker, Sr. / 1980*										
82$\frac{4}{8}$	16$\frac{3}{8}$	15$\frac{6}{8}$	6$\frac{4}{8}$	6$\frac{5}{8}$	14$\frac{1}{8}$	9$\frac{6}{8}$	5$\frac{3}{8}$	6$\frac{2}{8}$	949	37
◆ *Hudspeth County / Ernest Elbert, Jr. / Ernest Elbert, Jr. / 1985*										
82$\frac{4}{8}$	16$\frac{5}{8}$	16$\frac{6}{8}$	6$\frac{7}{8}$	6$\frac{7}{8}$	8$\frac{7}{8}$	5$\frac{3}{8}$	5	4$\frac{6}{8}$	949	37
◆ *Hudspeth County / Bruce Kettler / Bruce Kettler / 1993*										
82$\frac{2}{8}$	16$\frac{2}{8}$	16$\frac{2}{8}$	6$\frac{6}{8}$	6$\frac{6}{8}$	13$\frac{2}{8}$	10$\frac{5}{8}$	4$\frac{6}{8}$	4$\frac{6}{8}$	1058	42
◆ *Sierra Blanca / Charles Nichols / Charles Nichols / 1960*										
82$\frac{2}{8}$	16$\frac{7}{8}$	18	6$\frac{1}{8}$	6	11$\frac{1}{8}$	5$\frac{6}{8}$	5$\frac{1}{8}$	5$\frac{1}{8}$	1058	42
◆ *Brewster County / McLean Bowman / McLean Bowman / 1982*										
82$\frac{2}{8}$	15$\frac{7}{8}$	15$\frac{6}{8}$	6$\frac{1}{8}$	6$\frac{1}{8}$	12$\frac{6}{8}$	8$\frac{7}{8}$	6$\frac{3}{8}$	6$\frac{3}{8}$	1058	42
◆ *Hartley County / Ernie Davis / Ernie Davis / 1984*										
82	14$\frac{6}{8}$	14$\frac{6}{8}$	6$\frac{5}{8}$	6$\frac{6}{8}$	11	6$\frac{3}{8}$	6$\frac{5}{8}$	6$\frac{2}{8}$	1157	45
◆ *Hartley County / Walter O. Ford, Jr. / Walter O. Ford, Jr. / 1964*										
82	15$\frac{2}{8}$	15$\frac{2}{8}$	5$\frac{7}{8}$	6	11$\frac{2}{8}$	7$\frac{1}{8}$	4$\frac{1}{8}$	4$\frac{3}{8}$	1157	45
◆ *Brewster County / Joseph W. Burkett III / Joseph W. Burkett III / 1972*										
82	16	16	6	6	9	6$\frac{2}{8}$	5$\frac{4}{8}$	5$\frac{4}{8}$	1157	45
◆ *Hartley County / John A. Wright / John A. Wright / 1977*										
82	17$\frac{1}{8}$	17$\frac{4}{8}$	6$\frac{4}{8}$	6$\frac{4}{8}$	0	0	4$\frac{2}{8}$	4$\frac{4}{8}$	1157	45
◆ *Culberson County / Charles Seidensticker / Charles Seidensticker / 1978*										
82	16$\frac{4}{8}$	16$\frac{4}{8}$	6$\frac{2}{8}$	6$\frac{2}{8}$	8$\frac{7}{8}$	4	5$\frac{1}{8}$	5$\frac{2}{8}$	1157	45
◆ *Hudspeth County / Luther V. Oliver / Luther V. Oliver / 1978*										
82	17	17	6$\frac{4}{8}$	6$\frac{3}{8}$	8$\frac{6}{8}$	6$\frac{4}{8}$	4$\frac{6}{8}$	5$\frac{1}{8}$	1157	45
◆ *Brewster County / Peggy F. Brady / Peggy F. Brady / 1979*										
82	17$\frac{6}{8}$	17$\frac{4}{8}$	6$\frac{3}{8}$	6$\frac{1}{8}$	8$\frac{7}{8}$	4$\frac{4}{8}$	5$\frac{4}{8}$	4$\frac{5}{8}$	1157	45
◆ *Hudspeth County / E. Scott Smith / E. Scott Smith / 1990*										
81$\frac{6}{8}$	16$\frac{1}{8}$	16$\frac{5}{8}$	6	6$\frac{4}{8}$	11$\frac{7}{8}$	7$\frac{2}{8}$	6	5$\frac{7}{8}$	1276	52
◆ *Hudspeth County / Ken E. Moreland / Ken E. Moreland / 1984*										
80$\frac{6}{8}$	17	16$\frac{3}{8}$	6$\frac{2}{8}$	6$\frac{1}{8}$	12$\frac{1}{8}$	6$\frac{7}{8}$	5	5$\frac{1}{8}$	1327	53
◆ *Hudspeth County / Mel Reichert / Mel Reichert / 1986*										
80$\frac{2}{8}$	15	16$\frac{5}{8}$	6$\frac{1}{8}$	6$\frac{1}{8}$	12$\frac{4}{8}$	10	6$\frac{2}{8}$	5$\frac{3}{8}$	1360	54
◆ *Hudspeth County / Jarl E. Hanson / Jarl E. Hanson / 1991*										
80	15$\frac{3}{8}$	15$\frac{3}{8}$	5$\frac{6}{8}$	5$\frac{7}{8}$	11$\frac{5}{8}$	6$\frac{5}{8}$	4$\frac{5}{8}$	4$\frac{4}{8}$	1386	55
◆ *Hudspeth County / Will Ross / Will Ross / 1985*										

Photograph Courtesy of Charles A. Grimmett

UTAH STATE RECORD
PRONGHORN
SCORE: 89⁴⁄₈
Locality: Uintah Co.   Date: 1988
Hunter: Charles A. Grimmett

PRONGHORN

Score	Length of Horn		Circumference of Base		Inside Spread	Tip-to-Tip Spread	Length of Prong		All-Time Rank	State Rank
	R	L	R	L			R	L		
♦ Locality / Hunter / Owner / Date Killed										
89⁴⁄₈	17⁷⁄₈	17⁵⁄₈	7⁴⁄₈	8¹⁄₈	10⁴⁄₈	5	5³⁄₈	5⁴⁄₈	23	1
♦ Uintah County / Charles A. Grimmett / Charles A. Grimmett / 1988										
88²⁄₈	18²⁄₈	18²⁄₈	6⁷⁄₈	7	16⁴⁄₈	12¹⁄₈	5³⁄₈	5⁶⁄₈	59	2
♦ Carbon County / James M. Machac / James M. Machac / 1989										
87	17	17	6⁶⁄₈	6⁷⁄₈	10⁴⁄₈	8²⁄₈	6¹⁄₈	6⁶⁄₈	101	3
♦ Millard County / Duane Stanworth / Duane Stanworth / 1984										
86	17	16⁶⁄₈	6⁵⁄₈	6⁵⁄₈	10⁶⁄₈	5⁶⁄₈	5⁶⁄₈	6⁶⁄₈	182	4
♦ Garfield County / Lynn M. Greene / Lynn M. Greene / 1991										
85⁶⁄₈	16³⁄₈	16⁵⁄₈	6²⁄₈	6²⁄₈	8	1⁷⁄₈	6⁵⁄₈	6⁶⁄₈	211	5
♦ Emery County / Jerry L. Oveson / Jerry L. Oveson / 1991										
85⁴⁄₈	16⁶⁄₈	16⁴⁄₈	6⁶⁄₈	6⁷⁄₈	9²⁄₈	5¹⁄₈	5⁴⁄₈	5¹⁄₈	238	6
♦ Millard County / David J. Carter / David J. Carter / 1989										
85²⁄₈	17¹⁄₈	17²⁄₈	6⁴⁄₈	6⁴⁄₈	7¹⁄₈	2⁴⁄₈	6⁶⁄₈	6²⁄₈	268	7
♦ Emery County / Marvin L. Thayn / Marvin L. Thayn / 1986										
85	17	17²⁄₈	6²⁄₈	6²⁄₈	11⁷⁄₈	8⁴⁄₈	6¹⁄₈	6³⁄₈	301	8
♦ Millard County / Scott C. Rowley / Scott C. Rowley / 1984										
84⁴⁄₈	17³⁄₈	17³⁄₈	6¹⁄₈	6²⁄₈	7⁵⁄₈	1⁷⁄₈	5⁷⁄₈	5⁷⁄₈	390	9
♦ Emery County / Bruce Gordon / Bruce Gordon / 1986										
84²⁄₈	15⁵⁄₈	15⁴⁄₈	6⁷⁄₈	6⁶⁄₈	9¹⁄₈	4¹⁄₈	6⁴⁄₈	5⁶⁄₈	436	10
♦ Box Elder County / O. Brent Maw / O. Brent Maw / 1991										
83⁶⁄₈	15⁶⁄₈	16¹⁄₈	6⁶⁄₈	6⁵⁄₈	12	7²⁄₈	5²⁄₈	5²⁄₈	565	11
♦ Millard County / Mitchell S. Bastian / Mitchell S. Bastian / 1985										
83⁴⁄₈	15⁷⁄₈	15⁶⁄₈	6³⁄₈	6³⁄₈	10²⁄₈	6⁴⁄₈	7	6³⁄₈	624	12
♦ Carbon County / John R. Stevens / John R. Stevens / 1989										
83²⁄₈	15⁵⁄₈	15²⁄₈	6⁷⁄₈	6⁶⁄₈	13⁶⁄₈	11³⁄₈	5⁵⁄₈	5⁷⁄₈	690	13
♦ Box Elder County / Larry D. Elliott / Larry D. Elliott / 1994										
83	16⁴⁄₈	16⁶⁄₈	6⁶⁄₈	7	10¹⁄₈	6	6¹⁄₈	5⁶⁄₈	775	14
♦ Emery County / Dennis G. McElvain / Dennis G. McElvain / 1987										
83	15⁵⁄₈	15³⁄₈	6²⁄₈	6³⁄₈	10²⁄₈	5³⁄₈	6¹⁄₈	5⁷⁄₈	775	14
♦ Juab County / Alan L. Pfiefer / Alan L. Pfiefer / 1992										
82⁶⁄₈	16²⁄₈	16¹⁄₈	6⁵⁄₈	6⁴⁄₈	9	4¹⁄₈	5⁵⁄₈	5²⁄₈	868	16
♦ Juab County / David B. Nielsen / David B. Nielsen / 1992										
82⁶⁄₈	16⁴⁄₈	16³⁄₈	7¹⁄₈	7	13²⁄₈	10¹⁄₈	6⁴⁄₈	6	868	16
♦ Rich County / Robby Aston / Robby Aston / 1992										
82⁴⁄₈	15⁴⁄₈	15⁵⁄₈	6⁶⁄₈	6⁴⁄₈	9⁴⁄₈	4⁵⁄₈	5³⁄₈	5³⁄₈	949	18
♦ Millard County / William R. Houston / William R. Houston / 1979										

Score	Length of Horn		Circumference of Base		Inside Spread	Tip-to-Tip Spread	Length of Prong		All-Time Rank	State Rank
	R	L	R	L			R	L		
	◆ *Locality / Hunter / Owner / Date Killed*									
$82\frac{4}{8}$	$15\frac{2}{8}$	$15\frac{1}{8}$	$6\frac{4}{8}$	$6\frac{2}{8}$	$14\frac{1}{8}$	$12\frac{6}{8}$	$5\frac{4}{8}$	$5\frac{4}{8}$	949	18
◆ *Box Elder County / Curtis K. Blasingame / Curtis K. Blasingame / 1989*										
$82\frac{4}{8}$	$17\frac{1}{8}$	17	6	$5\frac{7}{8}$	$13\frac{6}{8}$	$9\frac{7}{8}$	$6\frac{3}{8}$	6	949	18
◆ *San Juan County / Wayne A. Hines / Wayne A. Hines / 1990*										
$82\frac{4}{8}$	$16\frac{3}{8}$	$16\frac{4}{8}$	$6\frac{7}{8}$	7	$10\frac{1}{8}$	$5\frac{6}{8}$	5	$4\frac{7}{8}$	949	18
◆ *Box Elder County / Roudy Christensen / Roudy Christensen / 1991*										
$82\frac{2}{8}$	$15\frac{2}{8}$	$15\frac{3}{8}$	$7\frac{1}{8}$	$7\frac{2}{8}$	$8\frac{7}{8}$	$5\frac{7}{8}$	$6\frac{1}{8}$	$6\frac{2}{8}$	1058	22
◆ *Duchesne County / David L. Peterson / David L. Peterson / 1976*										
82	$15\frac{5}{8}$	$15\frac{4}{8}$	7	7	$10\frac{3}{8}$	$6\frac{4}{8}$	$5\frac{2}{8}$	$5\frac{3}{8}$	1157	23
◆ *Rich County / William B. Bullen / William B. Bullen / 1993*										
$81\frac{2}{8}$	$16\frac{3}{8}$	17	$6\frac{1}{8}$	$6\frac{1}{8}$	$9\frac{3}{8}$	$7\frac{1}{8}$	$6\frac{3}{8}$	6	1290	24
◆ *Emery County / Monte E. Tucker / Monte E. Tucker / 1989*										
$81\frac{2}{8}$	$15\frac{4}{8}$	$15\frac{2}{8}$	$6\frac{4}{8}$	$6\frac{3}{8}$	11	$7\frac{7}{8}$	$5\frac{4}{8}$	$5\frac{3}{8}$	1290	24
◆ *Rich County / Gary M. Larsen / Gary M. Larsen / 1992*										
81	$16\frac{3}{8}$	$16\frac{2}{8}$	$6\frac{2}{8}$	$6\frac{1}{8}$	$10\frac{6}{8}$	$6\frac{3}{8}$	$5\frac{5}{8}$	$5\frac{6}{8}$	1310	26
◆ *Wayne County / Ronald K. Lowe / Ronald K. Lowe / 1985*										
81	$16\frac{1}{8}$	16	$6\frac{6}{8}$	$6\frac{5}{8}$	$8\frac{7}{8}$	$4\frac{1}{8}$	$5\frac{3}{8}$	5	1310	26
◆ *Uintah County / Ben M. Murray / Ben M. Murray / 1989*										
$80\frac{6}{8}$	$15\frac{2}{8}$	15	$6\frac{1}{8}$	$6\frac{2}{8}$	$9\frac{1}{8}$	6	$5\frac{6}{8}$	$5\frac{6}{8}$	1327	28
◆ *Box Elder County / Merrell A. Hurd / Merrell A. Hurd / 1989*										
$80\frac{4}{8}$	$15\frac{4}{8}$	$15\frac{4}{8}$	7	$6\frac{6}{8}$	$10\frac{2}{8}$	$8\frac{1}{8}$	$5\frac{7}{8}$	5	1345	29
◆ *Rich County / Steven J. Larsen / Steven J. Larsen / 1994*										
$80\frac{2}{8}$	$15\frac{5}{8}$	$15\frac{3}{8}$	$6\frac{4}{8}$	$6\frac{3}{8}$	$10\frac{2}{8}$	$4\frac{4}{8}$	$5\frac{6}{8}$	$5\frac{5}{8}$	1360	30
◆ *Box Elder County / Carol Conroy / Carol Conroy / 1988*										
80	$15\frac{6}{8}$	$15\frac{5}{8}$	$6\frac{2}{8}$	$6\frac{2}{8}$	$9\frac{2}{8}$	$2\frac{6}{8}$	$4\frac{5}{8}$	$4\frac{6}{8}$	1386	31
◆ *Tooele County / Jack F. Newman / Jack F. Newman / 1987*										

John L. Anderson was guided to this trophy pronghorn, scoring 83 points, by Norm Heater in Carbon County, Wyoming, in 1994.

Photograph Courtesy of Fred Starling

WYOMING STATE RECORD (TIE)
PRONGHORN
SCORE: 91
Locality: Rawlins   Date: 1967
Hunter: Fred Starling

WYOMING
PRONGHORN

Score	Length of Horn R	L	Circumference of Base R	L	Inside Spread	Tip-to-Tip Spread	Length of Prong R	L	All-Time Rank	State Rank
91	16 6/8	16 4/8	7 6/8	7 7/8	10 3/8	3	7 2/8	7 4/8	8	1
	◆ Carbon County / J. Ivan Kitch / J. Ivan Kitch / 1964									
91	16 2/8	15 6/8	7 1/8	7 1/8	14 1/8	11 7/8	5 6/8	5 5/8	8	1
	◆ Rawlins / Fred Starling / Fred Starling / 1967									
90 6/8	16 2/8	16 4/8	7 4/8	7 4/8	17 2/8	15 2/8	7 5/8	7 5/8	11	3
	◆ Weston County / Allen Douglas / Richard J. Macy / 1943									
90 6/8	16 3/8	16 4/8	7	7 3/8	13 2/8	8 6/8	5 7/8	6 1/8	11	3
	◆ Natrona County / Richard J. Guthrie / Richard J. Guthrie / 1989									
89 6/8	17 5/8	17 5/8	7 3/8	7 3/8	11 1/8	6 5/8	6 1/8	6 2/8	17	5
	◆ Rawlins / Mary C. Kircher / Mary C. Kircher / 1961									
89 4/8	17 6/8	17 4/8	7 2/8	7 1/8	10	3 2/8	6 3/8	6	23	6
	◆ Ferris / John T. Peddy / John T. Peddy / 1957									
89 4/8	17 2/8	17 4/8	7	7 1/8	13 5/8	9 7/8	6 1/8	6 1/8	23	6
	◆ Laramie County / Roy Vail / Roy Vail / 1958									
89 2/8	17 4/8	17 1/8	6 6/8	6 6/8	8 1/8	2 4/8	6 6/8	6 6/8	28	8
	◆ Lincoln County / Harold P. Wales / Harold P. Wales / 1991									
89	16 1/8	16	7 3/8	7 4/8	11 2/8	8	6 5/8	7 1/8	36	9
	◆ Sweetwater County / Willis E. Haines / Willis E. Haines / 1985									
89	16 3/8	16 2/8	7 5/8	7 5/8	10	5	6 2/8	6 5/8	36	9
	◆ Sweetwater County / Douglas G. DeVivo / Douglas G. DeVivo / 1993									
88 4/8	16 6/8	17 1/8	7	7	10	5 4/8	5 7/8	6 2/8	51	11
	◆ Fremont County / Terry N. TenBoer / Terry N. TenBoer / 1974									
88 2/8	16 1/8	15 7/8	7 2/8	6 6/8	13 7/8	11 5/8	7 4/8	7	59	12
	◆ Goshen County / William P. Price / William P. Price / 1991									
88 2/8	17 2/8	17 4/8	7	7	13 1/8	10 5/8	6 7/8	7	59	12
	◆ Natrona County / John J. Heidel / John J. Heidel / 1992									
88	16 1/8	16 1/8	7	7	13	9 4/8	6 1/8	6	66	14
	◆ Uinta County / John V. Lockard / John V. Lockard / 1990									
88	16 7/8	16 7/8	6 6/8	6 7/8	11 3/8	8	6	6 2/8	66	14
	◆ Natrona County / F. Miles Hartung / F. Miles Hartung / 1992									
87 7/8	17	16 7/8	7 4/8	7 4/8	15 2/8	12 1/8	5 3/8	5 2/8	74	16
	◆ Fremont County / William I. Crump / William I. Crump / 1963									
87 7/8	15	15 2/8	7 2/8	7 2/8	10 4/8	6 3/8	7 2/8	7 1/8	74	16
	◆ Fremont County / Frank Schuele / Frank Schuele / 1975									
87 7/8	15 3/8	15 3/8	7 6/8	7 6/8	13 6/8	11 2/8	7 1/8	7	74	16
	◆ Fremont County / Karey H. Stebner / Karey H. Stebner / 1991									

Score	Length of Horn		Circumference of Base		Inside Spread	Tip-to-Tip Spread	Length of Prong		All-Time Rank	State Rank
	R	L	R	L			R	L		
◆ Locality / Hunter / Owner / Date Killed										
87⁴⁄₈	17⁵⁄₈	17³⁄₈	6⁴⁄₈	6³⁄₈	11⁵⁄₈	6³⁄₈	6⁴⁄₈	6³⁄₈	79	19
◆ Gillette / Stanley Scott / Stanley Scott / 1961										
87²⁄₈	16³⁄₈	16¹⁄₈	6⁵⁄₈	6⁴⁄₈	13⁵⁄₈	11	7⁴⁄₈	7⁵⁄₈	85	20
◆ Fremont County / Scott A. Trabing / Scott A. Trabing / 1973										
87²⁄₈	17⁵⁄₈	17⁴⁄₈	6⁷⁄₈	6⁶⁄₈	10⁷⁄₈	4²⁄₈	6⁷⁄₈	6⁴⁄₈	85	20
◆ Sweetwater County / Jay R. Anderson / Jay R. Anderson / 1975										
87²⁄₈	16⁵⁄₈	16⁵⁄₈	7⁴⁄₈	7²⁄₈	14²⁄₈	10²⁄₈	6	5⁷⁄₈	85	20
◆ Carbon County / Lee Miller / Lee Miller / 1976										
87²⁄₈	16	16¹⁄₈	7²⁄₈	7¹⁄₈	12¹⁄₈	9	6³⁄₈	6⁴⁄₈	85	20
◆ Niobrara County / Stephen M. Cameron / Stephen M. Cameron / 1976										
87	15⁷⁄₈	15⁷⁄₈	7¹⁄₈	7	10⁵⁄₈	5	6¹⁄₈	6⁴⁄₈	101	24
◆ Sweetwater County / Dell J. Barnes / Dell J. Barnes / 1976										
87	16³⁄₈	16⁴⁄₈	6⁵⁄₈	6⁴⁄₈	11⁴⁄₈	7⁴⁄₈	7²⁄₈	6⁵⁄₈	101	24
◆ Sweetwater County / William S. Salisbury / William S. Salisbury / 1983										
87	16³⁄₈	16³⁄₈	8¹⁄₈	8	11⁵⁄₈	11	6	6⁴⁄₈	101	24
◆ Lincoln County / Jim S. Vilos / Jim S. Vilos / 1991										
86⁶⁄₈	17⁴⁄₈	17³⁄₈	6⁴⁄₈	6⁶⁄₈	15⁵⁄₈	13⁴⁄₈	7⁴⁄₈	6	114	27
◆ Rock Springs / Stanley Sinclair / Stanley Sinclair / 1952										
86⁶⁄₈	16⁴⁄₈	16⁵⁄₈	7²⁄₈	7²⁄₈	9⁷⁄₈	6⁵⁄₈	6²⁄₈	6¹⁄₈	114	27
◆ Rawlins / C.M. Chandler / C.M. Chandler / 1953										
86⁶⁄₈	16³⁄₈	16³⁄₈	7	7	11⁶⁄₈	9⁴⁄₈	6	6¹⁄₈	114	27
◆ Carbon County / Chuck Sanger / Chuck Sanger / 1968										
86⁶⁄₈	16⁵⁄₈	16⁵⁄₈	7	7	8⁴⁄₈	2⁵⁄₈	6⁴⁄₈	7	114	27
◆ Fremont County / Richard A. Fruchey / Richard A. Fruchey / 1973										
86⁶⁄₈	15³⁄₈	15⁶⁄₈	6³⁄₈	6²⁄₈	9³⁄₈	6	7⁶⁄₈	8²⁄₈	114	27
◆ Sublette County / Mrs. Arvid J. Siegel / Mrs. Arvid J. Siegel / 1974										
86⁶⁄₈	18³⁄₈	18¹⁄₈	6⁵⁄₈	6⁵⁄₈	8⁷⁄₈	5⁶⁄₈	4⁶⁄₈	5³⁄₈	114	27
◆ Sublette County / Glenn A. Eiden / Glenn A. Eiden / 1983										
86⁶⁄₈	15⁵⁄₈	15⁵⁄₈	7³⁄₈	7³⁄₈	11²⁄₈	10⁵⁄₈	6⁵⁄₈	7	114	27
◆ Albany County / Lloyd D. Kindsfater / Lloyd D. Kindsfater / 1983										
86⁶⁄₈	15⁵⁄₈	15⁵⁄₈	7⁶⁄₈	7⁶⁄₈	11	7⁶⁄₈	6²⁄₈	6¹⁄₈	114	27
◆ Carbon County / Troy T. Hall / Troy T. Hall / 1987										
86⁶⁄₈	16⁶⁄₈	16³⁄₈	6⁴⁄₈	6⁷⁄₈	13³⁄₈	11¹⁄₈	6⁵⁄₈	6¹⁄₈	114	27
◆ Fremont County / Glen H. Taylor / Glen H. Taylor / 1991										
86⁶⁄₈	16	16¹⁄₈	7	6⁷⁄₈	13⁵⁄₈	10¹⁄₈	6⁵⁄₈	6⁵⁄₈	114	27
◆ Carbon County / Gary L. White / Gary L. White / 1993										
86⁴⁄₈	17	16⁷⁄₈	7⁴⁄₈	7⁶⁄₈	11	6⁷⁄₈	6	5⁶⁄₈	140	37
◆ Sweetwater County / Rex A. Behrends / Rex A. Behrends / 1980										

Score	Length of Horn		Circumference of Base		Inside Spread	Tip-to-Tip Spread	Length of Prong		All-Time Rank	State Rank
	R	L	R	L			R	L		
	♦ *Locality / Hunter / Owner / Date Killed*									
86 4/8	17 2/8	17 4/8	7 2/8	7 2/8	9	6 6/8	4 1/8	5 3/8	140	37
	♦ *Sweetwater County / Richard E. Hueckstaedt / Richard E. Hueckstaedt / 1982*									
86 4/8	16 6/8	16 4/8	7	6 7/8	11 2/8	7 5/8	6 6/8	6 5/8	140	37
	♦ *Fremont County / Gerald G. Korell / Gerald G. Korell / 1989*									
86 4/8	15 6/8	15 7/8	7 2/8	7 2/8	9 3/8	5 3/8	5 5/8	6 1/8	140	37
	♦ *Uinta County / Randy L. Mair / Randy L. Mair / 1992*									
86 2/8	16 6/8	16 2/8	6 4/8	6 3/8	11 4/8	10	7	6 1/8	155	41
	♦ *Manville / J.J. Hartnett / Roy Vail / 1952*									
86 2/8	15	15 2/8	7 6/8	7 6/8	9	5 6/8	6	5 6/8	155	41
	♦ *Casper / William W. Brummet / William W. Brummet / 1963*									
86 2/8	16 7/8	16 1/8	6 5/8	6 6/8	12 1/8	7 2/8	6 6/8	6 4/8	155	41
	♦ *Carbon County / Mike Davich / Mike Davich / 1974*									
86 2/8	16 6/8	16 2/8	6 4/8	6 4/8	12 3/8	9 4/8	6	6	155	41
	♦ *Big Horn County / Robert Temme / Robert Temme / 1974*									
86 2/8	17 2/8	17	7	7	12 6/8	10 7/8	5 6/8	5 7/8	155	41
	♦ *Carbon County / Harold J. Rollison / Harold J. Rollison / 1975*									
86 2/8	16 4/8	16 5/8	7 7/8	7 7/8	14 3/8	9 6/8	5	5 1/8	155	41
	♦ *Fremont County / Douglas B. Stromberg / Douglas B. Stromberg / 1976*									
86 2/8	17 3/8	17 3/8	6 7/8	7	13 7/8	13 7/8	5	5	155	41
	♦ *Carbon County / James Poydack / James Poydack / 1977*									
86 2/8	17 4/8	17 1/8	7 5/8	6 6/8	7 5/8	5	6 1/8	6 3/8	155	41
	♦ *Sweetwater County / J. Robert Tigner / J. Robert Tigner / 1980*									
86 2/8	15 1/8	15 1/8	7 6/8	7 4/8	10 6/8	10 1/8	7	6 6/8	155	41
	♦ *Sweetwater County / Kurt A. Mari / Kurt A. Mari / 1988*									
86 2/8	15 3/8	15 4/8	7 1/8	7 1/8	12 1/8	10	7 1/8	6 6/8	155	41
	♦ *Sweetwater County / Brian T. Gabbitas / Brian T. Gabbitas / 1990*									
86 2/8	17	16 3/8	7 3/8	7 4/8	9 2/8	2 6/8	6 1/8	6 2/8	155	41
	♦ *Sweetwater County / Geraldine Hazzard / Leonard L. Arnold / 1991*									
86 2/8	16 4/8	16 4/8	7 3/8	7 3/8	9 2/8	4	6 2/8	5 3/8	155	41
	♦ *Sweetwater County / Daniel Daugherty / Daniel Daugherty / 1991*									
86	15 4/8	15 1/8	7	7 2/8	6 6/8	4 2/8	6	6	182	53
	♦ *Medicine Bow / Jack R. Campbell / Jack R. Campbell / 1959*									
86	15	15	7 2/8	7 1/8	13 6/8	11 6/8	6 7/8	6 6/8	182	53
	♦ *Fremont County / Robert Hall / Robert Hall / 1973*									
86	17	17 3/8	7 1/8	7 1/8	10 1/8	4 2/8	6 5/8	6 4/8	182	53
	♦ *Sweetwater County / F.A. Oliver / F.A. Oliver / 1981*									
86	16 1/8	16	7 1/8	7	9 4/8	4 2/8	5 7/8	5 6/8	182	53
	♦ *Natrona County / David H. Crum / David H. Crum / 1983*									

Score	Length of Horn R	L	Circumference of Base R	L	Inside Spread	Tip-to-Tip Spread	Length of Prong R	L	All-Time Rank	State Rank
	◆ *Locality / Hunter / Owner / Date Killed*									
86	16⁶⁄₈	16⁷⁄₈	6⁷⁄₈	6⁵⁄₈	10²⁄₈	6	6	6¹⁄₈	182	53
	◆ *Sweetwater County / Jason K. Faigl / Jason K. Faigl / 1991*									
86	16²⁄₈	16⁴⁄₈	7	7	8⁷⁄₈	8²⁄₈	6⁴⁄₈	6⁴⁄₈	182	53
	◆ *Sweetwater County / William H. Miller / William H. Miller / 1991*									
85⁶⁄₈	16⁵⁄₈	16⁴⁄₈	6⁴⁄₈	6⁴⁄₈	13⁶⁄₈	10⁶⁄₈	6	6	211	59
	◆ *Carbon County / B.L. Holman / B.L. Holman / 1953*									
85⁶⁄₈	18	17⁵⁄₈	6⁴⁄₈	6⁴⁄₈	7⁷⁄₈	3⁴⁄₈	5³⁄₈	5⁶⁄₈	211	59
	◆ *Chugwater / Louis C. Morrison / Louis C. Morrison / 1955*									
85⁶⁄₈	15²⁄₈	15²⁄₈	7²⁄₈	7²⁄₈	13⁴⁄₈	10⁶⁄₈	7	6⁷⁄₈	211	59
	◆ *Rock Springs / C.J. McElroy / C.J. McElroy / 1969*									
85⁶⁄₈	16³⁄₈	15⁷⁄₈	6²⁄₈	6²⁄₈	10	9	4⁴⁄₈	4⁴⁄₈	211	59
	◆ *Sweetwater County / E. Tom Thorne / E. Tom Thorne / 1969*									
85⁶⁄₈	16⁵⁄₈	16⁵⁄₈	6²⁄₈	6²⁄₈	9⁷⁄₈	5⁶⁄₈	5²⁄₈	5³⁄₈	211	59
	◆ *Sweetwater County / Roger A. Perkins / Roger A. Perkins / 1971*									
85⁶⁄₈	18³⁄₈	18²⁄₈	6⁶⁄₈	6⁴⁄₈	7⁷⁄₈	4⁷⁄₈	5²⁄₈	4³⁄₈	211	59
	◆ *Carbon County / Robert F. Johnston / Robert F. Johnston / 1977*									
85⁶⁄₈	16¹⁄₈	16	7	7¹⁄₈	11²⁄₈	8⁷⁄₈	6²⁄₈	6¹⁄₈	211	59
	◆ *Natrona County / Terrie L. Morrison / Terrie L. Morrison / 1980*									
85⁶⁄₈	15⁷⁄₈	16	6⁷⁄₈	6⁷⁄₈	9⁴⁄₈	4³⁄₈	5⁴⁄₈	5⁵⁄₈	211	59
	◆ *Sweetwater County / Mark E. Nedrow / Mark E. Nedrow / 1981*									
85⁶⁄₈	15⁴⁄₈	15⁵⁄₈	7³⁄₈	7⁴⁄₈	7⁴⁄₈	3	5⁵⁄₈	5⁶⁄₈	211	59
	◆ *Carbon County / James M. Jagusch / James M. Jagusch / 1981*									
85⁶⁄₈	16	16²⁄₈	6⁴⁄₈	6⁴⁄₈	9	3	6⁷⁄₈	6⁷⁄₈	211	59
	◆ *Sweetwater County / Steven J. Vanlerberghe / Steven J. Vanlerberghe / 1988*									
85⁶⁄₈	15⁷⁄₈	15⁷⁄₈	7⁶⁄₈	7⁶⁄₈	8⁶⁄₈	2³⁄₈	5⁵⁄₈	5⁵⁄₈	211	59
	◆ *Sweetwater County / Duane M. Smith / Duane M. Smith / 1989*									
85⁶⁄₈	16⁶⁄₈	16⁶⁄₈	6⁵⁄₈	6⁵⁄₈	10⁶⁄₈	9⁴⁄₈	6	6	211	59
	◆ *Carbon County / Herman A. Hatfield / Herman A. Hatfield / 1990*									
85⁶⁄₈	15⁴⁄₈	15⁴⁄₈	7²⁄₈	7²⁄₈	8³⁄₈	3	6⁴⁄₈	6²⁄₈	211	59
	◆ *Sweetwater County / Robert C. Sexton / Robert C. Sexton / 1992*									
85⁴⁄₈	16⁶⁄₈	16⁵⁄₈	7⁵⁄₈	7⁴⁄₈	11⁶⁄₈	8⁴⁄₈	7³⁄₈	6⁵⁄₈	238	72
	◆ *Rawlins / Paul C. Himelright / Paul C. Himelright / 1960*									
85⁴⁄₈	17²⁄₈	16⁵⁄₈	6¹⁄₈	6²⁄₈	10⁷⁄₈	6²⁄₈	6²⁄₈	6²⁄₈	238	72
	◆ *Campbell County / Eugene D. Springen / Eugene D. Springen / 1962*									
85⁴⁄₈	15⁴⁄₈	15³⁄₈	7²⁄₈	7²⁄₈	7⁶⁄₈	4¹⁄₈	6²⁄₈	6³⁄₈	238	72
	◆ *Saratoga / Carlyn J. Ourada / Carlyn J. Ourada / 1969*									
85⁴⁄₈	16	16	6⁷⁄₈	7	7³⁄₈	3³⁄₈	6⁵⁄₈	6⁴⁄₈	238	72
	◆ *Sweetwater County / Lee Frudden / Lee Frudden / 1982*									

Score	Length of Horn		Circumference of Base		Inside Spread	Tip-to-Tip Spread	Length of Prong		All-Time Rank	State Rank
	R	L	R	L			R	L		
◆ Locality / Hunter / Owner / Date Killed										
85⁴⁄₈	16⁴⁄₈	17¹⁄₈	7	6⁷⁄₈	13	9³⁄₈	5⁵⁄₈	5⁷⁄₈	238	72
◆ Fremont County / Jerry A. Martin / Jerry A. Martin / 1982										
85⁴⁄₈	15⁵⁄₈	15⁶⁄₈	6⁷⁄₈	6⁷⁄₈	8⁴⁄₈	2³⁄₈	6³⁄₈	6³⁄₈	238	72
◆ Fremont County / Roger E. Udovich / Roger E. Udovich / 1982										
85⁴⁄₈	17	16⁶⁄₈	6⁷⁄₈	6⁷⁄₈	9³⁄₈	6	5³⁄₈	5⁷⁄₈	238	72
◆ Sweetwater County / E. Jay Dawson / E. Jay Dawson / 1983										
85⁴⁄₈	17	16⁶⁄₈	6⁵⁄₈	6⁶⁄₈	12⁴⁄₈	8²⁄₈	6	5⁶⁄₈	238	72
◆ Campbell County / Ronald R. Mobley / Ronald R. Mobley / 1993										
85²⁄₈	16³⁄₈	16⁴⁄₈	7¹⁄₈	7¹⁄₈	12⁴⁄₈	8⁶⁄₈	5⁶⁄₈	5⁴⁄₈	268	80
◆ Saratoga / Russell Cutter / Russell Cutter / 1957										
85²⁄₈	15⁴⁄₈	15⁴⁄₈	7¹⁄₈	7¹⁄₈	12²⁄₈	11¹⁄₈	6	6	268	80
◆ Lower Sweetwater / John Kereszturi / John Kereszturi / 1963										
85²⁄₈	14⁴⁄₈	14³⁄₈	6⁶⁄₈	6⁶⁄₈	14	11⁵⁄₈	6⁴⁄₈	6³⁄₈	268	80
◆ Sublette County / Mike Wilson / Mike Wilson / 1966										
85²⁄₈	17¹⁄₈	16⁶⁄₈	6²⁄₈	6³⁄₈	11¹⁄₈	5⁶⁄₈	6³⁄₈	6¹⁄₈	268	80
◆ Sweetwater County / Mario Shassetz / Mario Shassetz / 1968										
85²⁄₈	15⁶⁄₈	16	6³⁄₈	6³⁄₈	10³⁄₈	7⁴⁄₈	7⁴⁄₈	7⁴⁄₈	268	80
◆ Johnson County / Robert P. Murphy / Robert P. Murphy / 1968										
85²⁄₈	14⁴⁄₈	14⁴⁄₈	7⁶⁄₈	7²⁄₈	11⁷⁄₈	9⁷⁄₈	4⁶⁄₈	4⁶⁄₈	268	80
◆ S. Wamsutter / William G. Hepworth / William G. Hepworth / 1970										
85²⁄₈	15⁷⁄₈	15⁶⁄₈	7²⁄₈	7¹⁄₈	8³⁄₈	3⁶⁄₈	6⁴⁄₈	6⁴⁄₈	268	80
◆ Carbon County / Daryl L. Frank / Daryl L. Frank / 1973										
85²⁄₈	15⁶⁄₈	15⁶⁄₈	6⁶⁄₈	6⁶⁄₈	12⁵⁄₈	8²⁄₈	7¹⁄₈	6⁷⁄₈	268	80
◆ Lincoln County / James R. Gunter / James R. Gunter / 1976										
85²⁄₈	16⁴⁄₈	16³⁄₈	7	7¹⁄₈	8⁵⁄₈	4³⁄₈	5⁶⁄₈	5²⁄₈	268	80
◆ Carbon County / Paul M. Ostrander / Paul M. Ostrander / 1977										
85²⁄₈	14⁴⁄₈	14⁴⁄₈	5⁷⁄₈	5⁷⁄₈	9⁷⁄₈	6⁷⁄₈	6	5⁷⁄₈	268	80
◆ Carbon County / Roland W. Anthony / Roland W. Anthony / 1978										
85²⁄₈	16	15⁵⁄₈	6⁴⁄₈	6⁵⁄₈	12	8⁴⁄₈	6	6²⁄₈	268	80
◆ Fremont County / Richard A. Fruchey / Richard A. Fruchey / 1981										
85²⁄₈	17⁴⁄₈	17³⁄₈	6¹⁄₈	6¹⁄₈	9³⁄₈	6⁵⁄₈	5⁴⁄₈	5⁷⁄₈	268	80
◆ Natrona County / Margery H.T. Torrey / Margery H.T. Torrey / 1981										
85²⁄₈	16³⁄₈	16³⁄₈	7	6⁷⁄₈	14³⁄₈	10⁵⁄₈	6²⁄₈	6²⁄₈	268	80
◆ Carbon County / Patrick R. Adams / Patrick R. Adams / 1982										
85²⁄₈	16¹⁄₈	16¹⁄₈	7	6⁷⁄₈	10⁵⁄₈	7¹⁄₈	5⁵⁄₈	6¹⁄₈	268	80
◆ Sweetwater County / L. Bill Miller / L. Bill Miller / 1982										
85²⁄₈	16⁴⁄₈	16⁴⁄₈	6⁶⁄₈	6⁴⁄₈	7⁵⁄₈	2⁶⁄₈	7	5⁴⁄₈	268	80
◆ Natrona County / J. Brendan Bummer / J. Brendan Bummer / 1990										

WYOMING PRONGHORN *(continued)*

Score	Length of Horn R	Length of Horn L	Circumference of Base R	Circumference of Base L	Inside Spread	Tip-to-Tip Spread	Length of Prong R	Length of Prong L	All-Time Rank	State Rank
	♦ *Locality / Hunter / Owner / Date Killed*									
85 1/8	17 4/8	16 5/8	6 6/8	6 5/8	20 5/8	20	7 2/8	6 4/8	300	95
	♦ *Sweetwater County / Annette D. Lynch / Annette D. Lynch / 1983*									
85	16 5/8	16 4/8	6 5/8	6 5/8	13 2/8	9 6/8	5 2/8	5 3/8	301	96
	♦ *Campbell County / O.P. Nicholson / Johnson Co. Museum / 1937*									
85	15 3/8	14 7/8	7 4/8	7 4/8	11 1/8	6 1/8	6	5 6/8	301	96
	♦ *Douglas / Floyd Bishop / Floyd Bishop / 1937*									
85	15 5/8	15 6/8	6	6	9 6/8	8 1/8	4 5/8	5 3/8	301	96
	♦ *Sage Creek Basin / Robert A. Hill / Robert A. Hill / 1959*									
85	16	15 7/8	7 1/8	7	8 6/8	4 6/8	5 6/8	5 7/8	301	96
	♦ *Rawlins / Clarence J. Becker / Clarence J. Becker / 1965*									
85	14 5/8	14 4/8	8 1/8	7 6/8	11 5/8	10 2/8	5 7/8	5 6/8	301	96
	♦ *Saratoga / Benny E. Bechtol / Benny E. Bechtol / 1968*									
85	16 2/8	16 2/8	6 6/8	6 6/8	14 1/8	9 1/8	5 7/8	6	301	96
	♦ *Rawlins / H.H. Eighmy / H.H. Eighmy / 1969*									
85	15 4/8	15 6/8	7 2/8	7	13 2/8	8 7/8	6 5/8	6 1/8	301	96
	♦ *Uinta County / Joan Beachler / Joan Beachler / 1974*									
85	16 5/8	16 6/8	6 4/8	6 4/8	10 2/8	5 2/8	5 6/8	5 6/8	301	96
	♦ *Lincoln County / Ross M. Wilde / Ross M. Wilde / 1980*									
85	16 2/8	16	6 6/8	6 6/8	12 7/8	9 4/8	6 1/8	6 1/8	301	96
	♦ *Carbon County / Kelly W. Hepworth / Kelly W. Hepworth / 1982*									
85	15 5/8	15 3/8	6 6/8	6 7/8	9 4/8	4 3/8	6 6/8	6 6/8	301	96
	♦ *Sweetwater County / Ronald L. Barber / Ronald L. Barber / 1989*									
85	15 7/8	15 1/8	7 3/8	7 2/8	7 3/8	4 5/8	6 4/8	6 3/8	301	96
	♦ *Sweetwater County / Mary A. Barbour / Mary A. Barbour / 1990*									
84 6/8	17 1/8	16 7/8	6 1/8	6 3/8	12 2/8	10 5/8	6 2/8	6 7/8	336	107
	♦ *Slate Creek / Jim Calkins / Jim Calkins / 1956*									
84 6/8	16 4/8	16 4/8	6 5/8	6 5/8	8 3/8	3 4/8	6 1/8	5 5/8	336	107
	♦ *Laramie / Roger D. Ramsay / Roger D. Ramsay / 1958*									
84 6/8	16 3/8	16 4/8	6 1/8	6	11 3/8	7 4/8	4 5/8	4 7/8	336	107
	♦ *Laramie Peak / Elmer Rupert / Elmer Rupert / 1961*									
84 6/8	16 3/8	16 4/8	6 5/8	6 6/8	11 1/8	7	5	5	336	107
	♦ *Sinclair / John Kastner / John Kastner / 1963*									
84 6/8	17 3/8	16 7/8	7 1/8	7 1/8	14 6/8	12 4/8	5 4/8	4 4/8	336	107
	♦ *Fremont County / Dick Cone / Dick Cone / 1963*									
84 6/8	16 6/8	16 5/8	6 7/8	7	12	11	5 2/8	4 7/8	336	107
	♦ *Johnson County / John G. Carroll / John G. Carroll / 1965*									
84 6/8	15 7/8	15 7/8	6 2/8	6 2/8	10 6/8	6 2/8	7	7	336	107
	♦ *Rock Springs / W. Daniel English / W. Daniel English / 1966*									

WYOMING PRONGHORN (*continued*)

Score	Length of Horn R	L	Circumference of Base R	L	Inside Spread	Tip-to-Tip Spread	Length of Prong R	L	All-Time Rank	State Rank
♦ Locality / Hunter / Owner / Date Killed										
84⁶⁄₈	15⅝	15⅞	7⅞	7⁶⁄₈	10²⁄₈	5⅞	5⁶⁄₈	5⅝	336	107
♦ Poison Spider Creek / Robert Ziker / Robert Ziker / 1966										
84⁶⁄₈	16	16	6⁶⁄₈	6⁴⁄₈	11²⁄₈	5⁴⁄₈	6⁴⁄₈	6⁴⁄₈	336	107
♦ Casper / John E. Mohritz / John E. Mohritz / 1966										
84⁶⁄₈	15⁴⁄₈	15⁶⁄₈	6⅜	6⅜	8⅝	3²⁄₈	6⅝	6⁴⁄₈	336	107
♦ Natrona County / W. Bruce Mouw / W. Bruce Mouw / 1980										
84⁶⁄₈	14⅛	14⅛	7⅜	7⅜	9²⁄₈	7⁴⁄₈	5	5⅛	336	107
♦ Fremont County / James E. Egger / James E. Egger / 1981										
84⁶⁄₈	16⅞	16⅜	6⅝	6⅝	11⁴⁄₈	8⁴⁄₈	7⅛	6⅞	336	107
♦ Carbon County / Robb D. Hitchcock / Robb D. Hitchcock / 1981										
84⁶⁄₈	15⁴⁄₈	15⁴⁄₈	7⅜	7²⁄₈	11⅝	7⁶⁄₈	6⅝	6⅝	336	107
♦ Sweetwater County / David L. Thompson / David L. Thompson / 1982										
84⁶⁄₈	16⅜	16²⁄₈	6⁴⁄₈	6⁴⁄₈	9⅜	4²⁄₈	5²⁄₈	5⅜	336	107
♦ Carbon County / Paul Herring / Paul Herring / 1983										
84⁶⁄₈	16⅜	16⅛	6⅜	6²⁄₈	13²⁄₈	11²⁄₈	6⅞	6⅞	336	107
♦ Sweetwater County / Melvin E. Killman / Melvin E. Killman / 1989										
84⁶⁄₈	15⁶⁄₈	16	6⅞	6⅞	7⁶⁄₈	3⅞	6⁶⁄₈	6⅝	336	107
♦ Natrona County / Warren N. Pearce / Warren N. Pearce / 1990										
84⁶⁄₈	15²⁄₈	15⅜	7⅜	7⁴⁄₈	11⅜	9⁶⁄₈	6	5⅞	336	107
♦ Carbon County / Myron J. Wakkuri / Myron J. Wakkuri / 1990										
84⁶⁄₈	16⅜	16⁴⁄₈	6⁴⁄₈	6⁴⁄₈	7²⁄₈	1²⁄₈	4⁶⁄₈	5⅜	336	107
♦ Fremont County / Karen L. Jenson / Karen L. Jenson / 1991										
84⁶⁄₈	15⅝	15⅝	7⅛	7	12	8²⁄₈	5⅜	5⅜	336	107
♦ Carbon County / Brian T. King / Brian T. King / 1991										
84⁶⁄₈	14⁶⁄₈	15	7⅛	7⅛	14⅝	11⅞	5⁶⁄₈	5²⁄₈	336	107
♦ Converse County / Michael R. Land / Michael R. Land / 1991										
84⁴⁄₈	16⅜	16⅜	7⅛	7⅛	9⁶⁄₈	6	5⅜	5⅜	390	127
♦ Carbon County / A.A. Carrey / A.A. Carrey / 1944										
84⁴⁄₈	16	16	5⅝	5⅝	14⁴⁄₈	13⅞	5⅛	5	390	127
♦ Fremont County / Ernest R. Novotny / Ernest R. Novotny / 1954										
84⁴⁄₈	15⁶⁄₈	15⅞	7⅝	7⅝	14²⁄₈	10⅜	5⁶⁄₈	5⅞	390	127
♦ Rawlins / Eloise Kees / Eloise Kees / 1962										
84⁴⁄₈	14⅞	14⁶⁄₈	7⁴⁄₈	7⁴⁄₈	9⅛	5⅞	5⅞	6²⁄₈	390	127
♦ Baggs / Tom Elberson / Tom Elberson / 1966										
84⁴⁄₈	17	17⅛	6⁴⁄₈	6⅝	11⅛	5⅛	5⁶⁄₈	5⁶⁄₈	390	127
♦ Sweetwater County / Harvey B. Bartley / Harvey B. Bartley / 1970										
84⁴⁄₈	16²⁄₈	16²⁄₈	6	6	13	8	7⅛	7	390	127
♦ Carbon County / William G. Mackey / William G. Mackey / 1972										

351

Score	Length of Horn		Circumference of Base		Inside Spread	Tip-to-Tip Spread	Length of Prong		All-Time Rank	State Rank
	R	L	R	L			R	L		
	♦ *Locality / Hunter / Owner / Date Killed*									
$84\frac{4}{8}$	16	16	$6\frac{4}{8}$	$6\frac{5}{8}$	$12\frac{3}{8}$	$7\frac{3}{8}$	$6\frac{6}{8}$	$6\frac{6}{8}$	390	127
	♦ *Lincoln County / George Kirkman / George Kirkman / 1973*									
$84\frac{4}{8}$	15	$15\frac{3}{8}$	$7\frac{5}{8}$	$7\frac{2}{8}$	$6\frac{5}{8}$	$4\frac{6}{8}$	$6\frac{6}{8}$	$5\frac{6}{8}$	390	127
	♦ *Carbon County / Stephen C. LeBlanc / Stephen C. LeBlanc / 1976*									
$84\frac{4}{8}$	$15\frac{6}{8}$	16	$7\frac{4}{8}$	$7\frac{4}{8}$	$10\frac{4}{8}$	$6\frac{6}{8}$	$5\frac{1}{8}$	$5\frac{3}{8}$	390	127
	♦ *Carbon County / John C. Sjogren / John C. Sjogren / 1976*									
$84\frac{4}{8}$	$16\frac{3}{8}$	$16\frac{3}{8}$	7	$6\frac{7}{8}$	$14\frac{6}{8}$	$12\frac{5}{8}$	6	$5\frac{4}{8}$	390	127
	♦ *Sweetwater County / Frankie Miller / Frankie Miller / 1979*									
$84\frac{4}{8}$	$17\frac{2}{8}$	17	$6\frac{5}{8}$	$6\frac{5}{8}$	$8\frac{3}{8}$	$4\frac{1}{8}$	$5\frac{5}{8}$	6	390	127
	♦ *Sweetwater County / Lee Frudden / Lee Frudden / 1981*									
$84\frac{4}{8}$	$16\frac{1}{8}$	$16\frac{4}{8}$	$6\frac{6}{8}$	$6\frac{5}{8}$	15	$12\frac{2}{8}$	$5\frac{5}{8}$	$5\frac{5}{8}$	390	127
	♦ *Carbon County / Jack A. Berger / Jack A. Berger / 1982*									
$84\frac{4}{8}$	15	15	$6\frac{4}{8}$	$6\frac{5}{8}$	$9\frac{6}{8}$	$7\frac{3}{8}$	7	$6\frac{6}{8}$	390	127
	♦ *Carbon County / William J. Stokes / William J. Stokes / 1982*									
$84\frac{4}{8}$	$15\frac{4}{8}$	$15\frac{2}{8}$	$7\frac{4}{8}$	$7\frac{4}{8}$	$13\frac{6}{8}$	10	$5\frac{6}{8}$	$5\frac{5}{8}$	390	127
	♦ *Fremont County / Michael P. Hauffe / Michael P. Hauffe / 1983*									
$84\frac{4}{8}$	$16\frac{6}{8}$	$16\frac{7}{8}$	$7\frac{3}{8}$	$7\frac{2}{8}$	$14\frac{4}{8}$	$8\frac{6}{8}$	$4\frac{5}{8}$	$4\frac{5}{8}$	390	127
	♦ *Fremont County / William R. Suranyi / William R. Suranyi / 1983*									
$84\frac{4}{8}$	16	$16\frac{2}{8}$	$7\frac{2}{8}$	$7\frac{4}{8}$	$8\frac{4}{8}$	$4\frac{4}{8}$	$5\frac{5}{8}$	$5\frac{5}{8}$	390	127
	♦ *Natrona County / Joe L. Ficken / Joe L. Ficken / 1985*									
$84\frac{4}{8}$	$16\frac{4}{8}$	$16\frac{5}{8}$	$6\frac{7}{8}$	$6\frac{7}{8}$	$8\frac{3}{8}$	4	$5\frac{1}{8}$	$5\frac{7}{8}$	390	127
	♦ *Sweetwater County / Mike D. McKell / Mike D. McKell / 1986*									
$84\frac{4}{8}$	$14\frac{7}{8}$	$15\frac{1}{8}$	$7\frac{3}{8}$	$7\frac{2}{8}$	$8\frac{6}{8}$	$4\frac{6}{8}$	$5\frac{6}{8}$	$5\frac{6}{8}$	390	127
	♦ *Fremont County / Lyle D. Fruchey / Lyle D. Fruchey / 1990*									
$84\frac{4}{8}$	16	$15\frac{6}{8}$	$7\frac{2}{8}$	7	$13\frac{7}{8}$	14	$4\frac{5}{8}$	$4\frac{7}{8}$	390	127
	♦ *Natrona County / Barry N. Strang / Barry N. Strang / 1991*									
$84\frac{4}{8}$	$16\frac{6}{8}$	$16\frac{4}{8}$	$7\frac{2}{8}$	$7\frac{1}{8}$	$8\frac{7}{8}$	$2\frac{5}{8}$	6	$5\frac{2}{8}$	390	127
	♦ *Sweetwater County / Clint N. Gibson / Clint N. Gibson / 1992*									
$84\frac{4}{8}$	$15\frac{6}{8}$	$15\frac{5}{8}$	7	$6\frac{7}{8}$	$10\frac{3}{8}$	9	$6\frac{4}{8}$	$6\frac{5}{8}$	390	127
	♦ *Carbon County / Kirby C. Hornbeck / Kirby C. Hornbeck / 1992*									
$84\frac{4}{8}$	$16\frac{5}{8}$	$16\frac{7}{8}$	$7\frac{1}{8}$	$7\frac{1}{8}$	$10\frac{7}{8}$	$6\frac{1}{8}$	$4\frac{5}{8}$	$4\frac{4}{8}$	390	127
	♦ *Fremont County / Jeff A. Schweighart / Jeff A. Schweighart / 1992*									
$84\frac{4}{8}$	$15\frac{6}{8}$	16	$7\frac{2}{8}$	$7\frac{1}{8}$	$7\frac{4}{8}$	4	$5\frac{6}{8}$	$6\frac{2}{8}$	390	127
	♦ *Fremont County / Stuart W. Shepherd / Stuart W. Shepherd / 1992*									
$84\frac{2}{8}$	$16\frac{6}{8}$	$16\frac{4}{8}$	$6\frac{6}{8}$	$6\frac{6}{8}$	$10\frac{2}{8}$	$5\frac{7}{8}$	$5\frac{4}{8}$	$5\frac{2}{8}$	436	150
	♦ *Sweetwater River / Kermit Platt / Kermit Platt / 1952*									
$84\frac{2}{8}$	$15\frac{4}{8}$	15	$6\frac{3}{8}$	$6\frac{3}{8}$	$11\frac{4}{8}$	11	$4\frac{3}{8}$	$4\frac{4}{8}$	436	150
	♦ *Pumpkin Buttes / John B. Miller / John B. Miller / 1957*									

Score	Length of Horn R	Length of Horn L	Circumference of Base R	Circumference of Base L	Inside Spread	Tip-to-Tip Spread	Length of Prong R	Length of Prong L	All-Time Rank	State Rank
$84^2/_8$	$16^4/_8$	$17^1/_8$	$6^4/_8$	$6^3/_8$	$10^2/_8$	$6^1/_8$	$4^6/_8$	$4^4/_8$	436	150
◆ *Sage Creek Basin / Aydeen Auld / Aydeen Auld / 1959*										
$84^2/_8$	$16^6/_8$	$16^5/_8$	7	$6^7/_8$	$7^5/_8$	$1^7/_8$	6	6	436	150
◆ *Natrona / William Fisher / William Fisher / 1960*										
$84^2/_8$	16	$16^3/_8$	7	7	$11^5/_8$	$7^6/_8$	$6^1/_8$	$6^2/_8$	436	150
◆ *Uinta County / Ross Lukenbill / Ross Lukenbill / 1965*										
$84^2/_8$	$15^7/_8$	16	7	$7^1/_8$	$10^2/_8$	$5^1/_8$	$6^1/_8$	$6^1/_8$	436	150
◆ *Rawlins / Armin O. Baltensweiler / Armin O. Baltensweiler / 1966*										
$84^2/_8$	$16^2/_8$	$16^1/_8$	$7^3/_8$	$7^1/_8$	$12^3/_8$	$8^6/_8$	$5^6/_8$	$5^5/_8$	436	150
◆ *Fremont County / Edward S. Friend / Edward S. Friend / 1967*										
$84^2/_8$	$14^6/_8$	$14^7/_8$	$6^5/_8$	$6^5/_8$	$7^2/_8$	$7^1/_8$	$6^6/_8$	$7^1/_8$	436	150
◆ *Big Piney / Lawrence M. Kick / Lawrence M. Kick / 1967*										
$84^2/_8$	15	15	$7^6/_8$	$7^5/_8$	$13^4/_8$	$11^7/_8$	8	8	436	150
◆ *Fremont County / Lee Arce / Lee Arce / 1968*										
$84^2/_8$	$15^2/_8$	15	6	6	$11^6/_8$	$8^2/_8$	$4^7/_8$	$4^7/_8$	436	150
◆ *Natrona County / Donald F. Mahnke / Donald F. Mahnke / 1971*										
$84^2/_8$	$16^4/_8$	$16^4/_8$	7	7	$15^1/_8$	$11^2/_8$	$5^2/_8$	$5^2/_8$	436	150
◆ *Albany County / George Panagos, Jr. / George Panagos, Jr. / 1972*										
$84^2/_8$	16	$16^1/_8$	$6^7/_8$	$6^7/_8$	$9^7/_8$	7	$4^5/_8$	$4^2/_8$	436	150
◆ *Carbon County / William O. Queen / William O. Queen / 1975*										
$84^2/_8$	$17^4/_8$	$17^4/_8$	$6^5/_8$	$6^5/_8$	$11^2/_8$	$8^1/_8$	$4^5/_8$	$4^3/_8$	436	150
◆ *Sweetwater County / Bill Jordan / Bill Jordan / 1976*										
$84^2/_8$	$15^2/_8$	$15^2/_8$	$7^3/_8$	$7^1/_8$	13	$12^1/_8$	$5^6/_8$	$5^6/_8$	436	150
◆ *Carbon County / Kenneth Mellin / Kenneth Mellin / 1976*										
$84^2/_8$	$15^5/_8$	$15^7/_8$	$7^3/_8$	$7^2/_8$	$14^2/_8$	13	$5^6/_8$	$5^7/_8$	436	150
◆ *Carbon County / Glenn F. Galbraith / Glenn F. Galbraith / 1977*										
$84^2/_8$	$15^4/_8$	$15^2/_8$	$7^4/_8$	$7^4/_8$	$12^3/_8$	8	$6^2/_8$	$6^2/_8$	436	150
◆ *Fremont County / William D. Baldwin / William D. Baldwin / 1980*										
$84^2/_8$	17	$17^3/_8$	$6^6/_8$	$6^5/_8$	$12^2/_8$	$10^2/_8$	$5^4/_8$	$5^6/_8$	436	150
◆ *Sweetwater County / John V. Wilgus / John V. Wilgus / 1980*										
$84^2/_8$	16	$15^6/_8$	$6^6/_8$	$6^6/_8$	10	$5^2/_8$	$5^5/_8$	$5^6/_8$	436	150
◆ *Carbon County / Ernest L. Tollini / Ernest L. Tollini / 1982*										
$84^2/_8$	$15^5/_8$	$15^5/_8$	$6^7/_8$	$6^5/_8$	$9^3/_8$	$4^5/_8$	$6^5/_8$	$6^1/_8$	436	150
◆ *Carbon County / Mike Clegg / Mike Clegg / 1983*										
$84^2/_8$	$16^5/_8$	$16^4/_8$	$7^4/_8$	$7^4/_8$	$9^2/_8$	$5^1/_8$	$5^1/_8$	$4^6/_8$	436	150
◆ *Natrona County / Allen J. Hogan / Allen J. Hogan / 1983*										
$84^2/_8$	16	$16^2/_8$	$6^5/_8$	$6^5/_8$	$13^2/_8$	11	$5^6/_8$	$5^6/_8$	436	150
◆ *Fremont County / John Monje / John Monje / 1985*										

Score	Length of Horn		Circumference of Base		Inside Spread	Tip-to-Tip Spread	Length of Prong		All-Time Rank	State Rank
	R	L	R	L			R	L		
	◆ *Locality / Hunter / Owner / Date Killed*									
$84\frac{2}{8}$	$15\frac{7}{8}$	$15\frac{1}{8}$	$7\frac{1}{8}$	$7\frac{1}{8}$	$10\frac{1}{8}$	$6\frac{3}{8}$	$6\frac{2}{8}$	$6\frac{2}{8}$	436	150
	◆ *Fremont County / Boyd E. Sharp, Jr. / Boyd E. Sharp, Jr. / 1989*									
$84\frac{2}{8}$	$15\frac{3}{8}$	$15\frac{5}{8}$	$7\frac{3}{8}$	$7\frac{2}{8}$	$9\frac{3}{8}$	$5\frac{1}{8}$	$6\frac{1}{8}$	$5\frac{5}{8}$	436	150
	◆ *Washakie County / Douglas D. Stinnette / Douglas D. Stinnette / 1989*									
$84\frac{2}{8}$	$15\frac{7}{8}$	$15\frac{7}{8}$	$7\frac{1}{8}$	7	$9\frac{3}{8}$	$8\frac{4}{8}$	$6\frac{2}{8}$	$6\frac{3}{8}$	436	150
	◆ *Sweetwater County / Kurt D. Olson / Kurt D. Olson / 1990*									
$84\frac{2}{8}$	$15\frac{2}{8}$	15	7	7	$11\frac{1}{8}$	8	$6\frac{4}{8}$	$7\frac{1}{8}$	436	150
	◆ *Carbon County / Robert G. Wimpenny / Robert G. Wimpenny / 1990*									
$84\frac{2}{8}$	16	$15\frac{5}{8}$	$7\frac{5}{8}$	$7\frac{5}{8}$	$12\frac{6}{8}$	$12\frac{6}{8}$	5	$5\frac{5}{8}$	436	150
	◆ *Fremont County / Carl A. Engler / Carl A. Engler / 1991*									
$84\frac{2}{8}$	$16\frac{4}{8}$	$16\frac{4}{8}$	$6\frac{6}{8}$	$6\frac{4}{8}$	$9\frac{6}{8}$	$6\frac{2}{8}$	$6\frac{2}{8}$	6	436	150
	◆ *Carbon County / Lynn Woodard / Lynn Woodard / 1991*									
84	$15\frac{6}{8}$	16	$7\frac{2}{8}$	$7\frac{2}{8}$	$14\frac{1}{8}$	$10\frac{6}{8}$	$3\frac{5}{8}$	$3\frac{3}{8}$	500	177
	◆ *Lost Cabin / Jack Henrey / Jack Henrey / 1955*									
84	$17\frac{1}{8}$	$17\frac{1}{8}$	$6\frac{4}{8}$	$6\frac{4}{8}$	$14\frac{2}{8}$	$11\frac{1}{8}$	5	$5\frac{2}{8}$	500	177
	◆ *Meadowdale / Mrs. Lodisa Pipher / Mrs. Lodisa Pipher / 1956*									
84	$14\frac{6}{8}$	$14\frac{4}{8}$	$7\frac{5}{8}$	$7\frac{5}{8}$	$14\frac{4}{8}$	$13\frac{6}{8}$	6	$5\frac{7}{8}$	500	177
	◆ *Pinedale / Edward Sturla / Edward Sturla / 1960*									
84	$16\frac{6}{8}$	$16\frac{4}{8}$	$6\frac{6}{8}$	$6\frac{4}{8}$	$11\frac{4}{8}$	9	$5\frac{5}{8}$	$5\frac{2}{8}$	500	177
	◆ *Sage Creek / Pat Swarts / Pat Swarts / 1960*									
84	$15\frac{6}{8}$	16	$6\frac{6}{8}$	$6\frac{6}{8}$	$11\frac{2}{8}$	8	$6\frac{4}{8}$	$6\frac{4}{8}$	500	177
	◆ *Campbell County / Fred J. Brogle / Fred J. Brogle / 1960*									
84	$17\frac{1}{8}$	$17\frac{4}{8}$	$6\frac{4}{8}$	$6\frac{5}{8}$	$13\frac{4}{8}$	$12\frac{5}{8}$	$5\frac{3}{8}$	$5\frac{1}{8}$	500	177
	◆ *Carbon County / Mrs. T.H. Green / Mrs. T.H. Green / 1964*									
84	$16\frac{5}{8}$	$16\frac{5}{8}$	$6\frac{3}{8}$	$6\frac{2}{8}$	$11\frac{2}{8}$	6	$6\frac{2}{8}$	$6\frac{1}{8}$	500	177
	◆ *Fremont County / Robert E. Novotny / Robert E. Novotny / 1964*									
84	16	$16\frac{1}{8}$	$6\frac{6}{8}$	$6\frac{5}{8}$	$8\frac{6}{8}$	$5\frac{2}{8}$	$5\frac{7}{8}$	$6\frac{2}{8}$	500	177
	◆ *Rawlins / John M. Sell / John M. Sell / 1964*									
84	$14\frac{4}{8}$	$14\frac{4}{8}$	7	$6\frac{6}{8}$	$11\frac{5}{8}$	$11\frac{5}{8}$	6	$6\frac{2}{8}$	500	177
	◆ *Red Desert / Fred Morgan / Fred Morgan / 1969*									
84	$16\frac{6}{8}$	$16\frac{1}{8}$	$6\frac{7}{8}$	$6\frac{7}{8}$	$7\frac{3}{8}$	$3\frac{5}{8}$	$4\frac{6}{8}$	$4\frac{6}{8}$	500	177
	◆ *Carbon County / Russ Allen / Russ Allen / 1970*									
84	15	$15\frac{2}{8}$	7	7	$14\frac{1}{8}$	$11\frac{4}{8}$	6	6	500	177
	◆ *Albany County / Andy Pfaff / Andy Pfaff / 1972*									
84	$18\frac{6}{8}$	$18\frac{2}{8}$	$6\frac{4}{8}$	$6\frac{4}{8}$	$17\frac{6}{8}$	$15\frac{7}{8}$	5	$4\frac{5}{8}$	500	177
	◆ *Sublette County / Dick Reilly / Dick Reilly / 1974*									
84	$14\frac{7}{8}$	$14\frac{5}{8}$	$7\frac{6}{8}$	$7\frac{3}{8}$	$11\frac{1}{8}$	10	$6\frac{3}{8}$	6	500	177
	◆ *Natrona County / Bill E. Boatman / Bill E. Boatman / 1980*									

Score	Length of Horn		Circumference of Base		Inside Spread	Tip-to-Tip Spread	Length of Prong		All-Time Rank	State Rank
	R	L	R	L			R	L		
◆ Locality / Hunter / Owner / Date Killed										
84	16⅛	16⁴⁄₈	6⅞	6⁶⁄₈	11²⁄₈	5⅞	6⁴⁄₈	5⁶⁄₈	500	177
◆ Fremont County / Joel E. Hensley / Joel E. Hensley / 1981										
84	15²⁄₈	15⅞	7²⁄₈	7⅛	15³⁄₈	13⁶⁄₈	6²⁄₈	6²⁄₈	500	177
◆ Fremont County / Victor M. McCullough / Victor M. McCullough / 1981										
84	16	15⁴⁄₈	7	7	12⁶⁄₈	9⅛	6²⁄₈	6³⁄₈	500	177
◆ Carbon County / Dudley R. Elmgren / Dudley R. Elmgren / 1982										
84	16⅞	16³⁄₈	7	6⁶⁄₈	10⁴⁄₈	6⁴⁄₈	5²⁄₈	5⁴⁄₈	500	177
◆ Sweetwater County / Richard H. Maddock / Richard H. Maddock / 1982										
84	16⅞	16⁴⁄₈	6⁶⁄₈	6⁶⁄₈	10⁶⁄₈	6	6⅛	6	500	177
◆ Sweetwater County / Lorio Verzasconi / Lorio Verzasconi / 1982										
84	16⁴⁄₈	16⁴⁄₈	6³⁄₈	6³⁄₈	11⁶⁄₈	7⁴⁄₈	5⁶⁄₈	5⅞	500	177
◆ Sweetwater County / Dennis W. Gallegos / Dennis W. Gallegos / 1983										
84	16⅞	16⁶⁄₈	6⅝	6⅝	10⁴⁄₈	6⁴⁄₈	6³⁄₈	6³⁄₈	500	177
◆ Natrona County / Dale A. Ableidinger / Dale A. Ableidinger / 1984										
84	15²⁄₈	15³⁄₈	6²⁄₈	6³⁄₈	12³⁄₈	8	7⅛	7²⁄₈	500	177
◆ Campbell County / Unknown / J. Michael Conoyer / PR 1986										
84	16²⁄₈	16²⁄₈	6⅝	6⅝	9⅞	6²⁄₈	5⅝	5³⁄₈	500	177
◆ Sweetwater County / Robert E. Bergquist / Robert E. Bergquist / 1991										
84	15	15²⁄₈	7²⁄₈	7²⁄₈	10⁴⁄₈	5²⁄₈	5³⁄₈	5⁴⁄₈	500	177
◆ Fremont County / John J. Weust / John J. Weust / 1991										
83⁶⁄₈	16	16	6⁴⁄₈	6⁴⁄₈	13	9⁶⁄₈	5⁶⁄₈	5⁴⁄₈	565	200
◆ Sheridan County / John T. Yarrington / John T. Yarrington / 1951										
83⁶⁄₈	16³⁄₈	16	7	7⅛	12⅞	11	5²⁄₈	4⁶⁄₈	565	200
◆ Saratoga / Bob Herbison / Bob Herbison / 1955										
83⁶⁄₈	15⁴⁄₈	15³⁄₈	7⅛	7	10⁴⁄₈	6³⁄₈	5⅞	5⅞	565	200
◆ Poison Spider / Robert Ziker / Robert Ziker / 1960										
83⁶⁄₈	15⅞	15⅞	7	7²⁄₈	8³⁄₈	5⁶⁄₈	5⅞	5⅞	565	200
◆ Alcova / Donald G. Gebers / Donald G. Gebers / 1964										
83⁶⁄₈	15	15	6⅝	6⅝	13⁴⁄₈	10⁴⁄₈	5⁴⁄₈	6³⁄₈	565	200
◆ Sweetwater County / R.L. Brown, Jr. / R.L. Brown, Jr. / 1970										
83⁶⁄₈	15	15⅛	7²⁄₈	7²⁄₈	14²⁄₈	11²⁄₈	5⁶⁄₈	5⅞	565	200
◆ Sweetwater County / Betty J. Oliver / Betty J. Oliver / 1974										
83⁶⁄₈	15⁴⁄₈	16	7⅛	7⅛	11⁴⁄₈	7	5⅝	5⁴⁄₈	565	200
◆ Sweetwater County / Dennis D. Seipp / Dennis D. Seipp / 1975										
83⁶⁄₈	15⁶⁄₈	16²⁄₈	6⁴⁄₈	6⁴⁄₈	10⁴⁄₈	10	6⅞	6⁶⁄₈	565	200
◆ Park County / D.F. & T. Holt / Don F. Holt / 1975										
83⁶⁄₈	16⁶⁄₈	17⁴⁄₈	6⁴⁄₈	6³⁄₈	11⁶⁄₈	7⅞	6³⁄₈	6⅛	565	200
◆ Wamsutter / James A. White / James A. White / 1980										

Score	Length of Horn		Circumference of Base		Inside Spread	Tip-to-Tip Spread	Length of Prong		All-Time Rank	State Rank
	R	L	R	L			R	L		
	◆ *Locality / Hunter / Owner / Date Killed*									
83 6/8	15 4/8	14 7/8	7 5/8	7 4/8	9 2/8	6	5 5/8	5 4/8	565	200
	◆ *Carbon County / Jack F. Schakel / Jack F. Schakel / 1981*									
83 6/8	17 2/8	16 3/8	6 5/8	6 6/8	7 1/8	2 5/8	6 4/8	6 1/8	565	200
	◆ *Natrona County / Ronald K. Morrison / Ronald K. Morrison / 1982*									
83 6/8	15 7/8	15 7/8	6 6/8	6 6/8	12 5/8	11	6 5/8	6 4/8	565	200
	◆ *Sweetwater County / Robert Gilbert / Robert Gilbert / 1983*									
83 6/8	16 2/8	16 5/8	7	6 6/8	12 6/8	8 4/8	5 6/8	5 5/8	565	200
	◆ *Carbon County / Douglas L. Hancock / Douglas L. Hancock / 1983*									
83 6/8	14 7/8	15	6 5/8	6 5/8	9 4/8	7 7/8	6 2/8	6 6/8	565	200
	◆ *Fremont County / Carl N. Anderson / Carl N. Anderson / 1987*									
83 6/8	14 3/8	14 3/8	7 5/8	7 5/8	7	3 3/8	5 7/8	5 7/8	565	200
	◆ *Carbon County / Thomas D. Widiker / Thomas D. Widiker / 1987*									
83 6/8	15 1/8	15	6 5/8	6 5/8	6	1 5/8	6 5/8	6 4/8	565	200
	◆ *Fremont County / Stuart W. Shepherd / Stuart W. Shepherd / 1990*									
83 6/8	16 4/8	16 6/8	6 5/8	6 5/8	9 6/8	6	5 6/8	5 7/8	565	200
	◆ *Carbon County / Rod F. Waeckerlin / Rod F. Waeckerlin / 1990*									
83 6/8	16 6/8	16 5/8	6 6/8	7	9 5/8	4 1/8	5	4 7/8	565	200
	◆ *Carbon County / John T. Johnson / John T. Johnson / 1992*									
83 6/8	17	17	6 4/8	6 3/8	10 3/8	5 3/8	5 4/8	5 4/8	565	200
	◆ *Campbell County / Loy D. Peters / Loy D. Peters / 1992*									
83 6/8	16 3/8	16 3/8	6 6/8	6 6/8	14	10 7/8	5 7/8	5 6/8	565	200
	◆ *Hot Springs County / Robert J. Ruiz / Robert J. Ruiz / 1992*									
83 4/8	17	16 2/8	6 4/8	6 2/8	14 1/8	11 1/8	6 4/8	6 1/8	624	220
	◆ *Farson / Geo. E. MacGillivray / Geo. E. MacGillivray / 1951*									
83 4/8	15 6/8	15 6/8	6 1/8	6 1/8	11 3/8	6 3/8	4 6/8	4 6/8	624	220
	◆ *Shoshoni / Collins F. Kellogg / Collins F. Kellogg / 1965*									
83 4/8	15 6/8	15 5/8	7	7 1/8	9 6/8	6 7/8	5 4/8	5 3/8	624	220
	◆ *Wamsutter / Kenneth L. Swanson / Kenneth L. Swanson / 1967*									
83 4/8	16 2/8	16 1/8	6 3/8	6 4/8	15 4/8	12 2/8	5 5/8	5 7/8	624	220
	◆ *Red Desert / David W. Knowles / David W. Knowles / 1970*									
83 4/8	16 2/8	16 2/8	6 6/8	6 6/8	12	10 1/8	5	5 1/8	624	220
	◆ *Carbon County / Billy C. Randall / Billy C. Randall / 1970*									
83 4/8	17 1/8	17	6 6/8	6 6/8	15 5/8	10 6/8	5	5	624	220
	◆ *Hoback Rim / F. Larry Storey / F. Larry Storey / 1973*									
83 4/8	15 3/8	15 6/8	7 2/8	7	8 1/8	2 2/8	5 3/8	5 1/8	624	220
	◆ *Fremont County / James G. Allard / James G. Allard / 1974*									
83 4/8	16	16	7 4/8	7 4/8	9	3 2/8	5 3/8	4 6/8	624	220
	◆ *Fremont County / Ruth Muller / Ruth Muller / 1974*									

Score	Length of Horn		Circumference of Base		Inside Spread	Tip-to-Tip Spread	Length of Prong		All-Time Rank	State Rank
	R	L	R	L			R	L		
◆ *Locality / Hunter / Owner / Date Killed*										
$83\frac{4}{8}$	$17\frac{3}{8}$	$17\frac{2}{8}$	$6\frac{3}{8}$	$6\frac{4}{8}$	$9\frac{5}{8}$	$5\frac{3}{8}$	$5\frac{5}{8}$	$5\frac{1}{8}$	624	220
◆ *Fremont County / Robert B. Cragoe, Sr. / Robert B. Cragoe, Sr. / 1975*										
$83\frac{4}{8}$	$15\frac{2}{8}$	$16\frac{1}{8}$	$6\frac{6}{8}$	$6\frac{5}{8}$	$10\frac{2}{8}$	6	$6\frac{2}{8}$	$6\frac{3}{8}$	624	220
◆ *Uinta County / Velma B. O'Neil / Velma B. O'Neil / 1978*										
$83\frac{4}{8}$	$16\frac{6}{8}$	$16\frac{7}{8}$	$6\frac{6}{8}$	$6\frac{5}{8}$	$8\frac{6}{8}$	$2\frac{4}{8}$	$5\frac{2}{8}$	$5\frac{2}{8}$	624	220
◆ *Sweetwater County / Otis T. Page / Otis T. Page / 1978*										
$83\frac{4}{8}$	$17\frac{5}{8}$	$17\frac{3}{8}$	$6\frac{1}{8}$	$6\frac{1}{8}$	$6\frac{7}{8}$	0	$6\frac{3}{8}$	$5\frac{7}{8}$	624	220
◆ *Natrona County / Gerald J. Ahles / Gerald J. Ahles / 1982*										
$83\frac{4}{8}$	18	18	$6\frac{7}{8}$	7	$9\frac{3}{8}$	$6\frac{2}{8}$	$4\frac{6}{8}$	$3\frac{1}{8}$	624	220
◆ *Carbon County / Ronald K. Pettit / Ronald K. Pettit / 1983*										
$83\frac{4}{8}$	$15\frac{5}{8}$	$15\frac{3}{8}$	7	$6\frac{6}{8}$	$11\frac{6}{8}$	$7\frac{2}{8}$	6	$6\frac{3}{8}$	624	220
◆ *Sweetwater County / Charles R. Monroe / Charles R. Monroe / 1989*										
$83\frac{4}{8}$	$14\frac{3}{8}$	$14\frac{4}{8}$	$7\frac{4}{8}$	$7\frac{4}{8}$	$13\frac{4}{8}$	$12\frac{1}{8}$	$6\frac{3}{8}$	$6\frac{2}{8}$	624	220
◆ *Natrona County / Jerry A. Stoll / Jerry A. Stoll / 1992*										
$83\frac{4}{8}$	$14\frac{5}{8}$	15	7	7	$9\frac{4}{8}$	7	$6\frac{1}{8}$	$6\frac{2}{8}$	624	220
◆ *Sweetwater County / Keith A. Dana / Keith A. Dana / 1994*										
$83\frac{3}{8}$	$15\frac{3}{8}$	$15\frac{3}{8}$	$7\frac{2}{8}$	$7\frac{2}{8}$	$16\frac{2}{8}$	$13\frac{4}{8}$	6	$5\frac{7}{8}$	689	236
◆ *Sweetwater County / Richard D. Ullery / Richard D. Ullery / 1980*										
$83\frac{2}{8}$	$16\frac{6}{8}$	$17\frac{1}{8}$	$6\frac{2}{8}$	$6\frac{1}{8}$	$16\frac{5}{8}$	$15\frac{3}{8}$	6	6	690	237
◆ *Arminto / Edward H. Bohlin / Edward H. Bohlin / 1951*										
$83\frac{2}{8}$	$16\frac{1}{8}$	16	7	$6\frac{7}{8}$	$12\frac{3}{8}$	$10\frac{4}{8}$	$5\frac{2}{8}$	$4\frac{7}{8}$	690	237
◆ *Newcastle / Rupert Chisholm / Rupert Chisholm / 1953*										
$83\frac{2}{8}$	$15\frac{3}{8}$	$14\frac{7}{8}$	$8\frac{2}{8}$	$8\frac{2}{8}$	$8\frac{5}{8}$	$6\frac{3}{8}$	$6\frac{3}{8}$	$6\frac{7}{8}$	690	237
◆ *Campbell County / Phillip M. Hodge / Phillip M. Hodge / 1955*										
$83\frac{2}{8}$	$15\frac{5}{8}$	$16\frac{1}{8}$	$6\frac{3}{8}$	$6\frac{2}{8}$	$9\frac{5}{8}$	5	$6\frac{4}{8}$	$6\frac{5}{8}$	690	237
◆ *Atlantic City / James S. Kleinhammer / James S. Kleinhammer / 1958*										
$83\frac{2}{8}$	$15\frac{2}{8}$	$15\frac{5}{8}$	$6\frac{2}{8}$	$6\frac{2}{8}$	$9\frac{6}{8}$	$6\frac{5}{8}$	$6\frac{6}{8}$	$7\frac{1}{8}$	690	237
◆ *Jeffrey City / Harry G.M. Jopson / Harry G.M. Jopson / 1961*										
$83\frac{2}{8}$	$16\frac{5}{8}$	$16\frac{3}{8}$	$6\frac{5}{8}$	$6\frac{5}{8}$	$8\frac{1}{8}$	$7\frac{6}{8}$	$5\frac{2}{8}$	5	690	237
◆ *Kaycee / R.B. Nienhaus / R.B. Nienhaus / 1961*										
$83\frac{2}{8}$	$16\frac{3}{8}$	16	$6\frac{4}{8}$	$6\frac{4}{8}$	$9\frac{3}{8}$	$4\frac{3}{8}$	6	6	690	237
◆ *Ferris Mt. / Ron Vance / Ron Vance / 1962*										
$83\frac{2}{8}$	$16\frac{7}{8}$	$16\frac{7}{8}$	$7\frac{1}{8}$	7	$14\frac{3}{8}$	$12\frac{4}{8}$	$5\frac{2}{8}$	5	690	237
◆ *Sweetwater County / Allen Tanner / Allen Tanner / 1970*										
$83\frac{2}{8}$	16	$16\frac{2}{8}$	$6\frac{1}{8}$	$6\frac{2}{8}$	11	$8\frac{4}{8}$	$7\frac{1}{8}$	$7\frac{2}{8}$	690	237
◆ *Carbon County / Ray Freitas / Ray Freitas / 1973*										
$83\frac{2}{8}$	16	$15\frac{6}{8}$	$6\frac{1}{8}$	$6\frac{1}{8}$	$8\frac{3}{8}$	$5\frac{5}{8}$	$5\frac{2}{8}$	$5\frac{2}{8}$	690	237
◆ *Park County / Dwight Brunsvold / Dwight Brunsvold / 1974*										

Score	Length of Horn R	Length of Horn L	Circumference of Base R	Circumference of Base L	Inside Spread	Tip-to-Tip Spread	Length of Prong R	Length of Prong L	All-Time Rank	State Rank

♦ *Locality / Hunter / Owner / Date Killed*

83²⁄₈	14⁶⁄₈	14⁶⁄₈	7¹⁄₈	7¹⁄₈	13	10⁶⁄₈	4²⁄₈	5¹⁄₈	690	237

♦ *Goshen County / William E. Patterson / William E. Patterson / 1976*

83²⁄₈	15²⁄₈	15²⁄₈	7¹⁄₈	6⁶⁄₈	14	10⁵⁄₈	6¹⁄₈	6¹⁄₈	690	237

♦ *Natrona County / Dean L. Johnson / Dean L. Johnson / 1977*

83²⁄₈	16	16	7	7	10¹⁄₈	5⁵⁄₈	5	6²⁄₈	690	237

♦ *Natrona County / Bill E. Boatman / Bill E. Boatman / 1981*

83²⁄₈	15¹⁄₈	15²⁄₈	6⁷⁄₈	6⁴⁄₈	9⁵⁄₈	6⁷⁄₈	6	5⁷⁄₈	690	237

♦ *Natrona County / Andy Van Patten / Andy Van Patten / 1981*

83²⁄₈	17²⁄₈	16⁴⁄₈	6⁴⁄₈	6⁴⁄₈	7²⁄₈	2²⁄₈	5³⁄₈	6	690	237

♦ *Fremont County / Benjamin T. Tonn / Benjamin T. Tonn / 1981*

83²⁄₈	17⁴⁄₈	17³⁄₈	6²⁄₈	6²⁄₈	8	2⁴⁄₈	5¹⁄₈	4⁶⁄₈	690	237

♦ *Campbell County / Dwayne A. Anderson / Dwayne A. Anderson / 1982*

83²⁄₈	16⁴⁄₈	16²⁄₈	6⁵⁄₈	6⁵⁄₈	8⁶⁄₈	3⁴⁄₈	6⁶⁄₈	6²⁄₈	690	237

♦ *Uinta County / Earl H. Heninger / Earl H. Heninger / 1983*

83²⁄₈	16⁶⁄₈	17	6⁶⁄₈	6⁴⁄₈	9⁵⁄₈	3⁷⁄₈	5²⁄₈	5³⁄₈	690	237

♦ *Sweetwater County / Donald W. Kramer / Donald W. Kramer / 1983*

83²⁄₈	15²⁄₈	15²⁄₈	7⁴⁄₈	7⁴⁄₈	12	11²⁄₈	4⁵⁄₈	5³⁄₈	690	237

♦ *Natrona County / Gary A. Campbell / Gary A. Campbell / 1983*

83²⁄₈	16⁵⁄₈	16⁷⁄₈	6³⁄₈	6³⁄₈	9³⁄₈	3⁷⁄₈	4⁷⁄₈	4⁷⁄₈	690	237

♦ *Sweetwater County / Rob M. Knight / Rob M. Knight / 1987*

83²⁄₈	15¹⁄₈	15¹⁄₈	6⁷⁄₈	6⁶⁄₈	6⁷⁄₈	1⁴⁄₈	5	4⁶⁄₈	690	237

♦ *Natrona County / Dean Albanis / Dean Albanis / 1990*

83²⁄₈	14⁵⁄₈	15	7	7	11⁴⁄₈	10⁵⁄₈	5⁴⁄₈	5	690	237

♦ *Uinta County / John W. McGehee / John W. McGehee / 1990*

83²⁄₈	16¹⁄₈	16⁴⁄₈	6⁷⁄₈	7¹⁄₈	13¹⁄₈	9⁷⁄₈	5⁵⁄₈	5⁶⁄₈	690	237

♦ *Carbon County / Thomas W. Popham / Thomas W. Popham / 1990*

83²⁄₈	16¹⁄₈	16¹⁄₈	6⁶⁄₈	6⁵⁄₈	9⁶⁄₈	6⁵⁄₈	5³⁄₈	5²⁄₈	690	237

♦ *Natrona County / Robert B. Poskie / Robert B. Poskie / 1990*

83²⁄₈	16¹⁄₈	15⁶⁄₈	6⁷⁄₈	6⁶⁄₈	13²⁄₈	9⁵⁄₈	5⁷⁄₈	5⁷⁄₈	690	237

♦ *Carbon County / Robert H. Ruegge / Robert H. Ruegge / 1990*

83²⁄₈	15¹⁄₈	14⁷⁄₈	6⁶⁄₈	6⁶⁄₈	10⁷⁄₈	10⁶⁄₈	6	6⁴⁄₈	690	237

♦ *Albany County / Shawn E. Dovey / Shawn E. Dovey / 1991*

83²⁄₈	17	16⁶⁄₈	7	6⁷⁄₈	11⁶⁄₈	6³⁄₈	5²⁄₈	5²⁄₈	690	237

♦ *Fremont County / John M. Dunsworth / John M. Dunsworth / 1991*

83²⁄₈	15²⁄₈	15³⁄₈	7	7	10²⁄₈	5²⁄₈	5⁵⁄₈	5⁶⁄₈	690	237

♦ *Natrona County / Sharnell I. Kamish / Sharnell I. Kamish / 1992*

83²⁄₈	17¹⁄₈	17	6²⁄₈	6²⁄₈	8⁴⁄₈	4³⁄₈	4⁶⁄₈	4⁷⁄₈	690	237

♦ *Carbon County / Kelly L. Sandry / Kelly L. Sandry / 1992*

Score	Length of Horn R	L	Circumference of Base R	L	Inside Spread	Tip-to-Tip Spread	Length of Prong R	L	All-Time Rank	State Rank
	◆ *Locality / Hunter / Owner / Date Killed*									
83	16²⁄₈	16⁵⁄₈	6⁴⁄₈	6³⁄₈	16²⁄₈	16⁴⁄₈	4¹⁄₈	5¹⁄₈	775	266
	◆ *Shirley Basin / Duncan G. Weibel / Duncan G. Weibel / 1946*									
83	15⁷⁄₈	15⁴⁄₈	7¹⁄₈	7	9¹⁄₈	3¹⁄₈	5⁵⁄₈	5⁴⁄₈	775	266
	◆ *Rawlins / Richard Eisner / Richard Eisner / 1951*									
83	14⁴⁄₈	15²⁄₈	7⁶⁄₈	7²⁄₈	10⁴⁄₈	8⁷⁄₈	6²⁄₈	6⁴⁄₈	775	266
	◆ *Casper / Tom R. Frye / Tom R. Frye / 1954*									
83	15²⁄₈	15¹⁄₈	6⁵⁄₈	6⁴⁄₈	14⁶⁄₈	13⁴⁄₈	6⁵⁄₈	6²⁄₈	775	266
	◆ *Saratoga / Dave Erickson / Dave Erickson / 1957*									
83	16⁴⁄₈	16¹⁄₈	6⁷⁄₈	6⁴⁄₈	13⁷⁄₈	11⁴⁄₈	5²⁄₈	5²⁄₈	775	266
	◆ *Rawlins / Melvin Birks / Melvin Birks / 1960*									
83	16³⁄₈	16²⁄₈	7	6⁶⁄₈	11	8⁵⁄₈	4⁶⁄₈	4⁴⁄₈	775	266
	◆ *Wamsutter / Marlene Simons / Marlene Simons / 1970*									
83	16	15⁵⁄₈	7	7	9	4²⁄₈	5⁷⁄₈	6	775	266
	◆ *Fremont County / Robert Cragoe, Jr. / Robert Cragoe, Jr. / 1974*									
83	16	16¹⁄₈	6⁴⁄₈	6⁴⁄₈	9⁵⁄₈	4²⁄₈	6¹⁄₈	6⁴⁄₈	775	266
	◆ *Sweetwater County / Douglas Grantham / Douglas Grantham / 1978*									
83	16²⁄₈	16²⁄₈	7	7¹⁄₈	9⁵⁄₈	5	6¹⁄₈	6²⁄₈	775	266
	◆ *Sublette County / Kenneth D. Knight / Kenneth D. Knight / 1978*									
83	17¹⁄₈	17¹⁄₈	6²⁄₈	6²⁄₈	8³⁄₈	2²⁄₈	5³⁄₈	5³⁄₈	775	266
	◆ *Sublette County / Thomas A. Scott / Thomas A. Scott / 1978*									
83	16	16²⁄₈	7⁵⁄₈	7⁵⁄₈	14⁵⁄₈	10⁵⁄₈	5³⁄₈	5⁴⁄₈	775	266
	◆ *Sweetwater County / Glen W. Coates / Glen W. Coates / 1979*									
83	15⁶⁄₈	15⁶⁄₈	7³⁄₈	7³⁄₈	8¹⁄₈	1⁷⁄₈	5⁶⁄₈	5⁶⁄₈	775	266
	◆ *Sweetwater County / Keith Penner / Keith Penner / 1980*									
83	15⁴⁄₈	15⁴⁄₈	6³⁄₈	6³⁄₈	7⁷⁄₈	4⁷⁄₈	5²⁄₈	5⁴⁄₈	775	266
	◆ *Campbell County / Richard S. Alford / Richard S. Alford / 1982*									
83	15⁶⁄₈	15⁶⁄₈	6⁶⁄₈	6⁶⁄₈	9	4⁴⁄₈	5⁵⁄₈	5³⁄₈	775	266
	◆ *Albany County / Mark T. Gleason / Mark T. Gleason / 1982*									
83	16	15⁷⁄₈	7¹⁄₈	7¹⁄₈	10¹⁄₈	8⁴⁄₈	5⁶⁄₈	5⁴⁄₈	775	266
	◆ *Carbon County / Frederick L. Proffit / Frederick L. Proffit / 1983*									
83	15⁵⁄₈	15⁵⁄₈	7¹⁄₈	7¹⁄₈	6⁶⁄₈	1²⁄₈	5⁴⁄₈	5⁶⁄₈	775	266
	◆ *Sweetwater County / Clifford Rockhold / Clifford Rockhold / 1985*									
83	15⁶⁄₈	15¹⁄₈	6⁶⁄₈	6⁵⁄₈	11⁷⁄₈	7⁷⁄₈	5⁶⁄₈	5⁶⁄₈	775	266
	◆ *Fremont County / Thomas A. Dremel / Thomas A. Dremel / 1985*									
83	15⁴⁄₈	15⁷⁄₈	7²⁄₈	7	11⁷⁄₈	9⁴⁄₈	5⁷⁄₈	5⁶⁄₈	775	266
	◆ *Natrona County / Gerald Utrup / Gerald Utrup / 1986*									
83	15⁷⁄₈	15⁶⁄₈	7	7¹⁄₈	8⁵⁄₈	4²⁄₈	5²⁄₈	5¹⁄₈	775	266
	◆ *Albany County / Robert J. Miller / Robert J. Miller / 1987*									

Score	Length of Horn R	L	Circumference of Base R	L	Inside Spread	Tip-to-Tip Spread	Length of Prong R	L	All-Time Rank	State Rank
83	16	16	$6\frac{4}{8}$	$6\frac{4}{8}$	$14\frac{6}{8}$	11	$5\frac{4}{8}$	$5\frac{4}{8}$	775	266
	Fremont County / Douglas R. Dow / Douglas R. Dow / 1988									
83	$16\frac{4}{8}$	$16\frac{2}{8}$	$6\frac{4}{8}$	$6\frac{4}{8}$	$16\frac{2}{8}$	$16\frac{4}{8}$	$4\frac{3}{8}$	$4\frac{5}{8}$	775	266
	Washakie County / Gordon E. Deromedi / Gordon E. Deromedi / 1988									
83	$15\frac{7}{8}$	$15\frac{7}{8}$	$7\frac{1}{8}$	7	$11\frac{1}{8}$	$7\frac{6}{8}$	6	$5\frac{7}{8}$	775	266
	Carbon County / Robert G. Wimpenny / Robert G. Wimpenny / 1989									
83	$16\frac{5}{8}$	16	7	$6\frac{7}{8}$	$13\frac{1}{8}$	$9\frac{7}{8}$	$6\frac{2}{8}$	$6\frac{3}{8}$	775	266
	Carbon County / Gary Duggins / Gary Duggins / 1989									
83	$16\frac{5}{8}$	$16\frac{3}{8}$	$6\frac{3}{8}$	$6\frac{3}{8}$	$16\frac{2}{8}$	$13\frac{7}{8}$	$4\frac{7}{8}$	$4\frac{5}{8}$	775	266
	Sheridan County / Tom W. Housh / Tom W. Housh / 1989									
83	$15\frac{4}{8}$	$15\frac{2}{8}$	$6\frac{4}{8}$	$6\frac{4}{8}$	$9\frac{4}{8}$	6	$6\frac{7}{8}$	$6\frac{4}{8}$	775	266
	Fremont County / Tom Covert / Tom Covert / 1990									
83	$16\frac{3}{8}$	$16\frac{2}{8}$	$6\frac{4}{8}$	$6\frac{4}{8}$	10	$5\frac{5}{8}$	$5\frac{6}{8}$	$5\frac{3}{8}$	775	266
	Carbon County / Roger M. Green / Roger M. Green / 1991									
83	16	16	$7\frac{3}{8}$	$7\frac{3}{8}$	$9\frac{3}{8}$	$3\frac{4}{8}$	$5\frac{7}{8}$	6	775	266
	Sweetwater County / Arnold DeCastro / Arnold DeCastro / 1991									
83	$16\frac{2}{8}$	$16\frac{4}{8}$	$6\frac{6}{8}$	$6\frac{5}{8}$	$10\frac{7}{8}$	$7\frac{3}{8}$	$5\frac{3}{8}$	$4\frac{7}{8}$	775	266
	Uinta County / Florence Kitchel / Florence Kitchel / 1991									
83	17	$17\frac{2}{8}$	$6\frac{7}{8}$	$6\frac{5}{8}$	$10\frac{3}{8}$	$5\frac{2}{8}$	$4\frac{6}{8}$	$5\frac{4}{8}$	775	266
	Carbon County / Gerald A. Steele / Gerald A. Steele / 1991									
83	$15\frac{6}{8}$	16	$6\frac{6}{8}$	$6\frac{7}{8}$	$10\frac{2}{8}$	$6\frac{4}{8}$	$5\frac{5}{8}$	$5\frac{6}{8}$	775	266
	Carbon County / Mark D. Gaines / Mark D. Gaines / 1992									
83	$15\frac{7}{8}$	$16\frac{2}{8}$	7	7	$6\frac{3}{8}$	$2\frac{4}{8}$	$5\frac{3}{8}$	$5\frac{3}{8}$	775	266
	Carbon County / John L. Anderson / John L. Anderson / 1994									
$82\frac{6}{8}$	$17\frac{2}{8}$	17	7	$6\frac{4}{8}$	$12\frac{1}{8}$	$5\frac{6}{8}$	$5\frac{7}{8}$	$5\frac{1}{8}$	868	297
	Natrona County / Unknown / G.S. Peterson / 1948									
$82\frac{6}{8}$	$15\frac{4}{8}$	$15\frac{4}{8}$	$6\frac{7}{8}$	$6\frac{7}{8}$	$14\frac{2}{8}$	11	6	$5\frac{6}{8}$	868	297
	Jelm Mt. / Guy Murdock / Guy Murdock / 1955									
$82\frac{6}{8}$	$14\frac{7}{8}$	$14\frac{6}{8}$	7	$6\frac{7}{8}$	$8\frac{3}{8}$	$2\frac{6}{8}$	$5\frac{3}{8}$	$5\frac{2}{8}$	868	297
	Gillette / R.R. Kirchner / R.R. Kirchner / 1961									
$82\frac{6}{8}$	$15\frac{6}{8}$	$15\frac{6}{8}$	$6\frac{7}{8}$	$6\frac{7}{8}$	$8\frac{3}{8}$	$5\frac{3}{8}$	$6\frac{2}{8}$	$6\frac{2}{8}$	868	297
	Sweetwater County / A.L. Bruner / A.L. Bruner / 1962									
$82\frac{6}{8}$	$15\frac{4}{8}$	$15\frac{7}{8}$	$6\frac{7}{8}$	7	$11\frac{3}{8}$	$8\frac{1}{8}$	$6\frac{2}{8}$	$6\frac{3}{8}$	868	297
	Natrona County / William S. Martin / William S. Martin / 1964									
$82\frac{6}{8}$	$15\frac{2}{8}$	$15\frac{3}{8}$	$6\frac{7}{8}$	$6\frac{6}{8}$	$15\frac{3}{8}$	$11\frac{7}{8}$	$6\frac{5}{8}$	$6\frac{2}{8}$	868	297
	Sweetwater County / James C. Klum / James C. Klum / 1965									
$82\frac{6}{8}$	$14\frac{2}{8}$	$14\frac{1}{8}$	$7\frac{6}{8}$	$7\frac{7}{8}$	$12\frac{5}{8}$	$10\frac{4}{8}$	$5\frac{5}{8}$	$5\frac{7}{8}$	868	297
	Alcova / J. & V. Johnson / New Park Hotel / 1965									

Score	Length of Horn		Circumference of Base		Inside Spread	Tip-to-Tip Spread	Length of Prong		All-Time Rank	State Rank
	R	L	R	L			R	L		

♦ *Locality / Hunter / Owner / Date Killed*

Score	R	L	R	L	Inside	Tip	R	L	All-Time	State
82⁶/₈	15⁶/₈	15⁶/₈	7⁵/₈	7⁵/₈	8⁶/₈	8³/₈	5	6	868	297

♦ *Converse County / Paul W. Tomlin / Paul W. Tomlin / 1965*

82⁶/₈	15²/₈	15⁴/₈	7	6⁷/₈	10⁵/₈	8¹/₈	6¹/₈	5⁶/₈	868	297

♦ *Fremont County / Terry N. TenBoer / Terry N. TenBoer / 1967*

82⁶/₈	16³/₈	16⁴/₈	6⁴/₈	6⁵/₈	10	4⁷/₈	5⁵/₈	5⁶/₈	868	297

♦ *Farson / Ronald O. West / Ronald O. West / 1967*

82⁶/₈	16	15⁷/₈	6⁷/₈	6⁷/₈	10²/₈	5¹/₈	5⁴/₈	5⁵/₈	868	297

♦ *Uinta Area / Barry Hyken / Barry Hyken / 1969*

82⁶/₈	15³/₈	15⁴/₈	6⁶/₈	6⁵/₈	8⁶/₈	5²/₈	6³/₈	6³/₈	868	297

♦ *Carbon County / John M. Sell / John M. Sell / 1969*

82⁶/₈	14⁴/₈	14	7⁵/₈	7⁵/₈	9	7⁶/₈	5⁶/₈	5⁴/₈	868	297

♦ *Sweetwater County / Keith F. Dunbar / Keith F. Dunbar / 1970*

82⁶/₈	16³/₈	16³/₈	6³/₈	6³/₈	8⁴/₈	2⁷/₈	6²/₈	5⁵/₈	868	297

♦ *Natrona County / Kenneth Niedan / Kenneth Niedan / 1971*

82⁶/₈	16¹/₈	15⁵/₈	6²/₈	6⁴/₈	10⁷/₈	8⁴/₈	6⁶/₈	6⁷/₈	868	297

♦ *Medicine Bow / Raymond Freitas / Raymond Freitas / 1973*

82⁶/₈	15⁴/₈	15⁴/₈	6³/₈	6¹/₈	9²/₈	4⁶/₈	5	4⁵/₈	868	297

♦ *Carbon County / Roger D. George / Roger D. George / 1975*

82⁶/₈	15⁶/₈	15³/₈	6⁵/₈	6⁵/₈	10⁵/₈	8²/₈	6⁵/₈	6¹/₈	868	297

♦ *Carbon County / Robert J. Smith / Robert J. Smith / 1980*

82⁶/₈	16¹/₈	16¹/₈	7⁴/₈	7³/₈	8⁷/₈	2¹/₈	5²/₈	5²/₈	868	297

♦ *Natrona County / Bill E. Boatman / Bill E. Boatman / 1982*

82⁶/₈	15	15	7²/₈	6⁷/₈	10	6	5³/₈	5⁵/₈	868	297

♦ *Carbon County / Dailen R. Jones / Dailen R. Jones / 1982*

82⁶/₈	15⁵/₈	16	6⁵/₈	6⁴/₈	9²/₈	6³/₈	6³/₈	5⁶/₈	868	297

♦ *Natrona County / Eugene Turner, Jr. / Eugene Turner, Jr. / 1982*

82⁶/₈	14⁶/₈	15	7⁵/₈	7²/₈	14⁶/₈	12³/₈	6³/₈	5⁶/₈	868	297

♦ *Carbon County / Kenneth E. Grail / Kenneth E. Grail / 1983*

82⁶/₈	16³/₈	16²/₈	6²/₈	6²/₈	8⁴/₈	2⁵/₈	6⁴/₈	6²/₈	868	297

♦ *Sweetwater County / Craig B. Argyle / Craig B. Argyle / 1985*

82⁶/₈	15⁷/₈	15⁵/₈	7²/₈	7³/₈	14⁵/₈	10⁶/₈	6²/₈	6	868	297

♦ *Natrona County / Michael L. Brownell / Michael L. Brownell / 1985*

82⁶/₈	15²/₈	15³/₈	7	7	8⁵/₈	3²/₈	5⁷/₈	6¹/₈	868	297

♦ *Natrona County / Tom Covert / Tom Covert / 1987*

82⁶/₈	16¹/₈	15⁴/₈	6²/₈	6²/₈	12⁴/₈	8²/₈	6²/₈	6⁶/₈	868	297

♦ *Sweetwater County / Roy D. Sessions / Roy D. Sessions / 1988*

82⁶/₈	16	15⁴/₈	6⁷/₈	6⁶/₈	8⁶/₈	4¹/₈	5⁷/₈	5⁷/₈	868	297

♦ *Campbell County / Richard H. Stasiak / Richard H. Stasiak / 1989*

Score	Length of Horn		Circumference of Base		Inside Spread	Tip-to-Tip Spread	Length of Prong		All-Time Rank	State Rank
	R	L	R	L			R	L		
	♦ *Locality / Hunter / Owner / Date Killed*									
82⁶⁄₈	17⁴⁄₈	17⁶⁄₈	6³⁄₈	6³⁄₈	11	5⁵⁄₈	6	4⁷⁄₈	868	297
	♦ *Fremont County / Ronald E. Cebuhar / Ronald E. Cebuhar / 1990*									
82⁶⁄₈	15⁴⁄₈	15¹⁄₈	6⁷⁄₈	6⁶⁄₈	9¹⁄₈	4⁶⁄₈	5⁶⁄₈	5⁶⁄₈	868	297
	♦ *Carbon County / Rebecca J. Miller / Rebecca J. Miller / 1991*									
82⁶⁄₈	15⁷⁄₈	15⁶⁄₈	6⁶⁄₈	6⁵⁄₈	12⁵⁄₈	9¹⁄₈	6	5⁷⁄₈	868	297
	♦ *Sweetwater County / Timothy L. Schuckman / Timothy L. Schuckman / 1991*									
82⁶⁄₈	15²⁄₈	16	7⁴⁄₈	7³⁄₈	8⁷⁄₈	2⁵⁄₈	6	5⁵⁄₈	868	297
	♦ *Fremont County / Lyle D. Fruchey / Lyle D. Fruchey / 1992*									
82⁶⁄₈	15⁷⁄₈	16	7⁵⁄₈	7³⁄₈	9⁷⁄₈	4²⁄₈	5¹⁄₈	5²⁄₈	868	297
	♦ *Sweetwater County / Joe Ingrao / Joe Ingrao / 1992*									
82⁶⁄₈	15⁶⁄₈	16	7	6⁷⁄₈	14	13²⁄₈	4⁶⁄₈	4⁷⁄₈	868	297
	♦ *Sweetwater County / Brian T. King / Brian T. King / 1992*									
82⁶⁄₈	16²⁄₈	16¹⁄₈	6⁶⁄₈	6⁶⁄₈	13⁵⁄₈	8⁴⁄₈	5⁷⁄₈	5³⁄₈	868	297
	♦ *Goshen County / Edward A. Greaves / Edward A. Greaves / 1992*									
82⁶⁄₈	15⁵⁄₈	15⁴⁄₈	6⁶⁄₈	6⁷⁄₈	11⁵⁄₈	8	5⁷⁄₈	6²⁄₈	868	297
	♦ *Sweetwater County / Tim A. Erich / Tim A. Erich / 1993*									
82⁶⁄₈	15²⁄₈	15⁴⁄₈	7⁴⁄₈	7⁴⁄₈	11⁵⁄₈	7³⁄₈	5³⁄₈	6³⁄₈	868	297
	♦ *Carbon County / Lawrence L. Searles / Lawrence L. Searles / 1993*									
82⁴⁄₈	16⁴⁄₈	16⁴⁄₈	6⁶⁄₈	6⁵⁄₈	9³⁄₈	4⁴⁄₈	5³⁄₈	5²⁄₈	949	332
	♦ *Saratoga County / Helen R. Peterson / Helen R. Peterson / 1945*									
82⁴⁄₈	14²⁄₈	14²⁄₈	7⁶⁄₈	7⁶⁄₈	12³⁄₈	11²⁄₈	6	5⁶⁄₈	949	332
	♦ *Ferris Mt. / Donald Anderson / Donald Anderson / 1959*									
82⁴⁄₈	16²⁄₈	16	6⁶⁄₈	6⁶⁄₈	10⁷⁄₈	7⁴⁄₈	4⁷⁄₈	5¹⁄₈	949	332
	♦ *Shirley Basin / Walter B. Hester / Walter B. Hester / 1960*									
82⁴⁄₈	16¹⁄₈	15⁷⁄₈	6⁵⁄₈	6⁶⁄₈	11¹⁄₈	8	5³⁄₈	5³⁄₈	949	332
	♦ *Campbell County / Fred J. Brogle / Fred J. Brogle / 1960*									
82⁴⁄₈	16²⁄₈	16⁴⁄₈	6⁵⁄₈	6⁴⁄₈	13¹⁄₈	8⁷⁄₈	3⁵⁄₈	3⁵⁄₈	949	332
	♦ *Poison Spider / Clarence Meddock / Clarence Meddock / 1961*									
82⁴⁄₈	16⁴⁄₈	16⁷⁄₈	6¹⁄₈	6	14²⁄₈	10	5³⁄₈	5⁶⁄₈	949	332
	♦ *Green Mt. / Forrest H. Burnett / Forrest H. Burnett / 1962*									
82⁴⁄₈	15⁵⁄₈	16	6⁴⁄₈	6⁵⁄₈	9	4³⁄₈	5³⁄₈	5	949	332
	♦ *Natrona County / Charles P. Weber / Charles P. Weber / 1965*									
82⁴⁄₈	15⁶⁄₈	15⁷⁄₈	6⁷⁄₈	7¹⁄₈	11	7¹⁄₈	5⁵⁄₈	6	949	332
	♦ *Laramie / Noel Weidner / Noel Weidner / 1966*									
82⁴⁄₈	16¹⁄₈	16	6⁵⁄₈	6⁵⁄₈	9⁷⁄₈	6³⁄₈	5²⁄₈	5⁶⁄₈	949	332
	♦ *Platte County / Dwight E. Farr / William R. Brewer / 1972*									
82⁴⁄₈	16⁴⁄₈	16⁵⁄₈	6²⁄₈	6	11⁷⁄₈	10⁶⁄₈	5⁵⁄₈	5⁴⁄₈	949	332
	♦ *Converse County / J.A. Merrill, Jr. & C. Davis / J.A. Merrill, Jr. / 1973*									

Score	Length of Horn		Circumference of Base		Inside Spread	Tip-to-Tip Spread	Length of Prong		All-Time Rank	State Rank
	R	L	R	L			R	L		
	♦ Locality / Hunter / Owner / Date Killed									
$82\frac{4}{8}$	15	15	$6\frac{4}{8}$	$6\frac{4}{8}$	$9\frac{4}{8}$	4	$6\frac{4}{8}$	$6\frac{4}{8}$	949	332
	♦ Sublette County / Larry W. Cross / Larry W. Cross / 1977									
$82\frac{4}{8}$	$16\frac{3}{8}$	$16\frac{4}{8}$	$6\frac{6}{8}$	7	$11\frac{1}{8}$	$5\frac{4}{8}$	$5\frac{6}{8}$	$5\frac{4}{8}$	949	332
	♦ Fremont County / Wayne D. Kleinman / Wayne D. Kleinman / 1977									
$82\frac{4}{8}$	16	$15\frac{5}{8}$	$6\frac{4}{8}$	$6\frac{6}{8}$	$14\frac{1}{8}$	$14\frac{2}{8}$	$5\frac{7}{8}$	$5\frac{7}{8}$	949	332
	♦ Washakie County / Greg Warner / Greg Warner / 1977									
$82\frac{4}{8}$	$16\frac{5}{8}$	$16\frac{3}{8}$	$6\frac{4}{8}$	$6\frac{3}{8}$	$9\frac{1}{8}$	$5\frac{3}{8}$	$5\frac{2}{8}$	$5\frac{1}{8}$	949	332
	♦ Sweetwater Co. Wyo. / Fred B. Keyes / Fred B. Keyes / 1978									
$82\frac{4}{8}$	$14\frac{6}{8}$	$14\frac{7}{8}$	$6\frac{6}{8}$	$6\frac{5}{8}$	$13\frac{7}{8}$	$11\frac{7}{8}$	$6\frac{4}{8}$	$6\frac{4}{8}$	949	332
	♦ Carbon County / Michael Boender / Michael Boender / 1979									
$82\frac{4}{8}$	$15\frac{1}{8}$	$15\frac{2}{8}$	$6\frac{6}{8}$	$6\frac{6}{8}$	$12\frac{1}{8}$	$10\frac{3}{8}$	$6\frac{1}{8}$	$6\frac{3}{8}$	949	332
	♦ Carbon County / Barry L. Alger / Barry L. Alger / 1980									
$82\frac{4}{8}$	17	$16\frac{6}{8}$	$6\frac{3}{8}$	$6\frac{4}{8}$	$9\frac{2}{8}$	$3\frac{3}{8}$	$5\frac{4}{8}$	$5\frac{4}{8}$	949	332
	♦ Sweetwater County / Donald R. Williamson / Donald R. Williamson / 1981									
$82\frac{4}{8}$	$14\frac{7}{8}$	$14\frac{6}{8}$	$6\frac{7}{8}$	$7\frac{2}{8}$	$9\frac{7}{8}$	$6\frac{6}{8}$	$6\frac{3}{8}$	$6\frac{4}{8}$	949	332
	♦ Campbell County / Larry L. Helgerson / Larry L. Helgerson / 1981									
$82\frac{4}{8}$	$16\frac{2}{8}$	$16\frac{1}{8}$	$6\frac{4}{8}$	$6\frac{4}{8}$	$9\frac{2}{8}$	$4\frac{5}{8}$	$5\frac{5}{8}$	$5\frac{3}{8}$	949	332
	♦ Natrona County / Edgar M. Artecona / Edgar M. Artecona / 1982									
$82\frac{4}{8}$	$15\frac{1}{8}$	$15\frac{1}{8}$	$6\frac{6}{8}$	$6\frac{6}{8}$	$10\frac{6}{8}$	$9\frac{1}{8}$	$5\frac{7}{8}$	$5\frac{7}{8}$	949	332
	♦ Carbon County / John T. Butters / John T. Butters / 1982									
$82\frac{4}{8}$	$16\frac{1}{8}$	$16\frac{1}{8}$	7	7	$5\frac{2}{8}$	2	$5\frac{2}{8}$	$5\frac{2}{8}$	949	332
	♦ Natrona County / Bill E. Boatman / Bill E. Boatman / 1983									
$82\frac{4}{8}$	$15\frac{5}{8}$	16	$6\frac{4}{8}$	$6\frac{3}{8}$	12	$10\frac{5}{8}$	$5\frac{6}{8}$	$5\frac{4}{8}$	949	332
	♦ Carbon County / Merlyn J. Kiel / Merlyn J. Kiel / 1983									
$82\frac{4}{8}$	$15\frac{6}{8}$	$16\frac{3}{8}$	$6\frac{6}{8}$	$6\frac{6}{8}$	$9\frac{4}{8}$	$5\frac{3}{8}$	6	$5\frac{6}{8}$	949	332
	♦ Sweetwater County / Richard E. Knox, Jr. / Richard E. Knox, Jr. / 1983									
$82\frac{4}{8}$	$15\frac{5}{8}$	$16\frac{1}{8}$	$6\frac{4}{8}$	$6\frac{5}{8}$	$8\frac{6}{8}$	$5\frac{2}{8}$	$5\frac{3}{8}$	$5\frac{4}{8}$	949	332
	♦ Sweetwater County / W.A. Chambers / W.A. Chambers / 1985									
$82\frac{4}{8}$	$15\frac{5}{8}$	$15\frac{5}{8}$	7	7	$9\frac{3}{8}$	5	$5\frac{6}{8}$	$5\frac{7}{8}$	949	332
	♦ Campbell County / Robert J. Anderson / Robert J. Anderson / 1987									
$82\frac{4}{8}$	$16\frac{1}{8}$	$16\frac{2}{8}$	$6\frac{6}{8}$	$6\frac{7}{8}$	$9\frac{4}{8}$	$3\frac{5}{8}$	$5\frac{7}{8}$	$6\frac{2}{8}$	949	332
	♦ Sweetwater County / Eric M. Berg / Eric M. Berg / 1988									
$82\frac{4}{8}$	$16\frac{5}{8}$	$16\frac{2}{8}$	$6\frac{5}{8}$	$6\frac{5}{8}$	$11\frac{4}{8}$	$7\frac{2}{8}$	$6\frac{2}{8}$	$6\frac{1}{8}$	949	332
	♦ Fremont County / Ben L. Adamson / Ben L. Adamson / 1989									
$82\frac{4}{8}$	$14\frac{5}{8}$	$14\frac{4}{8}$	$7\frac{1}{8}$	7	$12\frac{6}{8}$	$11\frac{5}{8}$	$6\frac{5}{8}$	$6\frac{6}{8}$	949	332
	♦ Fremont County / James M. Machac / James M. Machac / 1989									
$82\frac{4}{8}$	$14\frac{5}{8}$	$14\frac{5}{8}$	$7\frac{2}{8}$	$7\frac{2}{8}$	$13\frac{2}{8}$	11	$6\frac{1}{8}$	$6\frac{3}{8}$	949	332
	♦ Carbon County / Lance E. Novak / Lance E. Novak / 1989									

Score	Length of Horn R	L	Circumference of Base R	L	Inside Spread	Tip-to-Tip Spread	Length of Prong R	L	All-Time Rank	State Rank
	♦ Locality / Hunter / Owner / Date Killed									
82⁴⁄₈	14⁶⁄₈	15	6⁶⁄₈	6⁷⁄₈	12⅛	8⅜	6²⁄₈	6⅜	949	332
	♦ Converse County / Larry E. Zumbrum / Larry E. Zumbrum / 1989									
82⁴⁄₈	15⁴⁄₈	15²⁄₈	7⁴⁄₈	7³⁄₈	8⅜	3²⁄₈	5⁴⁄₈	5⅝	949	332
	♦ Natrona County / Robert W. Genner / Robert W. Genner / 1990									
82⁴⁄₈	15⅝	15⁶⁄₈	6⅝	6⁴⁄₈	12⅝	11⅞	5²⁄₈	5²⁄₈	949	332
	♦ Converse County / Farrell M. McQuiddy / Farrell M. McQuiddy / 1990									
82⁴⁄₈	15⁶⁄₈	15⁴⁄₈	7⅛	7	12²⁄₈	8²⁄₈	6⅛	5⁶⁄₈	949	332
	♦ Fremont County / James J. Person / James J. Person / 1990									
82⁴⁄₈	15⁴⁄₈	15⁶⁄₈	7⅛	7	12²⁄₈	8⁴⁄₈	6⅜	5⅝	949	332
	♦ Sweetwater County / Justin C. Shadrick / Justin C. Shadrick / 1991									
82⁴⁄₈	15⅝	16	7	6⁷⁄₈	15⁴⁄₈	15²⁄₈	6²⁄₈	6⅜	949	332
	♦ Sweetwater County / Robert S. Lund / Robert S. Lund / 1991									
82⁴⁄₈	15⅝	15⅝	7	7²⁄₈	9⁴⁄₈	4⅝	5⅞	6	949	332
	♦ Uinta County / Velma O'Neil / Velma O'Neil / 1991									
82⁴⁄₈	16⁴⁄₈	16⅝	6⁴⁄₈	6⁴⁄₈	12⁴⁄₈	9⁶⁄₈	5²⁄₈	5⅝	949	332
	♦ Hot Springs County / Brett W. Jones / Brett W. Jones / 1991									
82⁴⁄₈	17	15⅝	7	6⁷⁄₈	11²⁄₈	9⅞	5⅛	5	949	332
	♦ Natrona County / Hubert C. Wightman / Hubert C. Wightman / 1991									
82⁴⁄₈	15⁴⁄₈	15⁴⁄₈	6⅛	6	7²⁄₈	4⅛	6⅜	6⅜	949	332
	♦ Carbon County / David Shadrick / David Shadrick / 1992									
82⁴⁄₈	14⁶⁄₈	14⁴⁄₈	7⅛	7²⁄₈	11⅞	10⅜	5⁶⁄₈	5⁶⁄₈	949	332
	♦ Park County / Dan Barngrover / Dan Barngrover / 1993									
82²⁄₈	16⁶⁄₈	16⅝	6⁴⁄₈	6⁴⁄₈	15⅞	11⅛	5⅝	5⅞	1058	372
	♦ Split Rock / Herb Klein / Herb Klein / 1952									
82²⁄₈	16	16⁴⁄₈	6⁴⁄₈	6²⁄₈	8⁶⁄₈	5⅝	6⅜	5⅞	1058	372
	♦ Rawlins / Thomas B. McNeill / Thomas B. McNeill / 1955									
82²⁄₈	15⁴⁄₈	15⁴⁄₈	6⁴⁄₈	6⁴⁄₈	8⁶⁄₈	4⁴⁄₈	5	5	1058	372
	♦ Saratoga / J.E. Prothroe / J.E. Prothroe / 1955									
82²⁄₈	15²⁄₈	15⁷⁄₈	7	7⅛	13²⁄₈	8⁶⁄₈	6	6⅛	1058	372
	♦ Sage Creek / Glenn P. Anderson / Glenn P. Anderson / 1959									
82²⁄₈	16⅛	16²⁄₈	6⅜	6⅜	10²⁄₈	6	6²⁄₈	6⁶⁄₈	1058	372
	♦ Crook County / John P. Wood / John P. Wood / 1960									
82²⁄₈	16²⁄₈	16⁴⁄₈	6⁴⁄₈	6⅝	6⁴⁄₈	4⁴⁄₈	5⁶⁄₈	5²⁄₈	1058	372
	♦ Park County / Don A. Johnson / Don A. Johnson / 1960									
82²⁄₈	16⅛	16	6⁶⁄₈	6⁶⁄₈	14	9	5	5	1058	372
	♦ Shirley Basin / T.C. Gonya / T.C. Gonya / 1961									
82²⁄₈	16²⁄₈	16²⁄₈	6⅜	6⁴⁄₈	11²⁄₈	7⅛	5²⁄₈	5⅝	1058	372
	♦ Poison Spider / Unknown / Robert F. Ziker / 1961									

Score	Length of Horn		Circumference of Base		Inside Spread	Tip-to-Tip Spread	Length of Prong		All-Time Rank	State Rank
	R	L	R	L			R	L		
◆ *Locality / Hunter / Owner / Date Killed*										
82²⁄₈	15⁷⁄₈	15⁶⁄₈	7⁷⁄₈	7¹⁄₈	11⁴⁄₈	6⁴⁄₈	5²⁄₈	5³⁄₈	1058	372
◆ *Casper / Frank Gardner / Frank Gardner / 1963*										
82²⁄₈	16²⁄₈	16¹⁄₈	6⁶⁄₈	6⁶⁄₈	12	9⁴⁄₈	5	5	1058	372
◆ *Laramie / Susan W. Tupper / Susan W. Tupper / 1964*										
82²⁄₈	16⁴⁄₈	16³⁄₈	6⁵⁄₈	6⁷⁄₈	10³⁄₈	8¹⁄₈	5³⁄₈	6²⁄₈	1058	372
◆ *Natrona County / R.O. Marshall, Jr. / R.O. Marshall, Jr. / 1970*										
82²⁄₈	15	15²⁄₈	6	6	10²⁄₈	9⁴⁄₈	5²⁄₈	5²⁄₈	1058	372
◆ *Fremont County / Collins F. Kellogg / Collins F. Kellogg / 1974*										
82²⁄₈	15²⁄₈	15³⁄₈	6³⁄₈	6³⁄₈	7⁷⁄₈	3³⁄₈	5⁶⁄₈	5⁷⁄₈	1058	372
◆ *Gillette / Gary Simonson / Gary Simonson / 1975*										
82²⁄₈	17³⁄₈	17⁴⁄₈	6²⁄₈	6³⁄₈	14⁵⁄₈	11⁷⁄₈	5³⁄₈	5⁴⁄₈	1058	372
◆ *Niobrara County / W.L. McMillan / W.L. McMillan / 1981*										
82²⁄₈	14⁵⁄₈	14⁷⁄₈	6⁵⁄₈	6⁶⁄₈	9⁵⁄₈	6²⁄₈	6⁵⁄₈	6²⁄₈	1058	372
◆ *Sweetwater County / Gregg R. Landrum / Gregg R. Landrum / 1982*										
82²⁄₈	16²⁄₈	16²⁄₈	6⁴⁄₈	6³⁄₈	13²⁄₈	11	5⁵⁄₈	4⁷⁄₈	1058	372
◆ *Fremont County / Michael C. Meeker / Michael C. Meeker / 1982*										
82²⁄₈	15⁶⁄₈	15⁶⁄₈	6³⁄₈	6³⁄₈	14¹⁄₈	13⁶⁄₈	5⁶⁄₈	5⁶⁄₈	1058	372
◆ *Carbon County / Larry J. Thoney / Larry J. Thoney / 1982*										
82²⁄₈	16⁴⁄₈	16⁴⁄₈	6⁴⁄₈	6³⁄₈	13¹⁄₈	9²⁄₈	5⁵⁄₈	5⁶⁄₈	1058	372
◆ *Fremont County / Richard L. Bostrom / Richard L. Bostrom / 1983*										
82²⁄₈	16³⁄₈	16⁵⁄₈	6²⁄₈	6²⁄₈	13³⁄₈	8³⁄₈	5⁶⁄₈	5⁶⁄₈	1058	372
◆ *Fremont County / Evelyn A. Maxon / Evelyn A. Maxon / 1983*										
82²⁄₈	14	14³⁄₈	7⁶⁄₈	7⁷⁄₈	10⁴⁄₈	8⁴⁄₈	6²⁄₈	6²⁄₈	1058	372
◆ *Sweetwater County / Peter B. Shaw / Peter B. Shaw / 1983*										
82²⁄₈	15⁷⁄₈	15⁶⁄₈	6⁶⁄₈	6⁵⁄₈	10³⁄₈	10	5⁴⁄₈	5⁴⁄₈	1058	372
◆ *Washakie County / Carol Greet / Carol Greet / 1983*										
82²⁄₈	15¹⁄₈	15⁴⁄₈	6³⁄₈	6⁴⁄₈	10	4⁷⁄₈	6¹⁄₈	6	1058	372
◆ *Fremont County / Charles D. Day / Charles D. Day / 1984*										
82²⁄₈	15⁴⁄₈	16	6⁶⁄₈	6⁴⁄₈	13⁴⁄₈	12	6⁴⁄₈	6⁴⁄₈	1058	372
◆ *Sweetwater County / Carl Holland / William Holland / 1984*										
82²⁄₈	16	15⁶⁄₈	6²⁄₈	6³⁄₈	12¹⁄₈	8⁶⁄₈	6¹⁄₈	6²⁄₈	1058	372
◆ *Natrona County / Michael D. Samuelson / Michael D. Samuelson / 1984*										
82²⁄₈	15²⁄₈	15	7³⁄₈	7⁴⁄₈	10²⁄₈	7⁶⁄₈	5⁴⁄₈	4⁶⁄₈	1058	372
◆ *Natrona County / Steven N. Levin / Steven N. Levin / 1986*										
82²⁄₈	16²⁄₈	15⁷⁄₈	6⁴⁄₈	6⁵⁄₈	7⁷⁄₈	2⁶⁄₈	5⁶⁄₈	6³⁄₈	1058	372
◆ *Carbon County / Robert Depellegrini / Robert Depellegrini / 1989*										
82²⁄₈	16¹⁄₈	15⁶⁄₈	6⁴⁄₈	6⁵⁄₈	12¹⁄₈	5⁵⁄₈	6¹⁄₈	6²⁄₈	1058	372
◆ *Natrona County / Valentine Novicki II / Valentine Novicki II / 1989*										

Score	Length of Horn		Circumference of Base		Inside Spread	Tip-to-Tip Spread	Length of Prong		All-Time Rank	State Rank
	R	L	R	L			R	L		

♦ *Locality / Hunter / Owner / Date Killed*

Score	R	L	R	L	Spread	Spread	R	L	Rank	Rank
82²⁄₈	16²⁄₈	16⁶⁄₈	6	6	9⁵⁄₈	3⁴⁄₈	6³⁄₈	6⁴⁄₈	1058	372

♦ *Fremont County / John A. Monje / John A. Monje / 1989*

82²⁄₈	15⁶⁄₈	15⁵⁄₈	7⁴⁄₈	7²⁄₈	9⁷⁄₈	7⁷⁄₈	6²⁄₈	5⁴⁄₈	1058	372

♦ *Natrona County / Brian G. Elliott / Brian G. Elliott / 1991*

82²⁄₈	14⁵⁄₈	14⁶⁄₈	7	7¹⁄₈	10³⁄₈	6⁷⁄₈	6¹⁄₈	6¹⁄₈	1058	372

♦ *Carbon County / Roger T. Ralph / Roger T. Ralph / 1991*

82²⁄₈	16²⁄₈	16⁵⁄₈	6⁶⁄₈	6⁵⁄₈	9³⁄₈	7¹⁄₈	4⁵⁄₈	4⁶⁄₈	1058	372

♦ *Weston County / Scott H. Eia / Scott H. Eia / 1991*

82²⁄₈	16⁵⁄₈	16⁶⁄₈	6⁵⁄₈	6⁵⁄₈	17³⁄₈	14⁴⁄₈	5¹⁄₈	5	1058	372

♦ *Sweetwater County / Dan E. McBride / Dan E. McBride / 1992*

82²⁄₈	15⁷⁄₈	15⁷⁄₈	6⁷⁄₈	6⁷⁄₈	9	5²⁄₈	5	4⁵⁄₈	1058	372

♦ *Sweetwater County / Casey Hunter / Casey Hunter / 1994*

82²⁄₈	16	16	7	7	9⁴⁄₈	5⁷⁄₈	5¹⁄₈	4²⁄₈	1058	372

♦ *Carbon County / Richard D. Lumpkins / Richard D. Lumpkins / 1994*

82	16²⁄₈	16²⁄₈	6²⁄₈	6⁴⁄₈	13¹⁄₈	10⁴⁄₈	5⁶⁄₈	6	1157	406

♦ *Shirley Basin / Earl Fisher / Earl Fisher / 1951*

82	14⁷⁄₈	14⁶⁄₈	6⁶⁄₈	6⁷⁄₈	9⁴⁄₈	8¹⁄₈	6³⁄₈	5⁷⁄₈	1157	406

♦ *Sage Creek / Mrs. Ramon Somavia / Mrs. Ramon Somavia / 1960*

82	16	16⁴⁄₈	6⁵⁄₈	6²⁄₈	12²⁄₈	8²⁄₈	6	5⁷⁄₈	1157	406

♦ *Encampment / G.A. Surface / G.A. Surface / 1960*

82	15⁵⁄₈	15⁶⁄₈	6⁷⁄₈	6⁷⁄₈	10³⁄₈	6¹⁄₈	5²⁄₈	5	1157	406

♦ *Natrona County / Fred Deiss / Fred Deiss / 1961*

82	15⁴⁄₈	15⁴⁄₈	6¹⁄₈	6¹⁄₈	11¹⁄₈	6⁴⁄₈	6⁴⁄₈	6⁶⁄₈	1157	406

♦ *Shirley Basin / Norman Miller / Norman Miller / 1961*

82	16	16¹⁄₈	6⁶⁄₈	6⁶⁄₈	16⁵⁄₈	14²⁄₈	5⁶⁄₈	5⁶⁄₈	1157	406

♦ *Shirley Basin / G.C. Cunningham / G.C. Cunningham / 1962*

82	16¹⁄₈	16	6⁴⁄₈	6³⁄₈	9⁵⁄₈	7⁶⁄₈	5²⁄₈	5	1157	406

♦ *Shirley Basin / Henry Macagni / Henry Macagni / 1962*

82	15²⁄₈	15	6⁵⁄₈	6⁵⁄₈	10¹⁄₈	8²⁄₈	5⁷⁄₈	5⁵⁄₈	1157	406

♦ *Carbon County / C.W. Hermanson / C.W. Hermanson / 1968*

82	15⁵⁄₈	15²⁄₈	7¹⁄₈	7¹⁄₈	8	7	5	5⁴⁄₈	1157	406

♦ *Farson / Larry Nolan Garner / Larry Nolan Garner / 1969*

82	15³⁄₈	15³⁄₈	6²⁄₈	6²⁄₈	14³⁄₈	13¹⁄₈	6	6	1157	406

♦ *Albany County / Edwin J. Keppner / Edwin J. Keppner / 1969*

82	15³⁄₈	15³⁄₈	7²⁄₈	6⁷⁄₈	15	13	5⁵⁄₈	5²⁄₈	1157	406

♦ *Wamsutter / Frank Simons / Frank Simons / 1969*

82	16	16	6⁵⁄₈	6⁶⁄₈	12³⁄₈	8⁶⁄₈	5⁵⁄₈	5³⁄₈	1157	406

♦ *Carbon County / Martin J. Stuart / Martin J. Stuart / 1969*

WYOMING PRONGHORN *(continued)*

Score	Length of Horn R	Length of Horn L	Circumference of Base R	Circumference of Base L	Inside Spread	Tip-to-Tip Spread	Length of Prong R	Length of Prong L	All-Time Rank	State Rank
	♦ *Locality / Hunter / Owner / Date Killed*									
82	14 5/8	14 3/8	7 3/8	7 3/8	9 3/8	7 3/8	5 2/8	5 2/8	1157	406
	♦ *Sweet Rock / Alphonse Cuomo, Jr. / Alphonse Cuomo, Jr. / 1973*									
82	15 5/8	15 4/8	7	6 5/8	10 1/8	8	6 4/8	6	1157	406
	♦ *Sublette County / Gary D. Jorgensen / Gary D. Jorgensen / 1973*									
82	16 2/8	16 1/8	6 4/8	6 4/8	12	7 3/8	5 6/8	5 6/8	1157	406
	♦ *Carbon County / Reg. R. Smith / Reg. R. Smith / 1974*									
82	14 5/8	14 6/8	6 4/8	6 4/8	10 3/8	5 6/8	5 7/8	5 7/8	1157	406
	♦ *Campbell County / Gilbert Steinen, Jr. / Gilbert Steinen, Jr. / 1975*									
82	14 1/8	13 6/8	7	6 6/8	11 4/8	9 6/8	4 4/8	4 4/8	1157	406
	♦ *Sweetwater County / Starla L. Cairns / Starla L. Cairns / 1976*									
82	16 4/8	16 4/8	6 6/8	6 6/8	11 4/8	8 2/8	5 4/8	5 4/8	1157	406
	♦ *Fremont County / Daniel R. Hahn / Daniel R. Hahn / 1977*									
82	15	15	7 3/8	7 1/8	12 4/8	10 3/8	5 6/8	5	1157	406
	♦ *Carbon County / Peck Rollison / Peck Rollison / 1977*									
82	16 4/8	16 3/8	7 5/8	7	12 6/8	10 3/8	5 4/8	5	1157	406
	♦ *Fremont County / John J. Eichhorn / John J. Eichhorn / 1978*									
82	14 5/8	15 1/8	6 7/8	6 7/8	10 7/8	6 7/8	6 3/8	6 5/8	1157	406
	♦ *Sweetwater County / Dan B. Artery / Dan B. Artery / 1979*									
82	16 1/8	16	7	6 7/8	9	2 1/8	5 2/8	4 6/8	1157	406
	♦ *Fremont County / Steven E. Clingman / Steven E. Clingman / 1980*									
82	16 6/8	16 5/8	6 3/8	6 2/8	15	11 5/8	5 5/8	5 2/8	1157	406
	♦ *Natrona County / Theresa Fulfaro / Theresa Fulfaro / 1980*									
82	15 3/8	15 2/8	6 7/8	6 7/8	15 5/8	14 5/8	5 5/8	5 7/8	1157	406
	♦ *Carbon County / Jerry G. Hagen / Jerry G. Hagen / 1980*									
82	15 7/8	15 3/8	7 2/8	7 1/8	16 1/8	14 1/8	6 2/8	5 3/8	1157	406
	♦ *Natrona County / Wade Dumont / Wade Dumont / 1981*									
82	16 2/8	16 1/8	6 6/8	6 6/8	12	8 3/8	5 2/8	5 1/8	1157	406
	♦ *Natrona County / Joseph P. Prinzi / Joseph P. Prinzi / 1982*									
82	17	17	6 2/8	6 1/8	6 6/8	1 6/8	5 5/8	5 4/8	1157	406
	♦ *Lincoln County / Tom Crank / Tom Crank / 1982*									
82	15 5/8	15 3/8	6 2/8	6 2/8	10 4/8	6 3/8	6 2/8	6 4/8	1157	406
	♦ *Fremont County / Thomas O. Martens / Thomas O. Martens / 1982*									
82	15 2/8	15 2/8	6 5/8	6 4/8	10	6 4/8	5 2/8	5 4/8	1157	406
	♦ *Carbon County / Eric J. Swanson / Eric J. Swanson / 1982*									
82	14 1/8	14	7 2/8	7 1/8	10 6/8	7 5/8	6 2/8	6 1/8	1157	406
	♦ *Sweetwater County / Brett A. Ward / Brett A. Ward / 1982*									
82	15 6/8	15 6/8	7	7	8 4/8	2 6/8	5 2/8	5 2/8	1157	406
	♦ *Crook County / Jay D. Hacklin / Jay D. Hacklin / 1982*									

Score	Length of Horn		Circumference of Base		Inside Spread	Tip-to-Tip Spread	Length of Prong		All-Time Rank	State Rank
	R	L	R	L			R	L		
	Locality / Hunter / Owner / Date Killed									
82	15	14 5/8	7	7 1/8	12	10 6/8	5 5/8	5 5/8	1157	406
	Carbon County / Albert Gregg / Albert Gregg / 1983									
82	15 5/8	16 1/8	6 7/8	6 6/8	8 4/8	3	5 6/8	5 6/8	1157	406
	Carbon County / James A. Rademacher / James A. Rademacher / 1986									
82	16 4/8	17	6 3/8	6 4/8	10 2/8	7 4/8	5 3/8	5	1157	406
	Johnson County / Thomas F. Williams / Thomas F. Williams / 1986									
82	16 4/8	16 2/8	6 4/8	6 4/8	7 5/8	3 2/8	5 7/8	5 7/8	1157	406
	Sweetwater County / Jeffrey A. Schalow / Jeffrey A. Schalow / 1987									
82	17 1/8	16 6/8	6 4/8	6 3/8	11 5/8	6 5/8	5 5/8	5 4/8	1157	406
	Fremont County / Timothy A. Kiefer / Timothy A. Kiefer / 1988									
82	14 2/8	14 3/8	7 2/8	7 2/8	9 3/8	5 4/8	5 7/8	5 3/8	1157	406
	Carbon County / Donald L. Soderberg / Donald L. Soderberg / 1988									
82	14 3/8	14 3/8	7 2/8	7 2/8	11 5/8	10 2/8	6 3/8	6 2/8	1157	406
	Carbon County / Becky Strand / Becky Strand / 1988									
82	14 4/8	14 3/8	7 6/8	7 6/8	10 6/8	8 6/8	5 5/8	5 6/8	1157	406
	Sweetwater County / Mark E. Gillespie / Mark E. Gillespie / 1989									
82	16 2/8	16 2/8	6 4/8	6 4/8	9 5/8	5 5/8	6 3/8	6 4/8	1157	406
	Lincoln County / Michael H. Romney / Michael H. Romney / 1989									
82	15 3/8	15 2/8	6 4/8	6 3/8	8 2/8	4	5 6/8	5 5/8	1157	406
	Albany County / Phil Darnell / Phil Darnell / 1990									
82	15	15 1/8	7	7 1/8	8 4/8	4	6 5/8	5 6/8	1157	406
	Carbon County / Allen A. Ehrke / Allen A. Ehrke / 1990									
82	16	16	6 3/8	6 4/8	10 4/8	8 1/8	6 1/8	7	1157	406
	Albany County / James T. Sprinkle / James T. Sprinkle / 1990									
82	15 5/8	15 5/8	6 2/8	6 1/8	8 6/8	5	5 6/8	5 4/8	1157	406
	Natrona County / Victor Colonna / Victor Colonna / 1990									
82	16 2/8	16	7	6 7/8	9 6/8	5 5/8	5	5 3/8	1157	406
	Washakie County / Jake Hanson / Jake Hanson / 1990									
82	13 4/8	13 2/8	7 1/8	7 1/8	11 7/8	10 6/8	6 4/8	6 3/8	1157	406
	Carbon County / Andrew W. Serres / Andrew W. Serres / 1991									
82	16 3/8	16 4/8	6 6/8	6 5/8	9 7/8	4 2/8	5 3/8	5 4/8	1157	406
	Converse County / Rick P. Sakovitz / Rick P. Sakovitz / 1991									
82	15 4/8	15 7/8	6 4/8	6 4/8	8 3/8	6 3/8	5 3/8	6 2/8	1157	406
	Carbon County / Jeffrey L. Engel / Jeffrey L. Engel / 1992									
82	16 1/8	16 5/8	6 3/8	6 4/8	10 7/8	6 6/8	5 5/8	5 7/8	1157	406
	Sweetwater County / Dennis L. Haan / Dennis L. Haan / 1992									
81 6/8	15 5/8	15 2/8	6 6/8	6 7/8	8 3/8	4 4/8	5 3/8	5 3/8	1276	455
	Carbon County / Loren R. Tri / Loren R. Tri / 1990									

Score	Length of Horn		Circumference of Base		Inside Spread	Tip-to-Tip Spread	Length of Prong		All-Time Rank	State Rank
	R	L	R	L			R	L		
◆ Locality / Hunter / Owner / Date Killed										
81⁶/₈	16	16	6⁷/₈	6⁴/₈	9²/₈	2⁵/₈	5⁵/₈	5⁶/₈	1276	455
◆ Carbon County / Russell E. Tostenrud / Russell E. Tostenrud / 1992										
81⁶/₈	16¹/₈	16¹/₈	6¹/₈	6¹/₈	9⁵/₈	4⁷/₈	5⁶/₈	5⁵/₈	1276	455
◆ Campbell County / Fred I. White III / Fred I. White III / 1993										
81⁴/₈	16³/₈	16³/₈	6¹/₈	6²/₈	10	6⁴/₈	5⁶/₈	5⁴/₈	1283	458
◆ Sweetwater County / Jeffrey L. Hoving / Jeffrey L. Hoving / 1991										
81⁴/₈	14⁴/₈	14⁵/₈	7⁴/₈	7⁴/₈	14	11³/₈	6	5⁵/₈	1283	458
◆ Sweetwater County / Jon S. Mueller / Jon S. Mueller / 1992										
81²/₈	15²/₈	15⁴/₈	6⁵/₈	6⁵/₈	9⁶/₈	8⁷/₈	6	6	1290	460
◆ Sweetwater County / Bruce E. Cepicky / Bruce E. Cepicky / 1989										
81²/₈	16⁴/₈	16³/₈	6⁶/₈	6⁶/₈	12³/₈	7⁵/₈	5	5³/₈	1290	460
◆ Sweetwater County / Stanton E. Wilson / Stanton E. Wilson / 1991										
81²/₈	14⁷/₈	15²/₈	7²/₈	7¹/₈	12	9⁴/₈	5⁶/₈	5⁵/₈	1290	460
◆ Carbon County / Joseph R. Alcantara / Joseph R. Alcantara / 1992										
81²/₈	14⁶/₈	14⁶/₈	7⁵/₈	7⁵/₈	9⁵/₈	7	4⁶/₈	5	1290	460
◆ Carbon County / Andrew W. Serres / Andrew W. Serres / 1992										
81¹/₈	14¹/₈	14⁵/₈	7³/₈	7⁵/₈	15⁶/₈	14²/₈	6¹/₈	6	1309	464
◆ Converse County / Barbara Moore / Barbara Moore / 1987										
81	16	16	6²/₈	6²/₈	8³/₈	4⁶/₈	5³/₈	5⁶/₈	1310	465
◆ Carbon County / Raymond R. Thomma, Jr. / Raymond R. Thomma, Jr. / 1990										
81	14⁵/₈	14⁶/₈	7³/₈	7³/₈	7³/₈	3⁵/₈	5⁵/₈	4¹/₈	1310	465
◆ Natrona County / Todd C. Gould / Todd C. Gould / 1992										
81	16¹/₈	16	6³/₈	6²/₈	11¹/₈	5⁶/₈	5³/₈	6²/₈	1310	465
◆ Sweetwater County / John B. Nieman / John B. Nieman / 1993										
81	16	16¹/₈	6³/₈	6²/₈	14⁵/₈	10¹/₈	5¹/₈	5¹/₈	1310	465
◆ Fremont County / Mark A. Blake / Mark A. Blake / 1994										
80⁶/₈	16⁴/₈	16²/₈	6⁵/₈	6⁴/₈	17²/₈	17²/₈	4⁷/₈	4⁷/₈	1327	469
◆ Carbon County / Harry G. Flock, Jr. / Harry G. Flock, Jr. / 1981										
80⁶/₈	15	14⁶/₈	7¹/₈	6⁷/₈	13²/₈	8⁷/₈	6	5⁶/₈	1327	469
◆ Fremont County / J.R. Hansen / J.R. Hansen / 1989										
80⁶/₈	14⁶/₈	15¹/₈	7	7¹/₈	12	7²/₈	6	5⁷/₈	1327	469
◆ Uinta County / David J. White / David J. White / 1990										
80⁶/₈	15⁷/₈	16	6⁴/₈	6⁴/₈	7⁷/₈	4¹/₈	5²/₈	5²/₈	1327	469
◆ Natrona County / William E. Butler / William E. Butler / 1992										
80⁶/₈	15¹/₈	15⁶/₈	6⁴/₈	6⁴/₈	10⁴/₈	5⁶/₈	6	5⁷/₈	1327	469
◆ Fremont County / Jim C. Femrite / Jim C. Femrite / 1992										
80⁴/₈	16	16⁴/₈	6⁷/₈	6⁶/₈	11⁴/₈	8	5⁵/₈	5¹/₈	1345	474
◆ Niobrara County / John E. Howard / John E. Howard / 1982										

Score	Length of Horn		Circumference of Base		Inside Spread	Tip-to-Tip Spread	Length of Prong		All-Time Rank	State Rank
	R	L	R	L			R	L		
	♦ Locality / Hunter / Owner / Date Killed									
80⁴⁄₈	15⁵⁄₈	15⁷⁄₈	6⁴⁄₈	6²⁄₈	13	11	5⁴⁄₈	5⁴⁄₈	1345	474
	♦ Carbon County / Jim E. Jairell / Jim E. Jairell / 1991									
80⁴⁄₈	14³⁄₈	14⁴⁄₈	6⁶⁄₈	6⁶⁄₈	10³⁄₈	8	5²⁄₈	5²⁄₈	1345	474
	♦ Carbon County / James A. Blome / James A. Blome / 1991									
80⁴⁄₈	16²⁄₈	15	6¹⁄₈	6¹⁄₈	9²⁄₈	5⁵⁄₈	6	6²⁄₈	1345	474
	♦ Sweetwater County / Lawrence S. Robinson / Lawrence S. Robinson / 1993									
80⁴⁄₈	15⁴⁄₈	15	7	7	11⁵⁄₈	8⁷⁄₈	4³⁄₈	4⁴⁄₈	1345	474
	♦ Goshen County / Samuel Teeters / Samuel Teeters / 1994									
80²⁄₈	15³⁄₈	15²⁄₈	6⁴⁄₈	6⁴⁄₈	10²⁄₈	6	6	5⁶⁄₈	1360	479
	♦ Natrona County / Richard O. Burns, Jr. / Richard O. Burns, Jr. / 1979									
80²⁄₈	15³⁄₈	15³⁄₈	6⁴⁄₈	6⁴⁄₈	13²⁄₈	9³⁄₈	5⁶⁄₈	6¹⁄₈	1360	479
	♦ Fremont County / Gary P. Stewart / Gary P. Stewart / 1989									
80²⁄₈	15¹⁄₈	15⁴⁄₈	6⁷⁄₈	6⁶⁄₈	9	6	5	4⁷⁄₈	1360	479
	♦ Fremont County / Russell W. Korp / Russell W. Korp / 1990									
80²⁄₈	17²⁄₈	17⁵⁄₈	5⁴⁄₈	5⁴⁄₈	9⁷⁄₈	5⁴⁄₈	5⁴⁄₈	5³⁄₈	1360	479
	♦ Sweetwater County / David F. DeMello / David F. DeMello / 1991									
80²⁄₈	16⁶⁄₈	16⁶⁄₈	6¹⁄₈	6¹⁄₈	13¹⁄₈	7⁵⁄₈	4⁵⁄₈	5	1360	479
	♦ Converse County / Clayton H. Maue / Clayton H. Maue / 1991									
80²⁄₈	14²⁄₈	14³⁄₈	6⁴⁄₈	6⁴⁄₈	10	6¹⁄₈	6⁵⁄₈	6⁷⁄₈	1360	479
	♦ Sweetwater County / Robert G. Hummel / Robert G. Hummel / 1992									
80²⁄₈	14⁷⁄₈	14⁶⁄₈	6⁷⁄₈	6⁷⁄₈	9⁴⁄₈	6¹⁄₈	5⁴⁄₈	5³⁄₈	1360	479
	♦ Campbell County / Donald G. Pike / Donald G. Pike / 1992									
80²⁄₈	15⁶⁄₈	15²⁄₈	6⁶⁄₈	6⁵⁄₈	9²⁄₈	5⁴⁄₈	5⁵⁄₈	5⁶⁄₈	1360	479
	♦ Carbon County / Robert L. Burderus / Robert L. Burderus / 1993									
80	14⁷⁄₈	14⁶⁄₈	7²⁄₈	7²⁄₈	10³⁄₈	5⁶⁄₈	5¹⁄₈	5²⁄₈	1386	487
	♦ Natrona County / John F. Druschba / John F. Druschba / 1983									
80	17	16⁷⁄₈	6⁴⁄₈	6⁴⁄₈	12³⁄₈	9	4⁶⁄₈	5	1386	487
	♦ Carbon County / Stanley K. Ash / Stanley K. Ash / 1987									
80	14⁶⁄₈	14²⁄₈	7³⁄₈	6⁷⁄₈	10¹⁄₈	6¹⁄₈	6	5⁶⁄₈	1386	487
	♦ Natrona County / David M. Crum / David M. Crum / 1990									
80	15⁷⁄₈	16	6⁵⁄₈	6⁵⁄₈	11	4⁷⁄₈	5⁵⁄₈	5⁶⁄₈	1386	487
	♦ Carbon County / Ron Duckworth / Ron Duckworth / 1992									
80	15¹⁄₈	15¹⁄₈	6⁵⁄₈	6⁵⁄₈	12⁴⁄₈	11	3⁷⁄₈	3⁶⁄₈	1386	487
	♦ Carbon County / Kenneth L. McCoy / Kenneth L. McCoy / 1992									
80	14⁶⁄₈	14⁶⁄₈	6⁴⁄₈	6⁶⁄₈	12³⁄₈	9⁶⁄₈	5⁴⁄₈	5³⁄₈	1386	487
	♦ Converse County / Kevin L. Stier / Kevin L. Stier / 1992									
80	14⁴⁄₈	14⁴⁄₈	6⁷⁄₈	6⁷⁄₈	9³⁄₈	5⁶⁄₈	5⁴⁄₈	5⁵⁄₈	1386	487
	♦ Carbon County / Andrew W. Serres / Andrew W. Serres / 1994									

Score	Length of Horn		Circumference of Base		Inside Spread	Tip-to-Tip Spread	Length of Prong		All-Time Rank	State Rank
	R	L	R	L			R	L		
◆ Locality / Hunter / Owner / Date Killed										
91²⁄₈	16²⁄₈	16⁴⁄₈	7⁴⁄₈	7⁴⁄₈	13⁴⁄₈	9	6⁶⁄₈	6⁴⁄₈	*	*
◆ Fremont County / Bill E. Boatman / Bill E. Boatman / 1988										
89⁴⁄₈	17	16⁷⁄₈	7¹⁄₈	7	11	6⁵⁄₈	6³⁄₈	6⁵⁄₈	*	*
◆ Sweetwater County / Richard D. Ullery / Richard D. Ullery / 1983										
89²⁄₈	15⁷⁄₈	15⁵⁄₈	8	7⁶⁄₈	9⁷⁄₈	7³⁄₈	5⁵⁄₈	5⁵⁄₈	*	*
◆ Carbon County / Sharon M. Carson / Sharon M. Carson / 1991										
87²⁄₈	16⁶⁄₈	16⁶⁄₈	7⁵⁄₈	7⁵⁄₈	12⁶⁄₈	9	5⁴⁄₈	6¹⁄₈	*	*
◆ Sweetwater County / Stanley L. Ackerman / Stanley L. Ackerman / 1980										
87	16⁷⁄₈	16⁴⁄₈	7⁵⁄₈	7⁵⁄₈	14⁵⁄₈	10⁵⁄₈	6²⁄₈	6	*	*
◆ Fremont County / Ronald K. Morrison / Ronald K. Morrison / 1980										

Photograph Courtesy of Howard M. Stephens

ALBERTA NUMBER THREE
PRONGHORN
SCORE: 85²⁄₈
Locality: Bow City   Date: 1964
Hunter: Howard M. Stephens
Owner: Eric Wilson

ALBERTA
PRONGHORN

Score	Length of Horn		Circumference of Base		Inside Spread	Tip-to-Tip Spread	Length of Prong		All-Time Rank	State Rank
	R	L	R	L			R	L		
◆ Locality / Hunter / Owner / Date Killed										
86²/₈	16⁷/₈	16⁶/₈	6⁷/₈	6⁵/₈	13⁵/₈	10	5⁴/₈	5⁷/₈	155	1
◆ Brooks / S. Prescott Fay / Boston Mus. Science / 1913										
85⁶/₈	16²/₈	16¹/₈	6⁵/₈	6⁶/₈	12⁵/₈	9⁶/₈	6²/₈	6¹/₈	211	2
◆ Brooks / Oliver Ost / Oliver Ost / 1964										
85²/₈	17	17	6⁶/₈	6⁴/₈	10⁶/₈	8	5¹/₈	5³/₈	268	3
◆ Bow City / Howard M. Stephens / Eric Wilson / 1964										
84⁶/₈	17	17⁴/₈	6⁶/₈	6⁶/₈	14⁶/₈	11¹/₈	6¹/₈	5³/₈	336	4
◆ Jenner / J.E. Edwards / J.E. Edwards / 1964										
84⁴/₈	16¹/₈	15⁷/₈	7	7	11⁷/₈	10⁴/₈	5²/₈	5²/₈	390	5
◆ Cutbank Creek / Cameron C. Owen / Cameron C. Owen / 1990										
84	17	17²/₈	7¹/₈	7¹/₈	12²/₈	6⁷/₈	4⁷/₈	4⁷/₈	500	6
◆ Milk River / George Vandervalk / George Vandervalk / 1966										
83⁴/₈	17²/₈	17⁴/₈	6³/₈	6⁵/₈	8⁴/₈	1⁶/₈	4⁶/₈	4⁶/₈	624	7
◆ Foremost / Brian J. Gathercole / Brian J. Gathercole / 1988										
83⁴/₈	16³/₈	16²/₈	6¹/₈	6¹/₈	16¹/₈	13⁷/₈	6	6	624	7
◆ Wildhorse / Ralph L. Cervo / Ralph L. Cervo / 1989										
83²/₈	16⁴/₈	16²/₈	6	6¹/₈	10⁶/₈	4¹/₈	6³/₈	6⁵/₈	690	9
◆ Rolling Hills / Dennis A. Andrews / Dennis A. Andrews / 1975										
83²/₈	15⁶/₈	15²/₈	6	6¹/₈	11	4¹/₈	7²/₈	7⁵/₈	690	9
◆ Medicine Hat / Roger H. Stone / Roger H. Stone / 1975										
83²/₈	17	16⁶/₈	6⁴/₈	6²/₈	11⁵/₈	6⁵/₈	5⁷/₈	5⁵/₈	690	9
◆ Sage Creek / Leslie C. Wall / Leslie C. Wall / 1993										
83	15²/₈	15³/₈	6⁶/₈	6⁶/₈	13³/₈	10¹/₈	5⁷/₈	5⁶/₈	775	12
◆ Manyberries / Rae E. Cervo / Rae E. Cervo / 1986										
83	16⁶/₈	16⁶/₈	6	6	13⁵/₈	10⁶/₈	5²/₈	5²/₈	775	12
◆ Milk River / Lyle G. Andersen / Lyle G. Andersen / 1993										
82⁶/₈	16	16²/₈	6⁴/₈	6⁴/₈	10²/₈	5²/₈	5	5³/₈	868	14
◆ Milk River / Darryl D. Bartos / Darryl D. Bartos / 1993										
82⁴/₈	15²/₈	15²/₈	6⁷/₈	6⁷/₈	11¹/₈	7²/₈	6¹/₈	5⁷/₈	949	15
◆ Medicine Hat / Nick Mandryk / Nick Mandryk / 1963										
82⁴/₈	15⁷/₈	15⁷/₈	6⁵/₈	6⁴/₈	8⁵/₈	3⁵/₈	6¹/₈	6	949	15
◆ Milk River / Carey Karl / Carey Karl / 1992										
82²/₈	15⁷/₈	16	7	7	11⁷/₈	7⁶/₈	5²/₈	5¹/₈	1058	17
◆ Hanna / Rita Shumka / C.W. Edwards / 1964										
82²/₈	16³/₈	16²/₈	6²/₈	6²/₈	13²/₈	9¹/₈	5⁴/₈	5²/₈	1058	17
◆ Knappen / Ken Bosch / Ken Bosch / 1965										

Score	Length of Horn		Circumference of Base		Inside Spread	Tip-to-Tip Spread	Length of Prong		All-Time Rank	State Rank
	R	L	R	L			R	L		

♦ *Locality / Hunter / Owner / Date Killed*

82²⁄₈	16⁴⁄₈	16²⁄₈	6³⁄₈	6³⁄₈	10²⁄₈	4¹⁄₈	5³⁄₈	5²⁄₈	1058	17

♦ *Foremost / Les Gordon / Les Gordon / 1966*

82²⁄₈	17³⁄₈	17²⁄₈	6⁷⁄₈	7²⁄₈	7¹⁄₈	3¹⁄₈	4⁷⁄₈	4⁷⁄₈	1058	17

♦ *Wild Horse / Adam Schmick / Adam Schmick / 1970*

82²⁄₈	17	16⁷⁄₈	6¹⁄₈	6²⁄₈	16³⁄₈	12¹⁄₈	5	5⁶⁄₈	1058	17

♦ *Middle Creek Res. / Donald P. Penner / Donald P. Penner / 1989*

82	15	14⁶⁄₈	6⁷⁄₈	6⁷⁄₈	10³⁄₈	7⁶⁄₈	5⁶⁄₈	5⁵⁄₈	1157	22

♦ *Bow Island / R.F. Dunmire / R.F. Dunmire / 1957*

82	15⁴⁄₈	15⁴⁄₈	6⁶⁄₈	6⁶⁄₈	8⁴⁄₈	5⁷⁄₈	5⁶⁄₈	4⁶⁄₈	1157	22

♦ *Alberta / Peter M. Parkyn / Peter M. Parkyn / 1987*

82	15⁴⁄₈	15³⁄₈	6⁴⁄₈	6⁴⁄₈	13⁵⁄₈	9	6⁴⁄₈	7	1157	22

♦ *Milk River / Lance Hartley / Lance Hartley / 1993*

80⁶⁄₈	15	15²⁄₈	6⁶⁄₈	6⁶⁄₈	7⁵⁄₈	7⁴⁄₈	5³⁄₈	5⁵⁄₈	1327	25

♦ *Orion / John Luthi / John Luthi / 1989*

80	15	15	6⁵⁄₈	6³⁄₈	8²⁄₈	6²⁄₈	5⁶⁄₈	6²⁄₈	1386	26

♦ *Forty Mile Coulee / Ronald M. Steels / Ronald M. Steels / 1989*

Photograph Courtesy of William P. Price

This gnarly-horned pronghorn, scoring an impressive 88-2/8 points, was taken in Goshen County, Wyoming, by William P. Price in 1991. Wyoming produces more pronghorns, including trophy specimens, than any other state or province in North American.

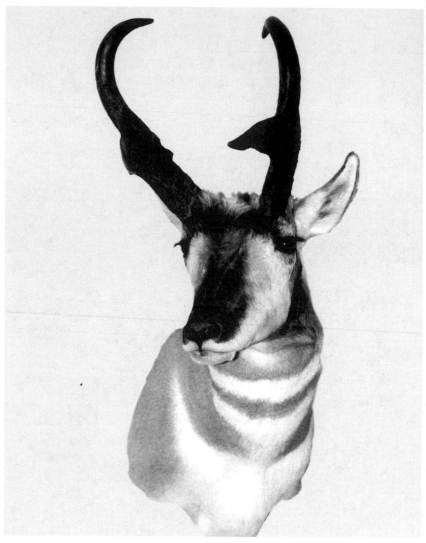

Photograph Courtesy of Gerald W. Bien

**SASKATCHEWAN PROVINCE RECORD
PRONGHORN
SCORE: 86⁴⁄₈**
Locality: Hay Lake   Date: 1990
Hunter: Gerald W. Bien

SASKATCHEWAN

PRONGHORN

Score	Length of Horn		Circumference of Base		Inside Spread	Tip-to-Tip Spread	Length of Prong		All-Time Rank	State Rank
	R	L	R	L			R	L		
◆ Locality / Hunter / Owner / Date Killed										
86 4/8	16 1/8	16	6 7/8	6 6/8	8 7/8	5 7/8	6	6 1/8	140	1
◆ Hay Lake / Gerald W. Bien / Gerald W. Bien / 1990										
85 2/8	16 3/8	16 2/8	6 5/8	6 3/8	12 1/8	8	6 1/8	6 1/8	268	2
◆ Maple Creek / Glen A. Lewis / George Hooey / 1964										
83 6/8	14 4/8	14 3/8	6 5/8	6 6/8	10 6/8	7 4/8	6 2/8	6 2/8	565	3
◆ Divide / Leslie Banford / Leslie Banford / 1975										
83 4/8	17 2/8	17 2/8	6 2/8	6 2/8	10	4 3/8	6	5 2/8	624	4
◆ Maple Creek / Lynn P. Needham / Lynn P. Needham / 1989										
82 6/8	16 3/8	16 2/8	6 1/8	6 2/8	8	1 6/8	5 2/8	5 7/8	868	5
◆ Cypress Lake / Jack Clary / Jack Clary / 1991										
82	15 2/8	15	6	6	8 4/8	7	6 7/8	7	1157	6
◆ Eston / Dennis Crowe / Dennis Crowe / 1966										
82	16 1/8	16 2/8	6 1/8	6 1/8	9 5/8	3 7/8	5 5/8	5 4/8	1157	6
◆ Frenchman River / Larry Schmidt / Larry Schmidt / 1991										
81 2/8	15 2/8	15 1/8	6 4/8	6 4/8	11 6/8	8 7/8	5 5/8	5 2/8	1290	8
◆ Burstall / Duncan L. MacEachern / Duncan L. MacEachern / 1993										
80 2/8	15 5/8	15 5/8	6 1/8	6 2/8	12	8 1/8	5 7/8	6	1360	9
◆ Cypress Lake / Jack Clary / Jack Clary / 1992										

Photograph Courtesy of Juan A. Saenz

MEXICO RECORD
PRONGHORN
SCORE: 85⅝
Locality: Chihuahua   Date: 1955
Hunter: Juan A. Saenz

MEXICO
PRONGHORN

Score	Length of Horn		Circumference of Base		Inside Spread	Tip-to-Tip Spread	Length of Prong		All-Time Rank	State Rank
	R	L	R	L			R	L		
	◆ Locality / Hunter / Owner / Date Killed									
85⁶⁄₈	15¹⁄₈	16³⁄₈	6⁶⁄₈	7	12⁵⁄₈	7³⁄₈	6	5³⁄₈	211	1
	◆ Chihuahua / Juan A. Saenz / Juan A. Saenz / 1955									
84⁴⁄₈	16⁴⁄₈	16²⁄₈	6²⁄₈	6²⁄₈	12⁷⁄₈	9²⁄₈	7⁶⁄₈	7⁵⁄₈	390	2
	◆ Chihuahua / Julio Estrada / Julio Estrada / 1945									

ISBN 0-940864-26

RECORDS OF N AMERICAN SHEEP SOFT

This book was:

Data compiled with the able assistance of:
C. Randall Byers
Theodore J. Holsten, Jr.
Sandra Poston
Chris Tonkinson
Philip L. Wright

Book designed by:
Jack and Susan Reneau

Photographic scans by:
Julie Tripp

Cover designed by:
Julie Tripp

Sketch of bighorn sheep by:
Hayden Lambson
Pocatello, Idaho

Typeset by:
Colorado Typographics
Loveland, Colorado
(statistics)
and
Meerkat Graphics
Lolo, Montana
(text)

Printed and bound by:
Royal Book Manufacturing, Inc.
Norwich, Connecticut
(softcover and hardcover trade editions)

Limited edition binding by:
Campbell-Logan Bindery
Minneapolis, Minnesota